Exploring Marriages and Families

Exploring Marriages and Families

Karen Seccombe
Portland State University

Allyn & Bacon

Boston   Columbus   Indianapolis   New York   San Francisco   Upper Saddle River
Amsterdam   Cape Town   Dubai   London   Madrid   Milan   Munich   Paris   Montreal   Toronto
Delhi   Mexico City   Sao Paulo   Sydney   Hong Kong   Seoul   Singapore   Taipei   Tokyo

Editor-in-Chief: Dickson Musslewhite
Publisher: Karen Hanson
Development Editor: Deb Hanlon
Associate Editor: Mayda Bosco
Editorial Assistant: Christine Dore
Executive Marketing Manager: Kelly May
Marketing Assistant: Janeli Bitor
Production Project Manager: Roberta Sherman
Manufacturing Buyer: Debbie Rossi
Cover Designer: Kristina Mose-Libon
Editorial Production and Composition Service: PreMediaGlobal Inc.
Interior Design: Joyce Weston
Photo Research: Kate Cebik

Credits appear on page 537, which constitutes an extension of the copyright page.

Cataloging-in-Publication data unavailable at press time

Many of the designations by manufacturers and sellers to distinguish their product-sare claimed as trademarks. Where those designations appear in this book, and the publisher was aware of a trademark claim, the designations have been printed in ini-tialcaps or all caps.

10 9 8 7 6 5 4 3 2 1   CIN-V   14 13 12 11 10

Allyn & Bacon
is an imprint of

www.pearsonhighered.com

ISBN-10:   0-205-71779-9
ISBN-13: 978-0-205-71779-8

Brief Contents

Contents

Chapter 2
Social Status:
Sex, Gender, Race, Ethnicity, and Social Class
36

PART II: The Foundations of Relationships

Chapter 3
Building Relationships
68

Chapter 4
Love and Loving Relationships
94

⊙ **Watch** the **Video** *Arranged Marriage: Rati and Subas* on **myfamilylab.com**

Chapter 5
Sexual Identity, Behavior, and Relationships
122

Watch the Video *Perspectives on Sexual Identity and Behavior: Kayla and Chris on* **myfamilylab.com**

Chapter 6
Communication, Conflict, and Power in Our Relationships
154

Watch the **Video** *Communication in Relationships* on **myfamilylab.com**

Chapter 7
Marriage
182

PART III: Parents and their Children

Chapter 8
Thinking about Parenthood
212

Chapter 9
Raising Children
240

▶ Watch the Video *Same Sex Parents Raising Children: Karen and Betsy* on **myfamilylab.com**

Chapter 10
Families and the Work They Do
270

👁 **Watch** the **Video** *Balancing Work and*
Family Life: Lisa and Chris on **myfamilylab.com**

PART IV: Family Strengths, Challenges, and Reorganization

Chapter 11

Family Stress and Crisis: Violence among Intimates
300

👁 ▶Watch the Video *Intimate Partner*
Violence: Shannon on **myfamilylab.com**

Chapter 12
The Process of Divorce
332

Chapter 14
Families in Middle and Later Life
390

👁 [Watch the Video *The Sandwich Generation: Amy* on **myfamilylab.com**

Chapter 15

Looking Ahead: Helping Families Flourish
420

👁 Watch the **Video** *A Comparison of Family Policies: France and the United States: Sophie and Alain on* **myfamilylab.com**

Preface

MARRIAGES AND FAMILIES is my favorite course among the many I have taught over the past twenty years. Students crave information about love, sex, dating, relationships, marriage, and children. However, they tend to see these issues in individualized terms, which makes the course a constant challenge to teach.

My goal, therefore, is to offer students a fresh perspective—*one that places individual relationships in their social context so that students can more fully understand why they make the choices they do.* Throughout the text I illustrate the ways in which historical, cultural, social, and political factors influence our personal experiences, beliefs, privileges, constraints, and choices. Our likelihood of marrying, bearing children, or divorcing; our family values, lifestyles, and opportunities; and our health and well-being (and stressors upon them) are all influenced by these structural factors. With a strong focus on assessment, theory, and research, a celebration of diversity, a rich look at how history shapes both our present and future, an emphasis on family resilience and empowerment, and an engaging visual presentation (including video segments for each chapter opening), this introductory text will help students make more informed decisions about their relationships by better understanding the social context in which they live and the relevance of social science to their lives.

I introduce the following key themes in the opening chapter, provide provocative examples of each throughout subsequent chapters, and revisit the themes in the concluding chapter: (1) the best way to truly understand families is to link micro- and macro-level perspectives; (2) families are not monolithic or static, but ever-changing; and (3) social science theory and research help us understand families and relationships.

The Best Way to Truly Understand Families is to Link Micro- and Macro-Level Perspectives.

While all of us experience relationships and family life as individuals, we will not understand these experiences without an appreciation of the social environment in which they happen. Our relationships are shaped in large part by our culture and elements of social structure, including our statuses (e.g., race, ethnicity, social class, gender, and sex) and our institutions (e.g., the economy, religion, and the political system). Thus at every appropriate opportunity in the text the relationship between macro-level factors and micro-level personal choices, experiences, opportunities, and constraints is highlighted. For example, social structure may influence who is considered an appropriate mate, how we communicate with our partners, our sexual experiences, benefits that accrue from marriage, the division of household labor between husbands and wives, decisions about children and childrearing, our likelihood of divorcing and repartnering, and many other family experiences.

Families Are Not Monolithic or Static, But Are Ever-Changing.

People construct families to meet their needs for warmth, companionship, economic cooperation, and as a way to raise children. Therefore, families take many different forms that continue to evolve, sharing historical, cultural, and subcultural differences in family life. The text suggests there is not one "right" type of family—one size does not fit all—and each chapter celebrates the diversity of families in the United States and around the world. For example, extensive coverage of topics such as gay and lesbian families, cohabitation, single parents, racial and ethnic differences in family structure and interaction, and social class differences are fully integrated throughout the text. Also included are documented changes in relationships and families advanced by technology such as cell phones, laptops, and networking sites like Facebook, Twitter, and MySpace. These technologies have changed the way people meet, communicate, and carry on their daily lives.

Social Science Theory and Research Help Us Understand Families and Relationships.
Everyone holds "common sense" opinions about families based on personal experience or information filtered through the mass media, peers, or parents. However, a scientific perspective can provide a more objective and factual window on the world, and can help us form opinions, develop our values, and make sound personal choices. Theories and methods of social research are introduced in Chapter 1. Each subsequent chapter provides solid theoretical grounding in key issues, demonstrates the value of research, and includes the most recent quantitative and qualitative interdisciplinary scholarship available. Finally, the boxed feature *Why Do Research?* illustrates how family scientists conduct research, the methods they use, the dilemmas they face, and how conclusions of research champion common sense perceptions about families.

:: Visual Style and Assessment Tools

Many college students today are *visual learners*, reading more websites, magazines, graphic novels, emails, and text messages than ever before. They learn and absorb information differently, thriving in an environment awash in information technology, where fast delivery and visually rich presentations are expected.

Professors, myself included, have been challenged by students' seeming disinterest in traditional textbooks. Many perceive textbooks as boring, outdated, and irrelevant. They find the material too intimidating to master. Many would rather consult a study partner, a classmate, or even Google rather than struggle with their textbook if they have a question.

This text has been designed with these concerns in mind. Based on a sound scholarship, the text is written in a conversational tone to help grab and hold students' attention. Each chapter begins with an engaging video from our *Exploring Families* video series (found on **www.myfamilylab.com**) and opening vignette about a couple or family whose story illustrates the chapter's main ideas. The video is then recalled at the end of the chapter as students answer questions applying what they have learned. A **Video Discussion Guide** is provided at the end of the text for further review of the video and chapter topics. Instructors have access to a wide selection of video samples online at **www.myfamilylab.com** and can tailor these openers to match their teaching preference.

Graphs, charts, and tables are attractively designed to deliver key information quickly and engagingly. Students can easily become overwhelmed with data. The tables and graphs here are not simply add-ons, rather they are fully integrated within the text itself and are strategically designed to help students process information more efficiently. Key points are specifically identified in each visual so that students are not left wondering, "What am I supposed to learn from this chart?"

The flow of each chapter is easy to follow, and includes a variety of assessment tools for students. They can test their knowledge and apply the information they have learned to their own lives. Each chapter begins with important numbered learning objectives (**Questions that Matter**), which are repeated and answered in the **Chapter Review**. Self-reflection questions can be found peppered throughout the chapter in the margins, as well as at the end of the boxed features (**What Do You Think?**). The **Getting To Know Yourself** boxed feature contains self-assessment tests and inventories students can take on their own time. The last paragraph of each chapter (**Bringing It Full Circle**) asks students to think critically about what they have learned and apply it to the *Exploring Families* video from the chapter opener. (All of these features, and more, are explained in detail in the next section of the Preface.)

Our overall goal is to present the material in a lively and appealing format, with 15 chapters to grab and retain students' attention as they work through their Marriages and Families course.

- For professors, this academic journey is grounded in solid theory and research.
- For students, it is accessible, relevant, and engaging.
- For both, the text captures the compelling family issues of our time.

:: Pedagogical Features

The features in each chapter are specifically designed to make learning easier and more rewarding, and to highlight the themes of the text:

Opening Vignette and Video Clip: *Grabbing students' attention immediately.* Each chapter begins with a compelling personal narrative and accompanying video clip (found in our *Exploring Families* video series on **www.myfamilylab.com**) that chronicles an individual's or couple's experience which is relevant to the chapter. Students can identify with these real stories; they bring the material to life, revealing the micro- and macro-level connections in our relationships while stimulating students' critical evaluation of the material. Questions appear at the end of each video that feed directly into the MyFamilyLab Gradebook, allowing the videos to be assigned as homework assignments. Instructors also have access to a wealth of additional video samples in MyFamilyLab they can choose from to match their teaching preference. Examples of vignettes and video clips include a couple describing the benefits of their arranged marriage; a young couple discussing their decision to cohabit; insights into the double standard from both a male and female perspective; a moving account of an international adoption; how one family juggles work and family responsibilities; a heroic confrontation of intimate partner violence; a young woman's painful remembrance of her parents' divorce; and the story of caring for a frail elderly parent while also carrying for a young child at home. Vignettes and video clips use humor, emotion, and curiosity to engage students and immediately draw them into the chapter. A **Video Discussion Guide** at the end of the text provides mulitple choice and critical thinking questions to promote further review of the *Exploring Families* videos and chapter themes.

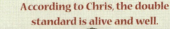

According to Chris, the double standard is alive and well.

◉ **Watch** the **Video** *Perspectives on Sexual Identity and Behavior: Kayla and Chris* on **myfamilylab.com**

Questions that Matter: *Allowing students to measure their understanding.* Each chapter opens with 12-15 specific numbered learning objective questions drawn from the key concepts of the chapter. These questions identify the key points of the chapter and allow students to test and measure their degree of understanding of the material. Detailed answers to these questions are provided at the end of each chapter in the Chapter Review.

Q UESTIONS *That Matter* • • • • • • • • • • • • • • • • • • •

5.1 Is sexuality purely biological?
5.2 How do macro-level factors influence sexuality?
5.3 What is the difference between "sex" and "gender"?
5.4 Do sex and gender go together?
5.5 What do we mean by "sexual orientation"?
5.6 What are sexual scripts, and where do we learn them?

5.7 Are sexual scripts different for men and women?
5.8 What are some important studies that have been done on human sexuality?
5.9 When do we become sexual?
5.10 How big a social problem is teenage pregnancy?
5.11 How prevalent is nonmarital sex among young adults?

5.12 What are some common sexual trends in marriage?
5.13 Do people remain sexual throughout their lives?
5.14 What is the most common STI?
5.15 Hasn't the issue of HIV and AIDS been resolved by now?

Questions for Reflection: *Encouraging students to form and analyze their own opinions.* Provocative critical thinking questions are strategically placed in the margins throughout the chapters to challenge students to think about controversial issues, form opinions, and analyze the factors that shape their opinions. This feature integrates all three themes, so that students think about macro-micro linkages, diversity, and how research findings can challenge our "common sense" ideas. Students are encouraged to use the information in the text to help them reflect on their own lives, take a stand, and to defend their position.

G *iven what you have learned about sex differences in general and sex differences in communication, do you think there are also differences in men's and women's methods of self-disclosure? What evidence can you provide for your answer?*

sexual orientation: The sexual and romantic pattern of partners of choice.

heterosexual: Having an attraction and preference for developing romantic and sexual relationships with the opposite sex.

Key Terms and Glossary: *Keeping students organized.* To help students better retain important information, key terms and concepts appear in boldface within the chapter text, and a marginal definition is included for reinforcement. Key terms are repeated again at the end of the chapter in the Chapter Review, with corresponding page references, and a full glossary concludes the book.

:: Boxed Features:

Tying It All Together: Factors That Shape. . . *Explicitly identifying the macro and micro links.* Students often have difficulty identifying the importance of culture and social structure, and how these influence personal relationships. This feature highlights the first theme by explicitly identifying macro- and micro-level influences upon our marriages, families, and close relationships. Students benefit from the insights of each perspective and their interrelationship. Within each chapter, this feature shows how culture, history, social institutions, and social status shape personal choices and constraints, including sexual scripts; dating and mate selection practices; the decline in marriage rates; the division of household labor; and the decision to have a child.

Tying It All Together

The Interrelationship of Micro-level and Macro-level Factors

What do we mean by micro-level and macro-level factors, or perspectives? Both are important for understanding marriage, families, and intimate relationships. At a micro-level, the focus is on the individual, and his or her social interactions. Opportunities, choices, and constraints are made or experienced by the individual, without much thought given to the social and cultural context in which that person lives. In contrast, a macro-level understanding reveals that our personal relationships are interconnected with the rest of society. Social structure influences the opportunities, choices, and constraints that we experience in all realms of life, including the intimate relationship.

Micro-level Factors

The focus is on the individual and his or her social interactions:

• Personal choices
• Behaviors
• Feelings
• Communication
• Decisions
• Constraints
• Values

Macro-level Factors

The focus is on the way our personal relationships interconnect with the rest of society, the recognition that our social structure influences our marriages and families:

• Culture
• History
• Power and inequality
• Social institutions, including the economy, political system, or dominant religion
• Social status, including sex, race, ethnicity, and social class
• Social movements and social change

What Do You Think?

1. Can you think of three ways in which our culture has shaped your personal attitudes or values about specific family or intimate relationships?
2. How would a social institution such as the dominant religion affect you personally if you do not practice that religion? For example, how would Christianity affect you if you are Jewish?

Policy and You: From Macro to Micro: *Connecting social structure to our personal lives.* This feature, supporting the text's first theme, critically examines programs or policies designed to strengthen families and focuses on how social structure creates specific needs within families, and how social policy can address those needs. Chapters include specific examples of "best practices," here in the United States and abroad, to show students what is happening, and what is *possible*. Examples include: maternity and family leave policies in the United States compared with other developed nations; the history of domestic partnerships and issues surrounding same-sex marriage; budgeting choices families living in poverty must make; and a look at family allowances, are available in over 80 countries to help families with the costs of raising children.

Policy and You: From Macro to Micro

Domestic Partner Benefits

One clear way in which societal definitions of family affect our individual relationships can be seen in our marriage laws. In most places around the country unmarried adults in long-term, committed relationships are routinely denied important benefits, such as spousal health insurance or dental care, bereavement leave, relocation benefits, or the benefit of filing joint tax returns or receiving Social Security. Unmarried adults, homosexual and heterosexual, face a number of obstacles simply because they lack the legal status of marriage. These obstacles affect the security and well-being of millions of families.

However, employers are beginning to recognize that denying benefits to partners in committed relationships may be not only unjust, but also bad for business. In 1982, the New York City weekly *The Village Voice* became the first employer to offer "domestic partner benefits." Since that time, over 9,300 employers have chosen to offer domestic partner benefits to an employee's unmarried partner, whether of the same or opposite sex. These employers include nearly 300 Fortune 500 companies, along with city, county, and state agencies.

Why do a growing number of employers offer benefits to domestic partners? One reason is simple fairness. Many employers believe that offering benefits to their employees' legally married partners, but not to nonlegal married partners, discriminates on the basis of sexual orientation and/or marital status. Because same-sex couples cannot legally marry in most states, their partners have traditionally been excluded from receiving benefits on the grounds that they are not part of an employee's legal family.

A second reason that more employers are offering domestic partner benefits has to do with the competition in today's labor market. In order to attract and retain a high-quality, diverse work force, employers need to offer a comprehensive benefit package. Offering domestic partner benefits is simply a sound business practice.

Several states have passed or are passing laws that establish domestic partnerships for committed same-sex couples. These laws provide all of the same state-granted privileges, immunities, rights, benefits, and responsibilities for same-sex couples entering a domestic partnership that are granted to married couples. Other states, under pressure from conservatives, are restricting these benefits, at least for state employees. And regardless of state policy, unmarried persons are not eligible for specific federal benefits such as filing joint tax returns and cannot receive Social Security as a spouse. This example shows that our laws and definition of what constitutes a "family" can be powerfully felt at the personal level.

Source: Employee Benefit Research Institute. February 2009; Human Rights Campaign. 2009, 2010.

What Do You Think?

1. Should an employer's domestic partner benefits cover both homosexual and heterosexual relationships? Why or why not?
2. Should we leave it to employers or to the state or federal government to decide whether to offer domestic partner benefits?

My Family: *Relating personal narratives that reveal how macro-level factors shape our micro-level experiences, choices, and constraints.* Family narratives bring the material alive for students. These boxes allow students the opportunity to see all three text themes in action: the effect of social structure on families, the diversity of family experience, and the importance of systematic research. Examples of this feature include stories of delaying marriage; living in a stepfamily; dating violence; growing up poor; and the experience of being widowed at a young age.

My Family

Not Married—Yet

The holidays are coming up and I've made my usual plans to drive down from Boston to see my family in Maryland. I haven't seen my parents, kid sisters, and grandma for about six months, so it will be great to see them all again. That is, until they start up on the "single thing."

What is it with the older generations, anyway? I'm 34, and they act like my life is nothing without a husband and kids. Last time I saw my mom she actually cried, and told me that if I don't hurry and get married, no one will be left for me. I'm too picky, she said. Another time she suggested that my eggs were "drying up" and I was sentencing myself to a life without children. My dad isn't much better, and grandma just smirks.

What they don't seem to understand is that I like being single right now. I have a great job in publishing, and enjoy the perks of a pretty good salary, a wonderful loft in a cool part of town, lots of travel, and the freedom to take some terrific vacations. Last year I went to Morocco and Egypt with a friend for three weeks. I'm not sure I could swing any of this with a husband and kids.

Of course, this doesn't mean that I never want to get married, or never want to have a baby. Okay, I admit that sometimes I'm lonely. Sometimes I do wonder if "he" is out there for me. I'm just not in any rush. I've had a few serious boyfriends. In college I even lived with my boyfriend for a couple of years, but then we split. He moved for a job and I left for graduate school, and we just realized we were going in different directions emotionally as well as geographically.

Right now I feel like I have a lot of friends, male and female, and we enjoy hanging out on weekends, you know, going out for dinner and drinks, sailing, or going to the latest gallery opening. I'm also training for a half-marathon, and have a good group of folks for my long run on Sundays.

My parents get none of this. "Hurry up, hurry up," they say. It bothers me because, sure, I want to get married, someday, just not yet.

—**Mariah, Age 34**

An increasing number of people in their 20s and 30s are single, using this opportunity to focus on their work, education, and their social life, but this does not mean that they will never marry.

What Do **You** Think?

1. What age do you think is ideal to marry? The average age for first marriage is increasing. Do you think delaying marriage is good or bad for society?
2. Is the pressure to marry and have children the same for men and women? Would Mariah have received more or less pressure if she were a man? Explain your answer.

Diversity in Families: *Showing the diversity of experience around the world, and within our own country.* This feature illustrates a variety of diverse family experiences and traditions, and emphasizes the text's second theme: families are not monolithic or static, but ever-changing. Examples include stories of social class differences in the way parents socialize their children; teaching children about racism; sex trafficking of children; patriarchy and divorce laws in Egypt; and father-headed single families.

Diversity in Families

Profile of U.S. Families

What do families look like today? Let's examine some of the key statistics from the U.S. Census Bureau, Current Population Reports, and other governmental sources that we will discuss in more detail throughout the text. First, however, be aware that government statistics have a number of limitations. For example, they use catchall categories like "Hispanic" or "Asian," but these groups are far from homogeneous. Although Cuban Americans, Mexican Americans, and Puerto Ricans share a common language, their cultures are significantly different. Nonetheless, government statistics, while imperfect, provide an important source of demographic information about our population.

Hispanics are now the largest minority group in the United States. By the year 2050, they may comprise nearly one-third of the population. How will this change American culture?

1. Both men and women are postponing marriage. Because of expanding opportunities and changing norms, women now marry at an average age of 25 years, compared to 21 years in 1970. Men now marry at an average age of 27 years, compared to 23 years in 1970.
2. Family size is shrinking. It is likely that nearly one in five women of childbearing age today will not have children, some by choice, and some because of infertility. Those who do have children are more likely to opt for just one or two.
3. The divorce rate has declined in recent decades. In the 1960s the divorce rate began to rise rapidly, peaking around 1980, but since that time it has steadily declined.
4. Single-parent households have been on the rise, particularly among men. Since 1970 there has been a 300 percent increase in single-parent households headed by mothers, and a 500 percent increase in those headed by fathers. Today, about one-quarter of White families are headed by one parent, as are over half of Black families and one-third of Hispanic families.
5. Mothers are increasingly likely to be employed outside the home. Today nearly two-thirds of mothers are employed outside the home.
6. Hispanic groups are now the largest minority in the United States at about 16 percent of the population. Because the birth rate and rate of immigration are higher among Hispanics than among other groups, their presence in the United States will continue to grow at a fast rate. By 2050, about 30 percent of all Americans will likely be of Hispanic descent.
7. The teenage birthrate has declined significantly over the past couple of decades. The birthrate among teenagers has declined by about 20 percent since 1990. This decline is occurring among all racial and ethnic groups, although it has been fluctuating in recent years.
8. Unmarried couples living together is common. The number of unmarried couples has almost doubled since 2000 to nearly 7 million today. This trend is found among all age groups, including the elderly.
9. The percentage of people living in poverty has fluctuated in conjunction with economic trends and is now on the rise. Poverty rates among families, single adults, and children were down in the 1990s; however, since then the poverty rate has risen. Today about 14 percent of Americans live in poverty, including over 20 percent of children.
10. The elderly population has been increasing almost four times as fast as the population as a whole. In 1900 only a small portion of people—one in 25—were aged 65 or older. This has certainly changed. Moreover, people who are 85 and older—referred to as the "oldest old"—constitute the most rapidly growing elderly cohort in the United States.

What Do **You** Think?

1. What other changes do you see occurring in families? Do you think these changes are for the better or for the worse? Why?
2. Do you think that any of these trends will be reversed over the next decade? If so, what will cause them to be reversed?

Why Do Research?

How to Study Families from the Past

Piecing together the history of family life has become an active topic of research. Drawing on a variety of historical documents, including diaries, letters, birth, marriage, and death registers, and immigration records, historians attempt to weave together a social history of the United States to reveal the daily lives, customs, and lifestyles of ordinary citizens. This is a radical departure from the work of most historians who focus on events such as wars, economic downturns, or other large-scale social events. Because the field of social history is relatively new, and many historical documents have been lost or are unavailable, there are significant gaps in our understanding of history, especially with regards to the dynamics of early minority families.

Historians and family scholars get creative as they piece together the past. Historical records can provide an aggregate record about immigration trends, age at first marriage, or the average length of time between marriage and first birth. Slave auctions, ledgers, and other transactions help us understand what, and who, was being bought and sold. Diaries and letters can reveal what was on the minds of ordinary people, including how they saw the world and how they expressed their views. Newspapers and magazines can reveal fads, fashions, and the mood of the era. All of

these records can provide insightful clues into the lives of ordinary people.

Finally, many scholars rely on "family reconstitution," in which attempts are made to compile all available information about significant family events and everyday life. Members of each generation who are still alive are interviewed in depth, and they are asked to reconstruct their family history. Recreating the past is not easy. Historical researchers work as "detectives" and try to obtain the greatest number of sources possible as they reconstruct the past. Sometimes numerous sources are available, but unfortunately, sometimes only a few clues remain.

What Do **You** Think?

1. Think about your own family's history. How far back does your information reliably go? Who are the oldest members of your family? Could you conduct a family reconstitution?

2. If your books, magazines, computer, or other important artifacts were saved in a time capsule, what would someone a hundred years from now learn about you? About your lifestyle? About your relationships?

Why Do Research? *Demonstrating the relevance of research.* Bolstering the text's third theme, students learn the logic behind quantitative and qualitative research. All chapters are grounded in research, and include many articles, books, and reports published in 2009 and 2010. This box offers specific theoretical or methodological insights so that students can better evaluate research findings and see the relevance to their lives. For example, students will read about the distinction between correlation and causation by using the example of successful men who were raised by single parents. Specific methodologies are highlighted, such as content analysis to see how adoption is portrayed in college textbooks or how art can be used to understand children's views of divorce. Additionally, the feature shows how research findings can challenge our stereotypes, such as whether women are really more talkative than men.

Getting to Know Yourself

How Do You Define 'Family'?

What is a family? Opinions differ. Let's see what you think. Please answer how you feel regarding each statement. There are no right or wrong answers here, just your opinions. Your answers can include:

1=Yes; 2=Unsure; 3=No

____ 1. Elian and Rosa have been living together for two years, but are not married, nor have they seriously discussed marriage. Are they a family?

____ 2. Jake and Tina have a child together, but they live in separate cities and see each other about once every month or two. Are they a family?

____ 3. Soolyn and Tran are married and have two young daughters. Are they a family?

____ 4. Jonathan and Patrick have been together for almost a year, and spend all their time together. They each have their own place to live, but Patrick has his house up for sale and as soon as it sells he will move in with Jonathan. Are they a family?

____ 5. William and Jenica have cohabited for seven years and have no children. Are they a family?

____ 6. Janie, Helen, and Rachel live with a man who legally married to only one of them, yet all 3 of the women consider themselves married to him, a practice known as polygamy. Are they a family?

____ 7. Hannah, 16, ran away from her parents' home last summer and has been living on the streets. She has since met up with a group of runaway and homeless youth. Together they beg or steal food, and some of the young people prostitute themselves to earn money for the group. They take care of one another. Are they a family?

____ 8. Corey, 8, has lived in four different foster homes since he was taken away from his drug-addicted and violent parents when he was 3. He has lived in

his current foster home for two years, and has a good relationship with the family in which he lives. His foster parents treat him just like they treat their other children. He does not know how much longer he will stay there, but hopes it is for a long time. Are they a family?

____ 9. Dee has five children fathered by five different men. She has never been married. The fathers rarely if ever pay child support and only a few come around sporadically to see her or their child. Are Dee and her childrens' fathers a family?

____ 10. Lucas and Emma are a married couple who are firmly committed to not having children. Are they a family?

Tally up your answers. The lower the score, the broader your definition of family. The higher your score, the more narrow your definition of family. Compare your answers with others. How do you compare?

What Do **You** Think?

1. What is your score? Do you have a broad or narrow definition of family, or are you somewhere in between?

2. Where do you think your views have come from? Do they reflect the values of your parents, your culture, or your peers? Which of these influences is the strongest, and why?

Getting to Know Yourself: *Employing self-tests and inventories that allow students to assess their own attitudes and compare their opinions with others.* This feature includes fun and engaging self-tests so that students can identify their own opinions, and compare themselves to others. Self-tests include both adapted classic scales, such as Bem's Sex Role Inventory or the Holmes and Rahe Life Events Stress Scale, as well as newly created self-tests, such as ones that assess attitudes toward divorce, sex differences in communication styles, and attitudes toward homosexuality. These self-tests can be taken individually, or completed in class to springboard discussion.

Bringing It Full Circle: *Revisiting and Reinforcing student learning.* Each chapter's concluding section revisits the opening narrative and *Exploring Families* video clip, and prompts students to think critically about it in the context of what they have learned in the chapter. For example, the opening story in Chapter 12, The Process of Divorce, presents a child's view of her parents' divorce. In the *Bringing it Full Circle* feature we return to this case, and pose several questions that draw upon the chapter content.

Bringing It Full Circle

Divorce is common in American society, although the divorce rate has declined significantly over the past several decades. The fluctuating divorce rate has many macrolevel and micro-level explanations, which are interrelated because macro-level factors shape our personal experiences and choices. As we saw in the opening vignette, conflict and divorce affect many relationships within the family, and families must sort through the emotional, legal, economic, co-parental, community, and psychic dimensions of separation and divorce. Children like Melanie are particularly affected by conflict and divorce, and they are more likely than other children to experience social and emotional challenges. Programs like mediation can offer a helping hand as couples move through the process of divorce. But, as we will see in the next chapter, sometimes divorce does not just end a relationship. With high rates of remarriage, it can also mean the beginning of a new family unit. Let's return a moment to Melanie's experience with her parents' divorce in the opening vignette. With the information you have learned in this chapter, consider the following questions:

- How would you describe Melanie's experiences with the different stations of her parent's divorce: emotional, legal, economic, co-parental, community, and psychic?
- Since the research shows that children do better if they remain in close contact with their noncustodial parents, should children like Melanie be required to stay with their fathers even if they don't really want to?
- Do you think that Melanie's family had a "good divorce"? Explain your answer.
- If you or someone close to you divorced, how would you explain it to your child? Would you focus only on micro-level issues, or would any macro-level issues be relevant?

Chapter Review: *Engaging and detailed question-and-answer format.* Each chapter concludes with a series of answers that summarize the important concepts introduced in the *Questions that Matter* learning objectives in the opening of the chapter. The Chapter Review also contains a list of key terms with corresponding page references, and instructions on additional assets and videos students can access on **www.myfamilylab.com**.

Video Discussion Guide: *Promoting further thought about the* **Exploring Families** *video clips.* At the end of the text, the Video Discussion Guide contains additional questions for each video in the *Exploring Families* video series, which can be used as assignments or for classroom discussion. Written by the author, these questions help students connect what they have seen in the videos with main themes and topics in the chapters. The *Exploring Families* videos can be accessed through MyFamilyLab (**www.myfamilylab.com**).

:: Supplements

Instructor's Manual and Test Bank (ISBN 0-205-01749-5): Each chapter in the Instructor's Manual includes the following resources: Chapter Summary, Chapter Outline, Learning Objectives, Critical Thinking Questions, Activities for Classroom Participation, Key Terms, and a Video User's Guide. A grid opens each chapter that correlates the detailed chapter outline to its corresponding video. Designed to make your lectures more effective and to save preparation time, this extensive resource gathers together useful activities and strategies for teaching your Marriage and Family course.

The Test Bank, written by Karen Seccombe, contains over 1400 questions. Each question is organized by its corresponding Learning Objective and classified according to Bloom's Taxonomy. An additional feature, currently not found in any other Marriage and Family test bank, is the inclusion of rationales for the correct answer in the multiple-choice questions. The rationales help instructors reviewing the content to further evaluate the questions they are choosing for their tests and give instructors the option to use the rationales as an answer key for their students.

This first edition Test Bank has been thoroughly developed in response to market feedback. It has also been analyzed by a developmental editor and a copy editor in order to ensure clarity, accuracy, and delivery of the highest quality assessment tool.

MyTest (ISBN 0-205-84245-3): This computerized software allows instructors to create their own personalized exams, to edit any or all of the existing test questions, and to add new questions. Other special features of this program include random generation of test questions, creation of alternate versions of the same test, scrambling question sequence, and test preview before printing. For easy access, this software is available within the instructor section of the MyFamilyLab for *Exploring Marriages and Families* by Seccombe, or at **www.pearsonhighered.com**.

PowerPoint Presentations (ISBN 0-205-84246-1): The PowerPoint presentations for Exploring Marriages and Families are informed by instructional and design theory. You have the option in every chapter of choosing from any of the following types of slides: Lecture & Line Art, Clicker Response System, and/or Special Topics PowerPoints. The Lecture PowerPoint slides follow the chapter outline and integrate images from the textbook. The Clicker Response System allows you to obtain immediate feedback from your students regardless of class size. The Special Topics PowerPoint slides allow you to integrate rich supplementary material into your course with minimal preparation time. Additionally, all of the PowerPoints are uniquely designed to present concepts in a clear and succinct manner that allow you to customize them with your own clip art or color ideas. They are available to adopters at **www.pearsonhighered.com**.

MyFamilyLab (ISBN with eText: 0-205-18359-X): MyFamilyLab is a state-of-the-art interactive and instructive solution for the Marriages and Families course, designed to be used as a supplement to a traditional lecture course, or to completely administer an online course. MyFamilyLab provides access to a wealth of resources all geared to meet the individual teaching and learning needs of every instructor and every student. We believe in learning - all kinds of learning for all kinds of people, delivered in a personal style. Because wherever learning flourishes, so do people.

Combining an eText, streaming audio-files of the chapters, video and audio-based activities, interactive flash cards, practice tests and exams, research support, and a guide for improving writing skills, and more, MyFamilyLab engages students by giving them the opportunity to explore important concepts in the study of the family, and to enhance their performance in this course.

Exploring Families video clips are found in MyFamilyLab. Each video is accompanied by a short quiz. Three other exciting new features in MyFamilyLab are Social Explorer, MySocLibrary, and Core Concepts Videos. Social Explorer provides easy access to U.S. Census data from 1790 to the present, and allows for exploration of Census data visually through interactive data maps. MySocLibrary includes over 200 classic and contemporary readings, all with assessments, and linked to the specific text in use. Core Concepts videos feature sociologists in action, exploring important concepts in the study of Marriage and the Family.

MyFamilyLab is available at no additional cost to the student when an access code card is packaged with a new text. It can also be purchased separately. Visit **www.myfamilylab.com** for more information.

ClassPrep makes lecture preparation simpler and less time-consuming. It collects the very best class presentation resources--art and figures from our leading texts, videos, lecture activities, classroom activities, demonstrations, and much more--in one convenient online destination. You may search through ClassPrep's extensive database of tools by content topic (arranged by standard topics within the sociology curriculum) or by content type (video, audio, simulation, Word documents, etc). You can select resources appropriate for your lecture, many of which can be downloaded directly. Or you may build your own folder of resources and present from within ClassPrep.

:: Acknowledgments

This book has been a long journey, and, fortunately for me, I have had support every step of the way. Thank you to everyone who helped to make this dream a reality. First and foremost, there is my family, husband Richard and daughters Natalie (age 10), and Olivia (age 8), who provided zany distractions and steadfast love that both drove me nuts and kept me grounded. While many authors write of the sacrifices their families made, I think writing this book actually enhanced our lives. What a great way to combine theory, research, and practical experience. For example, I know Richard really appreciated all that I learned in writing the chapter on communication!

I also want to thank my friends and academic colleagues who provided their ideas, listened to mine, and challenged me to do my best work. In particular, Becky Warner provided invaluable help and camaraderie on an earlier manuscript prior to her becoming Vice Provost at Oregon State University. Karen Pyke, with her keen insights and generous heart, always invigorates me intellectually and kept me moving forward. Mentors Gary Lee, Kathy Kaiser, and Manley Johnson sparked my intellectual curiosity about families.

Then, of course, there are many friends who, at first blush, had nothing to do with this book but helped me more than they will ever know. Natalie Birk took charge in the summer of 2009 and led me towards calm, and I will be forever grateful to her. I also thank Cordie Tilghman and Ali Cook, who took me to movies, discussed *other* books at our book club, or shared glasses of wine in cool Portland venues when I needed a break. I am genuinely grateful to the entire Oregon Episcopal School community for providing Natalie, Liv, and our whole family with a safe harbor.

Many reviewers took time from their busy schedules to read earlier drafts of this manuscript, and provided important feedback. I want to thank the following reviewers for their suggestions:

Margaret Bader, Nunez Community College
Chuck Baker, Delaware County Community College
Cheryl Boudreaux, Grand Valley State University
Wanda Clark, South Plains College
Mark Dickerson, Panola College
Jessica Eckstein, Western Connecticut State University
Stephen Glennon, Iowa Eastern Community College
Scott Hall, Ball State University
Soohyun Kim, Idaho State University
Claire Kimberly, University of Kentucky
Nicole Loftus, Saddleback College
Timothy Loving, The University of Texas
Brian Masciadrelli, SUNY Fredonia
Patricia Missad, Grand Rapids Community College
Aurea Osgood, Winona State University
Romana Pires, San Bernadino Valley College
Margaret Preble, Thomas Nelson Community College
Kami Schwerdtfeger, Okahoma State University
Joanne Sommers, Bowling Green State University
Elissa Thormann Mitchell, University of Illinois at Urbana-Champaign
Sterling Wall, University of Wisconsin – Stevens Point
Erica Yeager, West Virginia University

I'd also like to thank the families and couples featured in the *Exploring Families* video series for graciously sharing their stories with us:

Becca, Taylor, Meghan, Jono, Rati, Subas, Kayla, Chris, Scherazade, Roderick, Tracey, Juan, Cassandra, John, Karen, Betsy, Jayla, Henry, Fred, Lisa, Chris, Christopher, Shannon, Melanie, Jane, Daneen, Jim, Connor, Kate, Lindsay, Jamie, Amy, Sophie, Alain, Hugo, and Noe.

Special thanks to those who sent in a family photo to be considered for the inside front and back covers. I loved the family stories they represent! Specifically, thank you to:

Diona Brown, Flor Cerda, Stephanie Freas, David Glen, Amie Goff Harris, David Hartman, Michele Hertel, Kelsey Love, Simone Rico, April Vincent, Keli Wherritt, and Melissa Young.

I also appreciate the tremendous help I received from my friends at Allyn & Bacon who took my words and actually turned them into a beautiful book. A round of applause goes to Karen Hanson (Publisher), Deb Hanlon (Development Editor), Roberta Sherman, Claudine Bellanton, and Karen Mason (Production Editors), Mayda Bosco (Associate Editor) and Christine Dore (Editorial Assistant).

Now, to the readers—faculty and students alike—if you have questions or comments, please send them my way. I want to hear from you: seccombek@pdx.edu.

All my best,

Karen Seccombe

About the Author

Karen Seccombe is a professor in the School of Community Health at Portland State University, located in Portland, Oregon. She received her B.A. in sociology at California State University, Chico, her M.S.W. in health and social welfare policy from the University of Washington, and her Ph.D. in sociology from Washington State University. Her research focuses on poverty, welfare, access to health care, and the effects of social inequality on families. She is the author of *"So You Think I Drive A Cadillac?": Welfare Recipients' Perspectives on the System and its Reform*, 3rd edition (Allyn & Bacon); *Families and Their Social Worlds*, 2nd edition (Allyn & Bacon); *Just Don't Get Sick: Access to Healthcare in the Aftermath of Welfare Reform*, with Kim A. Hoffman (Rutgers University Press); *Families in Poverty* (Allyn & Bacon); and *Marriages and Families: Relationships in Social Context* with Rebecca Warner (Wadsworth). She is a fellow in the National Council on Family Relations, and a member of the American Sociological Association and the Pacific Sociological Association, where she has held elective offices. Karen lives in Portland, Oregon with her husband Richard, a health economist, her ten-year-old daughter, Natalie Rose, and her eight-year-old daughter, Olivia Lin. In her spare time she enjoys hiking with her family near their cabin in the Oregon Cascades, kayaking and cycling in the San Juan Islands, and exploring the kid-friendly attractions in Portland, of which there are many.

1

Why Study Families and Other Close Relationships?

CHAPTER OUTLINE

Top: Karen and Betsy with their children, Jayla and Henry. Center: Meghan and Jono. Bottom: Tracey and Juan with their adopted children, John and Cassandra.

What is a family? This seems a fairly simple question, but it can have a surprisingly complex answer.

Throughout this text you will meet people in different types of relationships: married couples, cohabiting couples, same-sex couples, and stepfamilies, to name just a few. Let's introduce a few of these families to you now.

Becca is a 31-year-old single mother of seven-year-old Taylor. Raised in poverty, homeless as a young adult, she has struggled successfully to overcome the odds against her. She is no longer homeless, has completed her degree in community college, and is a loving mother to her daughter, Taylor. Becca has no relationship with her mother and other relatives. Unfortunately, Becca had to give up a son for adoption before she had Taylor. Today, Becca and Taylor have a good relationship with him and his adoptive family. Are Becca and her mother "family"? Are Taylor and her half-brother "family"?

Melanie, a young woman in her twenties was devastated by her parents' divorce when she was ten years old. Like other children whose parents divorced, she harbored dreams that they would one day get back together, even though both parents remarried other people. She had little use for her stepparents at the time, but finally realized that her parents would never remarry when her father and his wife had a baby together. Are Melanie and her stepparents family? Are her half-brother and her mother family?

Meghan and Jonathon—"Jono" as he is called, are a young couple happily in love. They have lived together for a couple of years, and both think they will probably get married some day, even though there has been no explicit discussion of marriage.

Are Betsy and Karen a family?

Watch the **Video** *What is a Family?* on **myfamilylab.com**

They believe it is important for her to finish her education first, and begin her career. Are Meghan and Jono a family?

Tracey and Juan, unable to have biological children, have adopted two beautiful children from Colombia. Juan was born in Colombia, and still has family residing there, so it seemed a natural place to pursue adoption. Tracey and Juan have some information on the birth mother of their son John, and know virtually nothing about the birth mother of their daughter Cassandra. The adoptions are closed—there will be no contact with either birth mother. So, are John and Cassandra's birth mothers part of the family?

Karen and Betsy have been together for thirteen years. They talked early on about wanting to raise children together. Today they have two children: Henry, eight, and Jayla, three. Karen gave birth to Henry, and although Henry's father does not live close by, he still plays a role in his life. Jayla was adopted and came to them just before her first birthday. Are Karen and Betsy a family? Are Betsy and Henry a family? Are Henry's father and Jayla a family?

Becca, Melanie, Meghan, Jono, Tracey, Juan, Karen, and Betsy represent some of today's families. The number of "traditional" two-parent heterosexual families has declined, while the number of nontraditional families is on the rise. Together we will examine these trends, look at their causes, and discuss their implications.

QUESTIONS *That Matter* •

1.1 How does this text define "family" and how does it differ from a legal perspective?

1.2 Why is the definition of "family" so important?

1.3 What are the functions that families provide?

1.4 What is the difference between a micro-level and a macro-level perspective for the study of families?

1.5 What is social structure and why is it important?

1.6 What types of marriage and kinship patterns exist around the world?

1.7 How would we characterize the changes in China's families and family policy in recent generations?

1.8 How have families changed throughout history, and what are the macro-level factors that have contributed to that change?

1.9 How does social science research help us understand families?

1.10 What methods do family scholars use to study families?

1.11 How can theory help us understand families and family research?

1.12 Are Americans rejecting marriage and families?

What is a family? Who would guess that such a commonly used word could generate disagreement? We all probably come from some kind of family. Students of all ages crave information about families, including love, sex, relationships, marriage, and children. Unfortunately, most students have a very individualized view of these issues. They tend to emphasize personal choices without focusing on the broader social, cultural, and historical conditions that shape these choices. This chapter will show you how our personal experiences are shaped by the social structure in which we live.

:: How Do We Define *Family?*

Welcome to the study of families! This text will take you on a journey of personal self-discovery and greater social awareness. We will learn about love and dating, cohabitation and marriage, parenting, aging families, divorce and remarriage, families and work, and family crises. Like all journeys, families encounter bumps along the road: miscommunication, jealousy, economic problems, discrimination, violence, and other stressors. However, we will also encounter sources of strength that help families cope with these stressors: education, legislation to help families, and cultural change that has led to greater acceptance of diversity in family life.

Today we are surrounded by childfree married couples, multigenerational families, unmarried adults who cohabit and sometimes have children, stepparents whose stepchildren reside with them only part-time, and gay and lesbian partnerships. These types of living arrangements are increasing, while the more traditional type of family—husband, wife, and children all living together—is on the decline (U.S. Census Bureau, January 14, 2010).

With such a variety of relationships, how can we define *family*? Some people believe that a couple must be legally married to be considered a family. Others think that children must be present—certainly you have heard people ask, "So, when are you going to start a family?" They mean, of course, when are you going to have children? And still others believe that gay and lesbian partners do not really qualify as a family regardless of their level of commitment to one another.

Legal versus Social Science Definitions

How would *you* define "family"? With all these different possibilities, it is important to stop and reflect on your own views for a moment. The feature box *Getting to Know Yourself: How Do You Define "Family"?* gives you the opportunity to think about your definition and then, perhaps you can compare it to the way other people think.

The U.S. Census Bureau defines a family as two or more people living together who are related by birth, marriage, or adoption. Heterosexual or homosexual unmarried partners are excluded from this definition. The U.S. government continues to use this traditional definition as the basis for many social programs and policies. However, many people object to the Census Bureau's definition because it excludes groups who *consider* themselves to be families. They suggest that government should expand its definition of *family* because it does not adequately reflect the reality of the rich diversity of family life in our society today (Allen, 2004; Boss, Doherty, LaRossa, Schumm, & Steinmetz, 2008; Lloyd, Few, & Allen, 2009; Scanzoni, 2004; Trask & Hamon, 2007). If people *feel* that they are a family, these feelings should not be ignored because of rigid definitions.

The leading scholarly journal about families, published by the National Council on Family Relations, changed its name from *The Journal of Marriage and the Family* to *The Journal of Marriage and Family* (deleting the word *the*), reflecting the growing recognition that families come in many forms. This text will also opt for a broader, more inclusive definition, proposing that a **family** is a relationship by blood, marriage, or affection, in which members may cooperate economically, may care for children, and may consider their identity to be intimately connected to the larger group. It can include a **family of orientation**, which is the family that you are born into, and a **family of procreation**, which is the family you make through marriage, partnering, and/or parenthood.

family: A relationship by blood, marriage, or affection, in which members may cooperate economically, may care for children, and may consider their identity to be intimately connected to the larger group.

family of orientation: The family that you are born into.

family of procreation: The family you make through marriage, partnering, and/or parenthood.

Getting to Know Yourself

How Do You Define "Family"?

What is a family? Opinions differ. Let's see what you think. Please answer how you feel regarding each statement. There are no right or wrong answers here, just your opinions. Your answers can include:

1 = Yes; 2 = Unsure; 3 = No

__3__ **1.** Elian and Rosa have been living together for two years, but are not married, nor have they seriously discussed marriage. Are they a family?

__1__ **2.** Jake and Tina have a child together, but they live in separate cities and see each other about once every month or two. Are they a family?

__1__ **3.** Soolyn and Tran are married and have two young daughters. Are they a family?

__3__ **4.** Jonathan and Patrick have been together for almost a year, and spend all their time together. They each have their own place to live, but Patrick has his house up for sale and as soon as it sells he will move in with Jonathan. Are they a family?

__3__ **5.** William and Jenica have cohabited for seven years and have no children. Are they a family?

__3__ **6.** Janie, Helen, and Rachel live with a man who is legally married to only one of them, yet all 3 of the women consider themselves married to him, a practice known as polygamy. Are they a family?

__3__ **7.** Hannah, 16, ran away from her parents' home last summer and has been living on the streets. She has since met up with a group of runaway and home-less youth. Together they beg or steal food, and some of the young people prostitute themselves to earn money for the group. They take care of one another. Are they a family?

__1__ **8.** Corey, 8, has lived in four different foster homes since he was taken away from his drug-addicted and violent parents when he was 3. He has lived in his current foster home for two years, and has a good relationship with the family in which he lives. His foster parents treat him just like they treat their other children. He does not know how much longer he will stay there, but hopes it is for a long time. Are they a family?

__3__ **9.** Dee has five children fathered by five different men. She has never been married. The fathers rarely if ever pay child support and only a few come around sporadically to see her or their child. Are Dee and her childrens' fathers a family?

__1__ **10.** Lucas and Emma are a married couple who are firmly committed to not having children. Are they a family?

Tally up your answers. The lower the score, the broader your definition of family. The higher your score, the more narrow your definition of family. Compare your answers with others. How do you compare?   *22 of 30*

What Do You Think?

1. What is your score? Do you have a broad or narrow definition of family, or are you somewhere in between?

2. Where do you think your views have come from? Do they reflect the values of your parents, your culture, or your peers? Which of these influences is the strongest, and why?

This text includes **fictive kin** in its definition of family. Fictive kin are nonrelatives whose bonds are strong and intimate, such as the relationships shared among unmarried homosexual or heterosexual partners, or very close friends. Fictive kin can provide important services and care for individuals, including financial assistance or help through life transitions such as the birth of a child or a divorce (Muraco, 2006). Nonetheless, fictive kin are routinely passed over for critical benefits that more traditional family members have come to expect, such as health insurance or tax advantages.

fictive kin: Nonrelatives whose bonds are strong and intimate.

There are many different kinds of families, including traditional married couples, same-sex couples, and even fictive kin.

Why Are Definitions so Important?

What is this concern with definitions? How our society defines a family has important consequences with respect to rights, including access to a spouse's or partner's Social Security benefits, pensions, and health insurance (Employee Benefit Research Institute, 2009; Human Rights Campaign, 2010). For example, unmarried partners cannot file jointly on federal taxes. And many employer health insurance plans cover only a worker's spouse and dependent children. Unmarried partners may be excluded from coverage. Therefore, if an unmarried couple has children, the children may be covered under their employed parent's health insurance plan, but the partner may be excluded. These decisions involve billions of dollars in employer and government benefits and affect millions of adults and children each year, as shown in the feature box *Policy and You: From Macro to Micro*. In addition, special membership discounts to a wide variety of organizations are available to families, but not to people who are roommates or friends.

:: The Functions of Families

Why do people marry? Why do we live in families? While some of the functions of marriage and families might differ from one society to another, what is more remarkable is how *similar* these are across time and place. All societies have **marriage**, an institutional arrangement between persons to publicly recognize social and intimate bonds. There are clear norms that specify who is eligible to be married, to whom and how many people an individual can marry, what the marriage ceremony should be like, and how married persons should behave. Anthropologist William Stephens provided a broad definition of marriage: (1) it is a socially legitimate sexual union, (2) begun with a public announcement, (3) undertaken with some idea of permanence, and (4) assumed with a more or less explicit marriage contract that,

marriage: An institutional arrangement between persons to publicly recognize social and intimate bonds.

Policy and You: From Macro to Micro

Domestic Partner Benefits

One clear way in which societal definitions of family affect our individual relationships can be seen in our marriage laws. In most places around the country unmarried adults in long-term, committed relationships are routinely denied important benefits, such as spousal health insurance or dental care, bereavement leave, relocation benefits, or the benefit of filing joint tax returns or receiving Social Security. Unmarried adults, homosexual and heterosexual, face a number of obstacles simply because they lack the legal status of marriage. These obstacles affect the security and well-being of millions of families.

However, employers are beginning to recognize that denying benefits to partners in committed relationships may be not only unjust, but also bad for business. In 1982, the New York City weekly *The Village Voice* became the first employer to offer "domestic partner benefits." Since that time, over 9,300 employers have chosen to offer domestic partner benefits to an employee's unmarried partner, whether of the same or opposite sex. These employers include nearly 300 Fortune 500 companies, along with city, county, and state agencies.

Why do a growing number of employers offer benefits to domestic partners? One reason is simple fairness. Many employers believe that offering benefits to their employees' legally married partners, but not to nonlegal married partners, discriminates on the basis of sexual orientation and/or marital status. Because same-sex couples cannot legally marry in most states, their partners have traditionally been excluded from receiving benefits on the grounds that they are not part of an employee's legal family.

A second reason that more employers are offering domestic partner benefits has to do with the competition in today's labor market. In order to attract and retain a high-quality, diverse work force, employers need to offer a comprehensive benefit package. Offering domestic partner benefits is simply a sound business practice.

Several states have passed or are passing laws that establish domestic partnerships for committed same-sex couples. These laws provide all of the same state-granted privileges, immunities, rights, benefits, and responsibilities for same-sex couples entering a domestic partnership that are granted to married couples. Other states, under pressure from conservatives, are restricting these benefits, at least for state employees. And regardless of state policy, unmarried persons are not eligible for specific federal benefits such as filing joint tax returns and cannot receive Social Security as a spouse. This example shows that our laws and definition of what constitutes a "family" can be powerfully felt at the personal level.

Source: Employee Benefit Research Institute. February 2009; Human Rights Campaign. 2009, 2010.

What Do You Think?

1. Should an employer's domestic partner benefits cover both homosexual and heterosexual relationships? Why or why not?
2. Should we leave it to employers or to the state or federal government to decide whether to offer domestic partner benefits?

---

spells out reciprocal obligations between spouses, and between spouses and their children (Stephens, 1963). Marriages and families in all cultures include such functions as:

- *Regulation of Sexual Behavior:* Every culture, including your own, regulates sexual behavior, including who can have a sexual relationship with whom, and under what circumstances they can do so. One virtually universal regulation is the *incest taboo* that forbids sexual activity (and marriage) among close family members. The definition of who qualifies as a "close family member" differs, but includes at least parents and their children, and siblings. The incest taboo reduces the chance of inherited genetic abnormalities, and it also forges broader alliances by requiring marriage outside of the inner family circle.

- *Reproducing and Socializing Children:* Each society must produce new members and ensure **socialization**, teaching children the rules, expectations, and culture of the society in which they live. Societies generally prefer that reproduction be done within the confines of an established family, rather than randomly among unrelated partners so that birth parents will be responsible for socializing children.

In thinking about your family of orientation, how did your own family fulfill these functions? For example, how did your family socialize you and teach you about the culture in which you live? How did your family care for, love, and nurture you? What type of identity and social position did your family give you?

socialization: The process by which people learn the rules, expectations, and culture of the society.

- *Property and Inheritance:* For much of human history, when people were nomadic hunters and gatherers, families owned little or nothing of their own; therefore, there was nothing to pass down or to inherit. However, with the invention of agriculture it was possible for people to own property, or to obtain a surplus beyond what they needed for survival. Thus, it became important to identify heirs. Monogamy ensured that men would know who were their heirs; without monogamy, paternity was uncertain (Engels, 1902, original 1884).

- *Economic Cooperation:* A family is the group that is responsible for providing its members with food, shelter, clothing, and other basic necessities. Family members cooperate with one another to provide these necessities. Often there is a gendered division of labor, although what constitutes "male tasks" and what constitutes "female tasks" varies from one society to the next.

- *Social Placement, Status, and Roles:* Families provide their members with an identity and social position in society. Members find their place in the complex web of *statuses* (the social positions that people occupy in a group or in a society) and *roles* (the behaviors associated with those positions). For example, families give us our initial social class position, provide us with a religious affiliation, and give us a racial and ethnic identity. ◉—Watch on **myfamilylab.com**

- *Care, Warmth, Protection, and Intimacy:* Humans need far more than food, shelter, and clothing to survive. Families are intended to provide the emotional care needed to survive and thrive. Although romantic love might not be a basis for marriage in many societies, spouses are expected to care for and protect one another, and to love and nurture their children.

Most of us have lived in some sort of family, so we naturally think of ourselves as "experts" on the topic. Yet our personal experiences are part of a larger picture. While all of us experience family life as individuals, we cannot fully understand this experience without an appreciation of the environment in which it takes place. The remainder of this chapter will focus on introducing the three key themes that will be the focus of this text.

◉—Watch the **Video**
Core Concepts: Social Interaction and Social Roles on
myfamilylab.com

Families have many functions in society. One of the universal functions of families is to care for and nurture the children.

:: Theme 1: Linking the Micro-level and Macro-level Perspectives on Families

First, *the best way to truly understand families is to link two perspectives: the micro-level and macro-level perspectives.* While we may initially think of our relationships solely in personal terms, they are shaped in large part by the **social structure** found in our society. Social structure refers to the patterns of social organization that guide our interactions with others. Let's discuss this topic further.

We live in a society with hundreds of millions of other people, most of whom also have families. Most of the time, we tend to focus on the uniqueness of our own relationships: "I love him because. . . ." "We get along so well because. . . ." "I chose to marry her because. . . ." "We decided not to have children because. . . ." Many people focus primarily upon this **micro-level** perspective, concentrating exclusively on individuals' interactions in specific settings. People who use this perspective focus on individual uniqueness, personal decision making, and the interactions between small groups of people in specific situations. For example, if you were taking a micro-level perspective on family problems, you might conclude that divorce would be reduced by teaching couples better communication skills, that violence can be controlled by learning to manage anger more effectively, or stressed families balancing the demands of work and family must find a way to improve time management

social structure: A stable framework of social relationships that guides our interactions with others.

micro-level: Focus on the individual and his or her interactions in specific settings.

skills. In other words, a micro-level perspective emphasizes the importance of relationship dynamics, including personal choices or constraints, but does not place those family dynamics into their social context.

Although each relationship is certainly unique, families also behave in remarkably predictable ways. For example, if your female cousin told you that she is getting married next year, could you guess the color of her wedding dress? Of course, her dress could be any color of the rainbow, or even black with pink stripes! However, you would probably guess that her dress will be white.

Our relationships are fairly predictable because they operate within the larger social structure. One important theme you will find throughout this text is *that elements of social structures shape our daily experiences, privileges, and constraints.* The personal choices that we make, such as who we marry, whether we decide to have children and, if so, how many, how we divide household labor, what type of job we get, or the childcare we arrange are all affected by the structure of our society.

A **macro-level** perspective examines the ways in which marriage, families, and intimate relationships are interconnected with the rest of society and with other social institutions. Families are not isolated entities. Realizing how social, cultural, economic, and political forces influence families helps us to understand why we make the supposedly "personal" choices that we do. Dating, marriage, divorce, domestic violence, work-family stress, and teen pregnancy are social processes that are rooted in our social structure. To understand these processes, we need to examine the organization of that social structure.

Chances are that these sisters do not spend a lot of time thinking about the macro-level factors that brought them together and continue to shape their relationship. They are too busy having fun with one another.

Family as a Social Institution

Because families and close relationships fulfill many of our personal needs, it is easy to forget that families are also a **social institution**: a major sphere of social life, with a set of beliefs and rules organized to meet basic human needs. Therefore, in addition to discussing *your* specific family, throughout this text we will discuss the social context of families. Families are a social institution in much the same way that political, economic, religious, healthcare, and educational systems are social institutions. In early human civilizations, the family was the center of most activities. Within families, people learned and practiced religion, educated their young, and took care of the sick. Over time other institutions took on many of these family functions. Today people worship in churches, educate children in schools, and go to hospitals when they are sick.

People still want to marry, despite a high divorce rate in the United States. Most individuals agree on some fundamental expectations between a husband and a wife such as marital fidelity. For example, a 2009 Gallup Poll, based on a large representative sample of adults, found that 92 percent of Americans believe that it is morally wrong for married men or women to have an affair (Newport, 2009).

Like other social institutions, families cannot be understood without examining how they influence and are influenced by social institutions. Religious customs, the type of economy, the structure of education, and the political system all shape family patterns, as do our attitudes, behaviors, and opportunities. For example, until recently in Afghanistan, the Taliban did not allow girls to go to school or women to work outside the home. Women had virtually no power inside or outside the family (Oxfam International, 2006; Revolutionary Association of the Women of Afghanistan, 2009).

Social Status and Families

In addition to social institutions, another aspect of social structure is **status**, which is the social position(s) that we occupy. You hold many statuses; you may be a daughter or son, a student, an employee, a friend, a roommate, or a parent, to name just a few. A **master status** is a status that tends to dominate the others. Most of us hold several master statuses, each with a set of privileges or constraints. Sex, race, ethnicity, and social class represent some of the major organizing constructs in our society, as we shall see in Chapter 2.

macro-level: Focus on the interconnectedness of marriage, families, and intimate relationships with the rest of society.

social institution: A major sphere of social life, with a set of beliefs and rules that is organized to meet basic human needs.

status: The social position that a person occupies.

master status: The major defining status or statuses that a person occupies.

Tying It All Together

The Interrelationship of Micro-level and Macro-level Factors

What do we mean by micro-level and macro-level factors, or perspectives? Both are important for understanding marriage, families, and intimate relationships. At a micro-level, the focus is on the individual, and his or her social interactions. Opportunities, choices, and constraints are made or experienced by the individual, without much thought given to the social and cultural context in which that person lives. In contrast, a macro-level understanding reveals that our personal relationships are interconnected with the rest of society. Social structure influences the opportunities, choices, and constraints that we experience in all realms of life, including the intimate relationship.

Micro-level Factors

The focus is on the individual and his or her social interactions:

- Personal choices
- Behaviors
- Feelings
- Communication
- Decisions
- Constraints
- Values

Macro-level Factors

The focus is on the way our personal relationships interconnect with the rest of society, the recognition that our social structure influences our marriages and families:

- Culture
- History
- Power and inequality
- Social institutions, including the economy, political system, or dominant religion
- Social status, including sex, race, ethnicity, and social class
- Social movements and social change

What Do You Think?

1. Can you think of three ways in which our culture has shaped your personal attitudes or values about specific family or intimate relationships?
2. How would a social institution such as the dominant religion affect you personally if you do not practice that religion? For example, how would Christianity affect you if you are Jewish?

For example, when the Gallup Poll surveyed adults about how satisfied they are with their lives, two-thirds of Whites claimed to be "very satisfied" with their lives, as compared to only 41 percent of Blacks and 53 percent of Hispanics (Gallup News Service, 2007). Why do you think that there is such a large racial and ethnic difference in something as fundamental as happiness? Are Blacks and Hispanics just negative by nature, or could there be some structural reasons for their unhappiness, such as racial discrimination?

How do micro-level and macro-level perspectives together shed light on families? The feature box *Tying It All Together* shows the interrelationship between these two perspectives. Next, you will read about one detailed example of how macro-level issues can influence our personal choices—unemployment and marriage rates—and throughout this text you will see many more ways that the micro-level and macro-level issues are linked.

An Example of the Interrelationship of Macro-level and Micro-level Perspectives: Unemployment and Marriage Rates

Many people are concerned about the number of single-parent households headed by women. People often wonder why these women keep having children outside of the institution of marriage. Terry Lynn is one of these women, and upon closer scrutiny you can see that her life choices are grounded in a social context.

Terry Lynn is a single mother who has never married and is raising a six-year-old daughter alone, with the temporary help of cash welfare assistance (Seccombe, 2011). She is a shy young woman, yet at the same time she is eager to tell her story. Terry Lynn works part-time at a bowling alley, a good job considering her weak reading and writing skills. She takes the bus to work, and various shifts sometimes keep her at work well into the night. She is savvy about the additional help she needs to support her child, and therefore must deliberately keep her employment hours below a certain threshold so that she and her daughter will continue to qualify for Medicaid, the government-sponsored health insurance program. Her employer does not offer health insurance, and even at the age of 24, Terry Lynn knows that providing coverage for her daughter is vital. She and her daughter live with a sister in a cramped, rundown two-bedroom apartment in an unfashionable part of town. The furniture is secondhand, and the couch is threadbare. Nonetheless, Terry Lynn is proud of herself and her daughter for "making it" on their own. You may wonder where the child's father is. He comes around now and then, she says, usually when he wants money or sex from her. Does Terry Lynn ever plan to marry him? Her answer is a definite "no".

Single-parent households have been blamed extensively for a wide variety of social ills. They are far more likely than other families to be poor (DeNavas-Walt, Proctor, & Smith, 2010). Why are so many women, especially poor and low-income women like Terry Lynn, having children without marrying their children's fathers?

We might initially be tempted to look at micro-level factors and ask what is happening within intimate relationships, specifically the personal aspects of these relationships, including the couples' values, choices, and communication. Certainly these are important. But many people have found that poor women seem to value marriage quite highly. In fact, if anything, perhaps they value it *too highly*. They believe that their own relationships will never meet the "gold standard" that they have set for themselves such as a partner with a steady job, the chance to own their own home, and a reasonably lavish wedding ceremony, and because of this they shy away from marriage (Edin & Kefalas, 2005; Seccombe, 2011).

Therefore, we must look at macro-level factors for an explanation as to why poor women are often hesitant to marry their partners. William Julius Wilson has suggested that the high unemployment rate of inner-city urban dwellers contributes to their low marriage rate. In his well-known books, *The Truly Disadvantaged* (1987) and *When Work Disappears* (1996), Wilson pointed out that many poor women see marriage to inner-city men as risky because the men cannot support families on their meager wages (Wilson, 1987; 1996). Furthermore, as factories and businesses move out to the suburbs or overseas, unemployment and poverty rates escalate. Consequently, there is a shortage of employed men whom these women see as good marriage prospects. Wilson shows us that our changing economy (macro-level factor) has a significant effect on individual relationship choices (micro-level factor). In addition to high unemployment, or perhaps interrelated with it, are many other reasons why poor women may have difficulty in finding a suitable mate. For example, homicide, violence, drug addiction, and incarceration have all taken a tremendous toll on young black men. In Terry Lynn's case, the father of her child was unemployed and has been in and out of jail, so she did not see him as a reliable "good catch." Although she cared for him, why would she want to marry him?

These concerns are found among many poor women, regardless of race or ethnic background (Edin & Kefalas, 2005; Seccombe, 2011). Clearly, the "choices" that people make in their personal relationships occur in conjunction with other larger developments in society. These may include economic conditions, crime rates, immigration policies, technological advances, changes in women's opportunities, new conceptions of fatherhood, and a wide variety of social and political movements.

Although macro-level forces that may seem outside of our immediate control shape our personal micro-level interactions, we are not passive recipients of these forces. **Human agency** is the ability of human beings to create viable lives, even when they are constrained or limited by social forces (Baca Zinn, Eitzen, & Wells, 2008). Rich, poor, male, female, young, or old—we are

human agency: The ability of human beings to create viable lives even when they are constrained or limited by social forces.

Why do you think that people rush to micro-level explanations and interpretations of family life, and forget to think about the macro-level? Can you give some examples of specific issues when you have done this?

all actively directing our lives, even though powerful social forces help shape our opportunities. We do have free choice, but we need to be aware of the ways that social structure influences our lives and choices.

:: Theme 2: Families Are Always Changing

A second theme you will see throughout this text is that *families are not monolithic or static, but instead are ever-changing.* People have constructed families to meet their needs; therefore, change should be anticipated and not feared. To illustrate this concept, let's first see how families are arranged throughout the world in terms of patterns of authority, rules of descent, and patterns of residence. Second, let's examine the changes in marriage and family patterns in China, a country in the midst of rapid economic and social transformation. Third, let's review marriage and family patterns in U.S. history. Taken together, these examples will illustrate the second theme of this text that the singular, monolithic family structure is largely a myth; *families have always been, and always will be, changing.*

monogamy: Marriage between one man and one woman.

polygamy: A system that allows for more than one spouse at a time (gender unspecified).

polygyny: The marriage pattern in which husbands can have more than one wife.

polyandry: The marriage pattern in which wives are allowed to have more than one husband.

Marriage Patterns

How do you imagine a marriage? Like many people, you probably assume that a marriage consists of only two people. This is a marriage pattern called **monogamy**. Monogamy is found widely, although not exclusively, throughout the world.

Other societies practice **polygamy**, which allows either a husband or wife to have more than one spouse at a time. There are two types of polygamy. The most common of these is **polygyny**, in which a husband can have more than one wife (Omariba & Boyle, 2007; Westoff, 2003). Although illegal in the United States, there may be about 37,000 American families who currently practice polygyny, primarily in the western states (Adams, 2005). Altman and Ginat (1996) found that, on average, polygamous families in the United States contained four wives and 27 children.

Polygyny is legal in several regions of the world today, including parts of Africa, the Middle East, and South America, and is often supported by religious custom. Researchers Charles Welch and Paul Glick examined 15 African countries and found that between one in five and one in three married men had more than one wife. Obviously, not all men can have more than one wife, given existing sex ratios. They found that those who practiced polygyny tended to have two, or occasionally three, wives (Welch & Glick, 1981). Having numerous wives is a sign of family wealth, education, and other dimensions of high status. Men use it as a way to increase fertility within a family, since having more than one wife increases the number of children born within the family.

The second type of polygamy is **polyandry**, where one wife is married to multiple husbands (Stone, 2006; Monger, 2004). This type of marriage pattern is rare and is more likely to occur in societies that experience harsh environmental conditions where poverty is widespread, such as among nomadic Tibetans in Nepal or in parts of rural northern China or India. Multiple husbands are often brothers or otherwise related to one another, and the marriage occurs to provide economic advantages. Brothers may live together as adults to share resources, and children are more likely to survive if they have the contribution

Although polygamy is illegal in the United States, there are thousands of families practicing one specific type—polygyny, with one man married to multiple women.

of many fathers. Often in these societies there is a shortage of women with which to marry because of female infanticide, as the birth of an infant girl may be seen as burdensome to families.

Patterns of Authority

In countries that practice **patriarchy**, which means "rule of the father," the expectation is that men have a natural right to be in positions of authority over women. In such a society, patriarchy is manifested and upheld in legal, educational, religious, economic, and other social institutions. The legal system may prevent women from voting; the educational system may provide an unequal education for girls or even refuse to offer them a formal education; and religious institutions may attribute male dominance to "God's will." Patriarchy is widespread throughout the world. The opposite of patriarchy is **matriarchy**, which is a form of social organization in which the power and authority in society would be vested in women. This is referred to as a "theoretical alternative" because no known cases of true matriarchies have ever been recorded.

In between these two extremes are authority patterns that could best be described as approaching **egalitarian**. In these societies, the expectation is that power and authority are equally vested in both men and women. While the United States and many other developed countries are headed in this direction, it would be wrong to assume that all vestiges of patriarchy have been eliminated, as you will see in Chapter 2.

Patterns of Descent

Where did you get your last name? How is property passed down from one generation to another? Whom do you consider to be your legal relatives? Developed nations most commonly use a **bilateral** pattern of descent, in which descent can be traced through both male and female sides of the family. For example, in the United States it is widely recognized that both your mother's parents *and* your father's parents are related to you—you have, potentially, two sets of grandparents.

In a **patrilineal** pattern, lineage is traced exclusively (or at least primarily) through the man's family line. If you lived in a patrilineal society, you would recognize your father's relatives as your kin, but you would have only minimal connections with your mother's side of the family. Even though the United States uses a primarily bilateral model in establishing descent, vestiges of patrilineal descent are still evident: (1) last names almost always reflect the father's lineage rather than the mother's; and (2) sons are sometimes given their father's first names as well and are then referred to as "Jr." or by a number (III, IV). Notice that there is no semantic equivalent for girls; they are not referred to as "Maria Gonzales, Jr." or as "Emma Smith III."

Finally, a few societies, including some Native American tribes, can be characterized as having **matrilineal** descent patterns because the lineage is more closely aligned with women's families than with men's families. This pattern is not the mirror opposite of a patrilineal pattern, however. In a matrilineal descent pattern women pass their lineage on through their brothers or other male members of the family.

Residence Patterns

With whom do you expect to live with after you marry? In industrial societies like the United States, most couples plan to live separately from either set of parents, which is referred to as a **neolocal** residence pattern. Families in other parts of the world practice **patrilocal** residence, which means it is expected that the couple will live with the husband's family. Less common is a **matrilocal** pattern, where the newly married couple routinely lives with the wife's family.

These different marriage and family patterns, summarized in Table 1.1 (p. 14), have real consequences for the way we experience family life, including whom and how we

patriarchy: A form of social organization in which the norm or expectation is that men have a natural right to be in positions of authority over women.

matriarchy: A form of social organization in which the norm or expectation is that the power and authority in society would be vested in women.

egalitarian: The expectation that power and authority are vested in both men and women, equally.

bilateral: Descent that can be traced through both male and female sides of the family.

patrilineal: A descent pattern where lineage is traced exclusively (or at least primarily) through the man's family line.

matrilineal: A descent pattern where lineage is traced exclusively or primarily within women's families.

neolocal: The expectation that a newly married couple establishes a residence and lives there independently.

patrilocal: The expectation that a newly married couple will live with the husband's family.

matrilocal: The expectation that a newly married couple will live with the family of the wife.

Table 1.1	Marriage and Family Diversity around the World

Can you identify the marriage and family patterns found in the United States?

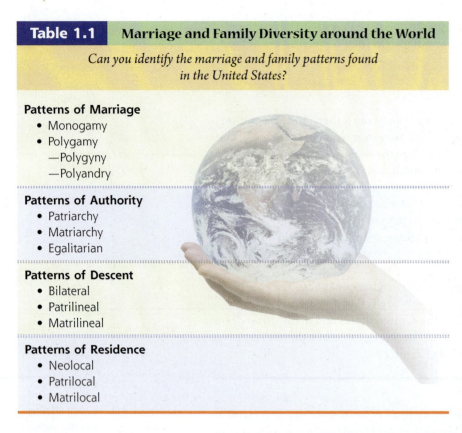

Patterns of Marriage
- Monogamy
- Polygamy
  - —Polygyny
  - —Polyandry

Patterns of Authority
- Patriarchy
- Matriarchy
- Egalitarian

Patterns of Descent
- Bilateral
- Patrilineal
- Matrilineal

Patterns of Residence
- Neolocal
- Patrilocal
- Matrilocal

marry, where we should live, who should have power, and how we inherit and trace our lineage.

How do these marriage and family patterns begin, and how do they change? A look at modern-day China shows the influence of a changing society.

Families in Transition: China

Yue Jiang Wang, who is 60 and lives in the largely rural Yunnan Province of China, is perplexed by young people today. He believes they want too much freedom, and with that freedom will come too many costly mistakes. "They even want to choose their own spouses," he sighs. Jiang married his wife Chang Mei Lin when he was 17 and she was 16. Their marriage was arranged by their parents, with the help of a matchmaker. Together they had seven children—three boys and four girls. Jiang met Mei Lin for the first time during their wedding ceremony. Their marriage began with "respect," but Jiang believes that they grew to love one another.

Jiang is confused by many aspects of life he observes in today's China, a country which has undergone many revolutionary changes within the past few decades. The new market-based economy is rapidly developing, education levels are rising, and cars and the infrastructure they require are dramatically altering the rural landscape. All of these changes have affected many traditional beliefs, including those surrounding women's roles, marriage, and children.

Jiang and Mei Lin married in 1959, and a study conducted of people just like Mei Lin—women who married in China between 1933 and 1987—found that more than 70 percent had not had any other boyfriends and more than 90 percent had not considered marrying anyone besides their husbands (Xu & Whyte, 1990). Today many Chinese men and women, especially those from urban areas, date and socialize with many partners before they marry, and they are sexually active and cohabit (Wang & Davidson, 2006; Higgins, Zheng, Liu, & Sun, 2002). They want to choose their own mates. They are likely to meet their spouse at school, at work, through a mutual friend, or even through the Internet, rather than through parents, relatives, or matchmakers.

Yet, despite these new freedoms to choose their own mates, couples in China still cannot marry freely. The central government requires people who plan to marry to apply for permission and to register officially on a waiting list with the local government. The government regulates when a couple can marry because it is one way to regulate births (Leeder, 2004). China had a large and exploding population, and beginning in the late 1970s the government decided to control the number of births so that the country would be able to feed and care for all its members (Fitzpatrick, 2009). With few exceptions, families are permitted to have only one child. When a couple wants to have children, they must again ask the government for permission to do so. A couple cannot simply "get pregnant" without facing grave consequences, such as a heavy fine or strong encouragement to have an abortion.

The one-child policy has made possible a tremendous increase in the standard of living for the Chinese people. The population has been reduced by 300 million people—the size of the entire U.S. population—compared to what it would have been had the policy not been in effect (Rosenberg, 2009). Chinese families can offer their single child the best of everything: the best education, their undivided attention, a more spacious house, and more disposable income.

Unfortunately, the one-child policy has also had many horrific side effects. Millions of baby girls have virtually disappeared. In a patriarchal country where people place a higher value on boys because they carry on the family lineage and take care of aging parents, and girls are considered an economic liability, should we be surprised that, if couples are allowed only one child, they prefer a boy? Female fetuses have been aborted, and baby girls have been killed or abandoned. Other girls are kept hidden by their parents, and their births are not recorded in birth registries so that their parents can try again for a boy. Therefore, these hidden girls are ineligible for government benefits like health care or education. As a result, sex ratios in China are becoming exceedingly imbalanced, with 120 young boys for every 100 girls (Zhu, Lu, & Hesketh, 2009).

Many people around the world have become alarmed by this situation, as have Chinese government officials. In a country that cherishes family, the disappearance of girls is seen as a failure of what was intended to be a policy to strengthen families. As a result, the Chinese have banned elective amniocentesis tests and have restricted the use of ultrasound scanners so that families cannot determine the sex of a fetus. They have also implemented a mass education effort to promote the idea that the birth of a girl is "just as good" as the birth of a boy (Zhu, Lu, & Hesketh, 2009).

There is some evidence that their efforts may be working. China now has fewer abandoned girls available for adoption. In 2009, 3,000 Chinese-born girls were adopted in the United States, down from 7,900 in 2005 (U.S. Department of State, 2010), as discussed in Chapter 8.

Meanwhile, Jiang and Mei Lin, who had an arranged marriage and seven children many years ago, are proud that their children heed the government's call to have only one child. They remain, however, quite confused about many other decisions of their children, including their move to urban areas, their daughters' desire to go to college, their plans to share housekeeping and childcare with spouses, and their use of new gadgets and technology.

China is currently undergoing rapid social change, fueled in part by the one-child policy that has been in effect for a generation.

History of Family Life in the United States

To further understand how families are continually changing, one only needs to look at families throughout our own history. But how do we learn about families in the earlier times, if no one is alive today to tell us about them? The feature box *Why Do Research? How to Study Families from the Past* (p. 16) gives us some clues about how historians can learn about some of the dynamics of these early families.

Family Life in Colonial America: European Colonists
Family historians have shown that families were the cornerstone of colonial society (Demos, 1970; Laslett, 1971; Mintz, 2004; Coontz, 2005). They were the primary social institution, helping early immigrants adapt to life in the New World. Families acted as:

- *Businesses.* They were the central focus of economic production. Each household was nearly self-sufficient, and men, women, and children worked together at productive tasks to meet their material needs, including producing food, clothing, furniture, and household goods.

Why Do Research?

How to Study Families from the Past

Piecing together the history of family life has become an active topic of research. Drawing on a variety of historical documents, including diaries, letters, birth, marriage, and death registers, and immigration records, historians attempt to weave together a social history of the United States to reveal the daily lives, customs, and lifestyles of ordinary citizens. This is a radical departure from the work of most historians who focus on events such as wars, economic downturns, or other large-scale social events. Because the field of social history is relatively new, and many historical documents have been lost or are unavailable, there are significant gaps in our understanding of history, especially with regards to the dynamics of early minority families.

Historians and family scholars get creative as they piece together the past. Historical records can provide an aggregate record about immigration trends, age at first marriage, or the average length of time between marriage and first birth. Slave auctions, ledgers, and other transactions help us understand what, and who, was being bought and sold. Diaries and letters can reveal what was on the minds of ordinary people, including how they saw the world and how they expressed their views. Newspapers and magazines can reveal fads, fashions, and the mood of the era. All of

these records can provide insightful clues into the lives of ordinary people.

Finally, many scholars rely on "family reconstitution," in which attempts are made to compile all available information about significant family events and everyday life. Members of each generation who are still alive are interviewed in depth, and they are asked to reconstruct their family history. Recreating the past is not easy. Historical researchers work as "detectives" and try to obtain the greatest number of sources possible as they reconstruct the past. Sometimes numerous sources are available, but unfortunately, sometimes only a few clues remain.

What Do **You** Think?

1. Think about your own family's history. How far back does your information reliably go? Who are the oldest members of your family? Could you conduct a family reconstitution?

2. If your books, magazines, computer, or other important artifacts were saved in a time capsule, what would someone a hundred years from now learn about you? About your lifestyle? About your relationships?

- *Schools.* Formal schooling conducted away from home was extremely rare. Instead, parents educated their children, teaching them how to read and write, as well as the vocational and technical skills necessary to become productive adults.
- *Churches.* Families worshiped and prayed together in their homes because churches were usually far away. Parents and children read the Bible together, one of the few books and sources of moral instruction that were readily available.
- *Correctional institutions.* Jails were rare in colonial times, and therefore courts sentenced criminals and so-called idle people to live with more respected families in the community. These families were considered the best setting to not only impose discipline but also to encourage reform.
- *Health and social welfare institutions.* Because there were no hospitals and few doctors during this period, families, and women in particular, took on the role of caring for the sick and infirm. Families also took care of the aging, the homeless, and orphaned children (Demos, 1970).

Most people in colonial America lived in **nuclear families**, comprised of adults and their children. **Extended families**, including grandparents or other relatives, were the exception. Because couples tended to be relatively older at first marriage and people did not live very long, older adults may have died before their grandchildren were born.

Families were large by today's standards, often containing six or more children. Siblings could be as much as 25 years apart in age. Husbands or wives may have married two or even three times because people died young (Laslett, 1971). Children often had stepsiblings or half-siblings. Some households also included servants or slaves, and they were sometimes counted as household family members in statistical records.

nuclear family: A family comprised of adults and their children.

extended family: A family comprised of parents, children, and other relatives such as grandparents.

Marriage and family were central events in people's lives. Although marriages were often undertaken to further business or financial interests, husbands and wives considered themselves a team and anticipated that love and affection would develop between them. However, a wife was considered her husband's helpmate, but not his equal. The husband was the head of the family, and it was his wife's duty to obey him. Women had crucial economic roles inside and outside the family, including cooking, sewing, cleaning, gardening, and certain farm chores, and they produced many products for the family. They raised and cared for many children. Husbands did the planting and harvesting, but women also helped at crucial times of the agricultural year.

Parents tended to be very strict with their children. They believed that children were born with "original sin" and needed firm discipline and severe religious training to break their innate rebellion and selfishness, and to ensure that children would grow up to be productive members of society. Excessive tenderness, they felt, could spoil the child. Children were treated as miniature adults; there was no concept of adolescence, as there is today. As soon as children were old enough to labor on the family farm or in the household, they were put to work.

Colonial America: African Americans and Slavery   The first Africans forcefully brought over to the colonies were indentured servants, and after serving a specified amount of time they were considered "free" and able to marry and purchase their own land. But by the late 17th century, the slave trade was well underway, with a million Africans captured and brought to the American colonies against their will. Some prominent Americans, including Thomas Jefferson, primary author of the Declaration of Independence and the third President of the United States, publicly denounced slavery but supported it privately. In addition to owning slaves, it is now generally agreed that he fathered children with a slave identified as Sally Hemings (Gordon-Reed, 2008).

For years, slavery has been used to explain the strong-female family patterns among contemporary Blacks. But today, instead of seeing slave families as incomplete or emasculated, historians are noting the resiliency of slave families (Wilkinson, 1997; Sudarkasa, 1999). African family ties were strong and relationships created by "blood" were considered more important than those created by marriage (Gutman, 1976; Sudarkasa, 1999).

By the early 1800s, the United States prohibited the importation of new slaves, and owners began to recognize the value of encouraging family relationships and childbearing among the slaves they owned. Some of these relationships were forced for "breeding" purposes. At other times real love developed between slaves. Yet slave marriages were fragile; one study conducted in several southern states revealed that over one-third of slave marriages were terminated by selling off either the husband or wife to another party elsewhere (Gutman, 1976). Even when slavery tore apart families, kinship bonds persisted. Children were often named after lost relatives as a way to preserve family ties.

Prior to the Civil War, there were approximately 150,000 free African Americans living in the south, and another 100,000 living in the northern part of the United States (Mintz & Kellogg, 1989). Yet, even "free" African Americans were not necessarily allowed to vote, attend White schools and churches, or be hired for jobs. Consequently, many free African Americans were poor, unemployed, and barely literate. Moreover, free women outnumbered free men in urban areas. Together, the high rates of poverty and the sex imbalance among free African Americans made it challenging for them to marry and raise children. It is therefore not surprising that many children were reared in female-headed households. One study indicated that when property holdings, a key measure of income, are held constant, the higher incidence of one-parent families among African Americans largely disappears (Mintz & Kellogg, 1989).

Industrialization, Urbanization, and Immigration   Family life in the United States changed considerably in the 19th and early 20th centuries because of three primary factors. First, *industrialization* transformed the economy from a system based on small family farms to one of large urban industries. "Work" became something that people did away from the

Immigrants to the United States in the 19th century were often poor, and worked in the dangerous and dirty factories that characterized the Industrial Revolution.

home. More and more goods and services were produced for profit outside the home, and families purchased these with wages they earned at outside jobs.

Second, people started moving from rural areas and farms to urban areas in search of jobs, a process known as *urbanization*. This process tore extended families apart, as the vast distances between farm and city made frequent contact impossible.

Third, the large waves of *immigration*, in which people from Europe and Asia came to the United States with the hopes of a better life, provided the cheap labor that fueled this industrialization. Between 1830 and 1930, over 30 million immigrants came to the United States from all parts of the world, including Europe, the Slavic countries, and China. In packinghouses, steel mills, textile mills, coal mines, and a host of other industrial settings, nearly half of the workers were immigrants to the United States (Steinberg, 1981).

The Poor and Working Classes   Most immigrants were poor or nearly so. Doris Weatherford, in her book, *Foreign and Female: Immigrant Women in America, 1840–1930* (1986), and Upton Sinclair's *The Jungle* (1906) describe the appalling conditions in which many immigrant families lived and worked. Housing was crowded, substandard, and often lacked appropriate sanitation facilities. Raw sewage was strewn about, causing rampant epidemics in immigrant neighborhoods. Early industrial working conditions were exceedingly dangerous, unsanitary, and inhumane and many workers died or became disabled or disfigured. There were few safety mechanisms in place, the lighting and ventilation systems were woefully inadequate, and people routinely did hard manual labor for 60, 70, or 80 hours a week.

The strain of family life under these abysmal working and living conditions was severe and took its toll. Alcoholism, violence, crime, and other social problems stemming from demoralization plagued many families. Yet immigrants continued to crowd cities in search of work because they hoped that it would lead eventually to a better life for their children.

Middle and Upper Classes   In the middle and upper classes, ideally the husband was the breadwinner while the wife reared the children and took care of the home. Children were no longer seen simply as miniature adults, perhaps because middle- and upper-class families no longer had to rely on their labor. Instead, children were seen as innocents who could be molded into good or bad citizens, a view that emphasized the important role that mothers played at home (Degler, 1980). Experts elevated women's childrearing responsibilities and frowned upon women working outside the home because this was seen as taking women away from their primary, natural, and most important work of all—motherhood.

The Rise of the "Modern" Family—The Twentieth Century   Many events occurred in the early to mid-1900s, including two World Wars, a Depression, and the relative affluence of the 1950s and 1960s, and all of these had an impact upon families. Families faced new daunting hardships during the Depression with increased unemployment, poverty, and homelessness. The World Wars separated families and many men were injured or killed on the battlefield. World War II ushered women into the labor market as never before; their employment was deemed a "patriotic duty." After World War II and throughout the 1950s and early 1960s, women were encouraged to give up their wartime jobs to men returning from the battlefield, and many female workers were fired if they failed to resign voluntarily.

It was also during these decades that technological innovations increased at a rapid pace. The popularity of the automobile changed the ways families traveled and increased their mobility. New suburban residential patterns and migration to the cities in search of work increased travel and commuting time and decreased the amount of time that fathers spent with their families. Kitchen appliances were designed to reduce the amount of time women spent on domestic labor.

A **companionate family** based on mutual affection, sexual attraction, compatibility, and personal happiness emerged. Young adults freely dated without chaperones and placed a greater emphasis on romantic love and attraction in their search for mates as compared to their parents and grandparents.

Betty Friedan, in her influential book, *The Feminine Mystique* (Friedan, 1963), documents a push towards domesticity during this period. Interviews with female college students revealed that their primary reason for attending college was to find a suitable husband rather than a career. College women who were unattached by their senior year felt like they had failed in their ultimate mission—to get their "MRS. Degree." Friedan's content analyses of women's magazines found that few women had jobs or careers; in fact, those who did were often portrayed as cold, aloof, and unfeminine. The "normal" or "natural" role for women was portrayed as a wife and helpmate to her husband, and eventually as a mother to a large number of children.

During this period the average age at first marriage dropped to an all-time low since records had been kept—barely 19 for women and 20 for men—and the birth rate exploded. To keep up with the move towards domesticity, the federal government underwrote the construction of homes in the suburbs, undertook massive highway construction projects that enabled long commutes from home to work, and subsidized low-interest mortgage loans with minimal down payments for veterans. Families, growing in size, craved the spaciousness and privacy of the new suburbs where they could have their own yards instead of community parks for their children. In the suburbs, women cared for their children in isolation, volunteered in their children's schools and within the community, and chauffeured their children to various lessons and events. Television programs, women's magazines, and other media sources glorified the new domesticity. But in reality, this cultural image was not attainable for many families. Working-class and poor women, including many minority women, often worked full- or part-time because their husbands did not earn enough to support the family. Nonetheless, this cultural image was a powerful one.

companionate family: A marriage based on mutual affection, sexual attraction, compatibility, and personal happiness.

Families Today

As we have seen from our look at family history, families are never isolated from outside events and the social structure in which they live. For example, the economy greatly affects family lifestyles, opportunities, and constraints. Over the past few decades our economy has shifted from relatively high-paying manufacturing jobs to lower-paying jobs in the service sector. This has made it very difficult to support a family on one income, and therefore, growing numbers of married women with children began to return to the labor market.

We also see evidence of increasing social inequality, and this, too, affects families. The rich have made tremendous gains during the past few decades, while the middle- and lower-income classes have experienced stagnation or a decline in real earnings when adjusted for inflation (Sherman, 2009). Increasingly, middle-class families are feeling the squeeze of the current recession. Although the 2010 economic forecast looked better than that of 2009, unemployment continued to hover around nearly 9.5 percent by June 2010 (Bureau of Labor Statistics, July 2, 2010) and home foreclosures continued (Christie, 2009).

Many workers are finding that temporary jobs with few benefits are the best that they can find. Between one-third and one-half of workers have shifts in the evening or on

Many middle-class families have fallen on hard times during the current recession. Unemployment hovers around 10 percent, causing many families to lose their homes in foreclosure.

FORECLOSURE

Figure 1.1	**Inflation-adjusted Value of the Minimum Wage, 1950–2010, in 2010 Dollars**

The value of minimum wage declined until 2007, when the minimum wage was raised again.

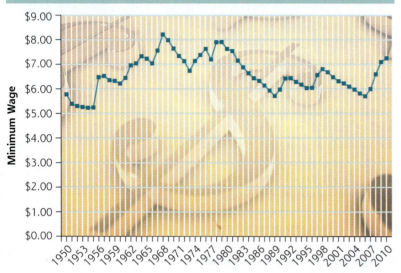

Source: Nine Years of Neglect: Federal Minimum Wage Remains Unchanged for Ninth Straight Year, Falls to Lowest Level in More than Half a Century by Jared Bernstein & Isaac Shapiro. August 30, 2006. EPI Issue Brief #227. Economic Policy Institute.

In your conversations with your grandparents or other older adults about "the good old days," what stories have you heard about family life? What information have you obtained about dating, marriage, or raising children? How is it similar or different from what you have learned in the history portion of this chapter?

weekends, or they have rotating schedules, which can wreak havoc on families and childcare arrangements (Presser, 2003; Joshi & Bogen, 2007; Gornick & Ratzdorf, 2009). Among couples with children, the risk of divorce increases up to six times when one spouse works between midnight and 8 A.M., as compared to daytime hours. Children whose mothers have nonstandard schedules are at great risk for depression, delinquency, or aggressive behaviors (Han, 2005; Joshi & Bogen, 2007).

Many modern families have noticed that their purchasing power has steadily declined because their incomes have failed to keep up with inflation. This problem is especially true for the lowest-income workers. The minimum wage does not allow parents to adequately support their children. Half of workers making the federal minimum wage are adults age 25 and over; most are often working in the service industry doing food preparation or serving (Bureau of Labor Statistics, March 11, 2009). Figure 1.1 illustrates the erosion in the value of the minimum wage, even with the increase to $7.25 per hour (Bernstein, 2007). The Center on Budget and Policy Priorities estimates that a minimum wage of $7.25, which translates into an annual salary of $14,500, will lift a family of four out of poverty only if they also receive $4,464 in food stamps, a $334 child care credit, and $4,926 from the Earned Income Tax Credit (EITC), a tax refund available to low-income working families (Furman & Parrott, 2007).

In addition to lower real incomes, housing costs remain unaffordable for many people hoping to buy their first home. The average price of a single-family home in June 2009 was $171,000 ($213,000 in the western United States) (National Association of Realtors, 2009). While this represents a considerable drop from a few years ago, many Americans are still forced to rent. Nationally, a modest 2-bedroom apartment averages $900 a month, according to estimates from the Department of Housing and Urban Development. In fact, over 16 million households pay more than half of their income in housing (Parrott & Schott, 2009). How do families cope with high housing costs? A Harvard University study found that people who struggle to pay for housing are likely to reduce their spending on food, transportation, clothing, and other necessities (Joint Center for Housing Studies, 2006). Others who struggle with high housing costs become homeless. About 750,000 Americans are homeless on any given night, and 3.5 million are estimated to be homeless at some point over the course of a year (National Coalition for the Homeless, 2009).

Because of these increased expenses, many families today not only work longer hours, but also have both spouses employed full-time outside the home. Unfortunately, many still find themselves in alarming debt as credit cards such as Visa, MasterCard, or American Express are tempting to people with economic difficulties.

In this brief review of historical and cross-cultural differences in family life, you can see that marriage, families, and close relationships are constructed by humans, and therefore their structures are not monolithic. Families are always changing and adapting to a wide variety of historical and cultural traditions.

What do American families look like today? The feature box *Diversity in Families: Profile of U.S. Families* draws on the U.S. Census as well as other government information to present key demographic facts about families today, at least as families are defined by the government.

Diversity in Families

Profile of U.S. Families

What do families look like today? Let's examine some of the key statistics from the U.S. Census Bureau, Current Population Reports, and other governmental sources that we will discuss in more detail throughout the text. First, however, be aware that government statistics have a number of limitations. For example, they use catchall categories like "Hispanic" or "Asian," but these groups are far from homogeneous. Although Cuban Americans, Mexican Americans, and Puerto Ricans share a common language, their cultures are significantly different. Nonetheless, government statistics, while imperfect, provide an important source of demographic information about our population.

Hispanics are now the largest minority group in the United States. By the year 2050, they may comprise nearly one-third of the population. How will this change American culture?

1. Both men and women are postponing marriage. Because of expanding opportunities and changing norms, women now marry at an average age of 25 years, compared to 21 years in 1970. Men now marry at an average age of 27 years, compared to 23 years in 1970.

2. Family size is shrinking. It is likely that nearly one in five women of childbearing age today will not have children, some by choice, and some because of infertility. Those who do have children are more likely to opt for just one or two.

3. The divorce rate has declined in recent decades. In the 1960s the divorce rate began to rise rapidly, peaking around 1980, but since that time it has steadily declined.

4. Single-parent households have been on the rise, particularly among men. Since 1970 there has been a 300 percent increase in single-parent households headed by mothers, and a 500 percent increase in those headed by fathers. Today, about one-quarter of White families are headed by one parent, as are over half of Black families and one-third of Hispanic families.

5. Mothers are increasingly likely to be employed outside the home. Today nearly two-thirds of mothers are employed outside the home.

6. Hispanic groups are now the largest minority in the United States at about 16 percent of the population. Because the birthrate and rate of immigration are higher among Hispanics than among other groups, their presence in the United States will continue to grow at a fast rate. By 2050, about 30 percent of all Americans will likely be of Hispanic descent.

7. The teenage birthrate has declined significantly over the past couple of decades. The birthrate among teenagers has declined by about 20 percent since 1990. This decline is occurring among all racial and ethnic groups, although it has been fluctuating in recent years.

8. Unmarried couples living together is common. The number of unmarried couples has almost doubled since 2000 to nearly 7 million today. This trend is found among all age groups, including the elderly.

9. The percentage of people living in poverty has fluctuated in conjunction with economic trends and is now on the rise. Poverty rates among families, single adults, and children were down in the 1990s; however, since then the poverty rate has risen. Today about 14 percent of Americans live in poverty, including over 20 percent of children.

10. The elderly population has been increasing almost four times as fast as the population as a whole. In 1900 only a small portion of people—one in 25—were aged 65 or older. This has certainly changed. Moreover, people who are 85 and older—referred to as the "oldest old"—constitute the most rapidly growing elderly cohort in the United States.

What Do You Think?

1. What other changes do you see occurring in families? Do you think these changes are for the better or for the worse? Why?

2. Do you think that any of these trends will be reversed over the next decade? If so, what will cause them to be reversed?

:: Theme 3: The Importance of Social Science Theory and Research

A third theme of this text is *an appreciation for the role that social science theory and research play in helping people understand families and close relationships.* Think for a moment about how you know what you know about families. We all have opinions about families based on our own experience or on information filtered through the mass media, peers, parents, religious teachings, or laws. Because virtually all of us were raised in families, we may feel that we are experts on the subject. In other words, we often just rely on our "common sense," a combination of political, legal, social, economic, and religious norms!

However, a scientific perspective can provide a more objective window on the world because common sense differs from one place to another, and from one point in time to another. The norms that underlie so-called common sense can also change. Instead, social science research can inform us about the structure of families, the experiences people have within them, and the meanings that they attach to their relationships (Neuman, 2009; Salkind, 2009). Research offers a firmer basis upon which to form opinions and choose our values. After all, common sense allowed men to beat their wives throughout most of our history, because women were considered inferior. In fact, the phrase "rule of thumb" comes from the belief that the switch that a husband used to beat his wife should be no wider than his thumb. Today it is against the law in the United States (and many other countries) for husbands to beat their wives (and vice versa).

However, violence among intimates is not illegal in many parts of the world. In certain countries, both husbands and wives believe that violence can be justified and it is the husband's prerogative to beat his wife. A World Health Organization study of 24,000 women in ten countries found that the prevalence of physical and/or sexual violence by a partner varied from 15 percent in urban Japan to 71 percent in rural Ethiopia, with most areas being in the 30–60 percent range (World Health Organization, 2009).

empirical approach: An approach that answers questions through a systematic collection and analysis of data.

If so-called common sense is subject to historical and cultural whims, then what can we depend upon to help us understand family dynamics? Sociologists and other family scientists use an **empirical approach**, which answers questions through a systematic collection and analysis of data. Uncovering patterns of family dynamics can be extremely important for building stronger families.

The goals of family research can (for example, in the case of violence among intimates):

- *describe* some phenomenon (how many women have been physically assaulted by someone close to them; how this compares to the number of men who are assaulted by their partners each year), or

Social science research can tell us a lot about social problems, including how to create programs and policies to best serve vulnerable people.

- *examine the factors that predict or are associated with* some phenomenon (what factors are associated with violence among intimates; what factors predict, whether a victim will report the assault to the police), or
- *explain the cause-and-effect relationships* or provide insight into why certain events do or do not occur (the relationship between alcohol and violence among intimates; the relationship between attitudes of male dominance and domestic violence), or
- *examine the meanings and interpretations* of some phenomenon (how abused women and men interpret the reasons for the assault, what does the label "victim" mean, and how might that meaning differ for women and men).

Because of research, we know that violence among intimates is a serious and pervasive social problem. Nearly one in four women in the United States report being physically assaulted by someone close to them (National

Coalition Against Domestic Violence, 2009). How can social science research help women who are battered by their partners? Family scholars conduct basic and applied research to understand the phenomenon, striving to reveal information about the incidence, predictors, social factors associated with violence, or the experience of violence that psychologists, social workers, and politicians could use to develop programs to prevent violence, assist victims, and treat the perpetrators. Violence among intimates is a social problem, not simply an individual one, and research can uncover the social patterns that underlie it.

How Do We Know What We Know? Methods of Social Research

There are a number of different methods that family scientists use to systematically collect and analyze data. Provided here is a brief introduction of six primary ways of collecting data, and Table 1.2 on page 24 offers a summary of these methods. Throughout this text you will see these research methods in action. ◉⊶Watch on **myfamilylab.com**

◉⊶Watch the **Video** *Core Concepts: Research Tools and Techniques* on **myfamilylab.com**

A **survey** is used to gather information about attitudes or behaviors through the answers that people give to questions. You have probably completed many surveys throughout your life. They are a popular research method because they can cover most topics from politics to sexuality to consumer marketing. If used correctly, a survey can produce results that can be generalized to the population.

A **random sample** is the key to being able to generalize your survey findings. A random sample allows every "person of interest" an equal chance of being selected for your research study. For example, let's say we wanted to survey registered voters to see how they felt about same-sex marriage. If we put every registered voter's name "in a hat" (or more likely, enter it into a computer program), and randomly chose 1,500 names, we could say that we had a representative sample. Or, let's say we wanted to survey college seniors at your university about their experiences with cohabitation. We could easily get a list of college seniors from the administration and randomly select 150 of them to survey.

However, in many contexts, finding a complete list of everyone of interest is impossible. Suppose that we wanted to survey people who have had a same-sex experience. Or men who plan to remain virgins until married? Or teenagers who don't get along with their parents? Where would we find a complete list of persons of interest for these surveys? Sometimes, we need to use other sampling strategies. For example, perhaps I can identify a young man who plans to remain a virgin until marriage, and he can introduce me to others who share this value, who then each introduce me to even more people. This would be called a snowball sample as the list grows larger.

Surveys can be done in a number of ways. They can include mail surveys, which are self-administered questions that are mailed to respondents. A mail survey may be appropriate if the number of questions is short and the questions themselves are simple such as, "How many children do you have?" or, "Do you smoke more than one cigarette a day?" However, if the questions require too much detail, respondents are unlikely to complete the survey on their own and it will be thrown away.

With a telephone survey, an interviewer calls respondents and asks them the questions over the telephone. These are becoming increasingly popular, but many people find them annoying and hang up immediately. However, if the interviewer can keep the person on the line, telephone surveys can be a quick and effective means of gathering information.

In-person surveys are done in a conversational setting. The interviewer asks a series of questions that the respondent answers. Since they are sitting down together, the interviewer may be free to probe further or clarify anything that may be confusing to the respondent. This type of survey can work very well unless the topic is extremely sensitive and embarrassing, such as surveys on sexuality, for which the respondent may want a bit more privacy.

In-depth interviews are also conducted in person, and allow an interviewer to obtain detailed responses to questions such as, "How does your family cope when there is not enough food to eat?" or, "What does it mean to you to be a father?" Sometimes the questions follow a set pattern and every respondent is asked the same questions in the same order. Other in-depth interviews follow a different approach, where every interview is

survey: A form of research that gathers information about attitudes or behaviors through the answers that people give to questions.

random sample: A sample in which every "person of interest" has an equal chance of being selected into your research study.

in-depth interview: A research method that allows an interviewer to obtain detailed responses to questions.

Table 1.2	Six Research Methods: A Summary		
Family researchers use a variety of methods to learn about families and close relationships.			
Method	**Application**	**Advantages**	**Limitations**
Survey	For gathering information about issues that are not directly observed, such as values, opinions, and other self-reports. Can be administered by mail, telephone, or in person. Useful for descriptive or explanatory purposes; can generate quantitative or qualitative data.	Sampling methods can allow researcher to generalize findings to a larger population. Can provide open-ended questions or a fixed response.	Surveys must be carefully prepared to avoid bias. A potential for a low return or response rate. Can be expensive and time-consuming. Self-reports may be biased.
In-depth Interview	For obtaining information about issues that are not directly observed, such as values, opinions, and other self-reports. Useful for getting in-depth information about a topic. Conducted in person, conversation is usually audiotaped and later transcribed. Generates qualitative data.	Can provide detailed and high-quality data. Interviewer can probe or ask follow-up questions for clarification or to encourage the respondent to elaborate. Can establish genuine rapport with respondent.	Expensive and time-consuming to conduct and transcribe. Self-reports may be biased. Respondent may feel uncomfortable revealing personal information.
Experiment	For explanatory research which examines cause-and-effect relationship among variables. Several types: Classical Experimental Design and Quasi-experimental Designs based on degree of controlling the environment. Generates quantitative data.	Provides greatest opportunity to assess cause and effect. Research design is relatively easy to replicate.	The setting may have an artificial quality. Unless experimental and control groups are randomly assigned or matched on all relevant variables, and the environment is carefully controlled, bias may result.
Focus Group	For obtaining information from small groups of people who are brought together to discuss a particular topic. Often exploratory in nature. Particularly useful for studying public perceptions. Facilitator may ask only a few questions; goal is to get group to interact with one another. Generates qualitative data.	Group interaction may produce more valuable insights than individual surveys or in-depth interviews. Research can obtain data quickly and inexpensively. Good at eliciting unanticipated information.	Setting is contrived. Some people may feel uncomfortable speaking in a group and others may dominate.
Observational Study	For exploratory and descriptive study of people in a natural setting. Researcher can be a participant or nonparticipant. Generates qualitative data.	Allows study of real behavior in a natural setting. Does not rely on self-reports. Researchers can often ask questions and take notes. Usually inexpensive.	Can be time-consuming. Could be ethical issues involved in certain types of observation studies, i.e., observing without consent. Researcher must balance roles of participant and observer. Replication of research is difficult.
Secondary Analysis	For exploratory, descriptive, or explanatory research with data that were collected for some other purpose. Diverse. Can be large data sources based on national samples, e.g., U.S. Census, or can be historical documents or records. Generates quantitative or qualitative data, depending on the source of data used.	Saves the expense and time of original data collection. Can be longitudinal, with data collected at more than one point in time. Good for analyzing national attitudes or trends. Makes historical research possible.	Because data were collected for another purpose, the researcher has no control over what variables were included or excluded. Researcher has no control over sampling or other biases in the data.

a conversation. The basic issues are covered, but much of the interview is emergent. The interviewer, with permission, records the interview, and later transcribes it verbatim.

An **experiment** is a controlled method for determining cause and effect. It is used often in evaluation research or psychological research, which may ask such questions as, "Does abstinence-based sex education reduce teenage sexual activity?" or, "Does premarital counseling reduce the likelihood of divorce?"

There are many different types of experimental designs. The classical experimental design randomly divides individuals into two groups, an experimental group and a control group. The researchers might administer a pre-test to each group to ensure that the groups are similar and to use the information as a baseline to assess any future changes. Then, the researchers introduce a stimulus to the experimental group, such as the abstinence-based sex education program or the premarital counseling program. The control group does not receive the stimulus. Then, the two groups are compared again, referred to as the post-test. If there is a difference in the two groups, it is assumed that it was caused by the stimulus. We can say that the stimulus caused the effect.

A **focus group** obtains information from a small group of people who are brought together to discuss a particular topic. It is a group interview and works well when a researcher is looking for exploratory information. The moderator may have only a few questions. The goal is to get the group members to interact, brainstorm, and exchange ideas with one another: "What types of responses have you had to your interracial relationship?" or, "Have you found online dating to be a worthwhile experience?" The researcher may then use ideas generated in focus groups to develop other types of research plans.

Observational studies go to the natural setting and observe people in action. A researcher may observe children in a day care center to answer the question, "How do four-year-old boys and girls express gender?" Or a researcher may visit nursing homes to answer the question, "How do nursing home staff treat people with Alzheimer's disease?" Researchers can be participant observers, which means that they actively participate in the group they are studying. They may even go undercover, and pretend to be a staff member while watching others in the nursing home, or they may take a teacher's aide job to more thoroughly watch the children. Other researchers are non-participants. In these cases the researcher may simply stand by, watch, and take notes. These non-participant researchers may observe children through a two-way mirror. Or they may walk around the nursing home, jotting down their observations.

Finally, many researchers rely upon **secondary analysis**. This means that the data were collected for some other purpose, but still prove useful to the researcher. These can be large sources of data from the U.S. Census Bureau or the U.S. Department of Justice to answer questions across the population such as, "How many single-parent households are poor?" or, "What were the racial and ethnic backgrounds of crime victims last year?" We can also conduct secondary analyses using other, smaller sources of data. The hallmark is that you are using data collected by someone else for a different purpose. Although this is the least expensive method, it often means you have to compromise your study because the original researchers may not have collected the data in exactly the same way you would have.

As you can see from these various research methods, some researchers focus on **quantitative research**, where the focus is on data that can be measured numerically. Examples of this method might be found in surveys, experiments, or doing a secondary analysis on available statistics from the government (such as the U.S. Department of Justice) or some other source. Others use **qualitative research**, and focus on narrative description with words rather than numbers to analyze patterns and their underlying meanings. Examples of qualitative research methods include in-depth interviews, focus groups, observation studies, or conducting a secondary analysis using narrative documents (such as letters or diaries).

◉—|Watch| on **myfamilylab.com**

None of these research methods is inherently better or worse than the others. The method used depends on the research questions that are posed. For example, if we want to better understand what family life was like in the 19th century, we would not want to conduct a survey. How would people who are alive today best inform us of what happened

experiment: A controlled method for determining cause and effect.

focus group: A small group interview of people who are brought together to discuss a particular topic.

observational study: A research method that goes into the natural setting and observes people in action.

secondary analysis: A research method in which the data were collected for some other purpose but still are useful to the researcher.

quantitative research: Research that focuses on data that can be measured numerically.

qualitative research: Narrative description with words rather than numbers to analyze patterns and their underlying meanings.

◉—|Watch| the **Video**
Core Concepts: Qualitative vs. Quantitative Research on **myfamilylab.com**

200 years ago? The best method would be to conduct a secondary analysis of documents that were written during that time period. Diaries, letters, or other lengthy correspondence between people of that time period could help us understand the common everyday experiences between families. Historical records could give us a picture of immigration trends, age at first marriage, or the average length of time between marriage and first birth.

However, if we are trying to assess attitudes or opinions about people today, perhaps a survey or in-depth interviews would be best. If we want to ask the same questions of everyone, and offer a standard set of answers from which they can choose from, such as "How many children do you personally want to have? Would you say it is zero, one, two, three, four, or five or more?", then a survey might be best. We can easily quantify the information. However, if we are interested in broader questions about which each person in our study will elaborate on the answers in his or her own way, such as, "How did you come to decide on the number of children that you would like to have?", we would likely use in-depth interviews, which then yield qualitative data.

Theories: Helping Us Make Sense of the World

Research is guided by **theory**, which is a general framework, explanation, or tool used to understand and describe the real world (Finlay, 2007; Smith, Hamon, Miller, & Ingoldsby, 2009; White, 2008). Theories are important both before and after data have been collected because they help us decide what topics to research, what questions to try to answer, how to best answer them, and how to interpret the research results. Before collecting data, theories can help us frame the question. When data have been collected and patterns emerge, theories can help us make sense of what was found.

There are many theoretical perspectives that make different assumptions about the nature of society. Table 1.3 summarizes the most common theories for studying families.

theory: A general framework, explanation, or tool used to understand and describe the real world.

Table 1.3	Summary of Family Theories

Theories range from macro-level to micro-level.

LEVEL OF ANALYSIS			
MACRO	Structural Functionalism	←→	The family as an institution and how it functions to maintain its own needs and those of society.
	Conflict	←→	Social inequality results in unequal resources resulting in inevitable conflict.
	Feminism	←→	Investigation of family life as experienced by those with minority status, especially women.
MICRO	Social Exchange	←→	Family life as a rational exchange designed to maximize rewards and control costs.
	Symbolic Interaction	←→	Family interaction governed by symbolic communication that defines reality.
	Developmental Theory	←→	Family life predicted by passage through normative stages and the accomplishment of corresponding tasks.
	Systems Theory	←→	Circular interactions among the system members resulting in functional or dysfunctional outcomes.

Source: From Smith, Hamon, Ingoldsby, & Miller, Exploring Family Theories 2e. (c) 2008 Oxford University Press.

Some theories are more macro in nature, and attempt to understand societal patterns; these include structural functionalism theory, conflict theory, and feminist theory. Others theories are more micro in nature, such as social exchange theory, symbolic interaction theory, developmental theory, and systems theory, and focus on personal dynamics and face-to-face interaction.

Structural Functionalism
The **structural functionalism theory** (often abbreviated to "functionalism") attempts to determine the structure, systems, functions, and equilibrium of social institutions, in this case, the family. A popular theory in the 1940s and 1950s, the focus is on how the family is organized, how it interacts with other social systems, the functions that the family serves, and how it is a stabilizing force in a culture (Parsons, 1937; 1951). For example, Parsons and Bales (1955) focused on the division of labor in families, noting the ways in which separate spheres for men and women contributed to the stability and functionality of families. The expressive roles and tasks fell to women, whereas the instrumental roles fell to men, which contributed to smooth family functioning (Parsons & Bales, 1955). Functionalists rarely note the tensions, conflicts, or the political ideologies behind their ideas, which may explain why it has fallen out of favor in more recent decades among sociologists.

Conflict Theory
Conflict theory emphasizes issues surrounding social inequality, power, conflict, and social change; in this case, how these factors influence, or are played out in families. Those who follow the writings of Karl Marx, a 19th-century philosopher, focus on the consequences of capitalism for families, such as the tensions and inequality generated by the distribution of wealth and power associated with capitalism (Marx & Engels, 1971, original 1867). Other conflict theorists focus on a broader array of issues surrounding conflict, inequality, or power differentials. For example, a conflict theorist might ask why virtually all elderly persons, regardless of income, receive government-subsidized health care that covers many of their health care needs (Medicare) when there is no similar program for children. Is this different treatment due to the fact that the elderly represent both a large special interest group and a powerful voting block, whereas children as a group are virtually powerless?

Feminist Theory
Feminist theory is related to conflict theory, but the difference between the two is that gender is seen as the central concept for explaining family structure and family dynamics (Osmond & Thorne, 1993). It focuses on the inequality and power imbalances between men and women and analyzes "women's subordination for the purpose of figuring out how to change it" (Gordon, 1979). It recognizes that *gender* is a far more important organizing concept than is *sex* because the former represents a powerful set of relations that are fraught with power and inequality. For example, research indicates that women do more household labor than men even when both partners are employed full-time. Feminist theorists see the gendered division of household labor as a result of power imbalances between men and women that are embedded in larger society and have virtually taken on a life of their own. This is an example of "doing gender," when gender differences become embedded in our culture (West & Zimmerman, 1987). We will discuss this further in Chapter 10.

Social Exchange Theory
Social exchange theory draws upon a model of human behavior used by many economists. It assumes that individuals are rational beings, and their behavior reflects decisions evaluated on the basis of costs—both direct and opportunity costs—and benefits (Nye, 1979; Becker, 1981). Exchange theorists would suggest that a particular type of family structure or dynamic is the result of rational decisions based upon evaluating the social, economic, and emotional costs and benefits compared to the alternatives.

Symbolic Interaction Theory
Symbolic interaction theory emphasizes the symbols we use in everyday interaction—words, gestures, appearances—and how these are interpreted by others (Mead, 1935). Our interactions with others are based on how we interpret these symbols. Some symbols are obvious—an engagement ring, a kiss, a

structural functionalism theory: A theory that attempts to determine the structure, systems, functions, and equilibrium of social institutions.

conflict theory: A theory that emphasizes issues surrounding social inequality, power, conflict, and social change.

feminist theory: A theory in which gender is seen as the central concept for explaining family structure and family dynamics.

social exchange theory: A theory that draws upon a model of human behavior used by many economists. It assumes that individuals are rational beings, and their behavior reflects decisions evaluated on the basis of costs—both direct and opportunity costs—and benefits.

symbolic interaction theory: A theory that emphasizes the symbols we use in everyday interaction—words, gestures, appearances—and how these are interpreted.

smile. We know how to interpret these symbols. Others are less obvious and may be more confusing to interpret, thereby causing tension or conflict in a relationship. For example, we have a general agreement about what a "mother" is supposed to do, but what is the role of a "stepmother"?

Developmental Theory   **Developmental theory** suggests that families (and individual family members) go through distinct stages over time, with each stage having its own set of tasks, roles, and responsibilities. These developmental changes include (1) getting married; (2) having children; (3) experiencing the preschool years; (4) experiencing the school-age years; (5) living with teenagers; (6) launching your children into adulthood; (7) being a middle-aged parent; and (8) aging (Duvall & Miller, 1985). Early development theorists claimed that the stages were inevitable and occurred in a relatively linear fashion, although most now recognize that people might move in unpredictable ways. For example, some families never have children. Other families have children later in life, so that parents may be facing tasks associated with middle age (such as saving for retirement) before children are launched. The developmental theory uses both micro and macro approaches to describe and explain family relationships and stages (Rodgers & White, 1993).

A related perspective, called the "life course perspective," examines how the lives of individuals change as they pass through events, with the recognition that many changes are socially produced and shared among a cohort of people (Elder, 1998; Schaie & Elder, 2005). For example, sociologist Glen Elder's longitudinal study followed a cohort of American children through the Great Depression and afterwards to see how an historical event of such large proportions affected them (Elder, 1999).

Systems Theory   A system is more than the sum of its parts. Likewise, **systems theory** proposes that a family system—the family members and the roles that they play—is larger than the sum of its individual members (Broderick & Smith, 1979). Collectively it becomes a system, but it also includes subsystems within it, such as the married couple subsystem, the sibling subsystem, or the parent-child subsystem. All family systems and subsystems create boundaries between them and the environment with varying degrees of permeability. They also create "rules of transformation" so that families function smoothly and know what to expect from another member. All systems tend toward equilibrium so that families work toward a balancing point in their relationship, and they maintain this equilibrium by feedback or control. Therefore, systems theory is particularly useful in studying how the family (or subsystems within the family) communicates with one another and the rippling effects of that communication.

Throughout this text you will read about and analyze the results of many scientific research studies and will see how theory informs our research. These studies are important because they show us important facts and meanings associated with family life. Understanding these facts and meanings helps shape our choices and our values. Next, let's look at a detailed example of how research can inform our values about families.

Family Decline or Not? What Does the Research Reveal?

Today some people are concerned that the family is in trouble (National Marriage Project, 2009; 2007), citing "the neglect of marriage," "lack of commitment by men," "loss of child centeredness," "the rise in cohabitation," and "fatherless families." Popular television shows, newspapers, and magazines bombard us with stories about the demise of the family. We hear that in the "good old days," there were fewer problems; life was easier, family bonds were stronger, families had more authority to fulfill their functions, and people were generally happier. People who feel that families are being threatened worry that (1) Americans are rejecting traditional marriage and family life; (2) family members are not adhering to roles within families; and (3) many social and moral problems result from the changes in families.

In contrast to this pessimistic perspective, others remind us that these golden years of the past never really existed. They argue that families have always faced challenges, including desertion, poverty, children born out of wedlock, alcoholism, unemployment, violence, and child abuse (Coontz, 1997; Abramovitz, 1996). Yet, despite these recurring

developmental theory: A theory that suggests families, and individual family members, go through distinct stages over time, with each stage having its own set of tasks, roles, and responsibilities.

systems theory: A theory that proposes that a family system—the family members and the roles that they play—is larger than the sum of its individual members.

problems, attempts to strengthen families through improved social services and financial assistance have been met with resistance. Providing families with services such as adequate childcare, educational opportunities, jobs, health care, and housing is at odds with the emphasis in the United States on "rugged individualism." Instead, we are a nation that encourages all of our citizens to "pull themselves up by their own bootstraps."

Which view is correct? To answer this question, we return to the third theme of this text: Rather than relying on common sense or personal experience alone to inform us about families, we should examine the information that research can provide. For example, you should not make sweeping statements that divorce is good or bad for children, that women on welfare neglect or do not neglect their children, that teenage pregnancy is increasing or decreasing, or that lesbians or gay men make bad or good parents on the basis of your personal opinion without looking at what research reveals about these issues. You may find that your own opinions are confirmed, or you may find that they are clearly refuted. **Read** on **myfamilylab.com**

Read the **Document** *The Way We Weren't: The Myth and Reality of the Traditional Family* on **myfamilylab.com**

Are We Rejecting Marriage and Family Relationships? Attitudes

Studies looking at attitudes toward family life over the course of several decades show both change and consistency over time. A national Gallup Poll reveals a long-term trend towards endorsing sex and gender equality, and a greater tolerance for different types of families and lifestyles. People now are less likely to make blanket statements that "this is what all people should do" (Gallup.com, 2008). Nonetheless, there is also a continued emphasis on and commitment to marriage, children, and family life. Both younger and older Americans devote or plan to devote much of their lives to children and spouses. They see marriage as a lifetime commitment that should not be terminated except under extreme conditions, and they view both marriage and having children as highly fulfilling. There is no evidence that this commitment has eroded over the past several decades.

Researchers from the University of Michigan have collected data from high school seniors since the mid-1970s, and the results indicate very little, if any, decline in the way young people value marriage and family. Figure 1.2 reports the percentage of high school

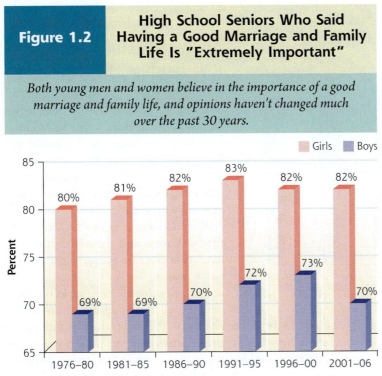

Figure 1.2

High School Seniors Who Said Having a Good Marriage and Family Life Is "Extremely Important"

Both young men and women believe in the importance of a good marriage and family life, and opinions haven't changed much over the past 30 years.

Girls ■ Boys

	1976–80	1981–85	1986–90	1991–95	1996–00	2001–06
Girls	80%	81%	82%	83%	82%	82%
Boys	69%	69%	70%	72%	73%	70%

Source: The National Marriage Project. 2009. The State of Our Unions: Marriage in America 2009. Charlottesville, VA: University of Virginia.

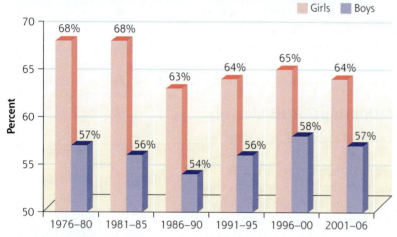

Figure 1.3

High School Seniors Who Expected to Marry, or Were Married, Who Said It Is "Very Likely" They Will Stay Married to the Same Person for Life

There has been very little change in attitudes among young married men and women over the past 30 years.

Source: The National Marriage Project. 2009. The State of Our Unions: Marriage in America 2009. Charlottesville, VA: University of Virginia.

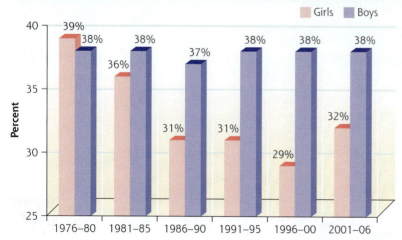

Figure 1.4

High School Seniors Who Said They Agreed or Mostly Agreed That Most People Will Have Fuller and Happier Lives If They Choose Legal Marriage

Young women today see more options for themselves than did young women 30 years ago.

Source: The National Marriage Project. 2009. The State of Our Unions: Marriage in America 2009. Charlottesville, VA: University of Virginia.

seniors over time who said that having a good marriage and family life is "extremely important." The vast majority of young men and women strongly believe in the importance of a good marriage and family life. It appears that the opinions of young men and women in recent years are no different from those who graduated between 1976 and 1980.

The majority of high school seniors also agree that it is "very likely" that they will stay married to the same person for life, as Figure 1.3 shows. Young women are more likely than their male counterparts to agree with this statement, and students' attitudes have changed little over time.

Figure 1.4 reports the percentage of high school seniors who said they agreed, or mostly agreed, that "most people will have fuller or happier lives if they choose legal marriage rather than staying single or just living with someone." Again, the researchers compared the answers across different cohorts of high school seniors. Despite the fact that young people value marriage and family life for themselves and hope to stay married forever, they are also becoming more tolerant of other lifestyle options. Interestingly, young men are somewhat more likely than young women to believe that most people will have happier lives if they choose legal marriage. Young women, especially, increasingly recognize that cohabitation and singlehood could indeed be viable options for people, even if they themselves would prefer to marry.

Are We Rejecting Marriage and Family Relationships? Behaviors

Data from the U.S. Census Bureau show that the percentage of people who are currently married has declined. But is it fair to assume that we are rejecting marriage and family relationships? Figure 1.5, see page 32, shows the marital status of the population aged 15 and over by sex for the years 1970 and 2009. First, note that the percentage of people over age 15 who had "never married" has risen only five or six percentage points for both men and women in thirty years. Moreover, this increase is due to the *delayed age at marriage*, not an increased likelihood of remaining single over the life course. Women now marry at an average age of 25 and men marry around age 27, compared to 21 and 23, respectively, in 1970. In fact, the percentage of people aged 65 and over who report never marrying is actually lower than it was in 1970. In other words, *people are still marrying, but marrying later* (U.S. Census Bureau, January 14,

My Family

Not Married—Yet

The holidays are coming up and I've made my usual plans to drive down from Boston to see my family in Maryland. I haven't seen my parents, kid sisters, and grandma for about six months, so it will be great to see them all again. That is, until they start up on the "single thing."

What is it with the older generations, anyway? I'm 34, and they act like my life is nothing without a husband and kids. Last time I saw my mom she actually cried, and told me that if I don't hurry and get married, no one will be left for me. I'm too picky, she said. Another time she suggested that my eggs were "drying up" and I was sentencing myself to a life without children. My dad isn't much better, and grandma just smirks.

What they don't seem to understand is that I like being single right now. I have a great job in publishing, and enjoy the perks of a pretty good salary, a wonderful loft in a cool part of town, lots of travel, and the freedom to take some terrific vacations. Last year I went to Morocco and Egypt with a friend for three weeks. I'm not sure I could swing any of this with a husband and kids.

Of course, this doesn't mean that I never want to get married, or never want to have a baby. Okay, I admit that sometimes I'm lonely. Sometimes I do wonder if "he" is out there for me. I'm just not in any rush. I've had a few serious boyfriends. In college I even lived with my boyfriend for a couple of years, but then we split. He moved for a job and I left for graduate school, and we just realized we were going in different directions emotionally as well as geographically.

Right now I feel like I have a lot of friends, male and female, and we enjoy hanging out on weekends, you know, going out for dinner and drinks, sailing, or going to the latest gallery opening. I'm also training for a half-marathon, and have a good group of folks for my long run on Sundays.

My parents get none of this. "Hurry up, hurry up," they say. It bothers me because, sure, I want to get married, someday, just not yet.

—**Mariah, Age 34**

An increasing number of people in their 20s and 30s are single, using this opportunity to focus on their work, education, and their social life, but this does not mean that they will never marry.

What Do You Think?

1. What age do you think is ideal to marry? The average age for first marriage is increasing. Do you think delaying marriage is good or bad for society?

2. Is the pressure to marry and have children the same for men and women? Would Mariah have received more or less pressure if she were a man? Explain your answer.

2010). While this may look like a rejection of marriage, a closer look reveals that this is not the case, as shown in the feature box *My Family: Not Married—Yet.*
❋ **Explore** on **myfamilylab.com**

Figure 1.5 also reveals that between 1970 and 2009, the number of people who claimed to be currently divorced or separated more than doubled for both men and women. Divorce was on the rise in the 1970s for many reasons that we will explore in Chapter 12. However, the divorce rate began to level off in the early 1980s and has declined significantly since then (Hamilton, Martin, & Ventura, 2010). In other words, *divorce is declining, not increasing.* If you consider the fact that most divorced people eventually remarry, it is difficult to make the argument that Americans are rejecting marriage and family life.

❋ **Explore** the **Concept**
Social Explorer Report: Patterns within the Married Population on **myfamilylab.com**

Figure 1.5	Marital Status of the Population 15 Years and Over, by Sex

More people today have never married, but this reflects a delay in the age at marriage, not a rejection of marriage.

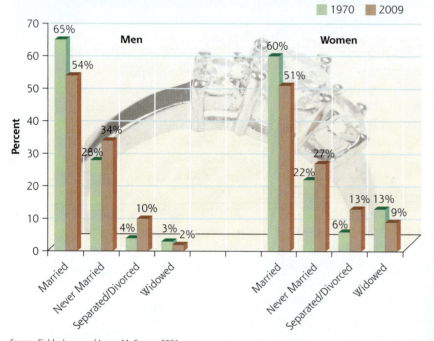

Source: Fields, Jason and Lynne M. Casper. 2001. "America's Families and Living Arrangements: March 2000." In Current Population Reports, P20–537. Washington DC: U.S. Census Bureau.

What are some common-sense assumptions about the family? Can you think of examples of family issues that you assumed to be true, but then you later learned the facts that showed you were wrong? How did you respond to this new information—did you welcome, deny, or accept it immediately?

Other national data show that an increasing number of adults do not have children. Today, about 20 percent of women approaching the end of their childbearing years are childfree, double the rate of only a generation ago (Dye, 2008). While you might conclude that our society is deciding against having children, it is important to understand that about 40 percent of childfree women aged 40–44 are *involuntarily* childfree, and assisted reproductive technology is big business these days (Centers for Disease Control and Prevention, 2009). Another 16 percent of women report that they are only postponing parenthood.

Nonetheless, more women are reporting that they do not want to have children. But let's ask ourselves, is that such a bad thing? In the past, many women who did not want children were pressured to have them anyway. In other words, although fewer people are having children, we do not know whether the percentage of people who do not want children has increased or whether it has remained constant.

Finally, some people consider the rise in the number of single-parent households to be a cause for concern. Single-parent households, which comprise about 30 percent of all families (U.S. Census Bureau, January 14, 2010), have been blamed for a variety of family problems, including poverty, delinquency, teen pregnancy, and school dropouts. Most of these single-parent households are headed by single mothers; however, the composition of single-mother families is beginning to change. They are increasingly made up of older, higher educated women while the number of births by teenagers has been declining significantly, although the trend has been fluctuating over the past few years, as you will see in Chapter 5 (Kreider & Elliott, 2009; Hamilton, Martin, & Ventura, 2010). In addition, the number of single-mother households has not increased appreciably since the mid-1990s. Rather, it is the number of *single-father* families that is on the rise.

Let's pause to consider why so many single-parent households are vulnerable to a variety of social problems. Most studies do not find that it is single parenthood, *per se*, that accounts for these problems. Rather, other issues *associated* with single parenthood seem to be responsible, such as an increased likelihood of poverty. Almost a third of single, female-headed households are poor, compared to only about 13 percent of all families (DeNavas-Walt, Proctor, & Smith, 2010). In other words, single parenthood may make poverty more likely to occur, but if we could do something to help fight poverty as a society, then many social problems could be reduced.

An international comparison may shed some light on what could be done to eliminate poverty and improve outcomes for children who grow up in single-parent households (Baker, 2006; Hill, 2006; Warner, 2005). Houseknecht and Sastry (1996) examined the relationship between the decline of traditional families and the well-being of children in Sweden, the United States, the former West Germany, and Italy. "Family decline" was measured by such factors as the divorce rate, the rate of nonmarital births, and the percentage of mothers with young children in the labor force. "Child well-being" was measured by the percentage of children in poverty, deaths of infants from abuse, and juvenile delinquency rates.

The researchers found that children seemed to fare best in both Italy and Sweden. But interestingly, Italy had low levels of family decline, while Sweden had significantly higher levels. Thus, it appears that changes in the family structure do not necessarily have negative effects on children.

Why did Italy, with low levels of family decline, and Sweden, with high levels, both report high levels of "child well-being"? The researchers concluded that both countries have many social policies and programs designed to help children and their families to keep them out of poverty, such as universal health insurance, subsidized childcare, a dependent child grant from the government, expanded paid maternity leaves, and many other programs that help families stay strong. The authors concluded that *poor child outcomes are the result of weak social policies that do not provide the support that our naturally evolving family structure requires.* In other words, poor child outcomes do not simply happen because of change, *per se*, and they are not inevitable.

Bringing It Full Circle

In the beginning of this chapter, we introduced you to several groups of people and for each group posed the question, "Are they a family?" With the new information presented in this chapter, you now know how important the answer to this question can be. Our definitions of family and our views about family relationships reflect both micro-level and macro-level factors. Micro-level factors include issues of personal choice and interpersonal dynamics. Macro-level factors include broader social structures, such as social institutions and the statuses of sex, race and ethnicity, class, and sexual orientation. Rather than relying on common sense, personal opinion, or "It has always been that way . . . ," family scientists are interested in systematically uncovering the patterns of our relationships and answering intriguing questions using social science research methods.

Armed with your new information about families, reflect back on the opening vignette.

- Do you think that all of the individuals, couples, and groups introduced are a family? Why or why not?

- Which are more accepted as families in our society, and why? Which are less accepted?

- Choose one of the families in the opening vignette, and explain how both micro-level and macro-level factors shape how society views this family type, and influences their family patterns and interactions.

- What questions do you have about the families in the opening vignette, and how could social science research help to answer these questions?

For further review, turn to the Video Discussion Guide, on page 449, to answer additional questions about how the chapter opening video relates to what you have learned in this chapter.

Chapter Review

1.1. How does this text define "family" and how does it differ from a legal perspective?

This text defines a family more broadly than the federal government. We define family as a relationship by blood, marriage, or affection, which may cooperate economically, may care for any children, and may consider their core identity to be intimately connected to the group. Thus, this definition may include unmarried homosexual or heterosexual partners.

1.2. Why is the definition of *family* so important?

How our society defines a family has important consequences with respect to many different rights, privileges, and responsibilities. Only married persons are eligible for federal benefits, such as Social Security benefits, or the ability to file taxes jointly. These decisions involve billions of dollars in employer and government benefits and affect millions of adults and children each year.

1.3. What are the functions that families provide?

Families provide many functions, including marriage; regulation of sexual behavior; reproducing and socializing children; property and inheritance; economic cooperation; social placement, status, and roles; care, warmth, protection, and intimacy.

1.4. What is the difference between a micro-level and a macro-level perspective for the study of families?

While people often initially think of our relationships solely in personal terms, which is a micro-level perspective, relationships are also shaped by the social structure. Our attitudes and behaviors, likes and dislikes, are not completely random, but are formed by the social forces operating in the society in which we live. A macro-level perspective examines the ways in which marriage, families, and intimate relationships are interconnected with the rest of society and with other social institutions.

1.5. What is social structure and why is it important?

Social structure refers to the patterns of social organization that guide our interactions with others. Part of this social organization includes our social institutions and our social statuses. Social structures shape our daily experiences, privileges, and constraints.

1.6. What types of marriage and kinship patterns exist around the world?

Marriage patterns include monogamy (including serial monogamy), and the two types of polygamy (polygyny and polyandry). Patterns of authority include patriarchy, egalitarian, and, theoretically at least, matriarchy. Patterns of descent include bilateral, patrilineal, and matrilineal, and residential patterns include neolocal, patrilocal, and matrilocal.

1.7. How would we characterize the changes in China's families and family policy in recent generations?

Interrelated with the changes in China's economy, China's families have moved from a large amount of parental involvement and supervision to greater individual freedom of choice. However, the Chinese people must adhere to strict governmental rules regulating marriage and fertility. Couples must request permission both to marry and to have a child. Families are generally only allowed one child.

Key Terms

1.8. How have families changed throughout history, and what are the macro-level factors that have contributed to that change?

Families evolved from being largely economic units to being based on mutual affection, sexual attraction, compatibility, and personal happiness. Several macro-level factors contributed to these changes, including urbanization, industrialization, immigration, social events such as wars and the Great Depression, and the rise of new technologies.

1.9. How does social science research help us understand families?

An empirical approach can describe some phenomenon, examine the factors that predict or are associated with some phenomenon, or explain the cause-and-effect relationships or provide insight into why certain events do or do not occur.

1.10. What methods do family scholars use to study families?

Many different methods are used to study families. Depending on the research question, studies can be based on surveys, in-depth interviews, experiments, observation, focus groups, or the analysis of secondary data.

1.11. How can theory help us understand families and family research?

Research is guided by theory, which is a general framework, explanation, or tool used to understand and describe the real world. Theories are important both before and after data have been collected because they help us decide what topics to research, what questions to try to answer, how to best answer them, and how to interpret the research results. Before collecting data, theories can help us frame the question. When data have been collected and patterns emerge, theories can help us make sense of what was found.

1.12. Are Americans rejecting marriage and families?

Families are changing, but there is little evidence that Americans are rejecting marriage and families. If we look at both attitudes and behaviors, we can see that most Americans do marry and do have children. However, the age at marriage has risen and more women are remaining childfree.

PEARSON
myfamilylab
www.myfamilylab.com

Experience, Discover, Observe, Evaluate

MyFamilyLab is designed just for you. Each chapter features a pre-test and post-test to help you learn and review key concepts and terms. Experience Marriage and Family in action with dynamic visual activities, videos, and readings to enhance your learning experience.

Here are a few activities you will find for this chapter:

Watch Core Concepts video clips feature sociologists in action, exploring important concepts in the study of Marriage and the Family. Watch:
- Social Interactions and Social Roles
- Research Tools and Techniques
- Qualitative vs. Quantitative Research

Explore Social Explorer is an interactive application that allows you to explore Census data through interactive maps. Explore the Social Explorer Report:
- Patterns within the Married Population

Read MySocLibrary includes primary source readings from classic and contemporary sociologists. Read:
- Coontz, "The Way We Weren't: The Myth and Reality of the 'Traditional' Family"

2

Social Status: Sex, Gender, Race, Ethnicity, and Social Class

Above: Becca with her daughter, Taylor (age 8).

What are the long-term effects of growing up in poverty?

Poverty involves more than just the absence of money. It can affect the way you see yourself, and how you are able to negotiate the broader world. Becca's story provides a close-up glimpse of what it is like to be poor.

Today Becca is a vibrant thirty-something-year-old mother on the path to success. But her life has had more than its share of dark periods and eroded self-esteem. Becca was born into poverty, and raised in the dismal housing projects of an urban city. Her mother was mentally ill, bounced from boyfriend to boyfriend, and could not properly care for herself or for Becca. Becca was left mostly on her own, unsupervised, dodging the addiction and violence that consumed her family. Becca loved school and did well; school was her refuge. There she was safe, loved, and well cared for. She graduated from high school with honors, despite her personal turmoil, and soon left for a prestigious university that she paid for herself with grants, loans, and her own hard work. She carried the baggage of her past with her to college, a place where she didn't feel comfortable. This discomfort caused her to make poor choices, including becoming too dependent on a man who took advantage of her—a pattern that she would repeat for several years. She became pregnant, and wanting a better life for her son she gave him up for adoption. This infuriated her family, and they virtually disowned

👁—**Watch** the **Video** *Raising Children in Poverty: Becca* on **myfamilylab.com**

her. By this time Becca had dropped out of school, had nowhere to live, and was homeless from ages 19 to 23, moving from shelter to shelter. Looking for love and some semblance of security she again found a boyfriend, but he too was abusive. Together they lived under a bridge, begging for spare change to those passing by. Although she felt that she was giving up her pride, she says that part of living in poverty is blocking out how others might judge you. Becca became pregnant again, and this time was determined to provide a good life for her child, a daughter she named Taylor. The next few years offer a story of hope and renewal, as she struggles to leave her alcoholic abusive partner, find housing for herself and Taylor—who has special needs and developmental delays—and continue with school. These paths are not easy for a person in poverty, as our social service system is cumbersome and difficult to navigate. For example, most landlords will not take her Section 8 subsidized housing voucher, but how can a poor person amass first and last month's rent? However, despite the numerous obstacles in her path, Becca is searching for, and finding her way.

As this story illustrates that our choices—even personal ones—do not exist in a vacuum. Sex, race, ethnicity, and social class affect a wide variety of opportunities, privileges, constraints, and choices available to us (Andersen & Collins, 2007; Bakanic, 2008; Chancer, 2006; Johnson, 2005). This chapter introduces the importance of sex and gender, race, ethnicity, and social class for our family relationships. Why a separate chapter? Shouldn't coverage in the subsequent chapters—dating, intimacy, marriage, children, divorce—suffice? You will learn the particulars in later chapters, but here we will introduce these signature concepts, provide useful definitions, and illustrate their importance in our lives. This chapter reveals the linkages between our micro-level private experiences and the macro-level social structure in which we live.

QUESTIONS *That Matter* • • • • • • • • • • • • • • • •

2.1 Why are gender, race, ethnicity, and social class important?

2.2 What is the difference between "sex" and "gender"?

2.3 How do we learn our gendered expectations?

2.4 What is patriarchy, and why is it important to the study of gender?

2.5 What is the difference between race and ethnicity, and which term is generally more useful?

2.6 What is the difference between individual and institutional discrimination?

2.7 Is the United States becoming more diverse?

2.8 How many social classes are there?

2.9 How does social class affect our lives?

2.10 How is poverty calculated?

2.11 Who is most likely to be poor?

2.12 What are the consequences of poverty?

2.13 Why are the intersections of sex, gender, race, ethnicity, and class important?

:: The Link between Private Experiences and Social Structure

Sex, race, ethnicity, and social class are social statuses that, alone and together, have a strong influence upon us throughout our lives (Bakanic, 2008; Hurst, 2010). They are also dimensions of **social stratification**, or the hierarchical ranking of categories of people within society. Not all categories are treated equally. Some people have more, less, or at least different opportunities because of their sex, race, social class, or a combination of these. Yet, we generally hesitate to acknowledge the stratification of our society. In this chapter, we encourage you to look further at the link between private experience and social structure. Do our statuses really influence our lives, or have things changed? Because we tend to associate with people who are similar to us, we sometimes fail to understand the real power of social structure.

"Why can't we all just be equal?" students have asked. Shouldn't we just pretend that race and ethnicity, and the differences we experience because of them, do not exist in our society? Likewise, aren't we all really middle-class? These questions ignore the fact that women and men, Whites and minorities, and the rich and the poor can have quite different experiences. For example, low-income families have significant difficulties finding even something as basic as housing. The median wage needed to pay for a two-bedroom rental unit was $17.84 per hour in 2009, more than double the minimum wage and far more than many families earn. In seven states—Hawaii, California, Massachusetts, New Jersey, New York, Connecticut, and Maryland—along with the District of Columbia, the average wage needed for a two-bedroom unit is over $20 per hour (Wardrip, Pelletiere, & Crowley, 2009). The lack of affordable housing forces many families to live in dilapidated dwellings without appropriate ventilation or heat, to live in dangerous neighborhoods that are unsafe for children, or to be homeless.

Thus, the rich and the poor, women and men, minorities and Whites often have different social experiences. Acknowledging differences allows us to concede that our private lives and family relationships are affected by what is happening in society. This recognition is called the **sociological imagination** (Mills, 1959). Certain categories of people are more likely to experience certain events than are others. It is not simply a coincidence, for example, that Whites are more likely to marry than are Blacks, that persons with lower incomes are more likely to divorce, that Hispanics have more children than do other groups, that racial or ethnic minority members have significantly higher unemployment rates, or that women are more likely to experience sexual harassment on the job than are men. These patterns are shaped, at least in part, by social and cultural forces, rather than by individual whim or random events.

But haven't things really changed for the better, you ask? Isn't our society more progressive now? There have been many social changes during the past decades, but let's not exaggerate the *degree* of social change. For example, in fiscal year 2009, the U.S. Equal Employment Opportunity Commission (EEOC) received over 26,000 sex discrimination charges, as shown in Table 2.1 (U.S. Equal Employment Opportunity Commission, 2010a). Likewise, the EEOC received over 33,000 charges of racial or ethnic discrimination (U.S. Equal Employment Opportunity Commission, 2010b). These charges represent an increase of more than 20 percent since 2005.

Despite reports of discrimination, some students are reluctant to acknowledge sex, race, or ethnicity as organizing constructs in our society. They may agree that men and women differ in sexuality and reproductive roles, but they are less likely to believe their personal relationships, goals, aspirations, expectations for marriage, job prospects and pay, and current and future roles are considerably shaped by their sex. However, economic data reveal that women still earn only 80 percent of men's earnings, even when both work full-time (Bureau of Labor Statistics, September 2009). It is easy to make the

social stratification: The hierarchical ranking of categories of people within society.

sociological imagination: The recognition that our personal experiences are, in large part, shaped by forces within the larger society.

Table 2.1	Race-Based and Sex-Based Charges of Discrimination		
Charges of discrimination have increased.			
	FY 2000	FY 2005	FY 2009
Race-Based	28,945	26,740	33,579
Sex-Based	25,194	23,094	28,028

Source: U.S. Equal Employment Opportunity Commission, 2010a; 2010b.

claim that "things have changed for the better," but social science research can reveal important trends and patterns.

Quite naturally, we tend to spend time with others most like us—people who live in the same neighborhoods, go to the same churches and schools, and share the same interests as we do. For example, many neighborhoods remain racially segregated (Census-Scope, 2008). In Chicago, Illinois, Whites live in neighborhoods that average 80 percent White, despite being only 60 percent of the population. Blacks live in neighborhoods averaging 75 percent Black, yet they comprise only 20 percent of the population in Chicago. As you might expect, people in the same neighborhood who attend the same schools and churches are likely to be of the same social class, and share similar values.

Lack of contact with individuals outside our social class, race, and ethnicity can foster misconceptions about these individuals. The poor, for example, are often denigrated by the middle class and blamed for their own economic circumstances. Welfare recipients in particular are criticized for living off the "public dole," despite the fact that most of them are children (Lindsey, 2011). Yet, many college students also live off the "public dole"; public state universities charge tuition rates that cover less than half of the real costs of a college education. Taxpayers, including people who have no college-age children, make up much of the difference.

Understanding the ways in which race and ethnicity, sex and gender, and social class shape our lives allows us to make rational choices about our own lives and our relationships with others. Acknowledging differences does not have to make us feel superior or inferior. Rather, it can help us better understand ourselves and the ways in which our society both empowers and constrains us. These privileges and constraints follow us as we mature and develop intimate relationships.

Throughout this text you will see many ways that these statuses shape our marriages and families, including how we develop intimacy, our marriage and partnering patterns, how we raise children, issues surrounding aging, and how we face challenges and transitions such as a divorce or remarriage. This chapter will introduce and define these signature concepts so that you can better understand the social context in which we live and how this context influences our relationships.

Do you think that the increase in charges of sex, racial, and ethnic discrimination represents an increase in incidents of discrimination? Or do you think that women and minorities are now more comfortable identifying when they have been discriminated against?

:: Sex, Gender, and Patriarchy

Most of us would be shocked if someone suggested women should no longer vote or be allowed to drive a car, should eat only after the men in their families had finished their meal, and should be under the authority of men at all times. But people hold these beliefs in many countries around the world. For example, women in Saudi Arabia generally must obtain permission from a guardian—a father, husband, brother, or son—to work, travel, study, marry, or even access health care (Pew Research Center, 2008).

Who we are—men or women—profoundly affects our experiences within our relationships and families, even here in the United States. As you will see in subsequent chapters:

- Girls and boys are treated differently by their parents, and parents hold different expectations for them.
- Males begin sexual relationships earlier than do females, and have a larger number of sexual partners.
- Although women are more likely to graduate from college than are men, they are less likely to have careers, and they earn less money.
- Wives are more likely than their husbands to do most of the housework and childcare.
- Husbands are more likely to bear the responsibility of supporting the family.
- If a couple divorces, the man is more likely to remarry.
- Wives are more likely to be widowed than are their husbands.

Biological sex differences are important, but so is the way that men and women are *treated* within their culture. **Sex** refers to biological differences between men and women and their role in reproduction; **gender** describes the culturally and socially constructed differences between males and females that we find in the meanings, beliefs, and practices associated with "femininity" and "masculinity." Gendered expectations can vary a lot, as we shall see.

Sex and Gender Differences

A popular Mother Goose nursery rhyme goes,
"What are little boys made of, made of?
What are little boys made of?
Frogs and snails
And puppy-dog tails,
That's what little boys are made of.
What are little girls made of, made of?
What are little girls made of?
Sugar and spice
And all things nice
That's what little girls are made of."

Poems, nursery rhymes, and songs often accentuate the traditional differences between men and women. Historically, people have viewed masculinity and femininity as a set of different, or even opposite, traits (Kramer, 2007; Lindsey, 2011). Men are often considered to be naturally more aggressive, strong, and independent, whereas women may be considered to be more emotional, nurturing, and sensitive. ◉─Watch on **myfamilylab.com**

The *Getting to Know Yourself* box offers a self-test you can use to assess your own personality traits. Are you more traditionally masculine, more feminine, or do you lean towards **androgyny** (having both masculine and feminine traits in near equal proportion)? Remember, there are no right or wrong answers; just take a look at yourself.

Researchers note some important biological differences between men and women beyond those needed for reproduction. For example, males are diagnosed with a wider variety of physical illnesses despite being stronger, more active, and more aggressive on average (Centers for Disease Control and Prevention, 2008; National Center for Health Statistics, 2009). In contrast, females are more likely to be diagnosed with an emotional illness such as depression.

On average, males and females also solve intellectual problems differently. Although no overall differences in intelligence are found (according to IQ tests), men tend to perform better on certain types of mathematical reasoning tests. And women outperform men in the precision with which they perform certain manual tasks. Women also tend to excel on tests measuring recall or matching.

◉─Watch the **Video**
Core Concepts: Similarities between Men and Women on **myfamilylab.com**

sex: Biological differences between men and women, and their role in reproduction.

gender: Culturally and socially constructed differences between males and females found in the meanings, beliefs, and practices associated with "femininity" and "masculinity."

androgyny: Possessing both masculine and feminine traits in near equal proportion.

Getting to Know Yourself

Gender Traits Test

Below is a Gender Traits Test, which is a way of judging how traditionally "male" or "female" you are in your behavior and feelings. It is adapted from the work of Dr. Sandra Bem, a psychologist who has written extensively on the subject of gender. There are no right or wrong answers, so just assess yourself on the characteristics listed, using the following scale:

1 = Never or Almost Never True; 2 = Usually Not True; 3 = Sometimes but Infrequently True; 4 = Occasionally True; 5 = Often True; 6 = Usually True; 7 = Always or Almost Always True

1.	Adaptable	1	2	3	4	5	6	7
2.	Affectionate	1	2	3	4	5	6	7
3.	Aggressive	1	2	3	4	5	6	7
4.	Conceited	1	2	3	4	5	6	7
5.	Compassionate	1	2	3	4	5	6	7
6.	Assertive	1	2	3	4	5	6	7
7.	Conscientious	1	2	3	4	5	6	7
8.	Eager to soothe hurt feelings	1	2	3	4	5	6	7
9.	Defend own beliefs	1	2	3	4	5	6	7
10.	Conventional	1	2	3	4	5	6	7
11.	Gentle	1	2	3	4	5	6	7
12.	Dominant	1	2	3	4	5	6	7
13.	Jealous	1	2	3	4	5	6	7
14.	Love children	1	2	3	4	5	6	7
15.	Forceful	1	2	3	4	5	6	7
16.	Moody	1	2	3	4	5	6	7
17.	Sensitive to the needs of others	1	2	3	4	5	6	7
18.	Have leadership abilities	1	2	3	4	5	6	7
19.	Reliable	1	2	3	4	5	6	7
20.	Sympathetic	1	2	3	4	5	6	7
21.	Independent	1	2	3	4	5	6	7
22.	Secretive	1	2	3	4	5	6	7
23.	Tender	1	2	3	4	5	6	7
24.	Have a strong personality	1	2	3	4	5	6	7
25.	Tactful	1	2	3	4	5	6	7
26.	Understanding	1	2	3	4	5	6	7
27.	Willing to take a stand	1	2	3	4	5	6	7
28.	Truthful	1	2	3	4	5	6	7
29.	Warm	1	2	3	4	5	6	7
30.	Willing to take risks	1	2	3	4	5	6	7

Scoring

Step 1: Beginning with **number one**, delete every third answer (e.g., 1, 4, 7, 10, 13, etc.)—these are "dummies" in order to keep you from skewing the test while you are taking it.

Step 2: Total up, beginning with **number two**, every third answer (e.g., 2, 5, 8, 11, 14, etc.). Let's call this "Score A."

Step 3: Total up, beginning with **number 3**, every third answer (e.g., 3, 6, 9, 12, 15, etc.). Let's call this "Score B."

Step 4: Subtract Score B from Score A for the "Difference Score." For instance, if your A Score is 90 and your B Score is 70, your Difference Score is $90-70 = +20$ (positive 20); if your A Score is 70 and your B Score is 90, your Difference Score is $70 - 90 = -20$ (negative 20).

Interpreting Gender Traits Scoring

Masculine: -20 and under

Nearly Masculine: -19 to -10

Androgynous: -9 to $+9$

Mostly Feminine: $+9$ to $+19$

Feminine: $+20$ and over

What Do You Think?

1. How did you score? Can you think of the micro- and macro-level factors that have influenced your score?

2. Do you think a test created more than two decades ago is still a useful inventory? Why or why not?

Source: Adapted from The International Foundation for Androgynous Studies, 2004; Bem, 1975, 1981.

Cognitive sex differences appear in very young children, and are evident among other types of animals used in research, even rats. What accounts for these sex differences? Research is still in its infancy because of the complexity of sex differences, but studies in the last few decades suggest that the size, shape, and use of the brain may differ somewhat between men and women in regions involved in language, memory, emotion, vision, hearing, and navigation (Becker, Berkley, Geary, Hampson, Herman, & Young, 2008). Women also seem to use more parts of their brain at once. Hormonal differences may be the cause of some of the dissimilarity, as women have higher levels of estrogen and progesterone, and men have higher levels of testosterone (Kimura, 2002; Hines, 2005; Onion, 2005). Exposure to different hormones begins when we are in our mother's womb and may help explain the way the brain is "wired."

It is intriguing to think about how men and women are different, and whether these differences are innate and biological, or whether we learn them in the social environment. How much is fixed, and how much is flexible? We may never have definitive answers, but we do know that social and cultural factors, alongside biology, are very powerful (Kramer, 2007; Lindsey, 2011). What one culture defines as feminine behavior, another may see as quite masculine. Thus, gender is socially constructed.

Gender Learning

We learn expected gender behavior through a process called **gender socialization**, which teaches us the cultural norms associated with being male or female. It may be a conscious effort, as in a parent scolding a young son for displaying his emotions—"big boys don't cry"—or less consciously, as in a parent providing different toys for children—dolls for daughters and trucks for sons. Gender socialization also occurs in our social structure; our religious institutions or the mass media, for example, teach us about what it means to be male or female. ⊙ Watch on **myfamilylab.com**

Gender socialization also has an important *evaluative component*. We learn that many traits associated with men or boys are considered "better" than the ones associated with women or girls. Here are two examples: When I ask my female students to raise their hands if they were considered "tomboys" when growing up, the hands eagerly and proudly shoot up. When I ask the male students how many were "sissies" as children, the class breaks into laughter. In other words, women have no trouble identifying with traditionally defined masculine behavior, but men are embarrassed to identify with that which is traditionally feminine. When I ask my female students to raise their hands if they have cried (with visible tears) during the past week, about half will raise their hands. When I then ask my male students the same question, again I hear mostly laughter. No man wants to admit to being seen as "weak," which is, in turn, seen as feminine.

⊙ Watch the **Video** *Core Concepts: Gender Socialization* on **myfamilylab.com**

gender socialization: Teaching the cultural norms associated with being male or female.

agents of socialization: The primary groups responsible for gender socialization.

Agents of socialization are the social groups responsible for gender socialization and include parents, schools, toys, peers, and the mass media, as shown in Table 2.2.

Parents   Parents provide the first exposure to a particular culture, and consciously or not, they may treat their sons and daughters differently (Lindsey, Cremeens, and Caldera, 2010). They hold baby girls more gently and cuddle them more than boys. Parents of infant girls describe their children as more dainty and delicate than will parents of infant boys, and the choice of dress usually reflects this (Leaper & Friedman, 2006). Differential treatment continues throughout childhood, repeating itself in a self-fulfilling prophecy beyond any true biological differences. Solely on the basis of sex, parents may

Table 2.2	Agents of Socialization and How They Work
Parents	Differential treatment becomes a self-fulfilling prophecy
Schools	Hidden curriculum encourages sex-typed behavior and teaches girls to fear academic success
Toys	Books show boys as leading characters and girls in stereotypical roles; toys are sex-typed
Peers	Same-sex play reinforces different interaction styles that carry over into adulthood
Mass Media	Television, music videos, and computer games tend to focus on boys and present girls in stereotypical ways

assign rules, toys, expected behavior, chores, hobbies, and a multitude of other cultural values or artifacts differently (Raffaelli & Ontai, 2004). When girls and boys are treated differently, not surprisingly they become more different.

Schools   From daycare through high school, schools present a **hidden curriculum** that informally teaches girls to value compliance (Orenstein, 1994). School textbooks and readers often have stories of boys or men as main characters, relegating girls and women to the sidelines or showing them in a limited number of roles or occupations (Etaugh, 2003). Even college textbooks often reveal gender stereotyping (Yanowitz, 2004). As recently as a decade ago, girls excelled over boys during grade school, but the situation reversed in middle and high school. A 2006 study involving 518 boys and girls from fifth to seventh grade found that girls were more successful than boys in the younger grades in math and on math achievement tests, but these differences tended to disappear among the older children. One study found that girls began to lose their academic confidence as they became teens (Kenney-Benson, Pomerantz, Ryan, & Patrick, 2006).

However, it appears that today many girls and young women have a strong achievement ethic, are doing well in school, and are surpassing boys and young men. More young women apply to, attend, and graduate from college now than young men. Fifty-four percent of undergraduate students are women, up from only 36 percent in 1970, as are 60 percent of graduate students (Fry & Cohn, 2010). Many college majors, however, remain sex-typed. Students in nursing, elementary education, and social work are overwhelmingly female, while students in engineering and computer science are primarily male. Nonetheless, among married couples under age 45 (born in the United States), wives are now likely to have more education than their husbands, as shown in Figure 2.1 (Fry & Cohn, 2010). 📖—Read on **myfamilylab.com**

Toys   Children's toys, books, and games also reflect our gendered culture and teach children important cultural messages about what it means to be a boy, girl, man, or woman (Diekman, 2004). If you visit any children's toy store, you will see that pink aisles specialize in "girl toys" (dolls and their accessories, arts and crafts, domestic toys), whereas other aisles are for "boy toys" (war games, sport accessories, action figures). Boys' favorite toys are manipulation-based, while girls' favorites are dolls (Cherney & London, 2006). Even a toy as gender-neutral as a bicycle takes on gender significance by its color; bicycles for boys are *not* painted pink with white wheels!

A content analysis of the best-selling and award-winning children's books published from 1999 to 2001 found that gender stereotyping was alive and well (Diekman, 2004). Reviewers of these books included male and female professors and students, and they found

📖 Read the **Document**
Too Many Women in College?
on **myfamilylab.com**

hidden curriculum: Gender socialization which is taught informally in school.

Figure 2.1	**Who Has More Education: Husbands or Wives?**

Married women now have more education than their husbands.

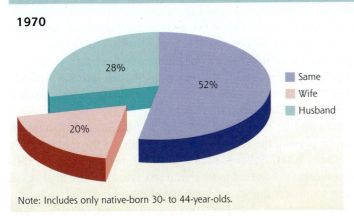
1970
28% 52% 20%
Same · Wife · Husband
Note: Includes only native-born 30- to 44-year-olds.

2007
19% 28% 53%
Same · Wife · Husband
Note: Includes only native-born 30- to 44-year-olds.

Source: Fry, Richard and D'Vera Cohn. 2010. "New Economics of Marriage: The Rise of Wives." Retrieved 20 January 2010(pewresearch.org/pubs/1466/economics-marriage-rise-of-wives).

There are many different agents of socialization. Can you see how children's toys teach them about what it means to be a boy or a girl in our culture?

that stories were nearly twice as likely to feature males as characters. When girls and women were portrayed, they were more than three times as likely to be shown as nurturing or caring for others as compared to boys and men. Female characters were more likely to be found indoors, while males were more likely to be outdoors. Males were found in a range of 32 different jobs, as compared to 12 for females. Of 23 female adult characters shown with an occupation, 21 had stereotypically feminine occupations. Even another survey of children's books evaluated as "nonsexist" by a group of independent raters reveals that the books still portray housework as women's work. Although the books showed women and girls at work or playing in active ways, they also showed women and girls doing domestic chores, unlike boys who were rarely portrayed doing housework (Diekman, 2004).

Peers   The influence of peer groups begins early, reaching its peak in adolescence. Psychologist Eleanor Maccoby found that children between the ages of two and three tend to sort themselves into same-sex play groups when given the opportunity to do so (Maccoby, 1998), and are more social with children of the same sex. She also noted that when girls were playing with other girls, they were as active as were boys playing with other boys. However, when girls were playing with boys, they frequently stood back and let the boys dominate the toys or games. Maccoby speculated that boys' rougher play and greater focus on competition was unattractive to girls, and girls responded by pulling back rather than by trying to exert their own play style. These different interaction styles tend to carry over into adulthood: boys' groups reinforce a more competitive, dominance-oriented style of interaction, which becomes adult male communication patterns that include greater interrupting, contradicting, or boasting. Girls' cooperative groups reinforce a style that contributes to adult female communication patterns including expressing agreement and acknowledging the comments of others, and asking questions rather than making bold pronouncements.

The Media   The mass media, including television and video games, represent an increasingly important mechanism for socializing children. More than two-thirds of American households play computer or video games; 60 percent of these players are male (Entertainment Software Association, 2010). In a study titled *Girls and Gaming: Gender and Video Game Marketing*, a look at 27 popular games found that many promoted "unrealistic body images and stereotypical female characteristics, such as provocative sexuality, high-pitched voices, and fainting" (Media Awareness Network, 2008).

t hink about the influence these agents of socialization had upon your own childhood. Which ones had the most influence on your gender?

Boys, especially middle-class White boys, are at the center of most television programming, playing the most roles and engaging in the most activity (Aubrey & Harrison, 2004; Baker & Raney, 2007). A review of recent children's television shows reveals that male characters are still more likely than female characters to answer questions, boss or order others, show ingenuity, and achieve a goal (Aubrey & Harrison, 2004). A study of morning commercials showed that half of the commercials aimed at girls spoke about physical attractiveness, whereas none of the commercials aimed at boys referenced attractiveness (National Institute on Media and the Family, 2009). Incidentally, females are less likely than males to be shown eating, not an insignificant finding given the high rates of eating disorders among girls and women (National Institute of Mental Health, 2009).

How Do Race, Ethnicity, and Class Shape Gender Socialization?

Let's be careful not to overgeneralize because people's experiences differ widely and because the intersections of gender, race, ethnicity, and class are complex. However, it does appear there are significant class, racial, and ethnic variations in the gender socialization process (Hirsch, 2003; Hill, 2002, 2005; Wallace, 2007). For example, Hill's in-depth interviews with a small sample of 35 Black parents examined the extent to which parents think gender influenced the ways in which they socialize and treat their children. All parents expressed some belief in gender equality, but middle-class Black parents expressed the strongest support.

In another example, Black women and girls are found to be more satisfied with their body types than are their White counterparts (Bailey, 2008). Blacks have a more flexible standard of attractiveness, believing that curves and a fuller body are more desirable than supermodel thinness. Black girls are more likely than White girls to say that they are beautiful, that they like their bodies, and that they like themselves the way they are (Bailey, 2008).

Gender's Influence on Our Family and Close Relationships: Division of Household Labor

While gender is forged into all aspects of social life, it is particularly evident within families and close relationships. A striking example is how work chores are divided in the home, which you will read about in depth in Chapter 10. Cooking, cleaning, grocery shopping, yard work, and laundry are critical functions, and take increasing time when a family has children. Household labor has been traditionally defined as "women's work" and was not deemed worthy of scientific study 20 or 30 years ago. Yet, a 2007 poll by the Pew Research Center reveals many people are adamant that sharing household chores is "very important for a successful marriage." This sentiment is growing, as shown in Figure 2.2. In fact, there was very little change between 1990 and 2007 in the survey items, except for sharing chores! The only other change was the decline in the percentage of people who believe children are very important for marital success (Pew Research Center, 2007).

We now know that women average up to two to three times the amount of time on household tasks that men do (Hook, 2006; Galinsky, Aumann, & Bond, 2009; Bureau of Labor Statistics, May 8, 2008). A similar although less dramatic pattern occurs with childcare (Finley, Mira, & Schwartz, 2008). These differences continue to hold when the wife is employed, or when both partners are retired, and they persist at all income levels. In fact, marriage has been shown to increase women's time spent in housework, while it reduces men's time (Gantert, 2008).

One explanation for why women do a disproportionate share of household labor is that society has defined such work as simply part of being a woman (Lachance-Grzela & Bouchard, 2010). We often view gender as a reasonable and legitimate basis for distributing rights and responsibilities. We define housework as a part of women's "essential nature," whereas a man's "essential nature" is *not* to engage in it (West & Zimmerman, 1987).

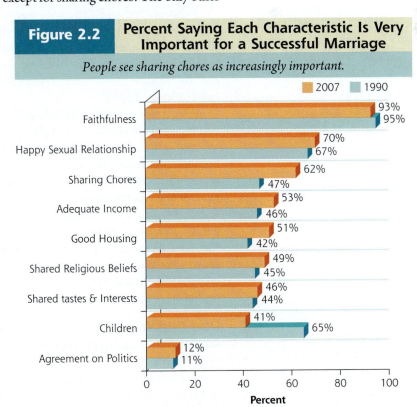

Figure 2.2 **Percent Saying Each Characteristic Is Very Important for a Successful Marriage**

People see sharing chores as increasingly important.

2007 | 1990

Characteristic	2007	1990
Faithfulness	93%	95%
Happy Sexual Relationship	70%	67%
Sharing Chores	62%	47%
Adequate Income	53%	46%
Good Housing	51%	42%
Shared Religious Beliefs	49%	45%
Shared tastes & Interests	46%	44%
Children	41%	65%
Agreement on Politics	12%	11%

Percent

Source: From Pew Hispanic Center and Kaiser Family Foundation, March 2004.

Male Privilege: Patriarchy

Patriarchy, introduced in Chapter 1, is found in a wide variety of social institutions, including legal, educational, religious, and economic ones. Traditional religious texts are filled with passages demeaning women, although their interpretations may be softened in modern-day texts. Christianity advocates patriarchy, as witnessed in the following passages in the New Testament (1 Tm. 2:11-15):

> Let a woman learn in silence with all submissiveness. I permit no woman to teach or to have authority over men; she is to keep silent. For Adam was formed first, then Eve; and Adam was not deceived, but the woman was deceived and became a transgressor. Yet woman will be saved through bearing children, if she continues in faith and love and holiness, with modesty.

Patriarchy is widespread and found in every society to some degree. As women improve their economic status, male-female relationships tend to become more egalitarian. Nonetheless, as we will see shortly, clear patterns of male dominance continue to exist even in the United States.

But let's first consider an example of patriarchy found in other parts of the world, female genital cutting. It is often easier to identify patriarchy and social inequality elsewhere than it is within our own culture.

Female Genital Cutting   "Female circumcision," "female genital cutting," or "female genital mutilation" is commonly practiced in over two dozen countries in Africa, the Middle East, and among some immigrant communities in North America and Europe (World Health Organization, 2009). In one form, clitoridectomy, the clitoris is literally cut out of the body. In the more extreme form, infibulation, a girl's entire external genital area is removed, including the vaginal lips, and the outer portion of the vagina is stitched together, leaving only a miniscule opening for menstrual blood and urine to escape. The girl's knees are bound together for several weeks for the incision to heal. The procedure is excruciatingly painful, has many serious side effects, and eliminates women's ability to experience sexual pleasure. This procedure has no known health benefits.

Between 100 and 140 million girls and women today have had their genitals cut or mutilated, and the practice appears to be spreading (World Health Organization, 2009). Even those women who privately oppose it undergo the procedure and intend to continue it with their daughters. They believe that failure to do so will make their daughters "different" or "promiscuous" and perhaps unmarriageable as a result (Yount, 2002; Amnesty International, 2004).

Why is this practice of female genital mutilation so widespread, and why has it continued for so many years? It is deeply rooted in the patriarchal traditions of societies where it is found. Although no religion formally endorses female genital mutilation, it is widespread because of customs demanding that women be virgins at the time of marriage and remain sexually faithful thereafter. Removing the clitoris, the source of a woman's sexual pleasure, ensures she will not experience orgasm, and thus the likelihood of engaging in or enjoying sexual relationships outside marriage is lessened. Among women whose entire external genital area has been removed, the opening that remains is so small as to forbid penetration. Female genital mutilation persists because women's status is low, and their options in society are few. Marriage and motherhood are the primary ways in which they receive recognition. Virginity is highly valued, and this procedure helps to ensure they will not have sex before marriage, thus bringing the family honor, and help in finding a suitable mate.

Does Patriarchy Exist in the United States?   After reading the previous example about female genital mutilation, it is easy to say, "Whew, I'm glad I live in the United States." However, the United States has its own set of patriarchal norms and customs. Do any come to mind? How many U.S. presidents have been women? Vice presidents? Senators? How many heads of Fortune 500 companies are women? How does women's pay compare to that of men? How do standards of beauty vary for men and women—some with potentially

In more than 200 years of history, the United States has yet to elect a female President or Vice President of the United States. Is this just a coincidence, or does it reflect patriarchy?

dangerous or painful repercussions (think of cosmetic surgery, breast implants, waxing, or even high-heeled shoes)? Over 12 million cosmetic surgery procedures are performed each year in the United States, a 60 percent increase since 2000 (American Society of Plastic Surgeons, 2009a, b). Ninety-one percent of cosmetic surgery patients are women, and one-quarter of these are teenagers. Table 2.3 lists the top five surgical cosmetic procedures in 2008 (American Society of Plastic Surgeons, 2009c). These procedures should be cause for concern, as these surgeries are not risk-free, and can have both short- and long-term side effects. It is believed that women who have cosmetic surgery have internalized the media messages about the body image of the "ideal" woman, and are dissatisfied with their own bodies (Markey & Markey, 2009).

Let's look at an example even closer to home—where did you get your *last name*? Most children carry their father's last name. When they marry, most women take their husband's last name (Jayson, 2005; Keen, 2005; Powell, 2005). Based on almost 7,000 wedding announcements published in *The New York Times*, only about 17 percent of women kept their own names, down from 23 percent in 1990 (Jayson, 2005). The women who keep their own last names are more likely to have graduated from more prestigious colleges, have more advanced degrees, marry later, hold more feminist attitudes, and have greater career commitment (Hoffnung, 2006).

Why do most women change their last names upon marriage? The reasons are summarized in the *Tying It All Together* box (p. 48). There are many micro-level reasons, for example, "It's easier this way…." But let's think of the macro-level reasons. The changing of women's names is a carryover from older patriarchal and patrilineal customs dictating that, upon marriage, the wife became the legal property of her husband. Last names clarified paternity so that a man could be certain of passing his property on to his heirs. These continuing patriarchal traditions tell us something about women's roles in society.

Dr. Ben Barres, a neurobiologist and professor at Stanford University, has something to say about male privilege. Barres has the unique experience of living as both a woman and a man. He was born a woman, but from an early age felt that he was really a man trapped in a woman's body. As an adult, Barres had a sex change operation, and has now lived as a man for over a decade. What did he learn from this experience? He is adamant that women and men are treated very differently, and that women are routinely discriminated against in ways that most of us are unaware of. As a man, Barres believes he is afforded more respect than when he was a woman, is thought to be more intelligent, has greater access to other physician and science colleagues, and is interrupted less in conversation. For example, after

Table 2.3	Top Five Surgical Cosmetic Procedures in 2008
Why is breast augmentation the most frequently performed surgical cosmetic procedure?	
Breast augmentation	307,000
Nose reshaping	279,000
Liposuction	245,000
Eyelid surgery	221,000
Tummy tuck	122,000

Source: American Society of Plastic Surgeons. 2009a. "2000/2007/2008 National Plastic Surgery Statistics: Cosmetic and Reconstructive Procedure Trends." Retrieved 20 January 2010 (www.plasticsurgery.org/Media/stats/2008-cosmetic-reconstructive-plastic-surgery-minimally-invasive-statistics.pdf).

Tying It All Together

Factors That Shape Why Most American Women Change Their Last Names upon Marriage

In the United States, you can really have any name you want. When you marry, you can keep the one your parents gave you, you can take your partner's name, you can hyphenate your name with that of your partner, or you can even invent one of your own. Given all these different options, have you noticed a pattern? Women usually take their partner's name or use a hyphen with both names. In contrast, men usually keep their own names, and rarely even hyphen their name with their partner's. What's behind this? At first glance, our choice of names seems personal, and we therefore draw upon micro-level explanations, "Oh, it's easier that way. . . ." Yet, why is it only "easier" for women, but not for men? There must be more going on to explain our choice of last name, and we must look for macro-level explanations to see the whole story.

Micro-level Explanations

- "It's easier this way. . . ."
- "It helps make us a family to have the same last name. . . ."

- "Why burden children with parents who have different last names from one another, or a long hyphenated name?"
- "It works out better this way for the children's school and medical records. . . ."

Macro-level Explanations

- It is a carryover from patriarchal and patrilineal customs in which, upon marriage, the wife became the legal property of her husband.
- Last names clarify paternity.
- It demonstrates that women have found a husband to avoid the stigma associated with being unmarried.

What Do You Think?

1. What do you plan to do with your last name if you marry, and why?
2. Why do you think that fewer women retain their last name when they marry despite greater equality nowadays? Do names no longer reflect patriarchy or paternity? What do they represent?

---

giving a lecture he overheard a colleague say, "Ben Barres gave a great seminar today, but then his work is much better than his sister's," unknowingly referring to him prior to his sex change operation (Science Daily, 2006; Vedantam, 2006).

How would your life be different if you were of the opposite sex? Assume you were raised in the same family, went to the same schools, and lived in the same neighborhood. Think about the ways in which your experiences, opportunities, or choices might be different or similar.

Sex and gender are firmly rooted in our social structure and affect a wide variety of opportunities, privileges, constraints, and choices available to us as we form families and intimate relationships. The task here has been to introduce these signature concepts. In addition to sex and gender, the aspects of race, ethnicity, and social class are an important part of our social structure, and also shape our relationships. Although many Whites have the luxury of rarely thinking about racial or ethnic issues, and many Americans believe that we live in a generally middle-class society, I want to impart a greater sensitivity toward how and why these aspects shape the structure of, and interactions within, marriages and families. These concepts are introduced next, so that you may have a fuller understanding when they are revisited in upcoming chapters.

:: Race and Ethnicity

Like sex and gender, race and ethnicity are also statuses that deeply influence our relationships and families. We will see many examples of this throughout this text, including:

- Blacks are more likely than Whites to live in extended families.
- Hispanics have the largest number of children, while Asian Americans are most likely to be childfree.

- Blacks are less likely than other groups to remarry.
- Teenage pregnancy and birth rates are declining among all racial groups, but the declines have been the largest among Blacks.
- Whites are least likely to live in poverty, while Native Americans are most likely to do so.
- Hispanics, in particular Mexican Americans, are least likely to have health insurance.
- Asian Americans are the least likely to divorce.
- Blacks begin sexual activity earlier than other groups.

Let's first step back and ask ourselves, what is race? What is ethnicity? Why are these concepts so important for understanding family patterns, interactions, and dynamics?

The Population Is Growing More Diverse

Race, ethnicity, and *minority* are often-used terms (Parrillo, 2008; Farley, 2010; Schaefer, 2011). But do we know what they really mean? Theoretically, **race** is a category describing people who share real or perceived physical traits that society deems socially significant, such as skin color. Nineteenth-century biologists created a three-part classification of races: Caucasian, individuals with relatively light skin; Negroid, individuals with darker skin and characteristics such as coarse curly hair; and Mongoloid, individuals with yellow or brown skin and folds on their eyelids (Simpson & Yinger, 1985). However, over the last half century or so, due to tremendous growth in our knowledge of genetics, race has ceased to be a useful construct (Lewontin, 2006). An increasing number of people are biracial, further leading most social scientists to suggest that narrow conceptions of race are not particularly accurate, nor are they a useful way to understand differences.

Ethnicity is a more useful concept than race because it reflects cultural traditions such as language, food, and celebrations, as shown here.

Ethnicity, or shared cultural characteristics such as language, place of origin, dress, food, religion, and other values, is a more useful concept. Ethnicity represents culture, whereas race attempts to represent biological heritage. People who share specific cultural features are members of an **ethnic group**. There are many different ethnic groups in the United States, and hundreds of these groups throughout the world. Even Caucasians may identify themselves as members of ethnic groups, such as Polish, German, or Italian, if they share interrelated cultural characteristics with them.

Usually when we talk about **minority groups**, we are not really referring to the size of the group, but rather, to a category of people who have less power than the dominant group, and who are subject to unequal treatment. Members of a minority group tend to earn less money and have less representation in politics and other social disadvantages. Most people would agree that women and people of color are members of minority groups; however, other ethnic groups such as Irish Americans are probably not. In some cases, minority groups may actually represent the statistical majority, as is the case for Blacks in South Africa, or for women in most societies around the world.

The United States is a nation with many minority groups, and is becoming even more diverse, as shown in Figure 2.3, see page 50 (U.S. Census Bureau Population Division, 2009). About one person in three is a member of a minority group, and in Hawaii, New Mexico, California, Texas, and the District of Columbia, minorities outnumber non-Hispanic Whites. By 2050, minority groups are likely to comprise about 54 percent of the U.S. population (U.S. Census Bureau Population Division, 2009). The largest increases will occur among Hispanics. The term *Hispanic*, rather than *Latino*, will be used in this text because, among those with a preference, *Hispanic* is the preferred term (Suro, 2006). Hispanic groups, now 16 percent of the population, will nearly double to 30 percent by the year 2050. Asians will increase to 8 percent of the population. The percentage of Blacks and

race: A category describing people who share real or perceived physical straits that society deems socially significant, such as skin color.

ethnicity: Shared cultural characteristics, such as language, place of origin, dress, food, religion, and other values.

ethnic group: A group of people who share specific cultural features.

minority group: A category of people who have less power than the dominant group, and who are subject to unequal treatment.

Figure 2.3

Resident Population by Race and Hispanic Origin Status—Projections: 2010 to 2050

Hispanics are the fastest-growing portion of the U.S. population.

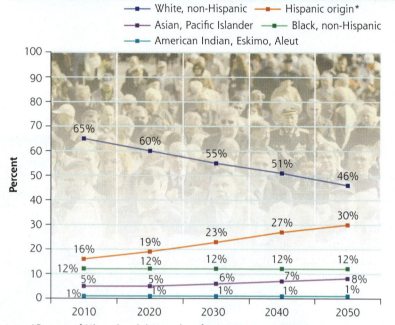

Legend:
- White, non-Hispanic
- Hispanic origin*
- Asian, Pacific Islander
- Black, non-Hispanic
- American Indian, Eskimo, Aleut

Percent	2010	2020	2030	2040	2050
White, non-Hispanic	65%	60%	55%	51%	46%
Hispanic origin*	16%	19%	23%	27%	30%
Black, non-Hispanic	12%	12%	12%	12%	12%
Asian, Pacific Islander	5%	5%	6%	7%	8%
American Indian, Eskimo, Aleut	1%	1%	1%	1%	1%

*Persons of Hispanic origin may be of any race.

Source: U.S. Census Bureau Population Division 2009.

✳**Explore** the **Concept**
Social Explorer Map:
The Mixed Race Population on
myfamilylab.com

social capital: Social networking connections, which can be a valuable source of information, such as a resource for job leads.

prejudice: A negative attitude about members of selected racial and ethnic groups.

stereotypes: Oversimplified sets of beliefs about a group of people.

discrimination: Behaviors, actions, or practices based on racial or ethnic preferences that have harmful impacts.

American Indians (Native Americans)/Alaska Natives will stabilize at 13 and 1 percent of the population, respectively.

Throughout its history, people have immigrated to the United States. Some came willingly, fleeing persecution or seeking better opportunities while others were coerced or brought as slaves or indentured servants. Together, these immigrants joined the Native Americans and Mexicans who were already living here and flourishing with many different cultures and languages. Today, about 13 percent of our population, or 38 million people, immigrated to the United States as either children or adults. They most likely came from Mexico and Latin America rather than Europe, which was the case for much of our history (Department of Homeland Security, 2010). There are also an estimated 8.3 million undocumented migrants in the United States (in 2008), a significant decline from several years ago (Hoefer, Rytina, & Baker, 2010; Passel & Cohn, April 14, 2009).

Minority groups are sometimes devalued and treated with suspicion and contempt by other members of society. The next section discusses these forms of treatment. ✳**Explore** on **myfamilylab.com**

Prejudice and Discrimination: Pervasive Problems

Let's say you are a manager for a medium-size company and you want to hire someone for a job. You receive four interesting applications from the following people: Emily, Greg, Lakisha, and Jamal. Who are you going to contact for an interview?

Researchers at the University of Chicago submitted fictitious resumes to over a thousand ads in Boston and Chicago newspapers. Resumes were randomly assigned Black- or White-sounding names, but other aspects of their resumes were similar. Those resumes with White-sounding names received 50 percent more telephone calls for interviews. This racial gap was found across different occupations, industries, and employer size (Bertrand & Mullainathan, 2004).

However, we also know that many jobs are never posted in newspaper want ads, but are advertised informally through "word of mouth" or through social networking connections. These connections, referred to as **social capital**, can be a valuable source of information about job leads. A study using a nationally representative survey found that minorities and women have much less social capital than do White men, and therefore miss many employment opportunities (McDonald, Lin, & Ao, 2009).

Prejudice is a negative attitude about members of selected racial and ethnic groups (Bakanic, 2008). It often comes from **stereotypes**, or an oversimplified set of beliefs about a group of people. For example, the stereotype that Black teenage girls are always having babies outside marriage, that Mexican Americans do not want to learn English, and that Jews are stingy represent widespread stereotypes prevalent in the United States.

Discrimination is a behavior that has harmful effects, such as refusing to hire or promote someone because of his or her race or ethnicity. Discrimination remains widespread in the United States today, as noted by the Equal Employment Opportunity Commission (EEOC) (U.S. Equal Employment Opportunity Commission, 2010a). A number of studies by scholar Ian Ayres found overwhelming evidence that in a variety of markets, Blacks and females are consistently at a disadvantage. For example, when Ayres sent agents of different races posing as potential buyers to more than 200 car dealerships in Chicago, he found that dealers regularly charged Blacks and women more than they charged White men. He also found that minority male defendants are frequently required to post higher bail bonds than their White counterparts. Consequently, only 55 percent of Blacks believe that relations between Whites and Blacks are "very good" or "somewhat good," compared to 75 percent of Whites (Gallup News Service, 2007).

We tend to think of discrimination at the individual level. For example, the Collins family does not want to sell their home to the Juarez family because they are Mexican, so they have their realtor falsely tell them that they already have a buyer. This form of discrimination, called **individual discrimination**, is widespread and problematic, although illegal. However, we should also recognize that another form of discrimination exists at the macro-level: **institutional discrimination**. This occurs when social institutions, such as the government, religious groups, and schools create policies and practices that are systematically disadvantageous to certain groups. Often such discrimination is unintentional, but difficult to detect and eradicate because the policies and practices are woven into the fabric of our culture as "the way we always do things." No one individual or group can be held accountable for these discriminatory policies and practices, and they are not questioned by most people.

For example, students are routinely taught that Christopher Columbus "discovered" America, and opened the New World to Western civilization. Every year in the United States we celebrate Columbus Day in his honor. Yet this "truth" is really a social construction. Many Native American groups had been living rich and meaningful lives in this region long before Columbus and his associates sailed across the Atlantic Ocean from Europe.

It is important to recognize the diversity of experiences in the United States. Next, we will briefly highlight some of the largest racial and ethnic groups in the United States— Hispanic, Black, Asian, and Native American/Alaska Native—so that we can better understand their marriage and family histories and current experiences in upcoming chapters.

We like to think that things have changed, but prejudice and discrimination are still a part of American culture. How do minority parents prepare their children?

Hispanic Families

The label "Hispanic" contains so many diverse ethnic groups that it may not make much sense to combine them into one category. A Mexican American, a Puerto Rican, and a Cuban American have little in common ethnically, except that they can trace their ancestry to Latin America or Spain. Their food, clothing, socioeconomic status, and even their language differ from one another. Yet the U.S. Census Bureau and other organizations often place these groups together for statistical purposes. As a group, Hispanics comprise about 16 percent of the U.S. population, and are the largest and fastest growing minority group (Bernstein & Edwards, 2008).

In the past, the growth in the Hispanic population was primarily fueled by immigration, but today only 11 percent of Hispanic children are first generation, i.e., were born elsewhere and immigrated here (Fry & Passel, 2009). Instead, the rapid growth of the Hispanic population is attributable to its high birthrate. Hispanic women have the highest fertility rate among all racial and ethnic groups, at about 99 births per 1,000 women, compared to a national average of 69 births per 1,000 women (Hamilton, Martin, & Ventura, 2010). In other words, the population is now expanding not only because of immigration, but because of the increase in the number of children born to those immigrants.

This change poses many new and intriguing questions for the Hispanic population. How will the lives of the second generation be different from those of their parents? How will families change? Will the second generation do better economically? Will they retain

individual discrimination: One person exhibiting a negative behavior towards another person.

institutional discrimination: Social institutions such as the government, religion, and education create policies and practices that are systematically disadvantageous to certain groups.

their Spanish language and Hispanic culture? How will the second generation change the dominant U.S. culture?

Differences between first- and second- or third-generation Hispanics are very pronounced, and the future of U.S.-born children of Hispanic immigrants looks bright (Pew Hispanic Center, January 23, 2008; Pew Research Center, January 21, 2010). Although the second generation is still young, many are moving beyond poverty or the working-class jobs more typical of their parents, and they are twice as likely to be joining the ranks of the middle class. They are better educated and more likely to speak English—many see it as their primary language. Second- and third-generation Hispanics are also more likely to hold mainstream U.S. values than the more conservative and traditional values of their parents. For example, they are more likely to support a woman's right to choose an abortion, to see divorce as an acceptable solution to an unhappy marriage, and to believe that undocumented immigration hurts the economy (Pew Hispanic Center, January 23, 2008; Pew Research Center, January 21, 2010).

Second- and third-generation Hispanics are becoming increasingly assimilated and often blend in easily with Whites. However, there are so many new adult Hispanic arrivals that assimilation may not be very visible to the casual observer. Nonetheless, many second-generation Hispanics report personal experience with discrimination; in fact, they are more likely than their parents to believe that they have been discriminated against. Their incomes are still significantly below those of Whites, and many do not have health insurance (Livingston, Minushkin, & Cohn, 2008; DeNavas-Walt, Proctor, & Smith, 2010).

Black Families

Blacks, comprised primarily although not exclusively of African Americans, make up about 13 percent of the U.S. population. On average, Black families tend to be somewhat larger than those of Whites. Although married Black couples have a similar number of children to their married White counterparts (about 1.9 per family), Black female-headed households have more children than do their White counterparts (U.S. Census Bureau, January 14, 2010).

Black families are also larger because they more likely contain extended family members, including grandparents, aunts, and uncles (Taylor, Passel, Fry, Morin, Wang, Velasco, & Dockterman, 2010). Over one in five Black children lives in an extended family, a rate nearly double that for Whites. Extended families can provide critical resources to family members, such as the ability to pool finances or share childcare, and yet they have sometimes been denigrated in American culture as a characteristic of only poor families. However, extended families offer considerable strengths, and Blacks are more likely than Whites, at all income levels, to live in extended families, in part because they have a rich cultural heritage of drawing upon and sharing aid with other family members (Hill, 2005).

Black families are more likely than any other racial or ethnic group to be headed by females. Forty-eight percent of Black children live with single mothers, compared with 16 percent of White children, 25 percent of Hispanic children, and 13 percent of Asian children. Few children live with single fathers (about 4–5 percent) and the differences across racial and ethnic groups are small. Single-parent families have been maligned and referred to as "broken homes." They are disadvantaged financially, and are overrepresented among those living in poverty; 30 percent of female-headed households are impoverished, compared to 6 percent of married couple families (DeNavas-Walt, Proctor, & Smith, 2010). But the problem with such a sweeping generalization is that there are different types of single-parent families with different circumstances—the situation of a pregnant teenager vastly differs from that of a 40-year-old single female professional with children.

Asian American Families

The term "Asian" or "Asian American" is a catchall for many different groups who had their origins with the early peoples of the Far East, Southeast Asia, or the Indian subcontinent. Often combined with these diverse groups are Pacific Islanders who have origins in Hawaii, Guam, Samoa, or other Pacific islands. As is the case with Hispanics, these groups represent great diversity with respect to food, culture, language, and socioeconomic conditions.

They came to the U.S. for different reasons, at different time periods, and had different opportunities for assimilation. Some, like Japanese or Chinese Americans, may have been in the United States for generations, while others, such as the Vietnamese or Cambodians, may have arrived as refugees from the Vietnam conflict in the 1970s (Reeves & Bennett, 2003). It may make little sense to combine them, but, nonetheless, for statistical purposes most government agencies combine these groups into one large category labeled "Asian American."

Asian Americans have been sometimes nicknamed a "model minority." This is because their families tend to be stable, their parents are highly educated and work in professional jobs, and they have the highest family incomes of any group, surpassing that of Whites. Although the rate of high school graduation is similar to other racial or ethnic groups, a much higher number of those graduates go to college and graduate, and go on to graduate or professional school, as shown in Table 2.4 (Crissey, 2009). Asian American families also have the lowest rate of divorce, and their children are more likely to reside in married-couple households than are any other racial or ethnic group (DeNavas-Walt, Proctor, & Smith, 2010; U.S. Census Bureau, 2010).

There are very few Asian Americans on television, and of these, they tend to play roles of well-educated professionals, illustrating their "model minority" status, such as B.D. Wong's role in *Law & Order: Special Victims Unit.*

Many important factors help to explain why Asian American families are considered to be so successful (Farley, 2010; Schaefer, 2011). Many who came to the U.S. were from privileged social classes in their countries of origin; they were professionals with college degrees, and often had considerable wealth to invest in their employment or educational opportunities in the United States. Certainly this is not the case of all Asian Americans, as some recent immigrants fleeing Vietnam, Cambodia, and Laos, for example, were from poor rural villages. Perhaps even more important is the long-standing emphasis on education, learning, and family primacy that characterizes Asian cultures. Individuality is de-emphasized and the well-being of the family is of primary concern. Parents invest heavily in their children's education, and the children tend to take their studies seriously because they believe that their success reflects honor upon the entire family.

Despite their overall positive record, it is important that we not overgeneralize about Asian Americans (Zhou & Bankston, 2006). Not all Asian American families are doing well on social and economic indicators. In particular, some of the more recent immigrants lack the resources of other Asian Americans, and therefore have low incomes and high rates of

Table 2.4	Educational Attainment By Race and Ethnicity			
	Asian Americans are more likely than other groups to go to college and earn an advanced degree.			
	High school graduate or more	Some college or more	Bachelor's degree or more	Advanced degree
White	87%	57%	29%	11%
Non-Hispanic White	89%	59%	31%	11%
Black	80%	46%	17%	6%
Asian	86%	68%	50%	20%
Hispanic	61%	32%	13%	4%

Source: Crissey, Sarah R. 2009 January. Educational Attainment in the United States: 2007. Current Population Reports No. P20–560. Washington, DC: U.S. Census Bureau.

poverty. For example, immigrants from Vietnam, Cambodia, and Laos have high poverty rates and have among the highest rates of welfare use in the United States (Huang, 2002). Other families struggle with acculturation, with children adapting to the culture faster than parents, or even other siblings, as revealed in the feature box *Why Do Research? The Challenge of Acculturation* (Pyke, 2000, 2005).

Native American and Alaska Native Families

Native Americans and Alaska Natives comprise about 1.5 percent of the U.S. population, at about 4.9 million people (U.S. Census Bureau, December 16, 2009). They have origins with many of the early peoples of North, Central, and South America who maintain tribal affiliation or community attachment. Three-quarters identify themselves as belonging to a specific tribe; Cherokee is the largest with nearly 900,000 members. Eskimo is the largest Alaska Native tribe, with nearly 50,000 members. About one-third live on designated American Indian Areas, which include reservations and off-reservation land trusts; 2 percent live in Alaska Native Village Statistical Areas; and nearly two-thirds live outside tribal areas (Ogunwole, 2006).

About three-quarters of Native American and Alaska Native households are family households, which is significantly higher than for other racial or ethnic groups. About a third of the Native American and Alaska Native population is under age 18, compared to 26 percent in the total population, and the median age is seven years younger, revealing their higher than average birth rates (U.S. Census Bureau, December 16, 2009).

Extended families are the cornerstone of Native American family life, and children enjoy close relationships with their grandparents, particularly grandmothers. More than half of Native Americans and Alaska Natives live with their grandchildren (U.S. Census Bureau, 2006). There is a strong ethic of social, emotional, and financial support among relatives, and relationships are less rigid than in other groups—aunts and uncles often refer to their nieces and nephews as "daughter" or "son" and families may live together temporarily or permanently. Fifty-six percent of Native American or Alaska Natives age 30 and over live with their grandchildren (U.S. Census Bureau, October 15, 2009). They provide hands-on care to children and families, which is particularly helpful to the 28 percent of single-parent families—twice the national average. Kinship is also an important component of political organization because of the ties it establishes to a specific tribe.

The elderly of Native American and Alaska Native groups have traditionally held high status in their families and communities, reinforcing their cultural identity. Although the value of this to younger generations has waxed and waned, there has been a resurgence in recognizing the importance of Native American and Alaska Native spirituality, language, values, and cultural traditions. Eighteen percent report speaking a language other than English "very well" compared to only 10 percent of the general population (Ogunwole, 2006). And among Alaska Natives, 85 percent believe that subsistence is "important" or "very important" to their household (McDowell Group, 2003).

Native American families do face many challenges. Infant mortality rates are comparatively high and life expectancy is low. Unemployment and poverty rates are high, and many live in inexpensive and substandard housing (U.S. Census Bureau, December 16, 2009). For example, 10 to 20 percent of housing on reservations lacks basic indoor plumbing. Smoking and alcoholism rates are high, as are violence and suicide (National Center for Health Statistics, 2009). However, despite these difficulties, tribal leaders have implemented numerous strategies to improve social and economic conditions. For example, highly profitable (and sometimes controversial) gambling establishments fund critically needed education programs and social services, create jobs, and provide individual tribal members with cash stipends that have considerably improved their economic circumstances.

extended families: Families that include not only parents and children, but also other family members, such as grandparents, uncles, aunts, or cousins.

All people have a racial and ethnic background, although Whites have the privilege of rarely thinking about this. How might these differences influence the Pitt-Jolie family?

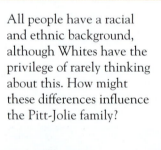

Why Do Research?

The Challenge of Acculturation

Research on immigrant families often finds a generational gap between children who acculturate, or adapt, faster to the new society than slower-changing parents. My interviews with second-generation Asian Americans suggest another acculturation divide also occurs in many immigrant families.

The Study Unfolds: When I chose to study college-age children of Korean and Vietnamese immigrants, there was little research that captured the family lives of most of my students who are second-generation Asian Americans. I set out to do such a study so that these students would no longer be invisible in our course materials. Many students on my campus eagerly volunteered to participate, from whom I collected face-to-face interviews, asking them to describe their subjective experiences growing up in immigrant families, with a focus on their relationships with parents and siblings. More specific research questions emerged over the course of collecting the first 73 interviews (Pyke, 2000).

As expected, respondents often described acculturation gaps with parents who were more likely than their children to maintain traditional ethnic practices and experience difficulty learning English. I was intrigued, however, when several respondents described deep acculturative differences with a sibling. To learn more, I embarked on a new study of families with acculturative divides between siblings. I gathered a sample of 32 college-age Korean and Vietnamese Americans who had at least one sibling they regard as more ethnically traditional or more assimilated ("Americanized") than themselves. Respondents ranged in age from 18 to 26 and averaged 21 years; they were born in the U.S. or immigrated at an average of 5 years. Of the 32 respondents, 15 were the oldest sibling, 7 the youngest, and 10 had at least an older and younger sibling. During the face-to-face interviews, I asked them to describe the nature of their acculturation differences with their siblings, relationships with their parents and between their siblings and parents, and how they and their siblings were raised.

More Traditional Older Siblings: In 28 of the 32 families I studied, the more traditional sibling was older than the assimilated sibling, and typically the first-born child. I wondered if perhaps older siblings had spent more time in the parents' homeland prior to immigration and thus had more contact with the ethnic culture. However, upon comparing the length of time siblings spent in the United States, I found little difference—both spent most, if not all, of their childhood in the United States. Instead, it appears the practice in many Asian families of affording greater power and responsibility to the eldest child contributes to a sibling acculturative divide.

Asian Family Structure: Older siblings in the families studied commonly assisted parents with English translation, financial matters, household tasks, and caring for younger siblings. They were often expected to also care for and live with their parents as they aged. Parents closely monitored their older children in preparing them to serve as role models and disciplinarians to their younger siblings, and socialized them with greater intensity to the ethnic beliefs and practices they were expected to pass on. They tended to be more lax with and interacted less frequently with their younger children, who were under the care of older siblings. Older siblings thus interacted more with their parents and had a greater need to maintain fluency in their ethnic language, while younger siblings, who were assigned fewer responsibilities, were freer to assimilate. Indeed, many younger siblings could not speak Korean or Vietnamese well and depended on older siblings to translate conversations with their parents. As one respondent said, "My sister is kind of the connection, the middle person, between me and my parents. She kind of holds us together."

The big acculturative gap in these families was not between parents and children. Rather, more ethnic older siblings and parents stood on one side of the acculturative divide and younger, more assimilated siblings on the other. Some assimilated children felt like outsiders in their family, like one young woman who said, "I know if I … tried to sit and talk with [my parents and sister], it wouldn't work. I wouldn't fit in."

From Pyke, Karen, 2005, 2000.

What Do You Think?

1. Immigrant parents sometimes complain that American society influences their children to let go of ethnic beliefs and practices and become Americanized. How does the family structure of Asian immigrant families encourage younger siblings to adopt more Americanized ways?

2. This study finds that immigrant parents get much assistance from older children who maintain ethnic practices. In what ways might immigrant parents also derive benefits from having younger children who are more Americanized?

Interracial and Interethnic Families

So far we have discussed race and ethnicity as though they are discrete categories, but millions of people in the United States have a clear and unequivocal connection to two or more racial or ethnic groups. As the taboos against interracial or interethnic marriage begin to break down, the growth in the number of children with multiple races or ethnicities is inevitable.

Parents of multiracial or multiethnic children continue to face issues that other parents do not experience (Smith & Hattery, 2009). For example, when both parents are White, despite good intentions, they may know very little about how prejudice and discrimination really operate, or how it really feels to be discriminated against. But in a multiracial or multiethnic family, the White parent must address these issues head on because his or her spouse and children may likely have been affected by prejudice and discrimination (Rockquemore & Laszloffy, 2005). Recent books speak to these issues and the challenges of forming a multiracial identity, including President Barack Obama's *Dreams from My Father: A Story of Race and Inheritance* (Obama, 2007).

*D*escribe your racial or ethnic background. Can you provide some examples of the ways in which your background has influenced your life? Why do you think that Whites have the privilege of rarely thinking about race or ethnic issues?

We all have a race and an ethnicity, whether we think a great deal or only rarely about these aspects of ourselves. Each group has a rich history and culture and draws upon them in meaningful ways to create relevant family structures and relationships. We will see more specific examples of this throughout the following chapters. However, there is another important aspect of our lives worthy of discussion here because it also powerfully shapes our families and intimate relationships. Let's now turn to a discussion of social class.

:: Social Class

While social class is less visible than race, ethnicity, or sex, we are probably all aware, to some degree, that social class can have a significant impact upon our lives. Class is an important focus of such well-known novels as *The Great Gatsby* (Fitzgerald, 1925, reprinted 1999), which focused on the lives of the wealthy, or *The Grapes of Wrath* (Steinbeck, 1939, reprinted 2002), which portrayed the desperate lives of sharecroppers from Oklahoma who migrated to California to escape the ravages of the Dust Bowl.

Today we are bombarded by images of the rich and famous cavorting in Hollywood, and by the poor in the most desperate of situations, such as Haitians after the earthquake of 2010. In the United States social class is often downplayed or denied (Lareau & Conley, 2008), but you know that where you come from does matter. Social class is not just about money; it encompasses an entire way of seeing and experiencing the world (Eitzen & Smith, 2009; Hurst, 2010; New York Times, 2005; Weininger & Lareau, 2009). Social class shapes your worldview, and influences those so-called "personal choices" you make. Think back to Becca in the opening vignette. How do you think that poverty influenced her sense of self and her self-esteem?

Approaches to Measuring Social Class

Social class is an abstract concept compared to sex, race, or ethnicity because we cannot always identify social classes or who are members of these classes. Social classes are based most obviously on income and wealth, but also on other resources, such as educational level and your occupational prestige. Social class boundaries in the United States are theoretically open, so people who gain schooling, skills, or income may experience a change in their social class position; however, there is much less movement across social classes than people imagine (Hurst, 2010; Lareau & Conley, 2008).

Today researchers often define class as some combination of education, occupation, and income, and we sometimes call this combination **socioeconomic status** or **SES**. Dennis Gilbert and Joseph A. Kahl (1993) have developed a widely used model of social class based

social class: A social position based primarily on income and wealth, but occupational prestige and educational level may be relevant as well.

socioeconomic status (SES): Some combination of education, occupation, and income.

on SES. Their model includes six categories updated with data from the 2006 Congressional Budget Office (Sherman & Aron-Dine, 2007): (1) the upper class; (2) the upper middle class; (3) the middle class; (4) the working class; (5) the working poor; and (6) the underclass.

The Upper Class

The upper class is the wealthiest and most powerful social class in the United States and consists of only about 3–5 percent of the population. Although few in number, its members have a tremendous influence upon the economy and the rest of society, often sitting on boards of major corporations or being active in politics. They may have very high incomes, averaging about $1,200,000 per year (Sherman, 2009). More importantly, they sustain substantial wealth.

Some upper-class families, nicknamed "old money" or "bluebloods," have been wealthy for generations, such as the Kennedys, Bushes, and Hiltons. They may belong to the exclusive *Social Register*, an annual listing of elites that has been published since the late 1800s, and prefer to socialize only with their peers. There is very little mixing with other social classes; private schools and the Debutante Ball, which brings unmarried young men and women together to meet each other, carefully control socializing.

Other members of the upper class, sometimes nicknamed "new money," have acquired their great wealth within one generation and therefore lack the prestige of the "bluebloods." The media mogul Oprah Winfrey and Microsoft founder Bill Gates are examples, and many people see them as having fulfilled the "American dream."

The Upper Middle Class

Approximately 15–20 percent of the U.S. population is categorized as "upper middle class." Members of the upper middle class tend to be highly educated professionals, including physicians, dentists, lawyers, college professors, and business executives. Household income may be in the range of $100,000 to $200,000, possibly more if both people in a couple are employed (Sherman, 2009; Sherman & Aron-Dine, 2007). These families generally have accumulated some wealth, have nice homes in well-respected neighborhoods, and play important roles in local political affairs. They strongly value education, and the vast majority of their children go on to college and graduate school, often at private institutions.

The Middle Class

Most people say they are "middle-class" but this is not exactly true. With incomes of about $40,000 to $100,000 a year, only 40 percent are really "middle class" (Sherman, 2009; Sherman & Aron-Dine, 2007). The median household income is little over $50,000 for all households, $72,000 for married couples, and $33,000 for female-headed households (DeNavas-Walt, Proctor, & Smith, 2010).

The middle class have a distinctive set of values, and prioritize security at home and at work as being very important (Taylor, Morin, Cohn, Fry, Kochhar, & Clark, 2008). College is valued by the middle class, and many work in white-collar jobs that require a college degree, such as teaching, nursing, or business, while others may be in highly skilled blue-collar jobs, such as electronics or construction. Traditionally, middle-class jobs have been secure and provided a variety of opportunities for advancement; however, with corporate downsizing, and a generally rising cost of living, many middle-class families are finding their lifestyles tenuous. For example, young middle-class families may find it difficult to purchase their first home in many U.S. cities, and older middle-class families find that saving for both retirement and their children's college bills stretches their budget beyond its means.

The Working Class

The term "working class" is somewhat misleading because just about all adults work. Therefore, some people refer to this group as the "lower middle class." They earn less than middle-class families, approximately $20,000 to $40,000. About 20 percent of the U.S. population falls into this group (Sherman & Aron-Dine, 2007). Jobs may include factory and custodial work and semiskilled labor. Members of the working class report less satisfaction in their jobs than do those in higher social classes, as their jobs are often more routine and require following specific directions rather than exercising creativity (Kohn, 1977, 2006). Family members face insecurity (Yates, 2009); they must plan carefully to pay their monthly bills, as unexpected doctor bills or car repair bills can wreak havoc on the family budget. Working class

There are two very different Americas—one for the wealthy and one for the poor. Think about the different opportunities, challenges, and constraints that children in each group faces.

social mobility: Movement from one social class to another.

I dentify what social class you were born into—what evidence do you have to help you decide? How has your social class shaped your world-view, your opportunities, your choices, and your constraints? What social class do you think you will be a member of for most of your adulthood? If these classes are different, how will this mobility be possible?

Social Mobility and the Lack of It   Tommy Johnson and Randall Simmons, as shown in the *Diversity in Families* box, are two young men who live in large metropolitan areas, and could not lead more different lives. Although both work long hours and are highly motivated, the social class in which each was born has substantially shaped opportunities, goals, and achievements. While theoretically people in the United States can be anything they want to be, in reality there is little upward **social mobility**, or movement from one social class to another. People usually live out their lives in the same social class in which they are born because of the norms they learn and the constraints and privileges they experience (Hurst, 2010).

If Randall had been born poor, his likelihood of going to law school would be small. He may have attended poorly funded and inferior public elementary and secondary schools. Chances are, Randall would have met few people who went to college, and even fewer people who went to law school—he would not have felt that it was a real opportunity for himself. But let's take this further. Had Randall been born an upper-class *female*, her family may have steered her to other, more "feminine" pursuits instead of law. Perhaps she would be the non-employed wife of a lawyer, rather than a lawyer herself. Or perhaps she would be an elementary school teacher at a private school, earning about 15 percent of Randall's salary. If Randall had been born a working-class minority female, the likelihood of attending law school diminishes even further.

Why would Randall's chances of being a successful lawyer be so different? With financial aid available to all students, we must look beyond sheer financial considerations. Many women, ethnic and racial minority groups, and those within the lower social classes are discouraged from attaining these goals by family, peers, and school counselors. For example, women may actively (or more subtly) be discouraged from graduate or professional school because of fears that a career will interfere with their ability to raise a family. When we add racial discrimination or social class barriers such as having fewer role models or inadequate preparation at poor secondary schools, it is not surprising that entering classes in professional schools tend to reflect the background of Randall Simmons rather than that of Tommy Johnson (Eitzen & Smith, 2009; Lareau, 2003; Lareau & Conley, 2008).

Let's now look at the bottom of the social class scale—poverty. Poverty touches the lives of millions, with serious consequences.

:: Poverty

Dee is a single mother who left an abusive marriage to begin anew with her 11-year-old daughter. She works the evening shift to support the two of them, while her daughter stays home alone. Kate was a middle-class woman, who left her husband after his infidelity. She now lives in a small, seedy apartment, trying to support herself and her two young children on a low-paying job without child support. Robert and Maria are a happily married couple who face a crisis because Robert's serious illness caused him to lose his job, cutting off the primary source of support for them and their four children. What do these three families have in common? They are all poor (Seccombe, 2007).

Poverty comes in many shapes, sizes, and colors—big families, small families, two-parent families, single-parent families, White families, and minority families—all have the potential to slip into poverty for a month, a year, or a lifetime (Edin & Kissane, 2010). In fact, by age 65, over half of us will likely have spent at least one year of our adulthood in poverty (Rank, 2009).

The Social Security Administration established the official *poverty threshold* (sometimes called the "poverty line") in 1964 as a way to measure the number of people living in poverty (Orshansky, 1965). Survey data in the early 1960s indicated that families spent approximately one-third of their income on food. Therefore, we calculate the poverty line from the estimated annual costs of a minimal food budget designed by the U.S. Department of Agriculture (USDA), which we then multiply by three. This food budget parallels the current "Thrifty Food Plan," which forms the basis of food assistance programs and is the least expensive food plan developed by the USDA (Center for Nutrition Policy and Promotion, 2009). It is far below the amount most middle-class families spend on food. Individuals or families with annual incomes below this established threshold of "food costs multiplied by three" are counted as "poor."

The poverty threshold varies by family size (and a few other features) and is revised yearly based on inflationary changes in the Consumer Price Index. The 2010 **poverty guidelines** in the 48 contiguous states and the District of Columbia were $18,310 for a family of three, and $22,050 for a family of four (U.S. Department of Health and Human Services, January 23, 2009), as shown in Table 2.5. Poverty guidelines in Alaska and Hawaii were slightly higher.

The quick budgeting exercise shown in the *Policy and You: From Macro to Micro* boxed feature (p. 62) illustrates that the poverty guideline is inadequate to meet the basic needs of families.

poverty guidelines: Guidelines established in 1964 as a way to measure the number of people living in poverty; based on a thrifty food budget, multiplied by three (sometimes called the "poverty line").

Table 2.5	The 2010 Poverty Guidelines for the 48 Contiguous States and the District of Columbia
Can you easily live on a poverty-level budget?	
Persons in Family	**Poverty Guideline**
1	$10,830
2	$14,570
3	$18,310
4	$22,050
5	$25,790
6	$29,530
7	$33,270
8	$37,010

For families with more than 8 persons, add $3,740 for each additional person.

Source: U.S. Department of Health & Human Services, 2009.

Who Is Poor?

About 43.6 million people, or 14.3 percent of the U.S. population, lived in poverty in 2009, an increase of 4 million people from 2008 due to recession. Twenty-one percent of children—more than one in five—live in poverty (DeNavas-Walt,

Policy and You: From Macro to Micro

What Does the Poverty Threshold Buy?

The 2010 poverty guideline for a family of three is $18,310 a year, which comes to $1,526 a month. This means that a family of three people—a single mother and two children, or two parents and one child—are only counted as poor if they live on less than this amount. Does this seem reasonable? Let's find out by examining a sample budget.

The costs in this budget are from reports by the USDA, HUD, the Center on Budget and Policy Priorities, and other consumer expenditure reports estimating the price of a "low-cost" food plan, the fair market rent for a two-bedroom apartment, and a cost estimate for childcare and other expenditures. The cost of living varies somewhat from one community to another; for example, rents may be higher (or lower) where you live than in the estimate below. You can substitute numbers from your own community if you prefer.

The question is: Is it reasonable to assume a family of three can live on $1,526 a month in the United States? Keep in mind that someone who works full-time, year round, at approximately $8.53 an hour would earn this amount.

Sample Expenses

Rent (two-bedroom apartment and utilities):	$800
Food:	$425
Child Care:	$620
Health Care:	$65
Clothing:	$60
Transportation:	$416
Miscellaneous:	$100
TOTAL:	**$2,486/month or $29,832/ year before taxes**

Already we have gone over budget. How can we cut back?

- Find a cheaper apartment, or one in a less desirable part of town? Don't forget that children live here.

- Lower the utility bill by keeping the house colder? This is one reason why poor children are sick more often.
- Eliminate the telephone? This could be dangerous in an emergency.
- Cut back on toiletries? Toilet paper, shampoo, and tampons are basic needs.
- Eliminate car maintenance? How will the family get to work, school, or run errands? A bus system may not be available or feasible with children.

We are over budget and we have not yet included other basic needs for this family:

School Supplies:	$25
Health Insurance:	$300
Entertainment:	$100
Laundry:	$25
NEW TOTAL:	**$2,936/month or $35,232/year before taxes**

Assumption Even this revised budget assumes the family already has an established household. There is no money included to buy furniture, a car, or household items like towels or dishes. In other words, even $2,936 a month is unrealistically low. As you can see, the poverty line is an inadequate measure of poverty.

What Do You Think?

1. If the poverty line is as inadequate as it appears, why doesn't the federal government increase it to a more realistic level? What should the poverty line be based on? What are the implications of changing it?

2. How can a family make ends meet if a parent earns poverty-level wages?

Source: Adapted and updated from Seccombe, 2007.

Proctor, & Smith, 2010). Table 2.6 shows which groups of people are most likely to be poor.

Consequences of Poverty

Poor families face a higher degree of stress, disorganization, and other problems. These are difficult for all family members, but in particular, weigh heavily on children's physical, social, and emotional health (Lovell & Isaacs, 2010). For this reason, let's first look at the consequences of poverty on children.

Poor children exhibit more antisocial behavior and are more likely to drop out of school or become teenage parents, are more likely to suffer from depression, and are in poorer health (Federal Interagency Forum on Child and Family Statistics, 2009; Linden, 2009; Evans, Gonnella, Marcynyszyn, Gentile, & Salpekar, 2005). Naturally, not all poor children suffer these outcomes; many poor children are the models of success. Nonetheless, they are more likely than other children to face a host of serious challenges. How does poverty exert its influence? Figure 2.4, on page 64, summarizes the pathways through which poverty hurts children (Seccombe, 2007). Poverty contributes to:

- inadequate health and nutrition
- lower-quality home environment
- parental stress and mental health problems
- fewer resources for learning
- housing problems
- poor-quality neighborhoods.

Inadequate Health and Nutrition   Research is clear about the relationship between poverty and health. Poverty puts the health of children at risk in many ways, including the likelihood of having low birth weight, which in turn increases chances of serious chronic and acute illness, along with emotional and behavioral problems (Breslau, Paneth, & Lucia, 2004; Federal Interagency Forum on Child and Family Statistics, 2009; Gray, Indurkhya, & McCormick, 2004). Poor children also may receive inadequate food and nutrition. Nearly 15 percent of households experienced **food insecurity** at some point during 2008, defined by the USDA as not having enough nourishing food available on a regular basis (Nord, Andrews, & Carlson, 2009). Twenty-two percent of households with children are food insecure. Children suffer the immediate pain of hunger, and the longer-term consequences of malnutrition. They run the risk of more frequent colds, ear infections and other infectious diseases, impaired brain function, and stunted growth, and are more vulnerable to lead and other environmental toxins.

Quality of the Home Environment   Warm loving relationships with parents, in conjunction with rich opportunities for learning, help children thrive. The Home Observation of the Measurement of the Environment (HOME) is a widely used interview and observation tool of parent-child interaction. It shows that poverty has a significant negative effect on the quality and stimulation of the home environment (Yeung, Linver, & Brooks-Gunn, 2002). One study of the linguistic capabilities of young children found that poor children on welfare between the ages of 13 and 36 months hear only half as many words per hour as the average working-class child, and less than one-third the average of a typical child in a professional family (Children's Defense Fund, 2005). Obviously, parents cannot teach their children what they themselves do not know. Moreover, poor parents are also less nurturing and more authoritarian, and they use more inconsistent and harsh physical discipline as a family's economic situation worsens.

Parental Stress and Mental Health   What else about an impoverished family environment may increase the likelihood of negative outcomes for children? One likely culprit is that parents who are living in poor conditions have a high level of stress, depression, and mental health problems related to their situation. For example, high levels of male unemployment are significantly associated with child abuse and deprivation. While child abuse occurs in many different type of households, poor children have a higher probability of being abused, neglected, and more severely injured by abuse than do their more affluent peers (Centers for Disease Control and Prevention, 2007; National Center for Health Statistics, 2009).

Table 2.6	People and Families in Poverty by Selected Characteristics, 2009
Children, Blacks, Hispanics, and female-headed households are most vulnerable.	

Total U.S. Population		14.3%
Age		
	Children Under 18	20.7%
	18–64	12.9%
	65 and Over	8.9%
Race		
	White (Non-Hispanic)	9.4%
	Black	25.8%
	Asian and Pacific Islander	12.5%
	Hispanic	25.3%
Family Type		
	Married Couple	5.8%
	Female-Headed	29.9%
	Male-Headed	16.9%

Source: DeNavas-Walt, Carmen, Bernadette D. Proctor, and Jessica D. Smith. 2008. September. Income, Poverty, and Health Insurance Coverage in the United States: 2007. Technical Report No. P60–235. Washington, DC: U.S. Census Bureau.

food insecurity: A lack of available nourishing food on a regular basis.

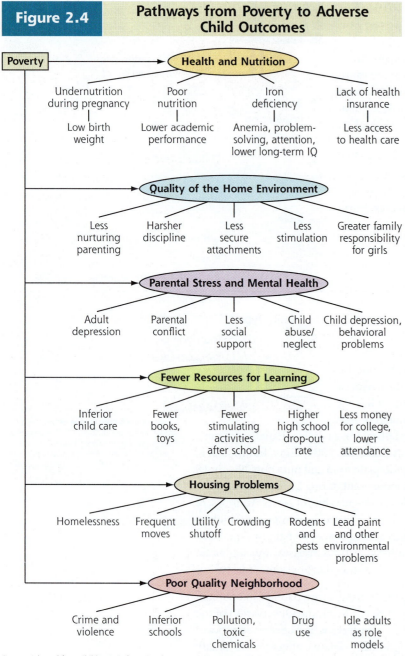

Figure 2.4 Pathways from Poverty to Adverse Child Outcomes

Source: Adapted from Children's Defense Fund 1994; Brooks-Gunn and Duncan 1997, from Seccombe, Families and their Social Worlds 1e. © 2007 Allyn & Bacon.

Fewer Resources for Learning On average, poor children have fewer resources for learning in the home, including books and educational toys. Therefore, high-quality childcare and preschool programs become very important to helping them overcome the disadvantages in their home environment. Unfortunately, childcare and preschool are very expensive, as you will see in Chapter 10, and far fewer subsidized spots are available than are needed. Full-time childcare can easily cost over $10,000 per year for each child (National Association of Child Care Resource & Referral Agencies, 2009). Thus, many poor children receive lower grades and lower scores on standardized tests; they are less likely to finish high school, and are less likely to attend or graduate from college than are other children (NICHD Early Child Care Research Network, 2005; Federal Interagency Forum on Child and Family Statistics, 2009).

Housing Problems The 2010 fair market rent for a two-bedroom apartment plus utilities, according to the Department of Housing and Urban Development (HUD), is about $1,056 in Seattle, $919 in Phoenix, $1,015 in Chicago, and $921 in Denver (U.S. Department of Housing and Urban Development, 2010). Poor families cannot afford to pay this rent, and so they often live in crowded and disease-ridden housing that may lack proper cooking, heating, or sanitation facilities. Moreover, a 2008 survey of 25 U.S. cities found that 23 of the cities reported a rise in homelessness among families (U.S. Conference of Mayors, December 2008).

Poor-Quality Neighborhoods Poor children are increasingly isolated from the nonpoor in their communities and live in inner cities where violence, crime, truancy, loitering, and a sense of despair predominate (Wilkenfeld, Moore, & Lippman, 2008; Massey & Denton, 1993; O'Hare, 1995). Guns kill over 3,000 children and teens each year, and homicide is the third leading cause of death among children ages 1 to 4, the fifth leading cause among children ages 5 to 14, and the second leading cause among teens ages 15 to 19. It is the leading cause of death among young Blacks ages 15 to 34 (Children's Defense Fund, 2008).

Poverty affects the entire family, and the potentially harmful health effects of poverty on adults are also numerous. For example, poor adults have significantly higher morbidity (sickness) and lower life expectancy than other adults (National Center for Health Statistics, 2009). They are more likely to work in dangerous occupations and live in unsafe neighborhoods, and their homes are more likely to be located near toxic sites.

One issue with far-reaching consequences for families is that poor men and women are less likely to marry (White & Rogers, 2000; Edin & Kefalas, 2005). Poverty undermines economic security and makes men less attractive marriage partners. For example, Wilson suggests that the key factor in explaining the falling marriage rate among inner-city Blacks is their declining employment opportunities as jobs move to the suburbs or overseas (Wilson, 1987, 1996). Poverty also undermines marital stability and leads to greater marital conflict because it increases stress or depression, which can then lead to anger, resentment, and hostility between partners, and difficulties among children (Conger & Conger, 2008; Cui, Donnellan, & Conger, 2007; Scaramella, Neppl, Ontai, & Conger, 2008).

:: The Intersections of Sex, Gender, Race, Ethnicity, and Class

Despite the statuses previously described, we are not simply male or female, Asian American or Hispanic, rich or poor. Our statuses intersect with one another (Anderson & Collins, 1995; Dill & Zambrana, 2009; Lobo, Talbot, & Morris, 2010; Segal & Martinez, 2007). For example, a person may be a White working-class male; a Chinese American upper-class male; a Black middle-class female; a White upper-class female, or any number of other racial, ethnic, gender, sex, and class combinations. We have multiple statuses, and they all interact to shape our lives.

A study by family scholar Charlotte Olsen (1996) analyzed the opinions of Black adolescent women about how their gender, race, and class related to their lives. Their lives reflected the fact that they were not simply "Black" or "women," but reflected the unique experiences associated with these multiple statuses. These young women, although acutely aware of times they had been discriminated on the basis of race, also felt they had experienced male domination and saw both as potential obstacles to achieving their own life goals. They reported many instances of prejudice and discrimination because of both their race and their sex. These included challenges associated with employment, and in finding a college-educated, middle-class Black husband, because far fewer Black men finish high school or go to college than do Black women (Children's Defense Fund, 2008). Thus, race, class, and sex are interwoven, and together they shape the nuances of our lives (Dill & Zambrana, 2009).

*W*hy does poverty persist? Do your reasons tend to focus more on micro or macro explanations? What kinds of programs do you think are really needed to end poverty? What are you doing today to ensure that you are not poor in the future? Do you feel that you can avoid poverty?

Bringing it Full Circle

Sex and gender, race and ethnicity, and social class, individually and together, shape a constellation of privileges and constraints that can affect our goals, opportunities, and choices. This chapter introduces these critical concepts. Throughout the remainder of the text you will see how they influence the family structure we are born into, the way our parents raise us, our choices and opportunities in intimate relationships, how we parent, and how we age. These statuses both shape us and the way others respond to us. As we saw in the opening vignette, Becca, a young woman born into poverty, violence, and addiction, is trying to beat the odds. She vividly shows us that social and emotional obstacles are real. Now that you have finished the chapter and have a greater understanding of these concepts, let's reflect on a few questions:

- What are some of the likely consequences of Becca's impoverished childhood? How did her childhood affect her adulthood?

- How do gender, race, ethnicity, and social class interact to influence Becca's situation?

- What pathways from poverty did you see in Becca's story?

- What are you doing today to ensure that you will never be homeless? Can you guarantee it?

For further review, turn to the Video Discussion Guide on page 449, to answer additional questions about how the chapter opening video relates to what you have learned in this chapter.

Chapter Review

2.1 Why are gender, race and ethnicity, and social class important?

These three social positions, referred to as statuses, have a strong influence throughout our lives. They represent significant categories that shape our worldview, including our opportunities, constraints, or privileges.

2.2 What is the difference between "sex" and "gender"?

Sex refers to biological differences between men and women, and their role in reproduction, whereas gender is the culturally and socially constructed differences between males and females found in the meanings, beliefs, and practices associated with "femininity" and "masculinity."

2.3 How do we learn our gendered expectations?

We learn gendered expectations through a process of gender socialization. Important agents of socialization include our parents, our teachers, toys, peers, and the media.

2.4 What is patriarchy, and why is it important to the study of gender?

Patriarchy is a form of social organization in which the expectation is that men have a natural right to be in control of women. Patriarchy is manifested and upheld in a wide variety of social institutions, including those in legal, educational, religious, and economic arenas. Vestiges are found in virtually every society.

2.5 What is the difference between race and ethnicity, and which term is generally more useful?

Race is a biological concept. Ethnicity is far more useful because it focuses on shared cultural characteristics, such as language, place of origin, dress, food, religion, and other values. Ethnicity represents culture, whereas race attempts to represent biological heritage (much of which has become mixed over the years).

2.6 What is the difference between individual and institutional discrimination?

Individual discrimination is a micro-level phenomenon that occurs when one person exhibits a negative behavior towards another individual. Institutional discrimination is a macro-level phenomenon that occurs when social institutions, such as the government, religious groups, and schools, create policies and practices that are systematically disadvantageous to certain groups. These are woven into the fabric of our culture so deeply that many people do not even notice them.

2.7 Is the United States becoming more diverse?

Yes. By the year 2050, projections are that minority groups will comprise more than half the U.S population. The largest increase will be among Hispanic groups.

Key Terms

agents of socialization (p. 42)

discrimination (p. 50)

ethnicity (p. 49)

ethnic group (p. 49)

extended families (p. 54)

food insecurity (p. 63)

gender (p. 40)

gender socialization (p. 42)

hidden curriculum (p. 43)

individual discrimination (p. 51)

institutional discrimination (p. 51)

minority group (p. 49)

poverty guidelines (p. 61)

prejudice (p. 50)

race (p. 49)

sex (p. 40)

social capital (p. 50)

social class (p. 56)

social mobility (p. 60)

social stratification (p. 38)

socioeconomic status (SES) (p. 56)

sociological imagination (p. 38)

stereotypes (p. 50)

2.8 How many social classes are there?

There is no exact way to measure social class. A common typology compares and contrasts six categories: upper, upper middle, middle, working class, working poor, and the underclass.

2.9 How does social class affect our lives?

Social class affects our lives in many ways, including our likelihood of being born; our health status and gender expectations; the values our parents hold for us; the likelihood of our attending and graduating from college; our dating and nonmarital sexual behavior; our likelihood of and age at marriage, our income and consumption patterns; and our hobbies and stress and coping mechanisms.

2.10 How is poverty calculated?

Poverty is calculated on the basis of the cost of a very low food budget developed by the USDA. This budget is then multiplied by three.

2.11 Who is most likely to be poor?

About 43.5 million people, or 14.3 percent of the U.S. population, lived in poverty in 2009, an increase of 4 million people from the year prior due to recession. Almost 21 percent of children—over one in five—live in poverty.

2.12 What are the consequences of poverty?

There are many social and health consequences for both adults and children, most of which are negative. For example, impoverished children suffer far more health risks from infancy on, including higher rates of infant mortality. They are also more likely to suffer from depression, have behavioral problems, and do poorly in school.

2.13 Why are the intersections of sex, gender, race, ethnicity, and class important?

We all have a race, ethnicity, sex, and social class, and these master statuses operate both individually and together. A person is not simply a man or a woman, but, for example, a poor White woman, or a middle-class Black man, or a wealthy Asian American. Together, these statuses interact to shape our experiences.

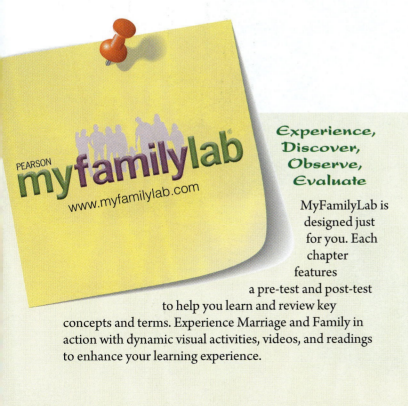

PEARSON
myfamilylab®
www.myfamilylab.com

Experience, Discover, Observe, Evaluate

MyFamilyLab is designed just for you. Each chapter features a pre-test and post-test to help you learn and review key concepts and terms. Experience Marriage and Family in action with dynamic visual activities, videos, and readings to enhance your learning experience.

Here are a few activities you'll find for this chapter:

Watch **Core Concepts** video clips feature sociologists in action, exploring important concepts in the study of Marriage and the Family. Watch:

- Gender Socialization
- Similarities and Differences between Men and Women

Explore **Social Explorer** is an interactive application that allows you to explore Census data through interactive maps. Explore the Social Explorer Map:

- The Mixed Race Population

Read **MySocLibrary** includes primary source readings from classic and contemporary sociologists. Read:

- Rosser, Phyllis, "Too Many Women in College?"

3

Building Relationships

CHAPTER OUTLINE

Above: Meghan and Jono

Ask your grandmother if she considered living with your grandfather before they were married, and you are likely to receive a rather surprised glare. Things have certainly changed.

Meet Meghan and Jonothan, who goes by the nickname Jono, a couple living together before marriage.

Meghan and Jono are among the nearly 7 million couples who cohabit. They are bright, well educated, madly in love, and as your grandmother might say, "living in sin." In your grandmother's day, people met, dated, got engaged, and then married quickly. Men and women—especially women—were expected to be virgins on their wedding day, so a four-year courtship was not very realistic.

Today, the progression towards marriage is quite different. Courtships often last much longer, as people do not seem to be in any particular hurry to marry. Instead of marrying first and then going to college, getting a job, saving money, buying a house, or having a baby, couples now expect to do many or even all of these things before marriage. Today's couples cohabit, and they do so for many reasons: as a prelude to marriage, as a relationship instead of marriage, and as another form of "going steady."

Meghan and Jono, both age 30, have been happily together for four years, the last two of which they have been cohabiting. She is in her final year of a nurse practitioner program, while he works full-

> "We're happy right now and we don't really need to get married for any particular reason."

👁 **Watch** the **Video** *Cohabitation: Meghan and Jono* on **myfamilylab.com**

time at a biotech company managing its lab. They met at a summer barbeque and quickly became very close. Fifty years ago, they would probably have become engaged and married within a short period. But today, what's the rush?

Like many other couples today, Meghan and Jono think of moving in together as normative: It is what you do when you are in love with someone. It is what all your friends are doing. It is how you take your relationship to the "next level". They had no specific plans to marry when they moved in together. As Meghan says, "I think I wanted to move in after about a year of being together, and it just seemed like the next step. We were really happy together and we had a really good thing going on. I had been in a probably four- or five-roommate situation for a long time and it was getting old. It was a great opportunity to get out of that and move in."

In addition to their friends, Meghan's parents cohabited, as did her aunts, uncles, and siblings, so her parents had no problem with their decision to move in together. Jono's parents were a bit

QUESTIONS *That Matter* •

3.1 How many people are single?

3.2 What does it mean to be "single"?

3.3 Why is friendship important in our lives?

3.4 How do friendships differ by sex, race, ethnicity, or social class?

3.5 Can men and women ever really be "just friends"?

3.6 How have the purpose and structure of dating changed over time?

3.7 How have macro-level factors shaped our micro-level choices with respect to dating?

3.8 What are some contemporary trends in dating?

3.9 How common is cohabitation?

3.10 How have attitudes regarding cohabitation changed over time?

3.11 How does cohabitation affect marriage?

3.12 What are the effects of cohabitation on children?

3.13 What are some differences and similarities between homosexual and heterosexual couples?

more reserved at first, but they have come around and accepted the situation.

Would Meghan and Jono ever consider marriage? Yes, but it is on the back burner. After two years of living together, they both now feel that they will eventually marry, but only when they are ready. As Jono explains, "All of our friends are getting married and everyone's asking us 'Are you going to get married? When are you going to get married?' So, it's definitely something we're starting to talk about. We're thinking, the timing has to be right, and we have to just feel good about it and know that we're secure in our lives with our careers and financially everything is set before we go there. Because we're happy right now and we don't really need to get married for any particular reason."

Relationships like this one begin and end every day. Quite naturally, Meghan and Jono believe that they have a relationship that is special, even magical. Yet, their relationship has followed a fairly predictable pattern—singlehood, dating, cohabitation, and possibly marriage—a pattern that has certainly shifted over time and varies from culture to culture. There is no one right way to build a relationship. The pattern popular in your parents' generation was different from their parents' generation, which also probably created considerable angst back then.

This chapter looks at where we have been and where we are going with respect to the processes by which we develop relationships with others. We will begin our discussion with singlehood, and then move to friendships, dating, and end with cohabitation. The goal of this chapter is to show you how many of our personal choices are shaped by macro-level social and cultural factors, including the choices we make as we build our relationships.

:: Singlehood

We may all be born single, but very few of us remain that way forever. Only about 4 percent of people never marry—a number that has remained stable for generations (U.S. Census Bureau, February 25, 2009). However, what is different today is the large and growing number of people who delay marriage, who prefer to cohabit instead of marrying, or who are divorced. Consequently, many people spend considerable amounts of time being single, but it is unfair to assume that they do not have close personal relationships. ✳ Explore on **myfamilylab.com**

How Many Stay Single? It Depends on How You Define It

Although "single" can mean different things to different people, the U.S. Census Bureau classifies people into one of several specific groups: "never married," "married," "separated," "divorced," and "widowed." Can you see a problem with this classification? It ignores the *social* meaning of being single. People like Jono and Meghan who live together are classified as "never married," implying that they are single even though they have a committed partner. Divorced and widowed persons, who are single, are not classified as such. In other words, these categories can be quite misleading.

Figure 3.1 shows the percentage of people who (1) never married and (2) who are "single"—defined as being unmarried for whatever reason. As you will note, there is little difference between the two groups when people are young. After all, what is the likelihood that a 17-year-old would be widowed or divorced? For young people, being never-married and being single mean about the same thing. However, this begins to change in our 20s, as we gain more life experiences. In our 20s, 30s, and 40s, many people get divorced (see Chapter 12). As we continue to age into our 60s, 70s, 80s, and beyond, many of us will be widowed (see Chapter 14). Therefore, we are single again, even though the label of "never married" no longer applies.

✳ Explore the **Concept**
Social Explorer Report:
Single Americans on
myfamilylab.com

voluntary temporary singles: Unmarried adults who may be delaying marriage while pursuing education or establishing a career.

voluntary stable singles: Unmarried adults desiring a single (unmarried) lifestyle.

involuntary temporary singles: Singles actively searching for a mate but unable to find a suitable one.

involuntary stable singles: Unmarried adults who can expect to be single for life even though they may not want to be.

Figure 3.1	Percentage "Never Married" versus Percentage "Single" (Defined as Unmarried for any Reason), Ages 15-85+, 2008

"Never married" and "single" are not the same thing. Young people are most likely to have never married and to be currently single, whereas older people may have married in the past, but are often single due to widowhood.

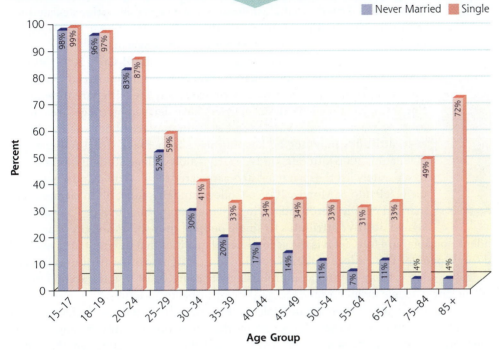

Source: U.S. Census Bureau, February 25, 2009.

What Does It Mean to Be Single? A Useful Typology

There are all kinds of single people. You may be single. A Catholic priest is single. A lesbian in a committed relationship living in Texas is single. My 10-year-old daughter is single. If we want to broaden our understanding of singles, we should ask two critical questions: (1) is it voluntary; and (2) is it temporary? Together these two dimensions yield four very different groups of singles (Stein, 1976, 1981):

- **Voluntary temporary singles**. Many so-called single people are really just delaying marriage. They may be pursuing higher education or establishing themselves in a career. However, this group is interested in marrying someday and will marry sometime in the future. The vast majority of people fit into this category.

- **Voluntary stable singles**. Voluntary stable singles want to be single, and want to be so for life. Catholic priests and nuns, for example, take a vow of celibacy. In most states, same-sex couples cannot legally marry, and therefore could be categorized as voluntary stable singles. Other people could marry but choose not to, including those who are committed to cohabitation or want to remain single for other personal reasons.

- **Involuntary temporary singles**. Involuntary temporary singles are those who would like to be married, but cannot seem to find a partner. Television programs and other media are full of images of single women (and men) desperate to find a spouse. Older women may be nicknamed "cougars," implying that they are hunting for a partner, preferably a younger man. Although the media stereotype single women (and single men), it is true that many women (and men) are actively "on the hunt" for a spouse.

If you are a single person now, which of the four categories of singles best describes you? Could you imagine a scenario in which you became a part of another category? For example, let's say you consider yourself a "voluntary temporary single," but over the course of your life you became an "involuntary stable single." How would you cope with such a change?

What are the stereotypes surrounding older single women? Either they are "old maids" or "cougars" on the hunt, like Courteney Cox's character on *Cougar Town*. How do these stereotypes differ from those of single older men?

- **Involuntary stable singles**. A small number of people who would like to be married never will be. Some "give up" and resign themselves to a single life, moving forward with their personal goals. For example, some women may adopt children on their own, deciding not to wait around for "Mr. Right" to come along and co-parent. Very few people fall into this category.

In previous generations, singles beyond a "certain age" were stigmatized. "Why isn't she married?" people would whisper among themselves. Women in particular experienced close scrutiny, as few viable options existed for them outside of marriage and motherhood. In contrast, many social clubs, organizations, and magazines were geared to the single man.

Attitudes have changed since then (Koropeckyj-Cox, 2005; Roark, 2009). Our attitudes reflect macro-level changes in our social structure. For example, many of us now experience family life with parents who are single (maybe they have never married, have delayed marriage, are cohabiting, or are divorced). Singlehood is commonplace in our society. However, attitudes may not be keeping pace with these structural changes (DePaulo, 2006). In one study, nearly 1,000 college students were asked to separately list the characteristics associated with married and single people (DePaulo & Morris, 2005). College students most often claimed that married people were kind, caring, giving, happy, and loving. They also assigned positive attributes to single people; they were thought of as independent, sociable, and fun. Yet it is the second tier of qualities that differentiated married and single people. The college students continued to assign positive attributes to married people, such as being faithful, compromising, or secure. However, the second tier of traits for single people included such things as being unhappy or lonely.

As previously described, there are multiple routes to singlehood, and the degree to which it is voluntary or permanent varies. Consequently, there is no one "identity" as single. Being single is only one part of a person's social identity, one that may be less important than other aspects. As shown in Chapter 2, our sex, gender, race, ethnicity, and social class also set the context for our family and intimate relationships (Pudrovska, Schiemann, & Carr, 2006). For example, an older, single Hispanic woman may experience reactions to her single status that are far different from those experienced by a White woman or a Black man. She has experienced her own unique patterns of gender and racial stratification and socialization over the life course based on her culture and the historical period in which she grew up. Both macro-level social and cultural contexts interact to shape our individual, personal experiences.

Whether single or not, we all know the importance of connecting with others. Being single hardly means we are all alone. One critical dimension of connecting and building relationships is through our friendships.

:: Friendships

Some of our most important and intimate relationships are with our friends. Even the youngest of children are ready to socialize (Dewar, 2009). Friendships not only provide companionship, but they are also good for our health (Sherman, Lansford, & Volling, 2006; Valeo, 2007). Having close friends that you can confide in may help you live longer. Friendships have been shown to lower blood pressure, heart rates, and cholesterol levels. One longitudinal study followed 61 women with advanced ovarian cancer and found that those with weaker friendships had higher levels of a particular protein linked to more aggressive cancers and that also inhibited the effectiveness of chemotherapy. Women with stronger, more extensive supportive networks fared considerably better (Costanzo, Lutgendorf, Sood, Anderson, Sorosky, & Lubaroff, 2005). Friendships perform a myriad of duties: they support us, help us build communities, enhance our self-esteem, and teach us about ourselves and others (Rawlins, 2008; Wissink, Dekovic, & Mejier, 2009).

Being Friends: Sex Differences

*O*ne of the things I really like about my girlfriends is that they love me no matter what. I can cry to them, and pour out my heart when I'm feeling depressed, and they always do their best to cheer me up.

—**Sophia, age 25**

*O*ne of the things that I really like about my friends is that they are always there for me no matter what. When I need to play some basketball to let off steam, or when I'm bored and want to go hang out, I can count on them.

—**Xavier, age 25**

Researchers looking at same-sex friendships have compared the quality and quantity of men's and women's attachments. Men and women have about the same number of friends, but men's friendships appear less personal or intimate than women's (Flood, 2008; Chu, 2005; Johnson, 2004). Women are more verbal and self-disclosing with their friends, while men spend time with other men engaging in activities. Because of cultural prescriptions about appropriate behavior for men, along with the fear of homosexuality that exists in our culture, men create close connections to other men through side-by-side physical activity. Instead of talking, as women do, men play sports and show signs of intimacy through back-slapping or "high-fives" (Kiesling, 2005).

A study of adolescents found several important differences in same-sex friendships (Johnson, 2004). The subjects included 95 eighth-graders, 54 tenth-graders, 55 twelfth-graders, and 66 first-year university students and both experimental and survey methods were used. Male adolescents reported knowing their friends longer than did females. Female adolescents reported spending more time with their friends, as well as experiencing more closeness and commitment in their friendships, than did males. This research tells us that males and females both consider their friendships important but they experience friendships in ways that are aligned with gendered norms. They enjoy their friendships, but expect different things out of them. Females expect greater closeness, commitment, and intimacy.

> Men and women tend to have about the same number of friends, but they relate to their friends differently. Women's friendships tend to be more intimate and personal.

Being Friends: Social Class and Race/Ethnicity

Friendships appear to differ across social classes (Walker, 1999). Members of the working class tend to have friendships that are longer-lasting than are those of the middle class. Walker found that working-class persons were more likely to have grown up in the same neighborhood and to continue living there as adults. The longevity of the friendships allowed more opportunity to become intimate and share much about themselves. Friendships among people in the middle class appeared to be of shorter duration. Occupations in the middle and upper middle classes often require geographic mobility. While friendships can be maintained over time, they are more likely to continue over the telephone or through the mail (or email), unlike friendships among the working class.

Another structural difference Walker noted is that those who were working-class experienced more crises in their lives. Unemployment, substance abuse, and family health problems were more frequent. Crises among those in the middle class were less severe on average, and of shorter duration. Intimacy in friendships often occurs by sharing problems.

The family is an important means of social support to ward off stress and depression, but so are friends (McAdoo, 2006). Clyde Franklin's (1992) early work on friendship among Black men also suggests that racial and ethnic, as well as social class, differences shape social relationships among men. "Because working-class black males experience greater isolation from mainstream society than upwardly mobile black men, they may not internalize the same taboos against male same-sex friendships, which result in non-self-disclosure, competitiveness, and nonvulnerability" (Franklin, 1992). Franklin found that working-class Black men expressed strong sentiments about their friends because they trusted them. They shared experiences, including being Black in a society with a long history of racism. Like Walker, Franklin suggests that upwardly mobile people are more temporary to a specific geographic area, and in their striving to succeed in life, have a more competitive relationship with others, including their friends.

Friendships between Women and Men: Just Friends?

Can men and women ever really be "just friends"? Friendship certainly is a good basis for a romantic relationship. But friendships *independent* of romance are sometimes suspect. Some people are concerned that men and women can never be "just friends." They assume that spending too much time together is bound to result in intimacy or sexual relations, or that misperceptions of sexual and romantic interests are bound to happen (Koenig, Kirkpatrick, & Ketelaar, 2007).

Historically, **cross-sex friendships**, a friendship between a man and a woman that is strictly platonic, have been rare, and they have been studied even more rarely because they were believed to be part of the developmental process of romantic engagement (friends become lovers or lovers later become friends). Some people also viewed cross-sex friendships as threatening to the heterosexual social order (Monsour, 2002).

cross-sex friendship: A friendship between a man and a woman that is strictly platonic.

Today, cross-sex friendships are far more common than they were in your parents' or grandparents' generation (Guerrero & Chavez, 2005; Harvey, 2003). Opportunities for women and men to meet are increasing in the workplace, schools, and in the community. Many women and men find they share mutual interests and enjoy similar activities. Cross-sex friendships can provide valuable insights into how the other sex thinks, feels, and behaves. Nonetheless, cross-sex friendships can contain elements of tension and are not always easy to maintain. The boxed feature *Why Do Research?* reveals that people can create a set of stories to help them maintain their cross-sex friendships.

Can women and men ever really be just friends? Do you have any cross-sex friendships? If so, what kinds of challenges do you experience, if any? How are these friendships different from same-sex friendships? If you do not have any cross-sex friendships, do you know why?

Friendships are important to our social, physical, and mental well-being. All friendships are valuable, but some do cross into new territory. We may see these friends in a new light and want to spend increasing amounts of time with them. They pique our romantic and sexual interests. Call it what you wish, "hanging out," "dating," or "going out," but in our society, pairing up is how we acquire our mates.

Why Do Research?

"Just Friends"

Like many people today, you probably have some opposite-sex friends who are just that—friends. Cross-sex friendships have some unique advantages, but also some potential challenges (Bleske-Rechek, 2008). A study by Vickie Harvey (2003) examined how people interpret the romantic challenges that cross-sex friendships can face.

Harvey asked 120 students enrolled in communication classes at two universities to keep a journal discussing the aspects of a cross-sex friendship. The journal entries were to answer three types of questions. The first type was questions about the friendship's emotional nature, such as, "What kinds of things do you typically do when you are together?" and "Is this an intimate relationship in terms of sharing experiences and confiding in each other?" The second type of question concerned the friendship's romantic nature, such as, "If ever, discuss the times when you felt you would like the friendship to become a romantic relationship," and "How do you communicate affection for each other?" The third type were audience-related questions such as, "How do you manage your public image as one of friends rather than as dating partners?" and "How have the reactions of other people affected your friendship?" Harvey collected the journals several times from the students over a 16-week period.

Cross-sex friendships have few guidelines and people are charting new territory, so they create myths to maintain these types of friendships as platonic rather than romantic. Harvey found the students' myths included the following themes (the answers are not mutually exclusive and therefore add up to more than 100 percent):

- *I'm not attracted to my friend.* Sixty-five percent of students acknowledged they had sent or received mixed messages about attraction.

- *We can remain just friends.* Forty-seven percent of the friends felt attracted to the other person at the beginning of the relationship when the other person assumed they were going to be just friends and struggled to remain so.
- *I could be attracted that way.* Thirty-two percent of the students reported their friend was attracted to them, but they did not feel the same way.
- *I don't discount my feelings.* Thirty percent reported they do not communicate their romantic interests in the other person because it has caused discomfort in the past, or they fear it will in the future.
- *Kissing doesn't count.* Twenty-six percent of the friendships included some romantic or sexual behavior, but it was considered only an extension of the friendship itself.
- *If we've been romantically involved, we can't be friends.* Nine percent of the students reported being romantically involved with their friend at some point and were now struggling to build a friendship.

Harvey's study, like others (Bleske-Rechek, 2008), reveals that cross-sex friendships are created and maintained without a clear set of guidelines, and the friends struggle to define and sustain these relationships.

What Do You Think?

1. Can you describe one of your closest cross-sex friendships? Do any of these myth constructions fit your situation?

2. Do you think men and women can be just friends? Why or why not? What micro- and macro-level factors help explain why cross-sex friendships are more common today than in the past?

Sources: Bleske-Rechek, 2008; Rawlins, 2008; Harvey, 2003.

:: Dating, Courtship, and Mate Selection

How do we decide who marries whom in our society? In some cultures it is easy—fathers or parents (often with the help of matchmakers) choose the mates for their children. But most people in the United States want to choose their own mates. And dating is the mechanism for finding a mate in Western culture. Dating serves many functions. It:

- Provides fun and recreation.
- Offers companionship.
- Allows intimacy.
- Confers social status.
- Assists in mate selection.

We generally assume in our "free" society that dating reflects our personal choices—*who, how,* or *why* we date is of our choosing. This reflects a micro-level orientation. Yet, we will see in the next section that our personal choices do not exist in a vacuum; they are embedded in macro-level historical, social, and cultural factors (Regan, 2008).

A Look at History: Macro-Level Influences on Our Micro-Level Choices

While in the past the ultimate goal of dating was to eventually select a mate, today we usually do not think of dating as being so narrowly focused. Meeting others and socializing can be fun in and of itself. But while we think of dating as a micro-level personal experience—e.g., "I hang out with whomever I like. . . ."—it is also shaped by larger, macro-level structural conditions in society. Over the last 200 years U.S. society has changed substantially, and along with those changes have come new ways of meeting and getting to know one another, falling in love, and selecting a mate. Let's look at some of these social and economic changes throughout our history.

Courtship in Early America
During colonial times, interactions between unmarried individuals of the opposite sex were highly supervised. This is not surprising when we consider the organization of social life prior to 1800 in the United States. Social life centered upon family and community, and the primary economic activity was agriculture. Therefore, opportunities for interaction occurred either at public social gatherings or in the homes of families. At social gatherings parents could influence who their daughters and sons met, and who might be later invited to their homes for a visit. The "date" was conducted in the parents' home. This practice was referred to as **calling** as in "Jed is going to come calling next week. . . ." Because distances between communities were often great and transportation was slow, it was not uncommon for the young man to spend days and nights at the home of the young woman's family.

Some people might believe that because women and their families could control who was allowed to call, women held more power in the development of romantic relationships than men. However, this is not really the case (Cott, 1978). Women were influenced not only by their parents, who had an incentive to encourage contacts with only certain men, but also by the men themselves, who were responsible for initiating contact. Women had to sit and wait to be called upon, and hope for the best. Since there were so few opportunities for women outside of marriage and motherhood, they knew that marriage was a necessity.

Industrialization, Consumerism, and the Emergence of Dating
Rapid industrialization in the mid-19th century resulted in rural to urban migration and the shifting of work from the farm to the factory. This change brought with it a higher standard of living and a cash economy that allowed people to save money for discretionary purposes. As automobiles became more affordable and popular in the 20th century, young couples had both a means of transportation and a place for intimacy. Likewise, urbanization brought with it a new set of social activities in places such as theaters or dance halls where young people could congregate.

Many other social changes also occurred in the early part of the past century that influenced interactions among unmarried young people. For example, labor laws limited the hours teenagers could work, and mandatory education required that they spend time in school. These two changes resulted in a period termed **adolescence**—a new developmental period between childhood and adulthood. Public schools were co-educational, which created an environment for adolescent girls and boys to interact socially. As relationships developed, couples could spend time together, away from parental supervision, at the movies or a dance club. Dating shifted focus from the family to the peer group.

We also see that young men and women played different roles in dating. Generally, it was the young man who initiated, planned, and paid for the date. It was the young woman's

calling: A dating practice of the 18th and 19th centuries in which a young man would visit a young woman in her parents' home.

adolescence: The period of life that occurs between childhood and adulthood.

responsibility to control the man's behavior, specifically his sexual advances, within the relationship.

The first major study of dating in college was conducted by Willard Waller in the 1930s at Penn State University (Waller, 1937). He found that, among the students, young men and women were rated in terms of their dating value; Waller's article was called "The Rating and Dating Complex." Men were at the top of the list if they had access to automobiles, could dance well, and had a lot of money. Women were held in higher regard if they dressed well, had good conversation skills, and were considered popular. Waller found that the goal was to be rated as high as possible, which would bring an enhanced reputation and the ability to get the most and the "best" dates. We can see how ideas about sex and gender (i.e., women should be pretty, and men should have money) were important components of the dating scene. Waller's research also compared the level of emotional attachment between dating partners. Waller coined the term **principle of least interest** referring to the idea that unequal emotional involvement between romantic partners has implications for the quality and stability of relationships.

Dating was a relatively new concept in the early 20th century, emerging alongside the new view of adolescence.

Macro Influences Today: Sex and Gender, Race/Ethnicity, Social Class, Sexual Orientation

Many macro-level influences have shaped dating and the choices we make. The 1970s ushered in many political movements, including a resurgence of the women's movement, and dating became less formal. The passage of the Education Amendments of 1972 and the famous Title IX, which included mandates that girls be allowed access to sports in ways comparable to boys, resulted in increased co-educational experiences. Sex segregation in the curriculum also declined. Colleges offered co-ed dormitories, increasing opportunities for social interaction. In the workforce, the opportunities for women and men to engage in similar types of occupations or jobs and to work together have also increased. [□●┤ **Read** on **myfamilylab.com**

Perhaps one of the biggest changes in dating over the past generation is that it is becoming more distinct from mate selection—dating may lead to partnering or marriage, but it may not and so we enjoy it for its own sake (Feiring, 2002; Furman, 2002). Rather than the pairing up of the past, dating today often involves simply "hanging out" or "getting together" with larger groups of people. There is less pressure to be paired off and more emphasis on group friendship, although obviously many people do pair off and eventually become partners.

[□●┤ **Read** the **Document** *The Balance of Power in Dating* on **myfamilylab.com**

Gender and Dating
Despite the increased informality of dating, researchers have found many young adults still behave in relatively traditional ways. Women and men often follow **dating scripts**, or sets of expectations about how to behave. The following scripts may be overgeneralized, but you will probably find them somewhat familiar. Women's dating scripts include waiting to be asked for a date, buying a new outfit, waiting for the date to arrive, eating lightly while out, going to the bathroom to primp, and calling a friend afterwards to discuss the date. Men's scripts include asking someone for a date, preparing the car, getting money, planning the date, picking up the date, opening doors for her, paying the bill, and walking her to the door when returning home. Both men and women have generally agreed on these gendered scripts. In other words,

principle of least interest: The idea that unequal emotional involvement between romantic partners has implications for the quality and stability of relationships.

dating script: A set of expectations around dating that are somewhat different for men and women.

Have you noticed that men do not wear engagement rings? Why do you think this is?

although attitudes about relationships have become less traditional and more egalitarian, these attitudes have not been fully translated into dating behavior.

It is not surprising that these scripts are still with us when we look at how the mass media presents ideas about dating. Television shows, books, music, and movies all perpetuate the idea that men and women approach dating in different ways. Men are told to be romantic, listen attentively, agree to do things with her family and friends, build her trust, spend time cuddling, and not to expect or demand sex. Women, on the other hand, are told not to expect a man to profess love too soon, or to push him into commitment.

Other rituals also reveal the ways in which dating is gendered. For example, how can we tell when a couple is dating exclusively? Your parents or grandparents may have known such rituals as "getting pinned," exchanging ID bracelets, or wearing a boyfriend's class ring or a "promise ring." These actions were especially important because they revealed to others that the young woman was in a relationship and had been chosen. Again, not that much has changed in this dating ritual. Exclusive relationships today are reinforced by the multi-million-dollar business of marketing engagement rings (Gona & Merry, 2007; Ingraham, 1999). About 75 percent of all first-time brides wear engagement rings at an average price of $5,800 (The Knot Inc., 2010). Notice that only women wear engagement rings, and they are purchased by the man. The diamond industry claims this is a good financial investment for the couple, but fails to mention that this habit reflects the patriarchal idea of male ownership of women. It signals "hands off—she's taken" to the larger society. It appears that despite the greater informality of dating, gendered norms persist.

Differences and Similarities in Dating Practices: Social Class, Race, Ethnicity, and Sexual Identity

Dating takes different forms and has different objectives across different social groups. Those who study the upper socioeconomic classes believe the wealthy control dating opportunities to maintain their distinctive place in society (Kendall, 2002). Private schools, private clubs, and gated communities are examples of the ways wealthy people segregate themselves by social class. Upper-class families also make sure their children fall in love with the "right" kind of people. Debutante balls, private schools, and social clubs serve as mechanisms to introduce young people to appropriate dating partners (Domhoff, 2005).

Dating ideals also reflect distinctive subcultures within racial or ethnic groups. One example is the *quinceañera*, a coming-out party for young Hispanic women (Miranda, 2004), as described in the feature box *Diversity in Families: I am 15 and a Woman Today!* A *quinceañera* is held at the time of a young woman's fifteenth birthday and includes a Catholic mass followed by a party. It is a festive event for both family and friends at which the young woman wears a special gown and a tiara, and gets to feel like a princess for a day. It is expected that she can begin dating after this celebration. Young Hispanic men are not given a *quinceañera* as this event is designed to signal the young woman's availability in Hispanic culture.

Some groups, including lesbians, gays, bisexuals, and transgender (LGBT) individuals, have a more difficult time meeting others because of social stigma. Public spaces created for LGBT individuals are limited, and many date by going to personal residences of friends or to gay-friendly bars and restaurants. In addition, because of discrimination at work, many gays and lesbians choose to stay "closeted" about their sexual identity and dating relationships to protect their jobs.

LGBT individuals share many similarities with heterosexuals in their relationships (Berzon, 2004; Kurdek, 2006, 2007, 2009). Those relationships last longest when the partners have a sense of greater equity. Research also suggests sex differences are similar to those

Diversity in Families

I Am 15 and a Woman Today!

A *quinceañera* is a special celebration given for a Hispanic girl by her family to indicate that she is growing up and can now begin dating. How does this celebration reflect gendered cultural values?

Maria was dressed in a beautiful new floor-length pastel gown, her hair swept up on top of her head, her rhinestone necklace and bracelet glittering in place around her neck and wrist. Her mother and godmother, beaming with pride, helped her with the final touch, placing the tiara on her head. Maria picked up her bouquet, ready to greet the 14 friends she had chosen for her court, other girls in their ball gowns, and boys in their tuxedos. Today was her special day—her *quinceañera*.

The passage from childhood to adulthood is a significant transition in many cultures. In Mexico, Puerto Rico, Cuba, and Central and South America, a girl's fifteenth birthday is the time for celebrating her journey into womanhood. The *quinceañera* is her coming-out party—she is presented to her peers and their families as a young woman approaching marriageable age.

The most important part of the celebration is the thanksgiving Mass (*Misa de acción de gracias*). The young woman takes a prominent place at the foot of the altar, kneeling on a special pillow personalized with her name, and after the Mass leaves her bouquet on the altar to honor the Virgin Mary. Afterwards, the party can begin, with food, drink, music, and dancing—few details are spared for this festive occasion. It is held in a banquet hall or home, depending on the size of the party and the economic means of the family. It resembles a wedding reception, with its formal invitations, guest book, photo album, gifts, cake and cake server set, and champagne glasses. The young woman's guests will toast her, offering their congratulations and best wishes for her future. The party also includes other traditions unique to the *quinceañera*, such as the Changing of the Shoes, in which the father ceremoniously changes the girl's shoes from flats to high heels, symbolic of her changing from a girl into a young woman.

The origins of the *quinceañera* celebration are unclear but it may come from the early Aztecs. Today among all social classes it is a girl's rite of passage that celebrates families and elevates traditional womanhood.

What Do You Think?

1. Why do you think that girls have a *quinceañera* celebration, but boys do not? How does this celebration reflect ideas about sex and gender in Hispanic culture?

2. How would you feel about having a *quinceañera* celebration or attending one? What macro-level and micro-level factors have shaped your opinions of this celebration?

Sources: Loeffler, 2008; Palfrey, 1997; Quinceañera-Boutique.com, n.d.

---

among straight women and men. Gay men tend to have shorter relationships with more partners, while lesbians tend more toward monogamy. Straight men are also more likely than straight women to have more partners and to have more than one partner at a time.

Clearly, dating takes place within a social context. Its purpose and structure are shaped by important macro-level historical, cultural, social, and economic conditions. How are men and women viewed in society, and what types of opportunities do they have? What are the existing economic conditions? What types of technologies are available? What is the support for gay, lesbian, bisexual, and transgender persons in the community? All these factors, and the ways in which they vary, influence the micro-level choices in selecting our mates.

A Micro View: Who Do We Date and Where Do We Meet?

Most people do not often focus on the broader, macro-level factors that shape who and how we date. We tend to take them for granted and focus instead on the here and now. Let's examine dating from this micro-level perspective. What are some contemporary dating trends?

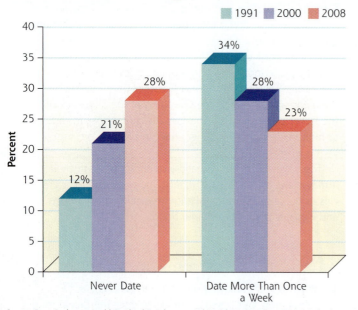

Figure 3.2

Percentage of 12th-Grade Students Who Never Date or Who Date Frequently (More Than Once a Week), 1991, 2000, 2008

Fewer high school seniors say that they go out on dates, or go out on dates frequently.

Source: From Bachman, Jerald G., Lloyd D. Johnston, and Patrick M. O'Malley. 1993. Monitoring the Future: Questionnaire Responses from the Nation's High School Seniors, 1991. Ann Arbor, MI: Institute for Social Research. 2001. Monitoring the Future: Questionnaire Responses from the Nation's High School Seniors, 2000. Ann Arbor, MI: Institute for Social Research. 2009. Monitoring the Future: Questionnaire Responses from the Nation's High School Seniors, 2008. Ann Arbor, MI: Institute for Social Research.

Online dating services are a big business, with over 1,400 different dating sites available.

Dating Trends Dating is viewed as a major developmental marker for teenagers. Those who date frequently have higher levels of self-esteem, rate themselves as more popular, and tend to have more autonomy than do other teens who date less frequently or not at all (Sneed, Hamagami, McArdle, Cohen, & Chen, 2007). Nonetheless, twelfth-grade students are less likely to date than they were in 1991, as shown in Figure 3.2. The percentage who claimed they never dated jumped from 12 percent in 1991 to 21 percent in 2000, and then to 28 percent in 2008 (Bachman, Johnston, & O'Malley, 1993, 2001, 2009). Those who claimed they date frequently (defined as more than once a week) declined significantly from 34 percent in 1991, to 28 percent in 2000, to only 23 percent in 2008. These differences could reflect the changing definition of dating itself; for instance, is "hanging out" with a group of people considered to be a date? A generation or two ago this situation might have been considered "double dating," but what do teens and young adults think today?

Another study of over 3,000 adults, all of them Internet users, found 16 percent of singles were "looking for a partner." Of these, 36 percent said they had been on no dates in the previous three months, 13 percent had been on one date, 22 percent had been on two to four dates, and 25 percent had been on five or more dates (Madden & Lenhart, 2006).

Who Do We Date? Relationships, including romantic ones, tend to be **homogamous**; we spend most of our time with people who look like us, act like us, and think like us. The majority of partners in both long-term and short-term relationships are similar with respect to:

- race and ethnicity;
- social class;
- education;
- age; and
- religion (Blackwell & Lichter, 2004; Wellner, 2005).

One reason for homogamy is **propinquity**, or geographic closeness. We tend to date (and eventually marry) people with whom we interact, and we are likely to interact with people who live in our neighborhoods and attend the same schools, churches, or other institutions. We share common interests: eating at the same restaurants, going to the same churches, and enjoying the same neighborhood activities. A wealthy young man from a rich and privileged family who went to elite schools may have a difficult time understanding the life of someone from the working class, as shown in the profiles of Randall Simmons and Tommy Johnson, introduced in Chapter 2 (p. 59). Likewise, a devout Muslim woman may have very little in common with, and thus not be particularly attracted to, a man actively committed to a Christian faith.

Another reason for homogamy is that parents may exert pressure on children to marry within their race. For example, although interracial marriages have now increased to over 8 percent of all couples (Passel, Wang, & Taylor,

2010), parents and other relatives often still disapprove of them. Forty-one percent of Black teens who have dated someone outside their race experienced parental disapproval (Wellner, 2005).

homogamous relationships: Relationships in which we spend most of our time with people who are very similar to ourselves.

Nonetheless, some people do date (and marry) outside their demographic categories. In fact, 14.6 percent of all marriages in 2008 were between people of different races or ethnicities (Passel, Wang, & Taylor, 2010). Why do these people defy tradition? One explanation is the size of the **pool of eligibles**, or the group from which you are likely to choose a mate. We tend to choose partners from a certain "pool" of people. Among Whites, the number of unmarried men and women is roughly equal across age groups. For other races, the pool is more limited. For example, eligible Black women far outnumber eligible Black men. Reasons for the skewed sex ratio include higher rates of crime and incarceration, crime victimization, and deaths from illness among Black men. According to the U.S. Bureau of Justice Statistics, about 10 percent of Black men are in jail, prison, or under criminal justice supervision compared to less than 1 percent of White men (U.S. Bureau of Justice Statistics, 2007; Pew Center on the States, 2009). In addition, unemployment is higher among Blacks than Whites, and wages are lower. These realities result in fewer opportunities for Black women to date or marry Black men (Edin & Kefalas, 2005).

Table 3.1	Where Dating Partners Meet
Most people meet partners at school or work, or through friends.	
Met at work or school	38%
Met through family or friends	34%
Met at a nightclub, bar, café, social gathering	13%
Met through the Internet	3%
Met at church	2%
Met by chance, such as on the street	1%
Met because they live in same neighborhood	1%
Met at recreational facility, gym	1%
Met on a blind date or through dating service	1%
Other	6%

Source: Pew Internet & American Life Tracking Survey, September-December, 2005, in Madden & Lenhart, 2006.

Where Do We Meet? As you may guess, most people meet each other at work, at school, and through friends or family, as shown in Table 3.1. The study of Internet users we described on page 80 found that, among people who are married or in committed relationships, over 38 percent met at work or school, and 34 percent met through family or friends, while only 3 percent met through the Internet (Madden & Lenhart, 2006). Most people who are married or in long-term relationships first met their partners the old-fashioned way—through face-to-face contact.

However, online dating services and websites have become an increasingly popular way to look for romantic partners even if only 3 percent of currently married or committed persons have met their partner on the Internet. There are approximately 1,400 online dating sites, the largest being eHarmony.com with over 20 million users and match.com with 15 million users (Scott, 2009). Nearly half of adults (49 percent) know at least one person who has dated someone he or she met online, according to a nationwide study conducted in July 2009 (Greenberg, 2009). This represents a significant increase from 2006 when only about a third said they knew someone who participated in online dating (Madden & Lenhart, 2006).

propinquity: Geographical closeness.

pool of eligibles: The group from which we are likely to choose our mates.

Among those who have tried online dating, almost two-thirds believe it is a good venue for finding a mate (Madden & Lenhart, 2006). Who participates in online dating services? As shown in Table 3.2 on page 82, they are somewhat more likely to be male, a racial or ethnic minority, urban, young, and to have lower levels of income and education, although these factors may be related to the fact that a high proportion of Internet daters are under age 30

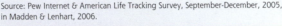

alk with your parents or someone from a previous generation about how they dated. Do you see a difference from your own style? Do you think recent changes in our patterns of dating, with an emphasis on informality, are a good thing or a bad thing for developing intimacy? Why or why not?

Table 3.2	Who Uses Online Dating?

Online daters are somewhat more likely to be male, a racial or ethnic minority, urban, young, and to have lower levels of income and education.

All Internet Users	11%
Sex	
Male	12%
Female	9%
Race/Ethnicity	
White	10%
Black	13%
Hispanic	14%
Geographic Location	
Urban	13%
Suburban	10%
Rural	9%
Age	
18–29	18%
30–49	11%
50–64	6%
65 +	3%
Household Income	
Less than $30,000	14%
$30,000–$49,999	13%
$50,000–$74,999	10%
$75,000 +	9%
Education Level	
Less Than High School	14%
High School Graduate	10%
Some College	11%
College +	10%

Source: Pew Internet & American Life Tracking Survey, September-December, 2005, in Madden & Lenhart, 2006.

(Madden & Lenhart, 2006). A study of over 3,300 people ranging in age from 19 to 89 found that those who use online Internet dating are more sociable, despite stereotypes to the contrary (Kim, Kwon, & Lee, 2009).

What is the current allure of online Internet dating? Many Internet users agree that it helps people find a better match because you can get to know a larger number of people. However, online daters themselves are divided as to whether this is the easiest and most efficient method of dating. Many daters see it as potentially dangerous and are somewhat wary of the risks, such as other people misrepresenting themselves (for example, by claiming they are single when they are really married) or trying to obtain personal information. Nonetheless, equal numbers of online daters report positive and negative experiences (Madden & Lenhart, 2006).

As you can see, macro-level factors can shape our personal micro-level choices about who we date, and why we choose to do so. These can be summed up in the boxed feature *Tying It All Together: Factors That Shape Dating*.

Some dating relationships become exclusive with a greater degree of commitment. Some people go on to marry, while others decide to cohabit. The next section examines these cohabiting relationships.

:: Heterosexual Cohabitation

It is tempting to think that this generation invented **cohabitation**, or living with your romantic and sexual partner without being married, but this is not the case. One hundred fifty years ago we may have spoken little of cohabitation, but it was a fact of life for many people, especially in rural areas. As a predominant rural nation, people were isolated from one another. A couple may have wanted to marry, but perhaps a minister was unavailable, or perhaps the couple was waiting until family could arrive for the wedding. Cohabitation was usually considered a temporary state until the couple could marry, and therefore others in the community usually treated them as a married couple (Cott, 2002).

However, as the U.S. began to develop and urbanize, these reasons for cohabitation became much less relevant. Distances were not so vast between communities, and methods of transportation improved. Consequently, cohabitation became less common in the early part of the 20th century. People who lived together without being married were considered sinful, deviant, or were branded as uncouth.

The attitude towards cohabitation changed again in the late 1960s and 1970s, when young people revolted against established norms and institutions (Popenoe, 2008). This was a period of new freedoms for a large baby-boom youth cohort—"the sexual revolution" and the availability of reliable birth control, and the "women's movement" with increasing numbers of women experiencing expanded access to education and the workplace. People no longer felt the need to marry young, and the average age at first marriage increased

The late 1960s and early 1970s were a period of great social change, including the so-called sexual revolution.

Tying It All Together

Factors That Shape Dating

It would seem that deciding who you spend time with and who you become intimate with are very personal issues. Why would you say that you are dating a certain person? Your answers may include reasons like, "He's cute." "She's smart." "I like his smile." "She's kind." But there is more to your reasons than this as shown below.

Macro-level Factors

- Cultural norms surrounding mate selection (Do you choose, or do your parents choose for you?)
- Technology
- Urbanization
- Development of an adolescent subculture
- Social and political movements
- Dating scripts based on sex
- Racial/ethnic cultural differences
- Economic considerations

Micro-level Factors

- Personal whims
- Friends, connections, and ways to meet new people
- Propinquity
- Size of your pool of eligible people

What Do You Think?

1. Can you see how any of these macro- and micro-level factors have operated in your own life?
2. Why do you think that most people just see the micro-level side of dating?

---

by several years. Divorce laws also changed, making it easier for married couples to divorce because of "irreconcilable differences," further increasing the number of single adults. These macro-level changes may have led people to ask, why not just live together?

Today, nearly 6.8 million U.S. households are maintained by heterosexual cohabiting couples, including Meghan and Jono from the opening vignette (U.S. Census Bureau, February 25, 2009). This number is about 10 percent of all couples (National Marriage Project, 2009). As you will note in Figure 3.3, this is more than double the number from 1990 alone and a more than five- to tenfold increase from a generation ago. It seems that today everyone knows someone who has, or is currently, cohabitating, as it is a typical pathway to marriage (Kennedy & Bumpass, 2008).

People cohabit for many reasons including convenience, economic considerations, as a way to assess compatibility for marriage or as a substitute for marriage, or as a way to avoid the expectations of marriage (Reed, 2006). In fact, unlike in the past, marriage may not be in the couple's future plans. Cohabitation may be an extension of dating or it may be an alternative to marriage itself (Sassler, 2010). A primary challenge of characterizing cohabitations is that partners may have differing motivations, their motivations may shift over time, or they may even disagree about whether or not they are in fact cohabiting (Seltzer, 2004). Let's say that you maintain an apartment with another friend, but you spend six nights a week, at least, at your boyfriend or girlfriend's place. Most of your clothes are stored there and you have designated closet space and dresser drawers in the bedroom, which you share. You cook, do laundry, and grocery shop with your boyfriend or girlfriend. Are you living together? Some would say yes; others would say no.

cohabitation: An arrangement in which two people live together without being married.

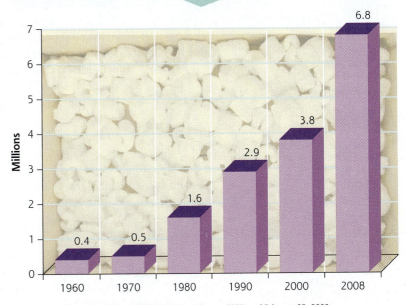

Figure 3.3   **Number of Cohabiting Couples of the Opposite Sex, 1960–2008**

Cohabitation has skyrocketed and is becoming increasingly normative.

Source: National Marriage Project, 2009; U.S. Census Bureau, 2006, and February 25, 2009.

Table 3.3	Characteristics of People Who Cohabit	
Cohabitation is very common, but research finds that men, Blacks, people with some college, and those who are less religious are more likely to have cohabited.		
	Yes	**No**
All Adults	36%	64%
Sex		
Male	39%	60%
Female	33%	66%
Race/Ethnicity		
White	34%	65%
Black	46%	53%
Hispanic	35%	65%
Education		
College Graduate	34%	66%
Some College	43%	56%
High School or Less	34%	66%
Attend Church		
Weekly or More	22%	77%
Monthly or Less	45%	55%
Seldom or Never	46%	53%
Religion		
White Protestant	30%	69%
Black Protestant	45%	55%
Catholic	31%	69%
Secular	56%	44%

Source: Pew Research Center. 2007a. "As Marriage and Parenthood Drift Apart, Public is Concerned About Social Impact: Generation Gap in Values, Behaviors" (pewresearch.org/pubs/526/marriage?parenthood).

Who Cohabits?

People who cohabit span all ages, races, and ethnic groups, and are found within all social classes. Over a third of adults say they have cohabited, currently or in the past. Among persons aged 30–49, nearly half have cohabited (Pew Research Center, 2007). In fact, today the majority of people who marry begin their union by cohabiting. Table 3.3 compares those who have cohabited with those who have not. You can see that men, Blacks, people with some college, and those who are not religious are more likely to have cohabited (Pew Research Center, 2007).

Some people argue that cohabitation and marriage have become indistinguishable in many respects but this, however, is not the case (Pew Research Center, 2007; Popenoe, 2008). How do cohabiters differ from married couples? Cohabiters tend to be more politically liberal, have more nontraditional ideas about gender, and are more likely to share housework and breadwinning responsibilities than are married couples (Seltzer, 2004; Kreider & Elliott, 2009; U.S. Census Bureau, February 25, 2009). Compared to their married counterparts, cohabiting men and women:

- are considerably younger;
- have less education and are significantly less likely to have graduated from college;
- earn less, on average;
- are somewhat less likely to have children residing with them, although the differences are not large;
- are nearly three times as likely to have a female partner who is six or more years older than the male partner, who earns more, and who is more highly educated; and
- are nearly twice as likely as married couples to be interracial, particularly with one Black and one White partner.

Attitudes toward Cohabitation: Is it still "Living in Sin"?

Along with changing behavior towards cohabitation, there is now a greater acceptance of cohabitation, as shown by the attitude of Meghan and Jono's parents at the beginning of this chapter. Before we look at the national trends, ask yourself how you feel about cohabitation. The boxed feature *Getting to Know Yourself: How Do You Feel about Cohabitation?* provides a short inventory of your views. It may be interesting to share these views with your partner, friends, or classmates. How are you similar? How are you different?

Now let's consider national trends of attitudes towards cohabitation. In a national survey, high school seniors were asked whether they agreed with the statement, "It is usually a good idea for a couple to live together before getting married in order to find out whether they really get along." Attitudes are considerably more favorable than those of a generation ago, with 65 percent of young men and 58 percent of young women agreeing that cohabitation is a good idea, compared to only 45 and 33 percent, respectively, in the late 1970s (National Marriage Project, 2009). Likewise, the General Social Survey, which is a large survey based on a nationally representative sample of adults, reports that 44 percent of adults agree or agree strongly with the statement, "Living together is an acceptable option."

But "acceptable" does not necessarily mean that cohabitation is seen as a "good" thing (Pew Research Center, 2007). Figure 3.4 (page 86) shows the results of a study by the Pew Research Center, which conducts research on many political and social values. This

Getting to Know Yourself

How Do You Feel about Cohabitation?

Please answer how you feel regarding each statement. Your answers can include:

1 = Strongly Agree 2 = Agree 3 = Neither Agree nor Disagree 4 = Disagree 5 = Strongly Disagree

	SA	A	N	D	SD
1. Living together without being married is immoral.	1	2	3	4	5
2. Cohabitation is a good way to have a trial marriage.	1	2	3	4	5
3. I have many friends who cohabit and I am comfortable with it.	1	2	3	4	5
4. I have cohabited before, and would never do it again.	1	2	3	4	5
5. It's a good idea for a couple who intends to marry to live together first.	1	2	3	4	5
6. It is all right for a couple to live together without intending to get married.	1	2	3	4	5
7. Cohabitation is harmful to children.	1	2	3	4	5
8. I currently live with someone.	1	2	3	4	5

	SA	A	N	D	SD
9. My family strongly disapproves of cohabitation.	1	2	3	4	5
10. Living together without getting married causes a lot of problems in society.	1	2	3	4	5

Scoring: First, transpose the answer categories of questions 2, 3, 5, 6, 8, and 9 so that Strongly Disagree is now worth 1 point, Strongly Agree is worth 2 points, etc. Keep questions 1, 4, 7, and 10 as is. Now, count up your points for each question. In general, the lower the score, the more negative you feel about cohabitation; the higher the score, the more positive you feel about cohabitation.

What Do You Think?

1. Do you think your attitudes differ significantly from your partner, friends, or classmates who might take this inventory? In what ways?

2. Can you identify any micro-level or macro-level factors that have shaped your views?

study found that overall, 10 percent of adults see cohabitation as a good thing for society, 43 percent believe that it makes no difference, and 44 percent feel it is bad for society. Interestingly, Blacks, who are most likely to cohabit, are also more likely than other racial or ethnic groups to believe that cohabitation is a bad thing for society. As you might expect, older persons and those who attend church regularly are more likely than younger persons and those who attend church rarely to believe that cohabitation is bad for society.

Nonetheless, cohabitation has become nearly institutionalized. It is now routine for surveys to ask about cohabitation and to include it as a separate category rather than combining it with the categories of "never married" or "unmarried."

Demographer Judith Seltzer notes three important demographic trends that indicate that the meaning of cohabitation is changing (Seltzer, 2004). First, although the majority of marriages today begin by cohabitation, cohabiting unions are less likely to be a prelude to marriage now than they were in past decades. Second, cohabiting couples are more likely to be parents. One or both may have a child from a previous union or the couple may have a child together. Third, single women who become pregnant are about as likely to cohabit today as they are to marry the child's father.

Some people voice grave concern over these issues. They may believe it is wrong for people to engage in sexual relationships outside of marriage, or they believe that living together is not a good way to start a healthy marriage. In particular, some people voice

Figure 3.4 Living Together without Getting Married

Most adults do not see cohabitation as a "bad thing for society," but, at the same time, not very many say that it is "a good thing."

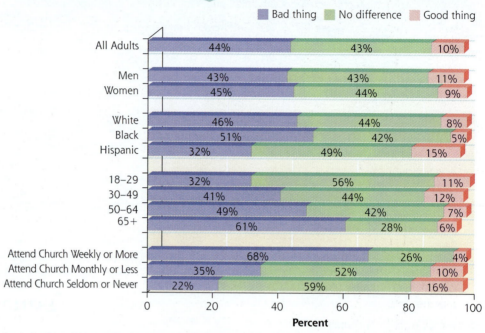

Source: Pew Research Center. 2007a. "As Marriage and Parenthood Drift Apart, Public is Concerned About Social Impact: Generation Gap in Values, Behaviors" (pewresearch.org/pubs/526/marriage?parenthood).

concern that cohabitation is harmful for children (Popenoe, 2008). David Popenoe, who is a leader in the National Marriage Project, says:

> "In the final analysis, the issue of cohabitation comes down to a conflict between adult desires and children's need. It seems a tragedy that, with all the opportunities that modernity has brought to adults, it may also be bringing a progressive diminution to our concern for the needs of children—and thus for the many generations to come" (Source: Popenoe, David. 2008. "Cohabitation, Marriage, and Child Well-Being: A Cross-National Perspective" (The National Marriage Project). Retrieved 28 August 2008 [http://marriage.rutgers.edu/Publications/NMP2008CohabitationReport.pdf]).

Do these concerns have a strong basis in reality? The next section examines the research on cohabitation, marriage, and children.

Cohabitation and Marriage

Rachel and Adam, both just out of college and beginning their careers, have been together for over a year. While in college they each had their own apartments that they shared with roommates, but over time they spent increasing numbers of days and nights at one another's places. Occasionally Rachel's roommate would complain, "Geez, he's practically living here . . ." and she let Rachel know that she did not care for a part-time third roommate (Adam) who was not paying rent. So, Rachel and Adam decided that once they were out of college and had more money of their own, they would get their own place. Why not, they asked? They would no longer be subject to the complaints of other roommates, it made good financial sense, and it would be a good way to test if they were compatible for marriage, although they had no specific plans to marry.

Cohabitation may ease roommate problems, and it may make good financial sense, but is cohabitation a good test for marriage compatibility? The answer to that question is complex. First, cohabiting relationships generally do not last very long. About half of cohabiting relationships break up in less than a year, and less than 10 percent last five years or more (Seltzer, 2004). However, these findings are highly correlated with age. Older cohabiters report significantly higher levels of relationship quality and stability than do younger cohabiters, although they are less likely to have plans to marry their partners, according to a study of 966 cohabiters in the United States (King & Scott, 2005). Older cohabiters are more likely to view their relationship as an alternative to marriage, whereas younger cohabiters are more likely to view their relationship as a prelude to marriage.

Second, despite the logic that living together prior to marriage gives partners the opportunity to test the relationship and therefore, to decrease their chances of divorce, people who cohabit are actually *more* likely to have unhappy marriages and to divorce (Hohmann-Marriott, 2006; Tach & Halpern-Meekin, 2009). This is true for all racial groups, especially Whites, although less so among Blacks or Hispanics (Phillips & Sweeney, 2005). Cohabitation after a divorce is also associated with reduced marital satisfaction in the remarriage and a higher rate of subsequent divorce (Xu, Hudspeth, & Bartkowski, 2006). Why are people who cohabit with their partners prior to marriage more likely to eventually divorce?

There are two primary reasons for the positive relationship between cohabitation and divorce. First, there may be a **selection effect** in operation (Lichter & Qian, 2008; Tach & Halpern-Meekin, 2009). The type of person who cohabits may be the same type of person who would willingly end an unhappy marriage. For example, someone who values personal freedom may be both more likely to cohabit and also more likely to divorce. Or a person who is less religious may be more likely to cohabit and also more likely to end an unhappy marriage. In other words, it is not the case that cohabitation *causes* the divorce, *per se*. Rather, the relationship between cohabitation and divorce is **spurious**, meaning that both cohabitation and divorce are really caused by a third factor—in these examples, the high value placed on personal freedom, or a weak sense of religiosity.

The second reason may be causal—perhaps there is something about the cohabitation experience that weakens a relationship and makes it more prone to divorce. Attitudes and behaviors developed through cohabitation may be at odds with long-term marriage. For example, couples who cohabit are more likely to maintain financial independence and keep their own separate checking accounts (Eggebeen, 2005), possibly emphasizing the couple's degree of separateness and undermining a feeling of unity. It is possible that cohabiting couples are living more like singles, with less of an emphasis on permanence, and therefore are not really "testing" the relationship as if it were marriage. Consequently, when they do marry, the social expectations that come along with being a husband, wife, son-in-law, and daughter-in-law remain new and uncharted territory. Is the relationship between cohabitation and divorce only spurious, or does cohabitation really cause divorce? It is likely that both are operating to some degree, but selection effects seem to receive the most support (Tach & Halpern-Meekin, 2009).

Why are there racial and ethnic differences in the relationship between cohabitation and divorce? Researchers Phillips and Sweeney (2005) speculate that it may be because Whites are more likely to characterize their relationship as trial marriages, whereas cohabitation for Blacks and Mexican Americans is more likely to function as a substitute for, or a precursor to, marriage. They suggest that more research is needed to truly understand the meanings of cohabitation across different racial and ethnic groups.

We do know that cohabiting relationships do not necessarily end easily nor are they free of problems. For example, after dissolution, the economic standing of formerly cohabiting women declines precipitously compared to that of men, leaving a substantial portion of women in poverty (Avellar & Smock, 2005). This problem is particularly pronounced for Black and Hispanic women. The economic inequality among men and women is primarily the result of women having custody of children (33 percent of formerly cohabiting women have children living with them, compared to 3 percent of men), and the lower earnings of women. Women cannot maintain the same standard of living as men after their relationship ends, and nearly one-third of them become impoverished (Avellar & Smock, 2005).

selection effect: An explanation for the fact that people who cohabit tend to be the same ones who later divorce.

spurious: When a relationship between two variables is actually caused by a third variable.

each state to deny constitutional marital rights between persons of the same sex that have been recognized in another state. Former President Bush emphasized, "I strongly believe that marriage should be defined as between a man and a woman. I am troubled by activist judges who are defining marriage." As a presidential candidate, President Obama said he would repeal the Act (Wilson, 2009), but by 2010 had failed to do so. 👁️—Watch on **myfamilylab.com**.

👁️—Watch the **Video**
Reaction to Gay Marriage Ban on
myfamilylab.com

Many gays and lesbians are in long-term committed relationships, despite our stereotypes to the contrary.

Commitment and Cohabitation

Despite popular stereotypes that homosexuals, particularly gay men, have frequent sex with multiple partners, in reality many gays and lesbians lead quiet and unassuming lives in committed monogamous relationships (Biblarz & Savci, 2010; Peplau & Beals, 2004). Estimating the number of same-sex couples is difficult; many fear identification because of discrimination or abuse. With this caveat in mind, the American Psychological Association suggests that between 40 and 60 percent of gay men and between 45 and 80 percent of lesbians are currently involved in a committed relationship. In addition, between 18 and 28 percent of gay couples and 8 to 21 percent of lesbian couples have lived together ten years or more (Kurdek, 2004; American Psychological Association, 2009). Another source of data is the U.S. Census Bureau. The 2000 U.S. Census began to compile data on unmarried households as a way to measure the number of cohabiting gays and lesbians, and reports that over 300,000 unmarried households were headed by a male partner, and nearly 300,000 unmarried households were headed by a female partner.

Similarities and Differences

We know that many gays and lesbians live together in committed, loving relationships despite the fact that they cannot marry in most states. This leads researchers to wonder if same-sex couples differ significantly from heterosexual couples, or whether gay relationships are structured differently from lesbian relationships.

Differences between Homosexual and Heterosexual Couples
To compare different types of relationships, the late family scholar Lawrence Kurdek collected data over time from gay, lesbian, and heterosexual married couples and compared many aspects of their relationships (Kurdek, 2006, 2007, 2009). He looked at relationship quality, level of commitment, level of satisfaction with the relationship, social support from family and friends, conflict and its resolution, and equality. He controlled for important sociodemographic variables (e.g., age, time living together, whether the couple had children) so that any findings could be attributed to sexual orientation rather than to other factors.

Kurdek found very few differences between same-sex couples and heterosexual couples, and most differences he did find were very small. For example, both gay and lesbian couples were more comfortable with closeness compared to their married counterparts, were more open with their partner, and were more autonomous in the relationship. Lesbians, in particular, reported greater levels of equality in their relationship and higher satisfaction. Gays and lesbians also reported receiving less support from family members than did the married couples, although lesbians reported greater support from friends. Overall, on three-quarters of the indicators, there were no significant differences between same-sex and heterosexual married couples. It would seem then that heterosexual and same-sex couples are more alike than they are different.

Differences between Lesbian and Gay Couples   Using the same set of variables from gay, lesbian, and married couples, Kurdek assessed how gay and lesbian couples differ from one another (Kurdek, 2003). He found even fewer differences between gay and lesbian couples than he did when he compared them to heterosexual married couples. There were virtually no differences between the two groups in the predictors of relationship quality, social support, and the likelihood of dissolution. The most significant results emerged in the relationship-related attitudinal questions, where there were differences in three of the eight variables. Lesbian couples reported stronger liking, trust, and equality than did gay couples. Again, it appears that differences among committed couples are generally minimal, whether gay, lesbian, or married heterosexual.

Do you know any gay or lesbian couples? If so, how are their relationships similar to or different from the heterosexual couples that you know? Since they probably had few role models to observe how gays or lesbians behave in committed relationships, where or how did they learn about what it means to be a couple?

Bringing It Full Circle

This chapter has explored how we build loving and intimate relationships. It has discussed our lives as singles and the friendships that we share. It then turned to a discussion of the changing nature of courtship, dating, and mate selection. The opening vignette focused on cohabitation, and the way in which it has become increasingly normative, and a normal, natural part of building a relationship—it may or may not lead to marriage. Upon first glance, this vignette seems to be the personal story of Meghan and Jono, and the choices they made. However, there is far more to the story than personal choice as many macro-level factors are at play. Did you notice that neither Meghan nor Jono feels stigmatized for being single at age 30, reflecting macro-level changes in the age at first marriage? We also saw that their cohabitation had an air of informality, a result of women's increasing social and economic opportunities which, in turn, offer more chances for men and women to meet and socialize. Finally, fifty years ago their cohabitation would have likely been a scandal. Today, because of many social movements, cohabitation has become an increasingly common feature of romantic relationships. As you can see, both micro- and macro-level factors can help us understand how we build relationships.

Now that you see things in a new light, let's review the information throughout the chapter in the opening vignette to see how it might relate to your life:

- How are dating and courtship today different from your parents' generation? How about your grandparents' generation? Can you think of specific ways that things have changed in your own family?

- What are your views of cohabitation? Would you cohabit, as Meghan and Jono do, or have you already? Why or why not?

- What evidence have you seen that cohabitation is becoming increasingly normative? Do you think it is becoming normative in all racial, ethnic, and social class groups? Why or why not?

For further review, turn to the Video Discussion Guide on page 449 to answer additional questions about how the chapter opening video relates to what you have learned in this chapter.

Chapter Review

3.1. How many people are single?

It depends on what you mean by single. Do you mean never-married? Or do you mean currently unmarried, which would include people who are also widowed or divorced? The difference between these two ways of defining single can yield very different results.

3.2. What does it mean to be "single"?

Single means different things to different people. It can include the never-married, divorced, and widowed people who are not in a committed relationship or cohabiting. If we want to broaden our understanding of singles, we can ask two critical questions: (1) is it voluntary; and (2) is it a temporary situation? Together these two dimensions yield four very different groups of singles: voluntary temporary singles, voluntary stable singles, involuntary temporary singles, and involuntary stable singles.

3.3. Why is friendship important in our lives?

Close friendships provide companionship, support, self-esteem, and teach us about ourselves and others. Some of our most important and intimate relationships are with our friends. Friends are also good for your physical and mental health. Having close friends who you can confide in has been shown to lower blood pressure, heart rate, and cholesterol level.

3.4. How do friendships differ by sex, race, ethnicity, or social class?

Our social statuses shape the types of our friendships. For example, although men and women have about the same number of friends, women's friendships are usually more personal or intimate in nature. We also find that friendships among lower-income and minority groups tend to be long-lasting and more intimate.

3.5. Can men and women ever really be "just friends"?

Historically, cross-sex friendships that were strictly platonic were rare and believed to be part of the developmental process of romantic engagement (friends become lovers or lovers later become friends). Today, cross-sex friendships are far more common than they were in your parents' or grandparents' generation. They are highly valued, but can contain some tensions as well.

3.6. How has the purpose and structure of dating changed over time?

One of the primary goals of dating is mate selection. In the past dating was more formal. A young gentleman "called" on a woman and remained under the watchful eye of her parents. With the rise of an adolescent subculture, where young men and women have more opportunities at school or work to interact with less supervision, they are now more able to date and socialize independently.

3.7. How have macro-level factors shaped our micro-level choices with respect to dating?

In the realm of dating, many macro-level factors influence our personal choices. Examples of these factors include women's status in society, the rise of an adolescent subculture, technology such as the automobile, and economic considerations.

3.8. What are some contemporary trends in dating?

Many people do not even use the term "date" today. High-school seniors for example, are far less likely than just a generation ago to say that they date. Today, dating is often conducted in informal groups, with the possibility of gradually pairing off. Many couples cohabit, with or without discussing marriage.

Key Terms

adolescence (p. 76)
calling (p. 76)
cohabitation (p. 82)
cross-sex friendships (p. 74)
dating script (p. 77)

homogamous relationships (p. 80)
involuntary stable singles (p. 72)
involuntary temporary singles (p. 71)

pool of eligibles (p. 81)
principle of least interest (p. 77)
propinquity (p. 80)
selection effect (p. 87)

spurious (p. 87)
voluntary stable singles (p. 71)
voluntary temporary singles (p. 71)

3.9. How common is cohabitation?

The number of people who cohabit has increased dramatically over the past few decades. In 1970, there were only about 500,000 couples cohabiting, but by 2008 there were nearly 7 million.

3.10. How have attitudes regarding cohabitation changed over time?

Our society began to have a more favorable view of cohabitation beginning in the 1960s and 1970s, and today, most of us know people who have cohabited and we consider it to be an acceptable lifestyle. However, few people say that cohabitation has been "good" for our society—most say that it either has made no difference or that it is actually bad for society.

3.11. How does cohabitation affect marriage?

Many cohabiting relationships do not lead to marriage; about half of cohabiting relationships break up in less than a year, and less than 10 percent last five years or more. Among those cohabiting couples that do marry, they have a greater chance of divorcing than do couples who did not cohabit. However, this may be a selection effect, or it may be a spurious relationship.

3.12. What are the effects of cohabitation on children?

Deciding whether cohabitation is good or bad for children largely depends on what alternatives exist. Cohabitation can be both good and bad, depending on the family make-up. Generally speaking, children do best when they live with two biological parents, but of course there are exceptions to this.

3.13. What are some differences and similarities between homosexual and heterosexual couples?

There are very few differences between homosexual and heterosexual couples, and the differences found seem to be rather small. In sum, these groups are far more alike than they are different.

PEARSON
myfamilylab
www.myfamilylab.com

Experience, Discover, Observe, Evaluate

MyFamilyLab is designed just for you. Each chapter features a pre-test and post-test to help you learn and review key concepts and terms. Experience Marriage and Family in action with dynamic visual activities, videos, and readings to enhance your learning.

Here are a few activities you'll find for this chapter:

Explore Social Explorer is an interactive application that allows you to explore Census data through interactive maps. Explore the Social Explorer Report:

• Single Americans

Read MyFamilyLibrary includes primary source readings from classic and contemporary sociologists. Read:

• Peplau & Campbell, "The Balance of Power in Dating"

4

Love and Loving Relationships

Above: Rati and Subas, a couple with an arranged marriage.

Would you consider allowing your mother to choose your marriage partner? In the United States, most young people would say, "No thanks."

However, arranged marriages are common in other parts of the world and most young adults would not have it any other way.

Rati and Subas are an educated and attractive young couple from Nepal, married here in the United States four years ago. What distinguishes them from other young couples is that their marriage was arranged. As Rati, the young woman, gratefully says, "I never had the thought that I would find my own partner because even though it was risky, I wanted to be on the safer side and have my parents make the major decision for me because their support has always worked. So in the big step of my life, I just let my parents decide."

In an arranged marriage, instead of the couple getting together and interacting with each other, parents or other family members bring a proposal to either the groom or the bride. In Rati and Subas's case, Rati's mother set up the meeting. She met Subas for an hour or so, and asked him a series of questions about himself, his occupation, and his family. She thought he might be an excellent match for her daughter. Rati said that her mother did not push her, but simply encouraged her to think about Subas as a possible husband. Rati and Subas met briefly on a few occasions, always supervised by others, and quickly agreed to be married.

> "I wanted to be on the safer side and have my parents make the major decision for me because their support has always worked."

▶ **Watch** the **Video** *Arranged Marriage: Rati and Subas* on **myfamilylab.com**

"In our culture, you don't have to appeal to each other before you get married," Rati explains. "You get married and start to get to know one another, and then you'll develop feelings."

Rati boarded a plane in Nepal for the United States, where Subas was living. She had never been to the United States before, or had even been on an airplane, so she was nervous. But when she saw him at the airport ready and waiting to greet her, she immediately felt comfortable. It was then, she says, that she started developing feelings for him.

Subas takes his role as a husband very seriously. He believes that it is his job to take care of his wife emotionally, financially, and socially. He has introduced Rati to American culture and has taught her how to cope with life in an American city. Rati thinks he is an excellent husband. Subas and Rati have been married for four years, are very happy, and hope to have children soon. They both agree that their arranged marriage now "is like a love marriage."

QUESTIONS That Matter

4.1 What do we mean by the term "love"?

4.2 How do we first learn to love?

4.3 What are the three primary attachment styles?

4.4 Does our attachment in infancy affect us as adults?

4.5 Have meanings of love changed over time?

4.6 What is the difference between romance and companionate love?

4.7 What do biological, micro-, and macro-level perspectives teach us about love?

4.8 Are women more interested in love than men?

4.9 What is the importance of same-sex love?

4.10 What is unrequited love?

4.11 Is jealousy always irrational?

4.12 What is stalking and how serious is this problem?

4.13 Why are breakups so difficult?

When we think about love, we usually see it as a micro-level phenomenon—full of warmth, intimacy, and passion. We care deeply about someone, and he or she in turn cares deeply about us. We *feel* love on this level, and we like it. However, our feelings do not exist in a vacuum. The way we experience love is also shaped by the macro-level social context in which we live. First, love is related to culture. In the United States, for example, the focus is on romantic love. In other cultures, this type of passion is thought to be foolish. It is seen as a poor reason for marriage because it is too fragile, and possibly too fleeting (Griffith, 2006). Instead, like Rati and Subas, many young people in these cultures opt for an arranged marriage.

Second, people have been socialized to see and experience love differently depending on their sex, social class, race, and ethnicity. The meanings attached to love and how we express them differ. For example, women often express their love with words, while men may express their love more with actions.

Third, love is also related to the relationship between the people who love, including parents and children, friends, and romantic partners. These relationships are profoundly different from one another, but contain an emotion that we all call "love." What is love then that it can encompass so many different relationships and distinct feelings within those relationships?

This chapter will address some of the complexities of the meanings and experiences of love. But first, let's try to define this ideal that we all seem to seek.

love: A strong affection for one another arising out of kinship or personal ties; attraction based on sexual desire; and affection based on admiration, benevolence, or common interests.

:: What Is Love?

The topic of love is everywhere, and is deeply fascinating, but providing a definition of love for all of our different types of relationships is complicated (Felmlee & Sprecher, 2006; Fehr, Sprecher, & Underwood, 2009). It is hard to imagine that the way we feel about our lovers, fathers, best friends, and daughters can be generalized to a "one-size-fits-all" definition.

The dictionary defines **love** as (1) a strong affection for one another arising out of kinship or personal ties; (2) attraction based on sexual desire; and (3) affection based on admiration, benevolence, or common interests (Merriam-Webster Online, 2010). We may be speaking of the love a parent feels for a child, the love a child feels for a sibling, the love between two friends, or the love experienced by romantic partners. Let's discuss a few components of this definition. First, love is an enduring bond between two or more people. Loving relationships are those we intend to be long-lasting. Second, love is based on affection and emotion. When we love another person, we feel something stronger towards him or her than we do towards others. In romantic partners, these feelings are usually sexual. Third, love includes a feeling of obligation toward another. When you love someone, you want to take care of that person and help him or her when he or she needs it, both physically and emotionally.

People who study love approach the concept in a variety of ways. Some have focused on our first description for love—a strong affection for one another arising out of kinship or personal ties. This refers to a bond or sense of attachment. How do we come to attach ourselves to others, and what are these

Love is based on mutual affection and emotion. When we love someone we feel something stronger toward him or her than we do toward others.

different types of attachments? Psychologists believe that we observe a biological component of bonding in early infancy, when dependent infants become attached to their primary caregivers (usually their mothers). As we will present in the next section, psychologists think that this initial bonding, or "attachment," then shapes the way we construct all other attachments throughout our lives, including those of romantic relationships.

Do you think it is possible to study love scientifically? Recalling what you learned in Chapter 1 about research methods, which approach, if any, might work best, and why? Which approach, if any, might be inappropriate, and why?

:: Love as Attachment

Humans are social beings and need interaction with others to survive. This notion forms the basis of **attachment theory** (Bowlby, 1969), which states the way infants form attachments early in life will affect their relationships throughout later life.

Attachment in Children

In the beginning, infants and children stay close to their parents or caregivers because they have to for survival. They are completely dependent on others for their physical and emotional care. Attachment theorists suggest these early attachments infants make with their primary caregiver will have implications for the way they make attachments to others throughout life.

How important are bonds and secure attachment early in life? You may have heard stories of children growing up in orphanages or children living in abusive families who have been denied opportunities to form secure and loving bonds with consistent caregivers. If a child's needs are frequently ignored, or the child is repeatedly given a harsh or inappropriate response, he or she may fail to develop a sense of trust. This lack of trust can lead to further problems in personal development and in social relationships (Mercer, 2006; Mooney, 2009). Children with insecure attachment patterns have difficulty forming close and intimate relationships, possibly throughout their lives, unless they receive help (Brisch, 2004; Lee, 2003).

One of the first case studies of the damage inadequate attachment can cause is the study of Anna, a girl born in the 1930s who lived her early life tied to a chair, alone in a room (Davis, 1940, 1947; Macionis, 2011). A social worker was called to a rural farmhouse to investigate a complaint about possible child abuse. In the house she was greeted gruffly by an elderly man and his obviously mentally challenged adult daughter. The daughter was dependent on her elderly father for help, but she showed no outward signs of abuse—so why was the social worker called? The answer was soon revealed. A noise, a search of the farmhouse, and there, in a dimly lit second-floor attic, was a girl about eight years old wedged into a chair with her arms tied. The girl was thin, dirty, and in diapers. She sat listlessly and stared into space. As the social worker approached her, speaking softly and kindly, the girl showed no sign of outward communication, such as eye contact or speech.

The social worker learned the little girl was called "Anna." Her mother had become pregnant out of wedlock as a young woman, and Anna's grandfather was so enraged about the pregnancy that at first he refused to allow the baby in the house. Anna was initially cared for elsewhere, but her mother could not afford this care and brought Anna home to the farmhouse. The little girl was shut away, with only enough food and water to keep her alive. She stayed in the attic for years until found by the social worker.

When sociologist Kingsley Davis heard of the child, he went to see her immediately. Although Anna was eight, she had the mental development of a two-year-old. She did not talk or even smile. Anna's deprivation and trauma were so severe they left her nearly devoid of human qualities. Davis visited her again after Anna had been in the care of social workers for ten days, and he found considerable improvement. Anna was somewhat

attachment theory: A theory postulating that the way in which infants form attachments early in life will affect relationships throughout later life.

Infants whose emotional needs are frequently ignored by their primary caregiver experience considerable stress, resulting in insecure attachments.

responsive and even smiled. Over the next year she learned to walk and to feed herself, but it took her nearly two years to begin to speak. Her years of isolation had done tremendous damage, but just how much of it was permanent we will never know. Tragically, she died of a blood disorder at the age of ten.

What is attachment and why is it so important? Psychologist Mary Ainsworth and her colleagues studied early interactions between infants and their mothers to answer these questions (Ainsworth, Blehar, Waters, & Wall, 1978). Using experiments to assess infants' reactions when their mothers were temporarily removed from their sight, they found three basic patterns of reactions, reflecting the quality of the infants' attachments with their mothers. About two-thirds of the infants had **secure attachments**, in which they felt safe when their mothers were out of sight. These attachments reflected children's confidence in knowing their mothers would be available when needed, an assurance that came from mothers having been warm, responsive, and consistently available to infants over time. In other relationships, mothers were less predictably warm and responsive to their infants, resulting in stress among infants who, in turn, developed insecure attachments. Some of these infants were characterized as **anxious/ambivalent**; they became nervous when their mothers left and then showed rejection of their mothers when they returned. An equal number of infants were characterized as **avoidant**, showing little attachment to their mothers at all. Ainsworth and her colleagues found that these mothers neglected the physical and emotional needs of their infants, and therefore the infants had no expectation that the mothers would be there for comfort.

Adult Romantic Attachments

Elicia and Damien met while working as counselors at a summer camp sponsored by their church. Elicia liked Damien immediately. They struck up a close friendship, but the rules at the camp prohibited them from developing much intimacy. Nonetheless, they spent a lot of time together, and genuinely enjoyed one another's company. Elicia told Damien that she was in love with him, and asked Damien if

... she panicked for fear that he would not want to see her when the summer ended and they went back to college.

he felt the same way. Damien felt flustered by her question, and told her that he liked her, but that he really did not know her well enough to think about being in love. This answer made Elicia insecure, and she panicked for fear that he would not want to see her when the summer ended and they went back to college. Elicia decided that she would try even harder to make Damien love her.

secure attachment: An attachment type where infants feel safe when their mothers are out of sight.

anxious/ambivalent attachment: An attachment type where infants become nervous when their parent leaves the room and can show rejection when the parent returns.

avoidant attachment: An attachment type where infants show little attachment to their primary parent.

Can our relationships as infants affect our relationships twenty, thirty, or forty years later? Infants and children develop a history of attachment that researchers and psychologists refer to as a "working model" (Cassidy, 2000). This history influences our friendships (Dwyer, Fredstrom, Rubin, Booth-LaForce, Rose-Krasnor, & Burgess, 2010) and adult relationships, for better or worse (Shaver & Mikulincer, 2009; Obegi & Berant, 2009;

Domingue & Mollen, 2009). Adult romantic relationships exhibit three distinct types of bonds, corresponding to the infant attachments described above (Mikulincer & Shaver, 2007; Shaver & Mikulincer, 2009). The three types, with some representative characterizing statements, are:

1. Secure attachments
   —*I find it relatively easy to get close to others.*
   —*I am usually comfortable depending on others and having them depend on me.*
   —*I generally don't worry about being abandoned.*
2. Anxious-ambivalent attachments
   —*Other people don't seem to want to get as close as I do, and it scares them away.*
   —*I often worry that my partner doesn't really love me or won't want to stay with me.*
   —*I tend to get close to a partner very quickly, usually before they do.*
3. Avoidant attachments
   —*I am just not that comfortable being close to someone.*
   —*It's difficult to trust people completely, and I'd rather not become too dependent on them.*
   —*Other people seem to want me to be more intimate and personal than I feel comfortable being, and that makes me nervous.*

Elicia, introduced in the story on page 98, demonstrates an anxious-ambivalent set of attachments. She wants to get close to Damien very quickly, and is worried that he does not love her or will abandon her after their summer camp experience.

As individuals create new relationships and romantic partnerships, they rely in part on earlier relationships to give them clues about what to expect from others. For example, a seven-year longitudinal survey following 112 adolescents as they entered adulthood found that individuals with secure working models experienced low stress in their relationships with parents, peers, and romantic partners and turned to their social network when they needed any help with their relationships. In contrast, those adolescents with more anxious working models experienced high relationship stress, especially with their parents, and used less effective coping mechanisms (Seiffge-Krenke, 2006).

Attachment reveals itself in other ways. A survey based on 53 couples (heterosexual and same-sex couples) who had been together for at least two years examined how the combination of attachment styles related to their conflict and communication patterns. Secure-secure couples reported the most mutually constructive communication (Domingue & Mollen, 2009). Researchers also note that securely attached adults tend to be more comfortable with their sexuality (Feeney & Noller, 2004). They are less likely to have casual sexual partners, one-night stands, or sex outside their primary relationships, and are less likely to use sex to avoid negative emotions or to bolster self-esteem (Cooper, Pioli, Levitt, Talley, Micheas, & Collins, 2006; Feeney & Noller, 2004).

Critique of Attachment Theory

While attachment theory can provide important insights into our marital and family relationships, some researchers question the degree to which we should apply research on infant attachments to explain the complexities of adult romantic attachments. First, for infants attachment depends on receiving protection and comfort from another. But in adult romantic relationships, both partners take the role of caregiver. At times one partner can be stressed and in need of comfort, while at other times the other partner is in need. From a structural functionalist theoretical perspective, introduced in Chapter 1, this mutual dependency provides the stabilizing bond in marriage (Nock, 1998).

Second, among adults, the love relationship is sexual, which further distinguishes it from infant attachment. Third, both positive and negative events happening in later

Can you identify the attachment model you had as a child? If so, can you point to specific instances where it has influenced your adult relationships? Was this attachment a positive or a negative experience?

childhood or adulthood, such as special mentoring, a parental divorce, or a sexual assault, can also shape attachment style (Hollist, 2005). Given these cautions, a review of a decade of theory and research on attachment concludes that studies in infant attachment cannot fully explain the dynamic nature of love in relationships over time (Fraley & Shaver, 2000).

Writings on love show it to be a complex and multi-dimensional concept. We will next examine a broad sweep of history to highlight some of the more powerful images of love that provide the source of our ideals that continue to influence us today.

:: Images of Love in History

Love and marriage—most people assume they go together "like a horse and carriage," as in the words of a popular rhyme. In fact, the assumption that love and marriage go together is a relatively recent phenomenon (Coontz, 2005). The way you view love is quite different from the way your great-grandparents probably viewed love. ▯●▮ **Read** on **myfamilylab.com**

▯●▮ **Read** the **Document**
Egalitarian Daters/Traditionalist Daters on **myfamilylab.com**

Some of the earliest stories of love come from ancient Greek and Roman mythology. The mythological figures of Venus, the Roman goddess of love, and her son Cupid, along with the Greek goddess Aphrodite and her son Eros, are familiar to us. The writings of the Greek philosopher Plato were infused with notions of love. Most classical stories of love were about passion and adoration, but they did not connect these romantic feelings to marriage. Greek men often kept their wives locked in their homes while they entertained prostitutes (Pomeroy, 1975). Marriage was more mundane and used for the purpose of reproduction. In fact, Plato wrote of the highest form of love as something that existed only between men—homosexual relationships were the only way to experience true love and romance (Dover, 1978). Women were not considered suitable partners for men's true love because they were thought to be intellectually inferior.

Throughout history there has been a high value on women's virginity. Chastity belts like this one helped to ensure that unmarried women would remain virgins.

Early Christianity also did not associate love with marriage. People—from nobles to peasants—married for practical or economic reason, or because they could not control their sexual desires (Searle, 1988). Erotic sexuality was considered immoral. Ideally, men and women were to deny all desire in order to obtain holiness (Queen & Habenstein, 1967). Protective devices like chastity belts helped to ensure that unmarried women would remain virgins; if a woman lost her virginity she was thought to be unmarriageable and useless (Williams, 1993). Although marriage was seen as the route for those who could not control their desires of the flesh, even sex in marriage was suspect (Hendrick & Hendrick, 1992). Newly married couples could be barred from church for a period of time, followed by a set penance. Men who had sex with their wives were required to bathe before entering church (Williams, 1993).

In the 12th century, during the Middle Ages, we begin to see some precursors to our own ideas about love—passion, desire, romance, intensity, idolizing the other, and jealousy (Collins, 1986). This was a period of time when society was highly stratified—most people were peasants, but families with successful warriors gradually established a system of hereditary knighthood. These knights, particularly minstrel knights called troubadours, focused on the lord and especially on his lady, offering gifts, writing poetry, and singing romantic songs of adoration for the beautiful, yet unattainable woman (Dickens, 1977). We call this **courtly love** (from which the term "courtship" is derived) because it was primarily engaged in by members of the royal court. As another sign of loyalty the knights would sometimes wear an item that belonged to the lord's wife, such as a scarf, into battle. These early forms of romantic love, as part of the concept of chivalry, placed women in a position of being idolized and adored.

A famous example of a relationship stirred by romantic courtly love is described in the legend of King Arthur, where his Queen Guinevere fell in love with Sir Lancelot. Many "illicit" romances among the ruling class were fueled by the quest for courtly love. In fact, one of the key characteristics of courtly love was that it was unattainable (de Rougemont, 1956). Poets wrote of passionate love for a woman who was unattainable because she was married to the lord. Yet, during the Middle Ages most people were peasants and did not have time for the rituals, rules, secrecy, and intensity of courtly love. Therefore, love was a phenomenon experienced primarily among the ruling class—the members of the courts across Europe (Alchin, n.d.).

By the 18th and early 19th centuries, ideas about romance expanded through the population, with an eye towards the marital relationship. People grew to value similarities between partners, sexual expression, and the emotional side of love. This "romantic love ideal" includes five core beliefs: (1) love at first sight; (2) there is one "true love" for each person; (3) love conquers all; (4) the beloved is (nearly) perfect; and (5) we should marry for love (Lantz, Keyes, & Schultz, 1975).

However, the Victorian period of the 19th century, and the accompanying Industrial Revolution changed much of this romantic love ideal (Cott, 1978). As we discussed in Chapter 1, people relocated from rural to urban areas to take paid work in shops and factories. As men were spending less time in the home, women became the heads of household and spent an increased amount of time caring for the needs of men and children. Along with these changes in gendered expectations, a new view emerged about men and women that historians call *the ideology of separate spheres*. The partnership-orientation between married couples began to break down. Women were seen as childlike, delicate, and less intelligent than men, in need of their protection (Cott, 1978; Haller, 1972). This 19th-century popular view, evident in magazines, political speeches, and religious sermons across the United States, claimed that men were better suited for the harsh, difficult world of the new economy, while women were best suited for the work of caregiving. This separate-spheres idea perpetuated the view that love was defined by what women did in the home.

This change led to the **feminization of love** in the 19th century (Cancian, 1987). Marriage manuals, popular magazines, and other writings noted a lack of intimacy between partners, as their lives were increasingly dissimilar. Women were thought to have little or no sexual desire. The purpose of sexual behavior was to reproduce, and therefore the only acceptable behavior was heterosexual vaginal intercourse, because only that behavior could result in conception. Thus, sexuality was tied to the family, which was seen as a system of marriage, kinship, and inheritance (Foucault, 1978).

By the early 20th century, numerous social and political changes occurred in the United States that encouraged new constructions of love and sexuality. Love and sexuality were not just important intimate bonds between husbands and wives, but were considered *mandatory* to a good relationship (Coontz, 2005; D'Emilio & Freedman, 1998). Marriage manuals during this era reveal a preoccupation with romantic love and sexual compatibility among partners. Sexual expression was no longer just a component of love, but the very basis of love itself. Falling *out* of love, or failing to experience sexual gratification, became defined as marital problems in need of help (Firestone, Firestone, & Catlett, 2008).

This brings us to our modern concept of love. In our culture, love has something to do with just about everything. "All you need is love," or so say the lyrics of the popular song by The Beatles.

courtly love: A poetic style of the Middle Ages when poets or troubadours would write songs of unrequited love and present them at the court of their aristocratic/royal masters.

feminization of love: The process beginning in the 19th century in which love became associated with the private work of women in the home, namely, nurturing and caring for family members.

Think back to your oldest relatives that you have known or have heard about. Do you think they equated marriage with love? Would you guess that they thought about love the same way you did when they were your age?

:: Contemporary Ideas about Love

How do we think about love today? Romantic love seems to get the most attention, but companionate love seems to last the longest.

Romance, Romance, and More Romance

We can easily see vestiges of courtly love in today's **romantic love**. It is a passionate, melodramatic, and exciting experience for all concerned. A look at fairy tales, movies, books, magazines, and television programs reveal countless images of beautiful "ladies" saved by strong "troubadour" knights. Think of the movies *Cinderella*, *Pretty Woman*, *Titanic*, and many of today's reality dating shows or MTV programming. Women bring their beauty to these relationships, get the attention of men through flirting, and win them over by being coy. Yet, this romantic "script" has a down side because it places women on a pedestal, promotes chivalry, and diminishes women to trophy status.

However, for most of us, romance also feels good, and we take it very seriously (Branden, 2008; Tennov, 1999; Sternberg & Sternberg, 2008). While other cultures may see romantic love as rather silly, we consider it the most basic prerequisite for dating, cohabiting, and getting married. In fact, when romantic love no longer exists, many people end their marriages.

When in the throes of romantic love, partners find it difficult to fully concentrate on study or work—they long for their partner. They care so passionately for one another that they may ignore their other friends and responsibilities, living in a two-person world (Sternberg & Sternberg, 2008; Hatfield, 1988). But let's pause and ask ourselves, does romantic love really last? Couples in long-term loving relationships do continue to mention the importance of romance (Acevedo & Aron, 2009; Masuda, 2003). However, long-term couples tend to focus on a deeper attachment that may not include physical passion. In fact, one researcher sought to conceptualize love by asking a group of people to freely list its various features or attributes (Fehr, 1988, 1993). After a long list of features was generated, a second group of people ranked them, and they are shown in Table 4.1. As you will note, romance is not even on the list of the top 12 features of love. This research was originally conducted in the 1980s, but do you think the list would be any different today?

Table 4.1	**Top Twelve Features of Love**
Do you see anything missing? What happened to romance?	

1. Trust
2. Care
3. Honesty
4. Friendship
5. Respect
6. Desire to promote the well-being of the other
7. Loyalty
8. Commitment
9. Accepting the other without wanting to change the other
10. Support
11. Desire to be in the other's company
12. Consideration of and interest in the other

Source: From Fehr, Beverly. 1988. "Prototype Analysis of the Concepts of Love and Commitment." Journal of Personality and Social Psychology 55(4): 557–79.

Companionate Love

Over time, the intensity of romantic love can begin to fade as people get to know one another. What may have seemed cute about someone at the beginning of a relationship can be downright annoying a few years later. Although people who are newly in love think this type of relationship will last forever, long-term love is deep, meaningful, and gratifying to those lucky enough to have it. **Companionate love** is based on strong commitment and trust that the other person will genuinely "be there" for you, no matter what. It grows over time as partners come to know and understand one another. They have learned one another's strengths, weaknesses, and quirks, and appreciate the feeling of connectedness and support they share (Knobloch-Fedders & Knudson, 2009). Long-term loving couples have a shared history, a sense of community, and likely have children together who solidify a strong family bond. Moreover, a long-term relationship does not necessarily have to kill

romantic love: A type of love that is characterized by passion, melodrama, and excitement, and which receives a lot of media attention.

companionate love: A type of love that grows over time, based on strong commitment, friendship, and trust.

We consider romantic love to be the most basic prerequisite for marriage, even though other cultures see our preoccupation with romantic love as silly.

Companionate love can also contain romance, but the emphasis is on companionship. It is based on strong commitment and trust that grows over time.

romantic love. In fact, romantic love, without the early obsession that so often goes with it, can make long-term relationships stronger and more rewarding (Acevedo & Aron, 2009).

If you are (or have been) in a loving relationship, would you guess that your relationship leans toward being more romantic or more companionate? The boxed feature *Getting to Know Yourself* gives you the opportunity to assess your relationship. Keep in mind that romantic and companionate relationships are not actually *dichotomies*; romantic relations certainly contain companionship, while companionate relationships contain romance. The difference is on the emphasis within each.

:: Theoretical Perspectives on Love

If you have ever been in love, do you ever wonder why you fell in love with that *particular* person, given the thousands of people you can expect to meet in your life? Next, we will discuss the different conceptions about love, how and why people fall in love, how love develops, and the different types of love that people experience. The theories fall into three categories: (1) biological perspectives; (2) micro-level perspectives; and (3) macro-level perspectives. Remember, there is no one *right* perspective. Each looks at different issues, and together they give us a broad picture of love.

Biological and Chemical Perspectives on Love

Many researchers are turning to biology to help us understand the role that love plays in our lives.

Sociobiology   **Sociobiology** is the study of how biology shapes our social life. Sociobiologists would argue that attraction and love are evolutionary processes that assist humans in passing on their genetic material and drawing them into long-term relationships to raise a child. When a woman bears a child, it is clear she is the biological mother (except in recent cases of surrogacy, which will be discussed in Chapter 8). There is little certainty, however, who is the biological father, and sociobiologists claim that this has led men and women to approach love and desire in different ways (Buss, 2009; Duntley & Buss, 2008). Historically, men may look to establish more than one romantic attachment because having

sociobiology: An evolutionary theory that all humans have an instinctive impulse to pass on their genetic material.

Getting to Know Yourself

Is Your Loving Relationship More Romantic or Companionate?

If you are in (or have been in) a loving relationship, let's see if it leaned more towards a passionate romance or comfortable companionship. Answer each question about this relationship honestly. Your answers can include:

1 = Yes, almost always; 2 = Sometimes; 3 = No, not really

_____ **1.** I feel included in my partner's life.

_____ **2.** We are very good friends, and I expect that we always will be.

_____ **3.** Our sex life is intense, satisfying, and very important to us.

_____ **4.** We were attracted to each other immediately when we met—love at first sight.

_____ **5.** I feel that my partner sees me as a best friend.

_____ **6.** I like to spend all my free time with my partner.

_____ **7.** Sometimes I get so excited about being in love with my partner that I cannot sleep.

_____ **8.** My partner admires me.

_____ **9.** My partner and I touch each other a lot.

_____ **10.** I like to know where my partner is all the time, so we call, text, or email each other several times a day.

_____ **11.** I get butterflies in my stomach when I think of my partner.

_____ **12.** I'm not really sure when our friendship turned to love.

_____ **13.** We have shared goals and future plans.

_____ **14.** My partner will always "be there" for me when I have difficult times.

_____ **15.** My partner and I spend a lot of time gazing into one another's eyes.

There is naturally some overlap between romantic and companionate relationships. However, in general, questions 3, 4, 6, 7, 9, 10, 11, and 15 lean towards the romantic, and questions 1, 2, 5, 8, 12, 13, and 14 lean towards the companionate. Were you more likely to score 1s or 2s on one set of traits versus the other?

What Do You Think?

1. Do you think that you and your partner would answer these questions in the same way? How might gendered expectations, which you learned about in Chapter 2, influence the way people answer this quiz?

2. Do you think these answers might vary across social classes, or among persons of different races or ethnicities? Why or why not?

---

multiple partners increases the odds of becoming a parent. Yet because women know their biological offspring, they are more selective about entering a relationship. Sociobiologists point to this as an evolutionary process that over the centuries has produced the behavioral patterns of dating and sexual relationships we continue to observe today (Thornhill & Gangestad, 2008).

Sociobiology also suggests that biology holds a clue to the *type* of people to whom men and women are attracted. Women tend to seek out older, larger men, who have a higher status than themselves so that the men can support and protect them when they are physically restricted through pregnancy, childbirth, and the child-rearing years. Men's attraction, on the other hand, tends toward younger women who are the most fertile. Interestingly, these age and status patterns persist today. Buss's research (1989) from more than 10,000 people spanning 33 countries found that men across cultures were more likely to value physical attractiveness and youthfulness in their potential mates, while good financial prospects appealed to women.

biochemical perspective of love:
Theories that suggest humans are attracted to certain types of people, at which point the brain releases natural chemicals that give us a rush we experience as sexual attraction.

Biochemical Approaches to Love A related approach that looks at biological and chemical factors to explain love is called a **biochemical perspective**. When we establish eye contact with, touch, or smell the scent of a person with features we see as desirable, our brain releases a flood of chemicals to the nerves and bloodstream that are natural amphetamines such as dopamine, norepinephrine, and phenylethylamine (PEA), which give us the rush we know as sexual attraction. These chemicals result in heavy breathing, flushed skin, dilated pupils, sweating, and stomach "butterflies," along with feelings of elation and euphoria. Biologists also point to another set of chemicals that help to maintain relationships after the initial excitement lessens. A new group of endorphins, chemically similar to morphine, help calm us and reduce anxiety.

This type of research is still in its infancy, but many interesting research projects point to the importance of biochemical influences on love (Fisher, 2010; Fisher & Thomson, 2007; Fisher, Egerton, Gershuny, & Robinson, 2006). For example, using a functional magnetic resonance imaging machine (MRI) on her subjects, Fisher found that the brain creates dramatic surges of norepinephrine, dopamine, and serotonin that fuel such feelings as passion, obsession, joy, and jealousy (Fisher, 2004). Others have noted that loss of a loved one, the feeling of having a "broken heart," is associated with psychological problems and stress that can bring on chest pain and even a heart attack (Wittstein, Thiemann, Lima, Baughman, Schulman, Gerstenblith, Wu, Rade, Bivalacqua, & Champion, 2005).

Before concluding that love is *all* a product of biochemical forces, however, let's look at other factors that help to explain the meaning and experience of love.

Micro-Level Perspectives on Love

A micro-level perspective focuses on the interpersonal nature of love. Several theorists can help us understand the different styles of love, its components, and the stages in the development of love.

Sternberg's Triangular Theory of Love   A second approach explores the many multi-dimensional components of love. Robert **Sternberg's triangular theory of love** (1986, 1988) suggests that love has three components: *passion, intimacy,* and *commitment,* which he views as a triangle, as shown in Figure 4.1 (page 106). *Passion* encompasses feelings of physical attraction, romance, and sexual arousal. Of the three components, passion is the most intense, but it peaks rather quickly, and can give way to a companionate love that is characterized by a calm, stable, and comfortable sense of attachment. *Intimacy* encompasses feelings of closeness and bonding, and includes such things as self-disclosure, respect, trust, and warmth. *Commitment* represents both the short-term decision to love one another, and the longer-term commitment to continue that love. It includes such feelings as loyalty, faithfulness, dedication, and devotion.

Sternberg argues that individuals can place different emphases on these three elements of love throughout their lives, and love is a process that undergoes change. When couples are complementary in these dimensions—when they want the same degrees of intimacy, passion, and commitment at the same time—relationships are stable and the couple is considered perfectly matched. Couples who vary just a little on these three dimensions may still be considered a close match. However, as individuals become more different from one another, their relationship becomes less stable.

Sternberg also suggests that various combinations of intimacy, passion, and commitment breed different kinds of love, as shown in Figure 4.2 (page 106):

- *Nonlove:* Many relationships really have no love in them. There is little or no intimacy, passion, or commitment.
- *Empty Love:* Sometimes people remain together solely because of a commitment—perhaps they stay together "for the sake of the children" or because they are also business partners and ending the relationship would be too complicated. These relationships are void of passion and intimacy.
- *Liking:* These relationships are intimate, such as good friendships, but typically there is no passion or commitment.

Sternberg's triangular theory of love: A theory that sees love as having three elements: intimacy, passion, and commitment.

Figure 4.3   Reiss's Wheel Theory of Love

Ira Reiss described love as an ongoing process that unfolds in four stages. Similar to a rolling wheel, the stages may be experienced many times, going frontward and backward.

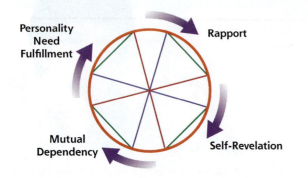

Naturally, the types of love we experience will develop and change over a lifetime. Singles are more likely to hold Manic and Ludic love attitudes than married adults, whose relationships are more likely to be represented by Storge. But few, if any, relationships are characterized in terms of only one type of love. The six types might be useful to help us understand how couples come together, and which couples may be the most, and the least, likely to have long-term relationships. Some researchers feel the styles match up with the categories of attachment we discussed earlier. For example, Agape and Storge are more secure types of love, while Mania is more anxious/ambivalent, and Ludus is closest to avoidant (Hendrick & Hendrick, 1992).

Reiss's Wheel Theory of Love   Ira Reiss's work examines the various stages in which love develops, and his contribution is called **Reiss's wheel theory of love** (1960). He describes four stages of love: building rapport, self-revelation, mutual dependency, and personality need fulfillment, as shown in Figure 4.3:

- In the beginning, people meet and establish *rapport* with one another. We are most likely to meet those who live near us, share our interests, and engage in the same activities that we like. As a result, we are also likely to share cultural, social, political, or religious values.
- After rapport is established, couples may move to a second stage of *self-revelation*. We become closer, more at ease, and begin to disclose more about ourselves. Over time our sharing becomes more personal, and we talk about our intimate thoughts, fears, and insecurities.
- As our relationship becomes more intimate, we may move to a third stage called *mutual dependence*. In this stage we open ourselves up even more, and begin to depend on our partner, as they do on us.
- As couples become dependent upon each other, they may move to the final stage of *personality need fulfillment*. In this stage the couple's lives become intertwined; they may make decisions together and they support one another's ambitions and goals.

Using an analogy to spokes on a wheel, these four stages may keep turning to develop into a deep and lasting relationship. The wheel can turn quickly or slowly, and it may move forward or backward or even stop at any stage. As we learn more about our partners, we may discover that we are incompatible in some way and so we end the relationship (Perillous & Buss, 2008) or step back a stage in its development.

Lee, Sternberg, and Reiss examine the micro-level factors associated with love—different types, how love develops, and how we experience love. Love is a personal emotion, but to fully understand how it develops and is experienced, we must continue our review of the research and examine our social environment.

Macro-Level Perspectives on Love

Love is more than just a personal emotion; it is also rooted in macro-level factors related to culture and social structure. For example, race, class, and sex all help to influence our ideas about and experiences with love. Love also has important implications for how societies are structured, as shown in the *Diversity in Families* feature box. In Iraq, among many other countries, a common pattern is for cousins to marry one another so that the family lineage can be kept intact. But for this to work, Iraqis must find a way to control or prevent their kin from falling in love with a stranger. How do they do this?

Reiss's wheel theory of love:
A developmental theory that shows relationships moving from the establishment of rapport, to self-revelation, mutual dependence, and finally, need fulfillment.

Diversity in Families

"It Is Safer to Marry a Cousin Than a Stranger"

Iqbal Muhammad does not recall her first glimpse of her future husband because they were both newborns at the time, but she remembers precisely when she knew he was the one. It was the afternoon her uncle walked over from his house next door and proposed that she marry his son Muhammad. "I was a little surprised, but I knew right away it was a wise choice," she said, recalling that afternoon nine years ago, when she and Muhammad were both 22. "It is safer to marry a cousin than a stranger."

Her reaction was typical in a country where nearly half of marriages are between first or second cousins, a statistic that is one of the most important and least understood differences between Iraq and the United States. The extraordinarily strong family bonds complicate virtually everything Americans have tried to do in Iraq, from finding Saddam Hussein to changing women's status to creating a liberal democracy.

"Americans just don't understand what a different world Iraq is because of these highly unusual cousin marriages," said Robin Fox of Rutgers University, the author of *Kinship and Marriage*, a widely used anthropology textbook. "Liberal democracy is based on the Western idea of autonomous individuals committed to a public good, but that's not how members of these tight and bounded kin groups see the world. Their world is divided into two groups: kin and strangers."

Iraqis frequently describe nepotism not as a civic problem but as a moral duty. The notion that Iraq's next leader would put public service ahead of family obligations drew a smile from Iqbal's uncle and father-in-law, Sheik Yousif Sayel, the patriarch in charge of the clan's farm on the Tigris River south of Baghdad. "In this country, whoever is in power will bring his relatives in from the village and give them important positions," Yousif said, sitting in the garden surrounded by some of his 21 children and 83 grandchildren. "That is what Saddam did...."

Saddam Hussein married a first cousin who grew up in the same house as he did, and he ordered most of his children to marry their cousins. Yousif said he never forced any of his children to marry anyone, but more than half of them chose to wed cousins. The patriarch was often the one who first suggested the match, as he did with his son Muhammad nine years ago. "My father said that I was old enough to get married, and I agreed," Muhammad recalled. "He and my mother recommended Iqbal. I respected their wishes. It was my desire, too. We knew each other. It was much simpler to marry within the family."

A month later, after the wedding, Iqbal moved next door to the home of Yousif. Moving in with the in-laws might be

Nearly half of marriages in Iraq are between first or second cousins. Iraqis put family first—nepotism is a moral duty. As Iqbal said, "It is safer to marry a cousin than a stranger."

an American bride's nightmare, but Iqbal said her toughest adjustment occurred five years later, when Yousif decided that she and Muhammad were ready to live by themselves in a new home he provided just behind his own. "I felt a little lonely at first when we moved into the house by ourselves," Iqbal said. Muhammad said he too felt lonely in the new house, and he expressed pity for American parents and children living thousands of miles from each other. "Families are supposed to be together," he said. "It's cruel to keep children and parents apart."

Yousif, who is 82, said he could not imagine how the elderly in the United States cope in their homes alone. "I could not bear to go a week without seeing my children," he said. Some of his daughters have married outsiders and moved into other patriarchal clans, but the rest of the children are never far away.

Muhammad and three other sons live on the farm with him, helping to supervise the harvesting of barley, wheat, and oranges and the dates from the palm trees on their land. The other six sons have moved 15 miles away to Baghdad, but they come back often for meals and in hard times. During the war in the spring, almost the whole clan took

(continued)

Diversity in Families (continued)

refuge at the farm, returning to the only institution they had been able to trust through the worst of Saddam's rule.

Cousin marriage was once the norm throughout the world, but it became taboo in Europe after a long campaign by the Roman Catholic Church. Theologians such as St. Augustine and St. Thomas argued that the practice promoted family loyalties at the expense of universal love and social harmony. Eliminating it was seen as a way to reduce clan warfare and promote loyalty to larger social institutions such as the church.

The practice became rare in the West, especially after evidence emerged of genetic risks to offspring, but it has persisted in some places, notably the Middle East, which is exceptional because of both the high prevalence and the restrictive form it takes. In other societies, a woman typically weds a cousin outside her social group, like a maternal cousin living in a clan led by a different patriarch. But in Iraq the ideal is for the woman to

remain within the clan by marrying the son of her father's brother, as Iqbal did.

Source: Tierney, John. 2003. "Iraqi Marriage Bedevils Americans." New York Times News Service. The Oregonian, 28 September, pp. A–2.

What Do You Think?

1. Why does Iraqi culture prefer that the woman remain in the clan by marrying the son of her father's brother, rather than marrying a cousin in a different clan? In other words, is the purpose of cousin marriage simply to ensure that children find a suitable spouse, or is there more involved than that?

2. How do American ideals of romance and love fit in with the Iraqi scheme? What would they think of our ideals?

Controlling the Development of Love   Many societies, both in the past and today, feel that love can be dangerous and must be monitored or controlled by parents or by society at large (Goode, 1959). Love, for example, has the ability to break up families, destroy communities, topple governments, and even cause wars. Sociologist William Goode claims that all societies, even our own in modern times, **control the development of love** to some degree through at least one of the following mechanisms:

- *Child marriage:* One way to control love is to have a child married or betrothed before feelings of love for another person can even develop. Marriage might even occur prior to puberty.

- *Kinship rules:* Another way to control love is to clearly define and restrict the set of eligible people that young people can and cannot marry, such as a cousin. As shown in the *Diversity in Families* box, this mechanism is widely practiced in Iraq, and has important political and economic consequences.

- *Isolation of young people:* A third way to control love is by segregating young people from one another. Boys and girls may go to different schools. Men and women may attend different religious services. Males and females are kept strictly segregated and isolated to eliminate opportunities for interaction.

- *Close supervision:* Short of isolation, some cultures watch over children and young adults very carefully, especially their girls and women. In many cultures a high value is placed on female virginity. Therefore, girls and women are highly supervised whenever they are in public to keep them men at a safe distance.

- *Formally free:* This mechanism of controlling love is found in our society today. Young people are considered free to choose their own mates based on love and attraction; however, their social environments can still be manipulated by their parents, such as sending children to private schools or living in a certain neighborhood to channel the influence of peers.

controlling the development of love: A macro-level perspective on love suggesting that all societies control or channel love.

A Modern-day Example: India   While people in the United States think of romantic love as a basis for partnering and marriage, in other countries people find their mates for different reasons: bringing families together, economic considerations, or other motivations (Medora, 2003; Leeder, 2004). Love may develop after the marriage (or it may not), as shown in the opening vignette with Rati and Subas, both from Nepal. Another good example is found in modern-day India.

In India, parents play an important part in who their children marry (Griffith, 2006). Many marriages are arranged by parents, and the children may know little or nothing about their future mate. These marriages have nothing to do with love in the way we think of love. In some Indian families, children have greater choice, but parental approval is mandatory.

Most Indians would find our belief in dating and romance as odd as we might find their idea of arranged marriage. They would suggest that we are too focused on passionate love, and on fun and games, to the detriment of building a solid and lasting relationship. "I want an arranged marriage," said a 22-year-old college student who considers himself a connoisseur of Western culture including National Basketball Association games and Arnold Schwarzenegger films. He continues, "but I fear that Fashion Television, MTV, and [music] Channel V are distorting the desires of the younger generation" (Derne, 2003). A recent survey of 15–34-year-olds living in Delhi, Mumbai, Kanpur, and Lucknow found that 65 percent said that they would obey their elders "even if it hurts." Over two-thirds of urban college students preferred to have their parents arrange their marriage. "Any girl I could find for myself would not be as good as the one my parents will find," says a 19-year-old college student (Derne, 2003).

Love is not a foreign concept to Indians. They simply have a different conception of it, influenced heavily by Hinduism, the caste system, and other norms in Indian culture. They hold that much of a person's life is predetermined by his or her karma. Marriage is out of the hands of the couple, and few would attempt to change fate. Some educated professionals prefer to choose their own mates, but for the most part, Indians anticipate that their parents will select their marriage partner for them.

Commonly, before two people from India can consider marriage, both sets of parents consult an astrologer to examine their zodiac signs to determine the couple's compatibility. The astrologer helps to determine whether the young man and woman are a proper match. If they are deemed to be a good match, then families can begin to discuss issues surrounding the dowry.

Despite their lower status in India's patriarchal society, women are important because of their fertility; large families and especially a large number of sons are still considered highly desirable by most Indians. Therefore, families spend considerable time negotiating a **dowry**, the financial gift given to a woman's prospective in-laws by her parents. The woman is generally not involved in the negotiations. Parents will spend considerable amounts on the dowry, depending on their caste or class standing, and may be left impoverished or in substantial debt as a result.

Child marriage was outlawed in 1978 in India; however, it still is a widespread practice in many parts of the country. In one province, Rajasthan, a 1996 survey of 5,000 women

Arranged marriages are common in India and in many other parts of the world, including among those who are well educated and wealthy. Adult children believe that something as important as selecting a spouse is too important to be left up to chance.

dowry: A financial gift given to a woman's prospective in-laws by her parents.

Tying It All Together

Factors That Shape Attraction and the Development of Love

There are many perspectives on the development and experience of love. These speak to biological and biochemical issues, micro-level dimensions such as relationship stages or choices, and macro-level factors such as the ways that love is controlled and channeled for mate selection.

Biological Theories	Basic Assumptions or Arguments
Sociobiology	• All humans have the instinct to pass on their genes.
Biochemical Perspective	• Men prefer younger and more physically attractive women. • Women prefer men who are more financially secure. • Attraction emits dopamine, norepinephrine, and phenylethylamine (PEA), which give us the rush we know as sexual attraction. • Another set of chemicals helps to maintain relationships by calming us and reducing anxiety.
Micro-level Theories	
Sternberg's Triangle Theory of Love	• Love has three primary dimensions: intimacy, passion, and commitment. • The weight of each dimension can vary and depends on the needs of the couple and the stage of their relationship.
Lee's Styles of Love	• There are six distinct styles of love: Eros, Storge, Ludus, Pragma, Agape, and Mania. • Relationships can be characterized by more than one style of love.
Reiss's Wheel Theory of Love	• Relationships develop in stages of rapport, self-revelation, mutual dependence, and need fulfillment. • Couples can move both forward and backward through the stages.
Macro-level Theories	
Social Structure and Control of Love	• Marriage has broad and important social, economic, and political implications, and children should not make their own decisions about who they marry. • Love is channeled in a number of ways, from "child marriages" to being "formally free."

*W*hat do you think might be some of the benefits of an arranged marriage? Answer the question from a parent's perspective and then from a child's perspective. Are the benefits different from these two perspectives? Explain.

revealed that over half of them were married prior to their eighteenth birthday. Some girls were married off as early as age four or five (Burns, 1998). Child marriages free a family from the obligations of supporting a girl, who is viewed as destined to leave the family anyway. In the eyes of the parents, it also decreases her likelihood of engaging in premarital sex or being exploited sexually, which would reduce her status.

Throughout this text thus far we have discussed the importance of how macro-level social forces shape our personal experiences. In this chapter, we have seen that love—what it means, its importance, and how it is achieved—varies considerably over time and place. The feature box *Tying It All Together: Factors That Shape Attraction and the Development of Love* summarizes the contributions of different perspectives on love.

:: How We Experience Love

Ryan and Kim were living in the dorms when they met in the dining hall one evening. The room was crowded with students trying to get a quick bite before studying or going to their social engagements for the evening. There was an empty seat next to Ryan, so Kim said rather matter-of-factly, "Okay if I join you?" They struck up a conversation, and quickly discovered they shared many interests, including their love of basketball, playing the violin, and travel. They laughed together as they shared some of their craziest travel stories. The next evening Ryan looked for Kim in the crowd of students in the dining hall, hoping to find a pal to go together to the basketball game.

As the semester went on, they found themselves spending more time together, and their conversations became more disclosing and personal . . . .

They spotted each other, and so began their friendship sharing conversation and laughs during meals, sporting events, and study breaks. As the semester went on, they found themselves spending more time together, and their conversations became more disclosing and personal; there was discussion of an alcoholic father, an assault during high school, their most embarrassing moments. Their relationship grew intense, passionate, sexual, and romantic. Ryan sent flowers when Kim received an "A" on a History exam. Kim would invite Ryan to stay the night when roommates were out of town. After many months, both expressed that they were in love.

Here is a simple story about a young couple falling in love while they are away at college. But the story takes on more complexity when we add contextual material to the story. What if Ryan and Kim are both males? What if they are "returning students" both 40 years old? What if they are of different racial or ethnic groups? What if Ryan's romantic feelings are not reciprocated? Let's look at a number of these aspects associated with experiencing love.

Sex, Gender, and Love

If we are to believe popular culture, women are more interested in love than are men. However, surveys show that men, in fact, are more likely than women to be in or looking for committed relationships (Madden & Lenhart, 2006; Madden & Rainie, 2006), and they report falling in love sooner and with more people than do women (Covel, 2003). Seventy-seven percent of men and 68 percent of women reported they are in love with someone right now (Saad, 2004). Twice as many men (24 percent) as women (11 percent) say they have been in love five or more times since turning 18.

We also note that men are more preoccupied with love. Table 4.3 reveals that single men are two and a half times more likely than single women to report they are looking for a partner.

If men actually fall in love more quickly than do women and are more focused on love, why does cultural rhetoric claim the opposite is true—that women are the ones obsessed with love? There may be several reasons for this myth. In reviewing the

Table 4.3	Single Men, Single Women, and Their Relationship Interests		
Men appear to be more interested in love and a committed relationship than do women.			
	All Singles	**Men**	**Women**
In a Committed Relationship	46%	30%	23%
Not in a Committed Relationship and Not Looking for a Partner	55%	42%	65%
Not in a Committed Relationship and Looking for a Partner	18%	23%	9%
Don't Know or Refused to Answer	3%	5%	3%

Source: From Madden, Mary and Lee Rainie. 2006. Not Looking for Love: The State of Romance in America. Pew Internet & American Life Project.

different styles of love, one study found that, in general, men were more *Ludic* (carefree), whereas women tend to lean towards *Storge* (comfortable and compatible) and *Pragma* (rational) (Hendrick & Hendrick, 1992). Not surprisingly then, some women are concerned that men are "afraid of commitment," or "commitment phobic" (Gerson, 2009; Whitehead & Popenoe, 2002).

Another reason we assume that women are more loving has to do with the different ways that men and women express love and our belief that women's expressions of this emotion are somehow innately better. This is referred to as the feminization of love (Cancian, 1987). The problem is not that men don't express love, but they often do not get credit for it because women ignore or minimize masculine-type expressions. Thus, the man who is a good provider, who takes his daughter to soccer, and who folds the laundry may be showing as much love as the woman who says "I love you" regularly. He may think that "actions speak louder than words," but his female partner is waiting for the words, and miscommunication can result.

Men and women fall in love for many of the same reasons—similar values, emotional maturity, dependability—but men are more likely than women to fall in love for reasons related to physical attractiveness (Eastwick & Finkel, 2008). Women are more cautious about love, taking longer and using a wider variety of factors in deciding whether they are in love. These factors include physical attractiveness and similarity in values and other traits but also ambition, industriousness, and financial prospects.

Reasons for falling in love appear to be associated with the ways that sex and gender are defined in our society. For most of history women have been financially dependent on men in marriage; therefore, it made good sense to closely examine a man's economic prospects before choosing a mate. But as the context changes, so do the reasons for choosing a mate. Since the 1970s, more married women are working outside the home and their financial dependence on men in marriage has declined (U.S. Census Bureau, January 14, 2010). Therefore, with less *need* for a husband as a provider, women focus on other qualities for their intimate relationships.

Same-Sex Love

We love many people of the same sex: our parents, other relatives, friends, and if you are gay or lesbian, your partner. As we discussed in Chapter 3, friendships are a valuable part of our lives. For most of history, friendships were almost exclusively between two men or two women (Caine, 2010; Schweitzer, 2006). Cross-sex friendships were thought to be threatening. Moreover, husbands and wives may have been partners, but they tended to work in different "spheres" and their same-sex friendships reflected the different worlds they inhabited. One interesting study of friendships between women from 1760 to 1880 focused on letters written between friends (Smith-Rosenberg, 1975). These letters may only reveal the lives of literate, middle-class women, but they show that women developed strong bonds with other women. The letters express love and tenderness and frequently describe a physical and emotional longing for the other. Some of these may have been "romantic friendships" as they were referred to then. Same-sex friendships were not seen as threatening, and terms such as "homosexual" were not really part of the vocabulary (Spenser, 1995).

✳ Explore on **myfamilylab.com**

✳ Explore the **Concept**
Social Explorer Map: Settlement Patterns of Unmarried Same-Sex Partners on **myfamilylab.com**

In your experience with love, does it seem that men and women want the same thing from love? Do they express love differently? What macro-level factors contribute to the way we express love?

Today, men and women can openly admit that their same-sex friends are not just friends but lovers or partners. The focus of this chapter how we define love, the importance of attachment, theoretical perspectives, and the experiences of love—are generally the same for same-sex couples as they are for heterosexual couples. Most gay, lesbian, and straight people want to be emotionally close to someone, share romance and companionship, and have a deep trusting relationship (Berzon, 2004; Clarke, 2010). Perhaps, the primary difference has to do with the prejudice and discrimination gays and lesbians experience on a regular basis. In many places around the country, same-sex couples are not free to show affection in public or acknowledge their love out of fear of being ostracized, attacked, or even killed (Gold & Drucker, 2008; Shepard, 2009). These issues will be explored further in Chapter 5.

Unrequited Love

Have you ever felt that you loved a person, but he or she did not love you? Or that someone loved you, but you did not feel the same way? This is referred to as **unrequited love**—one person's feelings are not reciprocated by the other (Merriam-Webster Online, 2010; Smit, 2005). Popular songs are full of examples of unrequited love, especially in country and western music. Unrequited love can occur any time during the process of a relationship. Sometimes it occurs in the beginning—one person is simply not interested in the other, and does not find him or her particularly attractive or interesting. Unrequited love can also occur as a relationship is being formed. Perhaps the motivations for the relationship are different—one is looking for a hook-up, while the other is looking for a lasting relationship. And finally, unrequited love can also occur in an established relationship. Couples break up or divorce, sometimes after many years of being together. Unrequited love can be a gut-wrenching, sad, and painful experience. Yet, the difficult fact is that we cannot control other people's feelings (Herbenick, 2009).

Unrequited love is when the feelings of love of one person are not reciprocated. In this case, her messages are ignored.

:: The Downside to Relationships and Love

Falling in love is a powerful emotion. For the most part, it feels wonderful, but there are a few "downsides" to relationships and love. And one of these is the emotion of jealousy.

Jealousy

"**W**e dated for three years—I devoted three years of my life to her trying to make her happy. I thought she was happy, I thought we were a good team. But then, out of the blue, she tells me that she wants to go out with a guy she works with.

. . . out of the blue, she tells me that she wants to go out with a guy she works with.

Who in the hell is this guy? He's younger than she is, and doesn't even earn that much money. Why on earth would she want to go out with him? She must be crazy. Really crazy. I'm so angry...."

This man is experiencing an emotion we have probably all felt at one time or another when threatened by the loss of an important relationship—that of jealousy (Shackleford, Voracek, Schmitt, Buss, Weekes-Shackleford, & Michalski, 2004; Fisher, 2009). He feels threatened, angry, sad, and resentful that a rival is competing for his girlfriend. He tries to make himself feel better by criticizing his girlfriend and his rival. **Watch** on **myfamilylab.com**

Jealousy can be rational, based on some real rival threat as in the case above, or it can be irrational, based on a perceived threat that is not real (Buunk, Massar, & Dijkstra, 2007). People can feel jealous for many reasons; men are more likely to focus on physical aspects of the

unrequited love: When one person's feelings are not reciprocated by the other person in the relationship.

Watch the **Video** *Internet Beating* on **myfamilylab.com**

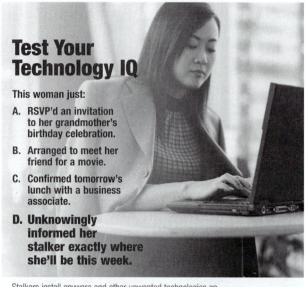

Test Your Technology IQ

This woman just:

A. RSVP'd an invitation to her grandmother's birthday celebration.

B. Arranged to meet her friend for a movie.

C. Confirmed tomorrow's lunch with a business associate.

D. Unknowingly informed her stalker exactly where she'll be this week.

Stalkers install spyware and other unwanted technologies on computers to capture information that can put victims at risk.

Stalking is a crime. If you or someone you know is a victim of stalking, **we can help.**

Stalking resource center www.ncvc.org/src

THE NATIONAL CENTER FOR **Victims of Crime** 1-800-FYI-CALL

This document was developed under grant number 2004-WT-AX-K050 from the Office on Violence Against Women (OVW) of the U.S. Department of Justice. The opinions and views expressed in this document are those of the author(s) and do not necessarily represent the official position or policies of the Office on Violence Against Women of the U.S. Department of Justice.

Cyberstalking or electronic monitoring is a growing form of stalking and can take a heavy personal toll on its victims.

threat, feeling jealous that their partner will be sexual with someone else, for example, while women more often focus on the emotional aspects, feeling jealous that their partner loves someone else (Groothof, Dijkstra, & Barelds, 2010; Rutley, 2001). Men and women show their jealousy in different ways, consistent with the way they have been socialized, as we saw in Chapter 3. Men are more likely to deny their jealous feelings, while women are more likely to acknowledge them.

Jealousy, especially if irrational, can come about from our own insecurities about our relationships and ourselves. It can be responsible for some very bad behavior, including physical or emotional abuse, as we will see in Chapter 11. How then can you deal constructively with jealousy?

- Make some agreements with your partner that you can both feel comfortable with about how you will behave.
- Try not to be too hard on yourself for feeling jealous. Jealousy can be a natural emotion; the trick is to be in control of your feelings rather than the other way around.
- Identify and isolate the specific reason for your jealousy. Is it something your partner is actually doing, or is it something you feel he or she *might* do? Once you know why you are jealous, you will have a better idea how to deal with it.
- Tell your partner your feelings in a calm, nonthreatening, and constructive manner. Then, listen to what he or she has to say in return. Communication is a two-way process. If you calmly discuss your feelings, you may find your partner can empathize and offer some measure of help.
- Depending on the cause of your jealousy, if you cannot negotiate a solution to the problem, or if you or your partner continually create situations that aggravate jealousy, you may need to find a counselor to help you resolve the problem (Sorgen, 2008).

Controlling Behavior

There are other types of controlling behavior besides jealousy. **Stalking** is conduct directed at a specific person that would cause a reasonable person to be fearful. The U.S. Department of Justice identifies seven types of stalking behaviors: (1) making unwanted telephone calls; (2) sending unsolicited or unwanted letters or emails; (3) following or spying on the victim; (4) showing up at places without a legitimate reason; (5) waiting at places for the victim; (6) leaving unwanted items, presents, or flowers; and (7) posting information or spreading rumors about the victim on the Internet, in a public place, or by word of mouth (Baum, Catalano, Rand, & Rose, 2009). By themselves these acts may not be criminal, but if done collectively or repeatedly, they may cause fear in the victim.

The federal government and all 50 states have laws criminalizing stalking, but it occurs frequently nonetheless—about 3.4 million adults are stalked each year, and the type of stalking that occurs is reported in Table 4.4. As you can see, the percentages add up to more than

Table 4.4	**Nature of Stalking Behaviors Experienced by Victims (3,424,100)**	
With over 3,000,000 known incidents of stalking, many victims report being stalked in multiple ways.		**Percent of Victims**
Unwanted phone calls and messages		66%
Unwanted letters and email		31%
Spreading rumors		36%
Following or spying		34%
Showing up at places		31%
Waiting for victim		29%
Leaving unwanted presents		12%

Note: Responses sum to more than 100% because multiple responses were permitted.

Source: Baum, Katrina, Shannan Catalano, Michael Rand, and Kristina Rose. 2009 January. Stalking Victimization in the United States. Bureau of Justice Statistics No. NCJ 224527. Washington, DC: U.S. Department of Justice.

100 percent because many cases of stalking involve multiple forms (Baum, Catalano, Rand, & Rose, 2009). About three-quarters of victims are women, and about two-thirds of stalkers are men, but there still are plenty of cases in which women are stalking men or other women, and men are stalking other men. Victims are most often ex-girlfriends/boyfriends or ex-spouses, but they can also be friends, roommates, neighbors, work colleagues, relatives, or even strangers.

Another relatively new, but very dangerous type of stalking is referred to as **cyberstalking** (or **electronic monitoring**), which involves stalking contact using electronic technology (Stalking Resource Center, June 2009). As shown in Table 4.5, 26 percent of stalking victims reported that some form of cyberstalking or electronic monitoring was used on them. Most commonly this took the form of unwanted email—82 percent of those who reported being victims of this form of cyberstalking reported unwanted emails, but they were also victims of instant messaging, blogs or bulletin boards, Internet sites about them, and chat room conversations. Those who had been stalked by electronic monitoring were most likely victims of video or digital cameras, listening devices/bugs, computer spyware, or even GPS tracking devices (Baum, Catalano, Rand, & Rose, 2009).

Stalking takes a heavy personal toll on its victims (Baum, Catalano, Rand, & Rose, 2009; Blaauw, Winkel, Arensman, Sheridan, & Freeve, 2002; Stalking Resource Center, June 2009). They fear not knowing what will happen next and worry that the stalking will never stop. Many suffer anxiety, insomnia, and severe depression. One in eight victims loses time from work because of the stalking, and one in seven feels forced to move for their safety.

Table 4.5	Involvement of Cyberstalking or Electronic Monitoring in Stalking
	Cyberstalking and electronic monitoring are on the rise. Sending unwanted emails are a form of stalking.

	Percent of Victims
Any type of cyberstalking or electronic monitoring	26%
Cyberstalking	22%
Percent of cyberstalking involving	
Email	83%
Instant messenger	35%
Blogs or bulletin boards	12%
Internet sites about victim	9%
Chat rooms	4%
Electronic monitoring	8%
Percent of electronic monitoring involving	
Computer spyware	34%
Video/digital cameras	46%
Listening devices/bugs	42%
GPS	11%

Note: Responses sum to more than 100% because multiple responses were permitted.
Source: From Baum, Katrina, Shannan Catalano, Michael Rand, and Kristina Rose. 2009 January. Stalking Victimization in the United States. Bureau of Justice Statistics No. NCJ 224527. Washington, DC: U.S. Department of Justice.

Breaking Up Is Hard to Do

A third possible downside to love is breaking up. When we are in love we think it will last forever. However, nothing about love is guaranteed, and most dating relationships break up within a few years (Regan, 2003). Some break up and renew again (and possibly break up again) (Dailey, Rossetto, Pfiester, & Surra, 2009).

Just like meeting a partner, breaking up with a partner is influenced by a host of macro-level and micro-level factors. On the micro-level, partners may stop communicating, discover different values or interests, or clash over differences in personalities. On the macro-level, socioeconomic conditions that affect employment or income may introduce friction into the relationship.

Given the significance that romantic partners have on each other's lives, the loss of a relationship is among the most distressing events we can experience as adults (Lewandowski, Aron, Bassis, & Kunak, 2006; Sbarra, 2006). Partners develop shared friends, activities, goals, and memories. They even have overlapping self-concepts, and are more likely to spontaneously use first-person-plural pronouns, such as "we," "our," and "us." After a breakup this self-concept can become unclear, generating considerable emotional distress (Slotter, Gardner, & Finkel, 2010).

stalking: Conduct directed at a specific person that would cause a reasonable person to be fearful.

cyberstalking (or electronic monitoring): Stalking contact using electronic technology.

Research has found that some couples break off relationships for the same reasons they were attracted to each other in the first place (Felmlee, 2001). Based on a sample of 125 undergraduates, some individuals were attracted to people who were "nice" or "considerate," but later these nice people were criticized as being unwilling to open up and be honest. Other undergraduates were attracted to people with "strong" personalities, only to feel later that these people were "stubborn." Many other changes in the evaluation of people's personalities occurred as well: what started out as "funny" later was seen as "flaky," "exciting" became "scary," and what was considered "successful" became "workaholic" (Felmlee, 2001).

Other research goes back to the pioneering work of Waller's principle of least interest, introduced in Chapter 3, and examines the consequences of unequal emotional involvement in romantic relationships. One study of 101 dating couples (college students) followed the relationships for over three years to determine the frequency and effects of unequal involvement (Sprecher, Christopher, & Cate, 2006). The researchers found that in 75 percent of the couples, at least one partner said that one partner was more emotionally involved in the relationship than the other partner. In 56 percent of the couples, both partners acknowledged that one person in the relationship was more involved than the other. Their research also found that the person who was least involved had more control over the relationship and whether or not it continued. The person who "loved the least" was also less satisfied in the relationship. Finally, relationships with unequal emotional involvement were more likely to break up over the course of the three-year study than were relationships based on more equal attachment (Sprecher, Christopher, & Cate, 2006).

Another theme in the research on love focuses on the individual benefits of romantic relationships. In Chapter 7 we will see that marriage brings some adults greater happiness and better health. Yet oddly, research on romantic attachments, at least during adolescence, finds just the opposite (Joyner & Udry, 2000). Using a survey tracking almost 8,000 seventh through twelfth graders for one year, the study found that those who entered into romantic relationships were more likely to experience an increase in depression compared to those who did not enter relationships. Adolescent girls, in particular, were more likely to become unhappy over time when they were involved romantically. And both boys and girls in romantic relationships had more alcohol and delinquency problems.

What do you think is responsible for the relationship between teenage romantic relationships and depression (and delinquency)? Is it a selection effect, or do teenage romantic relationships cause these negative outcomes? Can you draw from your own experiences?

Why would adolescent romance seem to have such negative consequences? It is not altogether clear if romantic relationships are causing the problem, or whether those with problems are more likely to get involved in relationships—a selection effect. One finding from this study is that over time those who enter romantic relationships tend to do more poorly in their schoolwork and experience problems with their parents. Romance includes a lot of emotional work, both positive and negative, which can affect the time and energy available for other relationships (Joyner & Udry, 2000).

Yet, it is also possible that adolescents who have problems at school or at home seek out romantic relationships, and therefore are already more likely to be depressed and unhappy. Another study looked at the associations between relationships and depression among over 300 adolescents and found that girls who engaged in sexual activity in short-term romantic relationships that were low in intimacy had a high frequency of depression, but that boys did not experience a high frequency of depression. In contrast, involvement in stable romantic relationships was not associated with depression for either boys or girls (Shulman, Walsh, Weisman, & Schelyer, 2009).

A basic reality of most relationships is that they eventually come to an end. One study found that nearly half of respondents said they have broken up with a partner at least twice, and almost one-quarter say that they have been "dumped" six to ten times. We usually feel very bad after a breakup. Men tend to feel worse, and, probably related to that, they resume dating more quickly than women (Fetto, 2003; Zinczenko, 2007). Nonetheless, recall that one of the positive functions of dating is to weed out unsuitable prospective mates. Breaking up allows us to open up to a larger group of people so we can make a more suitable and confident choice before we marry.

Bringing It Full Circle

The way people think about and experience love is very much shaped by the structure of society, its norms, values, and customs. Our culture glorifies romantic love, but ask people who are in a long-term loving relationship and they will tell you that love is about more than romance, and includes companionship, commitment, caring, and a sense of shared history. Rati and Subas, our married couple from Nepal in the opening vignette, understand this perfectly well. Romantic love, if it develops at all, is last on the list, not first, in establishing a loving, long-term commitment. There are many different theoretical perspectives that help us understand love in all its forms. Taken together, these biochemical, micro-level, and macro-level perspectives shed light on why and how we love.

Now let's reflect upon what you have learned from this chapter to answer the following questions:

- William Goode suggested that cultures try to control love in one of a number of ways. The arranged marriage of Subas and Rati, introduced in the opening vignette, would fall into which category? Into which category do love and marriage in the United States fall?
- Using Sternberg's triangle theory of love and Lee's styles of love, which styles best describe the relationship of Subas and Rati? How does this compare with the loving relationships you have experienced?
- Put yourself in Rati's position--she had never been to the United States before marrying Subas. Can you guess what she thinks of our cultural ideals about love?

For further review, turn to the Video Discussion Guide on page 449 to answer additional questions about how the chapter opening video relates to what you have learned in this chapter.

Chapter Review

4.1 What do we mean by the term "love"?

Love is: (1) a strong affection for another arising out of kinship or personal ties; (2) an attraction based on sexual desire; and (3) an affection based on admiration, benevolence, or common interests. We may be speaking of the love a parent feels for a child, the love a child feels for a sibling, the love between two friends, or the love experienced by romantic partners.

4.2 How do we first learn to love?

Psychologists suggest our first relationships in life, those with our primary guardian, shape the way we approach relationships with others.

4.3 What are the three primary attachment styles?

Secure attachments reflect children's confidence in knowing their mothers (or caregivers) are warm, responsive, and consistently available to them. Anxious/ambivalent attachment occurs when the mother is less predictably warm and responsive to her infant. These types of relationships result in stress among infants who, in turn, tend to develop insecure attachments. Avoidant attachments show little attachment by infants to their mothers. Avoidant infants may have been neglected by their mothers in terms of their physical and emotional needs, and therefore had no expectation the mothers would be there for comfort.

4.4 Does our attachment in infancy affect us as adults?

Yes, our attachment history can influence our friendships and intimate adult relationships throughout our lives, for better or worse. People with secure attachments may find it relatively easy to get close to others and do not worry about depending on others or fearing abandonment. People with anxious-ambivalent attachments may act needy and tend to get close too quickly or worry that their partner does not care for them. Those with avoidant attachments may not be comfortable with closeness and intimacy.

4.5 Have meanings of love changed over time?

The ways we define and experience love depend upon *whom* we love, *where*, and *when*. For instance, love has been constructed as occurring only between men in ancient Greece, as a sexual flirtation between men and women who cannot be together in the Middle Ages (courtly love), and as a feminine quality allowing the care of family members during the mid-19th century (feminization of love).

4.6 What is the difference between romance and companionate love?

A look at fairy tales, movies, books, magazines, and television programs reveals countless stories of romantic love, which is full of passion and excitement. We consider it the most basic prerequisite for dating, cohabiting, and getting married. Yet, over time the intensity of romantic love can begin to fade as people get to know one another. Companionate love is based on strong commitment and trust that the other person will genuinely "be there" for you, no matter what. It grows over time, as partners come to know and understand one another.

4.7 What do biological, micro, and macro-level perspectives teach us about love?

Biological perspectives such as sociobiology and biochemistry look at evolutionary properties of love and chemicals or hormones released during attraction; micro-level perspectives, such as the work by Steinberg, Lee, and Reiss, focus on the development or the experiences of love; and macro-level perspectives, such as the work by Goode, focus on the way that our social structure controls love.

4.8 Are women more interested in love than men?

The short answer is "no." Men, in fact, are more likely than women to be in or looking for committed relationships and they report falling in love sooner and with more people than do women. More men than women reported they are in love with someone "right now" and twice as many men as women say they have been in love five or more times since turning 18.

 Key Terms

anxious/ambivalent attachment (p. 98)
attachment theory (p. 97)
avoidant attachment (p. 98)
biochemical perspective of love (p. 104)
companionate love (p. 102)

controlling the development of love (p. 110)
courtly love (p. 101)
cyberstalking (or electronic monitoring) (p. 117)
dowry (p. 111)
feminization of love (p. 101)

Lee's styles of love (p. 106)
love (p. 96)
Reiss's wheel theory of love (p. 108)
romantic love (p. 102)
secure attachment (p. 98)
sociobiology (p. 103)

stalking (p. 116)
Sternberg's triangular theory of love (p. 105)
unrequited love (p. 115)

4.9 What is the importance of same-sex love?

Men and women's same-sex friendships have been an important source of love and affection, fostered by the fact that their lives have been segregated through most of history. Some of these same-sex friendships may have included a romantic and sexual component, but these were rarely discussed publicly. Today gays and lesbians are freer to acknowledge their romantic partners; however, many heterosexual people remain uncomfortable with their public displays of affection, sometimes even resorting to violence over it.

4.10 What is unrequited love?

Unrequited love is when a person's feelings of love for someone are not reciprocated. It can occur any time in the process of a relationship: in the beginning when one person is simply not interested in the other; as a relationship is being formed when the people have different intentions; and in a long-term relationship.

4.11 Is jealousy always irrational?

Jealousy occurs when we feel threatened by the loss of an important relationship. Jealousy can be rational, based on some real rival threat, or it can be irrational, based on a perceived threat that is not real.

4.12 What is stalking and how serious is this problem?

Stalking is conduct directed at a specific person that would cause a reasonable person to be fearful, and can include making unwanted telephone calls; sending unsolicited or unwanted letters or emails; following or spying on the victim; showing up at places without a legitimate reason; waiting at places for the victim; leaving unwanted items, presents, or flowers; and posting information or spreading rumors about the victim on the Internet, in a public place, or by word of mouth. About 3.4 million adults are stalked each year, increasingly through cyberstalking.

4.13 Why are breakups so difficult?

Breakups can occur at any stage of the relationship. Partners develop shared friends, activities, goals, and memories. They even have overlapping self-concepts, and are more likely to spontaneously use first-person-plural pronouns, such as "we," "our," and "us." After a breakup, this self-concept can become unclear, contributing to considerable emotional distress.

PEARSON
myfamilylab
www.myfamilylab.com

Experience, Discover, Observe, Evaluate

MyFamilyLab is designed just for you. Each chapter features a pre-test and post-test to help you learn and review key concepts and terms. Experience Marriage and Family in action with dynamic visual activities, videos, and readings to enhance your learning.

Here are a few activities you'll find for this chapter:

Explore Social Explorer is an interactive application that allows you to explore Census data through interactive maps. Explore the Social Explorer Map:

- Settlement Patterns of Unmarried Same-Sex Partners

Read MySocLibrary includes primary source readings from classic and contemporary sociologists. Read:

- Laner, "Egalitarian Daters/Traditionalist Daters"

5

Sexual Identity, Behavior, and Relationships

Top: Kayla; Center: Kayla and her friend, Zachary; Bottom: Chris and his friend, Kim.

Sex may be biological, but it occurs in a social context.

Chris and Kayla offer a glimpse of the social context of sexuality among young, unmarried adults.

Out of the blue, ask your parents or grandparents about the "double standard." Even if you provide no context, they will know exactly what you are talking about: that it is more acceptable in our society for boys and men to engage in nonmarital sex than it is for girls and women.

But that was then, and this is now. Does the double standard still exist? What is the social context of sexuality for young people today, and how is it different from in the past? I posed these questions to two young adults, Chris, a 23-year-old male graduate student studying physical therapy, and Kayla, a 26-year-old administrative assistant.

Both Chris and Kayla note the acceptance of casual sex, often called "hook-ups" today. People meet one another on social networking websites and through friends, but bars are a primary venue for casual hook-ups. Although men and women in earlier generations also engaged in nonmarital sex, it was more likely to occur within a committed relationship. Sure, some had so-called "one-night stands," but rarely did women talk about these casual encounters with the openness that surrounds today's "hook-ups." As Kayla told me, "I've had experience when I was hooking up with a friend of a friend and we both just said, 'this is fun, we like each other's company, and it doesn't have to be any more than that.' We were

both very clear from the start. As long as those expectations don't change, I think that it could be great."

But, the more things change, the more they also stay the same. According to Chris, the double standard is alive and well. First, he acknowledges that despite its shallowness, men still rank a woman's attractiveness as her most important attribute, at least initially—is she "hot" or not? Kayla, in contrast, refers to a man's sense of humor as "always the best part."

Chris also says that women who have casual sex are looked at more negatively than men who have multiple partners: "I think there is a double standard between men who have slept with tons of women and women who have slept with tons of men. For women it's a lot more negative. It's 'she's a whore, she's sexually promiscuous, she doesn't think highly of herself, or she doesn't have a lot of confidence.' For a guy it's almost like 'he's awesome, he's the man,' and you think 'this guy must just know everything.'"

Kayla sees things somewhat differently and feels that gender stereotypes are becoming less important. "There is still some stigma attached to women who have multiple casual sexual partners, but I also believe that there is a—maybe a less harsh stigma, but a stigma as well attached to men who have multiple casual sexual partners." What do you think?

According to Chris, the double standard is alive and well.

5:20 / 8:51

👁 **Watch** the **Video** *Perspectives on Sexual Identity and Behavior: Kayla and Chris* on **myfamilylab.com**

QUESTIONS That Matter

5.1 Is sexuality purely biological?

5.2 How do macro-level factors influence sexuality?

5.3 What is the difference between "sex" and "gender"?

5.4 Do sex and gender go together?

5.5 What do we mean by "sexual orientation"?

5.6 What are sexual scripts, and where do we learn them?

5.7 Are sexual scripts different for men and women?

5.8 What are some important studies that have been done on human sexuality?

5.9 When do we become sexual?

5.10 How big a social problem is teenage pregnancy?

5.11 How prevalent is nonmarital sex among young adults?

5.12 What are some common sexual trends in marriage?

5.13 Do people remain sexual throughout their lives?

5.14 What is the most common STI?

5.15 Hasn't the issue of HIV and AIDS been resolved by now?

Sexuality is a universal human experience. Even young children are keenly interested in their genitals and feelings of arousal (Thigpen, 2009). We know that sexuality has a biological basis, but we also think of sexuality as a highly personal matter. Our sexuality is so intimate that it is an integral part of our own identity—our feelings of *who* we are. We may have particular sexual preferences and personal desires. However, sex is more than just biological or personal; it is also *social*. We cannot understand sexuality until we look at macro-level factors. In previous chapters, we have stressed how human behavior varies around the world or at different times in history. We have emphasized how your membership in certain groups, such as your sex, race, or social class, shapes who you are, the values you hold, and the opportunities and constraints you encounter. These factors influence the realm of sexuality as well (Stombler, Baunach, Burgess, Donnelly, Simonds, & Windsor, 2010). This chapter will show you how the biological, personal, and social factors are intertwined in our sexuality.

You may vividly remember the first time you heard about how babies were "made." But learning about sex means more than just discovering its mechanics. It includes learning the *who, what, where, when, how,* and *why* of sexual behavior. With whom do we have sex? What is appropriate sexual behavior? Where do we have sex? When do we have sex? How do we have sex? Why do we have sex?

> Images of sexuality are found in all types of media, including those that are readily available to children. Parents say that they are very concerned about the messages their children are receiving.

The answers to these questions say a lot about how sex is accepted and practiced in a particular culture, and in a particular historical period (Rathus, Nevid, & Fichner-Rathus, 2011). For example, in your grandparents' era, sex was largely hidden from public discussion. Today, discussions of sex are very public, as Kayla and Chris show us in the opening vignette. Media depictions of sex are as close as the magazines in the check-out line at the grocery store. Mainstream women's and girls' magazines such as *Cosmopolitan, Redbook,* and *Seventeen* use sex to sell copies. *Sports Illustrated*'s annual swimsuit edition, featuring bikini-clad women in provocative poses, sells twice as many copies as any other issue. Television, radio, film, and the Internet also use sex to entertain and to increase their profits. Verbal and visual references to sexual activity bombard us with images of what it means to be sexual in mainstream U.S. culture. Nearly two-thirds of parents are "very concerned" about the amount of sexual content their children see on primetime television (Kim, Sorsoli, Collins, Zylbergold, Schooler, & Tolman, 2007).

:: Overview of Historical and Cultural Influences on Sexuality

Sexuality may be a universal and natural physiological experience, but sexual attitudes and behaviors can be quite different across cultures. For example, among the Mangaia people of Polynesia, both girls and boys are expected to have a high level of sexual desire in early adolescence. At the age of thirteen or fourteen, boys are given explicit instruction through personal experience with an older female teacher in how to please a girl through kissing, fondling, oral sex, and taught specific techniques for giving her multiple orgasms. It is critical that a boy quickly learn these techniques. Soon he will begin sexual relations with a girl his own age, and if he fails to satisfy her, she will likely publicly denounce him and his lack of sexual skill (Strong, DeVault, Sayad, & Yarber, 2002).

In contrast to the Mangaia, the Dani of New Guinea show little interest in sex beyond what is needed for reproduction. Sexual intercourse is performed quickly and female orgasm is virtually unheard of. After childbirth, mothers and fathers abstain from sex for five years. Sexual affairs are rare or nonexistent. These examples from two different cultures illustrate that many aspects of sex are far from innate.

We can also see differences *within* our own culture, including across historical periods, between racial and ethnic groups, social classes, and between women and men. For example, our images of early American sexuality are of prim and proper Puritans and sexually repressed Victorians. Religious and medical authorities of the time did not believe that women experienced sexual desires; those women who did were considered dangerous or evil (Ehrenreich & English, 1989).

Myths and stereotypes surrounded males as well. People believed sexual intercourse drained a man of his natural vitality, and therefore engaging in it too frequently—more than once a month—was not recommended. **Masturbation**—the rubbing, fondling, and stimulating of one's own genitals and other body parts—was considered perverse or dangerous for men, and virtually unheard of among women. The Reverend Sylvester Graham (1794–1851) preached that the loss of even an ounce of semen was equal to the loss of several ounces of blood (Bullough, 1976). Each time a man ejaculated, he was thought to be risking his physical health. Graham encouraged men to control their sexual feelings by adopting a diet based on whole-grain flour. His name is still identified with a cracker he developed in the 1830s to help men control their sexual urges—the Graham cracker!

The 20th century witnessed a number of new social trends that began to shape sexual behavior, marriage, and family life (Weis, 1998). Industrialization and the growth in jobs encouraged men and women to move away from their extended families in rural areas. In urban areas, away from their traditions, they experienced greater independence and opportunities. The growth in public schools allowed young men and women to spend time together with less parental supervision, and led to the creation of a new adolescent subculture. More women worked outside the home, which, together with required schooling, increased opportunities for both sexes to meet, interact, and socialize. The employment of women also increased a family's standard of living, and gave rise to a growing middle class that could afford some of the latest technologies, such as an automobile or telephone. These technologies increased opportunities for freedom and privacy for young people.

All of these changes led many people to question existing ideas about sexuality, and the traditional values began to give way to a search for personal fulfillment and satisfaction. Both men and women began to view sexual gratification as a right, and the availability of birth control offered women and men a degree of control over their lives that had been largely unavailable. Marriage was increasingly connected to romance as husbands and wives were seen as companions attending to each other's physical, emotional, and sexual needs.

Today our culture addresses sexuality more openly than a few generations ago. At the turn of the 20th century, it was illegal to provide unmarried people with information about birth control, while today many unmarried teenagers already know about and have used various methods of preventing pregnancy. Most American adults even approve of nonmarital sex (Pew Research Center, 2007). In fact, Americans now have more sexual partners over the lifespan, begin sexual activity at an earlier age, and are less likely to view sexual activity solely as an act of procreation. If pregnancy occurs, marriage is only one of several options available. Most Americans believe it is morally acceptable to have a baby outside marriage, and about 40 percent believe abortion should be legal under any or most circumstances (Juby, 2009; Gallup News Service, 2007).

We are single for longer periods of time, thereby increasing our likelihood of having nonmarital sex. Biology is interwoven with these social and cultural conditions. In 1890, the average age at **menarche**, or a woman's first menstrual period, was 15–17 years, and the average age of marriage for women was 22 years. Today, the average age at menarche is around 12 years, and the average age of marriage for women is about 26 years, resulting in five more years as an unmarried yet physically mature woman (Tanner, 1978; U.S. Census Bureau, January 2009). This provides a larger window of opportunity for young women and men to explore their sexuality.

masturbation: Sexually stimulating one's own body.

menarche: A woman's first menstrual period.

Why Do Research?

Researchers Note Earlier Onset of Puberty in U.S. Girls

The definition of "normal" development for U.S. girls is changing, and this vividly illustrates how the biological and social aspects of sexuality are intertwined. Girls' childhoods are growing shorter, with developmental milestones occurring at earlier ages. While the typical 8-year-old U.S. girl is enjoying third grade, practicing her cursive writing, and jumping rope on the playground, more and more of these young girls are also experiencing the process of becoming women.

Researchers are noting that signs of pubertal development can be seen in girls as young as 7 or 8. The blossoming of breast buds is the first sign of pubertal development in girls. Breast bud development used to be considered average between the ages of 10 and 12 years old, but now girls are experiencing this development change at an earlier age. In a study of 17,000 girls in North Carolina, almost 50 percent of Black and 15 percent of White girls showed breast buds by age 8.

The onset of menarche, or first menstruation, is also experienced at a younger age than in years past. Between 1890 and today, the average age of menarche has decreased from 15–17 to about 12. What is behind the trend of earlier pubertal development among girls?

Explanations have included growth hormones in our foods, better sanitation, easier access to good nutrition, and public health interventions that reduced the spread of disease. As the health of females improved, the chemical signals within the body began to initiate the process of puberty sooner because the body was better equipped to reproduce at earlier ages. In many ways, puberty has traditionally been a sign of good health and wealth, although early puberty does carry some health risks—longer exposure to estrogen over a lifetime may contribute to breast cancer, other forms of cancers, or other problems.

But why else should we be concerned? The combination of an 8- or 9-year-old girl with breast buds, along with societal messages telling young girls to dress and act sexy, may be dangerous for a young girl whose emotional and mental development has not caught up with her physical maturation. Sexy clothing and makeup are now heavily marketed to a new group called "tweens," children between the broad ages of 7–12. In fact, sales of thong underwear to "tweens" have quadrupled since 2000. Young girls are increasingly sexualized, and they feel social pressure from their peers to

The marketing industry has been accused of sexualizing young children, especially girls, as young as seven or eight.

look, act, and *be* sexy. Even their immature genitals are sexualized: many adult women have taken to waxing to remove their pubic hair to more closely resemble a prepubescent girl.

Although many young girls are biologically capable of having babies, they are still children themselves and need time to grow into adult women.

What Do **You** Think?

1. Compare and contrast the biological, micro-level, and macro-level factors associated with early pubertal development. Do you think these differ for boys and girls?

2. Have you seen evidence of the sexualization of "tweens"? What do you think are some of the consequences of this sexualization?

Written by Nicole K. Smith

Sources: Brink, 2008; Wells, 2003; Levin & Kilbourne, 2008.

Some people, however, are concerned that the age of physical development and menarche has decreased to a point at which children are not yet equipped emotionally to handle these changes. For example, as shown in the *Why Do Research?* feature box, some girls are experiencing breast development as young as eight. What are the implications of this early physical change? One implication is that businesses now heavily market sexually suggestive clothing and makeup to "tweens"—girls between the ages of 7 and 12. This marketing sexualizes young children in new and disturbing ways (Levin & Kilbourne, 2008; Lamb & Brown, 2006).

:: Our Sexual Selves: Biology and Culture Intertwined

*S*ince sexual attitudes and behaviors seem to change over time, do you think those of the next generation will be different from your own? If yes, in what ways? If not, why not?

Sex is biological, personal, and social. Let's begin our discussion of sexuality with the biological basics of who we are and show how biology and our social environment are intertwined to shape our personal identities, attitudes, and behaviors. **Read** on **myfamilylab.com**

Read the **Document**
Sex and Temperament in Three Tribes on **myfamilylab.com**

Sex and Gender

Recall from Chapter 2 that our definition of sex referred to biological differences and our role in reproduction. Typically people think of two sexes based on genitalia: male and female. But these categories are not always this obvious.

Some people are born **intersexed**, a term used for a variety of conditions in which a person has a reproductive or sexual anatomy that does not fit the typical definitions of what is considered female or male (Haas, 2010). For example, a person might be born with a female appearance, but have mostly male genitalia. Or a person may be born with genitals in between the usual male and female types—a girl may have a noticeably large clitoris or lack a vaginal opening, or a boy may be born with a notably small penis or a divided scrotum formed more like labia.

How common are these differences? It depends on the condition. A variation that is so atypical as to require surgery occurs only in about one or two in 1,000 births. However, many other people are born with subtler forms of sex anatomy variations (Intersex Society of North America, 2008).

In contrast to sex, recall that **gender** refers to the culturally and socially constructed differences between the meanings, beliefs, and practices associated with femininity and masculinity (Lindsey, 2011). Gender is social in nature and consists of learned attitudes and behaviors, not biological or physical qualities. We are *born* male or female, but we *learn* the cultural and socially prescribed traits associated with masculine or feminine patterns of behavior.

Not everyone fits so neatly into his or her prescribed category; sometimes a person's identity does not conform to his or her biological anatomy. **Transgender** individuals manifest characteristics, behaviors, or self-expressions associated typically with the other gender (American Psychological Association Online, 2009; PFLAG, 2009; Pardo, 2008). A man may feel as relaxed, comfortable, and normal engaging in feminine traits such as wearing certain clothing (dresses), following particular grooming practices (painting nails), or having typically feminine hobbies, as he does in engaging in masculine ones, or even more so. Transgender women are not usually as obvious to us because we allow women more leeway to behave in traditionally masculine ways, such as wearing men's clothing or acting aggressively.

Transgender issues have been largely ignored, but this is beginning to change (Pfeffer, 2010; Girschick, 2008; Schilt, 2006). It is not known how many transgender men and women exist because of the long-held stigma associated with being transgender (Grossman & D'Augelli, 2006). The American Psychological Association estimates that 2–3 percent of biological males may engage in cross-dressing, at least occasionally (American Psychological Association Online, 2009).

Some transgender individuals harbor a deep sense of discomfort about their sex and wish to live fully as members of the other sex. Usually referred to as **transsexuals**, these individuals may have sex reassignment surgery and hormone treatments, either male-to-female or female-to-male. Current estimates of the prevalence of transsexualism are about 1 in 10,000 for biological males and 1 in 30,000 for biological females (APA Task Force on Gender Identity and Gender Variance, 2008). Reassignment surgery is expensive, costing

intersexed: Those born with genitalia that do not clearly identify them as unambiguously male or female.

transgender: When a person feels as comfortable, if not more so, in expressing gendered traits that are associated with the other sex.

transsexual: An individual who undergoes sex reassignment surgery and hormone treatments.

up to $50,000, and the preparation is time-consuming and emotionally difficult. It is estimated that 100 to 500 sex reassignment surgeries are conducted each year in the United States, and two to five times this many worldwide. Perhaps 25,000 U.S. adults have undergone sex reassignment surgery (Encyclopedia of Surgery, 2009).

Sexual Orientation

Another aspect of who we are concerns our **sexual orientation**, which refers to an enduring pattern of romantic, emotional, and sexual partners we choose (American Psychological Association, 2009). It involves a person's *identity*, or how one sees oneself.

Although we now understand that sexual orientation ranges along a continuum, with many people somewhere in the middle (Kinsey, Pomeroy, & Martin, 1953), for ease of discussion many people still talk about sexual orientation in terms of discrete categories. A **heterosexual** identity, sometimes called "straight," refers to an attraction and preference for developing romantic, emotional, and sexual relationships with the other sex (i.e., a man and a woman). A **homosexual** identity refers to attraction and preference for relationships with members of one's own sex (i.e., two men or two women). Homosexual men may be referred to as "gay males," or just "gay." Homosexual women are often called "lesbians." The term **bisexual** refers to an orientation in which a person is attracted to both males and females (engaging in both heterosexual and homosexual partner choice) (Rathus, Nevid, & Fichner-Rathus, 2011).

Counting the number of persons who are gay, lesbian, and bisexual is challenging. One reason is that having a gay or lesbian *identity* can be a very different thing from having a gay or lesbian *experience* (Ward, 2010). Some people have had a gay or lesbian experience, or many experiences, yet still think of themselves as heterosexual (Vrangalova & Savin-Williams, 2010). The number of people who self-identify as gay or lesbian is quite a bit smaller. When researchers asked in one survey, "Do you think of yourself as heterosexual, homosexual, bisexual, or something else?" about 3 percent of men and slightly less than 2 percent of women claimed either a homosexual or bisexual self-concept (Vrangalova & Savin-Williams, 2010). Other studies suggest the number is a little higher. In a national survey that drew upon a large representative sample of adults ages 18–45, 4.1 percent of respondents identified themselves as gay, lesbian, or bisexual (Gates, 2006). In a CNN presidential exit poll, about 4 percent of registered voters reported being gay, lesbian, or bisexual (CNN.com, 2008).

Yet the likelihood of having a same-sex sexual *experience* may be two or three times higher (AVERT.ORG, 2010; Erens, McManus, & Prescott, 2003). Moreover, the number of people with same-sex *interests* is higher still (Vrangalova & Savin-Williams, 2010). One study of young adults ages 19–26 found that 10 percent of men and 25 percent of women reported having some homosexual experience, interest, or identity (Pedersen & Kristiansen, 2008). Thus, the number of persons who identify themselves as homosexual or bisexual is significantly smaller than the percentage of persons who have had, or have considered having, a same-sex sexual experience. ◉⊸Watch on **myfamilylab.com**

What Determines Sexual Orientation?
How do we come to have a specific sexual orientation? Are we the way we are because of biology, or because of social and environmental factors? Is our sexual orientation a choice? The question of what causes sexual orientation is an intriguing one that we cannot yet definitively answer. However, scientists are coming to the conclusion that a complex set of biological (genetics and hormones) and social factors shape who we are. In other words, sexual orientation is not really a choice (American Psychological Association, 2009).

There are probably many reasons for a person's sexual orientation and these reasons may differ for different people, but emerging evidence suggests the biological components are far greater than we once imagined. Psychologists, psychiatrists, and other mental health professionals generally agree that homosexuality is not an illness, mental disorder, or emotional problem. In 1973, the American Psychiatric Association removed homosexuality from the official manual that lists mental and emotional disorders. Two years later, the American Psychological Association passed a resolution supporting the removal (Conger, 1975).

◉⊸**Watch** the **Video**
Core Concepts: Alternative Sexual Orientation on
myfamilylab.com

sexual orientation: The sexual and romantic pattern of partners of choice.

heterosexual: Having an attraction and preference for developing romantic and sexual relationships with the opposite sex.

homosexual: Having an attraction and preference for relationships with members of one's own sex.

bisexual: An orientation in which a person is attracted to both males and females.

For most people, sexual orientation is shaped at an early age (American Psychological Association, 2009). One study of college students found that 17 percent of gay and bisexual men and 11 percent of lesbian and bisexual women reported knowing they were gay or bisexual as early as grade school (Elliott, Brantley, & Johnson, 1997).

Research that focuses on siblings can demystify the causes of sexual orientation. One study set out to determine whether identical twins, who share genetic material, were more likely to be gay or lesbian than other siblings. The researchers considered three types of sibling pairs, *in which one was known to be gay or lesbian*: (1) identical twins, who share genetic material; (2) fraternal twins, who share half their genetic material; and (3) adopted siblings, who share no genetic material. The researchers found that 52 percent of the male identical twin pairs and 48 percent of the identical female twin pairs were both homosexual, compared to only 22 percent of male fraternal twins and 16 percent of female fraternal twins. Adopted siblings were least likely to both be homosexual (11 percent and 6 percent for male and female adopted siblings, respectively) (Bailey & Pillard, 1991; Bailey, Pillard, Neale, & Agyei, 1993). These results suggest that homosexuality may contain an important biological component.

Another study examined the relationship between the sexual orientation of 55 gay or bisexual fathers and their 82 adult sons at least 17 years of age (Bailey, Bobrow, Wolfe, & Mikach, 1995). More than 90 percent of the sons were heterosexual. Furthermore, gay and heterosexual sons did not differ on potentially relevant variables, such as the length of time they had lived with their fathers. Thus, the researchers question environmental influences and suggest that they do not appear as important as previously assumed.

What explains our sexual orientation? Although the answers are not completely known, most scientists think that biology can give us important clues.

Some researchers suggest homosexuality is more common on the maternal side, fueling a discussion that homosexuality may be "passed" through women (Hamer & Copeland, 1994). Another researcher, a neuroscientist, performed autopsies on the brains of recently deceased men and women whose sexual orientation was established (LeVay, 1991). He found that a small region in the center of the brain involved with sexual response was smaller among gays than among heterosexual men. However, there were only 41 subjects in the sample and only 6 were women. Another study found that gay men's brains respond differently from those of heterosexual men's in some ways, and actually operate more like women's brains (Schmid, 2005). Scientists interpret these results with caution. Even if we could directly link specific genes or brain processes to sexual orientation, our behavior is also shaped and molded by our cultural and historical context.

Attitudes toward LGBT   Attitudes towards lesbians, gays, bisexuals, and transgender persons (LGBT) differ around the world. For example, in many countries in the Middle East and Africa, homosexuality is against the law and carries harsh penalties, such as imprisonment or even death. For example, in the African countries of Malawi and Kenya, homosexuality is punishable by up to 14 years in prison, and a lawmaker with the governing party in Uganda recently proposed executing people who are gay (Bearak, 2010; Gettleman, 2010). The *New York Times* recently reported that police broke up a same-sex wedding in Kenya; not only were they concerned about its illegality, but they were afraid that an angry mob would stone the couple to death (Gettleman, 2010).

In the United States, many people still disapprove of homosexuality, but attitudes are becoming more accepting. In 2009, according to a Gallup Poll, 49 percent of Americans believed homosexuality was "morally acceptable"—the first time that more people found

Getting to Know Yourself

Weigh Your Attitudes and Beliefs about Homosexuality

Answer the following questions truthfully. For the sake of ease, "gay" refers to both homosexual men and homosexual women.

1 = Strongly Agree; 2 = Agree; 3 = Neither Agree nor Disagree; 4 = Disagree; 5 = Strongly Disagree

____ **1.** I worry that gay people will try to seduce me.

____ **2.** Gay people are immoral.

____ **3.** Homosexuality is acceptable to me.

____ **4.** I would not be good friends with someone if I knew he or she was gay.

____ **5.** I think gay people should not be teachers.

____ **6.** I usually laugh at derogatory gay jokes.

____ **7.** Marriage between gays is acceptable.

____ **8.** It does not matter to me whether my friends are gay or straight.

____ **9.** I make jokes about gay people.

____ **10.** Gay people demand too many rights.

____ **11.** Organizations which promote gay rights are important and necessary.

____ **12.** I have called a gay person a name out loud to their face, like "queer."

____ **13.** I have damaged property of a gay person, such as scratching their car.

____ **14.** I would feel uncomfortable having a gay roommate.

____ **15.** Homosexual behavior should be against the law.

____ **16.** It would bother me to see gays kissing.

____ **17.** I have never met anyone who is gay.

First, transpose the answer categories of questions 3, 7, 8, and 11, so that Strongly Disagree is now worth 1 point, Strongly Agree is worth 2 points, etc. Now, count up your points for each question. In general, the lower the score, the greater the negative attitudes and beliefs about homosexuals; the higher the score, the more positive.

What Do You Think?

1. Do you think average scores of men and women differ? Why or why not? How about Whites, Blacks, Hispanics, Asian Americans, Native Americans, and other minority groups?

2. Can you identify any micro-level or macro-level factors that have shaped your views?

Figure 5.1	**Perceptions of the Morality of Homosexual Relations**

Attitudes are changing: more people now believe that same-sex relationships are morally acceptable rather than morally wrong.

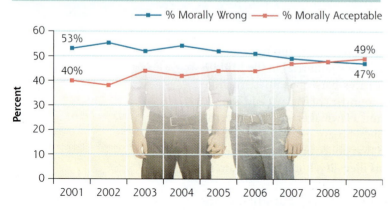

— % Morally Wrong — % Morally Acceptable

53%   40%   49%   47%

Percent: 60, 50, 40, 30, 20, 10, 0

2001 2002 2003 2004 2005 2006 2007 2008 2009

Source: Saad, Lydia. 2009. "Republicans Move to the Right on Several Moral Issues." Retrieved 14 February 2010. Gallup Poll (www.gallup.com/poll/118546/republicans-veer-right-several-moral-issues.aspx).

it "morally acceptable" than "morally wrong," as shown in Figure 5.1 (Saad, 2008, 2009). In particular, Blacks, older persons, those with less education, conservative Republicans, and those persons who attend church more often were more likely to believe that homosexuality was morally unacceptable or to hold other negative attitudes (Vincent, Peterson, & Parrott, 2009). The Gallup Poll also found that 89 percent believe homosexuals should have "equal rights in terms of job opportunities," although only 39 percent agree that "marriages between same-sex couples should be recognized by law as valid with the same rights as traditional marriage" (Saad, 2008). A CNN poll put the percentage of people favoring same-sex marriage as slightly higher at 44 percent (Steinhauser, 2009).

What are your attitudes toward homosexuality? The *Getting to Know Yourself* feature box offers a self-assessment survey that measures your thoughts, feelings, and behaviors with regards to homosexuality. How do you compare with your friends or others in class?

Some people experience very strong negative feelings toward homosexuality, called **homophobia (or anti-gay prejudice)**, a display of which can take many forms, including using derogatory names, making disparaging jokes, discriminating, or even causing violence (Pascoe, 2007). Much media attention was given to the plight of Matthew Shepard, a young gay man in Wyoming who was tied to a fence, pistol-whipped, and left to die in 1998 (Shepard, 2009). This horrendous crime outraged the public and led some state legislatures to add violence against gays and lesbians to their hate crime statutes. The U.S. Justice Department claims that, of all hate and bias crimes reported to the FBI, 17 percent involve sexual orientation (U.S. Department of Justice, November 2009).

Anti-gay prejudice adversely affects both homosexuals and heterosexuals. It creates fear, anxiety, misunderstanding, and hatred. Heterosexuals, for example, may restrict their same-sex friendships, or heterosexual males may act hypermasculine for fear they may be mistaken for gay men. The delay in our country's response to the HIV/AIDS epidemic has been attributed to anti-gay prejudice. In his best-selling book, *And the Band Played On: Politics, People, and the AIDS Epidemic*, Randy Shilts (1987) illustrated the ways in which the labeling of HIV/AIDS as the "gay" disease kept the government from acting as quickly or thoroughly as if another, more acceptable group had initially contracted the disease.

In summary, understanding our sexual selves leads us to closely examine our sex, our gender, and our sexual orientation, as shown in Table 5.1. For many, these three components operate together in predictable ways: if you are a woman, you behave in ways our culture considers feminine, and you are romantically and sexually attracted to men. Likewise, if you are a man, you act in ways deemed masculine, and you are attracted to women. However, as we have learned in this section, sex, gender, and sexual orientation are separate and distinct components and do not always operate in a predictable fashion.

We have seen some influences of biology in shaping who we are—our sex and our sexual orientation. Yet, our sexual attitudes and many of our sexual behaviors are learned. From where do we learn them?

Table 5.1	Sex, Gender, and Sexual Orientation	
Sex, gender, and sexual orientation are three distinct components of our identity. Often they go together in a predictable fashion, but because they are distinct, they can also be mixed. What are the possibilities?		
Sex:	Male	Female
Gender:	Masculine	Feminine
Sexual Orientation:	Heterosexual	Homosexual

- *A heterosexual feminine man*
- *A homosexual feminine man*
- *A heterosexual masculine man*
- *A homosexual masculine man*
- *A heterosexual feminine woman*
- *A homosexual feminine woman*
- *A heterosexual masculine woman*
- *A homosexual masculine woman*

Do you know anyone (including yourself) whose sex, gender, and sexual orientation do not conform to traditional expectations? For example, do you know anyone who is transgender, intersexed, or gay or lesbian? What have been some of their (your) experiences with respect to intimate relationships or with discrimination?

:: Sexual Scripts

We like to think that our sexual attitudes are distinctly our own, and our behavior represents uniquely individual likes and dislikes. Yet even these personal aspects of our lives are highly shaped by social and cultural factors. Our sexual attitudes and behaviors are organized and directed through **sexual scripts**, which are the norms or rules regarding sexual behavior. They govern the *who, what, where, when, how,* and *why* we have sex. For example, our culture prohibits sex with animals, children, and, unless you live in a few selected counties in Nevada, someone to whom you have paid money. It does not prohibit sex among unmarried people or those of different religious faiths, races, or ethnic backgrounds. As a society, we have decided that a married person should only have sex with his or her spouse. We have decided that sex can be enjoyed for pleasure rather than just for reproduction. Other cultures see things differently. Sexual scripts act as a blueprint, informing us

homophobia (or anti-gay prejudice): Having very strong negative feelings toward homosexuality.

sexual scripts: The norms or rules regarding sexual behavior.

what is expected and appropriate, and what is considered inappropriate or taboo with regard to our sexuality.

We learn our sexual scripts from at least three different sources (Laumann, Gagnon, Michael, & Michaels, 1994):

- The culture in which we live, including our parents, our friends, the mass media, and the dominant religion practiced.
- The interpersonal communication between us and our partner as we begin, and attend to, our personal relationship.
- Our personal views of sex, based on feelings, desires, and fantasies.

In other words, we must look beyond biology to explain our sexual rules and behaviors.

:: Gender and Sexual Scripts: The Double Standard

Traditionally, men are granted far more leeway in sexual behavior than are women, a situation called the **double standard**. Men are expected to be assertive in seeking sexual behavior, to always be ready for sex, and to have more sexual partners. They are rewarded socially for "scoring." Women, in contrast, are to walk a fine line by being "sexy," yet not "too sexy." They must make themselves desirable and attractive to the attention of men, but by becoming too desirable or attractive they risk being labeled "easy," "cheap," or a "slut." They must be careful to appear interested, but not too interested, in sex.

A recent content analysis of adolescents' top 25 primetime network programs reveals that sexual scripts are highly gendered (Kim, Sorsoli, Collins, Zylbergold, Schooler, & Tolman, 2007). The portrayals of boys and men showed a clear message: accumulating sexual experience is an important, desirable, and even necessary component of masculinity. Boys and men should attain sexual experience by whatever means available, including force or deceit. Television images of girls and women in these top primetime shows were more conflicted: girls and women walk the precarious line between making themselves sexually available and being appropriately demure. Feminine courtship strategies encouraged girls and women to seduce boys and men by exploiting their bodies and dressing in tight, revealing clothing, even though these same behaviors were then devalued and seen as a sign of their sexual indiscretion. Girls and women faced a challenge: how to conform to pervasive conventions of sexuality and be sexually available, while trying to control boys and men's "uncontrollable" sexual desire. In other words, these images give young viewers information about how girls, women, boys, and men are supposed to think, feel, and behave in romantic and sexual situations (Kim, Sorsoli, Collins, Zylbergold, Schooler, & Tolman, 2007).

*H*ave you seen any evidence that the double standard still exists?

Interestingly, both men and women uphold the double standard: Even women perceive other women more negatively if they have sex in an uncommitted rather than a committed relationship. People of all ages, including preadolescent boys and girls, middle and high schoolers, college students, and adults commonly use harsh terms to refer to sexually active girls (Bogle, 2008; Tolman, 2005).

Peggy Orenstein, in her book *School Girls*, found that the fear of being labeled a slut in middle school affects how girls see themselves and directly influences how they relate to both other girls and to boys. She describes one interview with Evie, a typical middle-school girl obsessed with pointing out the girls at school who are "sluts." Evie is learning the rules, or scripts, about sexuality. She explains to Orenstein in her middle-school language that sex "ruins" girls but enhances boys; that boys have far fewer constraints than do girls; and that sexual behavior for girls is controllable, but for boys it is inevitable and excusable: "Boys only think with their dicks" (Orenstein, 1994). Girls who fail to follow the scripts are shunned. If they dare to complain about the scripts, or confront a boy who is pressuring them for sex, *their* reputations are on the line. "The thing is, we don't have control," Evie explains.

double standard: The idea that men have been allowed far more permissiveness in sexual behavior than women.

"Hecould just say that we were asking for it or that we wanted it. Then everyone will think we're sluts" (Orenstein, Peggy. 1994. School Girls. New York, NY. Anchor Books).

Another study based on extensive interviews with teenage girls found that girls genuinely wrestled with their sexuality. In *Dilemmas of Desire* (2005), author Deborah Tolman describes how girls eagerly wanted to be desired by boys, but at the same time, they disassociated from their own bodies and did not seem to express any real sexual feelings themselves. They were content simply to be "objects of desire." Sex was something that just happened to them, and was not something they felt that they owned.

Components of the Male and Female Sexual Scripts

Let's examine male and female sexual scripts in our society. First, what are some components of the *male* sexual script? Keep in mind that these features are certainly modified in a relationship where people are able to break free from cultural stereotypes and experience true intimacy. Nonetheless, the male script, which will look familiar to you, emphasizes sex over intimacy (Seccombe, 2012):

- *A man's looks are relatively unimportant, but his status is enhanced if he is with a beautiful woman.* A woman is a trophy, and the more attractive the trophy, the more of a man he is perceived to be.
- *The man always wants sex and is ready for it.* It does not matter much what else is going on or what his feelings are towards a potential partner. A man is like a machine and can be "turned on" immediately.
- *A man is in charge.* He is the initiator, the leader, and knows more about sex than his partner does. He would not feel comfortable asking his partner what she really likes.
- *All physical contact leads to sex.* Because a man is a machine, ideally any physical contact should lead to sexual intercourse. Touching, caressing, and kissing are not pleasurable ends in themselves.
- *A man cannot easily stop himself once he gets turned on.* Men have greater sexual needs than women do, and they may not be able to stop once aroused, regardless of whether a man's partner asks him to stop.
- *Sex equals intercourse.* The focus of sex is on stimulating the penis. Hopefully, this will be satisfactory to his partner.
- *Sexual intercourse always leads to orgasm.* According to the male sexual script, the purpose of intercourse is for the male to have an orgasm. If one does not occur, the act is incomplete or a failure. However, it is less important that a female has an orgasm.

Males and females have different scripts in our society. What does this photograph from a scene of the sitcom *The Big Bang Theory* tell you about their sexual scripts?

In contrast, what are some components of the *female* sexual script? Again, these features may be modified in relationships in which people can truly be themselves and move away from rigid scripts. For women, we can see that the sexual script emphasizes feelings over sex:

- *Women should make themselves sexually attractive to men to get their attention, but they should not make themselves too attractive.* Women should dress "a certain way," so that they will gain the attention of men, but they also run the risk of gaining too much attention. It is up to women to sort out the appropriate type of dress, makeup, and demeanor to attract the right amount of male attention.

- *Women's genitals are mysterious.* Many girls and women know little about their bodies. They have been taught not to touch or explore them, and many have never even used a mirror to look at them. What they do know comes from media images that tell them that their genitals have odor, which must be controlled. Consequently, many women are very uncomfortable with their bodies.
- *Women should not know too much about sex or be too experienced.* Women walk a fine line today—they must not appear too uptight about sex, but they must not feel too comfortable with it either. Women should not be "too experienced," however it is quantified, because they run the risk of being labeled a "slut" or a "whore."

  - *Good girls do not plan in advance to have sex or initiate it.* To plan in advance (and take appropriate precautions) may look to her partner as though she is too experienced or likes sex too much. She cannot take the lead or she may risk her reputation.
  - *Women should not talk about sex.* Many women cannot talk about sex because they are not expected to be very knowledgeable or to feel very comfortable with it. Women may feel more comfortable *having* sex than having a simple conversation about it with their partner.

- *Men should know how to please a woman.* Although he may be primarily focused on his penis and his own orgasm, a woman feels it is his job to know how to arouse her. He is supposed to know what she wants, even if she does not want (or does not know how) to tell him.
- *Sexual intercourse is supposed to lead to orgasm and other stimulation should be unnecessary.* Studies indicate that between one-third and one-half of women do not have an orgasm in sexual intercourse; they need additional oral or manual stimulation of the clitoris. Nonetheless, many women believe that something is wrong with them if sexual intercourse itself does not produce an orgasm.

*H*ow *would a conflict theorist analyze the difference between male and female scripts? How does that compare to a functional theorist?*

The double standard is found throughout the world, in both developed and developing nations. Sometimes it even lays the foundation for government social policy. The *Diversity in Families* feature box illustrates how the double sexual standard has affected government policy in Japan. While the Japanese government took many decades to approve birth control pills to prevent pregnancy, the government offered no delays when it came to approving Viagra to help men with impotence. Many Japanese found this a flagrant example of sexism.

The Double Standard in Current Sexual Behavior

Given the strong gendered sexual scripts in our society, it is not surprising that researchers continue to find significant differences between men and women in their sexual behavior (Fryar, Hirsch, Porter, Kottiri, Brody, & Louis, 2007; Langer, Arnett, & Sussman, 2004). An ABC News survey (2004) of adults showed that men think about sex more often than women (70 percent of men versus 34 percent of women reported "thinking about sex every day"); more often enjoy sex "a great deal" (83 percent versus 59 percent); have visited a sex website more often (34 percent versus 10 percent); and have more sexual partners. Regardless of actual behavior, men and women have different *ideal* numbers of lifetime sex partners; if there were no risks or limitations on sexual activity, men say about 13 partners would be an "ideal number," whereas women report five would be "ideal" (Fenigstein & Preston, 2007).

The double standard permeates all aspects of society and illustrates important ideas about women, men, and how they should relate to one another. It contributes to a number of problems: it fosters a lack of knowledge about women's bodies and the mistaken idea that women have less important sexual needs; it perpetuates the notion that male sexuality should be the normative baseline for eroticism and sexual activity; and it objectifies women by keeping them as the "objects of desire." Here is an example of a problem exacerbated by this double standard: the lack of knowledge about women's bodies.

Diversity in Families

Quick Passage of Viagra in Japan Reignites the Birth Control Debate

Masako, a 32-year-old mother of two, was frustrated by the lack of reliable birth control available in Tokyo. Why was she concerned? In Japan, birth control pills were under government review for decades. Meanwhile, the Japanese government took only six months to approve the impotence treatment drug Viagra. This left many people asking why women's need for the birth control pill was less important than men's desire for Viagra.

Advocates of the birth control pill claimed that approval would serve more people and be of greater benefit than Viagra. Women's groups and the media accused the Japanese government of sexism. "When old guys want something, they get it. But when women want something, nothing happens. . . . Japan is still a male-dominated society," says Midori Ashida, who heads a Tokyo-based group that lobbied for acceptance of the birth control pill.

Advocates of the birth control pill finally met with success. Within a few months after the public outcry over the approval of Viagra, the Japanese government decided to allow limited sale of the birth control pill. However, it requires a doctor's prescription and is not covered by public health insurance.

The Health Ministry says the main reason the pill spent so long in review is that the government had concerns about possible side effects. However, more than 300 million women around the world already use birth control pills, and recent studies show few, if any, long-term ill effects.

The Japanese government also claimed to be concerned that acceptance of the birth control pill would cut into the use of condoms and contribute to the spread of HIV/AIDS. Others cited fears about the destruction of moral values. However, the government did not seem concerned with the possible side effects of Viagra for HIV/AIDS transmission, or for declining morality.

Why was Viagra approved so quickly? Takaichi Hirota, a spokesman for Pfizer (which makes the drug), believes the reason is that the company provided hard data on the drug. Others believe the quick passage of Viagra and the slow passage of the birth control pill were more likely related to the Japanese government's goal of raising the nation's rapidly declining birthrate. It is at an all-time low of 1.39 births per woman, and government officials are worried this will increase the proportion of elderly in the population and create a serious financial problem for Japan in the coming decades. Others see it as a vivid example of the sexual double standard in action.

What Do You Think?

1. If you were living in Japan, what would your reaction have been to the quick approval of Viagra, while approval of birth control pills was stalled?

2. What social and cultural factors do you think may account for these policy decisions?

Sources: Hayashi, 2004; Kageyama, 1999; Parker, 1999.

Example of the Double Standard: Confusion over the Source of Women's Pleasure

Sexual intercourse is often viewed as the ultimate sexual act; it is sometimes referred to as "having sex," as though other sexual activities are preliminaries or foreplay. While this makes sense from a procreative standpoint—since sexual intercourse is needed to make babies—it does not make sense to the many women who are more likely to have orgasms from manual or oral stimulation than from sexual intercourse itself.

Many women need additional clitoral stimulation beyond that which is provided in sexual intercourse in order to reach orgasm (Richters, de Visser, Rissel, & Smith, 2006). For example, as shown in Table 5.2 (page 136), a study based on a representative sample of over 19,000 Australians between the ages of 16 and 59 found that half of women did not have an orgasm during their most recent sexual encounter if they had only vaginal intercourse. However, if manual or oral stimulation was included, the odds of women having an orgasm significantly increased. In fact, orgasm was most likely if the sexual encounter did not contain intercourse at all!

This seems to confirm what some people have long suspected. The Hite Report, a nonrepresentative sample, but based on information from over 3,000 women, found that only 26 percent reported experiencing orgasm regularly during intercourse (Hite, 1977).

Table 5.2	**Combinations of Sexual Practices Received and Likelihood of Orgasm at Most Recent Heterosexual Encounter (Percent)**	
Which type of sexual activity is least likely to give women an orgasm?		
Practice	**Percent Who Had Orgasm**	
	Men	**Women**
Vaginal intercourse only	95	50
Intercourse + manual stimulation	95	71
Intercourse + oral stimulation	99	73
Intercourse + manual + oral stimulation	98	86
Manual stimulation only	82	79
Manual + oral stimulation	87	90
Oral stimulation only	Numbers too small to allow reliable estimate	

Source: Richters, Juliet, Richard de Visser, Chris Rissel, and Anthony Smith. 2006. "Sexual Practices at Last Heterosexual Encounter and Occurrence of Orgasm in a National Survey." The Journal of Sex Research 43(3): 217–26.

Yet, women felt so much pressure from their partners to have an orgasm during intercourse that the majority of women reported faking them (Muehlenhard & Shippee, 2009; Langer, Arnett, & Sussman, 2004). Historically, sexologists have often been confused over women's sexuality and the real source of women's pleasure. They have debated between vaginal and clitoral orgasms. Women who did not have orgasms in intercourse were thought to have a "female sexual dysfunction" requiring treatment. Although recent sex researchers have tried to clear up this confusion, even today people seem fairly ignorant about female anatomy, orgasm, and sexual response. If half to three-quarters of women need clitoral stimulation to have an orgasm, why is stimulation often not considered a normal part of sex?

How did you learn your sexual script? Can you think of people or events that shaped your script? Have you ever violated your sexual script? What were the consequences of that violation?

Research now shows us that the clitoris is, in many ways, the female counterpart of the penis. Both organs receive and transmit sexual sensations. However, in sexual intercourse, while the penis receives direct stimulation, the clitoris may receive only indirect stimulation. And while the penis is directly involved in reproduction, the clitoris is unique in serving no known purpose but providing sexual pleasure. It is ironic that many cultures both past and present have viewed women as unresponsive to sexual stimulation, when it is women, not men, who possess a sexual organ apparently devoted solely to providing pleasurable sensations. The double standard is powerful!

:: Studying Human Sexuality

Throughout this text we have shown the importance of research and described how research is conducted, but you might think that something as personal as sexuality would be too difficult to study. Will people really participate in experiments, respond to surveys, participate in lengthy interviews, or subject themselves to observation about sex? Next, let's focus on some of the key pioneers in sex research—**sexology**—and learn about the research methods they used in their work.

Early Pioneers

Sigmund Freud (1856–1939) focused much of his work on the study of the psychosexual development of children and how it affected adult life and mental condition. Freud

sexology: A field comprised of a multidisciplinary group of clinicians, researchers, and educators who study sexuality.

believed we are all born with biologically based sex drives. These drives must be channeled through socially approved outlets, he believed; otherwise, the individual will experience conflict within himself or herself, with the family, or with society at large. Although some of his work is controversial today, it has had a large influence on the field of psychology.

One of the first large surveys on human sexuality was the pioneering work of Alfred Kinsey (1894–1956) and his associates. Kinsey was a professor at Indiana University who was asked to teach a new course in sexuality and marriage in the 1930s. In preparing his lectures, Kinsey was frustrated by the lack of reliable research about sexuality and set out to change this. His work, which brought him great notoriety, includes *Sexual Behavior in the Human Male* (Kinsey, Pomeroy, & Martin, 1948) and *Sexual Behavior in the Human Female* (Kinsey, Pomeroy, & Martin, 1953) (otherwise known as *The Kinsey Reports*), published in the 1940s and 1950s. These reports are based on in-depth interviews with approximately 11,000 men and women and provide a complete sexual history of each respondent. Although they used a nonrandom and biased sample, these data served for decades as a major source of statistics on sexual behavior. The Kinsey Institute, located at Indiana University, remains a major center for research on sexuality today.

Perhaps Kinsey's greatest contribution is the way he moved the discussion of sexual orientation away from a simple dichotomy—the idea that you are either heterosexual or homosexual. Kinsey and his researchers developed a 7-point classification scheme, ranging from 0 (entirely heterosexual) to 6 (entirely homosexual) (Kinsey, Pomeroy, & Martin, 1953). His research showed that a surprising number of people are not really 0's or 6's— meaning entirely heterosexual or entirely homosexual, but instead are somewhat more towards the middle. Many people reported that they had some homosexual experiences, although they continued to think of themselves as heterosexual. Kinsey's work revealed that sexual identity is conceptually distinct from sexual behavior.

The groundbreaking research of William Masters and Virginia Johnson in the 1960s addressed several features of sexuality, including the physiology of human sexual response; a greater understanding of women's sexuality; and the treatment of sexual dysfunction. Rather than relying on Kinsey's survey methods, Masters and Johnson adopted observational designs within a laboratory setting (Maier, 2009). They used sophisticated instruments to measure the physiological responses of nearly 700 individuals during sexual activity. The married couples engaged in intercourse and other forms of mutual stimulation. The unmarried subjects participated in studies that did not require intercourse, such as masturbation. The participants experienced more than 10,000 orgasms in these controlled laboratory experiments! The findings were published in their book *Human Sexual Response* (Masters & Johnson, 1966).

In particular, Masters and Johnson are known for their understanding of the sexual response cycle, which they divided into four states—(1) desire; (2) excitement; (3) orgasm; and (4) resolution—and they found that men and women experience these states in a similar fashion. Their work enlightened us about the source of women's pleasure—the clitoris— and debunked previous myths that some women have orgasms originating in their vaginas. They taught us that, sexually, men and women are far more alike than different.

Contemporary Research in Human Sexuality

The field of sexology is now well developed, and a number of more recent studies offer important information about contemporary sexuality in the United States. In 1992, the National Opinion Research Center and the University of Chicago conducted a large research project based on face-to-face interviews with a random sample of 3,432 U.S. adults ages 18–59. The results are reported in *The Social Organization of Sexuality: Sexual Practices in the United States* (Laumann, Gagnon, Michael, & Michaels, 1994) and *Sex in America: A Definitive Survey* (Michael, Gagnon, Laumann, & Kolata, 1994). The respondents were selected using the same sophisticated sampling techniques as in other social and political research, and 80 percent of those contacted agreed to participate, ensuring findings that are

Popular magazines are consumed with sex—what you and others are or should be doing. Do you think they present a realistic image about sexuality?

far more representative and generalizable to the adult population than previous research. Their study focused on a wide variety of attitudes and behaviors—marital, non-marital, heterosexual, and homosexual—and examined differences by age, racial, ethnic, gender, and class subgroups. Although the sample omitted participants age 60 and over, and therefore does not tell us about the sexual activities of the elderly, it nonetheless gave us the first truly scientific study of sex among a representative sample of younger adults in the United States.

Several other excellent and more recent sources of data about human sexuality use surveys. For example, the *Youth Risk Behavior Survey* (YRBS), conducted every other year for the Centers for Disease Control and Prevention (CDC), measures the prevalence of many health-risk behaviors, including sexual behavior, contraceptive use, risking sexually transmitted diseases, and unintended pregnancy among 14,000 students in grades 9–12. The *National Health and Nutrition Examination Survey* (NHANES) is about the sexual behavior of over 6,000 adults ages 20–59 (Fryar, Hirsch, Porter, Kottiri, Brody, & Louis, 2007). The survey collects data by way of an audio computer-assisted self-interview, which allows respondents to answer questions about sensitive issues in complete privacy. The *National Survey of Family Growth* (NSFG) is another contemporary survey, based on personal interviews conducted in the homes of a national sample of women ages 15–44. Its main purpose is to provide reliable national data on marriage, divorce, contraception, infertility, and the health of women and infants in the United States. Public opinion polls such as *Gallup, NBC News,* and *ABC News* also conduct surveys with representative samples of U.S. adults or teens (Gallup, 2007; NBC News/People Magazine, 2005; ABCNews.com, 2004).

Altogether, these sources reveal important trends regarding sexual behaviors and their changes over time. Let's now turn to some of these trends.

:: Sexual Behaviors

When you are next at your neighborhood grocery store, look at the magazine covers on display. What titles do you read? Here are some examples:

"The Sex Skill Men Adore"
"You've Cheated, Should You Tell?"
"Faking Orgasms: Will He Really Know?"
"Love Your Breasts, Even If They Are Small"
"10 Sex Tips That Will Drive Him Wild"
"New Places to Make It"

Sex! Everybody seems to be doing it. Or are they? What are they doing, with whom are they doing it, and why? The vast majority of adults are monogamous and happy, expressing a desire for emotional commitment and a satisfaction with their sex lives. But what *are* we doing? Table 5.3, based on an *ABC News* poll, gives some interesting clues (Langer, Arnedt, & Sussman, 2004).

Once considered taboo, **oral sex**, oral stimulation of the genitals, has become nearly as common as intercourse among heterosexual, White, young, and more highly educated samples, including adolescents and college students (Chambers, 2007; Halpern-Felsher, Cornell, Kropp, & Tschann, 2005; Prinstein, Meade, &

Table 5.3	Americans' Sexual Behavior (by Percent)

What are Americans up to? More than half have had sex outdoors or discussed fantasies; nearly half of women report that they have faked orgasms.

Sex outdoors	57%
Discuss fantasies	51%
Faked orgasm (women)	48%
Sexually adventurous	42%
First-date sex	29%
Paid for sex (men)	15%
Paid for sex (single men, 30+)	30%
Cheated	16%
Threesome	14%
Sex at work	12%

Source: Langer, Gary, Cheryl Arnedt, and Dalia Sussman. 2004. "Primetime Live Poll: American Sex Survey." Retrieved 9 June 2007 (abcnews.go.com/print?id=156921).

Cohen, 2003). Whites are more likely to engage in and receive oral sex, both **cunnilingus**, oral stimulation of the woman's genitals by her partner, and **fellatio**, oral stimulation of the man's genitals by his partner, than are Blacks and Hispanics (Sterk-Elifson, 1994).

Table 5.4 reveals the number of sexual partners U.S. adults have had, according to a survey by *ABC News* (Langer, Arnett, & Sussman, 2004). Women report a mean (average) number of six sex partners in their lifetimes; men report an average of 20. However, these data are highly skewed because a few men report a very large number of partners. A better gauge is the median, or the midpoint between the high and low. Using this measure, we find that women have a median of three sexual partners, while men have eight.

Blacks report the greatest number of sexual partners. For example, 46 percent of Black men have had 15 or more sexual partners, compared to 27 percent of Whites, and 20 percent of Mexican Americans. In contrast, only 6 percent of Black men claim to have had no more than one sexual partner, compared to 17 percent of White men, and 24 percent of Mexican American men (Fryar, Hirsch, Porter, Kottiri, Brody, & Louis, 2007). Although persons with lower incomes and less education begin sexual activity at a younger age, there is little difference in the number of sexual partners across income and education levels (Fryar, Hirsch, Porter, Kottiri, Brody, & Louis, 2007).

Next let's turn to a discussion of sexual expression throughout our lives, from when we are infants until our old age.

Table 5.4	Number of Sex Partners (by Percent)		
Men have a greater number of sex partners in their lifetimes.			
	All	**Men**	**Women**
One	19%	12%	25%
2–4	25%	16%	33%
5–10	28%	26%	29%
11–20	12%	18%	6%
21+	12%	20%	4%
Mean	13	20	6
Median	5	8	3

Source: Langer, Gary, Cheryl Arnedt, and Dalia Sussman. 2004. "Primetime Live Poll: American Sex Survey." Retrieved 9 June 2007 (abcnews.go.com/print?id = 156921).

:: Sexual Expression throughout Our Lives

We tend to think that only young adults are sexually active. We do not like to acknowledge that our parents are sexual, and are even less inclined to think about our grandparents as sexual beings, or your seven-year-old kid sister. But in reality, we are sexual throughout our lives. ✳ **Explore** on **myfamilylab.com**

Childhood

We know that we become sexual very early in our lives—even infants have been observed to stimulate themselves. We do not just become sexual when we reach puberty (Rathus, Nevid, & Fichner-Rathus, 2011). Newborns have the physiological changes associated with sexual response. Boys as young as a few days can have erections, and girls secrete vaginal lubrication. Young infants and toddlers fondle their genitals for the pleasure it provides.

During early childhood (2 to 6 years), children develop a sense of who they are as girls or as boys and have a good understanding of gendered behavior. They are curious about their bodies and the bodies of others, perhaps even playing "doctor" as a way to explore the genitals of others.

In middle childhood (7 to 11 years), children experiment with masturbation. During the late part of this period, many children will develop their first "crush" or have their first sexual fantasies.

Adolescence (12 to 21 years) is a period when children sexually mature. Increased estrogen will cause girls' breasts and sexual organs to grow, and the average age of menarche is now about 12 years. Among boys the increased androgen sex hormones, testosterone in particular, cause hair growth, voice changes, and growth in size of sexual organs. By the end of middle school or the beginning of high school, most boys and girls have experienced the physiological changes necessary to begin sexual activity. Some do begin sexual activity at this time, although U.S. culture largely frowns upon it.

✳ **Explore** the **Concept**
Social Explorer Report: Lifespan Differences between Men and Women on **myfamilylab.com**

oral sex: The oral stimulation of the genitals.

cunnilingus: The oral stimulation of the woman's genitals by her partner.

fellatio: The oral stimulation of the man's genitals by his partner.

Teenage Sexuality, Pregnancy, and Motherhood

Jake and Lianne met six months ago at a party given by a mutual friend who was celebrating a milestone birthday. It was a warm summer night, and the air, the music, and the drinks were richly intoxicating. He first noticed her hair: long, silky, and nearly jet black. She first noticed his eyes, piercing and

"What began as a casual encounter—a little flirting, a sensuous smile, and a few laughs—has since evolved into much more."

blue. "Who is that?" they both asked themselves. Jake had to find out, and made his move. What began as a casual encounter—a little flirting, a sensuous smile, and a few laughs—has since evolved into much more. They began having a sexual relationship within a month. Jake and Lianne are fifteen.

Figure 5.2	Teenage Sexual Behaviors, Grades 9–12, by Sex

About half of high school students in grades 9-12 have had sexual intercourse, and about one-third are currently sexually active.

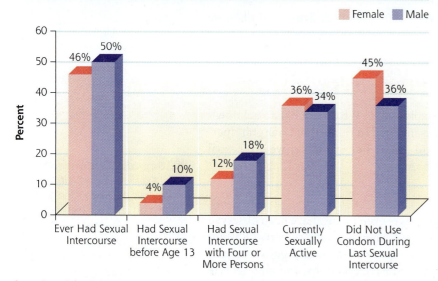

Source: Eaton, Daince K., Laura Kann, Steve Kinchen, Shari Shanklin, James Ross, Joseph Hawkins, William A. Harris, Richard Lowry, Tim McManus, David Chyen, Connie Lim, Nancy D. Brener, and Howell Wechsler. 2008 August 8. Youth Risk Behavior Surveillance—United States, 2007. Technical Report No. Morbidity and Mortality Weekly Report, v. 57, no. SS-4. Atlanta, GA: Centers for Disease Control and Prevention.

Many American adolescents are sexually active, as shown in Figure 5.2 and Figure 5.3. A large study conducted by the CDC with 14,000 students in grades 9–12 shows that 46 percent of girls and 50 percent of boys have had sexual intercourse, including 4 percent of girls and 10 percent of boys who had intercourse before age 13 (Eaton, Kann, Kinchen, Shanklin, Ross, Hawkins, Harris, Lowry, McManus, Chyen, Lim, Brener, & Wechsler, 2008). About one-third of high school boys and girls have a current sexual partner, and over one-third did not use a condom during their last sexual intercourse.

Black teens are more likely to be sexually active than are Hispanics or Whites, and they tend to begin having intercourse at younger ages than other teens. Two-thirds of Black students in grades 6–9 have had sexual intercourse, with 16 percent having intercourse before age 13. Nearly half report being currently sexually active. Reasons for racial and ethnic differences include environmental and socioeconomic issues; for example, Blacks are more likely to have lower incomes and live in poorer neighborhoods, and thus are less likely to be enrolled in supervised after-school programs (Eaton, Kann, Kinchen, Shanklin, Ross, Hawkins, Harris, Lowry, McManus, Chyen, Lim, Brener, & Wechsler, 2008).

By the end of high school, about two-thirds of young men and women have had intercourse. Perhaps surprisingly, among these young adults, boys are slightly more likely to be virgins than are girls (Eaton, Kann, Kinchen, Shanklin, Ross, Hawkins, Harris, Lowry, McManus, Chyen, Lim, Brener, & Wechsler, 2008).

With respect to oral sex, according to a national survey of 13- to 16-year-olds by *NBC News/People Magazine*, 12 percent of young teens have had oral sex. Girls, however, are far more likely to give than to receive: they are four times more likely than boys to report that their partner "never performs oral sex on them" (Chambers, 2007; *NBC News/People Magazine*, 2005). Interestingly, nearly half of young teens do not believe oral sex is "as big a deal" as intercourse and they do not see it as spoiling virginity, although fewer girls feel this way than do boys. Indeed, over one-quarter of adolescents reported oral sex was not even sex.

Teenagers engage in sex for a variety of reasons and in a variety of contexts. Some are in monogamous long-term relationships and see sexuality as a mechanism for expressing their love. Others are in short-term relationships, and some are not in relationships at all, but engage in sex with friends or even strangers for physical gratification, peer pressure, or a desire to be popular.

Most parents are concerned about teenage sexual activity. They worry that their teens are not mature enough to handle sexuality. They fear exploitation of young teenage girls by older boys or men. They are concerned about the spread of disease and infection. They also worry about teenage pregnancy. Unlike other cultures that consider it "normal" for teenage girls to have babies, teenage pregnancy and motherhood are considered major social problems in the United States. We want our teens to have a carefree adolescence—to finish high school, to go to college or complete other training, and to work. Having a baby during the teenage years makes these things difficult to accomplish.

Teenage Pregnancy and Motherhood Nonetheless, about 750,000 U.S. women under age 20 become pregnant each year, resulting in about 435,000 births (Hamilton, Martin, & Ventura, April 2010). The negative consequences of early parenting in the United States have been well documented (Levine, Emery, & Pollack, 2007; The Annie E. Casey Foundation, 2009). Teenage parents are disadvantaged compared to other teens and they are generally unprepared for the financial, social, and psychological challenges of raising children. Teenage mothers are more likely to die in childbirth than are older mothers; their infants are more likely to be of low birth weight and die within the first month of life. Further, teenage mothers are more likely to drop out of school than are other teens, are considerably poorer, and are more likely to receive welfare. Adolescent mothers are also less knowledgeable about child development, less prepared for childrearing, and more likely to be depressed than are other mothers.

Teenage births declined significantly during the 1990s and early 2000s. In 1991, there were 62 births per 1,000 women ages 15–19, but by 2005, births had declined to only 40 per 1,000 women ages 15–19. However, that number began slowly increasing over the next few years to 43 births in 2007. After a few years of rising teen birthrates, the trend is now heading downward again. In 2008 there were 42 births per 1,000 women ages 15–19, as shown in Figure 5.4 (Hamilton, Martin, & Ventura, April 2010). Thus, it appears that teenage birthrates are in a state of flux. However, teenage birthrates for all racial and ethnic groups remain well below what they were in the 1990s, and policymakers and researchers are keeping a close watch on future trends.

There is no single explanation as to why the teenage birthrate may be rising. A large study of high school youth sponsored by the CDC revealed that the likelihood of teens having sex has not changed. What has changed is that those teens who are sexually active are slightly less likely to use birth control, condoms in particular (Santelli, Orr, Lindberg, & Diaz, 2009). Researchers also point to several key factors, including a trend toward early puberty for girls, earlier and more frequent sexual activity, and a decline in contraceptive use

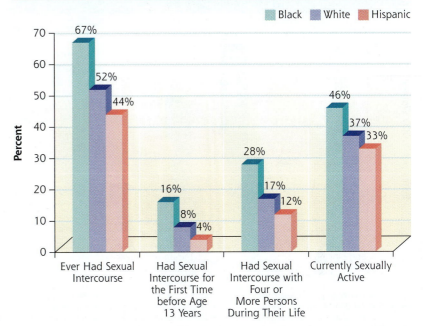

| **Figure 5.3** | **Teenage Sexual Behaviors, Grades 9–12, by Race/Ethnicity** |

Black high school students have the most sexual experience, while Hispanics have the least, with Whites somewhere in between.

Source: Eaton, Dance K., Laura Kann, Steve Kinchen, Shari Shanklin, James Ross, Joseph Hawkins, William A. Harris, Richard Lowry, Tim McManus, David Chyen, Connie Lim, Nancy D. Brener, and Howell Wechsler. 2008 August 8. Youth Risk Behavior Surveillance—United States, 2007. Technical Report No. Morbidity and Mortality Weekly Report, v. 57, no. SS-4. Atlanta, GA: Centers for Disease Control and Prevention.

The teenage birthrate declined among all race and ethnic groups in the 1990s, but has now started to fluctuate.

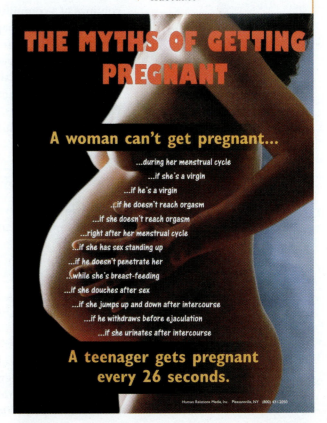

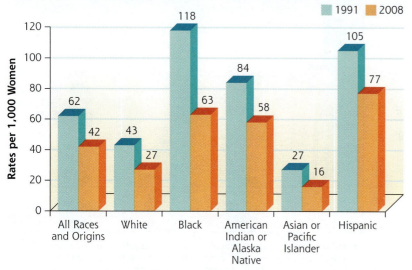

Figure 5.4	**Birthrates for Women Ages 15–19 Years by Race and Ethnicity, United States, 1991–2008**

Teenage birth rates have declined among all groups since 1991, especially among Black teens.

Source: Hamilton, Brady E., Stephanie J. Ventura, Joyce A. Martin, and Paul D. Sutton. 2006. "FInal Births for 2004." Retrieved 13 July 2006. Hyattsville, MD/National Center for Health Statistics (www.cdc.gov/nchs/products/pubs/pubd/hestats/finalbirths04/finalbirths04.htm). Hamilton, Brady E., Joyce A. Martin, and Stephanie J. Ventura. 2009. "Births: Preliminary Data for 2007." Vol. 57, No. 12. Retrieved 18 August 2009. Hyattsville, MD/National Center for Health Statistics (www.cdc.gov/nchs/data/nvsr/nvsr57/nvsr57_12.pdf).

Watch the Video
Core Concepts: Sexuality Education Debate on
myfamilylab.com

Males and females interact more casually now than they did in previous generations. This leads some to engage in casual sex, known today as "hook-ups."

hooking up: Sexual interactions without commitment or even affection for one another.

(The Annie E. Casey Foundation, 2009; Centers for Disease Control and Prevention, 2008). Other factors may include the decreased stigma associated with births outside of marriage and the highly publicized pregnancies of several celebrity teens, the changing economic conditions that diminish educational or job opportunities, and the complacency that followed the decade of progress in reducing teen pregnancy (Holcombe, Peterson, & Manlove, 2009; National Campaign to Prevent Teen and Unplanned Pregnancy, 2009).
Watch on **myfamilylab.com**

Nonmarital Sex and Young Adults

Although teenage sexuality is largely frowned upon in our society, people are far more accepting of nonmarital sex (often referred to as "premarital sex") among young adults. Fifty-nine percent of adults reported that premarital sex is only "sometimes or not at all wrong," according to a nationwide study based on over 2,000 adults. There is, however, a generational gap in these views: 70 percent of people ages 18–24 believe that premarital sex is only sometimes or not at all wrong, but only 40 percent of people age 65 and older agree with that sentiment (Pew Research Center, 2007).

As with teenagers, premarital sex among young adults takes place for a variety of reasons and in a variety of contexts. By age 25, 88 percent of women and 89 percent of men have engaged in premarital sex (Finer, 2007). Note this is higher than the number who believe that premarital sex is not wrong. Again, some young adults have done so within the confines of a committed relationship; others have engaged in more casual sexual encounters. As shown in Chapter 3, dating has evolved from more formal to more informal interactions in recent years, and therefore not surprisingly, sexual relationships have followed suit and sometimes become more casual as well.

One type of casual sexual experience has received widespread attention—**hooking up**, or the casual sexual interactions among people without any expectations of commitment. On college campuses, in dorms, fraternities, and sororities, "hooking up" parties are common, which give young adults the opportunities to engage in sexual acts which may include anything from only kissing to mutual masturbation, oral sex, or sexual intercourse (Bogle, 2008). These sexual encounters are an outgrowth of how young people socialize today. Instead of socializing in dating pairs, young people today socialize in groups. Male-female relations are more casual, sometimes leading to sexual activity among friends or acquaintances. While earlier generations saw dating as the beginning of an intimate relationship, with possible sex to follow, many young people today have sex first, and then possibly date afterwards (Bogle, 2008).

How common is the practice of hooking up? It may be almost as common as dating (Bradshaw, Kahn, & Saville, 2010). One study of over 600 students at a university on the west coast found that 40 percent of the students reported that they have hooked up (England & Thomas, 2007). Another study of 404 students enrolled in an introductory psychology course in a large Southern university noted that 52 percent of males and 36 percent of females reported having engaged in casual sexual relationships (Grello, Welsh, & Harper, 2006).

Potential partners range from strangers to good friends, the latter of which may be referred to as "friends with benefits." Over one-third of respondents in the Southern university study claimed that their most recent casual sexual encounter was with a stranger or someone that they did not know well. The west coast study found that half of the surveyed students had hooked up five or more times; a third said that they had hooked up more than 10 times. While about a third reported that their hook-up did not go any further than kissing and nongenital touching, nearly half reported that their hook-up included either oral sex or sexual intercourse. Alcohol is a big part of hooking up; it decreases inhibitions and encourages people to feel freer to do things they might not otherwise (Grello, Welsh, & Harper, 2006).

Despite the popularity of hooking up, women do not find it as satisfying as men. One study from a midsized university in the Southeast interviewed men and women about their preferences, and found that in most situations women preferred dating over hooking up, while the opposite was true for men—they preferred hooking up over dating (Bradshaw, Kahn, & Saville, 2010). However, let's not overgeneralize. Although men are often portrayed as happy beneficiaries of casual sex, many men, like many women, yearn for a greater emotional connection (Epstein, Calzo, Smiler, & Ward, 2009).

Gay and Lesbian Sexual Relationships

Gay men and lesbians are so often only defined by their sexuality that it is easy to get the mistaken impression that all they ever do is have sex! However, we know that all people—gay, lesbian, heterosexual, and bisexual—lead busy lives, and while sex is important, other things can also take center stage such as work, school, children, and life's daily routine (Peplau & Beals, 2004). Certainly, love, intimacy, and sexual relationships are important to most of us, regardless of sexual orientation. The late researcher Lawrence Kurdek collected extensive information over time to determine how gay and lesbian relationships differ from, or are similar to, heterosexual relationships (Kurdek, 2006, 2008, 2009). Overall, he found that the similarities between heterosexual and homosexual relationships far outweigh the differences. All people value love and commitment, and hope for a good relationship with open and strong communication. Likewise, gays and lesbians engage in the same sexual behaviors as heterosexuals—e.g., kissing, caressing, and oral sex—with the exception of penile-vaginal intercourse, and respondents report no differences in sexual satisfaction.

Nonetheless, research on the sexual and committed relationships of gays and lesbians does reveal some notable differences. First, while most gays and lesbians value monogamous intimate relationships, gay men are more accepting of nonmonogamous relationships than are lesbians or heterosexuals, and, on average, they have more casual sex (Christopher & Sprecher, 2000). Gendered expectations may play a part here, as men have been socialized to initiate sex. Second, lesbians may engage in sex less frequently than gay men or heterosexual women, although this may be a function of the way that "sex" is defined and tabulated (sometimes "sex" is defined as "sexual intercourse"). Third, while both lesbians and gay men link sex with intimacy, lesbians are more likely to emphasize this than are gay men.

Sex in Marriage

Sex in marriage is often the butt of jokes: "Sex in marriage? Now that's an oxymoron." A review of television primetime shows in the early 1990s revealed that less than one in ten sex scenes shown were between married couples (Hanson & Knopes, 1993). Instead, there were six times as many scenes of nonmarital sex. In fact, extramarital sex was portrayed four times as often as sex in marriage. For some reason, the topic of sex in marriage does not seem to be very interesting to most people.

However, most married people are indeed sexually active, and report being quite satisfied with the sexual aspects of their relationship. As one woman said, "As I'm growing older and my husband's growing older, and we're monogamous, it's so pleasant to have one other person that you trust completely. It's a treasure."

How frequently do married couples have sexual relations? While the frequency varies, married couples report having sexual relations about once or twice a week or about six to seven times per month (Christopher & Sprecher, 2001). Younger couples engage in sex more often, older couples less. Most married couples do not consider the decline in frequency of sex to be a major problem. They attribute it to a lack of time or energy because of work and family demands, and to becoming more "accustomed" to one another. A study by the American Association of Retired Persons (AARP) reports that, among men and women ages 45–49 who have a regular sex partner (presumably a spouse, but could be otherwise), 65 percent of men and 61 percent of women report that their sex lives are extremely or very physically pleasurable and 69 percent of men and 62 percent of women report that their sex lives are extremely or very emotionally satisfying. There was little variation across racial or ethnic groups (AARP, May 2005).

Extramarital Sex   Despite the pleasure and intimacy that sex provides to married couples, some married persons have engaged in **extramarital sex**, defined as sex while married with someone who is not your spouse. Other terms commonly used are "affair," "adultery," "infidelity," or "being unfaithful." Americans frown upon extramarital sex, with 78 percent saying that it is always wrong, and another 15 percent saying that it is almost always wrong. Only 2 percent believe that it is not wrong at all (General Social Survey, 2009). Two-thirds of Americans say that they would not forgive their spouse for having an affair, and two-thirds would also seek a divorce (Jones, 2008).

However, as we all know, there are *beliefs*, and there are *behaviors*, and these do not always correspond. The best estimates are that about 3–4 percent of currently married people have a sexual partner besides their spouse in a given year, and about 15 percent of women and 22 percent of men have had a sexual partner other than their spouse at some time while married (Smith, 2006).

Men are somewhat more likely to have extramarital sex, and the longer they live, the more likely they are to do so. According to the National Health and Social Life Survey, based on a representative sample of American adults, 37 percent of men ages 50–59 have had extramarital sex, compared with just 7 percent of men ages 18–29. The men's percentages went up steadily in each age range, whereas for women, differences across age groups were not as large. About 20 percent of older women reported having an affair, but in all other age ranges infidelity hovered between 11 and 15 percent (Downs, 2003). There are many reasons for extramarital sex, including sexual curiosity, a lost sense of fun and excitement in the marriage, an inability to communicate one's own needs and desires, sexual addiction, or boredom with marriage or life in general.

For those involved, especially the spouse of the person who had an affair, feelings of betrayal, hurt, and anger are common (Baucom, Snyder, & Gordon, 2009). Extramarital affairs can also hurt an entire family, including children who are usually incapable of understanding the situation or what led to it, and have little say in how their parents will deal with the aftermath. As the family systems theory introduced in Chapter 1 reminds us, family members are inextricably linked, and what happens between two members is likely to influence the whole group (Ingoldsby, Smith, & Miller, 2003).

Sex and the Elderly

My husband and I probably enjoy sex more today than we did when we were younger. All of our children are now grown up and out of the house, which I'm sure helps our sense of privacy and stress. I don't have to worry about getting pregnant anymore because I'm way past that stage. Also,

"Seriously, I think sex is better now."

our sex seems more affectionate now, if that's possible—what I mean is that the goal isn't just on having your own orgasm, but really relaxing and pleasing the other person. Our sense of love and commitment after all these years really shines through. Seriously, I think sex is better now.

—Carmen, age 62

extramarital sex: Sex, while married, with someone other than your spouse.

A common misperception about the elderly is that they are no longer sexually active. In the college classroom, any discussion of the sexuality of the elderly is largely met with snickers or looks of disbelief. In response, I ask students, "Well, at what age do you plan to give up sex?" Then, I hear gasps of astonishment.

Sexuality remains an essential element of the lives of the elderly (DeLamater & Sill, 2010). The vast majority of elders have a positive view of sexual relationships, and if married or partnered, it is quite likely that they are still sexually active (AARP, May 2005). The AARP conducted a large survey about sexuality in midlife and beyond, based on a sample of over 1,600 older adults. Three-quarters of men ages 60–69 who have a regular sexual partner reported engaging in sexual touching or caressing at least once a week over the previous six months, and nearly half reported engaging in sexual intercourse at least weekly. Among men age 70 and older, about one-third reported having sexual intercourse weekly or more. Many also engage in oral sex.

Another study based on a random sample of over 3,000 adults ages 57–85 reported similar conclusions, as shown in Figure 5.5 (Lindau, Schumm, Laumann, Levinson, O'Muircheartaigh, & Waite, 2007). Although the likelihood of sexual activity does decline with age, 39 percent of men ages 75–85 are still sexually active, as are 17 percent of women. A primary reason that the figures are not higher than this is simply that no partner is available: rates of widowhood are high.

It appears that it is time to debunk the myth that the elderly are asexual!

People often assume that the elderly are not sexually active, but that could not be further from the truth.

:: Sexual Satisfaction in Committed Relationships

How important is sex in a committed, loving relationship? For most men and women, there is a positive relationship between sexual satisfaction and overall relationship satisfaction, commitment, and stability regardless of whether we are talking about heterosexual, gay, or, lesbian relationships (Harvey, Wenzel, & Sprecher, 2004; Schwartz, 2007). Both the quality and quantity of sex in a committed relationship is associated with feelings of love for one's spouse or partner.

A large study with a random sample of the adult U.S. population (Schwartz, 2007) found that a large majority of married individuals reported feeling extremely or very satisfied in their sexual relationship and reported having feelings of love and intimacy after engaging in sexual behaviors. However, it appears that the relationship between sexual satisfaction and the quality of the overall relationship is somewhat stronger for men than for women. While men are more likely to feel that a poor sex life undermines the entire relationship, women are more likely to feel that a relationship can still be good even if the sex life is not so great.

Other differences between men and women exist as well, related to the gendered nature of our sexual scripts (Sprecher, 2002; Byers, 2005). For example, among women, increased relationship satisfaction leads to increased sexual satisfaction, but among men, increased sexual satisfaction leads to increased relationship satisfaction. Why the difference?

| Figure 5.5 | Elderly Who Have Been Sexually Active with a Partner in Last 12 Months |

The elderly are sexually active. Older males are more likely to be sexually active than are older females because females are often widowed.

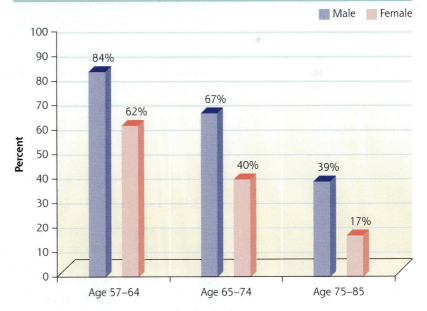

Source: Lindau, Stacy T., L. Philip Schumm, Edward O. Laumann, Wendy Levinson, Colm A. O'Muircheartaigh, and Linda J. Waite. 2007. "A Study of Sexuality and Health Among Older Adults in the United States." New England Journal of Medicine 357 (23 August): 762–74.

Why do you think that people find it hard to believe that the elderly are sexual? Where did these attitudes come from? Do you think these attitudes are found throughout the world? Why or why not?

Tying It All Together

Factors That Shape Teenage Sexuality

Why are so many teenagers sexually active? It's easy to just say, "because they want to be." While that may be true to some extent, the reason is far more complex. To really understand teenage sexuality, we must look at a number of different micro- and macro-level factors.

Micro-level Factors Influencing Teenage Sexuality

- Sexual desire
- Love, or the desire to please a partner
- Wanting to have a baby
- Manipulation
- Lack of information about how pregnancy is prevented

Macro-level Factors Influencing Teenage Sexuality

- Sexual attitudes and behaviors differ across cultures (the United States has the highest rate of teenage pregnancy of any developed country)
- Sexual attitudes and behaviors change over time (the teenage pregnancy rate has declined significantly since 1990)
- Social institutions channel and direct sexuality (the United States defines teenage pregnancy and births as problematic and tries to reduce them through sex education programs in the schools, yet at the same time our economic system sexualizes teens and children)

Men's sexual scripts focus on sexual behavior first, relationships second; while women are encouraged to think of the relationship first. Good communication is important to all aspects of a couple's relationship; their sex life is no exception. Open communication is not always easy, but it significantly contributes to both relationship and sexual satisfaction, and brings couples closer together. It is important that each partner feels comfortable expressing his or her sexual needs, wants, and desires. Openness, honesty, respect, and integrity are critical in strong intimate relationships (American Psychological Association, 2005).

An important theme in this chapter is that our sexual norms, attitudes, and behaviors are influenced by the social world in which we live and the human groups to which we belong. In other words, micro-level factors and macro-level factors intertwine with biology to influence how we engage sexually with others. Using teenage sexuality as an example, the *Tying It All Together* feature box summarizes the importance of these dual factors.

:: Sex as a Social Problem: Sexually Transmitted Infections

Millions of Americans currently have at least one sexually transmitted infection (STI), and an additional 19 million people become infected each year (Centers for Disease Control and Prevention, November 13, 2009). STIs include chlamydia, genital human papillomavirus (HPV), herpes, trichomoniasis, gonorrhea, syphilis, pelvic inflammatory disease (PID), and HIV/AIDS. About one in four girls between the ages of 14 and 19 in the United States is infected with at least one of the most common sexually transmitted diseases.

Although people might be inclined to think of STIs as personal problems, they affect large numbers of people and are social problems. Our ideas about family privacy and personal shame tend to exacerbate our misunderstanding of STIs, allowing them to spread at alarming rates and inhibiting effective treatment.

Despite the fact that STIs are widespread and can strike people of any age, sex, or sexual orientation, most people remain unaware of the risks and consequences of all but the most publicized—HIV and AIDS. However, other STIs are far more prevalent in the population. Genital HPV is estimated to be the most common STI, with at least 50 percent of sexually active men and women acquiring genital HPV infection at some point in their lives. Chlamydia is the most commonly reported STI, with 2.3 million people infected, and over one million new cases a year; however, even more go undiagnosed (Centers for Disease Control and Prevention, November 13, 2009).

Although STIs like chlamydia and genital HPV are widespread across all racial and ethnic groups, average STI rates tend to be higher among Blacks than Whites. We can attribute some of this difference to differences in risky behaviors (beginning sexual intercourse at an earlier age, having multiple partners, engaging in unprotected intercourse, having a higher level of drug use) and social conditions like poverty and limited access to health care. However, part of the disparity is because Blacks are more likely to seek health care in public clinics, which report STIs more thoroughly than do private providers (Centers for Disease Control and Prevention, November 13, 2009). Consequently, the statistics may actually underreport the rates among Whites.

How should education about STIs be targeted to young people to be most effective?

Genital HPV

Genital HPV is the most common STI in the United States, with about 20 million Americans currently infected, and another 6.2 million people becoming newly infected each year (Centers for Disease Control and Prevention, November 13, 2009). There are more than 40 different types of genital HPV infections, but in all cases the virus infects the skin and mucous membranes. You cannot see HPV symptoms; therefore, most people who become infected are not even aware they contracted the disease.

Fortunately, most people with HPV do not develop symptoms or health problems. In 90 percent of cases, the body's immune system clears the HPV infection naturally within two years. However, for others, HPV can cause genital warts or certain cancers, most commonly, cervical cancer. About 11,000 women develop cervical cancer each year (Centers for Disease Control and Prevention, November 13, 2009). It can also cause cancers of the vulva, vagina, anus, and penis, which usually are not detected until they are quite advanced.

How can genital HPV be prevented? One method is to avoid have sex with an infected person; however, most people do not know that they are infected, making this method extremely unreliable. Condoms may lower the risk; however, a condom may not fully cover the infected area. Another, more controversial method is a new vaccine that can protect females from the four types of HPV that cause most cervical cancers and genital warts—controversial because it is recommended for girls as young as 11 and 12 years old, and it is also expensive.

HIV and AIDS

Acquired immune deficiency syndrome (AIDS) is caused by infection with the human immunodeficiency virus (HIV) and passed from one person to another through blood-to-blood transmission, through sexual contact, and through pregnancy, delivery, or breastfeeding. HIV and AIDS receive more media attention than any other STI because they are so deadly, and because of the political implications surrounding their discovery and treatment (they were originally labeled a "gay" disease).

History and Development   In the early 1980s, physicians in a number of U.S. cities began to notice that numerous cases of rare diseases were occurring among otherwise strong and healthy men. Kaposi's sarcoma, a type of cancer of the blood vessels, and Pneumocystis carinii pneumonia, a usually mild lung infection, had become deadly diseases in the gay male population because of a breakdown in the immune system. It was given the name AIDS even before the virus responsible (HIV) was discovered.

At first AIDS seemed to be confined to few groups: gay men, people with hemophilia, and Haitians. Some have argued that because the disease seemed not to run through the entire population, but through groups that faced stigma and discrimination, the government was slow to act (Shilts, 1987). As Pat Buchanan, a conservative leader and former U.S. presidential hopeful said, "The poor homosexuals—they have declared war upon nature and now nature is exacting an awful retribution" (Strong, DeVault, Sayad, & Yarber, 2002).

Scientists identified a type of chimpanzee in West Africa as the source of HIV infection in humans. The virus most likely jumped to humans when they hunted these chimpanzees for meat and came into contact with their infected blood. Over several years, the virus slowly spread across Africa and later into other parts of the world. Since then, HIV/AIDS has become one of the greatest public health challenges both nationally and globally. Throughout the world, tens of millions of people have died, including nearly 600,000 in the United States (Centers for Disease Control and Prevention, November 13, 2009).

More than 1.1 million people in the United States have HIV/AIDS, about half with full-blown AIDS. No cure has yet been found, and many will die as a result.

Current Status   More than 1.1 million persons are living with HIV/AIDS in the United States, about half with full-blown AIDS. Some people mistakenly believe it is no longer a problem; however, the CDC estimates there are 56,000 new cases of HIV each year (Centers for Disease Control and Prevention, October 19, 2009). Nearly three-quarters of new HIV/AIDS diagnoses are males, who are most likely to get HIV/AIDS through male-to-male sexual contact, whereas females are most likely to contract the disease through heterosexual contact, as shown in Figure 5.6.

Minority groups have been particularly hard-hit by HIV/AIDS. For example, Blacks comprise only 12 percent of the U.S. population, but they represent about half of newly reported HIV/AIDS cases; Hispanics represent 14 percent of the population, but account for 18 percent of the new AIDS cases reported (Centers for Disease Control and Prevention, October 19, 2009). To be particularly effective in minority communities, the CDC recommends that prevention programs be culturally sensitive. While race and ethnicity alone are not risk factors for HIV and AIDS, underlying social and economic conditions such as higher rates of poverty, substance abuse, limited access to health care, cultural diversity, and language barriers may increase the risk of infection. Moreover, some Black and Hispanic men are in denial; because Black and Hispanic men who have sex with other men tend to identify themselves as heterosexual, they may not relate to prevention messages geared towards men who identify as homosexual (Centers for Disease Control and Prevention, August 3, 2008).

The number of AIDS deaths has decreased slightly, and the number of persons living with HIV/AIDS has increased because of promising HIV treatments that have slowed the progression from HIV to AIDS. Nonetheless, there remains no known cure, and about 14,000 men and women will die this year in the United States alone (Centers for Disease Control and Prevention, October 19, 2009).

As devastating as HIV/AIDS is in the United States, the picture here is dwarfed by that in other parts of the world, where 33.4 million people today are infected, and 25 million have already died (UNAIDS and World Health Organization, November 2009). Particularly hard hit is sub-Saharan Africa; with just over 10 percent of the world's population, it is home to more than 67 percent of persons with HIV (UN-AIDS and World Health Organization, November 2009). Five percent of the adult population in sub-Saharan Africa is infected, and the number is increasing.

Unlike the United States, where most HIV/ AIDS victims are men who have sex with other men, heterosexual women and girls are most vulnerable in sub-Saharan Africa. Power imbalances make it difficult for women to protect themselves from their husbands, who often have multiple sex partners. Moreover, young women and girls may become infected through "survival sex"—having sex with older men for a promise of food or shelter. Men seek out young girls because of the widespread myth that sex with a virgin can cure HIV. The United Nations insists that increasing the status of women and girls is a primary strategy for fighting HIV/AIDS throughout the world (UNAIDS and World Health Organization, November 2009).

Meanwhile, HIV/AIDS is wreaking havoc on families. More than 14 million children have been orphaned in sub-Saharan Africa alone because of AIDS, and this number is expected to jump to 18 million by the end of 2010. These children are fighting to survive, according to the United Nations Secretary-General Special Envoy for HIV/AIDS in Africa:

> ... in Zambia, we were taken to a village where the orphan population was described as out of control. As a vivid example of that, we entered a home and encountered the following: to the immediate left of the door sat the 84-year-old patriarch, entirely blind. Inside the hut sat his two wives, visibly frail, one 76, and the other 78. Between them they had given birth to nine children; eight were now dead and the ninth, alas, was clearly dying. On the floor of the hut, jammed together with barely room to move or breathe, were 32 orphaned children ranging in age from two to sixteen. . . . It is now commonplace that grandmothers are caregivers for orphans (cited in AVERT.ORG. 2010 "How May Gay People Are There?" Retrieved 14 February 2010 (www.avert.org/gay-people.htm)).

Many children are now cared for by aging and frail grandparents, while others are left to fend for themselves, as described in the feature box *My Family: Apiwe.*

Figure 5.6	**Transmission Categories of Adults and Adolescents with HIV/AIDS Diagnosed During 2007**

Most males contract HIV though male-to-male sexual contact; whereas most females contract HIV though heterosexual contact.

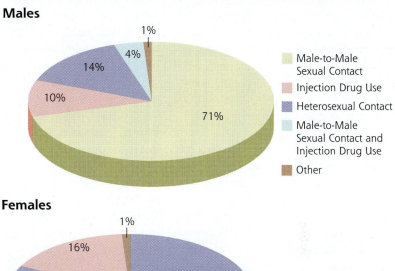

Males

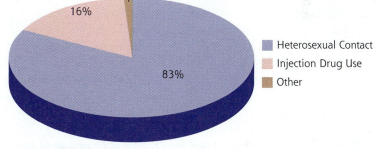

Females

Source: Centers for Disease Control and Prevention, August 21, 2009.

How has the world changed because of HIV/AIDS? How have relationships and families changed? On a micro-level, how do you think HIV/AIDS has affected your intimate relationships?

My Family

Apiwe

Apiwe is already a well-known thief in her community. She mostly steals food from gardens or from the local stores. Sometimes when people catch her they give her a good beating—many of them are hungry too—but Apiwe is lucky today. "Shoo, get away," said the farmer's wife, calling her a foul name, and chasing her with a broom, yet letting Apiwe keep what she has taken. All in all, it was a good day, and she and her sister will have food to eat tonight.

Apiwe is 12 years old and is responsible for the complete care of herself and her 7-year-old sister. They are two of the 14 million children who have been orphaned by AIDS in sub-Saharan Africa, and they are testimony to the devastation that HIV/AIDS is causing in this part of the world. They live in their parents' house, a one-room shack that was rickety in the best of times, but is decaying further from lack of care. Apiwe misses her parents and does not really understand

how they got "that" disease—the disease everyone whispers about. Her father died first, several years ago, withering away slowly and painfully. Her mother soon fell weak, and Apiwe quit school to care for her until she died last year. "That disease" is highly stigmatized and no one talks about why they died. Apiwe has no place to go for answers to her questions.

The number of children orphaned by AIDS is increasing at an unprecedented rate, as shown in Figure 5.7. Without AIDS, the percentage of children who are orphans would be expected to decline in number because of general improvements in health, but AIDS has changed all this. As more parents develop AIDS and die, the number of orphans will continue to rise rapidly.

Apiwe and her sister live in a resource-poor environment made even more perilous by the death of their parents. Basic needs like schooling, food, shelter, clothing, and healthcare have

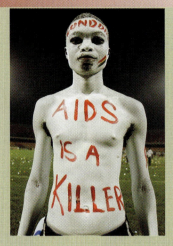

Five percent of adults in Sub-Saharan Africa have HIV/AIDS—that is one out of every 20 adults. When they die, they leave behind their children.

disappeared. The sisters beg on the streets, hoping for a coin here and there, and steal food when they can. Some days are more successful than others.

A "nice" older man has been paying attention to Apiwe lately. Apiwe thinks that he must be rich because he gives her two shiny coins every time he comes by. He has even invited her to his house, offering to "take care of her," he says with a sly grin. Apiwe does not want to go to his house. The man says her sister cannot come, and Apiwe will not leave her alone. Besides, she has an idea of what the man will do to her, and she does not want to make a baby. But some days, when she and her sister are really hungry, she wonders whether it would be so bad. Yes, there would be one more mouth to feed, but maybe this man would help all of them.

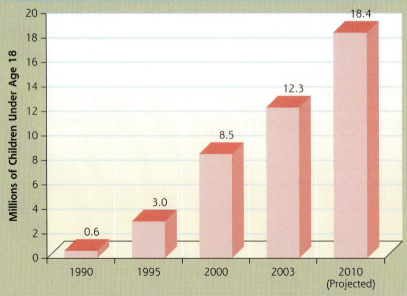

Figure 5.7

Increase in Children Orphaned by AIDS in Sub-Saharan Africa, 1990–2010

The number of AIDS orphans in sub-Saharan Africa is skyrocketing, increasing from 8.5 million to over 18 million in just 10 years.

Millions of Children Under Age 18

1990	1995	2000	2003	2010 (Projected)
0.6	3.0	8.5	12.3	18.4

Note: Estimate of children who lost at least one parent to an AIDS-related cause.

Source: UNAIDS, UNICEF, & USAID, 2004.

What Do You Think?

1. What type of stigma do Apiwe and her sister face? What types of dangers may lie ahead for them?

2. What can be done to help Apiwe, her sister, and the millions of other AIDS orphans? To what degree is the United States helping with this crisis?

Sources: AVERT.ORG, December 22, 2009; UNAIDS and World Health Organization, 2009.

Bringing It Full Circle

What could be more personal than sex? Yet on the other hand, what seems to command as much public attention? Television shows, blogs, magazines, and other media blare out their entertainment, opinions, and advice. They offer us a definition of normalcy—*who* we should have sex with, *what* we should do, *where* we should have sex, *how often* we should have sex, and *why* we should have sex. They influence Chris and Kayla, and they influence you. These sexual scripts are rooted in macro-level social, cultural, and historical arrangements. Based on what you have learned in this chapter, let's go back to the opening vignette and answer a few questions about our sexual scripts and the double standard:

- Chris believes that a double standard still exists, but Kayla has her doubts. Are your views more similar to Chris's or to Kayla's? In general, do you think that men and women see the double standard differently?

- What experience, if any, do you have with a double standard? What consequences have you experienced?

- If you wanted to research the double standard, which research method introduced in Chapter 1 would you use, and why?

For further review, turn to the Video Discussion Guide on page 449 to answer additional questions about how the chapter opening video relates to what you have learned in this chapter.

Chapter Review

5.1 Is sexuality purely biological?

Sexuality contains biological, personal, and social components. We cannot understand sex apart from our membership in human groups.

5.2 How do macro-level factors influence sexuality?

Human behavior, including norms surrounding sexuality, varies around the world and at different points in history. Your sex, race, and social class also shape your sexual values, behaviors, opportunities, and constraints.

5.3 What is the difference between "sex" and "gender"?

Sex refers to the biological differences and our role in reproduction, whereas gender refers to culturally and socially constructed differences associated with masculinity or femininity.

5.4 Do sex and gender go together?

What we define as feminine and masculine can vary dramatically from one culture to the next or from one historical period to the next. Also some people are transgender: their physical sex and their gendered feelings do not match in the predicted fashion.

5.5 What do we mean by "sexual orientation"?

We are referring to the sexual and romantic partner of choice. Kinsey's early work showed that sexual orientation exists on a continuum from completely heterosexual to completely homosexual. While the number of people who are exclusively homosexual is small, many people lie somewhere in between these two polar points. Those individuals who are bisexual are attracted to both males and females.

5.6 What are sexual scripts, and where do we learn them?

Sexual scripts are the norms regarding sexual behavior. They act as a blueprint, informing us what is expected and appropriate, and what is considered inappropriate or taboo. We learn our sexual scripts from the culture in which we live, including our parents, our friends, the mass media, and the dominant religion, as well as the interpersonal communication between us and our partner as we begin, and attend to, our personal relationship.

5.7 Are sexual scripts different for men and women?

Yes. We refer to this difference as "the double standard." Men are allowed far more latitude in sexual behavior than are women. Men are expected to be assertive in seeking sexual behavior, to be always ready for sex, and to have more sexual partners; they are rewarded socially for "scoring." Women, in contrast, are to walk a fine line between being "sexy," and yet not "too sexy." They must be careful to appear interested, but not too interested, in sex.

5.8 What are some important studies that have been done on human sexuality?

A number of excellent studies of human sexuality give us keen insights into values and sexual behaviors, including Freud's work in the late 19th century, Kinsey's work in the 1940s and 1950s, Masters and Johnson's work in the 1970s, and more recently, work by organizations such as the Centers for Disease Control and Prevention (CDC) and popular media polls. The most useful studies rely on large and representative samples.

Key Terms

bisexual (p. 128)
cunnilingus (p. 139)
double standard (p. 132)
extramarital sex (p. 144)
fellatio (p. 139)

heterosexual (p. 128)
homophobia (or anti-gay prejudice) (p. 131)
homosexual (p. 128)
hooking up (p. 142)

intersexed (p. 127)
masturbation (p. 125)
menarche (p. 125)
oral sex (p. 138)
sexology (p. 136)

sexual orientation (p. 128)
sexual scripts (p. 131)
transgender (p. 127)
transsexual (p. 127)

5.9 When do we become sexual?

We know that we become sexual very early in our lives—even infants have been observed to stimulate themselves. Newborns have the physiological changes associated with sexual response.

5.10 How big a social problem is teenage pregnancy?

Approximately 750,000 teens become pregnant each year in the United States, and about 420,000 give birth. However, there is much good news. The teen pregnancy, abortion, and birthrates are at their lowest points since they were first measured in the early 1970s. Declines are seen among both younger and older teens, and across all racial and ethnic groups.

5.11 How prevalent is nonmarital sex among young adults?

Nonmarital (or premarital) sex among young adults takes place for a variety of reasons and in a variety of contexts. By age 25, 88 percent of women and 89 percent of men have engaged in nonmarital sex. Some young adults engage in casual sex, or "hooking up." Studies of college students reveal that somewhere between 30-50 percent report to have engaged in "hook-ups."

5.12 What are some common sexual trends in marriage?

It may be the butt of jokes, but apparently most married people are sexually active on a regular basis and are happy with the frequency of sex and its intimacy.

5.13 Do people remain sexual throughout their lives?

Yes. If your grandparents are married or partnered, it is likely that they have remained sexually active. A study by AARP found, for example, three-quarters of men ages 60–69 who have a regular sexual partner reported engaging in sexual touching or caressing at least once a week over the previous six months, and nearly half reported engaging in sexual intercourse at least weekly.

5.14 What is the most common STI?

Genital human papillomavirus (HPV) is the most common STI, with over 20 million currently affected and over 6 million new cases a year; however, chlamydia is the disease most often reported.

5.15 Hasn't the issue of HIV and AIDS been resolved by now?

Unfortunately, no. In the United States alone there are about 56,000 new cases every year, and about 14,000 people die annually. HIV and AIDS are particularly devastating in sub-Saharan Africa.

PEARSON myfamilylab
www.myfamilylab.com

Experience, Discover, Observe, Evaluate

MyFamilyLab is designed just for you. Each chapter features a pre-test and post-test to help you learn and review key concepts and terms. Experience Marriage and Family in action with dynamic visual activities, videos, and readings to enhance your learning.

Here are a few activities you'll find for this chapter:

Watch Core Concepts video clips feature sociologists in action, exploring important concepts in the study of Marriage and the Family. Watch:
- Sexuality Education Debate
- Alternative Sexual Orientation

Explore Social Explorer is an interactive application that allows you to explore Census data through interactive maps. Explore the Social Explorer Report:
- Lifespan Differences between Men and Women

Read MySocLibrary includes primary source readings from classic and contemporary sociologists. Read:
- Mead, "Sex and Temperament in Three Tribes"

t one time or another we have probably all said:

> *"That's not what I said!"*
> *"You're not listening to me!"*
> *"That's not what I mean!"*
> *"I don't know what you're talking about!"*
> *"You don't understand!"*

We have been communicating since we were born, and using words combined into sentences to make our needs and wants known since we were toddlers. Why then is communication sometimes so tricky? Why do we find it difficult to express what we mean? Why do other people have such trouble receiving our messages? In addition to our verbal and nonverbal communication, we live in an increasingly fast-paced, technology-oriented, diverse society. On any given morning, you may have uploaded some pictures to Facebook, texted your friends, emailed your mom, Skyped your Spanish-speaking pen pal in Mexico, and sent a fax off for your graduate school application. What are we to make of all this communication?

:: The Importance of Communication

Communication is an interactive process, using symbols like words and gestures to both send and receive messages. Each person brings to the process his or her own life history, assumptions, and interpretations. We communicate verbally and nonverbally (Dunn & Goodnight, 2011; Tubbs & Moss, 2008), and these forms of communication do not always send the same messages; for instance, we may smile while criticizing someone. Communication professors Richard West and Lynn Turner have summarized the general concepts of communication (2006):

- *Communication is a transaction:* all human behavior is a continuous exchange, and partners are simultaneously senders and receivers of messages.
- *Communication is a process:* it is dynamic and always changing, and culture, race, ethnicity, and sex are critical.
- *Communication includes co-construction of meanings:* each partner speaks a language and interprets meaning in a way acquired from his or her family of orientation.
- *Communication uses symbols:* to construct meanings or definitions, we rely on symbols that can be verbal like words or nonverbal like gestures.

It is no wonder expressing yourself, being understood, and understanding others can be challenging at times! Yet good communication is particularly important for marriage and other intimate relationships (Galvin, Bylund, & Brommel, 2008; Smith & Wilson, 2009). Most marital problems stem from ineffective communication (Okun, 2002). The *Getting to Know Yourself* feature box gives you the opportunity to assess the communication in your current or most recent relationship.

When we think about communication as an interactive transaction, we are focusing on the micro-level aspects of the process. But communication is also steeped in our social structure.

:: The Cultural Context of Communication: Embracing Difference

In this text, we have discussed a few of the fundamental ways that people differ from one another, and the ways in which these differences manifest themselves in family and intimate relationships. Our sex, social class, race, and ethnicity, for example, contribute to an overall perspective that influences how we relate to others as friends, as partners, as spouses, and as parents. This includes how we communicate with each other.

communication: An interactive process that uses symbols like words and gestures to both send and receive messages.

Getting to Know Yourself

How Do You Communicate?

Think about the communication style you have in your current (or most recent) relationship. An answer of T (True) indicates that item usually applies to your relationship, (S) if it sometimes applies, and F (False) if it rarely or never applies. Consult the scoring key after you finish to get an assessment of your communication patterns.

1. Disagreements almost never occur in our relationship.   T S F
2. We consider ourselves to be best friends.   T S F
3. When we get angry, at least one of us uses profanity.   T S F
4. At least one of us tends to keep feelings bottled up inside until we cannot take it anymore.   T S F
5. We both feel free to talk about anything with each other.   T S F
6. I can trust my partner with my sensitive feelings, and he or she trusts me.   T S F
7. When we argue, someone ends up with hurt feelings.   T S F
8. We try to be truthful and honest with each other.   T S F
9. We mutually express our love for one another.   T S F
10. It is easy for us to forgive if we offend one another.   T S F
11. My partner always interrupts me, or complains that I interrupt.   T S F
12. We often blame and accuse one another.   T S F
13. There is give-and-take in our interactions.   T S F
14. At least one of us really hates conflict.   T S F
15. One of us inevitably gets his or her way even at the other's expense.   T S F
16. We are very competitive with one another.   T S F

Scoring Key

First, give yourself 2 points for each statement that you answered this way: 1=F; 2=T; 3=F; 4=F; 5=T; 6=T; 7=F; 8=T; 9=T; 10=T; 11=F; 12=F; 13=T; 14=F; 15=F; 16=F.

Second, give yourself 1 point for each S answer.

Then, total your points; the higher the score, the better the communication.

What Do You Think?

1. Look at the items you missed and discuss them with your partner. Would improvement in these areas enhance the overall communication in the relationship?
2. Do the findings from this assessment accurately reflect you, your expectations, and your experiences? Why or why not?

Race, Ethnicity, and Communication

Since we are more likely to interact with people who are like ourselves, it is not surprising that members of a particular social class, race, or ethnic group develop their own ways of communicating through words, gestures, or expressions (Allen, 2004). For example, linguists have documented substantial differences between Standard American English (SAE), variants of which are spoken by Whites and some Blacks in the United States, and African American English (AAE), variants of which are spoken by many Blacks, especially in the South. These linguistic differences include actual words, syntax, acoustics, and rules for subject-verb agreement (Clopper & Pisoni, 2004). Listeners can identify a speaker's race from his or her speech, even if only hearing short snippets of speech (Grogger, 2009; Thomas & Reaser, 2004), and this identification has been used to discriminate against Blacks. For example, a study that asked Black- and White-sounding telephone callers to

There are significant racial, ethnic, and social class differences in speech patterns and nonverbal communication.

📖 **Read** the **Document**
Talking Past Each Other: Black and White Languages of Race on **myfamilylab.com**

Sapir-Whorf hypothesis: The concept that language shapes our culture, and at the same time, our culture shapes our language.

inquire about an advertised apartment for rent found that Black-sounding callers were more likely than White-sounding callers to be told the apartment was already rented (Massey & Lundy, 2001).

Racial differences in speech patterns also help explain the gap in wages between Blacks and Whites (Grogger, 2009). Audio data from a random sample of 402 Black and White respondents from the National Longitudinal Survey of Youth were used to assess the relationship between the sound of a respondent's speech and his or her wages. Participants were recruited to listen to the audio excerpts and provide their perceptions of a number of speaker characteristics, including his or her race. Nearly 84 percent of the White speakers were accurately identified by the listeners, as were about 77 percent of the Black speakers. The study found that Blacks with racially distinct speech earned lower wages than did Whites. However, Blacks who did not use racially distinct speech had wages equal to those of Whites. The wage gap persisted even when taking skill level, education, family structure, and income into account (Grogger, 2009). The results show that speech patterns are highly correlated with wages among young Black workers.

Nonverbal messages also differ across racial and ethnic groups. Roberto, for example, is referred for special education testing by his fourth-grade teacher because he seems inattentive in class and barely makes eye contact with her when she speaks (McGee, 2008). She assumes that Roberto is "tuned out." However, Roberto is only being respectful as many children from Latin American, Native American, and Asian cultures avoid making eye contact with authority figures. Thus, to stare at a teacher could be construed as a sign of disrespect, or of "showing off." 📖 **Read** on **myfamilylab.com**

Social Class and Communication

The pioneering work of Basil Bernstein and William Labov on social class and linguistics also showed substantial differences in how language is used by different groups (Bernstein, 1960, 1973; Labov, 1966, 1972). For example, members of the working class tend to speak less Standard American English (SAE), use more words of simple coordination such as "like" or "but," and use fewer pronouns compared to the middle and upper-middle classes (Bernstein, 1973; Lakoff, 2000; Macaulay, 2005; Wardhaugh, 2010). The *Diversity in Families* feature box describes a young working-class woman's realization that she spoke differently from her college peers. Although some sociolinguists question the utility of traditional conceptualizations of social class (Mallinson & Dodsworth, 2009), it is widely recognized that people with different levels of income, education, and occupational prestige communicate in different ways. At the same time, groups sometimes "break code"—they know what SAE is and can weave in and out of it when it suits their interests (Bernstein, 1973). Even President Obama has given speeches with two different linguistic styles: one for a mostly upper-middle-class White audience in which he closely followed SAE, and one for an audience comprised of Black working-class "brothers," in which his accent, word choice, and tone all differed.

Cultural Differences

Culture is another macro-level factor that shapes our communication. In the early part of the 20th century, anthropologist Edward Sapir and his student Benjamin Whorf noticed that language shapes our culture, and at the same time, our culture shapes our language. This is known as the **Sapir-Whorf hypothesis** (Sapir, 1949). These anthropologists studied the language patterns of several different cultural groups and found, for example,

Diversity in Families

Learning to Speak SAE

Okay, here's the deal: I'm a working class girl done good. Please allow me to rephrase that. I would like to share that I am a highly successful woman who has roots in the working class. Do you see the difference in these two ways of speaking? My words, syntax, tones, even gestures change depending on the group I'm with. It hasn't always been that way.

I was raised in a working class family with notoriously bad grammar. Around them parts we said "ain't," as in "I ain't hungry no more," and "fixin," as in "Hey Janey, you fixin' to get to the store soon?" We all spoke this way in my family, as did many people within my community, so I really wasn't aware that my grammar was incorrect. I don't even remember my teachers calling me on it.

Things changed drastically when I went to college. Because I did well in high school, I had the fortunate opportunity to attend a prestigious college in the Northeast. I would like to say that I loved the experience, but the culture shock was so overwhelming that I might as well have landed on Mars. In particular, I noticed that people did not speak the same way I did. They didn't have my accent, they used different words, and they used those words in a different pattern. I immediately felt inadequate.

One incident stands out in particular: In one of my math classes I wanted to ask the professor to expand upon his explanation, so I simply asked "How come?" He stared at me. "How come?" he repeated. Then he said it again more loudly than the first, "HOW COME?" The class snickered. At first I didn't catch what they were laughing about. But then it came to me, "I mean, why?" I gulped. Later that day I withdrew from the class.

That same day I also went to the English department and asked the secretary if the department offered any English tutors "for, you know, people who talk differently." She was a sweet lady, "Oh, you mean for people who have English as a second language? Sure honey, let me get you a list." I didn't dare tell her that I was looking for a tutor for me. But I contacted the first name on the list, Darcy, and I am forever grateful. She taught me to speak "Standard American English," as she called it. We met weekly for an entire year, and I practiced almost daily. The drills included verbal and nonverbal communication, as well as the written word.

I can now easily pass as an upper-middle-class student at my college. I know how to "talk the talk." However, when I go back home to see my mama and pa, I'm just one of the working class girls done good.

By the way, I think I'll stop by to see my old math professor just to say "hey."

—Janey, Age 20

What Do You Think?

1. What is it about social class that contributes to different speech patterns? Can you think of specific issues that would cause these differences?

2. Why is an upper-middle-class speech pattern, Standard American English, more valued than other speech patterns? How would a conflict theorist answer this?

that Hopi Native Americans use one word for every creature that flies, except for birds. That may seem odd to modern-day English speakers, but for the Hopi, flying creatures occupy a single category.

Likewise, Native Alaskan groups have many different words for "snow." Given that their culture revolves around snow, this makes good sense. After all, snow can be soft, crunchy, wet, melting, or powdery, to name just a few descriptors, and how Native Alaskan groups are able to use this snow depends on the type. In comparison, residents of Miami, Florida, probably have few words in their repertoire for "snow" because it is not a meaningful part of their everyday lives.

Let's think about the Sapir-Whorf hypothesis in your world today. Our technology-driven culture has provided many new words—chances are, words like "cell phone," "texting," and even "PC" were not a part of the everyday vocabulary of your parents. And, our language also shapes our culture. New words like "Attention Deficit Disorder" or "gifted" have created new dimensions of our culture, with the fields of medicine and special education to go along with these labels. We used to label these people as "disruptive" or "smart," but now we have words that help to shape our culture's collective worldview (Beebe, Beebe, & Redmond, 2011).

Understanding how language influences, and is influenced by, culture is critical in our global world (Lustig & Koester, 2010; Asante, Miike, & Yin, 2007). Success at interpersonal relationships on the job, in our social life, and in personal relationships depends upon our ability to communicate with those who may have a different cultural orientation. We need to understand how cultures differ and how these differences influence our forms and styles of communication. Communication experts have discovered at least six cultural orientations. Keep in mind, however, that differences in each of these dimensions exist on a continuum rather than in discrete categories as presented below (Beebe, Beebe, & Redmond, 2011; Lustig & Koester, 2010; Hofstede & Hofstede, 2004; Hall, 1976):

A collectivist culture focuses on the needs of the group over the needs of the individual. China is an example of a culture with a collectivist orientation.

- *Individualist versus Collectivist Cultures:* An individualist culture values personal achievement and independence. The general belief is that people are responsible for themselves and should receive little help from outside sources, such as the government. Examples of individualist cultures include the United States, Australia, and the Netherlands. In contrast, a collectivist culture focuses more on the needs of the group—the family, the community, or the society. The goals of the group supersede the goals of the individual. Examples of collectivist cultures include China, Guatemala, and Pakistan. The potential for miscommunication between people of these two types of cultures are great because of the differing emphasis on individualism.

- *High- versus Low-context Cultures:* In high-context cultures, emphasis is placed on indirect and nonverbal communication. Communication is based on the context of the individual. High-context cultures are also collectivist cultures, such as Latin America or Japan where people may want to get to know one another well before engaging in any transactions. People tend to use more "feeling" in their expressions. In contrast, in a low-context culture like the United States or Germany, communication is more direct; because people do not know each other well, more emphasis is placed on formal transactions and everything must be explained explicitly. This directness may be perceived as being rude by someone from a high-context culture.

- *Masculine versus Feminine Cultures:* Some cultures emphasize stereotypical male values of achievement, assertiveness, and material success, while others emphasize traits that have been more traditionally aligned with the feminine, including caring for others, modesty, and enhancing overall quality of life. In masculine cultures, gender stereotypes tend to be more rigid and women have less power in society. Japan, Austria, and Mexico are examples of masculine cultures, whereas Sweden and Norway lean towards more feminine cultures. Feminine cultures are more likely to see compromise and negotiation as useful communication tools, where masculine cultures may see these tools as signs of weakness.

- *Centralized versus Decentralized Power:* In some cultures power is centralized, or in the hands of a few. There is usually a great distance between those few who have power and the masses that do not. Examples of these cultures include India, the Philippines, and Brazil. In cultures with a more decentralized power structure, such as Denmark and New Zealand, power is more evenly distributed and average people have a chance to participate. These differences also affect our worldview and our communication styles. If you are from a culture in which power is shared, you may feel comfortable complaining to your boss about your workload, talking with your professor about the "C–" you received on the last test, or telling your parents that you and your partner are going to cohabit. These conversations would be more difficult to have if you are from a culture with a centralized power.

- *High versus Low Ambiguity:* Tolerance for ambiguity is another cultural trait that is highly variable. Some cultures do not tolerate ambiguity well, and their members may experience anxiety about the future. These cultures, such as Greece, Portugal, or Serbia, tend to create clear-cut rules for behavior and communication. In contrast, people living in cultures that tolerate high levels of ambiguity are generally comfortable with unknown situations. They minimize the importance of strict rules governing relationships and communication. Examples of these societies include Hong Kong, Malaysia, and Sweden.

- *Short-term versus Long-term Time Orientation:* How a culture uses and values time is critical to understanding its worldview and patterns of communication. Cultures that focus on the long term, such as many Asian cultures, emphasize the future and tend to value traits like thrift, deferred gratification, and perseverance. Other cultures, such as Nigeria, the Czech Republic, and Pakistan, think in the short term. These cultures are more interested in spending rather than saving, place greater emphasis on social status, and look for quick results from their efforts.

These six cultural orientations provide a framework for the ways in which our culture influences us and shapes our thinking about the world. Thus, communication takes place within our cultural experiences.

Have you ever traveled to another country? Or do you know another culture well through conversations with a close friend, or from reading or watching television? Can you identify where this culture is along these six dimensions? Does the orientation of this culture differ from the one in which you were raised? Can you see how this might affect communication with people from this culture?

:: Types of Communication

There are many different kinds of everyday communication in which we participate. In this section, you will be introduced to several types, including listening, verbal communication, nonverbal communication, electronic written communication, and disclosure.

Are You Listening to Me?

Many students have taken a speech class in college, but how many have had a class on listening? Learning how to listen well is an acquired skill, and one that is very important for effective communication (DeVito, 2011b; Nadig, 2006). **Listening** is more complex than just hearing; it is the process of giving thoughtful attention to what we hear. Listening requires us to use more than just our ears. In fact, the Chinese character for the word "listening" includes the character for ears, eyes, and heart, as shown in Figure 6.1, because the Chinese believe that really listening involves all three structures.

Listening is a collection of skills that involves several components, as shown in Figure 6.2 (DeVito, 2011a). First, you need to receive, or hear, the message. You note not only what is said, but what is missing. Second, understanding occurs when you decode what the speaker is saying. You grasp both the words and the tone that accompanies the words, such as anger, joy, or boredom. Third, messages that you receive and understand must be retained for some period of time. Fourth, you evaluate the messages that you hear by asking yourself: Why are they saying this? Do I agree? What do I think? Finally, you respond to what has been said. Your responses can happen while the other person is speaking by nodding your head, saying "uh-huh," or it may be after they have finished. Note that the listening process is circular and continues in a loop—often within a split second. However, listening can also go wrong at any one of these five stages.

Figure 6.1	**The Chinese Character for "Listen"**

Listening is a key concept in communication, in any language.

listening: The process of giving thoughtful attention to what we hear.

Figure 6.2

Five-Stage Model of the Listening Process

Good listening is a collection of skills and occurs in a circular fashion.

Receiving
Hearing
Attending

Understanding
Learning
Deciphering
meaning

Responding
Answering
Giving feedback

Remembering
Recalling
Retaining

Evaluating
Judging
Criticizing

Source: Devito, 2011a.

We all know how to listen, right? Actually, being a good listener is more difficult than it sounds.

active listening: Extremely attentive listening, where the listener has good eye contact and body language, and encourages the other person to continue talking.

verbal communication: The spoken exchange of thoughts, feelings, or other messages.

At the heart of most communication problems is poor listening—not poor hearing—but not really focusing on and understanding what the other person is saying (Lane, 2010). For example, if a friend vents her frustration about a partner, a poor listener may interrupt, change the subject, or share one's own views about that person, *"Oh, I agree that Devan doesn't seem to get it. Do you know what he said to me? You won't believe it. . . ."* The listener might even wander off the topic to talk about her own partner, *"Oh yeah, you know what my boyfriend does? It drives me crazy. . . ."* This person is not truly listening to the friend. A good listener focuses on what the person is saying, and is not distracted in any manner or thinking of his or her own response. A good listener listens to both the content and the feelings that are associated with that content (Kelly, 2008).

One type of listening is referred to as **active listening** (Perkins & Fogarty, 2005). This occurs when you are extremely attentive, with good eye contact and body language, and encourage the other person to continue talking. As an active listener, you may also paraphrase what the person is saying, or ask for clarification or further details. Some examples of sentences that indicate active listening include:

"You seem to be frustrated about that. Is that because . . . ?"
"Tell me what happened next."
"How did that make you feel?"
"What do you think we should do?"

Active listening involves asking good questions, listening non-judgmentally, empathizing, and paraphrasing (Perkins & Fogarty, 2005). As summed up by Beebe, Beebe, & Redmond (2011), a good listener: (1) stops; (2) looks; (3) listens; (4) asks questions; and (5) reflects by paraphrasing.

Verbal Communication: It's All Your Fault

Verbal communication is the spoken exchange of thoughts, feelings, or other messages (DeVito, 2011a; Dunn & Goodnight, 2011). This type of communication includes the content of the words themselves, and the tone and the expression used. Were the words said in a playful bantering tone, in a heated exchange, or with an aggressive stance? One study compared three groups—happily married couples, couples seeking marriage therapy, and couples in the process of divorce—and found happily married couples showed more effective verbal communication skills in their daily lives than did the other two groups (Smith, Heaven, & Ciarrochi, 2008).

Words are symbols that represent something else. The word "dog," for example, triggers an image of a four-legged animal. However, drawing upon symbolic interaction theory, introduced in Chapter 1, we know that people attach meaning through their experiences and interactions with others. The word "dog" may conjure up a furry friend curled up on your bed, or a growling creature with sharp fangs. We cannot be in charge of the meanings that people derive from our messages; therefore, we need to communicate as clearly as possible.

Words have the power to create monumental misunderstandings as well as deeply felt connections (Kopecky & Powers, 2002). Some specific barriers to understanding verbal communication include (Beebe, Beebe, & Redmond, 2011):

- *Bypassing:* It is easy to misunderstand what someone is saying when one word has several meanings. The English language can be quite imprecise. The 500 or so words used most often in daily conversation have more than 14,000 different dictionary definitions. If someone says that they "love" you, what does that really mean?

- *Lack of precision:* We have all heard people mistake one word or phrase for another, e.g., "prescription" for "proscription," "literally" for "figuratively," or "I could care less" for "I could not care less." Sometimes this is humorous, as are using words out of context, or putting words in the wrong order. Consider these statements by former President George W. Bush: *"I know how hard it is to put food on your family," "For every fatal shooting there are roughly three nonfatal shootings. And folks, this is unacceptable in America," "I have opinions of my own, strong opinions, but I don't always agree with them"* (Allvoices.com, 2009). Whether funny or not, incorrect or unclear language can easily foster miscommunication.

- *Overgeneralizing:* Some people have a tendency to make sweeping generalizations, such as *"You always forget to unload the dishwasher," "You are never ready on time," "Why do you always drink too much when we have dinner at the Smiths' house?"* These statements imply that evidence has been collected to reach a definitive conclusion, when in reality this is probably not the case.

- *Static evaluation:* Think back to a time in your life when you did something silly or embarrassing. Don't you hate to be reminded of it? After all, the event may have occurred ten years ago and you have changed since then. Yet some people continue to make statements that do not allow for change such as, *"You've always been the wild one in the family, haven't you?" "You're pregnant? Why, I thought you didn't want children."*

- *Polarization:* Some people speak in extremes, or see the world in black and white terms such as, *"It's all your fault,"* or *"I didn't do it."* If you ignore the middle ground on issues, your language probably does not reflect reality.

- *Biased language:* Using words that reflect biases about race, ethnicity, sex, sexual orientation, religious faith, or other cultures can also foster miscommunication and conflict. Many people find this type of language offensive (Ivy & Backlund, 2008).

How can we improve our verbal communication in intimate relationships? In addition to paying attention to the barriers described above, we can create a supportive environment for speaking and listening. For more than three decades, communication researcher Jack Gibb studied groups of people in conversation, and noted that some exchanges created a supportive environment, while others created a more defensive one (Gibb, 1961). There are several ways to make the environment more of a true supportive dialogue rather than a debate shrouded in defensiveness (Beebe, Beebe, & Redmond, 2011):

- *Describe your own feelings rather than evaluate the behavior of others.* Few of us like to be judged or evaluated. It creates an environment of defensiveness, which makes good communication difficult. One way to avoid evaluating others is to focus on your own feelings, using "I" words. For example, instead of saying, *"Why are you always home late from*

How often do you hear biased language, such as a racist or sexist joke, or the use of disparaging terms? Do you find this language offensive? What do you do when you hear it?

work?" you can rephrase the question as an "I" statement, *"I find it hard to manage the kids when you come home late."*

- *Solve problems rather than try to control others.* We do not like to be judged, and we also do not like to feel that another person is controlling us. Open-ended questions such as, *"What should we do?"* create a more supportive environment than a judgmental statement such as, *"This is why you are wrong."*

- *Be genuine rather than manipulative.* Being a genuine person means that you strive to be yourself and that you take an honest interest in others. In contrast, a manipulative person has hidden agendas and focuses primarily on his or her own needs and desires. Those who strive to be more genuine in their interactions with others promote a more positive communication environment.

- *Empathize rather than remain detached.* Empathy, the ability to understand the feelings of others and predict their emotional responses, is a critical component of a supportive communication environment.

- *Be flexible rather than rigid.* We all have opinions, but when we express them in a rigid fashion it creates an environment that curtails rather than encourages communication. No one wants to hear you say to them, *"I know I'm right,"* even if this is a true statement. Another way of voicing your opinion could be, *"The way I see it is . . ."* or *"Here's one way to look at the problem. . . ."*

- *Present yourself as equal rather than superior.* We can antagonize others when we act as though we are superior to them. The statement *"Listen to me because I have a lot more experience than you do,"* might work if you are talking to a child (or it might not), but it will probably not be appreciated by your partner. When we communicate as equals, it creates a more supportive environment, *"We each bring our own perspective, and here is mine."*

These tactics can move us towards the goal of creating a supportive rather than a defensive communication environment. But as you know, not all communication is expressed through words as our nonverbal behavior can also reveal our feelings.

Nonverbal Communication: What Exactly Does That Smile Mean?

An awkward silence; a smile; eye contact; holding hands; a grimace; an erect posture; a squint; aggressive hand gestures; rolling the eyes—these are all forms of **nonverbal communication**, or ways we communicate without words (Seiler & Beall, 2011). We use nonverbal messages all the time to convey attitudes and express emotions, from love and affection to contempt and disdain, although we may not be conscious of these messages. In fact, we may use nonverbal messages more often than verbal messages when we want to discuss the state of our feelings within the relationship (Koerner & Fitzpatrick, 2002). For example, if a partner feels jealous of the attention given to another person, he or she is likely to communicate this nonverbally—rolling the eyes, being silent, or pulling away from touch—rather than saying, *"You know, I feel insecure when you talk with Pat at parties because I worry that you're rejecting me."*

In face-to-face communication we blend verbal and nonverbal messages to best convey our meanings (DeVito, 2011b). Nonverbal messages may accentuate or complement our spoken words. When we meet someone for the first time, we might not only say, *"It's nice to meet you,"* but we will say it with eye contact and a smile. But what if our verbal and nonverbal messages are not in agreement? For example, you may see your ex-boyfriend or ex-girlfriend while running errands and say with a grimace, *"Nice to see you."*

We have all heard the phrase "actions speak louder than words." It means that nonverbal communication is often more believable than verbal communication when the two are in conflict. Nonverbal communication is more difficult to falsify. Research shows that people who are lying tend to have reduced eye contact, pauses in their conversation, slower speech, a higher pitch to their voice, and more deliberate pronunciation and articulation of words (Zuckerman, DePaulo, & Rosenthal, 1981; Porter & ten Brinke, 2008, 2010).

nonverbal communication: Communicating without words, by using gestures, expressions, and body language.

One problem with nonverbal messages is that they are easily misunderstood. We have dictionaries to help us interpret words, but what do we use for help with interpreting gestures, posture, or expressions? Does the furrowed brow mean a person is deep in thought, or expressing disapproval? Does that smile represent happiness or nervousness? Is someone yawning from boredom or from sleepiness? Does that deliberate pronunciation and articulation mean that someone is lying or just trying to be clear?

The potential for misinterpretation is made even greater by cultural differences. Figure 6.3 shows how specific hand gestures have significantly different meanings from one country to another. What is a sign of support or friendliness in one place may be a crude or vulgar gesture elsewhere!

Another example of nonverbal messages is the degree of "personal space" we are comfortable with when interacting with the world. While we are not always conscious of how much space we need, researchers have analyzed the comfort level of Americans in different situations (Hall, 1966). In intimate relationships, our comfort zone of communication is between actual touch and 18 inches. In other social relationships, such as classmates working on a group project, the comfort zone is between 18 inches and 4 feet. In communication of a nonpersonal nature, such as a business meeting or an interaction with a sales clerk, the comfort zone is about 4 to 12 feet. Yet these distances vary among different racial or ethnic groups in the United States. For example, Hispanics in casual conversation stand or sit much closer to each other than do Whites (Kaleidoscope, 2003). Therefore, in a conversation between a White person and a Hispanic person, we may find the Hispanic person moving closer to talk, while the White person backs away because the closeness feels awkward.

Eye contact is another example of nonverbal messages. In the United States, direct eye contact is considered polite and shows interest in another person and his or her conversation. However, in many other parts of the world eye contact has a different meaning. In particular, eye contact between men and women is a sign of sexual suggestiveness and invitation.

Written Electronic Communication

Increasingly, people "talk" to each other electronically; in other words, they really do not talk at all, they write. Unlike the days when we relied solely upon the U.S. Postal Service to relay our messages, electronic messaging is instantaneous, which has changed the way we communicate. As of 2009, 125 million people had a MySpace or Facebook account (De-Wolfe & Anderson, 2009). A study conducted at the University of Texas reports that over four-fifths of students and staff have Facebook accounts (Baron, 2008). Some people use these so often that about one-third of students reported that they either agreed or strongly agreed with the statement, "I feel addicted to Facebook" (Vanden Boogart, 2006). Likewise, college students are required to have email accounts, so electronic messaging has become a requisite part of student life. ◉—Watch on **myfamilylab.com**

Figure 6.3	**Hand Gestures in Different Cultures**

Gestures are a very important component in communication, but they can mean different things across cultures.

OK sign

France: you're a zero; **Japan:** please give me coins; **Brazil:** an obscene gesture; **Mediterranean countries:** an obscene gesture

Thumbs up

Australia: up yours; **Germany:** the number one; **Japan:** the number five; **Saudi Arabia:** I'm winning; **Ghana:** an insult; **Malaysia:** the thumb is used to point rather than the index finger

Thumb and forefinger

Most countries: money; **France:** something is perfect; **Mediterranean:** a vulgar gesture

Open palm

Greece: an insult dating to ancient times; **West Africa:** "You have five fathers," an insult akin to calling someone a bastard

Something as simple as eye contact has very different meanings across cultures. In the United States, making eye contact is a form of politeness, but in many other regions of the world it is considered rude or even sexually suggestive.

◉—Watch the **Video** *Core Concepts: Social Interaction and Technology* on **myfamilylab.com**

Table 6.1 Electronic Shorthand

We communicate through words and symbols, and these are continually changing as our culture changes. If you read an English text written in the 18th century, you will see that word use, grammar, and spelling have changed significantly since that time period. For example, we no longer say "thou" or "thee."
Our reliance on electronic forms of communication is also changing our words, grammar, and spelling, as these examples reveal:

Acronyms		Emoticons	
2G2B4G	Too good to be forgotten	:-*	kiss on the cheek
2more	Tomorrow	:-@	screaming
9	Parent watching	I-o	yawning
AATK	Always at the keyboard	'-)	winking
BWL	Bursting with laughter	:-}	embarrassed
CM	Call me	%)	confused
ILY	I love you		
M4C	Meet for coffee		
GMAB	Give me a break		
OMG	Oh my god		
THX	Thanks		
Y	Why?		
P-ZA	Pizza		

Electronic communication is now how many of us communicate daily (Ramirez & Broneck, 2009). How has our increased reliance on the electronic written word changed communication? Linguist Naomi Baron suggests many changes have already or will occur in our society (2008):

Our electronic media allows us to share information right as it is happening. We can live in the moment. and share it with others.

- *Informality is the new norm.* We write more informally, are less concerned about grammar and punctuation, and are more likely to use slang or abbreviations for words, as shown in Table 6.1. We may become increasingly uncertain about how we use words, so we may make up our own language rules.

- *Our writing influences our speech.* The way we communicate electronically influences how we communicate face-to-face. We use more abbreviations in our speech patterns, and are less concerned about grammar. We even have new meanings for old words like "cookie," "worm," or "spam."

- *We have volume control over our messages.* We can see who is contacting us, and can better screen our communications: we decide when, where, and even if we will receive

messages, unlike the past when we answered a ringing telephone without knowing who was on the other end.

- *We have more relationships with less depth.* We communicate with more people, but we do so only very briefly, and we know less about each of them. In the past, you may have spoken by telephone a couple of times a day or written one or two letters a week; you may now send over a dozen electronic messages in a single morning.

- *We can live in the moment.* Unlike in the past when a letter or telephone call usually involved a synopsis of what *had* happened, communication today can be more of a running discourse. We can actually live in the other person's moment and "hear" the information as it is unfolds.

Electronic communication is likely to be a growing part of our culture, influencing how we communicate, access, and share information. Unfortunately, it also opens up a new way of miscommunication.

How might social class influence our different forms of communication? For example, are the poor as likely to have computers, Internet access, and cell phones? Likewise, how might social class affect verbal and nonverbal communication? If you think that there might be differences, what accounts for these differences? Money? Culture? Or something else?

:: Sex Differences in Communication

Do men and women communicate differently? Much media attention has been devoted to the idea that women and men have different communication patterns and are prone to miscommunication. Popular self-help books such as *Men Are from Mars, Women Are from Venus* (Gray, 1992) have widespread appeal because people are concerned about communication and genuinely would like to improve their communication skills.

Communication researchers have challenged many of Gray's assertions that men and women are really so different as to occupy different communication "planets" (Edwards & Hamilton, 2004; Barnett & Rivers, 2004; Wood, 2002). One of these challenges is revealed in the feature box *Why Do Research?* (p. 169) It describes a research study designed to investigate the stereotype that women talk more than men.

Linguists, however, have noted a number of sex differences in communication (Wood, 2009). One sex difference involves the way we self-disclose information. Women tend to be more verbal in disclosing their feelings about the relationship; men tend toward more physical displays. Yet the woman may complain that she wants more than just the presence of her partner in her life; she would like more regular verbal displays of affection from him: *"Tell me you love me,"* she says. *"I'm here, aren't I?"* he responds.

This sex difference in communication can lead to a misunderstanding between partners. Both styles are self-disclosing, but they do not always give the other credit, given their different styles. It may be the *perception* of disclosure that makes the difference in the quality of marriages (Richman & Rosenfeld, 1995; Uebelacker, Courtnage, & Whisman, 2003). Women do not see as much communication disclosure from their partners as they would like, which partly explains why women show lower rates of satisfaction in marriage than men do.

There are many other sex differences in communication as well, both verbal and nonverbal, as shown in Table 6.2 (Trenholm, 2008; Cameron, 1998; Tannen, 1990, 1994). What are some of these differences?

Jamal and Renée get lost driving to visit friends in another part of the city. Seeing they may be late, Renée suggests that they stop and ask for directions, but Jamal refuses. He is uncomfortable asking for help and believes there is no guarantee a stranger will give accurate

"He is certain that he can find the way himself and would rather just drive around until he does so."

information. He is certain that he can find the way himself and would rather just drive around until he does so. This does not make sense at all to Renée, who is getting angry. She is not embarrassed about asking for directions and believes that anyone who is lost should ask for help.

Table 6.2	Conclusions Drawn from Research on Sex Differences in Communication

It's not really correct to say that women talk more than men.
It's much more complicated than that.

Quantity of Talk: Who Talks the Most?
- In task-oriented cross-sex groups, men talk more than women.
- In friendly same-sex pairs, women prefer to spend time talking; men prefer to share activities like sports or hobbies.

Topics of Talk: What Do Men and Women Talk About?
- Women talk more about private matters, such as family, relationship problems, other women or men, clothing, and feelings.
- Men talk more about public matters, such as sports, money, and news, and they tell more jokes.

Vocabulary: Do Men and Women Use Different Words?
- Women more often use weak expletives ("Oh dear" or "oh my"), whereas men more often use stronger expletives, including obscenities.
- Women use more color detail terms than men ("mauve," "teal").

Grammatical Constructions: Do Men's and Women's Syntax Differ?
- Women use more qualifiers ("somewhat," "kind of," "I guess").
- Women use more disclaimers ("I'm no expert, but . . . ," "Don't get mad but . . .").
- Women are more likely to use polite forms of conversation, such as, "May I please have . . . ,", "I'm sorry about that. . . ."

Taking Turns: Who Controls Interaction?
- In cross-sex pairs, men interrupt women more than women interrupt men.
- Women ask more questions and men make more statements during conversation.
- Men successfully initiate topics more often than do women.

Source: Trenholm, S. 2008. *Thinking Through Communication.* Boston: Allyn and Bacon. Reprinted by permission of Pearson Education.

What causes these sex differences in communication? Linguist Deborah Tannen, who has extensively studied sex and gender differences in communication, believes that men and women grow up in different "cultures" (1990, 1994). Women's culture stresses intimacy and connection with others while men's culture values autonomy and individual achievement. These different perspectives influence men's and women's topics of conversation, communication styles, and interpretations of one another's messages. Throughout their lives men and women learn how to use behavior in line with their gender identities. Men learn that being competitive and strong is a way of expressing masculinity. Women learn that stressing connection and feelings is feminine. This explains why many men do not seem to mind driving around when lost, rather than asking for directions, which might reveal weakness (Trenholm, 2008).

Women's Patterns

Women are more likely to use conversation as a way to establish and maintain relationships. They tend to use communication for the purpose of connecting and relating to other people, whereas men tend to approach communication as an exchange of information.

Compared to men, women tend to smile more often, express a wider range of emotions through facial expressions and nonverbal behavior, and maintain more eye contact with others (Ivy & Backlund, 2008). When they speak, women use more qualifying, tentative

Why Do Research?

Who Really Has the Gift of Gab?

You know the stereotype: women talk more than men. But is it true? Whether or not women really do talk more than men is an empirical question, meaning that it is a question that can be answered using scientific research methods. "No one knows where this belief even came from, but it's been reported for years," says psychologist James Pennebaker, from the University of Texas at Austin.

To answer this question, a group of psychologists from the Universities of Arizona, Texas, and St. Louis set out to listen to men and women, and count their words. The researchers

placed microphones on 396 college students ages 17-29 from the United States and Mexico, for periods ranging from two to ten days. The researchers sampled their conversations and calculated how many words they used in the course of a day. The electronically activated recorder unobtrusively records snippets of conversation during a person's daily routine. The small device, the size of a cell phone, turns itself on every 12 minutes and records whatever it hears for 30 seconds. This digital technology is a far better approach than relying on the self-reported data from surveys that were done in the past.

The researchers then transcribed the recordings of the students, and calculated the words used per day. Any guesses on what they found? Men averaged 15,669 words per day while women used 16,215, which is such a small difference that it is not statistically significant. In other words, men and women use about the same amount of words. It's time to put to rest the myth that women have the gift of gab!

Sources: Brizendine, 2006; Dance, Mehl, Vazire, Ramirez-Esparza, Slatcher, & Pennebaker, 2007; Yong, 2007.

Who talks more, men or women? Any guesses?

What Do You Think?

1. Why did the stereotype that women talk more than men begin, and why does the myth persist?

2. If men and women talk about the same amount, do they talk about the same kinds of things?

---

statements, such as *"I think I would like to do this"* or *"It sort of seems like you would rather not do that."* These qualifiers weaken the message and add an element of uncertainty. Women are also more polite in tone, ask a greater number of questions, and are more likely to show interest and concern, using phrases such as *"Oh, really?"* or *"I know what you mean."* Women also offer more personal details and disclosures while referring to their feelings, *"I felt so bad when . . ."* or *"Wasn't it depressing when . . . ?"* These phrases serve to maintain and perpetuate conversations, fostering closeness and understanding. However, they also reflect the gendered patterns in our society—women are taught not to be too pushy, to be kind and accommodating, and to cooperate and build consensus.

Women and men also use their bodies differently when they communicate. For example, when talking with others, women are more likely to prefer side-by-side interactions than the more confrontational face-to-face style of interaction of men. Women also occupy less personal space than men.

Men's Patterns

Men tend to approach communication from a content orientation. They talk when they have something to say or need to receive or give information (Beebe, Beebe, & Redmond, 2011). Compared to women, men's nonverbal communication and speech are more direct

Men and women communicate verbally and non-verbally in different ways. One important difference is the way they use their bodies. Men are more likely to spread out their arms and legs and take up greater personal space than do women.

Now that you've learned about sex differences in communication, use this information to analyze your own communication style. Think about same-sex and cross-sex communication with friends, partners, family members, and even strangers or acquaintances. What kinds of patterns do you see? Where did you learn your communication style?

and assertive. Their speech is more instrumental and less likely to convey feelings or emotions. Men's speech tends to be more authoritative and absolute, *"I'll give you three reasons why it won't work . . . ,"* rather than women's more tentative style, *"I'm not sure this will work. . . ."* Communication experts have noticed that in most mixed-sex contexts men tend to dominate the conversation, speak more frequently and for longer periods of time, speak on topics of their interest, and interrupt more frequently (West & Zimmerman, 1983; Tannen, 1994).

Men tend to spread their bodies out and occupy more personal space around them than do women, and are more likely than women to talk face-to-face. They use more gestures, for example, "talking with their hands" while women will rest their hands on the arm of a chair while seated. Men are also more likely to touch others, especially women, when talking with them (Beebe, Beebe, & Redmond, 2011).

Why Do Women and Men Communicate Differently?

Given these distinctive styles of communication, it is easy to see why men and women often miscommunicate. What accounts for these differences? Are they biological, or are they social in origin?

This question cannot yet be definitively answered, but it is likely a combination of both factors. We have learned that males and females are socialized differently, but we have also learned of important brain differences. Women tested in such diverse countries as Japan, England, the Czech Republic, Nepal, and the United States use more words correctly, use better grammar and pronunciation, and in other ways, excel at verbal communication compared to men (Fisher, 2000). Certain regions of the prefrontal brain area are activated differently during language tasks performed by women and men. At least one study showed that both the left and right hemispheres of the prefrontal area were activated in women as they performed language tasks, while only the left hemisphere was activated in men. This suggests that it is easier for women, biologically, to articulate words (Baron-Cohen, 2003). And in the event of a stroke, men's verbal abilities are more likely to be impaired because women's right-hemisphere language areas take over some functions if the left-hemisphere language areas are damaged.

:: Communicating to Keep Your Relationships Strong: Self-Disclosure

One of the primary ways we can use communication to help create satisfying marriages and intimate relationships is through **self-disclosure**, or telling your partner something private about yourself that he or she would not otherwise know (Galvin, Bylund, & Brommel, 2008). Self-disclosure can range from insignificant or superficial topics, such as *"My favorite color is orange,"* to information that can be extremely personal and significant, such as sexual fantasies or childhood traumas. We have various layers of information about ourselves,

self-disclosure: Telling a person something private about yourself that he or she would not otherwise know.

Table 6.3	The Windows on Myself

A useful way of thinking about self-disclosure distinguishes how much information you know about yourself, how much others know about you, and how much you are willing to disclose.

	Known to Self	Unknown to Self
Known to Others	**Open Window Pane** known to self and others	**Blind Window Pane** blind to self, seen by others
Unknown to Others	**Hidden Window Pane** open to self, hidden from others	**Unknown Window Pane** unknown to self and others

Source: Luft, Joe. 1969. "Of Human Interaction." In Palo Alto. Retrieved 30 June 2008. Cited by Tim Borchers, 1999, Allyn & Bacon (www.abacon.com/commstudies/interpersonal/indisclosure.html). Reprinted by permission of Pearson Education.

and when we develop intimacy with another person, we allow that person to penetrate through the superficial layers to the core of deeply personal topics.

However, it is important to acknowledge that engaging in self-disclosure does not guarantee the success of a relationship (Lane, 2010). Disclosing disturbing information may even contribute to the demise of a relationship, because the other partner may be very uncomfortable hearing this type of information, such as *"Honey, I've been having an affair for the past three years. . . ."*

A useful way of viewing self-disclosure is shown in the so-called Johari window in Table 6.3. The Johari window distinguishes how much information you know about yourself, how much others know about you, and how much you are willing to disclose.

As you can see, the *Open Window Pane* includes information that is clearly visible or known, such as your physical appearance or where you live. The *Blind Pane* includes information others can see in you, but you cannot see in yourself. You might think you are a talented manager, yet others think you exhibit weak leadership skills. The *Hidden Pane* contains information you wish to keep private, such as your fantasies. The *Unknown Pane* includes everything neither you nor others know about you. For example, you may have hidden artistic talents you have not explored. Through self-disclosure, we open and close the window panes so we may become more intimate with others (Luft, 1969).

However, for self-disclosure to benefit a relationship there must be reciprocity and support (Galvin, Bylund, & Brommel, 2008), a tenet of the social exchange perspective introduced in Chapter 1. That is, both partners should feel free to be honest with each other and supportive of the feelings being shared. Disclosing feelings can be risky, for not all feelings are positive. But if partners support each other in sharing both the good and the bad, trust can develop. Lack of support, or a negative response to self-disclosure, can be detrimental to the quality of a relationship.

Given what you have learned about sex differences in general and sex differences in communication, do you think there are also differences in men's and women's methods of self-disclosure? What evidence can you provide for your answer?

:: Conflict, Communication, and Problem Solving

The potential for conflict is inherent in any relationship (Lane, 2010). You and a friend may disagree over what movie to watch; you and your partner may have different views of where to go on vacation; you and your fiancé may disagree about your type of wedding; you and your spouse may have different spending habits; and you and your child may disagree over whether fast food is a healthy meal choice.

Conflict occurs when members of the group disagree over two or more options to make a decision, solve a problem, or achieve a goal (Beebe & Masterson, 2006). It applies to all types of relationships, including friendships, romantic relationships, other family relationships, and even work-related relationships. Individuals who are involved in conflict have some degree of

conflict: Disagreements over decision making, problem solving, or achieving goals, which can result from differences between group members in personality, perception, information, tolerance for risk, and power or influence.

Culture not only shapes communication, but it shapes conflict. In the United States, extramarital sex creates a major source of conflict in marriage, but this is not the case everywhere. In many cultures, extramarital sex (at least for men) is tolerated, if not even expected.

dependence on the other person—why would we need to resolve a disagreement if we did not affect one another? Conflict can result from differences between group members in personality, perception, information, tolerance for risk, and power or influence.

Culture also influences the issues that people fight about and how people experience conflict. For example, a woman in the United States who loses her virginity prior to marriage probably faces little parental conflict, but a woman in Saudi Arabia would face the wrath of her angry parents. Conversely, an American man who engages in extramarital sex is likely to cause more conflict in his marriage than a married man living in Spain. In cultures that have a more collectivist orientation, conflict is likely to involve breaking the group rules or norms in some way. On a recent trip to Tokyo, I was advised to always stand towards the right on escalators. To stand towards the left or in the middle of an escalator is considered very rude and could cause tension or conflict. In more individualist cultures like the United States, conflict is more likely to arise because of a transgression or perceived transgression upon an individual. *You* didn't do something for *me*, and that made me angry.

Conflict, *per se*, is not unhealthy. In fact, people in stable, romantic relationships experience conflict about twice a week (Lloyd, 1987). The question is not how can you avoid conflict, but how can you best manage the inevitable conflict that occurs in any relationship?

Types of Conflict

There are many different types of conflict, and some are easier or more difficult to resolve than others. Figure 6.4 illustrates four types of conflict: pseudoconflict, content conflict, value conflict, and ego conflict, and each are discussed below (Lane, 2010; Miller & Steinberg, 1975).

Figure 6.4	**Types of Conflict**

Not all conflict is the same; this typology suggests four distinct types.

Pseudo Conflict → Content Conflict → Value Conflict → Ego Conflict

Easiest to Manage   **Most Difficult to Manage**

pseudoconflict: Falsely perceiving that our partner is interfering with our goals or has incompatible goals.

content conflict: A type of conflict where individuals disagree about information.

value conflict: A type of conflict that results from differing opinions on subjects that relate to personal values and issues of right or wrong.

Pseudoconflict occurs when we falsely perceive that our partner is interfering with our goal or has incompatible goals. This type of conflict is relatively easy to resolve once we realize that we actually do not disagree with one another. For example, suppose a friend teases you about a new item of clothing that you were wearing. You may become upset because you believe that this person's goal is to embarrass you, but perhaps their goal is only to acknowledge that you have something new.

Content conflict occurs when we disagree about information. This type of conflict can also be easy to resolve if the correct information is readily available. For example, suppose you believe the party begins at 8:00 PM, but your partner believes that it begins at 9:00 PM. How to resolve this disagreement? Find a credible source with the information—simply look at the invitation, or contact the host for the correct time.

Value conflict is more difficult to resolve because it results from differing opinions on subjects that relate to personal values and to issues of right or wrong. You may try to bring someone around to your way of thinking, which may or may not work. For example, suppose you want to adopt a baby from Ethiopia because you are concerned about the growing number of children orphaned by AIDS, but your partner is not at all comfortable adopting a child. While you want to save the world one child at a time, your partner does not share your sentiment. Can this conflict be resolved?

Finally, **ego conflict** may be among the most difficult type of conflict to resolve because it arises when individuals believe they must win at all costs to save face. The issue under discussion almost becomes secondary because the ego becomes involved and the real goal is simply to win. Perhaps in the midst of a conflict your partner told you, *"You're being ridiculous. . . ."* You may then find yourself becoming defensive and trying to prove your worth, even after the original source of the conflict is long forgotten.

How we deal with a conflict depends upon the type of conflict, how much concern we have for the relationship, and our own personal conflict styles. These styles include avoiding, accommodating, competing, compromising, and collaborating, as shown in Table 6.4 (Lane, 2010).

- *Avoiding* occurs when we remove ourselves from the conflict psychologically or physically. We may deny the existence of the conflict, refuse to discuss the issue, or walk away. This type of response can be labeled "lose-lose" because neither partner really accomplishes his or her goals. In fact, because the conflict is avoided, it may resurface later, and the tension may even increase.

- *Accommodating* is a strategy that entails satisfying our partner's needs at the expense of our own goals, and can therefore be labeled "lose-win." The accommodating partner chooses to lose and let the other partner win. Accommodating the other partner may be an effective strategy some of the time, but habitual accommodation signals a potential imbalance in the relationship.

- *Competing* is the opposite strategy: we attempt to meet our own goals without concerns for our partner's needs. We may use any tactic available to us, possibly even

ego conflict: A type of conflict where individuals believe they must win at all costs to save face.

Table 6.4	Personal Conflict Styles			
Researchers identify five conflict styles that show how much concern we have for our communication partner and how much concern we have for obtaining our own goals.				
Style	**Approach**	**Example**	**Advantages**	**Disadvantages**
Avoiding	Lose-Lose	"Just leave me alone."	Can reduce intense emotions; can be effective when used with unimportant issues	Increased relational tension and difficulty solving a dispute; may influence us to perceive a conflict as more serious than warranted
Accommodating	Lose-Win	"Whatever you say."	Can be effective when used with unimportant issues and when we give in for "social credit"	May lead to poor decision making; possibly being taken advantage of
Competing	Win-Lose	"It's my way or the highway!"	Can be effective in emergency situations and if an issue is critical to our own or our partner's well-being	Damage to a relationship
Compromising	Lose-Lose	"I'll do some of this if you do some of that."	Can be effective when we do not have the time to engage in a collaborative conflict style or when the use of other conflict styles are not successful	Lose a portion of what we desire; may accept a less effective solution to bring about the compromise; feeling dissatisfied with the solution
Collaborating	Win-Win	"Let's work on finding the best solution for both of us."	Goals of both self and other are achieved	Takes time and knowledge of win-win conflict resolution methods

Source: From Lane, Interpersonal Communication: Competence and Contexts, 2e. (Table 11.2, p. 290) (2010). Allyn & Bacon. Reprinted by permission of Pearson Education.

verbal attacks, lies, or threats. This has been called "win-lose" because we try to meet our own goals no matter what the cost is to our partner.

- *Compromising* occurs when both partners give up part of what they want to achieve partial satisfaction in meeting their goals. Both partners may walk away from the conflict feeling the resolution is not particularly satisfying; hence, it is called "lose-lose." However, compromising may work best when other styles are not successful.
- *Collaborating* is used when we attempt to satisfy both our own needs and those of our partner. This style is labeled "win-win" because the goals of both partners are attained. Using this style, conflict can actually strengthen a relationship.

Intimacy, Communication, and Conflict

Research on communication in relationships has focused primarily on its ability to help reduce conflict and improve problem solving. The way couples communicate about their differences has real implications for happiness and stability. Conflict in any marriage or personal relationship is normal and expected. The key is *how* we communicate and deal with conflict.

✳ Explore on **myfamilylab.com**

John Gottman presents how couples communicate and resolve their differences in his extensive body of work, including his book *Why Marriages Succeed or Fail* (1994). He distinguishes between **regulating couples**, who generally use communication to promote closeness and intimacy and use constructive comments even during arguments, and **nonregulated couples**, who have far more negative exchanges. Nonregulated couples may use the following techniques:

- *Contempt:* This is an attitude of feeling superior to your spouse such as rolling your eyes while he or she is talking.
- *Defensiveness:* This is an effort to defend yourself and your position when you feel attacked in an argument.
- *Criticism:* This includes making negative evaluations of your spouse's behavior or feelings.
- *Stonewalling:* This is a type of withdrawal technique in which some people show how they refuse to listen to their spouse.
- *Belligerence:* This challenging behavior is meant to establish power in the marital relationship (Gottman, 1994).

Gottman's research suggests there may be a pattern to conflict. He and his colleagues observed 130 couples at the beginning of their marriages, and then followed them for six years (Gottman, Coan, Carrere, & Swanson, 1998). At the end of six years there had been 17 divorces, and the communication patterns of those who divorced were different from those who had remained married. In particular, there seemed to be an initiation of conflict by the wife, perhaps as a result of something in the relationship she did not like or did not feel was fair. This was followed by the husband's refusal to accept input from his wife. The wife then reciprocated with negativity, and the husband made little or no effort to lower the negativity of his wife. The couples who finished the study in happy, stable marriages, however, had more positive exchanges, expressing humor, affection, and interest.

These research results should not be interpreted to mean wives start all the arguments in marriage! Rather, women are more likely to verbalize their feelings—one study of nearly 4,000 men and women found that 32 percent of men compared to 23 percent of women say they bottle up their feelings in a spat (Parker-Pope, 2007). Instead, Gottman's work suggests both husbands and wives can improve their communication styles to reduce the level of negativity, and hence, reduce the likelihood of unhappiness and divorce. Wives can think of better ways to communicate that soften the initiation of conflict, and husbands can learn to accept input from their wives and reduce their own negative comments. In other words, husbands can learn to share power with their wives in their marital relationships.

✳ **Explore** the **Concept**
Social Explorer Map: Divorce Rates Across the United States on **myfamilylab.com**

regulating couples: Couples who use communication to promote closeness and intimacy.

nonregulated couples: Couples who have many negative communication exchanges.

*W*e all have our own patterns for dealing with conflict. Chances are we use different communication styles at different times. Think about your current or a recent intimate relationship. What types of conflicts did you tend to have, and what types of patterns of resolving conflict emerged?

My Family

How My Parents Dealt with Conflict

Growing up I watched my parents argue a lot. Often the subject of their arguments were trivial—who gets to watch what television show; what to have for dinner; whose job it is to fold the laundry; and things of that nature—definitely not earth-shattering. But their fights followed a common pattern. My mom would say something really direct, often in an accusatory tone, and my father would ignore her. She would say something like, "I'm choosing the television show tonight because you always choose it." "I'm making tacos for dinner because I'm tired of all the hamburgers you make." "It's your turn to do the laundry because I always do it." My dad, in turn, would just ignore her, and flip on the show he wanted to watch, or just let the clothes pile up. My mom would then say something again about it, and then he would get defensive, "You're crazy, I do so much around here. You don't know the half of all I do." Blah-blah-blah.

Their arguments would escalate from there, sometimes lasting an hour or two. I remember my brother and me sitting in our rooms thinking, "Geez, the laundry could have been done by now," or "The T.V. show is long over so would you quit arguing?," or "We've lost our appetite and don't want tacos or hamburgers."

One night, after a really heated argument, again probably over something stupid, my dad yelled, "I'm leaving!" and grabbed his coat and ran out the door. He was gone for two days, without a word. My brother and I were only about eight and ten at the time, and we were scared. My mom didn't say anything, but apparently she was scared too. Despite all the arguing, I guess she really loved my dad, and was worried that he was going to leave us for good.

When he came back home, I remember her crying, and then he started crying too. They decided that they were going to see a marriage counselor to help them work on communicating better. I don't know exactly what they did in therapy, but whatever it was, it seemed to work.

In looking back over the years, I can see that my mom had a point: to be honest, my dad did hog the television, didn't do his share of the housework, and well, he did always cook the same thing when it was his night in the kitchen. But she approached it all wrong and therefore didn't get the results she was looking for. He responded in a way that made things even worse by ignoring her, then getting defensive when she repeated herself. He didn't get the result he was looking for either. In therapy they learned how to talk things over when they disagreed about something, without yelling, accusing, or being defensive. Whew, life at home became a lot more peaceful after that.

—**Geraldo, Age 24**

What Do You Think?

1. Do you think that Geraldo's parents were a "regulated" or "unregulated" couple, according to Gottman? Which techniques did they use in their disagreements?

2. How did their pattern of conflict compare to the other couples that Gottman studied?

Can you identify the pattern of conflict in the feature box *My Family: How My Parents Dealt with Conflict?*

:: Power, Control, and Decision Making

Keesha gets a promotion at work, but accepting it means that she and her family will have to relocate. Her husband, Clay, does not want to move.

Jody wants to take a vacation with her girlfriend to Hawai'i, but her husband thinks it is inappropriate for a married woman to go on a vacation without her husband.

Lee wants to put the family's tax refund towards the purchase of a new car, but Masako wants to use it to visit her grandmother in Japan.

Emma is tired of doing much of the housework, but she is afraid to discuss the issue with her partner.

Intimate partner power involves decision making, the division of household labor, and a sense of entitlement.

Each of these situations is related to the balance of power in the relationship. Even in the best of marriages and intimate relationships, partners may still have different attitudes, interests, or goals that require negotiation and compromise. Micro-level decisions about who does the household chores, what types of jobs spouses take, or how families spend their leisure time all must be negotiated.

Power is the ability to exercise your will. There are many different types of power. **Personal power** is the degree of autonomy a person has to exercise his or her will. It includes the ability to make choices about yourself, e.g., "Should I go to graduate school?" "Should I adopt a cat?"

A second type is **social power**, or the ability to exercise your will over another person. This kind of power can be found in many different arenas, including that of work, home, or social settings. When your boss tells you that a specific report is due immediately, you know to make it a priority. Failing to do so may cost you your job.

The third type of power is **intimate partner power** (sometimes known as conjugal power). This type of power involves decision making among intimate partners, their division of labor, and their sense of entitlement. Who gets to make the major decisions? Who does the housework? And who is allowed to complain? Most marriages may not include overt opposition—"We're doing it this way or else . . ."—but differences of opinion can be strong. Are the outcomes of negotiation random, or do some spouses have an edge in getting an outcome that is to their advantage?

Intimate partner power is a complex phenomenon. For example, true equity and the *perception* of equity are not necessarily the same thing. Does my husband have more power than me if he works outside the home to earn money and I stay home and do housework and take care of the children? What if he makes the major purchasing decisions while I make the day-to-day decisions around the house, and we both believe this arrangement to be fair?

Early social scientists acknowledged that power is not a one-dimensional concept. There are at least six sources of power, and each can bring a different aspect to the relationship:

- *Coercive power* is based on the ability to achieve your will by force, either psychological or physical. Spanking a child and withholding a child's food are examples of coercive power.

- *Reward power* comes from the ability to offer material or nonmaterial benefit to achieve your goal. Offering your teenage son a chance to go to a concert if he gets all "As" on his report card is an example of reward power.

- *Expert power* stems from a person's special knowledge or ability. Your doctor has the power to tell you to have a colonoscopy, even though you may find it to be an uncomfortable procedure.

- *Informational power* comes from the information that a person may use to persuade another to do something he or she would not otherwise do. A woman might be able to persuade her partner to wear a condom when they have sexual intercourse, not because the man wants to, but because she informs him of what might happen otherwise—pregnancy or a possible STI.

- *Referent power* stems from the emotional identification of the less dominant person towards the more dominant person. A wife might attend the football game with her husband not because she likes football, but because he wants her to go, and satisfying his desires are important to her.

- *Legitimate power* is based on a person's claim of authority or the right to exercise his or her will. For example, fundamentalist Christians may take the biblical passage literally that men are the head of the household just like Jesus Christ is the head of the Church.

power: The ability to exercise your will.

personal power: The degree of autonomy a person has to exercise his or her will.

social power: The ability to exercise your will over another person.

intimate partner power: A type of power that involves decision making among intimate partners, their division of labor, and their sense of entitlement.

Theories of Power

Sociologists and other family scientists have been studying marital power for years and can explain it with several theoretical approaches (Blood & Wolfe, 1960; Cancian, 1987; Cohen & Durst, 2001; Fenstermaker Berk, 1985; Thompson & Walker, 1989; Waller, 1937; West & Zimmerman, 1987).

Resource Theory   One of the first major studies about marital power, conducted by Blood and Wolfe (1960), reported that the socioeconomic status of a spouse is influential in making family decisions. **Resource theory** suggests that the spouse with the more prestigious or higher-paying job can use that advantage to generate more power in the relationship, and thereby influence decision making. As women entering the work force have increased their economic resources, so too has their power increased in relationships. In marriages where the occupational prestige, education, and income of spouses are more equal, resource theory suggests the relative power of each will be more equal as well.

A problem with resource theory, however, is that reality does not reflect this pattern. No matter what their occupational status is relative to that of their wives, husbands continue to have more power in marriage even if they are unemployed (Cohen & Durst, 2001; Thompson & Walker, 1989). Regardless of socioeconomic status, men have been more successful in bargaining to avoid tasks such as housework that offer no pay, carry minimal social prestige, and are not generally thought of as fun.

Principle of Least Interest   Another explanation of marital power draws upon the principle of least interest, introduced in Chapter 3 (Waller, 1937). Recall that this perspective acknowledges that power comes from sources other than socioeconomic status. Instead, the partner with the least commitment to the relationship has the most power. The spouse who loves or needs less, or who is more willing to end the relationship, can use his or her lack of interest as a bargaining tool to exert dominance and power. The spouse who feels that he or she has more to lose may be willing to acquiesce to the other spouse.

Relative Love and Need Theory   Like resource theory and the principle of least interest, the **relative love and need theory** suggests that each partner brings resources to the relationship. However, a strictly micro-level analysis of who contributes what does not allow for the understanding of more macro-level factors that contribute to the interpretation of the exchange. One of these factors is the way that love itself is defined and interpreted, as shown in Chapter 4. Love has been "feminized" according to Francesca Cancian; women are socialized to become more relationship oriented, to need love, and to express their feelings of affection, whereas men are socialized differently (1987). As Cancian notes, "Men's dependence on close relationships remains covert and repressed, whereas women's dependence is overt and exaggerated." Men dominate women in marriage and intimate relationships because they hold at bay the expressions such as talking, caressing, and disclosing that our society (and women in particular) have come to define as love.

Doing Gender   Another macro-level factor that can influence the nature of power in intimate relationships is the way that sex and gender are conceptualized in our society, and the fact that these conceptualizations affect nearly every aspect of our lives. This perspective, called "**doing gender**," suggests that we take power differentials among men and women for granted and continue to reproduce them simply because they are so ingrained (Fenstermaker Berk, 1985; West & Zimmerman, 1987). "Doing gender" reflects the fact that our culture has traditionally placed a higher value on the traditional activities of men, including their employment, while devaluing those of women. We often fall into traditional roles without even realizing it. For example, as you will see in Chapter 10, women do most of the housework because it has been culturally defined as "women's work." It is easier (and takes less effort) to fall back on traditional cultural definitions than it is to make up our own.

These five perspectives help us explain power, control, and decision making in intimate relationships. They are summarized in the feature box *Tying It All Together: Factors That Shape Power* (p. 178), and illustrate ways in which personal, micro-level family decisions

resource theory: A theory of power that suggests that the spouse with the more prestigious or higher paying job can use that advantage to generate more power in the relationship and thereby influence decision making.

relative love and need theory: A theory of power that looks at the way that love itself is feminized, defined, and interpreted.

"doing gender": A theory of power that suggests that we take power differentials among men and women for granted and continue to reproduce them.

Chapter Review

6.1 What are four general concepts that summarize communication?

First, communication is a transaction; all human behavior is a continuous exchange, and partners are simultaneously senders and receivers of messages. Second, communication is a process; it is dynamic and always changing, and culture, race, ethnicity, and sex are critical. Third, communication includes the co-construction of meanings; each partner speaks a language and interprets meaning in a way acquired from his or her family of orientation. Fourth, communication uses symbols; to construct meanings or definitions, we rely on symbols that can be verbal like words or nonverbal like gestures.

6.2 How does communication vary across racial and ethnic groups, and among social classes?

Members of different social classes or racial or ethnic groups develop their own ways of communication through words, gestures, or expressions. For example, linguists have documented substantial differences between Standard American English and African American English, variants of which are spoken by many Blacks. These linguistic differences include actual words, syntax, acoustics, and rules for subject-verb agreement.

6.3 What is the Sapir-Whorf hypothesis?

Linguists have noted vast cultural differences in language patterns. The Sapir-Whorf hypothesis suggests that language shapes our culture, and at the same time, our culture shapes our language.

6.4 What are the six dimensions of culture that can affect communication styles?

These six dimensions are: (1) individualist versus collectivist cultures; (2) high- versus low-context cultures; (3) masculine versus feminine cultures; (4) centralized versus decentralized power; (5) high versus low ambiguity; and (6) short-term versus long-term time orientation.

6.5 What are the components of listening?

First, you need to receive, or hear, the message. Second, you must understand, or when necessary, decode what the speaker is saying. Third, messages that you receive and understand must be retained for some period of time. Fourth, you evaluate the messages that you hear. Finally, you respond. The listening process is circular and continues in a loop—often in a split second.

6.6 What are some barriers to verbal communication?

(1) *Bypassing:* misunderstanding what someone is saying when one word has several meanings; (2) *lack of precision:* mistaking one word for another, or using incorrect or unclear language; (3) *overgeneralizing:* making sweeping generalizations; (4) *static evaluation:* making statements that do not allow for change; (5) *polarization:* speaking in extremes; (6) *biased language:* using words that reflect biases towards other groups.

6.7 How can we improve our verbal communication?

(1) Describe your own feelings rather than evaluate the behavior of others; (2) solve problems rather than try to control others; (3) be genuine rather than manipulative; (4) empathize rather than remain detached; (5) be flexible rather than rigid; (6) present yourself as equal rather than superior.

6.8 What do we mean by the phrase "actions speak louder than words"?

It means that nonverbal communication is often more believable than verbal communication when the two are in conflict. Nonverbal communication is more difficult to falsify.

6.9 How are electronic means of communication changing the face of communication?

(1) We write more informally; (2) our writing influences our speech, we use more abbreviations in our speech patterns, and are less concerned about grammar; (3) we have control over our messages because we can see who is contacting us, and therefore we can better screen our communications; (4) we have more relationships, but with less depth; (5) we can live in the moment and our communication today can be more of a running discourse.

Key Terms

active listening (p. 162)
communication (p. 156)
conflict (p. 171)
content conflict (p. 172)
"doing gender" (p. 177)
ego conflict (p. 173)
intimate partner power (p. 176)

listening (p. 161)
nonregulated couples (p. 174)
nonverbal communication (p. 164)
personal power (p. 176)
power (p. 176)
pseudoconflict (p. 172)

regulating couples (p. 174)
relative love and need theory (p. 177)
resource theory (p. 177)
Sapir-Whorf hypothesis (p. 178)
self-disclosure (p. 176)

social power (p. 176)
value conflict (p. 172)
verbal communication (p. 162)

6.10 How do men's and women's communication styles differ?

Without overgeneralizing, many differences have been noted. For example, compared to men, women tend to smile more often, express a wider range of emotions through facial expressions and nonverbal behavior, and maintain more eye contact. When they speak, women use more qualifying, tentative statements that weaken the message and add an element of uncertainty. Women are more polite in tone, ask a greater number of questions, and are more likely to show interest and concern. Women also offer more personal details and disclosures.

6.11 How does self-disclosure benefit intimate relationships?

When we develop intimacy with another person we allow that person to penetrate through the superficial layers to the core of deeply personal topics—this is self-disclosure. However, it is important to acknowledge that engaging in self-disclosure does not guarantee the success of a relationship because some types of self-disclosure can threaten the relationship.

6.12 What are four types of conflict?

Pseudoconflict occurs when we falsely perceive that our partner is interfering with our goals or has incompatible goals. *Content conflict* occurs when we disagree about information. *Value conflict* results from differing opinions on subjects that relate to personal values and issues of right or wrong. *Ego conflict* arises when individuals believe they must win at all costs to save face.

6.13 What theories explain the distribution of power and decision making in relationships?

Resource theory suggests that the spouse with the more prestigious or higher-paying job can use that advantage to generate more power in the relationship and thereby influence decision making. The *principle of least interest* acknowledges that power comes from other sources than just socioeconomic status, including having less investment in the relationship. The *relative love and need theory* is a macro-level perspective that looks at the way that love itself has been defined and interpreted as feminine. The "*doing gender*" perspective suggests that we take power differentials among men and women for granted and continue to reproduce them simply because they are so ingrained in us.

PEARSON
myfamilylab
www.myfamilylab.com

Experience, Discover, Observe, Evaluate

MyFamilyLab is designed just for you. Each chapter features a pre-test and post-test to help you learn and review key concepts and terms. Experience Marriage and Family in action with dynamic visual activities, videos, and readings to enhance your learning experience.

Here are a few activities you'll find for this chapter:

Watch Core Concepts video clips feature sociologists in action, exploring important concepts in the study of Marriage and the Family. Watch:
• Social Interaction and Technology

Explore Social Explorer is an interactive application that allows you to explore Census data through interactive maps. Explore the Social Explorer Map:
• Divorce Rates across the United States

Read MySocLibrary includes primary source readings from classic and contemporary sociologists. Read:
• Blauner, "Talking Past Each Other: Black and White Languages of Race"

7

Marriage

Scherazade and Roderick with their son, Arshan

What are the ingredients for a happy and sustaining marriage? While every marriage is different, that of Scherazade and Roderick provides us with some important clues. They show us that a good marriage is the result of shared values, commitment, and communication.

Scherazade and Roderick, married for 13 years, are a very happy couple in love with life, each other, and their family. They met 14 years ago when they were tenants in the same apartment building. Given their hectic but exciting schedules where 80-hour workweeks were the norm, they agree that it was a good thing that they shared a roof because otherwise, they would never have had the time to meet!

But meet they did and they quickly fell in love. Scherazade describes herself as ambitious and playful, a global citizen, and as someone who wants a full life. She wanted a partner who could keep up with her and share a lot of things—not only what she currently likes, but introduce her to new things as well. Roderick explains that he was looking for someone who shared his values: spirituality, family, and the desire to explore the world.

Their marriage is one of complete partnership. They speak of taking turns with their careers; first, Roderick finished his medical residency, then Scherazade fulfilled her dream of doing international work in Africa. Roderick then completed his master's degree in public health, and afterwards Scherazade started a nonprofit organization.

Scherazade and Roderick's marriage is one of complete partnership.

👁 Watch the Video *Marriage: Scherazade and Roderick* on **myfamilylab.com**

Roderick began a consulting practice and they then had a baby, and are currently expecting their second child. Now, Roderick and Scherazade work only 4 days a week so that they can spend alternate days with their 18-month-old son, Arshan, who is the light of their lives. "He just reminds us of playing, laughing, and being spontaneous—things that are a really big part of who I am, and he also reminds us to put these things back into our lives because I had gotten away from them," Scherazade says.

"Life is really busy right now. We just have all kinds of things happening, all at the same time," Roderick says, but neither of them would trade their lives for anything else. How do they maintain the intimacy of their relationship? As Scherazade explains, "Maintaining that same level, or more, of passion, romance, and excitement is a challenge when you have everything else going on, but we definitely pay attention to it because it's something we value." Consequently, they schedule a date night weekly, and after their son goes to bed each night, they make time to talk and share their feelings and ideas.

Q UESTIONS That Matter

7.1 Is marriage found in every society?

7.2 Is marriage a personal relationship or a social institution?

7.3 How has marriage changed over time?

7.4 How does the marital decline perspective compare with the marital resilience perspective?

7.5 How do we explain the decline in marriage rates?

7.6 How do Americans feel about same-sex marriage?

7.7 In what ways are attitudes toward marriage changing?

7.8 What is the marriage premium?

7.9 What is a selection effect?

7.10 Does marriage benefit everyone equally?

7.11 What factors are associated with marital satisfaction and success?

7.12 What is the marriage movement?

7.13 What is a "peer" marriage?

Their shared values, commitment, and communication are clear. As Roderick says, reflecting on their family's past and future, "We've had a very rich and exciting life, and now we have the opportunity to make it rich and exciting with children. So, we have ideas of living overseas and having them learn other languages and seeing what it's like to be in a different part of the world—the idea of having them grow up as global citizens. I think that is going to be fun and exciting and a new way to grow our family." Scherazade nods in agreement.

📖► **Read** the **Document**
Mate Selection and Marriage around the World on **myfamilylab.com**

M ore than two million women and men say their wedding vows each year as they move their relationships toward what they hope will be a lifetime commitment (Tejada-Vera & Sutton, 2010). Ninety-five percent of U.S. adults marry at least once (U.S. Census Bureau, January 14, 2010). Most adults who divorce eventually remarry. They all want a relationship full of passion, love, and sexual energy, and a spouse who is kind, attentive, and compassionate—a best friend. They expect marriage to ward off loneliness and be a safe haven in an increasingly impersonal world. This is a tall order to fill, especially over the course of fifty to sixty years! 📖► **Read** on **myfamilylab.com**

However, for many married couples, such as Scherazade and Roderick, marriage seems to work. While overall only about one quarter of unmarried U.S. adults consider themselves "very happy," 43 percent of married persons do (Taylor, Funk, & Craighill, 2006). Regardless of race, ethnicity, sex, or social class, most adults place marriage at the top of their priority list. Among high school seniors, 82 percent of young women and 71 percent of young men say having a good marriage and family life is "extremely" important to them (National Marriage Project, 2009).

In this chapter we explore two sides of marriage. Most of us see the micro-level aspects of marriage; this is a personal relationship full of fun and hard work. However, marriage is also a macro-level social institution with rules, rights, and responsibilities, some determined at the state or federal level. For example, you are not free to marry just anyone. Laws in all states say you cannot marry your sibling or your twelve-year-old neighbor; in most states you cannot marry your first cousin. And as of 2010, in only five states can you marry someone of the same sex (National Conference of State Legislatures, 2010). States also establish the rules for both marriage and its dissolution. Why is the government so involved in your personal relationships? Because society views marriage as a stabilizing force and the government views marriage as its business. Here, **marriage** is defined as *a legally and socially recognized relationship that includes sexual, economic, and social rights and responsibilities for partners.*

:: Marriage: Here, There, and Everywhere

We find marriage in every human society. As an institutional arrangement for publicly recognizing social and intimate bonds, it is an important factor in ensuring the success of a society. For example, because marriage is closely connected with the socialization of children, it can also serve as a way of ensuring intergenerational continuity (Farrell, 1999). Cultural norms and sanctions, often codified into laws, specify who is eligible to be married, to whom, what the marriage ceremony should consist of, and what behavior is expected of married men and women.

Marriage is a deeply meaningful micro-level personal relationship *and* an important macro-level social institution. It is likely to shape many aspects of our personal lives—where and with whom we live, with whom we have sex, our economic well-being, how much personal power we have, and our relationship to society.

In the mainstream culture of the United States today, we marry for love; most of us believe love is the priority for a good marriage. If we fall out of love, we may even end the marriage. In other countries, love is considered among the worst reasons to marry (Leeder, 2004). Instead, marriage in these countries is about forging new bonds among extended families, creating and raising children, or continuing family lineage. For example, extraordinarily strong family bonds influence all aspects of Iraqi society because to Iraqi people, the world is divided between

marriage: A legally and socially recognized relationship that includes sexual, economic, and social rights and responsibilities for partners.

strangers and kin. Through your kin you receive financial and emotional support, job opportunities, and social position, far too much to risk with a stranger. In Iraq, it is quite common and much safer to marry a first cousin (Tierney, 2003). In parts of Africa, young teenage girls are married to older men whom they have never met. As one 14-year-old girl living in a poor area of rural Kenya speculates about the 27-year-old man her parents have chosen for her:

I wonder whether he already has other wives. Will we live together, or will he live away from the family to work in the city? Does he have a job? I probably will not continue in school or have a job. Instead, I will be having and taking care of children. ...I wonder if he could have AIDS? If I become infected, who will care for our children? Will they have it? My mind is in a whirl of questions; I am excited, happy, nervous, and concerned (Wilson, Ngige, & Trollinger, 2003).

Parents are deeply involved in choosing their children's mates in many parts of the world. As you learned in Chapter 4, about 85 percent of marriages in India are arranged (Griffith, 2006). A survey of 15- to 34-year-olds living in Delhi found 65 percent said they would obey their parents' choice. *"Any girl I could find for myself would not be as good as the one my parents will find,"* says a 19-year-old college student (Derne, 2003).

Since families, communities, and the state all have an interest in marriage, they also have a hand in controlling whom people marry. They do so by channeling and restricting interactions (and the development of love) among young people in a number of ways that are specific to different cultures. Here is a review of some of these strategies, which were introduced in Chapter 4 (Goode, 1959):

- *Child marriage*—having the child betrothed or married prior to puberty before feelings of romantic love are likely to develop.
- *Kinship rules*—adopting specific kinship rules so there is little choice as to whom to marry.
- *Segregation*—separating men and women so there is little or no chance for interaction.
- *Close supervision*—short of isolation, strictly supervising and chaperoning of young people.
- *Relative freedom*—managing the social environment of young people through schools, neighborhoods, churches, and other organizations.

All societies mark the beginning of marriage with some type of publicly recorded ceremony, although features of the ceremony can be quite different.

What components of the wedding ceremony (or the reception) are unique to American culture? How do these components contribute to the high costs of weddings in our society? How do you think wedding guests would feel if some of these components were eliminated?

All societies mark the beginning of marriage with some type of publicly recorded ceremony. In some cultures, weddings are highly festive with a party-like atmosphere and plenty of food, drink, and dancing. Weddings and wedding receptions in the United States are big business, and cost an average of $20,398 (The Wedding Report, 2010). Many parents cannot afford this high cost, but lavish weddings are so much a part of American culture that one-third of brides and grooms will pay the costs themselves rather than opt for simplicity (Wong, 2005). Other cultures have weddings that are somber, and which may be an avenue for grieving the loss of a child. Some cultures include both men and women in the wedding or the reception, or both, while in other cultures, such as where Islam is practiced, men and women are strictly segregated. The women party together in one room, while the men party together in another.

:: Marriage in U.S. History

Wives, submit yourselves unto your husbands, as unto the Lord.

For the husband is head of the wife, even as Christ is the head of the Church; and he is the savior of the body. Therefore, as the Church is subject unto Christ, so let the wives be to their own husbands in everything.

This text from the Christian Bible offers a fascinating glimpse into the nature of marriage in the United States. In the prevailing Judeo-Christian model of marriage, husband and wife "shall be one flesh" and man shall be the "head" of his wife, as Jesus Christ was the head of the Church. We can see these themes in the story of marriage throughout U.S. history.

Colonial America: Marriage and the Formation of a Nation

The founders of the U.S. government established marriage as a free-choice, heterosexual union that put husbands at the head of the household. Husbands were required to support their wives and children, and to represent them legally. The marriage "union" literally meant the husband and wife were "one," and that "one" was the husband. Wives did not have the right to vote, own property, or enter into any legal agreements without the consent of their husbands. Because they did not hold independent legal status, wives also could not be tried for a crime. Their husbands, as their freely chosen representatives, would represent them and ensure their protection.

The early Native Americans held different ideas about marriage from the colonists. The Iroquois allowed polygamy and followed matrilineal descent and patterns of matrilocal residence. As you recall from Chapter 1, this means that the kinship was drawn from the mother's lines, and the family tended to live with or near her family. Since women were the primary farmers while men were migratory hunters, it made sense that families would organize themselves around the more geographically settled wives (Brown, 1975). Some Native American groups were also known to permit premarital sex, divorce, and remarriage. This posed a challenge to early European settlers, who considered premarital sex immoral and promiscuous behavior, and divorce as sinful. As Native Americans were forced into treaties and resettlement, government officials tried to impose Christian forms of marriage upon them by offering land for relinquishing their tribal affiliations and practices (Cott, 2000).

Because the early U.S. government did not establish a national church and instead formalized the separation of church and state, states were left to regulate marriage and family relationships. In a vast and growing nation, state laws about marriage varied, and many of these differences persist today.

Redefining Marriage in the 19th Century

The institution of marriage faced many challenges throughout the 19th century. A draft of the Thirteenth Amendment, intended to eliminate slavery, included the phrase "All persons are equal before the law, so that no person can hold another as a slave." Senators worried that such language could threaten the power of men as heads of household—some might argue that wives were not unlike slaves, given that they had no independent rights to vote or own property, even though they entered marriage voluntarily. The phrase was deleted from the Amendment, and "Neither slavery nor involuntary servitude . . . shall exist within the United States" was substituted (Cott, 2000).

The first wave of the women's movement began with women working for the emancipation of slaves, as some noticed that *their* equal rights had been passed over with the adoption of the Thirteenth Amendment. The first Women's Rights Convention was held in 1848 in Seneca Falls, New York, where a group of women, including Susan B. Anthony, Elizabeth Cady Stanton, and Lucretia Mott, formed their own constitution demanding equal civil rights for all citizens, regardless of sex. They urged a marriage standard of equal partnership and greater social, economic, and legal opportunities for women.

Marriage was also challenged by those who resisted monogamy. Mormons in the Utah Territory permitted polygamy, arguing that monogamous marriage could isolate couples from the broader community or leave some women without husbands, threatening the cohesion of society. Other alternative groups, such as the Oneida Community, sprang up in the Midwest and Northeast and allowed polygamy or group marriages using the same arguments.

Marriage after the Industrial Revolution

The Industrial Revolution not only carved separate spheres of work for men and women; it also moved families from farms and small communities to cities in search of work, weakening the community's influence on the married couple and bringing a focus to marriage that was more personal and based on companionship. The responsibilities of spouses were still largely differentiated and complementary; men worked outside the home while women took care of the children and the home. Other social changes influenced marriage as well including:

- *The changing experiences of youth.* As we learned in Chapter 3, relationships between young men and women underwent significant changes at the turn of the 20th century. Because young people spent increasing time in school, away from parents, there was more opportunity for personal growth and the development of romantic relationships (Coontz, 1992). This focus carried forward into marriage. Couples made decisions about marriage based more on love and less on the economic aspects of earlier generations.

- *A sexual revolution.* We often think of the "sexual revolution" occurring during the 1960s among college students. However, most historical research shows that nonmarital sex has been far more common throughout U.S. history than some have assumed. The early 1900s, for instance, ushered in a greater amount of leisure time away from parents, an emphasis on romantic love, opportunities for privacy in new places like the automobile, and the availability of birth control.

For most of history a person moved quickly from childhood to adulthood. But today people spend longer in school and are financially dependent for more years, and therefore, delay marriage. *How I Met Your Mother* is one of many television shows that depict this trend. When people do marry, they have high expectations for affection, intimacy, and friendship.

Tying It All Together

What Explains Blacks' Lower Rate of Marriage?

In the U.S., Blacks are far less likely to marry than are Whites. A snapshot in time reveals that only about 33 percent of Blacks were married in 2009, compared to 56 percent of Whites. Certainly more people postpone marriage; this partially accounts for why so few people today fall into the category of "married." However, there are several macro-level factors operating that influence our micro-level personal choices and values.

Micro-level Factors

- "I haven't yet met the right person . . ."
- "I don't want to get married . . ."
- "I like being single . . ."
- "I don't want to get married yet . . ."
- "I don't think I will ever get married. . . ."

Macro-level Factors

- Economic considerations: unstable work, low pay
- Imbalanced sex ratio
- Racism
- Levels of education

What Do You Think?

1. Can you think of specific ways that the macro-level factors might shape the micro-level choices about marriage?
2. Do you think these macro-level factors operate differently across different racial and ethnic groups? In other words, how might they operate differently for Hispanics, or what other macro-level factors might be uniquely pertinent for Hispanics? Asian Americans? Native Americans? Whites?

Blacks have lower rates of marriage than do other groups, but it is not because they do not value marriage; actually, they value marriage very highly. Many do not want to marry until important markers are in place, such as a good job or a nice house, or money for a wedding.

that they often cannot meet. They want employment, a secure home, and an expensive wedding; "I want a yard with grass, plus, I want a nice wedding" (Edin & Kefalas, 2005). Marriage is a sign of prestige: it comes *after* a certain level of attainment. Yet, these goals are difficult to obtain on low-wage work; therefore, many Blacks put off or forgo marriage. In other words, macro-level factors, such as economic conditions, can shape our micro-level choices, such as whether we choose to marry.

A second macro-level reason for lower marriage rates in the U.S., particularly among Blacks, is a skewed sex ratio in some Black communities which makes it difficult for women to find marriage partners. For example, the rate of incarceration among Blacks is six times that of Whites (Sabol, West, & Cooper, 2009). Even though the number of Blacks in prison declined by nearly 18,500 since 2000, Black men are 30 times as likely to be in jail as Black women, skewing the sex ratio for available mates.

These are only two challenges facing Black marriages, but there are many others. The high school dropout rate among Blacks is considerably higher than for Whites, which makes it more challenging for educated Black women to find partners (National Center for Education Statistics, 2009). Perhaps, it is not surprising that young Black people are significantly more likely to assume that they will never marry (Crissey, 2005). In other words, macro-level factors shape our opportunities and constraints.

Blacks who *do* marry are a select group; they are more likely to have stable jobs; they report more traditional attitudes about marriage, cohabitation, and premarital sex than Whites; and they are more religious (Brown, Orbuch, & Bauermeister, 2008; Wilcox & Wolfinger, 2007). In other words, despite the structural odds against marriage for this group, they believe so strongly in marriage that they are able to beat those odds.

As the number of years between reaching adulthood and marriage increases for all racial and ethnic groups, so does the opportunity for nonmarital sex and cohabitation. Rising rates of singlehood, cohabitation, nonmarital sex, and nonmarital childbearing are all seen as challenges to the institution of marriage. Nonetheless, most U.S. adults want to marry, and most eventually do. In fact, the likelihood of never having married by age 65 has not changed in over 100 years. Instead, the two primary reasons for the cross-sectional decline in the percentage of the population who is married at any given time is that (1) people are more likely to divorce—the percentage of persons divorced or separated in 2009 was more than twice that in 1970 (although most divorced people eventually remarry); and (2) people are delaying marriage until later in life. In other words, these people do eventually marry (sometimes even a second or third time), but because they marry when they are older, cross-sectional data portray a large number of unmarried individuals. ✴ ⌐Explore on **myfamilylab.com**

Delayed Marriage

✴ ⌐**Explore** the **Concept**
Social Explorer Report: Trends in Marriage Rates on
myfamilylab.com

Thais is 26, has a master's degree in education, is a teacher, and writes dramatic movie scripts in the evening. She is also developing a nonprofit tutoring organization so that she can someday have her own business. She is happy, and has a plan for where she is going over the next several years. It isn't down the aisle. "I don't see myself getting married until, maybe, when I'm over thirty. Well over thirty" (Malernee, 2006).

Ask your grandparents or any other older person about the 1950s (and early 1960s), and they will likely tell you that they married when they were about 20 or 21. During this period, there was a near-feverish push to get married and have a family. One psychiatrist wrote in 1953 that "a girl who hasn't a man in sight by the time she is 20 is not altogether wrong in feeling that she may never get married," and therefore, young women set their sights on finding a husband early (Coontz, 2007). Betty Friedan chronicled the emphasis on domesticity in her best-selling classic, *The Feminine Mystique* (1963). Even if your grandmother went to college, she understood that even more important than earning her B.A. degree was obtaining her "M.R.S." degree. Television shows, radio, and magazines seemed to glorify being a wife and mother to the exclusion of all other choices. The cheerful housewife was portrayed in her immaculate dress, wearing heels, and a necklace of pearls, happily cooking dinner for her husband and many children. Consequently, as shown in Figure 7.3, age at marriage dropped to an all-time low during the 1950s, to 20 years for women (with the greatest number marrying at 18) and 23 for men.

Since that period, the age at first marriage has been steadily increasing, particularly over the past few decades. Today, the average age for first marriage is 26 for women and 28 for men (U.S. Census Bureau, 2009); for those persons with advanced degrees, the age is even higher. The reasons for this increase include changes in occupational and educational opportunities—especially for women, broader cultural shifts in values associated with marriage and singlehood, and structural changes in the economy. Women and men are remaining unmarried not because marriage is less appealing, but because it is becoming more appealing to wait.

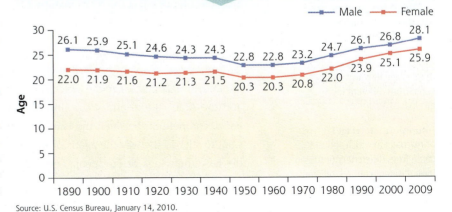

Figure 7.3 **Median Age at First Marriage, Ages 15 and Over, by Sex, 1890–2009**

The average age at which we marry has been increasing since 1960 for both men and women.

Source: U.S. Census Bureau, January 14, 2010.

Homogamous versus Heterogamous Marriages

People tend to marry others who look like them and have similar backgrounds, making **homogamous marriages**. A 70-year-old man marrying a 28-year-old woman or a woman on welfare marrying a millionaire may make gossip magazine headlines, but these types of relationships are rare. Still, our society has become more tolerant of **heterogamous marriages**, in which spouses do not share certain social characteristics, such as race, ethnicity, religion, education, age, or social class.

This section will discuss three ways in which marriages are becoming more heterogamous in our society: (1) interracial/interethnic marriages; (2) marriages between different social classes; and (3) interfaith marriages.

> In heterogamous marriages, spouses are significantly different from one another on a critical dimension, such as age, religion, race or ethnic background, or social class.

Interracial and Interethnic Marriages The number of persons of different races or ethnic background who marry is increasing (Passel et al. 2010). A record 14.6 percent of all marriages in 2008, and 8 percent of marriages overall, were between people of differing races or ethnicities, almost double the rate in 1990. Of marriages performed in 2008, Asians were most likely to marry someone of a different race or ethnicity, while Whites were least likely (Passel et al. 2010).

Interracial marriage, or marrying someone of a different race, once was illegal in the United States. During the 19th century, concerned by the impending emancipation of slaves, states created **antimiscegenation laws** forbidding interracial marriage, mainly to prevent marriage between Whites and those considered nonWhite, especially Blacks. Marriages between different nonWhite races such as between a Black and an Asian were generally not prohibited. The laws were meant to maintain the power and privilege of Whites and uphold popular beliefs about racial separation, difference, and purity (Lee & Edmonston, 2005). It was not until 1967 that the U.S. Supreme Court struck down such laws in *Loving v. Virginia*. Alabama was the last state to formally repeal its antimiscegenation law through a state constitutional amendment in 2000.

Interethnic marriages, with partners from different cultural or ethnic backgrounds, are more common than interracial marriages. Partners in interethnic marriages must be sensitive to cultural differences and the social and political forces that have created or perpetuated them. For example, a study about marriage between Western women and Palestinian men living in Palestinian cities on the West Bank found that patriarchy and east-west power relations and stereotypes affect the relationships. One man describes the importance of compromise:

homogamous marriage: A type of marriage in which spouses share certain social characteristics such as race, ethnicity, religion, education, age, and social class.

heterogamous marriage: A type of marriage in which spouses do not share certain social characteristics such as race, ethnicity, religion, education, age, and social class.

antimiscegenation laws: Laws forbidding interracial marriage, which existed at the state level until 1967.

interracial marriage: A type of marriage in which spouses come from different racial groups.

interethnic marriage: A type of marriage in which spouses come from different countries or have different cultural, religious, or ethnic backgrounds.

I understand differences we have between myself and Helen, between the Western culture and the Arab culture and it's a kind of, you know, competition between the two. And if I want to stick to the way the Arabs or the Middle Easterners look at Europeans, everything would be wrong. Just take women's lives, the way it is open in the West, the way women have rights, freedom, all this. It's different here and we have to accept these differences and take steps towards each other (Roer-Strier & Ben Ezra, 2006).

Attitudes toward interracial and interethnic relationships have become more favorable in the last 30 or 40 years (Rosenfeld, 2008). Seventy-seven percent of adults approve of Black-White marriages, up from only 48 percent in 1994 (Carroll, 2007). Despite potential challenges, partners in one study of interracial relationships reported significantly higher relationship satisfaction than those in same-race relationships (Troy, Lewis-Smith, & Laurenceau, 2006). A second study found no differences between interracial and same-race relationships in relationship quality, conflict patterns, coping style, and attachment. These studies cast doubt on the idea that interracial relationships are burdened with more problems, or break down in the face of challenges, more often than do more homogamous relationships (Troy, Lewis-Smith, & Laurenceau, 2006).

Marriage across Social Class Boundaries   The extent of opportunities to meet and marry others outside your social position influences the rate of heterogamous marriages. Certainly people are free to marry anyone they choose—rich or poor. The idea of marrying across class lines is a common theme in U.S. movies, but the movie-going public tends to marry within its own social class.

For example, a common way to meet a spouse is through college. Many of the very rich attend elite private colleges and universities to make connections for some of the best jobs; however, being accepted into these colleges depends upon far more than just grades. Most have *legacy preferences*—programs for admitting children of alumni—that account for 10 to 15 percent of the composition of every incoming class (Economist.com, 2004). The incoming classes are not particularly diverse; these schools perpetuate a way for the elite to meet other elites. Middle- and working-class students tend to go to state-funded universities, and meet other middle- and working-class students.

Moreover, some boundaries in the socioeconomic hierarchy are difficult to cross. In terms of occupations, someone who works with his or her hands—for example, in construction—is less likely to marry someone who works with ideas—for example, a college professor. With respect to education, intermarriage is also less likely between those with and those without a college education. The reason is that occupation and education serve as both indicators of preferences and tastes *and* predictors of economic success, and thus people choose spouses with whom they have things in common.

Interfaith Marriages   Marrying someone of a different religious faith is less frowned upon in society than marrying across other groups because faith is generally not as visible as race, age, or social class. Nonetheless, interfaith marriages can still face challenges.

Religion is important to many people. Seventy-one percent of U.S. adults are "absolutely certain" there is a God, and 56 percent claim their religion is very important in their lives (Pew Research Center, June 23, 2008). Religions provide beliefs about what is right and wrong, and different religions approach certain topics very differently, such as women's and men's roles in marriage, divorce, abortion, or how to raise children—all issues that may require considerable negotiation and compromise in a marriage. Therefore, it is not surprising that couples who hold similar religious beliefs and participate jointly in religious practice have, on average, happier and more satisfying marriages than those who do not (Curtis & Ellison, 2002; Myers, 2006). Shared religion can increase family cohesiveness and provide a unified approach to resolving marital and family issues.

There are many different types of interfaith marriages, including:

- a spouse who follows a specific religion and a spouse who follows a non-theistic ethical system (say, Judaism and Humanism)
- spouses of two religions that are totally different (such as Christianity and Buddhism)
- spouses of two religions that have at least some points of similarity (two Abrahamic religions that share Abraham as a Patriarch, including Christianity and Islam)
- spouses from different major divisions within the same religion (Roman Catholicism and Protestantism)

- spouses from different sects of the same religion (Evangelical and mainline Christian)
- spouses from different traditions within the same sects of the same religion (two conservative denominations such as Southern Baptist and Assemblies of God)

To make the marriage combination even more complex, one spouse could be an atheist. The degree of complexity in interfaith marriages largely depends on (1) the degree of difference between the partners' faiths and (2) how religious the partners actually are. A marriage between a devout Mormon and a committed Muslim would likely face far more differences and potential clashes of faith than would a marriage between two Protestant denominations, despite the fact that both religions are misunderstood by a substantial number of Americans (Pew Research Center, June 23, 2008; September 25, 2007). More than half of U.S. adults say they do not know very much or anything about Muslims or Mormons. Yet, seventy percent say the Muslim religion and 62 percent say the Mormon religion is "a lot different" from their own religion, and over one-quarter have an unfavorable attitude toward these two groups (Pew Research Center, September 25, 2007).

Overall, rates of intermarriage based on race, ethnicity, class, and religious differences have increased, both in the United States and in other developed nations. The mainstream U.S. view is that we are free to choose whom we marry, and the decision to marry should be based on love. At the same time, marriages do not exist in a vacuum. Prejudice still exists in U.S. society, and there are still consequences for those who marry someone significantly different from themselves. Macro-level factors continue to shape our micro-level choices.

Same-Sex Marriage

Another recent change in marriage is the legalization of same-sex marriage in Massachusetts, New Jersey, Connecticut, Iowa, and Vermont (National Conference of State Legislatures, 2010). California and Maine allowed same-sex marriage until ballot measures overturned the decisions. One of the most important policy issues of the day, same-sex marriage is also among the most controversial.

> Jack Baker, a lawyer, and Mike McConnell, a librarian who has been Jack's partner since 1967, are old fashioned romantics in the Midwestern tradition. Each believes the other is his soul mate, his "better half," the one person whose love makes his own life complete. Once you have found your soul mate, Baker and McConnell agree, you ought to commit your lives to one another. The institution within which you should do that—for spiritual, personal, and even civic reasons—is marriage, which they idealize as potentially perfect. Anything else is a cheap imitation (Eskridge & Spedale, 2006).

Why are gays and lesbians demanding the right to marry? Because marriage matters (Waite & Gallagher, 2000). There are at least 1,400 documented legal rights associated with marriage that are not guaranteed to cohabiting couples, including joint parenting and adoption laws, tax savings, immigration and residency, insurance benefits, crime victims' recovery benefits, and the right to make end-of-life decisions. Some of these rights are given to members of **civil unions**, a public policy designed to extend some benefits to partners who are not legally married, but as shown in Table 7.2, civil unions do not provide the same degree of protection as marriage. For example, partners in civil unions cannot file joint federal tax returns.

Vermont is credited as the leader of the same-sex marriage movement in the United States for its adoption of a civil union bill in 2000, which moved the debate to a new level. However, Massachusetts was the first state to actually allow same-sex marriage. How did

civil union: A public policy designed to extend some benefits to partners who are not legally married.

Table 7.2	The Benefits of Marriage versus Civil Unions		
	Marriage confers many benefits on a couple that civil unions do not.		
	Married Couples	**Unmarried Couples**	**Civil Unions**
Portability of rights	Union automatically recognized in all 50 states.	Can register as domestic partners in some states.	Usually only recognized in the state that approves them. But recently in New York, a civil union from Vermont was recognized in a wrongful-death suit.
Gifts and property transfers	May make unlimited transfers and gifts to each other.	Any gift or transfer worth more than $10,000 in a year requires filing a federal gift tax return.	Same as unmarried couples, larger gifts and transfers are subject to federal tax.
Income tax status	"Married filing jointly" generally works to the advantage of couples when one earns much more than the other, but creates a penalty when their incomes are similar.	Unmarried couples cannot file jointly, although an adult with custody of a child can file as "head of household."	A couple can file only state tax returns jointly, federal returns are filed individually.
Child or spousal support	Criminal penalties are imposed on spouses who abandon a child or a spouse.	Unmarried partners have no legal obligation to support their partners or partner's children.	In state where the union is granted, the courts can impose penalties on a partner who abandons a child or a spouse.
Medical decisions	A spouse or family member may make decisions for an incompetent or disabled person unless contrary written instructions exist.	A health-care proxy, prepared before a problem occurs, can designate anyone, including a partner, to make decisions.	Partners in the state where the union was granted can make health decisions, but in other states that authority may not be recognized.
Immigration	U.S. citizens and legal permanent residents can sponsor their spouses and other immediate family members for immigration purposes.	Not allowed to sponsor a partner or other immediate family members.	Not allowed to sponsor a partner or other immediate family members.

Source: "Majority Continues to Support Civil Unions: Most Still Oppose Same-Sex Marriage", October 9, 2009, Pew Research Center For the People & the Press and the Pew Forum On Religion & Public Life, projects of the Pew Research Center.

that law come about? In 2004 a lesbian couple filed a lawsuit in Massachusetts, claiming they, too, had a right to marry. Massachusetts courts sided with them and ruled that only full, equal marriage rights for gay couples, rather than civil unions, are constitutional. "The history of our nation has demonstrated that separate is seldom, if ever equal," one Justice claimed, evoking similarities to Blacks' struggle for equality (Peter, 2004). The lesbian couple is introduced in the *Diversity in Families* box.

Advocates see same-sex marriage as a civil rights issue, akin to equal rights for women, minorities, or the disabled. The Court's ruling repeatedly invoked the words "respect and dignity" and framed the marriage question as one that deeply affected not just couples, but also their children.

The opinions of opponents vary, but many feel same-sex marriage is immoral and in violation of God's teaching. Others believe marriage has always been defined as between a man and a woman, and changing the definition cheapens its fundamental meaning. Others say homosexuality is unnatural, and states should not sanction homosexual relationships or raising children in a homosexual household (Family Focus, 2008). Some opponents of

Diversity in Families

"I Don't Think We Ever Take Our Marriage for Granted"

"*Our marriage is even more precious to us because we had to work so hard for it.*"

Gina and Heidi, both 43, are the picture of domesticity. Together since 1990, they live and raise children together, and are upstanding members of their community, volunteering for such projects as adult literacy, fair housing, and mentoring a high school student. Gina works as a classroom aide for students with disabilities, and Heidi is an executive director of an emergency food pantry. They never intended to be in the limelight. Yet Gina and Heidi made history—they were

Massachusetts was the first state to allow same-sex marriage. In 2004, a lesbian couple filed a lawsuit in Massachusetts, claiming they, too, had a right to marry. Since then several other states have allowed same-sex marriage, allowing many same-sex couples like the one above to marry.

among the plaintiffs in the Massachusetts lawsuit against the State Department of Public Health after being denied a marriage license, which led to the legalization of same-sex marriage in 2004. With their sons by their side and 100 family members and friends in attendance, they were legally married in May 2004.

Why was it so important for Gina and Heidi to marry? Their answer resembles that of any couple in love, "*The most important reason we wanted to get married is that we love each other, and we wanted to be responsible for and to each other,*" said Gina. She continued, "*No one knows Heidi as I do—what her fears are, her hopes, her dreams. I know what she wants if she is unable to make decisions for herself. I know what she wants for our children. And she knows those things about me. Marriage makes us feel secure in our relationship and ensures that those wishes will be respected. It is a public statement of our love and commitment.*"

How do they address the concerns of others that somehow their marriage devalues traditional marriage? Gina continues, "*Some people think that we are not honoring marriage by pursuing the lawsuit. But the complete opposite is true, because we saw marriage as a way to protect our family and to stand up and have our community recognize us as a serious relationship.*" They do not see themselves as dishonoring marriage, but rather, as asking to be a part of something that they honor so deeply. Heidi adds, "*I don't think we ever take our marriage for granted.*"

Sources: WorldNetDaily, 2003; Redbook, June 2008; Gay & Lesbian Advocates & Defenders, 2008.

What Do **You** Think?

1. Some people may think same-sex marriage devalues traditional marriage. What is your opinion on the issue? How did you form this opinion?

2. Can you think of any issue that you would be willing to fight for in the courts?

What do you think about these various changes in marriage laws? Which ones do you think are good ideas, and which do you see as potentially problematic, and why?

same-sex marriage support civil unions or domestic partnerships for gays and lesbians, but shut the door on legal marriage. Former President Bush was an outspoken opponent of same-sex marriage and supported a national ban against it, ". . . If we're to prevent the meaning of marriage from being changed forever, our nation must enact a constitutional amendment to protect marriage in America. Decisive and democratic action is needed because attempts to redefine marriage in a single state or city could have serious consequences throughout the country" (The White House, 2004). Although a national ban never materialized, many states have passed laws prohibiting same-sex marriage. President Obama, while not actively working towards a ban, also does not support same-sex marriage.

Public support for same-sex marriage and civil unions is increasing, as shown in Figure 7.4. Overall, over half of U.S. adults now support civil unions, and 39 percent support same-sex marriage. As you can see in Table 7.3, women are more likely than men, and Hispanics are more likely than other racial or ethnic groups, to support same-sex marriage. Young adults and college graduates are now more likely to support than oppose same-sex marriage (Pew Research Center for the People and the Press, October 9, 2009).

When you think about marriage, do you think about it as a micro-level personal relationship, or as a macro-level social institution? What are your reasons for your views?

Changing Attitudes about Marriage

Americans are shifting the way they think about marriage and intimate relationships which, in turn, changes the nature of marriage in our country. As you learned in Chapter 3, we are becoming more tolerant of nonmarital sex, cohabitation, and nonmarital childbearing, and we are witnessing a change in attitudes about the gendered division of labor (National Marriage Project, 2009; Pew Research Center, July 1, 2007). In the opening vignette of this chapter, the depiction of Roderick and Scherazade show that breadwinning and domestic labor are increasingly being shared by married couples.

One area that has *not* changed much, however, is the value associated with marriage. Most people want to marry and view a "good" marriage as an important life goal. They believe marriage is a lifetime commitment and should not be terminated except under extreme circumstances. Nonetheless, most people believe there are other legitimate paths to happiness as well. This may explain why belief in a "decline" in the value of marriage is a misinterpretation: people do want a happy marriage, but they are also tolerant of different lifestyles.

Attitudes about Nonmarital Sex   There has been a strong shift in U.S. attitudes toward nonmarital sex, as noted in Chapter 5 (Pew Research Center, July 1, 2007). In 1970, about half of survey respondents believed nonmarital sex was "almost always" or "always" wrong. Most people, especially younger generations, now believe nonmarital sex is not wrong, and most have engaged in it (Axinn & Thornton, 2000; Carter, 2006). Therefore, people no longer need to turn exclusively to marriage early in life to fulfill their sexual needs.

Attitudes about Cohabitation   With nearly 7 million U.S. households maintained by cohabiting heterosexual couples, and countless more maintained by gay and lesbian couples, virtually all of us

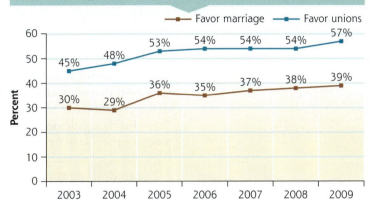

Figure 7.4	Support for Gay Marriage, Civil Unions, 2003–2009

Support for same-sex marriage and civil unions is on the rise, but it remains that civil unions have more widespread support.

— Favor marriage   — Favor unions

Favor unions: 45% (2003), 48% (2004), 53% (2005), 54% (2006), 54% (2007), 54% (2008), 57% (2009)

Favor marriage: 30% (2003), 29% (2004), 36% (2005), 35% (2006), 37% (2007), 38% (2008), 39% (2009)

Source: "Majority Continues to Support Civil Unions: Most Still Oppose Same-Sex Marriage", October 9, 2009, Pew Research Center For the People & the Press and the Pew Forum On Religion & Public Life, projects of the Pew Research Center.

Table 7.3	Percent Who Favor Same-Sex Marriage

Women, Hispanics, younger persons, those who have more education, and those who are less religious are more likely to support legalizing same-sex marriage.

	Favor
Total	39%
Men	34%
Women	43%
White	39%
Black	26%
Hispanic	45%
18–29	58%
30–49	38%
50–64	35%
65+	22%
College grad +	49%
Some college	42%
High school or less	32%
Attend services	
Weekly or more	22%
Monthly/yearly	47%
Seldom/never	54%

Source: "Majority Continues to Support Civil Unions: Most Still Oppose Same-Sex Marriage", October 9, 2009, Pew Research Center For the People & the Press and the Pew Forum On Religion & Public Life, projects of the Pew Research Center.

know someone who has or is currently cohabiting (National Marriage Project, 2009; U.S. Census Bureau, February 25, 2009). Marriage may or may not be a part of the couple's future plans. Today, people of all ages are more likely than in the past to approve of living together (Cunningham & Thornton, 2005; Manning, Longmore, & Giordano, 2007; Seltzer, 2004). Over half of high school seniors agree it is a "good idea for a couple to live together before getting married in order to find out if they really get along" (National Marriage Project, 2009). Young people may be including cohabitation in their life trajectories, but rarely do they see it as a substitute for marriage (Manning, Longmore, & Giordano, 2007).

Attitudes about Nonmarital Childbearing

About twenty years ago, Murphy Brown, a television character who epitomized the single professional woman of the time, shocked viewers by choosing to have, and raise, a baby outside marriage. Then-U.S. Vice President Dan Quayle condemned the controversial television show, saying Murphy Brown was mocking the role of fathers, and glorifying single motherhood. What do today's Americans think about single women having children?

Overall, most people do not think positively about single motherhood. While people are more tolerant than they were in the past, 66 percent of adults still believe that single women having children "is a bad thing for society" (Pew Research Center, July 1, 2007). Men and Whites are far more disapproving than women or minorities. Interestingly, there is little difference by age: 65 percent of adults ages 18–29 think that single women having children is bad for society, as do 68 percent of adults ages 50–64.

Although many Americans do not think single motherhood is a good idea, most do not have a problem with unmarried couples having children. The same survey by the Pew Research Center found that only about 43 percent of adults reported that it was "very important" for an unmarried couple to marry when they have a child together. Hispanics felt the most strongly that the couple should marry, as did older persons (Pew Research Center, July 1, 2007).

Attitudes about Shared Breadwinning

ran and Lan Li Li have been married for nine years and have two young sons, ages 6 and 7. Tran is an architect and Lan Li Li works as a librarian for the county courthouse. They always knew they would both work while raising their children and never seriously considered otherwise. Tran is happy to share the

They always knew they would both work while raising their children and never seriously considered otherwise.

responsibility of earning an income, "Of course Li Li works, this isn't the 1950s here. Besides, a family cannot really make it on one income anyway. I really wouldn't want all that responsibility on my shoulders. Sure, we scramble in the morning to get everyone ready for school and work, but Li Li and I do it together."

How do your attitudes about marriage differ from those of your parents? What do you think accounts for these changes? Can you identify any macro-level factors? What do your parents think of your attitudes toward marriage?

More married women are working outside the home than ever before. They work for many reasons: as the sole provider, to share the breadwinning role, for supplemental income, or for the fun of it. In previous generations women often quit work when they married, or at least when they had children. Marriage meant a complementary division of labor: husbands earned the family income and wives stayed at home and raised the children. Today women comprise nearly half the labor market, and the majority of U.S. adults believe both spouses should work outside the home (Paul, 2006). In fact, wives now have slightly more education than husbands, and nearly one-quarter of wives earn more than their spouse (Fry & Cohn, 2010). "There are fewer

Cinderella marriages these days. Men are less interested in rescuing a woman from poverty. They want to find someone who will pull her weight," says Dr. Stephanie Coontz, author of several books on families, including *Marriage, a History* (Coontz, 2006, cited in Paul, 2006). The man who is a physician, lawyer, or business executive is more likely to marry his peer rather than his nurse, legal secretary, or office assistant. This change has significantly reshaped marriage as an institution to include the allocation of power, decision making, and household labor.

Attitudes about the Division of Household Labor If men now want a woman who will "pull her weight financially," then, when both partners work, who should be responsible for cooking, cleaning, yard maintenance, and taking care of the children? As we will see in Chapter 10, housework and childcare are still primarily done by women, even when women work outside the home (Bianchi & Milkie, 2010; Bureau of Labor Statistics, May 8, 2008; Schiebinger & Gilmartin, 2010). Nonetheless, the time men spend on domestic tasks is increasing (Evertsson & Nermo, 2004; Galinsky, Aumann, & Bond, 2009). Younger men and women, in particular, believe housework should be shared and are learning to negotiate these important tasks.

In summary, attitudes about marriage and sexual relations have changed considerably over the past several decades. U.S. adults are now more accepting of nonmarital sex, cohabitation, having children outside marriage, and less traditional domestic practices. But despite views that challenge traditional notions of marriage, the majority continue to endorse marriage, want to marry, and eventually do. Marriage still holds a special place in people's lives. Their expectations have changed, but they still believe marriage is a good thing. What benefits accrue from marriage? 👁 Watch on **myfamilylab.com**

Although women still do more domestic labor than do men, things are changing, especially among the young, as depicted in this photograph.

👁 **Watch the Video**
Marriage and Family–Work
on **myfamilylab.com**

:: The Marriage Premium: Happiness, Health, and Economic Security

Arguments in favor of marriage include a **marriage premium**, meaning that married people are happier, healthier, and financially better off than those who are not married, including cohabiters (DeNavas-Walt, Proctor, & Smith, 2010; Fagan 2009; Manzoli, Villari, Pirone, & Boccia, 2007; Waite & Gallagher, 2000). But, does marriage *cause* people to be happier, healthier, and have a better economic situation? Or, in a **selection effect**, are people who are happier, healthier, and wealthier more likely to marry in the first place? Marriage is likely both a cause and a consequence of happiness, health, and stronger finances for the married couple. However, there is no denying that marriage seems to protect people and confers on them many real and important benefits (Manzoli, Villari, Pirone, & Boccia, 2007; DeNavas-Walt, Proctor, & Smith, 2010).

Psychological Well-being and Happiness

Married people are more likely to say that they are "very happy" with life in general than are those who are not married (43 percent versus 24 percent, respectively) (Taylor, Funk, & Craighill, 2006). This has been a consistent research finding over many years, for men as well as women, for young and old, although the marriage gap in happiness is not quite as great among the elderly. At the other end of the spectrum, married people are the least likely to say they are unhappy with their lives. Married people also benefit in other dimensions of

marriage premium: The concept that married people are happier, healthier, and financially better off than those who are not married.

selection effect: The hypothesis that people who marry may be different from those who do not marry; for example, they may be happier, healthier, and have more money.

Why Do Research?

Marriage Is Good Medicine for Those with Depression

Marriage, at least a good marriage, seems to boost levels of happiness, but what happens if you experience depression prior to getting married? Do people with depression also benefit from marriage? A research team from Ohio State University, Drs. Frech and Williams, pondered that question, and hypothesized that people who have depression would have worse marital quality and would therefore, experience fewer benefits from marriage, but that is not what they found.

The researchers used data from the National Survey of Families and Households, a large, nationally representative sample that included over 3,000 unmarried adults under age 55. After following their sample for five years, they identified people who

Unmarried people, on average, have higher rates of depression, lower levels of self-esteem, more distant personal relationships with others, a weaker sense of personal growth, and feelings of being less in control of one's life.

married during that period and asked questions about the quality of their marriage and their psychological well-being.

What they found surprised them: although marriage seems to provide benefits, it provides even greater psychological benefits to persons with depression than it does to the rest of the population. When they compared *all* the people who married with *all* the people who did not marry during this period, they found those who married were somewhat less likely to have depression than those who were unmarried. However, among the subgroup of persons with depression, the benefits of marriage were even greater, and they scored even lower on the depression scale. The study did find that persons with depression have marriages with greater conflict and report being less happy in their marriages. Nonetheless, apparently being in even a less-than-perfect marriage considerably increased their level of happiness. The researchers speculate that marriage might provide the companionship that singles with depression typically lack in their lives.

Sources: Frech & Williams, 2007; Health Behavior News Service, 2007.

What Do You Think?

1. Do you think the benefits of marriage might be different for men with depression and women with depression? Would the benefits be different for Blacks, Whites, Asians, Hispanics, or Native Americans? Why or why not?

2. Given what you have also learned in Chapter 3 on cohabitation, why do you think cohabitation does not lower depression or increase happiness in the same way marriage does?

psychological well-being, including having lower rates of depression, higher levels of self-esteem, closer personal relationships with others, a stronger sense of personal growth, and feelings of being more in control of one's life (Fagan, 2009; Frech & Williams, 2007; Lamb, Lee, & DeMaris, 2003). While some of the difference may be due to a selection effect—happy people are more likely to marry in the first place—researchers are quick to point out that marriage affords a number of protections such as social support and companionship that can significantly boost psychological well-being. People with depression may get the biggest boost of all from marriage, as shown in the *Why Do Research?* feature box.

Health

Married people, men in particular, are healthier than people who are unmarried (Hughes & Waite, 2009; National Center for Health Statistics, 2009; Schoenborn & Adams, 2010; Verbrugge, 1979a, b). They live longer and are less likely to die from the leading causes of death (coronary heart disease, stroke, pneumonia, cancer, cirrhosis, automobile accidents, murder, and suicide) (Manzoli, Villari, Pilone, & Boccia, 2007). Married persons are less likely to have depression or anxiety than their unmarried counterparts. They have better health habits, are more likely to have health insurance, and to receive more regular health care (Bernstein, Cohen, Brett, & Bush, 2008; National Center for Health Statistics, 2009).

Why do these health differences exist between married and unmarried people? It is generally thought marriage confers a health advantage by offering social support and decreased isolation, an incentive to behave in healthier ways, and an increased income for the couple. However, researchers have found that it is not only marriage that is associated with better health, but a *satisfying* marriage (Parker-Pope, April 12, 2010; Partenheimer, 2003). In a study of nearly 500 middle-aged women over a 13-year period, researchers found happy marriages were associated with good health, but unhappy marriages were linked to more depression, hostility, and anger—all risk factors for coronary heart disease and other health problems.

Economic Security

People who are married have more money and accumulate greater assets than those who are single or divorced, regardless of race or ethnic background (DeNavas-Walt, Proctor, & Smith, 2010). In particular, married men have higher earnings than their unmarried counterparts—by at least 12 percent. What accounts for this **wage premium** associated with marriage? The premium may be attributed to at least three factors: (1) married men may work harder knowing they are supporting others; (2) employers may discriminate in favor of "family men," whom they see as stable and good workers; and (3) wives still have most of the responsibility for housework and childcare, freeing men to focus on paid work. Women receive financial gains from marriage as well, although not necessarily in terms of their own earnings. They benefit indirectly because of the addition of their husbands' income and greater earning power to the household. Spouses pool their resources together and therefore have higher incomes, are more likely to have savings and assets, and health insurance and retirement benefits through employers.

It appears that a happy marriage conveys many important health and economic benefits, and being married is considered a positive ideal in the U.S. But again, is there a marriage premium in operation, or is it a selection effect? Even though both factors are likely in operation—that is, marriage is both a cause and a consequence of happiness, health, and stronger finances—there is no denying that marriage seems to protect people and confer on them many real and important benefits (Manzoli, Villari, Pilone, & Boccia, 2007).

One way in which marriage confers benefits is through producing **social capital**—the goods and services that are by-products of social relationships, such as connections, social support, information, and financial help. Marriage, through its obligations and bonds, is an important source of social capital. These social obligations and bonds exist not only between the married partners, but also between the couple and their extended families, and between the couple and their community.

t hink about yourself, or someone close to you who is married. What specific types of social capital are received in this marriage? How might this social capital be different from that received by a cohabiting couple or a single person?

:: Does Marriage Benefit Everyone Equally?

Marriage may confer considerable benefits upon the married couple, but we may not have the entire picture if the only comparison made is between people who are married and those who are not married. Another important point to consider is whether marriage benefits all married people equally. The answer is a complex one, but we are beginning to see that macro-level social factors such as sex, race, and ethnicity influence the benefits that we receive from marriage.

wage premium: Generally, married men earn more than their unmarried counterparts, particularly married men with stay-at-home wives.

social capital: The goods and services that are by-products of social relationships, including connections, social support, information, or financial help.

These different concepts reveal that marriage can be enduring without necessarily being particularly happy—or at least happy by traditional standards. Cuber and Haroff (1965) found 80 percent of the relationships in the study were in one of the first three categories. These marriages may come up short of conventional definitions of "happy," but the spouses consider them "good enough" with no real reason to end them.

Measuring Marital Satisfaction

Just as there are many different types of marriages, there are many different ways to measure satisfaction in marriage. These range from detailed evaluations about the relationship and interaction patterns to a single-item measure such as, "Would you say you are very happy, somewhat happy, somewhat unhappy, or very unhappy with your marriage?" Studies may also be cross-sectional (a snapshot in time) or longitudinal (following people over time to better capture the dynamic nature of marriage). Because of these different ways of measuring marital satisfaction, we should not be surprised to find that research has produced some mixed results on what makes a satisfying and enduring marriage.

Nonetheless, about 64 percent of men and 60 percent of women report that their marriages are "very happy" (Popenoe, 2007). Longitudinal data allow us to see the changing level of satisfaction with marriage over the life course as people experience the initial year of marriage, have children, raise teenagers, launch children into adulthood, or retire from work (Glenn, 1998; VanLaningham, Johnson, & Amato, 2001). Most marriages start out quite happy, but satisfaction begins to decline early in most marriages. As the marriage continues, many transitions foster the decline in satisfaction—children are born and therefore responsibilities increase and bills may mount. The couples' relationship may become more routine and utilitarian. However, as a couple ages and children grow up and leave home, marital satisfaction rises again, although it does not approach the high level from the beginning of the marriage.

What Makes a Successful Marriage?

Unfortunately, there is no guaranteed 12-step program for how to have a happy marriage. A study asked over 2,000 adults to evaluate the importance of several factors to marital success, and as you can see in Figure 7.5, "faithfulness" was most likely to be rated as "very important for a successful marriage." Next comes a happy sexual relationship followed by sharing household chores (Pew Research Center, July 1, 2007).

Figure 7.5 also reveals some interesting differences by race and ethnicity. Whites stand apart because, other than "faithfulness," they are less likely to rate various components of marital success as very important. For example, they are less likely to rate having a happy sexual relationship, sharing household chores, having an adequate income, having good housing, sharing religious beliefs, having similar tastes and interests, having children, and agreeing on political issues as very important. Blacks and Hispanics are remarkably similar in their evaluation of a successful marriage with two

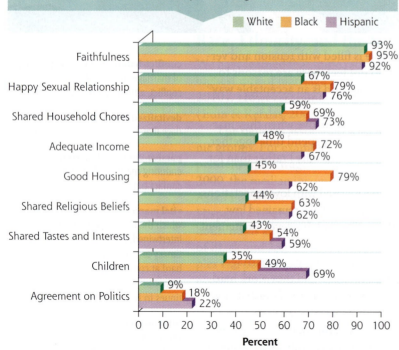

| **Figure 7.5** | **Rating Components of Marital Success, by Race and Ethnicity (Percent saying each is very important for a successful marriage)** |

Americans believe that faithfulness, a happy sexual relationship, and sharing household chores are the top three ingredients for a successful marriage.

■ White   ■ Black   ■ Hispanic

Component	White	Black	Hispanic
Faithfulness	93%	95%	92%
Happy Sexual Relationship	67%	79%	76%
Shared Household Chores	59%	69%	73%
Adequate Income	48%	72%	67%
Good Housing	45%	79%	62%
Shared Religious Beliefs	44%	63%	62%
Shared Tastes and Interests	43%	54%	59%
Children	35%	49%	69%
Agreement on Politics	9%	18%	22%

Percent (0 10 20 30 40 50 60 70 80 90 100)

Note: Whites include only non-Hispanic Whites. Blacks include only non-Hispanic Blacks. Hispanics are of any race.
Source: From Pew Research Center. 2007. "As Marriage and Parenthood Drift Apart, Public is Concerned About Social Impact: Generation Gap in Values, Behaviors" (pewresearch.org/pubs/526/marriage-parenthood).

exceptions: Blacks are most likely to rate good housing as very important, and Hispanics are most likely to rate having children similarly.

Other factors associated with happy and successful marriages include the backgrounds and characteristics people bring to marriage, the transitions they experience, and the way couples communicate and spend time together. Some of the factors people bring to relationships include:

- *Type of relationship with parents:* The relationship children have with their parents influences the relationship they develop with their spouses. Recall the discussion of attachments in Chapter 4—the type of attachment formed between parents and their children will carry forward into the children's relationships with others later in life. Marital quality is enhanced when spouses recall having secure attachments rather than avoidant or anxious attachment styles with their parents.

- *Quality and stability of parents' marriage:* Individuals whose parents have happy and stable marriages are more likely to have happy and enduring marriages themselves (Amato & Deboer, 2001; Teachman, 2002, 2004). Adult children model their own parents' behavior, both positive and negative. Parents who have strong communication skills, who value commitment in their marriage, or who believe physical or verbal abuse is an appropriate way to settle an argument, model these behaviors for their own children.

- *Shared values, goals, and characteristics:* Spouses with similar values and goals—like shared views about spending, childbearing, religion, or the integration of work and family—are more likely to have happy and enduring marriages. Similar personality traits are important as well (Partenheimer, 2005). One study found that people are attracted to mates with similar values, but once in a committed relationship and dealing with the challenges of daily life, personality factors, such as degree of extroversion or introversion, or the degree to which a person is fearful or secure, become at least as or even more important (Shanhong & Klohnen, 2005).

What makes a happy marriage? One factor is shared religious faith and practice.

- *Religious faith and practice:* People who are more religious, regardless of their age, sex, income, or the age at which they married, report higher levels of marital satisfaction and commitment to their partners, and fewer negative interactions (Myers, 2006; The Pew Forum on Religion and Public Life, June 2009). For example, one survey found that, among people who attend religious service one or more times per week, 73 percent report being very happy with their marriages, compared to 52 percent of persons who never or almost never attend service (Johnson, Stanley, Glenn, Amato, Nock, Markman, & Dion, 2002). Couples who are religious are also less likely to think of divorce as an option to an unhappy relationship (Proulx, Helms, & Buehler, 2007).

- *Frequency and satisfaction with sexual relationship:* Sexual activity obviously influences the quality of the relationship. Couples who report having regular or frequent sex, and who report enjoying their sex life, are more likely to evaluate their marriages as satisfying (AARP, 2005; Goodwin, 2009; Holmberg, Blair, & Phillips, 2010). For example, a study of women in both heterosexual and lesbian long-term relationships found that sexual satisfaction was linked to stronger relationship well-being and mental health for both types of couples (Holmberg, Blair, & Phillips, 2010).

Chapter Review

7.1 Is marriage found in every society?

Yes, but its structure may be very different. In mainstream U.S. culture, for example, we have a relatively free mate-selection choice, and we marry for love. Other societies may think that these are poor ways to structure a lasting or satisfying marriage.

7.2 Is marriage a personal relationship or a social institution?

It is both. Naturally, it is a personal relationship between two people, but state laws and regulations tell us who we can marry, how we marry, and what is expected of us afterwards.

7.3 How has marriage changed over time?

In colonial America, marriage was established as a monogamous relationship, entered into freely, with the husband as the head of the household. Today, marital relationships are more symmetrical than those of previous generations, with wives providing a greater share of the family income and husbands providing more domestic labor.

7.4 How does the marital decline perspective compare with the marital resilience perspective?

These are the two primary perspectives from which to view marriage today. The marital decline perspective suggests that the value society places on marriage is declining. The marital resilience perspective suggests that marriages have always faced challenges—the real threats to marriage are social problems such as poverty, discrimination, poor schools, and the lack of social services that families need to remain strong and resilient.

7.5 How do we explain the decline in marriage rates?

While the number of people who are married at any given time has declined, the main reason for the decline is that more people are delaying marriage and more are divorcing, although divorced people usually remarry.

7.6 How do Americans feel about same-sex marriage?

Attitudes toward same-sex marriage have become more accepting over time, although the majority of people still oppose it. However, certain groups, such as women, young adults, college graduates, and those who are less religious tend to be more supportive of same-sex marriage.

7.7 In what ways are attitudes toward marriage changing?

Americans are shifting the way we think about marriage and intimate relationships, and, naturally, this changes the nature of marriage. We are becoming more tolerant of non-marital sex, cohabitation, and nonmarital childbearing, and we are witnessing a change in attitudes about the gendered division of labor. One area that has *not* changed much, however, is the value associated with marriage.

7.8 What is the marriage premium?

The marriage premium explains the observation that married people live longer and are happier, healthier, and financially better off than their unmarried counterparts, including cohabiters. While we can attribute much of this difference to marriage *per se*, it is also likely that people who are happier, healthier, and have more money, are more likely to marry in the first place.

7.9 What is a selection effect?

We know that married people tend to be happier, healthier, and better off financially. However, does marriage provide these advantages, or do happier, healthier, and wealthier people self-select into marriage? The selection effect suggests that people who marry may be different from those who do not marry; for example, they may be innately happier, healthier, and have more money.

Key Terms

antimiscegenation laws (p. 192)

civil union (p. 194)

conflict-habituated marriage (p. 203)

covenant marriage (p. 207)

devitalized marriage (p. 203)

heterogamous marriage (p. 192)

homogamous marriage (p. 192)

interethnic marriage (p. 192)

interracial marriage (p. 192)

marital decline perspective (p. 188)

marital resilience perspective (p. 189)

marriage (p. 184)

marriage movement (p. 207)

marriage premium (p. 199)

passive-congenial marriage (p. 203)

peer marriage (p. 208)

selection effect (p. 199)

social capital (p. 201)

total marriage (p. 203)

vital marriage (p. 203)

wage premium (p. 201)

7.10 Does marriage benefit everyone equally?

In general, men benefit more from marriage than women, partly because men are more likely to significantly change their behavior when married, including taking fewer risks. There are racial and ethnic differences in the marriage premium as well, especially in terms of economic well-being.

7.11 What factors are associated with marital satisfaction and success?

While there is no clear formula for a happy marriage, people bring a number of personal background factors and characteristics to marriage, such as their parents' attachment style, whether their parents divorced, the degree to which they share values, goals, interests, and religious faith with their spouse, and their degree of satisfaction with the gendered division of labor. The way couples communicate and spend time together also affects marital satisfaction and success.

7.12 What is the marriage movement?

The marriage movement believes the decline of traditional marriage is responsible for many social problems that cost taxpayers considerable expense, such as poverty, crime, and delinquency. As a solution, they suggest the government should use taxpayer money to promote traditional marriage. The movement is controversial, and tends to be supported more fully by those who are religious and politically conservative.

7.13 What is a "peer" marriage?

These marriages involve relationships in which spouses consider themselves to have equal status or standing in the relationship, and equally and fairly share breadwinning, housework, and childrearing roles.

PEARSON
myfamilylab®
www.myfamilylab.com

Experience, Discover, Observe, Evaluate

MyFamilyLab is designed just for you. Each chapter features a pre-test and post-test to help you learn and review key concepts and terms. Experience Marriage and Family in action with dynamic visual activities, videos, and readings to enhance your learning.

Here are a few activities you'll find for this chapter:

Explore **Social Explorer** is an interactive application that allows you to explore Census data through interactive maps. Explore the Social Explorer Report:

• Trends in Marriage Rates

Read **MySocLibrary** includes primary source readings from classic and contemporary sociologists. Read:

• Ingoldsby, "Mate Selection and Marriage around the World"

8

Thinking about Parenthood

Juan and Tracey with their adopted children, Cassandra and John.

Tracey and Juan, a happily married couple, wanted children, but could not have them. Having no success with infertility treatments, they turned to adoption.

But seeing themselves as members of a global community, they adopted two children from Colombia.

Tracey and Juan dreamed about the time they would be parents. However, like growing numbers of couples they struggled with infertility, and underwent painful and invasive treatments to increase their odds of becoming pregnant. Still having no success, they began to expand their thinking about the issue: Why not adopt? After all, many children are in need of a loving home.

Thousands of American children need families, but that number is small compared to the number of children around the world who need families. Choose any region: China, Eastern Europe, India, Haiti, Africa, or South America, and you will find parents who are living in the vice-like grips of poverty, succumbing to AIDS, adhering to government policies allowing only one child, or being caught in the ravages of war and unable to take care of their children. Tracey and Juan looked to the world and found their children in Colombia.

Nearly 13,000 children were adopted internationally in 2009; 238 of these children were from Colombia. For Tracey and Juan, it is a natural fit because Juan is originally from Colombia, still has family there, and speaks fluent Spanish. They could teach their children

about their native culture, and provide some continuity in their children's lives.

Juan's family in Bogotá steered them to a reputable orphanage from where they first adopted Cassandra. They know very little about Cassandra's birth mother other than that she was very young, poor, had little education, and was overwhelmed caring for multiple children. She surrendered Cassandra to the orphanage at birth; Cassandra was only two months old when she joined Juan and Tracey.

◉—▯**Watch** the **Video** *Adoption: Tracey and Juan* on **myfamilylab.com**

Several years later they adopted John. His story is different; his mother was older, a high-school graduate, and she had only one other child besides John. She vacillated about what to do. She gave him to the orphanage to raise but did not immediately relinquish her parental rights. He finally joined Tracey and Juan's family when he was four months old.

How has Tracey and Juan's family fared since the adoptions? The children are bright, happy, well-adjusted, and display no particular issues associated with spending their first months in an orphanage. The research supports their experience: children adopted young usually adjust very quickly to their new family. Tracey and Juan have also adjusted quickly to

Q **UESTIONS** *That Matter* ●

8.1 What are population and fertility trends worldwide?

8.2 What factors have influenced fertility rates in the United States over the past century?

8.3 What is pronatalism?

8.4 What are current trends showing about the age at which people have children?

8.5 What are some of the costs associated with having children?

8.6 What are some of the benefits associated with having children?

8.7 How serious a problem is infertility?

8.8 Why are more couples choosing to remain childfree today?

8.9 How has childbirth changed and become medicalized in the United States?

8.10 What is the difference between open and closed adoptions?

8.11 What are some of the social contexts of adoption?

8.12 Why is the transition to parenthood challenging for new mothers and fathers?

8.13 How do other countries help to make the transition to parenting easier?

their new roles; they see themselves as parents, not simply as "adoptive parents." They treat adoption as a natural part of their family: *"From our standpoint, there is no difference. You give the same amount of love, the same amount of care, the same amount of everything that you would give any child. If there is any difference, it is that these* are wanted children, and I know not all biological children are as wanted or as welcome. Our children were anticipated, waited for, and there were great strides taken to get them here. So if there's any significant difference in being adopted, it's that they were truly wanted, and that makes all the difference in the world."

Most, but not all, adults become parents. How does the process of deciding if, when, and how we will be parents unfold? What kinds of decisions do we need to make along the way? What types of changes does parenting bring to our lives? This chapter focuses on the decisions surrounding fertility, infertility, and the life-changing process of becoming a parent. You will see that the transition to parenting can be surprisingly challenging, yet tremendously rewarding.

Fundamental changes are occurring today with the value associated with having children. As educational and economic opportunities for young women continue to expand, coupled with the increasing availability of relatively effective birth control and a growing acceptance of singlehood, cohabitation, and divorce, women and men are having fewer children than ever before. People are having children when they are older, and a growing number do not have children at all either by choice or because of infertility, as in the opening vignette with Juan and Tracey.

But before we discuss micro-level issues regarding becoming a parent, let's first look at the larger picture. What are some population and fertility trends around the world? An examination of these worldwide trends sets the stage for what is happening here in the United States.

:: Population and Fertility Trends Worldwide

The world's population is growing rapidly, but this has not always been the case. The population did not reach 1 billion people until about the year 1800. However, it increased to 1.6 billion only 100 years later. The world's population is about 7 billion in 2011, and is projected to be over 8 billion by 2025 (Bremner, Haub, Lee, Mather, & Zuehlke, 2009). If the concept of a billion is difficult to comprehend, consider the following:

- If you were 1 billion seconds old, you would be 31.7 years old.
- The circumference of the earth is 25,000 miles. If you circled the earth 40,000 times, you would have traveled 1 billion miles.

In some countries, such as Mexico, the size of the population could double in less than 35 years. In others, such as Japan, the population is not expected to double for nearly 500 years (Bremner, Haub, Lee, Mather, & Zuehlke, 2009). Why such a large difference between countries? Population change is linked to many important macro-level issues that affect families, including economic opportunities or constraints, geography, food production and distribution policies, health threats, infant mortality and life expectancy, status of women, and overall quality of life. ●▶ Watch on **myfamilylab.com**

Fertility and Mortality Rates: The Keys to Understanding Population Growth

Population statistics such as these reflect two important trends that occur at opposite ends of the lifespan. First, they represent **fertility rates**, which can be reported in different ways to yield somewhat different information:

●▶ **Watch** the **Video** *Core Concepts: Population Growth and Decline* on **myfamilylab.com**

fertility rate: A measure reported as: (1) average number of children born to a woman during her lifetime; (2) number of children born per 1,000 women ages 15–44 (some other countries use 49 as the cut-off age); or (3) number of children born per 1,000 population.

- *Total fertility rate:* Average number of children born to a woman during her lifetime. This is a direct measure of the level of fertility since it refers to births per woman. This indicator shows the potential for population change in the country. A rate of two children per woman is considered the replacement rate for a population, resulting in relative stability in terms of total numbers. Rates above two children indicate populations growing in size. This measure allows for useful historical and international comparisons.
- *General fertility rate:* Number of children born per 1,000 women ages 15–44 (some countries use 49 as the cut-off age). This refined method allows us to make international or historical comparisons because it relates birth to the age and sex group likely to give birth.
- *Crude fertility rate:* The number of children born per 1,000 population. Note that this does not take into consideration the age of the population. Obviously, if the average age of the population is young (e.g., Kenya), there will be more children born than if the average age of the population is old (e.g., Japan).

Globally, the "total fertility rate" (or average number of children born per woman) fell from 5.0 to 2.6 between 1950 and 2009; however, the fertility rate in developing nations far exceeds the rate in developed nations. In Niger, for example, an average woman bears 7.4 children, while in Taiwan she has only 1.0 (Bremner, Haub, Lee, Mather, & Zuehlke, 2009; Population Reference Bureau, 2010). In many developing nations, less than a third of married women use contraceptives, including 30 percent in Pakistan and 10 percent in Afghanistan (Population Reference Bureau, 2010). Contraceptive use is hindered by obstacles such as inadequate funds for supplies and a lack of comprehensive programs to educate women and their partners on their options. Also, large families are often valued as a means of social security. In reality, large numbers of children are likely to keep families impoverished.

In addition to fertility rates, population statistics also reflect a country's **mortality rates**, or death rates. Countries with high fertility rates (many births) also tend to have high mortality rates (many deaths) due to a lack of medical care and family planning services (e.g., most of Africa). Conversely, countries with the lowest fertility rates also tend to have low mortality rates (e.g., the United States, Canada, Western Europe) (Bremner, Haub, Lee, Mather, & Zuehlke, 2009).

However, in recent years we can see an important change: Those high mortality rates have begun to decline in the developing world. What has happened in these countries to decrease mortality? More people have benefitted from improved vaccinations, sanitation, and modern medicines, and have learned new ways to combat the spread of disease. This is very good news, but these factors also exacerbate population growth because fewer people are now dying. Therefore, when we speak of a population explosion in developing nations, the cause is not just too many babies being born (and, in fact, most such countries have actually reduced their fertility rates). The cause of spiraling population growth is also declining death rates, especially among infants and children.

The United States is a developed nation with great wealth. It is easy to assume that our fertility patterns do not reflect these kinds of macro-level influences, but that would be incorrect.

> Population trends reflect both fertility (birth) rates and mortality (death) rates. Countries that have high fertility rates tend also to have high mortality rates.

mortality rate (or death rate): A measure of the number of deaths in a population.

If the world's population reaches 8 billion by 2025—in your lifetime—what kind of social, environmental, and economic changes do you think will take place? How will these changes affect families? Will all these changes be bad for families, or will any be good?

:: Fertility in the United States

Pronatalism

A strong incentive towards having babies exists in just about every part of the world. Although each culture has its own values associated with childbearing and encourages fertility in its own unique way, **pronatalism**—a cultural value that encourages childbearing—is found virtually everywhere. In the United States, pronatalist values suggest that having children is a normal and natural part of a happy life, and that those who voluntarily remain childfree are selfish, immature, lonely, unfulfilled, insensitive, and more likely to have mental problems than do parents. About 40 percent of adults in one national survey thought it is "better to have a child than to remain childless" (Koropeckyj-Cox & Pendell, 2007). Older adults, men, and persons with lower levels of education were most likely to agree with pronatalist statements. Pronatalism is not just supported by your own parents and grandparents who may be pushing you to have a child; it is also supported by social institutions and policies here and around the world. For example, the Christian Bible exhorts us to "be fruitful and multiply."

Historical Fluctuation

We can observe many interesting patterns within U.S. fertility rates. One is the degree of fluctuation, as shown in Figure 8.1 (Martin, Hamilton, Sutton, Ventura, Menacker, & Munson, 2005; Hamilton, Martin, & Ventura, 2010). The U.S. birthrate shows remarkable highs and lows, often occurring in quick succession. In 1920, which was a period of relative affluence and limited birth control, the U.S. general fertility rate (defined as live births per 1,000 women ages 15–44) hovered around 118 per 1,000 women. Yet, only 15 years later the fertility rate plummeted, bottoming out in 1935 at 77 per 1,000 women. Why would such a steep decline occur in such a short amount of time? Birth control measures were still fairly limited in the 1930s, so this cannot be the primary factor.

pronatalism: A cultural value that encourages childbearing.

Such a sharp decline suggests that fertility rates are far more than simply biological phenomena. Personal choices are influenced by macro-level structural conditions and social trends. During the 1930s, the U.S. fell into a deep economic depression. Because of the dire consequences of this "Great Depression," fewer people were marrying, others were marrying later, and many families split up to pursue employment. Not surprisingly, the birthrate declined accordingly.

However, a decade later, as the Depression was ending and the United States moved into and out of World War II, the birthrate rose to a level not seen for decades. By 1950, the fertility rate increased to 106 per 1,000 women ages 15–44, a period that has since been described as the "baby boom." A look at macro-level economic trends helps explain this growth: The United States experienced a degree of affluence after the war. Therefore, couples married younger and the number of employed married women working outside the home declined. Women were

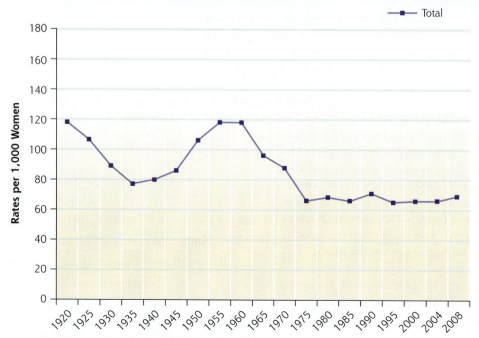

| **Figure 8.1** | **Fertility Rates per 1,000 Women Ages 15–44, 1920–2008** |

Fertility rates were low during the Depression, high after World War II, and then began declining sharply in the 1960s.

Sources: Martin, Hamilton, Sutton, Ventura, Menacker, & Munson 2005; Hamilton, Martin, & Ventura, 2010.

encouraged to find fulfillment as shown in a content analysis of the articles and advertisements in "women's magazines" (Friedan, 1963). Family, and particularly motherhood, became a primary cultural goal.

Yet, by the middle of the 1960s, the fertility rate began to drop again significantly. This period through the 1970s is sometimes called the "baby bust," and rates continued on a downward trend to 69 births per 1,000 married women today (Hamilton, Martin, & Ventura, 2010). Many macro-level reasons explain this rapid decline in fertility rates. One demographic explanation is that the number of women of childbearing age was lower in the 1970s as a result of the declining birthrates during the Great Depression, which generally translates into fewer children being born. Other reasons for the decline in fertility rates are more social in origin and represent changing attitudes about women's social and family roles. More women began going to college, including graduate and professional schools, and gained employment in new fields. Likewise, the number of married women employed outside the home increased. Women saw that additional options were available to them, so many chose to delay childbearing, or to not have children at all.

Today fertility rates differ across racial and ethnic groups in the United States, as illustrated in Figure 8.2 (Hamilton, Martin, & Ventura, 2010). Whites and American Indian/Alaska Natives have the fewest children on average (less than 60 and 65 births per 1,000 women ages 15–44, respectively). Hispanics have the highest fertility rate at nearly 99 births per 1,000 women. Again, these differences likely reflect macro-level issues, including cultural and economic considerations. For example, Hispanics are more likely to be Roman Catholic, and the church frowns upon the use of birth control. Hispanics also celebrate large families more so than do other groups.

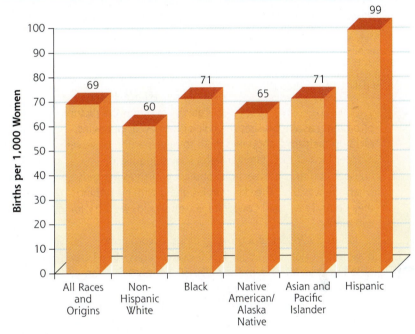

Figure 8.2   Fertility Rates by Race and Ethnicity, 2008

Hispanic groups have the highest fertility rates, and Non-Hispanic Whites have the lowest.

Source: Hamilton, Martin, & Ventura, 2010.

Delayed Parenthood

Another interesting and more recent pattern is that women and men are delaying the age at which they have their first child. In 1970, the average age at which women had their first birth was around 21, but today it is around 25 (Mathews & Hamilton, 2009). That may not sound like a huge increase, but it is more significant than you may realize. Perhaps another way of seeing the change is this: about 27 percent of women ages 30–34 do not have children today, compared to only 16 percent of women in the same age group in 1976 (U.S. Census Bureau, September 9, 2008). (The Census Bureau does not keep equivalent data on men.) It is likely that many of these women will eventually have one or more children; they are simply postponing the age at which they have them.

Delayed parenthood is, again, more than just a biological phenomenon. The reasons for later parenthood are often social in nature (e.g., women wanting to pursue education or careers; the rise in the number of second marriages). In other countries, the average age of a first-time mother is over 29, including the Netherlands, Japan, and Switzerland (Vienna Institute of Demography, 2008). A growing number of women and men are having their first child in their 40s or 50s, currently about 10 per 1,000 women ages 40–54. This delayed fertility takes on an interesting twist depending on the sex of the parent, as shown in the *Diversity in Families* feature box (page 218). While most people are not particularly

Diversity in Families

Having a Baby at 50 or 60

The average age at which we become parents is on the rise. A growing number of couples are having babies in their forties or fifties. What are the benefits and drawbacks of delayed parenthood?

Much public concern exists about teenagers being too young to have a baby, but when is a person *too old* to have a baby? Biology used to answer that question, at least for women. With the onset of perimenopause, few women conceive naturally after their early 40s. But modern technology has changed this, and with the help of donor eggs, women can now have children considerably later in life.

At first glance, Judith Cates's life seems the picture of ordinary as she brushes the hair of her 5-year-old twins, picks up their toys, and takes them to pizza parties. However, a closer look at their family reveals something highly unusual. Judith is 63 years old, and gave birth to her girls when she was 57. "They keep us laughing with everything they do and say," said Cates. "If I wasn't so old, we'd try for two more."

Judith is a leader of a growing trend. According to government statistics, about 7,500 women ages 45–54 gave birth last year. Women in their 40s, 50s, or even 60s can get pregnant with relative ease using eggs from younger women and can expect reasonably normal pregnancies and healthy babies. Age related fertility problems are related to the declining number of eggs an older woman produces, not the quality or condition of her uterus. Researchers tracked the fates of 77 women ages 50 to 63 who underwent in-vitro fertilization with donor eggs over a ten-year period. The women received, on average, three to four embryos each. Forty-two of the 77 women had live births—including three who each had two consecutive births—for a total of 45 births producing 61 babies (31 single children, 12 sets of twins, and two of triplets), all of them healthy. Some complications such as pregnancy-related high blood pressure do increase with age, but there is no definitive medical reason for excluding these women from attempting pregnancy on the basis of age alone.

Helping women in their 50s become pregnant has been controversial. The ethics committee of the American Society of Reproductive Medicine has concluded that the practice is not unethical but should be discouraged.

Others have echoed that view, warning against widely promoting the practice. "Just because you can do something doesn't mean you should," said Robert Stillman, medical director of the Shady Grove Fertility Reproductive Science Center in Rockville, MD. The Center has refused to treat women older than 50, the average age of menopause. However, there are no restrictions on men's ages for fertility treatment.

Furthering the debate is the research that shows that older women and men often make excellent parents. Brian Powell, a sociology professor at Indiana University, noted in a study of 30,000 households that people who had children in their 40s were better off financially, spent more time with their children, and had a closer connection to their children's friends than younger parents. He summarized his research with "the older you were as a parent, the better off the child." Powell was not able to analyze the results of parents who had children in their 50s because statistically there are so few of them, but the presumption is that the findings would be consistent.

Judith Cates does not worry about her age difference with her children or worry that she will die when they are young. "My mom lived to be 83. It was a wonderful life. I pray to God I will live to her age and have that much time with my girls and my husband. That's something nobody knows," Cates replied.

Sources: Hamilton, Martin, & Ventura, 2009; Hefling 2004; Weiss, 2002.

What Do You Think?

1. Some people claim that it is unethical or inappropriate to help women in their 50s or 60s have babies. What arguments can you make for and against a 50- to 60-year-old woman having a successful pregnancy by allowing her to use donor eggs? Do you think that these people would make the same argument against men in their 50s or 60s fathering babies? Why or why not?

2. A number of famous older men in recent years have fathered children while in their 50s and 60s, including Paul McCartney, Michael Douglas, Hugh Hefner, and Larry King. Have they (or their younger wives) experienced stigma because of their age? What if the reverse occurred—a 55-year-old woman had a baby with her 35-year-old husband? Is there a double standard?

concerned when a man becomes a father at age 50, the sentiment seems to be quite different if a woman wants to become a mother at the same age.

This section has shown that more than just personal choice affects how many babies are born. Now that we have explored the "big picture," let's look specifically at people who have children. In the next section, we will examine the costs and rewards associated with children.

:: The Costs and Rewards of Raising Children

There are two contrasting pictures of how children affect the lives of adults. One picture is very positive, emphasizing the emotional rewards. The other picture, in contrast, negatively emphasizes the emotional or financial costs. For many people, reality is a complex mixture of these pictures (Umberson, Pudrovska, & Reczek, 2010). Let's first discuss the costs of raising children.

Economic and Opportunity Costs

Raising children is costly in more than just economic terms. Parents experience more stress, have lower psychological well-being, and face greater declines in intimacy with their partner, compared to those couples without children (Doss, Rhoades, Stanley, & Markham, 2009; Evenson & Simon, 2006; Gorchoff, John, & Helson, 2008). And then, there is the economic cost.

Economists often talk about **direct financial costs** (e.g., out-of-pocket expenses for things such as food, clothing, housing, and education) and **opportunity costs** (e.g., lost opportunities for income by working only part-time, or not at all because of children). In many developing nations, children are a valuable source of labor. However, in developed nations like the United States, the cost of children is an important explanation of the decline in fertility rates. The U.S. Department of Agriculture estimates that it will cost middle-income families about $286,050 in food, clothing, shelter, and other goods and services for a child born in 2009 until his or her 18th birthday (Lino, 2010). Remember, this is only *one* child. And it does not include college tuition, which averages $7,020 at a *public* university during the 2009–2010 academic year, and rises over 6 percent annually (The College Board, 2009).

What exactly costs so much money? Figure 8.3 shows the average expenses for a typical American two-parent family with two children (estimates are for the youngest child). Housing is the largest category of costs.

With a financial picture such as this, one might wonder why anyone would want children at all! What are the rewards of being a parent?

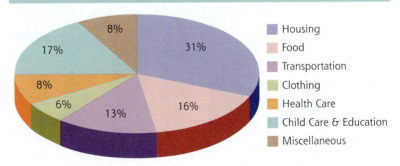

Figure 8.3

Expenditure Shares on a Child from Birth through Age 17 as a Percentage of Total Child Rearing Expenditures, 2009

Families spend approximately half of their expenses associated with children on two items: housing and food.

- Housing
- Food
- Transportation
- Clothing
- Health Care
- Child Care & Education
- Miscellaneous

Source: Lino & Carlson, 2010.

The Rewards of Parenting

Perhaps one reason studies conclude that the costs outweigh the rewards of parenthood is that the rewards are subjective and more difficult to measure. The emotional feelings of love and devotion towards children are harder to quantify. Children can bring tremendous joy and purpose into the lives of their parents. A nationwide Gallup Poll asked parents about what they gained the most from having children. Common responses included "children bring love and affection"; "it is a pleasure to watch them grow";

direct financial costs: Out-of-pocket expenses for things such as food, clothing, housing, and education.

opportunity costs: Lost opportunities for income by working only part-time or not at all because of children.

What fertility trends do you expect in the next few decades? For example, do you think that the age at which women have babies will rise, decline, or stay about the same as it is today? What about the number of children? If you expect to see some changes, can you explain why they will occur?

"they bring joy, happiness, and fun"; "they create a sense of family"; and "they bring fulfillment and a sense of satisfaction" (Gallup, 2001). Many parents feel a great deal of satisfaction and pride in seeing their child's accomplishments—excelling in the school spelling bee, singing in the choir, giving a first violin recital, scoring a first goal on the soccer field—and parents do take some measure of credit for their child's success.

A study by the Pew Charitable Trust asked people where they find the most fulfillment in their lives. Eighty-five percent of parents said the relationship with their minor children was most fulfilling, while only 23 percent with jobs or careers evaluated those as most fulfilling (Pew Research Center, July 1, 2007).

What do you think are the costs and benefits of having children for you personally? Do you think differences exist across sex, social class, racial, or ethnic groups in perceived costs and benefits? If so, can you explain why?

Another area of parental reward that has received attention is the degree to which children connect parents socially with others. Research shows that parents are more socially integrated than are adults without children (Gallagher & Gerstel, 2001; Nomaguchi & Milkie, 2003). Children provide parents with opportunities to interact in new ways with relatives, neighbors, and friends. Children also provide parental links to social institutions such as churches or schools, thereby providing further opportunities to develop relationships.

In weighing the costs and rewards, a small but growing number of adults are deciding that the costs associated with children outweigh the rewards. Others are finding that they cannot become pregnant. The next section reviews what we know about those adults who remain childfree.

:: Remaining Childfree

According to U.S. Census Bureau data, about 20 percent of women between the ages of 40 and 44 do not have children (see Figure 8.4), a jump from 10 percent in 1976 (Dye, 2008). It is possible that a few of these women may have children after age 44, but most will not. At first glance, the high number of childfree women seems a radical societal change. A look through history, however, reveals other time periods with similar or even higher rates of childlessness. For example, recall from earlier in the chapter that during the Great Depression of the 1930s, about 25 percent of women in their childbearing years did not have children, many by choice (Graybill, Kiser, & Whelpton, 1958).

Who is most likely to be childfree today? Women who do not have children are a diverse group; however, overall they tend to be among the most highly educated, having completed college or graduate school (Koropeckyj-Cox & Call, 2007), and live in central cities and metropolitan areas. Blacks and Whites are most likely to be childfree and Hispanics are least likely (Dye, 2008).

People have different reasons for remaining childfree (Koropeckyj-Cox, 2002). Some are childfree because of longstanding infertility or postponed childbearing until age-related infertility prohibited it; and others voluntarily chose to remain childfree. Let's look at these childfree groups. ✳ Explore on **myfamilylab.com**

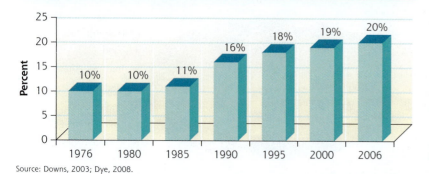

Figure 8.4 — **Percentage of Women Age 40–44 Who Do Not Have Children, 1976–2006**

One in five women between the ages of 40 and 44 do not have children. While some of these women may have children eventually, the majority will not.

Source: Downs, 2003; Dye, 2008.

✳ **Explore** the **Concept**
Social Explorer Report: Changing Household Size between 1970 and 2000 on **myfamilylab.com**

Infertility

Not all individuals without children are childfree by choice. For many people, the dream of having a child is not easily realized, as shown by Tracey and Juan in the opening vignette. **Infertility** is the inability to get pregnant after one year of trying (Centers for Disease Control and Prevention, November 11, 2009). It is a medical problem that affects about 12 percent of adults of childbearing age in the United States and occurs in all income groups and racial and

infertility: The inability to conceive a child.

ethnic categories. It affects men and women equally; roughly 30 percent of infertility difficulties can be attributed to a problem with the woman, 30 percent with the man, and in the remaining cases, it results from problems with both partners or from indeterminate causes (Resolve: The National Infertility Association, 2010). Infertility services include medical tests to diagnose infertility, medical advice and treatments to help a woman become pregnant, and services other than routine prenatal care to prevent miscarriage.

Medical Treatment Many treatment options are available to women and men trying to conceive a child from hormone treatments, sperm treatments and insemination, to more advanced technologies such as in vitro fertilization (IVF) (with or without egg or sperm donation, or both), and surrogacy. **Assisted reproductive technology (ART)** includes all fertility treatments in which both egg and sperm are handled. IVF is by far the most common form of ART, comprising about 99 percent of procedures. During IVF, a woman will use ovulation-stimulating drugs to produce an excess number of eggs. These eggs are then surgically removed and fertilized in a dish with sperm. If fertilization takes place, the physician implants the embryo(s) into the woman's uterus. Sometimes eggs from a donor are used instead of those from the woman herself.

IVF was first successfully performed in 1978 and resulted in the birth of Louise Brown, the first baby born on July 25, 1978. The world reacted as if she, and IVF, were a creation of science fiction. Children born from IVF were referred to as "test tube babies." However, given the widespread desire among infertile couples to have children and advancing ART technologies, much has changed. ◉─Watch on **myfamilylab.com**

Approximately 120,000 ART cycles were conducted in 2007 that used embryos from women's own eggs (rather than donor eggs), and another 16,000 that used donor eggs. About a third of these cycles resulted in a birth. In other words, it averages about three attempts to have a successful birth (Centers for Disease Control and Prevention, February 9, 2009). Success rates, however, differ by a woman's age as shown in Table 8.1, whether the embryos were fresh or frozen, and whether they belonged to the woman herself or were from a donor. This procedure can be extremely expensive, costing more than $12,000 per cycle. Many insurance companies only partially cover costs, and some insurers will not cover ART at all (American Society for Reproductive Medicine, 2009).

Many issues surrounding ART are controversial. For example, how many embryos can or should be implanted at one time? No U.S. laws cover this question, but the American Society for Reproductive Medicine recommends implantation of no more than two embryos.

◉─Watch the **Video**
Embryo Mix-Up on
myfamilylab.com

Table 8.1 Pregnancy Success Rates

As women age, in vitro fertilization is less effective.

Type of Cycle	Age of Women			
Fresh Embryos From Nondonor Eggs	**<35**	**35–37**	**38–40**	**41–42**
Number of cycles	42,119	23,503	20,608	9,535
% of cycles resulting in pregnancies	45.7	37.2	28.1	18.4
% of cycles resulting in live births	39.6	30.5	20.9	11.5
Average number of embryos transferred	2.2	2.5	2.8	3.1
% of pregnancies with twins	33.2	28.2	21.6	14.0
% of pregnancies with triplets or more	3.5	4.5	4.0	2.5
Frozen Embryos From Nondonor Eggs	**<35**	**35–37**	**38–40**	**41–42**
Number of transfers	10,515	5,386	3,518	1,125
% of transfers resulting in live births	33.6	29.9	25.0	20.8
Average number of embryos transferred	2.2	2.2	2.4	2.5

Source: Centers for Disease Control and Prevention, February 9, 2009.

assisted reproductive technology (ART): All fertility treatments in which either egg or sperm (or both) are handled.

However, some doctors will implant many more either because of parental wishes, or to increase the clinic's "success rate." This can result in shocking numbers of fetuses, which is dangerous for the fetuses and the mother. Couples must resort to selective abortion to increase the odds that at least one or two babies will survive, or take their chances with multiple births. This was the case with Nadya Suleman, the so-called "Octomom," who bore eight children (after already having six older children).

Another controversial issue is what happens to unused embryos. Should they be destroyed? Should they be donated to science? Should they be given or sold to other infertile couples? These are important ethical questions for which our society is only beginning to explore the answers.

Surrogacy Because of the high risk of ART failure and its controversies, or repeated miscarriages, some people instead turn to surrogacy. **Surrogacy** involves a relationship in which one woman gives birth to a child for another person or a couple who then adopts or takes legal custody of the child. One woman acts as a surrogate, or replacement mother for another woman, sometimes called the "intended mother," who either cannot produce fertile eggs or cannot carry a full-term pregnancy.

Many assisted reproduction technology (ART) procedures are controversial. For example, how many embryos should be implanted at one time? Nadya Suleman bore 8 children, after already having 6 others.

Surrogate mothering can be accomplished in many ways. Most often, the husband's sperm is implanted in the surrogate by a procedure called artificial insemination. In this case, the surrogate mother is both the genetic mother and the birth (or gestational) mother of the child. This method is sometimes called **traditional surrogacy**.

At other times, when the intended mother can produce fertile eggs but cannot carry a child to term, the intended mother's egg is removed, combined with the husband's or another man's sperm in IVF, and implanted in the surrogate mother. This method is called **gestational surrogacy**.

The issue of surrogate motherhood came to national attention during the 1980s with the *Baby M* case. In 1984, a New Jersey couple, William and Elizabeth Stern, contracted to pay Mary Beth Whitehead $10,000 to be artificially inseminated with William Stern's sperm and carry the fetus to term. Whitehead decided to keep the baby after it was born, refused to receive the $10,000 payment, and fled to Florida. In July 1985, the police arrested Whitehead and returned the baby to the Sterns.

Why would anyone want to be a surrogate mother? Who would carry a baby to term, only to hand him or her over to someone else moments after birth? Surrogacy arrangements are categorized as either commercial or altruistic. In *commercial surrogacy*, the surrogate is paid a fee plus any expenses incurred in her pregnancy. In *altruistic surrogacy*, the surrogate is paid only for expenses incurred or is not paid at all. The feature box *My Family: Why I Became a Surrogate Mother* tells the story of a woman who chose to be a surrogate.

Surrogacy, too, is not without ethical considerations (Hall, Bobinski, & Orentlicher, 2008). It challenges our most basic ideas about motherhood. States have conflicting statutes regarding surrogacy; some pose restrictions such as requiring at least one parent to have a genetic link to the child (Saul, 2009). Surrogacy also raises concerns about "renting out bodies" and the potential for exploiting low-income women. Rumors circulate about the wealthy who hire surrogates simply to avoid stretch marks or the "hassle" of pregnancy (Ali & Kelley, 2008). In some countries, such as India, surrogate motherhood for wealthy Americans is becoming a big business (Gentleman, 2008).

surrogacy: The act of giving birth to a child for another person or a couple who then adopts or takes legal custody of the child.

traditional surrogacy: A type of surrogacy where the man's sperm is implanted in the surrogate through artificial insemination.

gestational surrogacy: A type of surrogacy where the intended mother's egg is combined with the man's sperm and implanted in the surrogate through in vitro fertilization.

My Family

Why I Became a Surrogate Mother

I love being pregnant. I feel one with nature and I feel closer to God when I'm carrying a baby. I love the high with all those rushing hormones. But I don't really want to raise another child because I already have three and that's about all my husband and I can afford.

I'm built to have babies. I'm tall, relatively slim, but I have wonderfully wide hips—"birthing hips" I like to call them. The births of all three of my own children were pretty easy—well, I don't know if "easy" is the right word, but it's part of the pregnancy process and I love it.

I first started to think about surrogacy when my cousin couldn't carry a baby to term—she has had a total of six miscarriages. I am a religious person, and when I began to investigate what my faith would have to say about surrogacy I was pleasantly surprised. In the 16th chapter of Genesis, the infertile Sarah gives her servant Hagar to her husband Abraham, to bear a child for them. Later, Jacob fathers children by the maids of his wives Leah and Rachel, who raise them as their own.

So I went to my cousin and suggested that I could carry the baby for her, using her own egg and her husband's own sperm. At first she was unsure, but it only took them a week to decide, yes, let's do it! I did not charge them anything of course, but they did give me $5,000 to help cover some medical expenses and to pay for a

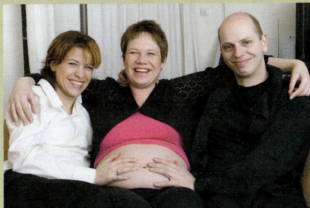

Some people turn to surrogacy to help them have a child—a woman gives birth to a child for another person or a couple who then adopts or takes legal custody of the child.

housekeeper so I could rest a little more. Everything worked out well, and their son Ben is now 7 years old. I don't feel like his mother at all, just a special cousin.

But then I got to thinking—why not do this again for someone else? To be honest, I could use a little money. And if I can earn some money while helping someone else have a baby, why not? What job would be better for me? So I contacted an agency and they did a number of psychological and physical tests. I passed with flying colors and then put together a portfolio so prospective families could learn more about me.

Over the last four years I have been a surrogate twice. I was paid about $30,000 by each of the families. The money has helped our family purchase day-to-day things. There is always some unexpected expense raising my three!

And we were able to treat our children to a first-class trip to Disney World as well.

Some people wonder, isn't it hard to give up the baby to someone else after I have carried it for nine months and given birth? No, not really. My family feels complete, so I don't really long for another baby to raise. Besides, at this point I have never used my own eggs, so the baby isn't really related to me genetically anyway. But, don't get me wrong. I have continued to have a relationship with each family and have been invited to baptisms and a few other family events. I have a special relationship with each of the babies I carried and birthed, but I just don't think of myself as their mother.

—*Terri, Age 35*

What Do You Think?

1. Could you envision being a surrogate mother, or a partner to a surrogate mother? Could you easily give up the baby? If you are male, how would you feel watching your spouse/partner's belly grow as she is carrying another couples' child?

2. Terri began as an altruistic surrogate, but her last two experiences were commercial surrogacy. Did you feel uncomfortable reading this narrative when she discussed financial issues?

The Hidden Emotions of Infertility   In addition to its financial costs, infertility can also be emotionally and physically exhausting. Infertility involves many losses for individuals, their loved ones, and society as a whole (Resolve: The National Infertility Association, 2010), including the:

- Loss of the pregnancy and birth experience
- Loss of a genetic legacy and loss for future contributing citizens of the next generation
- Loss of the parenting experience
- Loss of a grandparenting relationship
- Loss of feelings of self-worth
- Loss of stability in family and personal relationships
- Loss of work productivity
- Loss of a sense of spirituality and sense of hope for the future

Infertility can erode a person's self-esteem. Suddenly your life, which may have been well-planned and successful up to this period, seems out of control. Not only is the physical body not responding as expected, but it feels as if your entire life is "on hold." Facing the disappointment of not becoming pregnant month after month can lead to depression. Studies have shown that infertility depression levels can rival those of cancer (Resolve: The National Infertility Association, 2010). Because infertility often involves major personal life issues and decisions, it is often experienced as a private matter and is not ordinarily discussed in public forums. The personal nature of the infertility experience contributes to the failure of society to recognize infertility as a disease, thus creating a lack of sound knowledge about the issue (Resolve: The National Infertility Association, 2010).

Voluntarily Childfree

As a child, I usually preferred the company of adults, or at least older kids. As a teen I never wanted to babysit—boring! Today, I am much more interested in my career, travel, and hanging out with my boyfriend. Don't get me wrong—I'm a caring person. I volunteer for Meals on Wheels twice a month, and I am involved in a number of social issues in my community. It's just that, well, I don't want to have kids. My boyfriend is okay with that. I think he could go either way, but said the decision is up to me.

—Janine, Age 27

The decision to not have children is usually not made only once, but many times, as people undergo a *process* of deciding about children. They might think about whether or not to have children while in their twenties, like Janine, then revisit the issue in their thirties, and again in their forties.

Women usually have firmer opinions than men about forgoing parenthood, despite our thinking to the contrary (Koropeckyj-Cox & Pendell, 2007a, b; Koropeckyj-Cox, Romano, & Moras, 2007; Seccombe, 1991). It is men rather than women who are more likely to report "it is better for a person to have a child than to go through life childless." Men are more likely than women to want to have children, and look less favorably upon people who are childfree.

Common concerns that childfree people express are: "Will I regret my decision? Will I be lonely in my old age?" Research studies have examined the lives of older childfree people to answer these questions, and most studies conclude that they are not particularly

Tying It All Together

Factors That Influence Fertility

Having babies is part biology and part choice, but even our so-called choices exist in a social context. Let's examine the macro- and micro-level influences on fertility.

Macro-level Factors

- Pronatalist cultural views
- Dominant religion
- Cultural considerations: Are children a benefit or liability?
- Education and employment opportunities for women
- Level of technology to combat infertility

Micro-level Factors

- Biological considerations: Is the couple capable of reproducing?
- Perceived psychological benefits and costs associated with children
- Pressure from family or friends
- Personal desire for children
- Economic situation
- Willingness to adopt

---

disadvantaged. For example, older childfree adults have similar or lower rates of depression than do other older people (Bures, Koropeckyj-Cox, & Loree, 2009). They may have fewer relationships with friends or extended family, but they have strong ties to their partners (Zhang & Hayward, 2001). Older childfree adults may be more isolated than couples with children, and are more likely to live alone or in an institution, but their finances are generally better. However, it is important to distinguish between those individuals who are voluntarily childfree and those who are involuntarily without children, as their experiences are likely to differ.

Thus far, a number of macro-level and micro-level factors that might account for fertility rates have been discussed. The number of children born is not just related to personal choices. Our social structure also shapes our interest in parenting and ability to be parents, as summarized in the feature box *Tying it All Together: Factors that Influence Fertility.*

Do you plan to have children? Why or why not? If your answer is "no," what kind of pronatalist sentiment have you experienced, or believe you will experience in the future? If you do want children, how do you think you would react if you found out that you or your partner cannot get pregnant? How far would you go to have a baby?

:: The Interconnection of Micro and Macro: Childbirth

Although infertility and voluntary childlessness are on the rise, most women do become pregnant and have a child. The biological processes involved in these events are the same everywhere. Women get pregnant the same way in Bangladesh as they do in England, and babies are born the same way in Nigeria as they are in Canada.

Nonetheless, it would be a mistake to assume that pregnancy and childbirth are simply biological processes. There are many micro-level choices that we make along the way about how a baby is conceived, the experience of pregnancy, the process of giving birth, and the experiences we have as new parents. Yet, many macro-level social factors are intertwined with these micro-level choices and experiences. For example, historical, cultural, and social norms influence who should or should not get pregnant (ideal age, or importance of marital status); who should impregnate a woman (the qualifications necessary for a spouse or partner); conditions and habits of the pregnant woman (what foods or beverages to be consumed or avoided); the degree of medical intervention appropriate to deliver a baby (whether a baby is born in a hospital or at home); and what a baby is fed (breast milk or formula). How we conceive children, give birth to them, and care for them are choices highly influenced by structural conditions, historical period, and social and cultural norms.

Childbirth throughout History: Towards Medicalization

Children are born every minute in all parts of the world. However, what may be considered normal, healthy, and appropriate childbirth practices in one culture or historical period may be viewed as dangerous or barbaric in another. Even something as routine as the position in which a woman gives birth—laying down on her back or squatting—reflects how norms are woven into social structure (van Teijlingen, Louis, McCaffery, & Porter, 2004). As feminist theorists point out, the medical establishment, the economic system, the political culture, and the degree of technological sophistication all play a role in defining an event as intimate as a woman giving birth.

Until the 19th century, childbirth was considered largely "women's business," attended to by mothers, sisters, friends, and a midwife if one was available (Cassidy, 2007). Doctors were generally absent because childbirth was not considered a medical event. Midwives believed that for most women childbirth is a normal part of life, and that their job was to help women do what they innately know.

By the middle of the 19th century, physicians seeking to develop the medical specialization of obstetrics worked to eliminate midwives (Dawley, 2003; Sullivan & Weitz, 1988). To achieve their professional dominance, physicians began claiming that childbirth was inherently dangerous and required medical assistance, and that midwives were inadequately trained to deal with the complex nature of delivering babies. Their desire to eliminate midwives had more to do with professional turf battles and less to do with the safety of birth itself.

As providers shifted, so did the role of women in childbirth (Wagner, 2008). Instead of being largely in control, women surrendered to the power and authority of male doctors. Wealthy women were the first to flock to male doctors for childbirth, lured by the promise of new technology and painkillers. Thus, childbirth became a medical event in which drugs and technological intervention became routine—the **medicalization of childbirth**. In the early 1900s the German method of "twilight sleep" was introduced in the United States—a combination of morphine for pain relief and other drugs that caused women to have no memories of giving birth (Cassidy, 2007). Since it was difficult to apply technology to childbirth in the home, childbirth was moved to a hospital setting. In 1900, physicians in hospitals were attending approximately one-half of all births in the United States, largely along social class lines. But by 1970, virtually all births occurred in hospitals (Dawley, 2003; Rooks, 1997). With this change of venue childbirth had shifted from a normal, home-based event to a hospital-based and sickness-oriented model (McCool & Simeone, 2002; Rothman, 1991).

In hospitals throughout most of the 20th century, women routinely had their pubic areas shaved, were strapped down on their backs to cold metal labor and delivery tables with their feet in stirrups (a painful and unnatural position), were given drugs that fogged the mind of mother and baby, and were given enemas to empty the bowels (which often empty on their own in the early stages of labor). They were hooked up to IVs and external fetal heart monitors that limit a laboring woman's mobility (which can increase her pain), and were given episiotomies (cutting through the perineum toward the anus to enlarge the vaginal opening). Husbands and partners were barred from the birth event. This was the dominant birth paradigm throughout most of the 20th century, but it started to change slowly in the 1980s as more women began to ask for alternatives.

Childbirth Today: A More Natural Approach or Not?

By the 1980s, many Americans questioned whether hospitalization and such intense technological intervention were always needed to deliver healthy babies. Books circulated advocating more natural methods, arguing that while medical technology can indeed save lives, it is not without emotional, financial, and physical costs. A low-technology approach could have equally favorable results as a high-technology approach for low-risk women (e.g., women who are not diabetic, not having twins, or

medicalization of childbirth: The belief that childbirth is a medical event in need of drugs and technological intervention.

are without other identified fetal or maternal health problems) (Davidson, 2002). New alternatives to pain management came into vogue—breathing and stretching exercises were presented as more natural approaches.

Birth settings also began to change. Families demanded that hospital policies and the hospital environment change so that a mother's needs would have a greater focus. Most hospitals responded by making their birthing rooms more personal and cozy. A woman could now write her own birth plan, labor in water, and be free to use alternative positions for delivery. However, hospitals still largely treat childbirth as a medical event, and compared to other birth settings, use far more technology—technology that many claim is invasive without producing better results (Block, 2008; Wagner, 2008).

Some women choose to give birth outside of hospitals. **Birth centers** are freestanding facilities, usually with close access to, but not affiliated with, a hospital. Birth centers usually present a homelike setting, and offer clients a greater degree of autonomy to decide the conditions surrounding the birth, while at the same time offering a degree of medical security appealing to many couples. However, insurance companies are less likely to cover births in a birthing center as compared to those in a hospital.

A small number of women opt for home births, attended by trained midwives or naturopathic physicians. One study found that 91 percent of women who had their last baby at home said they would prefer to have their next baby at home. Among those who had experienced both a home birth and a hospital birth, 76 percent preferred the home birth, citing factors such as safety, avoiding medical interventions common in hospital births, previously negative hospital experiences, more control, and a comfortable and familiar home environment (Boucher, Bennett, McFarlin, & Freeze, 2009). With skilled attendants present, women with low-risk pregnancies have outcomes just as safe at home as in hospitals (de Jonge, van der Goes, Ravelli, Amelink-Verburg, Mol, Nijhuis, Bennebroek, & Buitendijk, 2009; NHS Knowledge Service, 2009).

Childbirth has become a highly medicalized event, usually occurring in hospitals surrounded by high technology. About one-third of births are by C-section. This does not improve birth outcomes, so some people are reconsidering a more natural approach to birth, including home births.

Yet at the same time, elements of the medicalization of childbirth may be as strong as ever (Block, 2008). The rate of caesarean delivery increased to about 33 percent of all U.S. births, rising more than 50 percent in the last decade alone (Hamilton, Martin, & Ventura, 2010). This is the highest rate ever recorded anywhere in the world. Caesarean section (C-section) operations are the leading operation performed in the United States. Some hospitals require a C-section for subsequent births if the first baby was delivered by caesarean, citing a higher risk of uterine rupture, although the risk may be only 1 percent (Cohen, 2009). The World Health Organization argues that many C-sections performed in the United States are medically unnecessary, potentially dangerous, and do not improve our infant or maternal mortality statistics, which are among the worst in the developed world (Population Reference Bureau, 2010).

In fact, an increasing number of C-sections are actually "elective" surgery (Korn, 2010), arranged for the convenience of the mother or the physician:

Courtney Mizel Green describes herself as a "total type-A personality and meticulous planner." So when it came to the birth of her first child, the Los Angeles lawyer was not willing to simply wait for nature to take its unpredictable course. Instead she decided to schedule a C-section for her baby's delivery. "I liked the idea of knowing what day and time my baby would arrive so I could schedule my parents to be here, a baby nurse, and furniture delivery," says Green (Korn, 2010).

birth centers: Freestanding facilities (usually with close access to, but not affiliated with, a hospital) where childbirth is approached as a normal, healthy process.

Elective C-sections are problematic. First, they can be dangerous, increasing the risk of injury and trauma for both mother and child (abcnews.go.com, January 7, 2009). A study in the *New England Journal of Medicine* found that 36 percent of women having elective C-sections scheduled their delivery before the recommended 39 weeks, making babies more likely to visit the intensive care unit, have infections, and develop respiratory distress (Tita et al., for the Eunice Schriver NICHD Maternal-Fetal Medicine Units Network, 2009).

If any of your friends or members of your family had children recently, what type of birth did they have? Was it at home, in a birthing center, or in a hospital? Did they choose a more natural method or one that used more technology? If you plan to have children, what type of birth would you like to have (or like your partner to have)?

Second, organizations such as Lamaze International, the American College of Nurse-Midwives, and the International Cesarean Network argue that birth is a natural physiological process that should be allowed to unfold naturally unless there is a strong medical reason for surgical intervention. Some critics even question how many so-called elective C-sections are really "convenience surgeries" pushed by medical professionals who do not want their vacations or weekends interrupted by a spontaneous delivery (Cosentino, 2006).

There are other paths to becoming a parent besides childbirth. Some people become parents through adoption. This next section examines the different contexts of adoption.

:: Other Paths to Parenthood: Adoption

Adoption is a mechanism by which adults legalize their parental relationship to nonbiological children (Jones, 2008). It provides parents to infants who are relinquished at birth, and parents for older children whose birth parents have died or had their parental rights revoked. It offers both individuals and couples a way to add children to their families when they cannot conceive or carry a pregnancy due to infertility. It provides an avenue for humanitarian assistance by offering a home to a child without one. And, it can provide a legal relationship between an adult and a nonbiological child for whom the adult is already caring, such as a stepchild or the child of a gay or lesbian partner.

Adoption touches the lives of many people. Although only about 4 percent of Americans are adopted, one survey based on a representative nationwide sample of 1,416 adults found that 64 percent reported a direct personal experience with adoption. They, a family member, or a close friend was adopted, had adopted a child, or had relinquished a child for adoption (National Adoption Information Clearinghouse, 2002).

Despite its prevalence, little attention is paid to adoption in current college texts that focus on family issues (Fisher, 2003). The feature box *Why Do Research? Teaching about Adoption* describes a content analysis of 21 family texts and 16 undergraduate readers, and reveals how adoption is portrayed.

Closed and Open Adoptions

Adoption was once stigmatized and often kept secret (Small, 2007). In the past most adoptions were **closed adoptions**, meaning that when an infant or very young child was adopted, all information about the birth parents remained sealed. The sealed records prevented the adoptee and the biological parents from knowing or discovering anything about each other, which at the time was thought to be in the best interest of everyone.

Today, while closed adoptions still exist, **open adoptions**, which include the sharing of information between birth mothers, the adoptee, and the adoptive parents, are more common. This type of adoption can take many forms along a continuum. An open adoption can mean as little as a birth parent providing basic information to the adoptee, or it can mean as much as a birth parent remaining actively involved in the child's life. Semi-open and open adoptions can have many advantages for the child, birth mother, and adoptive parents (Miall & March, 2005).

closed adoption: An adoption where identifying information is sealed and unavailable to all parties.

open adoption: A type of adoption that involves direct contact between the biological and adoptive parents.

Why Do Research?

Teaching about Adoption

Texts about marriages and families like this one are designed to give students the knowledge base and tools to better understand family types, processes, and interactions. The texts recognize diversity and multiple paths to building families. One such path is adoption. How do these texts cover this type of family?

Let's pause for a moment and think how to best answer this research question. With a survey? With an experiment? Perhaps the best way to address how marriage and family texts cover adoption is to look through the texts themselves. A **content analysis** closely and systematically examines the content of materials, in this case, college texts. A researcher can count up pages or words devoted to the topic of adoption to see how much coverage a text gives to the topic. Or, a researcher can tabulate the type of comments that are made about adoption.

One such study looked at marriage and family books, both texts and readers that were published between 1998 and 2001 (Fisher, 2003). Fisher found that four of the 21 texts reviewed (19 percent) and three of the 16 readers reviewed (19 percent) offered no coverage of adoption. Among those books that did discuss adoption, the texts devoted an average of 2.4 pages, and the readers devoted few more.

Moreover, as shown in Table 8.2, the researcher found that the negative points made about adoption far outnumbered the positive points. Books tended to comment on potential problems, such as the behavioral and psychological problems among adoptees; the unavailability of healthy children; the high costs of adoption; legal problems; the stigma surrounding adoption; the ideological or ethical problems associated with adoption; the long waits; or the unknowns about the child's genetic background or physical or emotional treatment. While these problems may exist, Fisher notes that the many positive aspects of adoption were far less likely to be discussed in these books, such as the changes in public policy that have made adoption less difficult and less expensive; the benefits of adoption for adopted children and adoptive parents; the decline in stigma towards adoption; the more

open, less secretive process of adoption; the humanitarian reasons that many adoptive parents offer for adopting; and the fact that despite the risks, most adoptions work out very well.

Table 8.2	Number of Positive and Negative Points Made about Adoption, by Type of Work	
Coverage of adoption in college textbooks have tended to overemphasize the negative and de-emphasize the positive.		
Type of Book	**Positive Points**	**Negative Points**
Texts (n = 21)	38	57
Readers (n = 16)	10	37
All books (N = 37)	48	94

Source: Fisher, Allen P. 2003. "A Critique of the Portrayal of Adoption in College Textbooks and Readers on Families, 1998-2001." Family Relations 52:154–60.

What Do You Think?

1. Why do you think that adoption is given so little attention in marriage and family texts? Is it simply an oversight, or is it because of the stigma once attached to adoption?

2. Content analysis is a useful research method for answering certain types of questions. What other research questions about marriages and families would lend themselves well to content analysis?

Source: Fisher, Allen P. 2003. "A Critique of the Portrayal of Adoption in College Textbooks and Readers on Families, 1998-2001." Family Relations 52:154–60.

Public and Private Adoptions

Public adoptions occur through licensed public agencies that specialize in placing children in adoptive families. **Private adoptions** are arranged directly between adoptive parents and the biological birth mother, usually with the assistance of an attorney. In a private adoption, the attorney may contact social workers, other attorneys, or doctors, or place a notice in a newspaper looking for a woman who intends to relinquish her child. Although "baby selling" is prohibited, the adopting couple will likely pay the birth mother's medical fees and often her living and other miscellaneous expenses. Private adoptions tend to be more expensive than public adoptions. However, they are more common because they are likely to result in the adoptive family obtaining an infant. Children in public adoptions are often older or have special needs.

content analysis: A research method that systematically examines the content of materials.

public adoption: An adoption that occurs through licensed public agencies.

private adoption: An adoption arranged directly between adoptive parents and the biological birth mother, usually with the assistance of an attorney.

Transracial Adoptions

Most adoptive parents are White, although 40 percent of children in the United States now available for adoption are Black. This raises a controversial issue: is it appropriate to place minority children with White families (Simon & Roorda, 2000, 2009)? In the 1970s, the Association of Black Social Workers and Native American activists strongly objected to placing Black and Native American children with White families, suggesting that transracial adoptions amounted to cultural genocide. Afterwards, the number of transracial adoptions declined dramatically. However, a longitudinal study conducted over 20 years found that minority children placed in White homes generally do develop positive racial and ethnic identities, and are knowledgeable of their history and culture (Simon & Alstein, 2000). Today, there is less stigma surrounding transracial adoptions.

Single-Parent Adoptions

A generation ago, if a single woman presented herself to an adoption agency to apply for an adoption, she would probably have been turned away. It was highly unusual (and in some states, illegal) for a single person to adopt a child. Much has changed in 30 years as today, single women are actively involved in adoption. Among adopters, 17 percent of women, and 6 percent of men, have never been married (Jones, 2008). In particular, single women and men tend to adopt children who are older, are racial or ethnic minorities, or are from other countries, although some countries, such as China, have recently imposed quotas or restrictions on single-parent adoptions. Single men often have difficulty adopting children. Despite the growing recognition of men as nurturers, there is still suspicion that a single man could not be sensitive to a child's needs and concern about what type of man would want to raise a child alone.

A common way for same-sex couples to have children is through adoption. On October 22, 2010, Florida, the final holdout, lifted its ban against gays and lesbians adopting.

Adoptions by Gays and Lesbians

Gay men and lesbians have always adopted, though in the past they usually hid their sexual orientation. Today, just as gays and lesbians are becoming more visible in all other aspects of American society, they are being considered more seriously as potential adoptive parents. As of late 2010, Florida, the final holdout, lifted its ban against gays and lesbians adopting children. Yet, only some states allow for same-sex *couples* to jointly adopt. Other states allow for one partner to first adopt the child, and then for the other partner to apply for a second-parent adoption. These second-parent adoptions create a second legally recognized parent for the adoptive child. These two methods are the only way for same-sex couples to both become legal parents of their children (Johnson, 2008). Yet, in some states the law is either unclear or contradictory from one region to another.

Concerns are frequently raised surrounding gay and lesbian adoption, many of which are based on stereotypes or myths about sexual orientation or homosexuality. What are these concerns, and what do research findings suggest (Biblarz & Stacey, 2010; Crowl, Ahn, & Baker, 2008)?

- *Homosexual parents will molest their children.* There is no scientific research that indicates a significant link between homosexuality and pedophilia. One study looked at 269 cases of child sexual abuse, and found only two cases in which the offenders were gay or lesbian. Indeed, the study found that a child's risk of being molested by his or her parent's (or other relative's) *heterosexual* partner was over 100 times greater than being molested by someone identified as homosexual (Jenny, 1994).

- *Children raised in homosexual households will become gay.* Stacey and Biblarz found that children of gay and lesbian parents are no more likely to identify themselves as gay, lesbian, or bisexual than the children of heterosexual parents. However, they are more likely to consider or experiment with same-sex relationships during young adulthood (2001).

- *Children raised in gay or lesbian households will suffer from depression or mental health problems.* Research reveals that children of same-sex parents show either no difference from those of heterosexual parents, or show a reduction in levels of anxiety, depression, or behavior problems (Stacey & Biblarz, 2001; Biblarz & Stacey, 2010). These children also score as high or higher on social performance, self-esteem, secure attachments, and affection and concern for younger children.

- *Children raised in gay or lesbian households will be teased and harassed.* Children of gay and lesbian parents *are* vulnerable to teasing and harassment, particularly as they approach adolescence. Courts have often viewed the stigma surrounding gay and lesbian parenting as possibly damaging to a child's self-esteem, and therefore side with the heterosexual parent in custody disputes. However, gay and lesbian parents are generally aware of this stigma and its effects, and go to great lengths to prepare and support their children. Although children of gays and lesbians do report teasing because of their parents' sexual orientation, their self-esteem levels are no lower than those of children of heterosexual parents (Garner, 2005; Huggins, 1989; Snow, 2004).

The leading medical society of pediatricians, the 65,000-member American Academy of Pediatrics, endorses the legal rights of homosexuals to adopt a partner's child, saying "children deserve to know their relationships with both parents are stable and legally recognized" (Hall, 2002).

Pretend that you are in a grocery store when your 5-year-old adopted daughter asks you, "Mommy/Daddy, you know that woman whose tummy I came out of? Why didn't she want to keep me?" How would you respond, right there, to your daughter's effort to understand her adoption?

International Adoptions

The number of Americans who are adopting children from other countries has declined sharply over the past few years. American parents adopted almost 13,000 foreign-born children in 2009, down from 23,000 in 2005 (U.S. Department of State, 2009). New standards have made adoption more difficult, including the Hague Adoption Convention, which adds many new regulations and restrictions (designed to ensure that inter-country adoptions are in the best interest of the child). Figure 8.5 shows how many children have been adopted in the United States over the last decade from China, Guatemala, and Russia, the top three countries for international adoptions (U.S. Department of State, 2009).

Political decisions or social problems often produce orphans who need families. For example, adoptions from China are in response to the strict one-child policy enforced by the Chinese

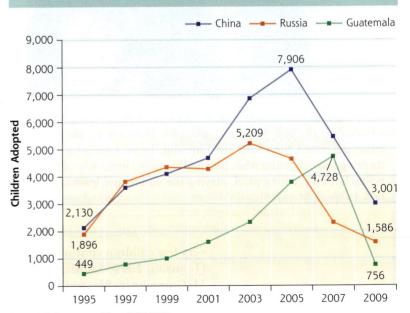

Figure 8.5	**Trends in International Adoption, 1995–2009**

The number of international adoptions has declined significantly since its peak in 2005.

Source: U.S. Department of State, 2006, 2009.

• *The transition to parenthood necessitates complex changes in the couple's relationship. Activities become more instrumental, and the division of labor becomes more gender-based. Most of the workload and lifestyle changes fall upon the woman.*

However, not all parents find the transition to parenthood so stressful. Several factors mediate the challenges faced by new parents. These factors include the baby's temperament, the parents' expectations about their baby, the support and assistance they receive from kin, their marital adjustment and communication skills, the father's parenting involvement, whether the baby was planned, and the baby's sex (Belsky & Rovine, 1990; Mulsow, Caldera, Pursley, Reifman, & Huston, 2002; Nomaguchi & Milkie, 2003; Simpson, Rholes, Campbell, Tran, & Wilson, 2003). For example, if a couple who enjoys their peace and quiet has an active, fussy baby who needs little sleep, and this couple does not have family around to help, especially while the father travels away from home on business, you can guess that the transition to parenthood will be a challenge. In contrast, a couple who has a so-called "easy" baby who cries or fusses little, who has flexible work schedules or family leave, and has family around to help will probably have an easier time adjusting to parenthood.

Sex Differences in the Transition to Parenthood

Few would disagree that women and men have different experiences as they transition into parenthood. Nonetheless, we know far more about how women are changed by becoming parents than we know about men.

In most families, babies spend considerably more time with their mothers than their fathers, as shown in Table 8.3 (Drago, 2009). Women retain most of the childcare responsibilities, and this is particularly true with an infant who may be nursing. With over half of mothers with children under the age of one in the labor force, work-family stress is a serious problem for many women, as you will see in Chapter 10.

Yet, as sociologist Susan Walzer explains, the transition to parenthood is far more than the logistics of juggling work and family. Her study of 25 couples who recently had a baby revealed that our image of what it takes to be a "good" mother or a "good" father is socially constructed and inextricably linked with our views about gender. Parenthood is a vivid example of "doing gender." Walzer writes:

"Mother" and "father" are social categories that existed before the individuals I interviewed became parents—or were born. These social categories have particular meanings attached to them—meanings that are socializing influences on new parents and that are institutionalized in cultural imagery associated with motherhood and fatherhood. New parents are channeled toward differentiation by social arrangements, and especially by cultural imagery that constructs what it means to be a "good" mother or father, wife or husband, woman or man (1998:7).

Table 8.3	**Time Spent in the Parenting of Infants under Age 1 Year (in hours and minutes)**		
	Mothers spend far more time caring for infants than do fathers, both on weekdays and weekends.		
		Partnered Mothers	**Partnered Fathers**
Total Childcare Weekdays		11:05	5:01
Solo Childcare		8:08	2:06
Primary Childcare (other parent helped)		3:15	1:25
Total Childcare Weekends		11:58	9:31
Solo Childcare		5:50	3:11
Primary Childcare (other parent helped)		3:19	1:52

Source: Drago, 2009.

These images set up a difficult situation for women because the image of a "good mother" is one who is always there and available for her child, yet the image of a "good woman" is to work and have a career. Balancing these two cultural images that are at odds with each other can be difficult. Men do not face this contradiction in roles. An employed father who has minimal caregiving tasks may still be perceived as a "good father." If a mother works outside the home, she and her husband usually frame her employment as something that should only minimally interfere with her mothering role.

Walzer suggests that mothers and fathers think about babies in different ways, and they analyze their thoughts so that they fit the culturally appropriate image of "good" mothers and fathers. Mothers are expected to expend considerably more mental energy on their babies than are fathers. For example, mothers worry more about their babies (and they worry about the way they are perceived by others), they buy and read the self-help books, they process the information and then translate it for their husbands or partners, and they manage and orchestrate childcare and the division of household labor.

What Can Help the Transition to Parenthood?

The transition to parenthood is a challenge for most families and is exacerbated by family policies that fail to recognize the structural pressures associated with a new baby. One such pressure involves time, including the ability to take time off from work after a baby is born. The feature box *From Macro to Micro: Maternity and Paternity Leaves* compares the leave policies in different countries, and as you will see, the United States is not highly ranked.

Family leaves are not the only things that can help new families. In her book, *Perfect Madness: Motherhood in the Age of Anxiety* (2005), Judith Warner describes the generous assistance available to her as a new mother living in France, and presents a jolting contrast after she returns to the United States:

> I was living in France, a country that has an astounding array of benefits for families—and for mothers in particular. When my children were born, I stayed in the hospital for five comfortable days. I found a nanny through a free, community-based referral service, then employed her, legally and full-time, for a cost to me of about $10,500 a year, after tax breaks. My elder daughter, from the time she was eighteen months, attended excellent part-time preschools, where she painted and played with modeling clay and ate cookies and napped for about $150 per month—the top end of the fee scale. She could have started public school at age three, and could have opted to stay until 5 P.M. daily. My friends who were covered by the French social security system (which I did not pay into), had even greater benefits: at least four months of paid maternity leave, the right to stop working for up to three years and have jobs held for them, cash grants after their second children were born starting at about $105 per month.
>
> And that was just the beginning. There was more: a culture. An atmosphere. A set of deeply held attitudes toward motherhood—toward adult womanhood—that had the effect of allowing me to have two children, work in an office, work out in a gym, and go out to dinner at night and away for a short vacation with my husband without ever hearing, without ever thinking, the word "guilt"(2005:9–10).

What is the impact of this collectivist orientation? French parents receive a great deal of government assistance when they have a baby. This assistance begins early in the child's life, made possible by three types of parent leaves: 16 weeks of paid maternity leave for the mother; 11 days of paid paternity leave for the father; and up to three years of unpaid leave for either parent with their job guaranteed (provided they have been on the job for at least one year) (Embassy of France, 2006).

If you have a child, do you think your transition to parenthood will be easier, more difficult, or about the same as it was for your parents? What types of macro-level changes would you like to see to help people transition more easily to parenthood? Do you think people who do not have children should pay to help those who do (through their taxes)? Why or why not?

Policy and You: From Macro to Micro

Maternity and Paternity Leaves

In Detroit, Michigan, Rhea, a first-time mother, is trying to get used to the thought of putting her 6-week-old son in daycare so she can get back to work. *"It's hard to imagine leaving him for 9 hours a day with a stranger, but I need the money,"* she laments. Across the border in Toronto, Canada, Kim is back at work after 14 months of paid maternity leave. *"It was terrific,"* she says. *"I was still making enough money to get by while I was at home with Ethan."* Across the ocean in Sweden, Nils is looking forward to sharing 16 months of parental leave at 80 percent pay with his girlfriend, whose baby will be born any day, *"It's great that we both have the time to bond with him."*

The United States has the least generous maternity and family leave policy of any developed nation. Other countries promote integration of work and family because they feel it is a benefit to everyone-child, parents, employer, and the society at large.

Longer leaves after childbirth are associated with better maternal and child health, lower stress, and greater well-being. Women are likely to breastfeed for longer periods if they have extended leave benefits. Employers themselves also benefit from longer parental leave; women are more likely to return to work after their leave expires rather than feel forced to quit. It is also more cost-effective to develop a well-planned parental leave policy than it is to rehire and retrain new employees.

What type of leave policies exists in the United States? Congress passed the **Family Medical Leave Act (FMLA)** in 1993, which requires employers with over 50 employees to provide 12 weeks of *unpaid* leave to eligible employees (both men and women) to care for themselves or their immediate families with specified medical conditions, including care of a newborn. Employees must have worked for the employer at least one year or 1,250 hours to be eligible for FMLA. Employers in small firms are not required by law to offer leaves.

Yet, in reality few people can afford to take unpaid leave. Therefore, many new mothers come back to work shortly after their short-term disability, vacation, or sick pay—if they have any—has been exhausted, often within a few short weeks.

In contrast to the United States, here are some examples of family support available in other countries:

- Japan offers 14 weeks of paid leave at 60 percent of salary.
- Denmark offers 18 weeks of paid maternity leave at 90 percent of salary.
- Spain offers 16 weeks of leave at 100 percent of salary.
- Switzerland provides 98 days at 80 percent of salary.

Parental leave is also more generous in poor or developing nations than it is in the United States. Even in Bangladesh, one of the poorest nations on Earth, women who work in *qualifying jobs* receive 12 weeks of maternity

The United States is unique in that it offers no national, paid maternity (or paternity) policy for new families. Most other peer nations offer new parents many months, or even years, off to relax and enjoy their new baby.

leave paid at 100 percent of salary. Mexico also offers 12 weeks of maternity leave at 100 percent of salary. In Iran, women receive 67 percent of their salary for 90 days. (Granted, many women in poor nations do not work in qualifying jobs because they work as maids, in the fields, or in the underground economy.)

However, the United States is one of two countries that do not guarantee paid leave at all for any of its workers (Australia also does not, although it does provide one year of unpaid leave). A recent report from the Families and Work Institute found that 16 percent of large firms in the United States with over 100 workers provide full pay during a maternity leave (usually six weeks); however, this is down from 27 percent in 1998 (Galinsky, Bond, & Sakai, 2008). If Americans have paid for optional short-term disability insurance with their employer, they can receive a partial salary for six weeks of leave. Yet, because the leave is "disability-related," it would not provide any pay for fathers, or for mothers of children who are adopted. Is this the best our government can do?

Source: Brown, 2009; Galinsky, Bond, & Sakai, 2008; United Nations Statistics Division, 2005, Table 5c.

What Do You Think?

1. It took the United States until 1993 to pass the Family Medical Leave Act, which provides only unpaid leave to certain qualified workers. Why do you think it took this long, and why is the FMLA less generous than the leave policies of other countries? Who would oppose the FMLA, and why? Who would support it, and why?

2. Do you think both males and females should be offered leave? Should it be paid for both? Why or why not?

Family Medical Leave Act (FMLA): An act that requires employers with over 50 employees to provide 12 weeks of *unpaid* leave to eligible employees (both men and women) to care for themselves or their immediate families with specified medical conditions.

Bringing It Full Circle

We began this chapter by meeting Tracey and Juan, the couple who adopted two children from Colombia. Families are created in many ways, and adoption itself touches the lives of people both in the United States and around the world. This chapter reveals that micro-level personal issues such as *whether, when, who,* and *how* to have a baby represent a complex intertwining of biological and macro-level structural and social forces. Cultural values such as pronatalism shape our attitudes and behaviors. Political, religious, economic, health care, and other social institutions also shape family life and policies about fertility, infertility, pregnancy, adoption, childbirth, and the transition to parenthood—dimensions of family life that many see as extremely personal. Reflecting upon what you have learned in this chapter, let's revisit the opening vignette with Juan and Tracey:

- Were the adoptions of Juan and Tracey's children private or public? Open or closed?

- What are some issues facing adopted children and their families that other families do not have? Think of the different contexts of adoption, including international adoption, transracial adoption, adoption by gays and lesbians, single-parent adoption, and closed versus open adoption.

- What transitions to parenthood might Tracey and Juan face, if they are typical parents? Would any of their transitions be different because their children are adopted?

- How do both macro-level and micro-level factors influence fertility patterns across cultures and across generations in your own family?

For further review, turn to the Video Discussion Guide on page 449 to answer additional questions about how the chapter opening video relates to what you have learned in this chapter.

Chapter Review

8.1 What are population and fertility trends worldwide?

The world's population could reach nearly 11 billion by 2050. Population growth occurs unevenly. Less developed countries have about 81 percent of the world's population, and in some countries the population may double in less than a generation. This is related to both birthrates and death rates.

8.2 What factors have influenced fertility rates in the United States over the past century?

Fertility rates have fluctuated throughout history. Trends are influenced by macro-level structural conditions, such as affluence, depression, war, and increasing opportunities for women.

8.3 What is pronatalism?

Pronatalism is a cultural value that encourages child-bearing. In the United States, pronatalism is manifested in the values that having children is a normal, natural part of a happy life, and that those who voluntarily remain childfree are selfish, immature, lonely, unfulfilled, insensitive, and more likely to have mental problems than parents. It is also supported by social institutions and policies around the world.

8.4 What are current trends showing about the age at which people have children?

Most people have children, but they have them later in life. The average age for women is now approximately 25, up from 21.4 years in 1970. Here is another way of understanding this trend: about 27 percent of women ages 30–34 do not have children today, compared to only 16 percent of women ages 30–34 in 1976.

8.5 What are some of the costs associated with having children?

Economists talk about direct financial costs (i.e., out-of-pocket expenses for food, clothing, housing, and education), which now amount to about $221,000 until a child's eighteenth birthday, and opportunity costs (i.e., lost opportunities for income by working only part-time, or not at all because of children).

8.6 What are some of the benefits associated with having children?

The emotional feelings of love and devotion may be more difficult to quantify; however, children can bring tremendous joy and purpose into people's lives. Parents love their children, take pride in them, and have fun with them. Children also connect parents socially with others.

8.7 How serious a problem is infertility?

Not all people who are childfree are so by choice. Infertility is the inability to get pregnant after one year of trying. It is a medical problem affecting approximately 12 percent of adults of childbearing age in the United States. It occurs in all income groups and racial and ethnic categories, and equally affects men and women.

8.8 Why are more couples choosing to remain childfree today?

With new educational and employment opportunities available to women, a growing number of couples opt to forgo parenthood. The decision not to have children is usually not made once, but many times, as people undergo a *process* of deciding about children. They might think about whether or not to have children while in their twenties, revisit the issue in their thirties, and again in their forties. Women usually have firmer opinions than men about forgoing parenthood because their lives would be most changed by parenthood.

 Key Terms

assisted reproductive technology (ART) (p. 221)
birth centers (p. 227)
closed adoption (p. 228)
content analysis (p. 229)
direct financial costs (p. 219)

Family Medical Leave Act (FMLA) (p. 237)
fertility rate (p. 214)
gestational surrogacy (p. 222)
infertility (p. 220)

medicalization of childbirth (p. 226)
mortality rate (or death rate) (p. 215)
open adoption (p. 228)
opportunity costs (p. 219)

private adoption (p. 229)
pronatalism (p. 216)
public adoption (p. 229)
surrogacy (p. 222)
traditional surrogacy (p. 222)

8.9 How has childbirth changed and become medicalized in the United States?

Until the 19th century, childbirth was "women's business," attended by midwives. To achieve their professional dominance, physicians began to claim that childbirth was inherently dangerous, required medical assistance, and that midwives were inadequately trained to deal with the complex nature of delivering babies. Women began to have their children in hospitals instead of at home, and birth was shaped by the latest technology. After a movement towards more holistic childbirth, the United States began to see an increase in elective caesarean births.

8.10 What is the difference between open and closed adoptions?

In an open adoption, information is shared between birth mothers, the adoptee, and the adoptive parents to varying degrees. In a closed adoption, popular in the past, all information about the birth parents is legally sealed.

8.11 What are some of the social contexts of adoption?

Many types of families adopt children, and each has its own unique reasons. For example, there are transracial adoptions, single-parent adoptions, adoptions by gays and lesbians, and international adoptions (in which the family usually has a different race or ethnic background from the adoptees).

8.12 Why is the transition to parenthood so challenging for new mothers and fathers?

Most new parents are shocked by the amount of work involved in caring for a new baby. This is because of many factors: Pronatalist sentiment may pressure people to become parents even though they may not really want to or be ready to parent; most parents have little or no experience in childcare; and becoming a parent is an abrupt change, unlike other adult roles. Expecting a baby is not the same thing as having one. New parents are suddenly on duty 24 hours a day, seven days a week; and the transition to parenthood necessitates complex changes in the couple's relationship.

8.13 How do other countries help to make the transition to parenting easier?

Other countries offer more extensive maternity and paternity leaves than does the United States. Longer leaves are associated with better maternal and infant health and well-being, and they are also good for business. In addition to leaves, many countries offer services to meet the needs of new parents. These services, along with personal social support, can make the transition to parenting more smoothly.

PEARSON
myfamilylab
www.myfamilylab.com

Experience, Discover, Observe, Evaluate

MyFamilyLab is designed just for you. Each chapter features a pre-test and post-test to help you learn and review key concepts and terms. Experience Marriage and Family in action with dynamic visual activities, videos, and readings to enhance your learning.

Here are a few activities you'll find for this chapter:

Watch Core Concepts video clips feature sociologists in action, exploring important concepts in the study of Marriage and the Family. Watch:

• Population Growth and Decline

Explore Social Explorer is an interactive application that allows you to explore Census data through interactive maps. Explore the Social Explorer Report:

• Changing Household Size between 1970 and 2000

Read MySocLibrary includes primary source readings from classic and contemporary sociologists. Read:

• Walzer, "Thinking about the Baby: Gender and Divisions of Infant Care"

9

Raising Children

Karen and Betsy with their two children, Jayla (age 3) and Henry (age 8).

What is it like to raise children? There is no simple answer to that question. Many aspects of parenting are similar across parenting contexts.

Yet there are unique differences as well. Meet Karen and Betsy, a same-sex couple raising their two children.

Karen and Betsy, who live in Massachusetts, have been together for 13 years. In 2005 they married, as Massachusetts is one of only a handful of states that allow same-sex couples to legally wed. Karen and Betsy spoke early on about wanting children, and today they are proud parents of Henry, who is eight years old, and Jayla, who is almost four. Henry is Karen's biological son. Henry's father does not live close by, but still plays a role in his life. Jayla is adopted, and joined their family just shy of her first birthday.

Karen and Betsy would tell you that in many ways raising children with two moms is no different from raising children in any other type of family. They worry about their children's health, safety, and happiness. But a closer look reveals that Karen and Betsy have to address issues that other families take for granted.

For example, while most parents simply move to any community convenient to work or school, Karen and Betsy had to make a concerted effort to find a community where other same-sex families lived, where the local public school reflected this diversity, and the community as a whole was inclusive. They wanted their children to grow up in an environment in which families like theirs are seen as normal. Karen and Betsy found such a community. Their children have grown up with other families with two moms, attend synagogue with other same-sex families, and attend a school with many families just like theirs.

Nonetheless, challenges remain. There have been some uncomfortable moments at Henry's school around mother's and father's day. Not all teachers recognize that such holidays or practices can be stressful to children and their parents. A preschool director insisted on having moms and dads visit the school on separate nights instead of just having one "parent night." If there are events or occasions that they anticipate, Karen and Betsy make a point of talking to the school administrators in advance. In other words, they must always be on guard, even in their relatively supportive environment.

Henry, at age eight, who until now had never given much thought to having two moms, is beginning to ask questions about their family. He is not so sure he likes being different. Karen and Betsy are aware he is experiencing a sense of "loss," but they reassure him that there are many types of families, and that he is very lucky to have two parents who love him dearly. Meanwhile, always aware of his needs, they have begun to add more male role models in his life. A high-school boy who is a friend of the family picks him

Watch the **Video** *Same Sex Parents Raising Children: Karen and Betsy* on **myfamilylab.com**

QUESTIONS *That Matter* •

9.1 Are there differences in parenting practices cross-culturally?

9.2 How has parenting changed over time?

9.3 What are some current trends in parenting found throughout the world?

9.4 What are some well-known theories of human development and socialization?

9.5 Who socializes our children?

9.6 How does socialization differ by social class, race and ethnicity, and gender?

9.7 What are three different parenting styles?

9.8 What does it mean to be a "mother," and how does that role differ from "father"?

9.9 How do children influence their parents?

9.10 What can be done to reduce the number of teen pregnancies?

9.11 Why should we be careful not to overgeneralize single parents?

9.12 How distinctive are gay and lesbian parents from heterosexual parents?

9.13 What are the unique strengths and challenges of grandparents raising grandchildren?

up from school once a week to "hang out" with him. Like all good parents, Karen and Betsy want to envelop their children with love, support, and self-confidence.

Being a parent is sure to be a labor of love, but it is also an emotional rollercoaster.

Parents have to take care of, nurture, and socialize their children. Some parents also have to teach their children about (and shield them from) the harsh realities of prejudice and discrimination.

In this chapter, we will explore many important issues about raising children. It is essential to remember that the journey is a two-way street: parents influence their children, but children also influence their parents. In particular, we will see that all parenting (and being parented) takes place in a social context.

:: Parenting: It's Not the Same Everywhere

▶ Read the **Document**
Parents' Socialization of Children
on **myfamilylab.com**

We know what parents are supposed to do: take care of, nurture, and socialize their children, right? Yes, but it is not that simple. These interactions between parents and children also take place within a broader social and cultural environment. Economic conditions, region of the country (whether it is urban or rural), cultural and religious traditions, gendered norms, job opportunities, and level of technology are just a few of the macro-level factors that set the stage for micro-level family interactions. For example, a couple living in an environment where reliable birth control is not readily accessible will have significantly more children than a couple with regular access to contraceptives. In much of the world, Africa, for example, families commonly have six, seven, or eight children (Population Reference Bureau, 2010). Think about how parenting in these families would differ from parenting in the United States, where having only one or two children is the norm. Technology and its access—in this case birth control— matter. ▶ Read on **myfamilylab.com**

Most people become parents, but *how* we parent our children, and what we consider *good parenting*, differs among cultures and across different times in history. In some countries, parents (usually the mother) literally *wear* their children for a few years. They strap them to their backs and work, play, cook, and do errands without a second thought. Think for a moment about parenting in the United States. Women usually give birth in hospitals away from family and friends, and this isolation sets the stage for our parenting. Our babies sleep in separate beds called cribs; they sleep in separate rooms away from their parents; and many are fed from bottles rather than their mother's breasts (Centers for Disease Control and Prevention, October 20, 2009). We place our children in strollers instead of carrying them close to our bodies. Within three months after giving birth, 40 percent of new mothers return to work because the United States has no paid maternity leave (Han, Ruhm, Waldfogel, & Washbrook, 2009). In contrast, in the United Kingdom, only 7 percent of new mothers return to work in three months.

Definitions of "good parenting" differ across cultures. In some cultures, parents would never think of putting their children in strollers, or having their babies sleep in cribs. Instead they strap their children to their backs, and sleeping together is routine.

As shown in Chapter 8, parents in many countries have an extensive array of maternity, paternity, and other benefits that allow them to stay at home while their children are young without losing their jobs, seniority, or pay. In fact, families often receive a cash benefit from the government to help with the costs of raising children. This benefit, known as a **family allowance** (or a **child allowance**), is available to all families—rich and poor—and is described in the feature box *Policy and You: From Macro to Micro*.

What is the *best* way to raise children? This question is difficult to answer because there may not really be one correct way. Although we have a strong sense of right and wrong, many of our childrearing rules are based on cultural and historical preferences rather than fact.

Policy and You: From Macro to Micro

Taking Care of Families

As April 15th approaches and American families with children fill out their tax returns, they will find some financial relief in the form of newly expanded child tax credits ($1,000 per child). While many families are delighted to have these expanded credits, how does the United States compare to other countries with respect to the financial help we give families?

Unfortunately, the United States is one of the few industrialized nations that do not provide families with child or family allowances. Eighty-eight countries provide cash benefits to families with children to help with the costs of raising their children. These are universal benefits, available to all families, regardless of income. The rationale is that all members of society benefit by having healthy, happy, and well-educated children, and therefore all members of society should share in the costs.

Many European countries began offering family allowances as early as the beginning of the 20th century. In Canada, family allowances were considered the first real social welfare program. In some countries, family allowances may be supplemented by many other cash programs or tax credits, including birth grants, school grants, child rearing or childcare allowances, adoption benefits, special supplements for single parents, guaranteed minimum child support benefits, and allowances for adult dependents and disabled children. By providing these cash benefits, governments are directly helping families with the costs of raising children and indirectly helping to lower the rate of child poverty.

Does the United States provide any similar program? Not exactly, but the United States does provide several tax benefits to families with children, particularly to low-income families. For example, low-income working families can apply for the refundable Earned Income Tax Credit (EITC) as long as their income was under $35,463 in tax year 2009 (with one qualifying child). The EITC is designed to partially offset taxes that low-income persons would otherwise pay, thereby serving as an inducement to work. Tax credits for families adopting a child, paying for a child's education, and for the costs of a child in eligible childcare are also available. All of these are designed to help low- and middle-income families, and all phase out as a family's income rises.

The problem is that applying for tax benefits can be confusing because it requires that a family be savvy enough to understand the tax system, available programs, and their eligibility requirements and ceilings. The net effect is that those American families who most need assistance are the least likely to apply for, or even be aware of, the benefits. For example, the Internal Revenue Service acknowledges that 25 percent of those eligible for the EITC do not receive this tax credit. Even when people do receive assistance, it arrives just on an annual, rather than on a regular monthly, basis. Given that poverty rates are significantly higher in the United States than in other developed nations, it might be worth taking a look at family allowances to determine how they could offset poverty for millions of families.

What Do You Think?

1. Why do you think that most Americans have never even heard of family allowances?

2. Do you think that family allowances help families by offering financial assistance to parents raising their children, or do they hurt families by creating dependency on the government?

Sources: Kamerman & Gatenio, 2002; Internal Revenue Service, April 13, 2009; Social Security Administration, September 2008; The Canadian Encyclopedia, 2005.

Our way of doing things today is virtually unheard of in many parts of the world. In other countries, parents and young children sleep together, children breastfeed for a few years, are carried by their parents in a sling, and mother and child are never separated for 40 hours a week (Han, Ruhm, & Waldfogel, 2009; Karraker, 2008; Kurchinka, 1998; Waldfogel, 2006).

Our guidelines for good parenting have changed throughout the years and what we think of as good parenting today was not always seen as such (Mintz, 2004). For example, compared to today's parents, parents in colonial America tended to be strict, emotionally distant, and expected unqualified obedience from their children. Some of this detachment may have been due to the high infant and child mortality rates during this period; parents were cautious about becoming too close with their children (Corsaro, 1997). Children were also thought to be born with "original sin," and therefore, needed firm discipline and severe religious training to discourage their innate rebellion and selfishness, and to keep them from literally going to hell. Excessive tenderness from the parents was thought to probably spoil the child.

family allowance (or child allowance): A cash benefit to families provided by the government to help offset the costs of raising children.

Children were treated as miniature adults in many ways (Mintz, 2004). There was little concept of adolescence, as there is today. As soon as children were old enough to labor on the family farm or in the household, they were put to work to help support the family.

There were, of course, differences by race, ethnicity, social class, sex, and religious orientation (Mintz, 2004). For example, Quaker families tended to be more emotionally attached to their children than were Puritans. Wealthy families tended to be more indulgent with their children than poorer families. Slave families faced the psychological burden of worrying about when and where their children might be sold. Boys were seen as belonging under the tutelage of a father, while a girl's training was the domain of the mother and included many domestic tasks, such as cooking, cleaning, and sewing.

During the Industrial Revolution, many families needed their children to work in the growing number of dangerous and dirty factories and other industries.

With industrialization, urbanization, and immigration during the 19th and early 20th centuries came sweeping changes in society (Handel, Cahill, & Elkin, 2007). Families moved from farms to cities in search of jobs, and record numbers of immigrants came from Europe with the hope of a better life. This period produced two views of childhood: the "protected child" among wealthy families, who was given education and leisure; and the "useful child" whose labor was needed by poor and working-class families to make ends meet (Mintz, 2004). Although a protected childhood was the cultural ideal for which most people strived, few families were able to attain this ideal for their children. Most families needed their children to earn a wage in the growing number of dangerous and dirty factories and other industries, as well as to cook, clean, and take care of younger siblings at home.

During the Progressive Era of the early 1900s, people became concerned about the increasing exploitation of children (Axinn & Stern, 2008; Day, 2009). Social reformers noted that there were few, if any, child labor laws, and many children toiled for ten hours a day, seven days a week, and never completed school. Because of the reformers' determination, many laws were finally passed protecting all workers, children in particular. With these workplace protections in place, the concept of childhood expanded to include a period that we now know as "adolescence."

This brief historical review reveals some of the macro-level aspects that influenced how we personally experienced families. Economic considerations and the need for child labor, dominant religious paradigms, the degree of industrialization and urbanization, slavery laws, and views about men and women all came together to shape our context of parenting.

Cultural and historical differences make us wonder: Is parenting so different everywhere that we can find no common ground? This section of the chapter began by noting that the primary job of parents is to take care of, nurture, and socialize children. Such parental responsibilities for children are found everywhere. Yet, there are other, newer themes beginning to emerge in the area of parenting. In looking at the evolution of *childrearing*, family scholars note at least three trends that exist in varying degrees in both industrial and non-industrial societies today (Adams, 2004; Adams & Trost, 2004):

- *First, although parents are central to childrearing, other people and social institutions are becoming increasingly involved in raising children.* These include grandparents and other relatives, daycare settings, governmental agencies, schools, and factories. Related to this is the rising tide of women's employment outside the home. Even in historically poor and patriarchal countries such as Bangladesh, increases in women's employment are changing the nature of families, the distribution of spousal power, and the care of children in profound ways (Ahmed & Bould, 2004).

- *Second, parents around the world increasingly encourage permissiveness and child independence.* There has been a decline in the value placed on obedience to parental authority, and more emphasis is now placed on independence and personal responsibility. Certainly not all cultures meet these changes with unabashed enthusiasm, but worldwide trends persist nonetheless (Adams, 2004; Adams & Trost, 2004).
- *Third, a higher value is placed on boys than on girls in most societies in the world.* The traditional preference for sons is based on family inheritance and the need for sons to care for aging parents. These values are very strong in countries such as China, Kenya, and India, but a preference for males is found in other countries as well (Banister, 2009; Pande & Astone, 2007; Pande & Malhotra, 2006). For example, a study conducted in India by the International Center for Research on Women showed that 46 percent of women said that they want more sons than daughters. Only 3 percent of women reported wanting more daughters than sons, and the remainder said that they wanted an equal number of sons and daughters or did not have a preference (Pande & Malhotra, 2006).

Next, let's explore some dimensions of parenting. First, we will focus on the process by which we learn about the rules of our culture and what is expected of us at different stages of our lives.

> *If you have had the opportunity to travel to other countries, compare and contrast the parenting there with what you are familiar with in the United States. If you witnessed any differences, what types of macro-level factors may contribute to those differences?*

:: Socialization: Learning to Be Human

Socialization refers to the lifelong process by which we acquire the knowledge, cultural values, and skills needed to function as human beings and participate in society. Socialization is unique to human beings because children are helpless at birth and have few instincts compared to other mammals. Although the debate about how much of "human nature" is biological and how much is social has not yet been definitely settled (and perhaps never will be), we do know that socialization is a powerfully complex process that imparts the qualities and cultural traits we think of as "human" (Rohall, Milkie, & Lucas, 2007).

Theoretical Approaches to How Children Develop

Social psychologists have elaborated on many theories to explain child development and the process of socialization (Aronson, Wilson, & Akert, 2010; Maccoby, 2007; Feldman, 2010). Four prominent social psychologists and their works are discussed below.

Sigmund Freud and the Psychoanalytic Perspective
Sigmund Freud (1856–1939) lived in an era when biological explanations of human behavior were prevalent. He proposed that human behavior and personality originate from unconscious forces within individuals: the id, ego, and superego. The **id** is the part of the personality that includes biological drives and needs for immediate gratification. The id is present at birth and readily visible in young children; however, this aspect of personality continues throughout our lives. The **ego** is the rational component of personality that attempts to balance the need for immediate gratification with the demands of society. It arises as we become aware that we cannot have all that we desire and that our needs must be balanced with the demands of society. The **superego** is our conscience, which draws upon our cultural values and norms to help us understand why we cannot have everything we want.

Jean Piaget and Cognitive Development
Jean Piaget (1896–1980) was a Swiss psychologist whose research focused on how people think and understand. He was particularly interested in how children come to understand the world and make meaning of their experiences. He identified four stages of cognitive development that are rooted in biology and based upon age. The first stage, which occurs in the first two years of life, is called the **sensorimotor stage**. Infants and toddlers understand the world primarily through touch, sucking, listening, and

socialization: The lifelong process by which we acquire the cultural values and skills needed to function as human beings and participate in society.

id: According to Freud, the part of the personality that includes biological drives and needs for immediate gratification.

ego: According to Freud, the rational component of personality that attempts to balance the need for immediate gratification with the demands of society.

superego: According to Freud, this is our conscience, which draws upon our cultural values and norms to help us understand why we cannot have everything we want.

sensorimotor stage: Piaget's first stage of cognitive development (from birth to age 2) in which infants and toddlers understand the world primarily through touch, sucking, listening, and looking.

looking. A child begins to organize and exercise some control over her life. The second stage, **preoperational thought**, occurs from ages two through seven as the child learns language, symbolic play, and symbolic drawing. They do not yet grasp abstract concepts and their knowledge is tied to their own perceptions. The third stage, **concrete operational thought**, occurs between the ages of seven and twelve. During this period, children begin to see the causal connections in their surroundings, and can manipulate categories, classification systems, and hierarchies in groups. The final stage of cognitive development is **formal operational thought**, which begins in adolescence and continues through adulthood. During this stage, children develop capacities for abstract thought, and can conceptualize more complex issues or rules that can be used for problem solving.

Charles Horton Cooley and George Herbert Mead: The Self

Charles Horton Cooley (1864–1929) and George Herbert Mead (1863–1931) turned attention to a sociological perspective by proposing that an individual cannot form a self-concept without social contact with others. They rejected or minimized Freud's claim of biological drives, and Piaget's assertion that individuals develop chronologically as they age. Instead, they believed that human behavior and our self-identity are shaped by interactions with others and the meanings we attach to those interactions. Cooley suggested that we come to see ourselves as others perceive and respond to us, a process he described as the **looking-glass self**. For example, we will see ourselves as thin or heavy, intelligent or less intelligent, attractive or unattractive, trustworthy or irresponsible, based on the way that other people perceive and respond to us.

Mead extended Cooley's sociological insight in several ways, including the view that social experience includes symbolic interaction. This was introduced in Chapter 1—we interact not just with words, but also with important symbols and meanings, such as eye contact or a wave of the hand. Mead also elaborated upon Cooley's work by focusing on **role taking**, which is the process of mentally assuming the role of another person to understand the world from his or her point of view and to anticipate his or her response to us. Role taking helps us to become self-reflective. Mead suggests that the self is divided into two components—the "I" and the "me." The "I" is the subjective element of the self and represents spontaneity and interaction that we initiate. The "me" is the objective element of self, reflecting the internalized perceptions of others towards us. Both the "I" and the "me" are needed to form the social self. In other words, the feedback loop is critical—we initiate behavior that is ultimately guided by the ways that others see us.

Social Learning Theory

Social learning theory, developed by Alfred Bandura (1973; 1977; 1997), expanded upon the idea that children learn by reinforcement. Bandura believes that children also learn by watching and imitating others. As he has argued, "learning would be exceedingly laborious, not to mention hazardous, if people had to rely solely on the efforts of their own actions to inform them what to do. Fortunately, most human behavior is learned observationally through modeling." In his famous "Bobo doll" studies, the child participants observed an adult acting violently toward a doll. When the children were later allowed to play in a room with the doll, they began to imitate the aggressive actions they had previously observed. The children received no encouragement or incentives to beat up the doll; they were simply imitating the behavior they observed. Therefore, when parents smile, hug, or hit their children, it is a powerful socialization process that sets an example for how children choose to interact with other people.

Who Teaches Our Children? Agents of Socialization

Chapter 2 introduced the various ways individuals, groups, or institutions, collectively referred to as agents of socialization, teach children about the norms and values of their particular culture. Let's briefly review these agents of socialization:

- *Family members, especially parents,* have the greatest impact upon socializing children because they provide the first exposure to a particular culture. Parents provide children with a place to live, food to eat, clothes to wear, vocabulary to learn, medical care when

preoperational thought: Piaget's second stage of cognitive development, occurring from ages 2 through 7, as the child learns language, symbolic play, and symbolic drawing, but does not grasp abstract concepts.

concrete operational thought: Piaget's third stage of cognitive development, which occurs between the ages of 7 and 12, when children begin to see the causal connections in their surroundings, and can manipulate categories, classification systems, and hierarchies in groups.

formal operational thought: Piaget's fourth stage of cognitive development, beginning at adolescence and continuing through adulthood, in which children develop capacities for abstract thought and can conceptualize more complex issues or rules that can be used for problem solving.

looking-glass self: Cooley's suggestion that we come to see ourselves as others perceive and respond to us.

role taking: According to Mead, the process of mentally assuming the role of another person to understand the world from their point of view and to anticipate their response to us.

social learning theory: Developed by Alfred Bandura, the theory that behavior is learned through modeling and reinforcement.

sick, and thus introduce the child to values and customs. They also pass on to the child his or her socioeconomic status and social position in terms of race, ethnicity, and religion.

- *Schools and childcare* enlarge children's worlds by introducing them to people and settings different from those of their immediate family. Schools organize and teach children a wide range of knowledge, skills, and customs, including the political ideology of the society.

- By the time children enter school, they are able to form *peer group* relationships without the direct supervision of family members and other adults. Peers usually reward conformity rather than deviations, so children learn to look, dress, talk, and act like others in their group. For example, young people learn which specific clothing styles are popular and which are not.

- *Toys and games* also reflect our culture and teach children important messages about what it means to be a member of society. For example, as shown in Chapter 2, toys and games tell children about what it means to be a boy, girl, man, or woman in our culture.

- *The mass media*, including television and the Internet, are increasingly important mechanisms for socializing children (Brooks-Gunn & Donahue, 2008; Calvert, 2008). Ninety-eight percent of households have at least one television, and over 80 percent have two or more. And over 77 percent of households— and 93 percent of married-couple households with children— have at least one computer in the home with Internet access, as shown in Table 9.1 (Kennedy, Smith, Wells, & Wellman, 2008).

In other words, socialization teaches children about the culture in which they live, but the socialization process is not completely uniform. Macro-level factors shape our families, the schools we attend, the peers we come to know, our toys and games, and our exposure to mass media. Next, we will look at how a few of these macro-level factors influence the socialization process.

Agents of socialization, particularly parents, teach children about the culture in which they live. Children imitate those around them, including their families, peers, and those they see in the media.

Socialization and Social Class

Your social class position has had a large effect on the ways you have been socialized (Crompton, 2006). First, social class affects how much money parents have to spend on their children. This in turn affects where they live, the quality of schools they will attend, the types of neighbors and friends they will have, the type of clothing they will wear, and the types and amount of toys, hobbies, and enrichment activities such as music lessons or sports. Participation in these programs costs money,

Table 9.1	Technology Ownership by Household Type (percent)

Technology is commonplace, especially in two-parent families with children.

	All adults (N = 2,252)	Married with child/ children (n = 482)
Cell phone(s) in household	84	95
Computer(s) in household	77	93
Internet household	77	94
2+ televisions	83	88
2+ home computers	39	58

Source: Report: Families, Mobile, New Media Ecology-Networked Families by Barry Wellman, Aaron Smith, Amy Wells, Tracy Kennedy. Oct 19, 2008. The Pew Research Center's Internet & American Life Project. Pew Research Center.

may require parental involvement, and may necessitate significant preparation time, all of which low-income families lack (or may have little of) (Weininger & Lareau, 2009). Yet, these programs can boost academic achievement and social development (Gardner, Roth, & Brooks-Gunn, 2008; Society for Research in Child Development, 2008).

But social class affects more than just material goods. It also affects the values, norms, and expectations that parents have for their children (Lareau, 2003; Seccombe, 2011). It is possible that the lower participation rates of low-income families also represent a different set of core values. Research studies have generally noted the following differences:

- When parents are asked to choose from a list of childhood traits they consider most desirable for their children, lower-income parents tend to choose traits such as obedience, conformity, staying out of trouble, and keeping neat and clean. In contrast, higher-income parents tend to choose traits such as creativity, ambition, independence, curiosity, and good judgment (Kohn, 1977; 2006).
- Lower-income parents tend to be more controlling, authoritarian, arbitrary in their discipline, and apt to use physical punishment, whereas higher-income parents tend to be more democratic and are more receptive to their children's opinions (Lareau, 2003; Berlin, Ispa, Fine, Malone, Brooks-Gunn, Brady-Smith, Ayoub, & Bai, 2009).
- Higher-income parents tend to show more warmth and affection to their children, talk to them more, and use more complex language than do parents from lower-income families (Berns, 2001; Ispa, Fine, Halgunseth, Harper, Robinson, Boyce, Brooks-Gunn, & Brady-Smith, 2004).

Sociologist Melvin Kohn suggested that parents value traits in their children that reflect the parents' world, particularly their world of work (1977). Lower-income parents tend to emphasize conformity and related traits because these traits will be useful in the working-class jobs their children are likely to hold in the future. For example, success on an assembly line requires obedience and conformity, not creativity, ambition, or curiosity. Those latter characteristics could actually sabotage good job performance. In contrast, higher-income parents are likely to have jobs that entail working with people or ideas, and involve self-direction and creativity. Higher-income parents value these characteristics and socialize their children to have them.

Therefore, it is likely that class differences in socialization reflect not only simple economic resources, but also the core values of parents as they prepare their children for their likely roles in society. We learn these values in our family of orientation, and we then reproduce these values in our families of procreation (Crompton, 2006).

To illustrate the power of social class, let's examine the work of sociologist Annette Lareau who studied 88 families of school-age children (Lareau, 2003; Weininger & Lareau, 2009). She spent time with these families during meals, on trips to school and extracurricular events, and on errands and appointments, visiting them about twenty different times over the course of her research. Lareau found strong social class differences in the ways parents interacted with their children. For example, middle-class parents enrolled their children in organized activities that they believe transmit important life skills. They disciplined their children by talking with them; they valued creativity and independent thought. As one middle-class father told her, "One of the things I think is important is just exposure. The more I can expose children to, with a watchful eye and supervision, the more creative they can be in their own thinking. The more options they will be able to see for themselves, the more they get a sense of improved self-esteem, self-worth, and self-confidence. I think it is something they will carry over into adulthood" (Weininger, Elliot B. and Annette Lareau. 2009. "Paradoxical Pathways: An Ethnographic Extension of Kohn's Findings on Class and Childrearing." Journal of Marriage and Family 71(3, August):680–95.

In contrast, children from working-class and low-income families engaged in fewer organized activities and were far more likely to spend their free time with their family and neighborhood friends. Working-class parents were more likely to see themselves as authority figures, and to issue directives rather than to try negotiating with their children. One mother spoke for many when she explained to her daughter why she must do something, "Because I said so and I'm your mother" (Weininger & Lareau, 2009:690). Lareau also found that working-class parents were more likely to discipline their children with physical punishment and spanking.

Despite these differences, let's be careful not to overgeneralize. Weininger and Lareau also found that middle-class parents routinely exercised subtle forms of control while attempting to instill self-direction in their children, whereas working-class and low-income parents tended to give children considerable autonomy in certain parts of daily life (Weininger & Lareau, 2009). Because working-class parents generally do not view life as a series of "teachable moments," they are less likely to try to manipulate or hover over their children. For example, one young girl, Katie, typically comes home after school, fixes a snack, and then decides by herself what to do for the rest of the afternoon. Sometimes she rides her bike; other times she watches television or plays with her younger brother or cousin. She has long stretches of unstructured leisure time and the choice to fill it spontaneously however she chooses. In contrast, her middle-class peers are given a structured menu of activities from which to choose.

Socialization, Race, and Ethnicity

As shown in Chapter 2, the United States is becoming more ethnically and racially diverse, creating a great need for sensitivity to values and customs that may differ among groups. The following story illustrates the importance of cultural values:

One day a fifth-grade teacher noticed that Juanita, normally a tidy youngster, had a brown smear of dirt on one arm. That day and the next, the teacher said nothing. However, when Juanita came to class with the mark on her arm the third day, the teacher told her to go wash her dirty arm. When Juanita said it was not dirty, the teacher told her not to argue and to do as she was told. Juanita complied. Several days later, her parents took Juanita out of school to attend the funeral of her sister. Two weeks had passed and Juanita had still not returned to school, so the principal went to her home to find out why. Juanita's mother told the principal that when

"We are one with nature. When someone is ill, that person is out of balance with nature."

someone is ill, each family member places a spot of oil and soil somewhere on the body. "We are one with nature. When someone is ill, that person is out of balance with nature. We use the oil and soil of our Mother, the Earth, to show her we wish our sick one to be back in balance with nature. When Juanita's teacher made her wash her arm, our oneness with nature was broken. That is why her sister died. The teacher caused her death; Juanita can never return to her class." (Berns, Roberta M. 2001. Child, Family, School, Community: Socialization and Support, 5th Ed. New York: Thomson Learning.)

Racial and ethnic families may differ from the majority culture in terms of how they practice religion or medicine, the primacy of their family ties and sense of family obligation, their gendered patterns of behavior, their emphasis on time and promptness, the degree of hierarchy and authority in their relationships, how strict parents are with their children, their views on the roles of the elderly, the importance placed on group cooperation or individual achievement, and the way they interact, nurture, and discipline their children (McLoyd, Cauce, Takeuchi, & Wilson, 2000). For example, the Japanese have more traditional views of gender than do most Americans. Because middle-class jobs often require very long hours, often extending well into the night, most Japanese mothers do not work outside the home. Japanese women do the majority of housework and childcare (Ishii-Kuntz, 2008; Ishii-Kuntz, Makino, Kato, & Tsuchiya, 2004). Japanese fathers are largely absent from the domestic world. When fathers are engaged with their children, it is most often in "fun" activities like eating, rather than in more mundane activities such as food preparation (Ishii-Kuntz, 2003). On a recent visit to Tokyo, I gave a lecture at a large university, and the female graduate students were shocked to learn that I have children and a career, and wondered how American women manage to have both.

One important difference between the socialization practices of White and minority parents is that the latter must teach their children about the importance of race, ethnicity, prejudice, and discrimination, while they provide their children with the coping skills necessary to develop and maintain a strong and healthy self-image (Barr & Neville, 2008; Bentley, Adams, & Stevenson, 2009; Hughes, Rodriguez, Smith, Johnson, Stevenson, & Spicer, 2006; Tamis-LeMonda, Way, Hughes, Yoshikawa, Kalman, & Niwa, 2008). Referred to as familial **racial (or ethnic) socialization**, parents' communication is important in shaping children's attitudes, beliefs, and self-efficacy in dealing with racial and ethnic experiences. Racial or ethnic socialization can instill a sense of identity, pride, and enculturation. Parents teach their children about religious traditions, cook specific types of foods, speak a particular language or dialect, and impart a set of values associated with their group identity. The feature box *Why Do Research?* reveals the importance of this socialization experience (Umaña-Taylor, Alfaro, Bámaca, & Guimond, 2009).

Racial and ethnic socialization also includes teaching the hard truths about racism in our society. When parents see instances of unfair treatment of their children, they become even more protective, and step up their cautions and warnings to them about racial and ethnic issues and relationships (Hughes & Johnson, 2001). This supportive parenting has been shown to reduce the harmful effects of racism, including anger, hostility, and aggressive behavior. For example, a study of over 300 Black adolescent males found that those with supportive parents were less likely to respond with anger or hostility to perceived discrimination, and when angered, were less likely to behave aggressively (Simons, Simons, Burt, Drummund, Stewart, Brody, Gibbons, & Cutrona, 2006).

Socialization and Gender

Chapter 2 identified many ways in which gender is constructed by families, social institutions (e.g., schools), and cultural artifacts (e.g., toys). Although there is no definitive answer as to how much of our gendered self is related to biology, most scientists suggest that gender differences probably are the result of biology and the social environment (Sax, 2006). Children learn about what it means to be a girl or a boy in a particular culture in a particular time first by the images, words, play, and rituals of their parents. Comments such as "Big boys don't cry," "You throw like a girl," "Let's play dress-up," "You're my little tomboy," "Help your mother with the dishes," and "Help your dad take out the trash," all teach us about how masculinity and femininity are defined across cultures and across different periods in history. ◉⫿Watch on **myfamilylab.com**

◉⫿**Watch** the **Video** *Core Concepts: Gender Socialization* on **myfamilylab.com**

racial (or ethnic) socialization: Teaching minority children about prejudice, discrimination, and the coping skills necessary to develop and maintain a strong and healthy self-image.

Think about your social class, racial or ethnic background, or your sex, and reflect upon specific ways that these statuses have shaped the way you were socialized by your parents. Of these three statuses, which had the most powerful influence on your socialization, and why?

Parents are a major force in shaping the gendered attitudes of their children. One such gendered attitude is that boys tend to evaluate themselves as more intelligent than girls evaluate themselves. A recent study based on nearly 500 eleventh and twelfth graders looked at whether boys' greater confidence is a result of actual sex differences in intelligence, or whether it may be due to sex-typed parental perceptions of their children's intelligence (Steinmayr & Spinath, 2009). All students were assessed for verbal, numerical, figural, and reasoning intelligence, and no differences were found. Yet the students' parents rated boys' numerical, figural and reasoning intelligence higher than that of the girls.

Parents also shape gendered attitudes of their children by their own behavior. For example, a longitudinal study that followed children for 30 years found that sons who grew up in a household in which their mothers stayed home while their fathers worked outside the home held more traditional gendered views as adults than did sons with dual-earner parents (Cunningham-Burley, 2001). Likewise, sons who saw their fathers doing stereotypical female labor in the home (e.g., washing dishes, cooking) were more likely to engage in those types of tasks as an adult than were other sons.

Parents have many different ways or styles of socializing their children. Let's explore these parenting styles in the next section.

Why Do Research?

The Importance of Ethnic Socialization for Hispanic Adolescents' Sense of Cultural Identity

The meanings that people make of their race, ethnicity, or culture are referred to as "cultural orientation," which includes the degree to which individuals (1) adhere to the values and behaviors of mainstream culture (i.e., acculturation); (2) adhere to the values and behaviors of the native culture (i.e., enculturation); and (3) explore and define their identity with respect to the native culture (i.e., ethnic identity). This study examines the importance of ethnic socialization to the enculturation and ethnic identity of adolescents. The researchers also wondered if ethnic socialization had different effects on adolescent boys and girls.

Hispanic students were recruited from five high schools with small Hispanic populations (only 8–16 percent), with an equal number of adolescent boys and girls participating. The study was longitudinal, meaning that the students were followed over time, in this case over the course of four years. Each student completed a 45-minute survey every year, and was paid for their participation. About 20 percent of the students dropped out over the course of the four-year study—they may have graduated, transferred schools, or were otherwise unavailable or unwilling to participate, but 80 percent were followed over the full four years.

The researchers asked students a wide variety of questions in their surveys to identify (1) their generational status; (2) the degree of ethnic socialization they experienced; (3) the depth of their enculturation; and (4) their ethnic identity. With respect to their generational status, adolescents reported the country of birth for themselves, each parent, and grandparent to produce an account of their generational status in the United States. With respect to ethnic socialization, students responded to a series of statements such as, "My family teaches me about our family's ethnic/cultural background," and "Our home is decorated with things that reflect my ethnic/cultural background." Enculturation was measured by students' fluency in reading, writing, and understanding Spanish, and students were asked about how frequently they used Spanish electronic media. Level of enculturation was also determined by a series of questions about traditional values, such as, "The family should consult close relatives (uncles and aunts) concerning its important decisions." Finally, with respect to ethnic identity, students were asked a series of questions that assessed the degree to which adolescents have explored and resolved what their ethnic identity means to them, such as "I have attended events that have helped me learn more about my ethnicity" and "I have a clear sense of what my ethnicity means to me."

Minority parents must teach their children about the importance of race, ethnicity, prejudice, and discrimination, while providing the skills necessary to instill pride and maintain a strong and healthy self-image.

Using sophisticated statistical techniques, the researchers concluded that generational status is an important predictor of ethnic socialization and Spanish fluency. The longer a family has lived in the United States, the less likely are parents to partake in ethnic socialization or to teach their children Spanish. Second, ethnic socialization is an important predictor of ethnic identity for both adolescent boys and girls. Students whose parents deliberately taught them about their ethnicity and culture were more likely to be interested in, explore, and feel comfortable with their ethnic heritage. Third, they found that adolescent girls experience more overt ethnic socialization than do adolescent boys. Parents assume that adolescent girls will be the carrier of the culture, and spend more time overtly teaching them about Hispanic issues. Taken together, this research identifies the central importance that families play in racial and ethnic socialization.

What Do **You** Think?

1. What do you think are the methodological strengths and weaknesses of this study? Think about things like the research method used (refer back to Chapter 1, pp. 23-26).

2. Do you think these findings would hold true for other racial or ethnic groups? Why or why not?

Sources: Umaña-Taylor, Alfaro, Bámaca, & Guimond, 2009; Umaña-Taylor, Yazedjian, & Bámaca-Gomez, 2004.

:: Parenting Styles

My daughter Ramona came home with a "C-" in algebra on her report card. I know that Ramona is capable of doing much better than this. Yes, I realize that her algebra homework takes extra time to understand and do correctly, and I am going to help her make the time in her busy day to devote to algebra. She will have to postpone one of her extracurricular activities until her grade improves. I will let her choose which one to postpone, and then we can assess the situation after her next report card.

My son Derek came home with a "C-" in algebra on his report card. I know that the subject is hard for Derek and he can't really help his poor grade. I don't want him to feel badly about it; I certainly don't want it to erode his self-esteem. I think we will all go out to dinner tonight and have fun, and try to forget about his "C-," after all, it's only a grade, isn't it? I'm sure he is doing his best.

My daughter Rebecca came home with a "C-" in algebra on her report card. What in the hell is that all about? That's it! She's grounded for a month. No child of mine is going to be a "C-" student. She can just get over herself. "Rebecca, come here right now because you have some explaining to do, do you hear me?"

Forty years ago researchers began to study parenting practices systematically. After careful observation and analysis of many different parents with their children, Diana Baumrind identified three general styles of parenting (1966; 1968)—a typology that remains widely used today. One style is reflected in the quote of Ramona's parent and is referred to as an **authoritative parenting style**. Parents are demanding and maintain high levels of control over their children, but they are also warm and receptive. These parents try to guide their children with compassion, while also setting limits on their behavior. Children are expected to follow the house rules, but at the same time parents are flexible, caring, and responsive.

In contrast, the quote of Derek's parent exhibits a **permissive parenting style**. Parents who adopt this style may be very nurturing, caring, and responsive to their children. They communicate well with their children, but they are, however, quite lenient. They put few controls or demands on their children and do not hold them accountable for their actions.

Finally, the quote of Rebecca's parent illustrates an **authoritarian parenting style**. In this style, parents are strict, punitive, less communicative, and offer less warmth and support. These parents love their children, but tend toward rigidity. They expect complete obedience as there is little room for compromise, and they offer little real communication with their children. These parents may also be more likely to use *corporal punishment* (spanking and physical discipline), an issue that will be covered more fully in Chapter 11. About three-quarters of parents agree that "it is sometimes okay to spank a child," down from 94 percent who agreed with that statement a generation ago (Cloud, 2009).

Can you guess which type of parenting style yields the best results? Both boys and girls tend to perform better in school and are more socially competent when raised by authoritative parents as compared to the other two types (Bradley, 2006; Brooks-Gunn & Markman, 2005). Children raised by authoritarian parents were more often fearful, while children raised by permissive parents were more likely to be aggressive and impulsive (Baumrind, 1966; 1968). In sum, developmental psychologists believe that the authoritative parenting style best predicts outcomes in children thought to be most desirable (Cheah, Leung, Tahseen, & Schultz, 2009; Dumas, Lawford, Tieu, & Pratt, 2009).

Let's now look at specific aspects of parenting—the identities of parents and their specific activities–and see how these identities and activities differ for fathers and mothers.

authoritative parenting style: A parenting style that is demanding and maintains high levels of control over the children, but is also warm and receptive.

permissive parenting style: A parenting style that places few controls or demands on the child.

authoritarian parenting style: A parenting style that is strict, punitive, and not very warm.

Which parenting style did your parents have? Did the style differ between your mother and father? How does their parenting style influence you today?

:: Mothering

"Mother" and "father" are nouns—these words identify biological lineage. But they also indicate legal and social ties, which are not always the same as biological lineage. For example, an adopted child may think of someone as "mom" even though the child has no biological connection to her. And, this child may have no real connection at all to the person who gave birth to her. Does the word "mother" describe the relationship between a child and the partner of her lesbian mother? Both women may see themselves as mothers, although the law may only recognize one of them. And just to make things more confusing, when a surrogate gives birth, who is the mother—the woman giving birth, or the woman who hired the surrogate? We can see from these examples that the seemingly simple nouns "mother" and "father" are not always so simple. They are both biological and social statuses.

But what do we mean when we say "mothering" or "fathering"? These terms are even more complex. They represent both an identity and a specific set of tasks.

"Mothering" as an Identity

What is "mothering"? Most people think it is the emotional and physical work involved with caring for children, but mothering takes place within specific historical and cultural contexts, and is framed by structures of gender, race, and class (Arendell, 2000; Warner, 2005; Pew Research Center, May 2, 2007). The expectations associated with mothering are socially constructed—they are never static, but are continually changing. What is seen as "good" or "appropriate" mothering in one place and time may be perceived quite differently elsewhere. Anthropological literature provides many examples of the variability in mothering, suggesting that it is primarily Western societies in which women (and their partners) raise children in isolation. Anthropologists illustrate other models that draw upon an extended circle of family, including older siblings, grandmothers, grandfathers, aunts, uncles, and cousins.

In the United States, motherhood is a powerful identity, more powerful than either marital status or occupation. Women with children report experiencing greater meaning in their lives than do childfree women (Ross & Van Willigen, 1996). Ironically, however, they also report greater distress and depression than do childfree women (Ali, 2008; Doss, Rhoades, Stanley, & Markman, 2009). This is because of the stresses associated with the extensive and ongoing emotional work; the increased household labor; the reduction in finances (e.g., a mother quitting work or working only part-time); the increased financial needs that accompany children; and the lack of social support and government assistance they receive for their mothering tasks.

Compared to other developed nations, American mothering is more intense and fraught with anxiety (Warner, 2005). In her book *Perfect Madness: Motherhood in the Age of Anxiety*, Judith Warner describes the "mess" that accompanies American motherhood—the unending anxiety about whether American women are perfect mothers wreaks havoc on their emotional well-being. Women in other countries are less likely to fret about the pros and cons of combining work with employment, or debate whether young children benefit from childcare or should stay at home. They are more able to relax and feel confident in their abilities as mothers. Much of this confidence comes from knowing that they are not mothering alone, but that they have a cadre of social and health professionals, midwives, physicians, nannies, and professional childcare providers, available at government expense, ready to help them and their children, as described in Chapter 8.

"Mothering" as an Activity

Mothering can bring tremendous personal satisfaction and growth, and boundless love. Most women want to become mothers; however, mothering, especially in the United States, is not without personal, financial, and social costs.

Mothers in the United States are typically more involved with their children than are fathers. Mothers do the majority of socialization, hands-on care, emotional work, discipline,

Did your mother work or stay home when you were a child? How did this arrangement affect you? What arrangement would you like to have if you have children, and why?

transporting, and management (e.g., remembering to make the twice-yearly dental appointment) (Craig, 2006; Jacobs & Kelley, 2006; Poortman & van der Lippe, 2009). Mothers spend over twice the amount of time per day caring for children under the age of six than do fathers, including about three times the amount of time per day spent on actual physical care. Among children of all ages, mothers are more involved than fathers, even when both work full-time outside the home (Sandberg & Hofferth, 2001).

How does employment affect the time a woman has to spend mothering? Employed mothers spend about 27 hours per week engaged with or accessible to their children as compared to 32 hours a week for full-time mothers (Sandberg & Hofferth, 2001). They engage in virtually the same activities with their children as do mothers who do not work.

Nonetheless, many employed mothers feel guilty about the time they spend away from home. There is a cultural contradiction: even though most mothers work outside the home, they must deal with critical judgments for doing so. Yet if a mother stays at home, she pays the price of being treated as an outsider to the larger world. As one woman laments:

I felt really torn between what I wanted to do. Like a gut-wrenching decision. Like, what's more important? Of course your kids are important, but you know, there's so many outside pressures for women to work. Every ad you see in magazines or on television shows this working woman who's coming home with a briefcase and their kids are all dressed and clean. It's such a lie. I don't know of anybody who lives like that (Hays, 2001:317).

It is no wonder that many women, especially women with children, are tired. A recent Gallup poll asked men and women if they felt "well-rested" yesterday (Pelham, 2010). Thirty-three percent of women said "no" as compared to only 26 percent of the men. Likewise, 34 percent of adults who had at least one child in the household did not feel well-rested, as compared to only 27 percent of childfree adults. But how do mothers with children and fathers with children compare to one another? The gap continues to grow, as shown in Figure 9.1.

:: Fathering

What about fathers? What are their identities, and what activities do they engage in? How are these identities and activities different from those of mothers?

"Fathering" as an Identity

Despite the popular stereotype of fathers as only "breadwinners," fathers have played other social roles throughout history, including moral overseer, nurturer, and a gender-model for their sons (Marsiglio & Pleck, 2005; Marsiglio, Roy, & Fox, 2005). However, specific details about the

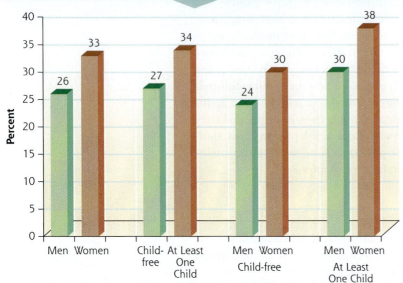

Figure 9.1

Percentage Saying They "Did Not Feel Well-Rested Yesterday" by Sex and Whether They Have a Child in the Home

Women are more likely than men to say that they are not well-rested. Why do you think this is the case?

Source: "Pelham, Brett W. 2010. "Rest Eludes Nearly 30% of Americans." Retrieved 2 March 2010. Gallup Poll (www.gallup.com/poll/125471/rest-eludes-nearly-americans.aspx?version=print).

Most people want to have children; however, "mothering" and "fathering" are really quite different roles and responsibilities. Mothers tend to spend far more time on their child's physical care, while fathers spend more time in play.

hands-on role they have had with their children are not as well-known. Sociologist Jessie Bernard (1973) traced the historical development of and the changes in male roles in U.S. families. She observed that the Industrial Revolution in the mid-19th century transformed men's roles into that of the "good provider," in which the focus shifted to primarily their breadwinning capabilities (Bernard, 1973). Instead of participating in the more nurturing and caretaking aspects of family life as they had done in the past, fathers were removed physically and emotionally from the work done at home. Being a good provider became the dominant concept of male identity. Moreover, having an employed wife was indicative of the father's failure to provide for his family, and threatened to undermine his position as "head of the household."

This model continued until the 1970s and 1980s, when the women's movement and other social movements ushered in ideological changes about men's and women's positions and activities within the family. As more married women with children have sought employment, families have begun to restructure themselves. Men are now becoming more involved in domestic life, and many are relieved that they no longer have the economic burden of being the sole breadwinner.

During the past twenty years there has been an explosion in research on fathering: what do fathers do with their children, what are the outcomes, and what are the meanings associated with being a father? We now believe that a father should be engaged with his children, and many programs exist to promote this relationship (Hawkins, Lovejoy, Holmes, Blanchard, & Fawcett, 2008; Cowan, Cowan, Pruett, Pruett, & Wong, 2009). Male-only social movements such as the "Million Man March on Washington" illustrates that men in our culture are wrestling with their roles as fathers, and many hope to increase public awareness about the meaning and importance of fathers in their children's lives (King, Harris, & Heard, 2004).

"Fathering" as an Activity

How involved are fathers in their children's lives? Mothers perform the majority of parenting tasks; however, fathers do play an important role, and their involvement appears to be

My Family

"What I Like About Being a Dad…and What I Don't"

I've always assumed I would have a few kids. While I've never been obsessed about it, I just figured that when I met the right person, we would get married and have two or three kids soon thereafter. I had to confront that image head-on when I was in a serious relationship after college. Amari was clear—she didn't want children. Not now, not ever. I didn't understand her decision at first—she spoke of how they would limit her career options, she would have to do most of the work, and she didn't really enjoy the company of children. Now, I'm a pretty enlightened guy, so I thought I could convince her that her number one and two concerns just really weren't issues. But my rational reasoning fell on deaf ears. So, I then considered forgoing kids for her sake. But that didn't last. We finally had to acknowledge that there really is no way to compromise on the issue, and so we ended our relationship.

Several years later I met Elyssa, several years after that we married, and voilà, today we have two fabulous kids. Nathan is now six, and Liza is five. What do I like about being a dad? I feel like I now have a greater purpose in life than just focusing on myself. I know that these two are going to make the world a better

place, and I am here to show them how to do it. Also, they are fun. I get a kick out of their silly antics. We love to work on model airplanes in the living room, eat ice cream for breakfast on Saturdays, and play on the swings at the park. They make me feel like I'm a kid again. I took Nathan canoeing last month, and I'm really looking forward to him getting a little older so we can do more things like that together. Elyssa and I also have a strong bond as parents, and I feel confident that it will never be broken.

Now that I've said all this, let me tell you that being a dad can also be a real drag. Okay, while I'm glad to focus on someone other than just myself, it would be nice to focus on me once in a while! Remember sleeping in late on Saturdays? Forget it. Liza is up every day at 6:00, and Nathan is up soon after. Elyssa usually gets up with them, but sometimes she's just so darn tired that I do it. And the house is usually a mess, with toys everywhere, dirty laundry piled up, and dishes in the sink. Speaking of which, the amount of housework that needs to be done is just ridiculous. I feel like I'm always cooking, cleaning, and soothing somebody, but to be honest, Elyssa is far more involved in it than

I am. One more thing, and this is a big one—our sex life has taken a turn for the worse. We're both so busy with work and kids that we almost have to pencil it in on the calendar—well, that's her excuse anyway. And, I never thought I'd be doing "date night"—an evening planned way in advance—there just isn't any spontaneity when you have to line up a teenage babysitter.

So, while I'm really glad I'm a dad, it is not all a party, believe me. It's hard work. But would I have it any other way? Not on your life.

—Cade, Age 34

What Do You Think?

1. Although you only read Cade's viewpoint, can you describe his family relationships? Look for clues throughout his story. What type of marriage do you think he has? Is he an involved parent? Describe the division of labor.

2. What macro-level factors affect Cade's experiences? Can you see macro-level influences with both Amari and Elyssa?

increasing (Smith, 2004). A generation ago fathers spent only about 2.5 hours a week in direct childcare, while today that figure has nearly tripled to seven hours a week (Bianchi, Robinson, & Milkie, 2006). Let's meet one of these "new" fathers, Cade, in the feature box *My Family: What I Like About Being a Dad . . .* and *What I Don't.*

The amount of time spent with children tends to decline as the child ages. Fathers with children ages two and under spend most of their time playing with children. As the child ages, fathers spend a greater portion of time on caregiving activities such as personal care or making meals; however, caregiving tasks still primarily fall to the mother.

Fathers who have more egalitarian, or equal, gender ideologies are more involved with their children—both sons and daughters—than are fathers with more traditional gender ideologies (Bulanda, 2004). Involved fathers take pride and pleasure in their participation, although they may try to justify why their participation is less than that of their wives, as these two men do (Gerson, 2001:335):

> I guess we both have to do some sacrificing; that's basically what it is to be a parent. It's probably not going to be fifty-fifty. . . . I think the mother would have a tendency to do a little more. But even sixty-forty is pretty good compared to the average.

> I wish I did more, but our time reference is quite different. I'll say, "Okay, I'll do that, but let me do this first." But she will frequently get frustrated and just not be able to stand the thought that it's not done, and then go ahead and do it.

How does involvement on the part of fathers affect their children? Father involvement can enhance children's social, emotional, and cognitive well-being (Bronte-Tinkew, Carrano, Horowitz, & Kinukawa, 2008; Sarkadi, Kristiansson, Oberklaid, & Bremberg, 2008). In a survey analysis of nearly 100 studies on parent-child relationships, father love (measured by children's perceptions of paternal acceptance/rejection and affection/indifference) was as important as mother love in predicting the social, emotional, and cognitive development and functioning of children and young adults (Rohner & Veneziano, 2001; Horn & Sylvester, 2006).

Many children do not live with their fathers because of divorce, separation, or because their parents were never married. Nearly one-half of U.S. children will experience living without a biological father for some period of their childhood. Some of these children see their fathers regularly, while others see their fathers sporadically or infrequently. Boys generally have more frequent contact with their nonresident biological father than do girls, at least with respect to overnight visits, sports, and movies (King, Harris, & Heard, 2004; Mitchell, Booth, & King, 2009). Racial and ethnic differences exist as well in specific activities—e.g., staying overnight, playing sports, going to religious services, talking about dating—however, no one racial or ethnic group stands out as being significantly higher or lower on father involvement (King, Harris, & Heard, 2004).

Thus far we have discussed the identities and activities of parents, but what about those of children? They are not passive recipients of their parents' behaviors as they, too, shape parent-child relationships. Socialization, mothering, and fathering occur in *interaction* with children. Children are not only influenced by their parents, but also influence them.

Think about your own father. To what degree was he involved in your life? What changes or similarities would you like to make in fatherhood for your own children, if you have them?

:: How Do Children Influence Their Parents?

From infancy to adulthood, children are actively engaged with their parents and help to influence their own family experience and the behaviors and attitudes of their parents (Warner, 2006). Parents do not simply socialize children. Children also influence this socialization through their own temperament, cognitive abilities, health and well-being, and sex. Systems theory, introduced in Chapter 1, is useful here because it reminds us that families are not just one unit, but are made up of many different subsystems (Broderick & Smith, 1979). Each of these subsystems operates to influence the whole. Parents influence children, and children influence their parents in the following ways:

- *Temperament*. "Oh, he's an easy baby," we hear a new parent say. "She was such a difficult child," we hear another parent report. What do they mean by their children being "easy" or "difficult"? All people have a certain behavioral style known as temperament (Gartstein & Rothbart, 2009; Rothbart & Sheese, 2007). Behavioral

Children's temperament, cognitive stages and intellectual abilities, health, and sex all work together to shape the parenting experience. This intelligent young man, Sameer Mishra, 13, is embraced by his father, while his sister watches, after winning the Scripps National Spelling Bee in Washington, DC. Mishra correctly spelled "guerdon," a word that means something one has earned or gained, to win the competition.

differences are present from birth, and they influence how babies and, later, children behave toward others and how they are affected by their environment. Temperament assessments often look at nine characteristics: activity level, regularity, adaptability, approach to novelty, emotional intensity, quality of mood, sensory sensitivity, distractibility, and persistence (Temperament.com, 2009; Thomas & Chess, 1957). A child who is often fussy; cries a lot; is highly sensitive to light, sounds, or scratchy clothing; does not respond well to change; and is very active is more difficult to parent than is the child who is usually in a good mood and smiles a lot; does not often cry; sleeps on a fairly regular schedule; and adapts well to transitions. Therefore, the "easy" child may give and receive lots of attention and affection, but the "difficult" child may receive less nurturance and affection, especially if the fit between child and parent temperament is poor (Bornstein, 2002). Temperament affects the views that parents have of the child and the views they have of themselves as parents.

- *Cognitive abilities.* Earlier, you were introduced to Piaget's work on the different stages of cognitive development. A child's stage of development has an important impact on how the parents socialize and interact with that child. For example, an infant or toddler in the sensorimotor stage understands the world primarily through touch, sucking, listening, and looking. A parent would not assume that their infant or toddler had capacities for abstract thought or could conceptualize more complex issues or rules for problem solving. Children go through these stages at approximately the same age.

However, other cognitive abilities, such as Intelligence Quotient (IQ) are far more variable, and also greatly influence how parents interact with and socialize their children (Kaufman, 2009). There are many arguments that IQ tests are culturally biased or ignore creativity or practical intelligence (Kaufman, 2009; Murdoch, 2007). Most researchers are aware that biases in test questions are possible and have made serious attempts to overcome them. They also are quick to acknowledge that IQ tests measure only one part of intelligence—cognitive abilities—and should not be interpreted to reflect global intelligence (Fletcher-Janzen, 2009). Nonetheless, if an IQ of 100 is average, what do we make of a child who scores 135 and is in the 99th percentile? This means that if 100 children were in the room, he or she would have scored higher on cognitive abilities than the other children. This child is as far from average as is the child who scored a 65—someone who is in the range of mental retardation or otherwise has such low cognitive abilities that they are in the first percentile, the lowest score in the room. The cognitive skills that children bring to a family can have a tremendous impact on the ways that parents and children interact, including the types of conversations they have, the games they can play, the chores children are given to do, the type of discipline used, and overall expectations for the child and his or her place within the family and society.

- *Health and well-being.* Today, pregnancy, childbirth, and infancy are relatively safe, with only six babies out of 1,000 live births failing to survive the first year of life in the United States (Central Intelligence Agency, November 2009). Immunizations and access to health care have improved children's chances of staying healthy and surviving to adulthood. Nonetheless, not all children are healthy. Asthma, chronic ear infections, lead

Diversity in Families

Sarah and Jake: Living Disability

I met Sarah several years ago when I was interviewing families for a research project about the health of low-income families, and whether they were able to get the health insurance and health care they need. I will always remember her. Before undertaking the "business" of the interview, it was clearly important to Sarah that I meet her son Jake. She carefully and lovingly presented Jake, an 8-year-old, who was lying on a blanket on the floor of her cramped living room, wearing nothing but a diaper. His skin was pale, as though he had never been exposed to sunlight. Although he is the size of a typical third grader, in all other respects, Jake is like an infant. He has severe cerebral palsy and developmental disabilities, which may have been caused by complications during Sarah's pregnancy and his birth. He was not breathing at birth, but was successfully revived; nonetheless, he suffered brain damage because of oxygen deprivation.

Sarah described for me what their lives have been like since Jake's birth:

He's eight years old and he doesn't talk. He makes sounds, more or less to indicate what he needs. He's in a wheelchair because he doesn't walk. So it's basically like having a three-month-old child that cries whenever it needs anything, and as a mom you do the same thing that any mother would. You go down a checklist: you've just eaten; you've just had your diaper changed, so it's a matter of a guessing game of what he needs or wants. His favorite sound is "uh" which sometimes means he wants a drink of water. But "uh" also means he can't reach his toy, or "uh" means you're watching TV and not feeding me.

My child is eight years old and the plain fact is, he's eight years old and he can't do anything for himself except play with his toys and his newspaper. If I set him

here on the floor he stays in this vicinity—he falls over on his side, he rolls on his tummy, he turns himself around a little, but he's subject to this part of the house because that's where I put him. Other than crying, I could leave him here all day long if I so desired and that would just have to work because there is nothing he could do about it. Not that I would, and let me tell you, that boy's got a great set of lungs.

Sarah went on to tell me of the difficulties raising Jake. She can take nothing for granted:

You can't have somebody come over and babysit at your house for five dollars. You're not talking about a kid who can say, "I'm tired, I want to go to bed," or "Can we watch a movie?" or "I'm hungry now." My fear of having any other sort of daycare take care of him is because of the fact that he doesn't complain about things. Does that mean he's going to sit in the corner for an hour and a half? There's no way of knowing, and in this day and age, God knows, he can't tell me if someone is doing anything unmentionable to him. I just pray to God every time he leaves the house that the person I'm sending him to school with is dependable and not some weirdo.

—Kim Hoffman and Karen Seccombe

What Do You Think?

1. In what ways do you think Jake's disability has affected Sarah's role as a mother?
2. How is Sarah's mothering—both the identity and the activity—similar to and different from other mothers who do not have a child with a disability?

paint poisoning, attention deficit disorder, diabetes, and disabilities are just some of the many ailments that millions of children suffer. Not surprisingly, parents of children with chronic conditions or disabilities must prepare their children for a unique set of challenges. For example, six million children alone have asthma, and there is no known cure (National Heart, Lung, and Blood Institute, September 2008). Parents must actively monitor their children, teach them about the factors that trigger their asthma, and develop a treatment plan for them, such as how to properly use an inhaler.

Parents face many stressors. The feature box *Diversity in Families: Sara and Jake: Living Disability* reveals the struggles that families of severely disabled children face every single day, including finding adequate childcare (Lee, Chen, Wang, & Chen, 2007), organizing critical social and health services (Seccombe & Hoffman, 2007), coping with the stigma attached to the condition, and managing the guilt that parents often feel when they see their child suffer.

• *Sex.* As you may recall, sex refers to biological categories—being female or male. But how does a child's sex affect parenting? First, parents react differently to sons and daughters. For example, parents are more verbal with daughters and more physical with sons, even when children are infants (Nokoff & Fausto-Sterling, 2008; Sax, 2005). Second, the amount of time that parents spend with sons and daughters, especially the father's time, differs (Lundberg, McLanahan, & Rose, 2007; Mammen, 2009). Fathers spend more time with sons than they do with daughters. And fathers who have all sons spend more time with them than do those fathers who have all daughters. In fact, fathers of boys are willing to reduce their own leisure time so that they will have additional time to devote to their sons. Finally, a child's sex also influences the parents' relationship with one another, increasing the quality and stability of their marriage. Parents report more satisfaction with their relationship after the birth of a son and are more likely to marry, if they haven't done so already (Raley & Bianchi, 2006). Likewise, married couples are less likely to divorce if they have sons than if they have daughters (Dahl & Moretti, 2008). These research findings reveal that a child's sex influences the parent-child relationship in many ways.

Changing family demographics have created new social contexts for raising children, including with teen parents, single parents, gay and lesbian parents, and even with grandparents. The next section reveals unique challenges and strengths of a number of different contexts.

> *I f you have siblings, think about the ways that each of them influenced your parents, their interactions with your parents, and the socialization process. Was their temperament, cognitive abilities, health, or sex a factor at all? Compare and contrast your siblings' experiences to your relationship with your parents. Are there any differences?*

:: Parenting and Family Contexts

The traditional family has given way to a variety of different family arrangements. Growing numbers of singles, gays and lesbians, grandparents, stepparents, cohabiting couples, and extended families have altered the social context of parenting and have fueled new legal debates over parental rights and responsibilities (Bianchi, Robinson, & Milkie, 2006). We will explore several of these contexts below.

Teen Parents

As you learned in Chapter 5, more than 400,000 teens may have babies this year, about 42 out of 1,000 young women in this age group (Hamilton, Martin, & Ventura, 2010). After years of decline, the number of teens giving birth is fluctuating, first rising and now declining again. Hispanics have shown the greatest recent decline, whereas Whites have shown the least decline, as found in Table 9.2. The trend is being carefully watched by public health and family professionals because of the deleterious social, physical, and financial costs associated with early childbearing (Advocates for Youth, 2009; The Annie E. Casey Foundation, 2009).

What can be done to help reduce the number of teen pregnancies? In its annual report *Kids Count*, The Annie E. Casey Foundation makes the following recommendations The Annie E. Casey Foundation. 2009. KIDS COUNT Indicator Brief: Reducing the Teen Birth Rate. Baltimore, MD: The Annie E. Casey Foundation, July:

• *Reinvigorate prevention efforts, intensifying the focus on underlying causes.* Most prevention efforts focus on

Table 9.2	Birth Rates per 1,000 Women Ages 15–19 Years: 2007–2008	

Teenage birth rates are in a state of flux. After a long period of decline they rose slightly in the mid-2000s, but have since declined again, and Hispanics now have the highest rate.

	2007	2008
All races and origins	43	42
Non-Hispanic White	27	27
Non-Hispanic Black	64	63
American Indian or Alaska Native	59	58
Asian or Pacific Islander	17	16
Hispanic	82	77

Source: Hamilton, Martin, & Ventura, April 2010.

young people's decision-making and behavior, but ignore broader macro-level social and environmental factors. Yet, the rates of teen pregnancy and childbearing are affected by race and ethnicity, family income, single parenthood, unemployment, neighborhood effects, and exposure to media (Advocates for Youth, 2009). Prevention efforts should be research-based, carefully targeted to those teens at greatest risk, and should consider protective factors such as social support networks as well as risk factors.

- *Help parents succeed in their role as sex educators.* Teen boys and girls who have strong emotional attachments to their parents and are closely supervised by them are much less likely to become sexually active and to use contraceptives when they do (The Annie E. Casey Foundation, 2009). Prevention efforts should build and sustain on-going parental involvement in all pregnancy prevention programs, and parents should be given the tools to effectively and confidently talk to their children.

- *Broaden the scope of pregnancy prevention efforts.* When prevention efforts are too narrowly focused, they miss critical opportunities to reach teens. For example, programs and policies aimed at preventing teen pregnancy should focus on both males and females because young men are also at risk for poor outcomes when they create unwanted pregnancies. Programs that focus on a wide spectrum of risk-taking behaviors, not just sex, are important because teens who drink or use drugs are more likely to have sex, to begin having sex at a younger age, and to forgo using contraceptives (Johnston, O'Malley, Bachman, & Schulenberg, 2009).

About 400,000 U.S. teens give birth each year. In our culture this is considered problematic because teens have not finished their education, have few job skills, and are not socially and emotionally well-equipped to be parents.

- *Provide accurate, clear, consistent, and ongoing information about how to reduce risk-taking behavior.* There is a large and growing body of research on effective sex education; the best programs focus less on reproductive biology and more on teaching adolescents correct information about pregnancy and prevention and giving them the skills they need to handle relationships, resist peer pressure, negotiate difficult situations, and make good decisions. Teens are eager for this information and want their parents to be involved (National Campaign to Prevent Teen and Unplanned Pregnancy, 2009).

- *Create a community-wide plan for teen pregnancy prevention, including adolescent reproductive health services.* Although most Americans want teens to refrain from having sex, most say that sexually active teenagers should have access to contraception (The Annie E. Casey Foundation, 2009). Reproductive health services should be located at sites that are accessible to teens and be low-cost or free. But community-wide plans should also address factors such as sex abuse and coercive sex, which play a greater role in teen pregnancy than has been commonly recognized (Logan, Holcombe, Ryan, Manlove, & Moore, 2007).

- *Give young people a credible vision of a positive future.* Young people should be given opportunities to imagine a broad range of experiences and options that are open to them if they delay childbearing and parenting. This may involve developing teen programs that show clear connections and pathways to college or jobs that give them hope and a reason to stay in school. It may also involve developing mentoring programs for at-risk youth that provide a rich combination of education, support services, service learning, employment opportunities, and a caring adult willing to listen and help.

An extensive plan such as this one outlined by The Annie E. Casey Foundation could get our society back on the track we were on in the 1990s and early 2000s when teen pregnancy declined significantly among all racial and ethnic groups.

❋ Explore the **Concept**
Social Explorer Map: The Increase of Single Women with Children on **myfamilylab.com**

Single Parents

Single-parent families are often seen as problematic and have even been referred to in the past as "broken homes." Today many people take exception to this negative term.

❋ Explore on **myfamilylab.com**

The vast majority of single-parent families are single-mother families, and the terms are often used interchangeably—if you say "single parent" people typically think of "single mother." These kinds of families have been maligned for causing juvenile delinquency, poverty, and a host of other social problems. The difficulty with such a generalization is that (1) there are different kinds of single-parent families with different kinds of circumstances (e.g., a teenage mother vs. a 40-year-old female executive); (2) there are different paths to becoming a single parent with varying consequences (e.g., never marrying, divorce, and widowhood); (3) the cause-and-effect relationship is unclear (e.g., does poverty cause single parenthood, or does single parenthood cause poverty?); and (4) single parenthood is less problematic in other industrialized nations because they have many social supports that are notably lacking in the United States (e.g., a higher minimum wage, nationalized health care, and childcare assistance).

Nonetheless, the number of single parents has risen in recent generations, as shown in Figure 9.2. In 1950, only 6 percent of households with children were maintained by a mother; now it is 23 percent. Only 1 percent of households in 1950 were maintained by single fathers, but that number has now jumped to 5 percent (Kreider & Elliott, 2009). Yet, the total number of single-mother and single-father families has been relatively stable over the past 15 years.

As Figure 9.3 reveals, Black children are far more likely to live with a single parent than are other racial or ethnic groups, regardless of the child's age. Thirty-five percent of Black children under the age of three live with a single parent, as do 45 percent of Black children ages 6–11. Asian American children are least likely to live with just one parent, with Hispanics and Whites somewhere in between.

The route to single parenthood can take many different paths. Some women have babies outside of marriage; other people become single parents because of a divorce; still others may be widowed. We can make some generalizations about single parents—they are more likely to be impoverished and on food stamps, they are less likely to own a home, and they have lower levels of education (DeNavas-Walt,

Figure 9.2 — Family Households with Children Under 18 by Type: 1950 and 2007 (Percent)

The number of single-parent households—both single mother and single father—has increased significantly since 1950.

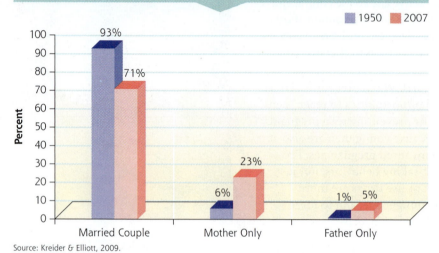

Source: Kreider & Elliott, 2009.

Figure 9.3 — Children Living with Sole Parent by Race and Hispanic Origin (Percent)

Black children are more likely to live with a single parent than are other racial or ethnic groups, regardless of the child's age. Asian American children are least likely to live with just one parent, with Hispanics and Whites somewhere in between.

Source: Kreider & Elliott, 2009.

Proctor, & Smith, 2010; Kreider & Elliott, 2009). Yet, we should be cautious with these generalizations because the different routes to single parenthood produce different results.

For example, 15 percent of single mothers have a bachelor's degree or higher. Much of the scrutiny and concern surrounding single-parent families is targeted towards *young* women having babies outside of marriage. But the rise in single-parent families is largely due to the rise in *older* unmarried women who are having babies, often by design. In 1970, only 8 percent of single mothers were age 30 or older when they gave birth. In fact, 50 percent were under age 20. Today, only 23 percent are teens and 17 percent are at least 30 years old (Ventura, 2009). Unmarried women in their thirties or forties offer a substantially different portrait of single parenthood than that of teens. A woman in her thirties or forties is likely to have completed her education and have a job, perhaps even a well-paying career.

Another important distinction is that, in some cases, what might first be viewed as a "single-parent" household is not really a single household at all. The single parent may be cohabiting with another adult (Kreider & Elliott, 2009). As cohabitation has increased, almost half of nonmarital births are to mothers living with their child's father (Osborne, 2005). The parents' partner in these families plays varying roles. Some have close, parent-like relationships with the children, while others are more distant.

However, some people remain concerned that so many children are being raised without a father present in the home, especially in light of the poor economic circumstances of single mothers overall (The National Marriage Project, 2009). Despite these concerns, not all the news about single-parent families is depressing. For example, one study based on a representative sample in the United States found that children from single-parent families report that they talk to their mothers more often than do children in two-parent families (McLanahan & Sandefur, 1994; Arditti & Madden-Derdich, 1997). After a divorce, mothers and their children often report greater equality, intimacy, and companionship (Arditti & Madden-Derdich, 1997). However, difficulties can arise because single parents are generally challenged by the lack of time as they juggle multiple roles and the absence of a "back-up" parent.

Children today grow up in many different types of families, and each type has its own strengths and challenges. Here, pop star Madonna sits with her adopted daughter, Mercy James, at the site of her Raising Malawi Girls Academy. How do macro-level social conditions contribute to our many different family forms?

Lesbian and Gay Parents

Lesbians and gay men are still fighting for a basic human right: to be recognized and accepted as families. Because they cannot yet marry in most states, the relationships of lesbians and gay men are often trivialized. The small amount of research on same-sex families tends to focus on lesbian families rather than families formed by gay males, enforcing the stereotype that gay men are not interested in committed relationships with partners and nurturing relationships with children (Biblarz & Stacey, 2010). However, these stereotypes are untrue (Kurdek, 2008; Spock, 2004). As you learned in Chapter 3, many gays and lesbians are partnered, and about 1 in 3 lesbian couples and 1 in 5 gay couples are raising children (Pawelski, Perrin, & Allen, 2006).

For the most part, same-sex parents have a great deal in common with heterosexual parents (Patterson & Hastings, 2007), as Karen and Betsy reveal in the opening vignette. Concerns that children growing up in gay or lesbian families will have difficulties with their own sexual identity, have difficulty in social relationships, or suffer psychologically have been largely unfounded. Instead, research studies find little or no significant difference in psychological well-being, performance in school, substance abuse, delinquency, or early sexual experiences (American Psychological Association, 2004; Biblarz & Stacey, 2010). Children growing up with same-sex parents are more likely to have had a homosexual experience or to envision that they could have one in the future, but as adults, they are no more likely than others to adopt a gay, lesbian, or bisexual identity.

There are many pathways for lesbians and gay men to become parents, including adoption and artificial insemination with a known or unknown sperm donor. However, most lesbian and gay families are formed as stepfamilies, in which the children were conceived in an earlier heterosexual relationship by one of the partners (Allen, 1997). Although most aspects of raising children are similar regardless of parents' sexual orientation (e.g., the daily tasks of getting children to school on time, taking children to soccer practice, or getting involved in the PTA), several specific features can affect the dynamics of lesbians and gays raising children (Spock, 2004; Stacey & Biblarz, 2001):

- *Because lesbians and gay men are stigmatized for having children, the decision to parent is generally a deliberate choice that reflects a strong commitment to raising children.* Studies tend to show either no difference among homosexuals and hetero sexuals in their fitness to parent, or that lesbian mothers and gay fathers may have an edge. For example, lesbian mothers exhibit more parenting skills and awareness of child development than heterosexual couples, and there is greater similarity between partners' parenting skills. Likewise, compared to heterosexual fathers, gay fathers go to greater lengths to promote their children's cognitive skills, are more responsive to their children's needs, and are more involved in activities with children. Lesbian and gay couples also tend to have a more egalitarian division of household labor than do heterosexual couples, and this is reflected in their joint division of childcare.

- *Lesbian and gay families are more likely to be affected by loss.* Lacking institutional constraints and support such as legalized marriage, lesbian and gay relationships are somewhat more likely to dissolve than are heterosexual ones. Yet because lesbians and gay men cannot legally marry in most states, their trauma may not be publicly recognized or as easily supported. Our society acknowledges the tremendous disruption caused by a divorce; however, a "breakup" may be trivialized. Lesbian and gay families may experience other losses as well. Lesbian and gay stepfamilies are created following a divorce (as are heterosexual stepfamilies), and children experience a loss of family members. Likewise, the HIV and AIDS epidemic has touched many lives, especially those in the gay male community. The Centers for Disease Control and Prevention estimate that over a million U.S. residents are living with HIV infection, one-quarter of whom are unaware of it (Centers for Disease Control and Prevention, October 19, 2009).

- *Lesbian and gay families must cope with homophobia and discrimination.* Homosexuality is stigmatized, and living openly as a family leaves them vulnerable to ridicule or discrimination. Although you have learned that attitudes are becoming more tolerant, many people still condemn homosexual relationships as unnatural or immoral. Violence against gays and lesbians is a possibility (Shepard, 2009). Just as racial and ethnic minorities must teach their children about racism, gay and lesbian parents must teach their children that some people have disparaging feelings toward them as well.

- *Lesbians and gay men often have a close network of friends whom they regard as an extended family who provide emotional and social support.* Social support is crucial from family and friends as a way to ward off oppression and to create a safe and supportive environment for lesbians, gay men, and their children (Oswald & Culton, 2003). They often have developed a close network of people who form a sort of extended family, or fictive kin, as introduced in Chapter 1. They are there to celebrate birthdays; participate in commitment ceremonies; babysit when needed; and in countless ways offer the love and support that are needed to keep a household and a family running smoothly. In fact, fictive kin are often more reliable and consistent in their support than biological families (Demo & Allen, 1996). Parents and families respond in a variety of ways, and organizations such as Parents, Families, and Friends of Lesbians and Gays (PFLAG) provide education, advocacy, and support to those in need.

Do you see any of these features in Karen and Betsy's family, from the opening vignette?

Grandparents Raising Grandchildren

Some children live with their grandparents. The U.S. Census Bureau estimated that in 2007 about 7 million children lived with their grandparents in their grandparents' own home (Kreider & Elliott, 2009). Sometimes the child's parent(s) also lives with the grandparent. But the greatest growth has occurred among children living with grandparents on their own without a parent present. About 3 million children are now under the care of grandparents.

Where are these children's parents? Mothers and fathers may be absent for many reasons, including incarceration, drug or alcohol problems, physical or mental illnesses, employment difficulties, child abuse or neglect, desertion, or even death. When parents are unable or unwilling to care for their children, grandparents often step in. Most arrangements are done privately, but in about one in six cases, child welfare agencies have intervened on behalf of the child. One study of 129 grandparents raising their grandchildren examined the situations that led to grandparents taking over their grandchildren's care and found multiple problems (Sands & Goldberg-Glen, 2000). The most commonly reported problem was substance abuse, but the parent's inability to care for the child, neglect, and psychological and financial problems were also cited as factors. Many of these problems are long-term issues for families. When the grandparents first began to care for their grandchildren, only one-third expected to be the caregiver until the grandchild grew up. But at the time of the study's interview, over three-quarters of grandparents had come to believe that they would be the caregivers.

Shane and Ricky came to live with me when they were four and five years old. Geez, what did I know about babies? It's been years since I had mine. But that mother of theirs was just awful to them. I think she even burned them with her cigarettes. And my son, Chris, well, he's so messed up with drugs. He's never even around. He just lives for meth. So, what could I do? I really have no choice. I love my grandsons and want to give them a better life.

—Barbara, Age 61

Grandparents raising grandchildren exhibit a unique set of challenges and strengths. Children separated from their parents experience trauma, but living with a grandparent, rather than a nonrelative or living in an institution, can minimize that trauma by providing a sense of continuity and family support (Dubowitz, Howard, Felgelman, Harrington, Starr, Zuravin, & Sawyer, 1994). Furthermore, many grandparents find meaning and satisfaction in caring for their grandchildren and want to provide the love and stability that is absent from the child's life.

Nonetheless, many of these families experience considerable strain and challenges (Goyer, 2006; Simmons & Dye, 2003; USA.gov, February 25, 2010; U.S. Census Bureau American Community Survey, August 2008). Some of these are revealed in Table 9.3 (p. 266). First, grandparents talk of physical exhaustion trying to keep up with their grandchildren. Forty-three percent of grandparents who take care of their grandchildren are 55 years or older, and 15 percent are 65 or older. Over half are single grandparents, yet many are caring for young children who require considerable energy. Second, the grandparents often have physical or mental health problems, which could make caring for a child difficult. Third, many of these families are poor, have difficulty paying housing bills, and suffer from food insecurity, defined as reducing the quality, variety, and desirability of a diet (USDA Economic Research Service, November 16, 2009).

think about your own grandparents. Would you have lived with them if your parents were unable to care for you? What would your life be like if you had lived with them? How would it have been different or similar?

Table 9.3	Demographics and Hardships for Children Living with Grandparents (n = 771)	
Can you identify the hardships that many grandparents and grandchildren face?		
Caregiver		
Under 45 years		12%
45 to 54 years		44%
55 to 64 years		28%
65+ years		15%
Married		48%
In fair or poor health or has a limiting condition		54%
Symptoms suggesting poor mental health		32%
Poor		37%
Low-income (200% of poverty line)		66%
For Low-Income Families		
Crowding or difficulty paying housing bills		31%
Food insecurity		48%
Receiving food stamps		43%
Child		
≤5 years		29%
6 to 11 years		41%
12 to 17 years		30%
High levels of behavioral or emotional problems (ages 6–17)		9%
In fair or poor health or has a limiting condition		19%
Low levels of school engagement (ages 6–17)		26%

Source: Demographics and Hardships for Children Living With Grandparents from Urban Institute Calculations. 1999 National Survey of America's Families. Urban Institute.

About 3 million children live solely with their grandparents—their own parents are not in the home. Parents are absent for many reasons, often because of neglect, abuse, incarceration, or drug addiction.

Despite these challenges, a growing number of grandparents continue to assume the responsibilities of caring for their grandchildren. As Barbara said, "I really have no choice. . . ." Out of love and out of duty, grandparents step in when parents fall short of their own responsibilities.

Parents usually see themselves as having the most important role in their child's socialization. However, our look at parenting reveals that the parent-child relationship does not exist in a vacuum. This chapter has shown you that many micro-level and macro-level factors shape parent-child relationships, and these are summarized in the feature box *Tying It All Together: Factors That Shape Parent-Child Interaction.*

Tying It All Together

Factors That Shape Parent-Child Interaction

Parenting takes place in a particular social context, and this affects the ways that parents socialize and interact with their children. Let's look at the macro-level influences and micro-level influences on this endearing intimate relationship.

Macro-level Factors

- Cross-cultural traditions
- Level of technology
- Economic considerations
- Social class, race and ethnicity, and sex
- Level and types of discrimination
- Types of programs and policies aimed at helping vulnerable families

Micro-level Factors

- Parenting style
- Personal characteristics of child
- Personal characteristics of parent

What Do You Think?

1. What theories introduced in Chapter 1 do you see as particularly useful for explaining parent-child interaction?
2. Do you think these micro- and macro-level factors differ for mothers and for fathers, given their different parenting identities and activities?

Bringing It Full Circle

This chapter has shown us the social context of raising children. Most parents are so busy with day-to-day activities that they rarely notice the way that social and cultural forces shape how we care for, nurture, and socialize our children. You have learned that parents are only one agent of socialization, although an important one. Schools, peers, and the media also shape who and what we are. All of these socialization influences, including parents, are shaped by macro-level social factors.

Let's review what we have learned as we reflect upon Karen and Betsy in the opening vignette, and apply this information to our own lives.

- How is parenting in same-sex families similar to, and different from, parenting in heterosexual two-parent families?
- Do agents of socialization operate differently for Karen and Betsy's children compared to children in other parenting contexts?
- Should they talk to their children about the prejudice and discrimination leveled at same-sex families? How is this different or similar to racial/ethnic socialization?
- If you decide to have children, what is likely to be your parenting context? What do you think will happen if that context suddenly changes? How will you and your children cope?

For further review, turn to the Video Discussion Guide on page 449 to answer additional questions about how the chapter opening video relates to what you have learned in this chapter.

Chapter Review

9.1 Are there differences in parenting practices cross-culturally?

Parents take care of, nurture, and socialize their children, but these interactions between parents and children take place within a broader social and cultural environment. Economic conditions, region of the country, whether it is urban or rural, cultural and religious traditions, gendered norms, job opportunities, and level of technology are just a few of the macro-level factors that set the stage for micro-level family interactions.

9.2 How has parenting changed over time?

Definitions of good parenting fluctuate greatly. For example, parents in colonial America tended to be strict, emotionally distant, and expected unqualified obedience from their children. The Industrial Revolution produced two views of childhood: the "protected child" whose family wealth offered education and leisure; and the "useful child" whose labor was needed by their poor and working-class families to make ends meet.

9.3 What are some current trends in parenting found throughout the world?

Three trends are emerging: (1) although parents are central to childrearing, there are other influences as well, including other people (e.g., babysitters, grandparents) and social institutions (e.g., schools, daycare centers); (2) parents increasingly encourage permissiveness and child independence; and (3) a higher value is placed on boys than on girls in most societies.

9.4 What are some well-known theories of human development and socialization?

Sigmund Freud believed that human behavior and personality originate from unconscious forces within individuals. Jean Piaget was interested in how children come to understand the world and make meaning of their experiences, and identified four stages of cognitive development. Charles Horton Cooley and George Herbert Mead believed that a person cannot form a self-concept without social contact and social experience with others—they learn to see themselves as others see them. Alfred Bandura claimed that children not only learn by reinforcement, but that children also learn by watching and imitating others.

9.5 Who socializes our children?

There are many "agents" of socialization, including parents, peers, toys, schools, and the media.

9.6 How does socialization differ by social class, race and ethnicity, and gender?

Social class affects not only how much money parents have to spend, but it also shapes values, norms, and expectations that parents have for their children. For example, working-class children are more likely socialized to be obedient and to conform. Racial and ethnic groups may have different cultural traditions, language, or food. One important difference between the socialization practices of White and minority parents is that the latter must teach their children about the importance of race, ethnicity, prejudice, and discrimination. Parents are very influential in teaching children about how masculinity and femininity are defined, and what appropriate roles are for girls and boys.

9.7 What are three different parenting styles?

An authoritative parenting style is one in which parents are demanding and maintain high levels of control over their children, but they are also warm and receptive. Parents who have a permissive parenting style may be very nurturing, caring, and responsive to their children; however, they put few controls or demands on the children. Parents who practice an authoritarian parenting style tend to be strict, punitive, less communicative, and offer less warmth and support to their children.

9.8 What does it mean to be a "mother," and how does that role differ from a "father"?

"Mother" and "father" are roles involving both an identity and specific actions. Mothers report experiencing greater meaning in their lives compared to childfree women, but also

Key Terms

authoritarian parenting style (p. 252)

authoritative parenting style (p. 252)

concrete operational thought (p. 246)

ego (p. 245)

family allowance (or child allowance) (p. 242)

formal operational thought (p. 246)

id (p. 245)

looking-glass self (p. 246)

permissive parenting style (p. 252)

preoperational thought (p. 246)

racial (or ethnic) socialization (p. 250)

role taking (p. 246)

sensorimotor stage (p. 245)

social learning theory (p. 246)

socialization (p. 245)

superego (p. 245)

report more distress and depression. Compared to fathers, mothers typically do more emotional labor and childcare.

9.9 How do children influence their parents?

Parent-child interaction is a two-way street, and children can influence their parents through their own temperament, cognitive abilities, health and well-being, and sex.

9.10 What can be done to reduce the number of teen pregnancies?

Prevention efforts focus on such things as reinvigorating these efforts; intensifying the focus on underlying causes of teen pregnancy; helping parents succeed in their role as sex educators; broadening the scope of pregnancy prevention efforts; providing accurate, clear, consistent, and ongoing information about how to reduce risk-taking behavior; creating community-wide plans for teen pregnancy prevention, including adolescent reproductive health services; and giving young people a credible vision of a positive future.

9.11 Why should we be careful not to overgeneralize single parents?

There are different kinds of single-parent families with different kinds of circumstances (e.g., a teenage mother vs. a 40-year-old female executive); there are different paths to becoming a single parent with varying consequences (e.g., never marrying, divorce, and widowhood); the cause-and-effect relationship is unclear (e.g., does poverty cause single parenthood, or does single parenthood cause poverty?);

and single parenthood is less problematic in other industrialized nations because of a wide array of social supports lacking in the United States.

9.12 How distinctive are gay and lesbian parents from heterosexual parents?

In most ways, there are very few differences. Research studies find no significant differences in psychological well-being, performance in school, substance abuse, delinquency, or early sexual experiences. Children growing up with gay or lesbian parents were more likely to have had a homosexual experience or to envision that they could have one in the future. But as adults, they were no more likely than others to have adopted a gay, lesbian, or bisexual identity.

9.13 What are the unique strengths and challenges of grandparents raising grandchildren?

Grandparents step in to raise their grandchildren because mothers and fathers may be absent due to incarceration, drug or alcohol abuse, physical or mental illness, employment difficulties, child abuse or neglect, desertion, or even death. Children separated from their parents experience trauma, but living with a grandparent can minimize that trauma by providing a sense of continuity and family support. Many grandparents find meaning in caring for their grandchild, but it is often not without emotional and financial cost.

PEARSON

myfamilylab®

www.myfamilylab.com

Experience, Discover, Observe, Evaluate

MyFamilyLab is designed just for you. Each chapter features a pre-test and post-test to help you learn and review key concepts and terms. Experience Marriage and Family in action with dynamic visual activities, videos, and readings to enhance your learning experience.

Here are a few activities you'll find for this chapter:

Explore **Social Explorer** is an interactive application that allows you to explore Census data through interactive maps. Explore the Social Explorer Map:

• The Increase of Single Women with Children.

Watch **Core Concepts** video clips feature sociologists in action, exploring important concepts in the study of Marriage and Family. Watch:

• Gender Socialization

Read **MySocLibrary** includes primary source readings from classic and contemporary sociologists. Read:

• Heath, "Parents' Socialization of Children"

10

Families and the Work They Do

CHAPTER OUTLINE

Above: Lisa and Chris, and their son, Christopher.

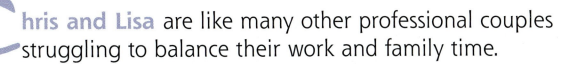

Chris and Lisa are like many other professional couples struggling to balance their work and family time.

As you read their story, ask yourself what could be done to make their lives, and the lives of millions of others, easier.

Most young adults say that they would like to marry, have children, and work at an interesting job. Is it possible to really "have it all"—an exciting career, a happy relationship, and the joy of parenthood? Ask Chris and Lisa. They are about as close to having it all as you can get, but they are also acutely aware of the stresses associated with their delicate balancing act.

Chris is the Chief Operating Officer for the Transit Authority of a large city. Lisa is a research administrator on the medical campus of a university. Both jobs are rewarding and very demanding. A forty-hour workweek easily spills over into evenings and weekends—there are always emails to answer, phone calls to make, and catching up on paperwork—often resulting in a fifty- or even sixty-hour workweek. While they are unhappy about how work encroaches on their private life, they feel there is little they can do about it. They might not be aware that the United States is among those countries with the longest workweek and the least amount of vacation. The time they do have

👁—|**Watch** the **Video** *Balancing Work and Family Life: Lisa and Chris* on **myfamilylab.com**

available is devoted to their delightful son, Christopher, who is now two years old.

Like most people, Lisa had minimal maternity leave and had to resume working five weeks after giving birth. "I was not happy about it," she said, but given that the United States has no national maternity policy, what choice did she have? She and Chris also began the overwhelming task of finding quality childcare for young Christopher. Luckily her mother lives nearby and was able to help care for Christopher. When he reached eight months of age, Lisa and Chris decided to give her mother a break and enroll Christopher in a daycare facility for a few days each week. Finding quality care, however, was not an easy task. There were few openings, many did not meet their quality standards, and those that did were surprisingly expensive. Again, unlike other countries, the United States generally does not help families with childcare costs, which are considered largely a personal responsibility.

QUESTIONS *That Matter* •

10.1 What is the history of work in early America?

10.2 How has participation in the women's labor force changed in the last century?

10.3 How have increased technology and globalization contributed to a changing occupational structure?

10.4 How has the rise in unemployment affected families?

10.5 How has the current recession contributed to unstable wages, working conditions, and a disposable workforce?

10.6 How serious a threat is losing health insurance?

10.7 What does research have to say about who is doing the housework and childcare?

10.8 What are three common explanations for the gendered division of labor?

10.9 What are three important concepts that help explain the causes of stress for adults when they combine work and family?

10.10 If balancing work and family can be stressful, why don't adults work part-time?

10.11 Who is taking care of preschool-age and school-age children while parents work?

10.12 What are the effects of childcare on child well-being?

10.13 What could the United States learn from other countries about early childhood education and childcare policies?

A lengthy search finally led to an ideal childcare situation in which little Christopher thrives. Nonetheless, the beginning was daunting, with their son screaming in fear as Lisa walked out the center's door. Wracked with "mother-guilt," Lisa wondered if she did the right thing. Is her son suffering? But, like virtually every child who has a rough beginning, he is now happy and enjoys his time at his home daycare.

Yet even after getting past this hurdle, Lisa and Chris still do not have an easy time. Both talk of wanting more time with their son, being sleep-deprived, having little time to themselves or for one another, feeling stressed, constantly rushing around, and feeling guilty. What would relieve some of these burdens? Given the dearth of policies in the United States to help working families, they look to individual solutions, such as working fewer hours, or starting their own business.

This chapter examines the work that families do inside and outside the home, and how these two domains interact and influence one another. We used to think of work as something that was done *outside* the home. Home and work were "separate spheres," and were largely segregated. Men went off to work, women stayed at home. Today we recognize that work and family are not separate domains, but are highly interrelated (Voydanoff, 2008; Whitehead, 2008). Several important issues speak to the overlap of these two concepts.

Every culture—in both developed and developing nations—has to find ways to combine work and family.

First, a majority of mothers now work outside the home, including mothers with preschool-age children. Women and men are no longer living in "separate spheres." Both are involved in work inside and outside the home, and dual-worker or dual-career families are common rather than the exception (Galinsky, Aumann, & Bond, 2009).

Second, the organization of work done inside the home has a tremendous influence on the work done outside the home. Issues such as how childcare, housework, or emotional labor is divided between partners influence stress level, which in turn can affect worker productivity, absenteeism, and retention (Parker, 2009). For example, how do parents negotiate who leaves work early to pick up a sick child from school? Who will routinely arrive at work a few minutes late to drop a child off at school?

Third, specific work policies have the ability to reduce work-family tensions and conflicts that parents experience—for example, the degree to which work policies allow for part-time or flexible work options, as well as offer health insurance, sick pay, parental leaves, and other important family-friendly fringe benefits (Hill, Yang, Hawkins, & Ferris, 2004; Whitehead, 2008). Yet, today families feel more economic pressure than ever. Work encroaches upon home life for a growing number of families as the number of single-parent households and dual-earner households continues to rise, hours on the job increase, and job benefits erode. Employment has not kept pace with the changing nature of the workforce by offering a family-friendly environment. Nonetheless, despite these problems, most adults want to have children; they are not willing to sacrifice having children for the sake of work. Children can bring great joy to adults, enriching their lives in many ways. This chapter examines key issues and challenges in the work that families do both inside and outside the home.

:: The Changing Dynamics of the Workplace

The context of work and family life has changed considerably over the course of U.S. history. Let's briefly review some of these work and family life changes.

Early America

In early colonial America, most families worked closely with the land. Their lives revolved around the seasonal work necessary for farming and ranching. The labor of men, women, and children was needed, and was considered invaluable to the success of the family enterprise. Men and women usually had different tasks, with men involved in the more physical agricultural work while women and children did the cooking, cleaning, weaving, and tending of small animals. However, at several crucial times of the year associated with planting and harvesting, the labor of all family members was needed in the fields. In other words, while sex may have been a central construct in the division of labor, the line between men and women's work often shifted.

In the 19th century, the U.S. economy was evolving from an emphasis on agriculture to an emphasis on industrialization. During this century, work was done away from home, and people were paid wages for this labor. There was considerable movement to urban areas in search of jobs, and over time, many small family farms could not support themselves and folded. An urban middle class emerged, with men going off to work outside the home, and women doing the unpaid work within. More and more goods and services were produced for profit outside the home and families purchased these with money earned from the wages they earned at jobs in factories and other places of work. An ideology emerged asserting that the man was supposed to earn the money and the woman was supposed to nurture her husband and family (Kimmel, 2006).

Women of the 19th century were consumers rather than producers of goods and services. Yet, the new industries needed expanding numbers of laborers so, in addition to recruiting men, young, poor, minority, and immigrant women and children were hired. By 1890, 17 percent of women were in the labor force. Most of these women were unmarried and were without children (Coontz, 2000). Much of the work in these factories was dangerous and dirty, as there were minimal occupational safety standards compared to today. Thus, women's roles became increasingly intertwined with class and race: poor or minority women *had* to work, whereas White middle-class women could enjoy "true" womanhood far away from the dangerous and unsafe world of work.

There have been short-term shifts in this ideology. For example, during World War II, because of a (male) labor shortage, entering into paid employment was seen as women's patriotic duty. Businesses and governments even helped create and pay for childcare so that mothers could more easily work outside the home. Once the war ended, women were fired or encouraged to quit their jobs. They were asked to return home to their role as wives and mothers and to focus on more domestic activities. The childcare facilities were closed.

During World War II, when many men were off to war, women were encouraged to take their jobs. Paid employment was seen as a woman's patriotic duty.

I'm Proud... my husband wants me to do my part

SEE YOUR U. S. EMPLOYMENT SERVICE
WAR MANPOWER COMMISSION

Trends in Child Labor

American children have often performed paid and unpaid labor, including indentured servitude. As industrialization took hold, and families moved from farms into urban areas in search of work, poor children often toiled beside their parents in dangerous factories, textile mills, canneries, and mines (Child Labor Public Education

Figure 10.1 Employment Status of Mothers by Marital Status: 1970–2007 (Percent)

Today, the majority of mothers work outside the home for pay, regardless of marital status, although there has been a slight decline in recent years.

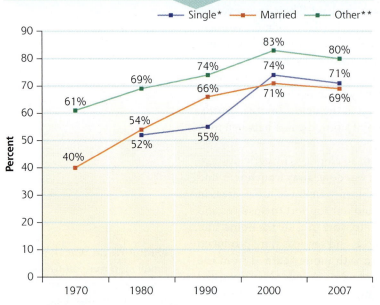

*Single data for 1970 not available.
**Widowed, divorced, or separated.

Source: U.S. Census Bureau, 2010 Statistical Abstract, December 17, 2009.

Watch the Video
Core Concepts: Women in the Workplace on
myfamilylab.com

Project, 2006). Poor families needed the labor of all members to earn enough for even minimal food, shelter, and clothing. In fact, children were often preferred as laborers because they were seen as less expensive, less likely to strike, and more docile. Thousands of children were employed in dismal working conditions doing hard labor for only a fraction of the wages paid to men or women. Opposition to child labor soon began to grow in the northern states. The first state child labor law in Massachusetts was passed in 1836 and required children under age 15 working in factories to attend school at least three months per year. In 1892, the Democratic Party platform voted to ban factory employment for children under age 15. Many factories moved South to avoid the growing protection of young workers in the North. By the early decades of the 20th century, the number of child laborers in the United States had peaked, and then began to decline as the labor and reform movements became more outspoken about the plight of many young workers. New protection laws were passed during this era, and by 1938, a minimum age of employment and maximum hours of work for children were regulated by federal law for the first time (Child Labor Public Education Project, 2006).

One important aspect of the changing dynamic of the workplace is the surge of women into the paid labor market in recent decades. We have witnessed a cultural shift in opportunities for women in work, education, and family life. Unlike in the past, many women now work because they *want* to work. And for many others, the "need" and "want" to work are virtually indistinguishable. In this next section, we will explore how macroeconomic, occupational, and cultural values have influenced the participation of women in the labor force. Watch on myfamilylab.com

Women's Labor Force Participation

You can really see how women's opportunities have changed by looking at my family. My grandmother, who never worked outside the home, is pretty adamant that mothers should not be working. She talks about that a lot, and is pretty worried about the state of families today. Meanwhile, my mom thinks it's okay for mothers to work as long as their

"My grandmother, who never worked outside the home, is pretty adamant that mothers should not be working."

children are in school. That's what she did—she waited until my brother and I were in first and third grade. Today, I feel differently. I'm planning to go to medical school, and I just assume that I'll be working when I have my children. I think women can have a fulfilling career and have children at the same time.

—Abby, Age 22

For most of the 20th century, most married women with children did not work outside the home. Even as recently as 1970, only 40 percent of married mothers worked, as shown in Figure 10.1 above (U.S. Census Bureau, 2010). However, by 1980 we began to see an important cultural shift: the majority of mothers, whether married, single, or divorced were employed outside the home. The change during this period likely reflected increasing job and educational opportunities for women, the popularity of feminist ideas of social and economic equality promoted by the women's movement, and changes in the economy. Women then worked for a variety of reasons, just as mothers do today: to put food on the table, to provide housing, to pay for vacations, or for personal fulfillment. Today, it is common for mothers to work outside the home: 69 percent of married mothers, 71 percent of single mothers, and 80 percent of divorced, separated, or widowed mothers were employed in 2007. The likelihood of mothers working has slightly decreased since the early 2000s.

Mothers with older children are more likely to work than are mothers with younger children, regardless of marital status, race, or ethnicity (Bureau of Labor Statistics, September 2009). Figure 10.2 shows the percentage of mothers who are employed, by the age of their youngest child, and their race or ethnicity. It shows that Asian American mothers are most likely to be employed, including when their children are young, and Hispanic mothers are least likely to be employed.

Yet, despite the fact that most families have a mother who is employed, *attitudes* toward working mothers are less positive than one might imagine. As depicted in Figure 10.3, a national survey based on a representative sample of adults asked, "Is the increase in working mothers with young children generally a good thing for society, a bad thing for society, or doesn't it make much difference?" Among adults, only 22 percent said that it was a good thing for society, while 41 percent said it was a bad thing. There were no real differences between men and women, but stark differences arose between the opinions of mothers who work and those who stay home, as shown in Figure 10.3. Younger adults are also more likely than older adults to view working mothers in a positive light (Taylor, Funk, & Clark, 2007; Morin & Taylor, 2008).

Next, let's take a look at both the recent changes that have occurred in the economy and with employment, and examine the consequences of these changes upon families. In particular, we will examine technological changes and global competition. How have these factors affected families?

The Changing Occupational Structure

American industries have undergone rapid restructuring in the past few decades in response to technological changes and global competition. First, the widespread use of personal computers (virtually unheard of 30 years ago), cell phones, fax machines, and pagers has changed the way we do business and how we conduct our personal lives. We regularly buy e-tickets for our flights, order groceries over the Internet, check our e-mail on our cell phones, and text our friends to see what's on the agenda for the weekend. Many companies also use these technologies to conduct business. More and more people can do their

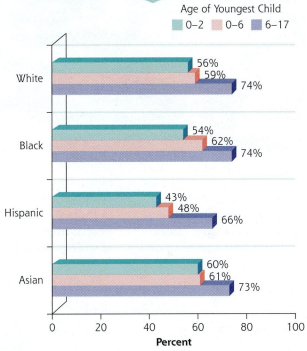

Figure 10.2 | **Mothers' Employment by Age of Youngest Child and Race/Ethnicity, 2008 (Percent)**

The majority of mothers with children 0–2 or 0–6 work outside the home, except among Hispanic groups.

Age of Youngest Child: 0–2, 0–6, 6–17

- White: 56%, 59%, 74%
- Black: 54%, 62%, 74%
- Hispanic: 43%, 48%, 66%
- Asian: 60%, 61%, 73%

Source: Bureau of Labor Statistics, September 2009.

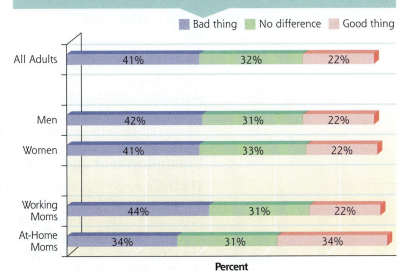

Figure 10.3 | **Is the Increase in Working Mothers with Young Children Generally a Good Thing for Society, a Bad Thing for Society, or Doesn't It Make Much Difference?**

Although the majority of adults say that working moms are either a good thing for society or do not make much difference, a sizable minority see working moms as a bad thing for society.

Bad thing | No difference | Good thing

- All Adults: 41%, 32%, 22%
- Men: 42%, 31%, 22%
- Women: 41%, 33%, 22%
- Working Moms: 44%, 31%, 22%
- At-Home Moms: 34%, 31%, 34%

Percent

Source: Is the Increase in Working Mothers with Young Children Generally a Good Thing for Society, a Bad Thing for Society, or Doesn't It Make Much Difference? Pew Research Center 2007.

The occupational structure is changing as many jobs are being outsourced to other countries because of cheaper labor costs or fewer labor or environmental protections.

*H*ow do you think your life has been affected by the changes in the labor force participation of women, new technologies, and globalization? Have these changes been good or bad for you? Are they good or bad for society? Why is it that sometimes what is good for you is at odds with what is good for society (and vice versa)?

Read the **Document**
The Time Blend: When Work Be-comes Home and Home Becomes Work on **myfamilylab.com**

living wage: Wages that are above federal or state minimum wage levels, usually ranging from 100 to 130 percent of the poverty line.

"work" from just about anywhere, including the dining room table as their children play nearby in the living room. Work now has entered our home. Likewise, our home life has entered the work arena: when we are at "work," we send a quick e-mail off to Mom. Thus, for many people the boundaries between work and family are becoming blurred. Sometimes there are benefits to this arrangement; maybe you can reduce your childcare costs if you can do some of your work at home. However, for others, the development of technology over the past few decades has increased their level of stress.

Second, many jobs are being outsourced to other countries as companies search for cheaper labor costs and fewer governmental restrictions (Galinsky, Aumann, & Bond, 2009; Whoriskey, 2009). Manufacturing, service, and sales jobs are now increasingly shipped overseas. Are you experiencing problems with your computer? When you telephone a call center for help, it is likely that a computer technician in India will answer the telephone. Consumers appreciate the 24/7 availability and we benefit from the lower cost of goods and services, but this outsourcing has contributed to widespread job loss in the United States. In particular, the number of workers in U.S. manufacturing has declined considerably over the past few decades. These "disappearing" jobs tended to pay relatively high wages because of union protections. Instead, the U.S. economy during the 1990s and early 2000s experienced an increase of jobs in the service sector, particularly in semi-skilled or unskilled positions characterized by job insecurity and low wages. The number of sales clerks, waitresses, and food service workers expanded quickly during this period.

These transformations have caused some major changes in how families conduct their work both inside and outside the home. Together with technology and globalization, many of today's working-class and middle-class families are facing a severe economic recession. Let's examine the current economic climate in the United States so that we can better understand the modern relationship between work and family. **Read** on **myfamilylab.com**

:: Life in a Recession

The recession that began in the late 2000s has caused financial hardship for many working-class and middle-class families in the U.S. The civilian labor force shrunk by well over a million workers between 2008 and 2009 alone. The proportion of workers who worked full-time, year round in 2009 was 64.8 percent, down from 68.4 percent in 2007, while the number of involuntary part-time workers (people whose work hours were reduced or who cannot find a full-time job) rose (Bureau of Labor Statistics, December 4, 2009; March 5, 2010).

Unemployment and Families

The U.S. unemployment rate averaged 9.6 percent in September of 2010, more than double the rate in late 2007 (4.7 percent), as shown in Table 10.1 (Bureau of Labor Statistics, October 22, 2010). The unemployment rates in 2009–2010 are the highest since late 1982, when unemployment skyrocketed to 10.8 percent. The unemployment rate is even higher for minority groups—Black unemployment was nearly 16 percent in 2010 (Bureau of Labor Statistics, July 2, 2010). However, the situation is really more serious: the number of persons who experienced *some* unemployment throughout the year more than tripled.

What these unemployment figures mean is that many bread-winners lost their jobs (or worry that they will) or had their income reduced, contributing to the rise in home foreclosures, personal bankruptcies, and the number of families who cannot access the health care system because they have lost their health insurance. Let's look at some of these financial problems and related issues in more depth.

What does it feel like to look for work week after week, and find no job offers? When even the lowest-tier jobs in our economy have stiff competition, many people who would like to work feel psychologically wounded by the lack of employment opportunities. Unemployment also affects personal relationships. For example, high unemployment tends to lower marriage rates—people are less likely to marry if they or their potential partner cannot find a job (Wilson, 1987, 1996; Edin & Kafalas, 2005). Other periods of high unemployment, such as the Great Depression, led to fewer children being born, as you learned in Chapter 8. The stress associated with unemployment can also endanger relationships, contribute to domestic violence, and harm children's social well-being (Aubry, Tefft, & Kingsbury, 2006). For example, a study based on 4,476 school-age children in 2,569 families across the United States found that when fathers are involuntarily unemployed, children have a greater likelihood of repeating a grade or getting suspended from school (Kalil & Ziol-Guest, 2007; Luo, 2009). We can see that these macro-level factors affect how we experience relationships. ✳ **Explore** on **myfamilylab.com**

Table 10.1	Unemployment Rates, November, Odd Years
The unemployment rate hovers around 10 percent, double what it was just a few years ago.	
1999	4.1%
2001	5.5%
2003	5.8%
2005	5.0%
2007	4.7%
2009	10.0%
September 2010	9.6%

Source: Bureau of Labor Statistics, 2009; October 22, 2010.

✳ **Explore** the **Concept**
Social Explorer Map and Report: Unemployment Rates between 1980 and 2000 on
myfamilylab.com

Unstable Wages and Working Conditions

Some families earn only the minimum wage or wages only slightly above the minimum wage. The federal minimum wage in the United States, at $7.50 per hour in 2011, does not enable even a small family to rise out of poverty. Working 40 hours per week at $7.50 an hour yields $300 a week, and $15,600 a year before taxes. And people working at minimum wage still pay taxes. So how does a person pay for rent, utilities, food, clothing, and other incidentals on a minimum wage? Because this rate is so low, 14 states have adopted state minimum wages that are higher than the federal wage. Washington and Oregon have the highest state minimum wages in the nation, at $8.55 and $8.40 an hour, respectively (Wage and Hour Division, January 1, 2010).

About 2.2 million hourly workers earned the minimum wage or even less in 2008. Half of these persons were age 25 or older. These low-wage workers are distributed evenly across racial and ethnic groups (except for Asians, who are more likely to have higher wages). Women are more likely to earn minimum wage (or less) than are men, and it is likely that many of these women are supporting children as well as themselves (Bureau of Labor Statistics, March 11, 2009). Recognizing that the minimum wage is too low to support a family, the concept of paying a **living wage** is taking hold. A living wage ordinance requires employers to pay wages that are above federal or state minimum wage levels, usually ranging from 100 to 130 percent above the poverty line. Only a specific set of workers are covered by living wage ordinances, usually those employed by businesses that have a contract with a city or county government or those who receive economic development subsidies from the locality. The rationale behind

Over two million people in the U.S. earn only minimum wage for their labor, not enough to support even a small family.

the ordinances is that city and county governments should not contract with or subsidize employers who pay poverty-level wages. Boston, Baltimore, Denver, Los Angeles, and Portland, Oregon are among nearly 100 cities around the country that make particular companies pay their employees wages that reflect the cost of living in the area, usually $3.00–$6.00 above minimum wage.

Part-Time, Nonstandard, and Temporary Work   In addition to pay, another concern is that many new jobs associated with economic restructuring are part-time, sub-contracted, temporary in nature, or have only evening hours. Some offer irregular work schedules. Employees working in these types of jobs, referred to as **nonstandard work schedules**, represent the fastest-growing category of workers in the United States (Gornick, Presser, & Ratzdorf, 2009; Presser, Gornick, & Parashar, 2008; Presser 2003). Since 1982, temporary employment has increased several hundred percent. In other words, millions of women and men begin the workday not knowing if, and for how long, their jobs are likely to continue. There is also a growing trend towards jobs that require weekend, evening, or variable nonfixed schedules, particularly those found in the lower-paying service sector.

Some part-time and contingency workers prefer this arrangement, especially highly paid professionals who value their freedom and independence on the job, or mothers with young children who would prefer to work only sporadically. But most American families prefer the assurance of a steady job with prearranged hours, and an established pay scale with fringe benefits. Families with nonstandard work schedules may find it difficult to organize childcare, as most childcare centers are only open between 7 A.M. and 6 P.M. Furthermore, childcare centers usually require a regular paid commitment to a particular schedule, such as a Monday through Friday schedule, or a Monday, Wednesday, Friday schedule. When a parent works full-time one week, three days the next week, and four half-days the next, it wreaks havoc upon childcare arrangements, school schedules, and many other dimensions of family life. It also affects the degree to which family, friends, and neighbors are able to provide childcare. This, in turn, creates tremendous stress for families (Davis, Goodman, Pirretti, & Almeida, 2008; Perry-Jenkins, Goldberg, Pierce, & Sayer, 2007).

Most women do not work these schedules out of personal inclination, but because these are the required working conditions of their jobs as cashiers, maids, nursing aides, cooks, or waitresses. Moreover, these occupations are likely to grow in the future.

Rhonda is one of many people who are looking for a good job with good pay (Seccombe, 2011). She has a high school diploma, but does not have a college degree. She is a single mother, and would like to raise her young son Bobby without relying upon government assistance. Rhonda wants a permanent full-time job, but she has been stymied by the tremendous growth in part-time, temporary positions, she explains (Seccombe, 2011: 177):

Hopefully I can get me a job. A permanent job. My sister's trying to get me a job where she works. I put my application in last week. And it would be a permanent job. When you go through those agencies, it's just temporary work. It's just whenever they need you, and it's unfair too. Every job I've found is through this temporary agency, like Manpower, but it's only temporary. And they cut my check and my food stamps, and when my job ends, it's like you're stuck again. So I'm trying to find a permanent steady job. But it's hard around here. I've been out looking for work, and hoping that something comes through.

nonstandard work schedules:
Job schedules that are part-time, sub-contracted, temporary in nature, occur at night, or offer irregular work schedules.

Rhonda may be surprised to learn that temporary agencies are doing very well in this recession economy. Manpower is one of the largest private employers in the United States, ranked 119 in the Fortune 500 list of large companies, and has revenues around $22 billion worldwide. They serve over 400,000 employer clients, and place four million workers a year in 82 countries and territories (Manpower Inc., 2009).

Disposable Workforce   Turnover rates in many low-tier jobs are high because they are the expendable workforce that consists of workers in the service industry, in clerical fields, and on assembly lines performing routine tasks. To the management of these industries, people in these largely unskilled or semi-skilled jobs are interchangeable. A high turnover rate is not a problem for management, and in fact, it may even be considered desirable so that health insurance premiums and payments of other benefits can be avoided. These disposable workers generally earn less than those on the regular payroll, and must live with the uncertainty that their jobs may permanently end today when they clock out at 5:00 p.m. Their anxiety level about their employment is high, and for many, unemployment insurance is not an option.

Eliza, a single mother of four children, epitomizes the plight of many people who are looking for work, but find they are at the mercy of employers that do not see that providing stable employment, reliable and sufficient work hours, and benefits for their employees as a priority. Eager to work, Eliza was delighted to find a job in a fast-food restaurant. She told the management that she was looking for 30 to 40 hours of employment per week. Knowing of her desire to work, the restaurant hired her, but instead of meeting her needs, her boss routinely asks Eliza to leave work early, unpaid, during the slow periods. She was hired to fill an organizational need, and released as soon as their need for her labor lessened. Because Eliza's income was so much less than she anticipated when being hired, she found that the job did not pay her bills. In addition, Eliza felt that the long commute was not worth her while, so she quit, returning to welfare (Seccombe, 2011: 206). She explained:

> *T*hat's something I need is a job. I've been looking. I just can't find the right one. I used to work at <fast food industry>, but I wasn't making much money. By the time I caught the city bus, went out there, by the time I got to my kids, I spent all the money that they gave me. I liked the job, but it was just that I had to pay 75 cents to get to work, and paid 75 cents to get back. If I missed the bus I had to give somebody $3.00 or $4.00 to take me. And they wouldn't give me enough hours. I told them when they gave me this job that I needed at least 30–40 hours a week. I just can't afford to work less. But I was wasting my time going out there. I had to be at work by 11 o'clock, but they would send me home by 2 o'clock. I didn't even get 20 hours a week. You hear what I'm saying? Ten or 12, maybe. I think what they were doing was hiring you for the busy hour, and once the busy hour passed, you was sent out of there. I had to quit because it was costing me too much to go way over there.

In other words, Eliza, a struggling single mother who is trying to work hard to support her children, was thwarted by the uncertainty associated with being part of a "disposable workforce."

The Threat of Losing Health Insurance

In 2010, sweeping reforms to the U.S. healthcare system were passed by Congress and signed into law by President Obama. Many of these reforms will be eased in through 2014. In sum, the new legislation will make the following changes (Kaiser Family Foundation, April 2010):

- Most individuals will be required to have health insurance by 2014.
- Individuals who do not have access to affordable employer coverage will be able to purchase coverage through a health insurance exchange with "credits" available to make coverage more affordable to some people. Small businesses will be able to purchase coverage through a separate exchange.

- Employers will be required to pay penalties for employees who receive credits.
- New regulations will be imposed on health plans that will prevent health insurers from denying coverage to people for any reason, or for charging higher premiums based on health status or sex.
- Medicaid will be expanded to 133 percent of the federal poverty level ($14,404 for an individual and $29,327 for a family of four in 2009 for all individuals under age 65).

This healthcare legislation was hotly contested by many groups, vehemently supported by others, and criticized by some who said it did not go far enough. Why was this proposed legislation so controversial?

Many Americans have difficulties getting the health care they need when they are ill because they are without health insurance. Unfortunately, by 2009 over 50 million Americans had no health insurance, a number rising quickly as shown in Table 10.2 (Commonwealth Fund Commission on a High Performance Health System, February 2009; DeNavas-Walt, Proctor, & Smith, 2010). The number of uninsured would continue to rise if the system was not substantially reformed. But that figure is a low estimate because it calculates the number of people who had no insurance *throughout* the year. If we look at how many people were without insurance *at some point in time* over the last two years, the number would be nearly 90 million, or one out of every three persons under age 65 (Pifer-Bexler, 2009).

Table 10.2	How Many Uninsured in the U.S.? 2000–2009
The number of people without health insurance rose sharply between 2008 and 2009 due to the recession.	
2000	40 million
2004	43 million
2008	46 million
2009	51 million

Source: DeNavas-Walt, Proctor, & Smith, 2010; Kaiser Family Foundation, October 2009; Commonwealth Fund, 2009.

The uninsured delay or forgo needed health care because of the out-of-pocket cost (Kaiser Family Foundation, September 2010). As a result, they experience unnecessary suffering, and even death. How can this problem exist in a country as wealthy as the United States?

The brief answer to this question is that the United States has traditionally had a *fee-for-service* health care system; in other words, if you get sick or injured, you must *pay* to go to the doctor. Other countries "roll" the price of health care into their taxes so that there is little or no additional cost when their citizens are sick or injured and seek medical help.

During World War II, when wage freezes were in effect, some large U.S. companies decided to offer health insurance as a fringe benefit. Insurance was cheap to purchase because healthcare costs were relatively inexpensive and there were few drugs available. People appreciated the fact that they did not have to pay taxes on health insurance, unlike income. Over time, most large U.S. businesses began to offer health insurance to their workers and their families. To compete for labor, medium-sized and small businesses decided to get into the insurance act as well (Blumenthal, 2006).

By the 1950 and 1960s, Americans began to equate health insurance with employment—you get a job and health insurance is part of the benefits package. We tend to forget that this connection began through a simple historical accident, e.g., wage freezes, and we also tend to forget that no other industrialized nation has tied health insurance to employment. In all other developed nations, access to healthcare is a guaranteed right of citizenship, much like education or access to police protection.

However, by the 1970s and 1980s, healthcare costs began to rise substantially in the United States. Offering health insurance to workers and their families became an expensive benefit, not a cheap one. Small businesses were the first to complain about the increasing costs of health care. Soon medium-sized and large businesses began to feel the financial strain as well. Today, companies of all sizes are completely dropping health insurance coverage, asking workers to pay more of the insurance plan costs, or to be on the job for six months or a year before becoming eligible for insurance, or are covering workers but not their families (Kaiser Family Foundation and Health Research & Educational Trust, 2010). Less than 60 percent of Americans receive health insurance from an employer, either as a worker themselves or as a dependent (spouse or child) (DeNavas-Walt, Proctor, & Smith, 2010). Among low-income workers who earn up to 200 percent of the poverty line—around

$35,000 a year—only about one-third receive employer-sponsored insurance. Clearly, there has been an erosion of the connection between health insurance and employment that was so embedded in our collective consciousness.

Why not just purchase the insurance yourself if you cannot get it from an employer? Many cannot afford the higher costs, as the average price of family health coverage is over $13,700 a year (Kaiser Family Foundation and Health Research & Educational Trust, 2010). Also, many people are turned down by health insurance companies because of a pre-existing condition. Moreover, most Americans do not qualify for **Medicaid** (the federal-state health care program for the eligible poor) or **Medicare** (the federal health care program for the elderly) because they do not meet the economic or age requirements.

About 50 million people were left without any health insurance by 2009, yet the consequences of being without this insurance can be devastating, as shown in the feature box *My Family: "It's not What We Had Planned for Our Family"* on page 282. Compared to those with health insurance, the uninsured:

- Are twice as likely to postpone seeking health care, are over four times as likely to forgo needed care, and are more than twice as likely to have a needed prescription go unfilled (Kaiser Commission on Medicaid and the Uninsured, September 2010).
- Pay large sums of their own money for their limited care, thereby reducing the amount of money for food, heat, and other necessities (Schwartz, 2007). A third of uninsured patients and one-half of low-income uninsured patients reveal that doctors make them pay upfront before any health care is rendered (Schwartz, 2007). Medical bills are a major financial hardship, and contribute to personal debt and bankruptcy (Kaiser Commission on Medicaid and the Uninsured, September 2010).
- Are less likely to receive any care, are twice as likely to receive no recommended follow-up care, and are more likely to report not fully recovering after an accidental injury (Hadley, 2007).

We have discussed how the changing occupational structure and our current economy—including health care—directly touch the lives of families every day. However, these macro-level factors *indirectly* influence families as well, for example, by encouraging women to join the labor force. Unlike a generation or two ago, many more women now feel that they *need* to work to make ends meet for their families. Alone or together with their partners, women in the workforce provide an important financial resource for the family.

Given that most parents—fathers and mothers—work outside the home now whether because of need, choice, or some combination thereof, we must ask ourselves how this has changed the nature of work done *inside* the home. How has the context of housework and childcare changed? Who is doing what chores? What new challenges, opportunities, and stressors does this bring?

*D*o you know anyone who has suffered economically during the recession? What happened to them? Did they lose their job, have their pay reduced, or lose their health insurance? How did they cope and how are they coping now?

:: Family Work at Home

The family work that feeds, clothes, shelters, and cares for both adults and children is just as important to the maintenance of society as the work that occurs in the labor market (Coltrane, 2000). Unfortunately, household labor and childcare have traditionally been considered "women's work," and therefore were not considered worthy of scientific study until 20 or 30 years ago. Since then, a tremendous amount of research has examined who does what in the home, under what circumstances and why, and how housework is embedded in complex social processes related to the social construction of gender.

The Division of Household Labor

How is **household labor** defined? This is an important question because it may be defined differently from one context to another. Generally, it refers to "unpaid work that is done to

Medicaid: The federal-state health care program for eligible poor of all ages.

Medicare: The federal health care program for the elderly.

household labor: In general, the unpaid work done to maintain family members and/or a home.

My Family

"It's Not What We Had Planned for Our Family"

Roberto and Maria virtually grew up together in the same working-class neighborhood. They came from modest means, but both grew up surrounded by parents and family who loved and cared for them. Although they had known each other all of their lives, they began to see something special in each other during high school, and married a few years later.

Before marriage both had gone to a community college near their home, but Roberto dropped out after a year for a full-time job in construction. Maria received a degree in cosmetology, and then began work in a hair salon. Together they earned "good money," saved what they could, and soon were able to buy a small, but cozy home in the neighborhood in which they grew up. Next, they decided to save money so that they could begin a family. They did not care about fancy cars or extravagant vacations; a stable home and family life were what mattered most to this couple.

Maria had their first child a few years later when she was 25, whom they named Adrian. She quit her job immediately; their plan was for Roberto to be the breadwinner and Maria to stay at home with their children. Two years later Sarah was born. Three years after that their twins, Levi and Jake, were born, and their family now felt complete.

Life was good for this family. Roberto's earnings fluctuated somewhat month to month, but he usually earned about $4,000 a month which was enough to support the growing family on a frugal budget. Their family life was stable and predictable.

Stable and predictable, that is, until the recession occurred. In an effort to reduce costs, Roberto's employer laid off a few of the most newly hired workers. Luckily, Roberto had some seniority, and was not personally affected. However, as a second cost-saving measure, his insurance benefits were reduced, requiring Roberto to pay several hundred dollars extra per month to cover his family. Later, this health insurance coverage was eliminated completely. His boss apologized profusely to Roberto, but said that it was just too expensive for his company to purchase any longer.

That evening when Roberto told Maria that their health benefits were now gone, she felt a stab of terror. With four active kids still under the age of nine, someone always needed to go to the doctor. In the past year alone, Adrian had broken his arm, Sarah had needed stitches, and Levi had been to the doctor several times for recurring ear infections. *"You just can't imagine the fear unless you've been in this situation. . . . We can get food from relatives, and they can help us with school clothes and this and that. But how are we supposed to pay for all those high-priced doctor bills?"* Maria asked.

Maria's fears were quickly realized. She developed a bladder infection and was wracked with pain. She put off going to the doctor and tried home remedies instead until she could wait no longer. The doctor scolded her for waiting so long to come in, and sent her home with some medicine and a hefty bill. The next month Levi had another ear infection and the doctor recommended extensive tests to determine the cause of his medical problems. Maria and Roberto wanted to know how much these tests were going to cost. Were they all necessary? Could we have a few tests now and a few tests next month? These medical tests for their son drove Roberto and Maria deeper in debt.

Life for the family continued in this pattern for a few years—forgoing routine medical care and postponing needed medical care until the ultimate crisis happened. Roberto suffered a burst appendix. Still, he tried to minimize his pain, fretting over how much a doctor's visit would cost. When he could stand the pain no longer, Maria drove him to the emergency room where he was immediately prepped for surgery. The surgery cost over $19,000, and the delay in care almost cost Roberto his life.

Roberto's recovery was slow, and his construction job could not be held for him. Maria was forced to go back to work as a stylist, but given that she had no clientele, she worked at a drop-in salon. Her earnings barely lifted the family out of poverty. She found working at odds with her values and she dreams of being a stay-at-home mother. They had to borrow money from her parents to pay their mortgage so that they would not lose the house. *"Where would the six of us go, anyway?"* Maria asked herself. They pieced together childcare as cheaply as they could—Monday with Roberto, Tuesday with Grandma, Wednesday with a babysitter, and who knows about Thursday and Friday?

As you can see, losing their health insurance has wreaked havoc on this family and their dreams for the future.

What Do You Think?

1. Why do you think our country links insurance with employment? What are the strengths and weaknesses of this approach?

2. Whose "fault" is it that Roberto and Maria lost their health insurance? Who can we blame? His employer? The insurance company? Our healthcare system? Do you think their situation is unique?

maintain family members and/or a home" (Knodel, Loi, Jayakody, & Huy, 2004). House-hold labor sometimes excludes childcare and other types of emotional labor and caregiving.

The number of studies on the topic has exploded over the past two decades. Household labor is researched in many different ways, including self-reports made by one partner (usually the woman) or both partners, or by time diaries that are kept over a specific period. Not surprisingly, there is often a discrepancy between partners in their assessments of how much time each spends on housework (Lee & Waite, 2005).

According to national surveys, the five most time-consuming household tasks are (1) meal preparation or cooking; (2) housecleaning; (3) shopping for groceries and household goods; (4) washing dishes and cleaning up after meals; and (5) laundry, including washing, ironing, and mending clothes. Sociologist Scott Coltrane refers to these tasks as **routine household labor**, because they are repetitive and less able to be postponed than are other tasks (Coltrane, 2000). Although some people enjoy some or all of these activities (Poortman & van der Lippe, 2009), many people say that they do not enjoy routine household labor, or do not enjoy a significant number of specific tasks because they are seen as boring (Kroska, 2003). Other tasks, called **occasional labor**, occur less frequently and have more flexibility in timing such as gardening, paying bills, household repairs, or servicing the car.

Who Does What? Housework

Regardless of the way that housework is defined or measured, research indicates that women do significantly more housework than do men. The size of men's and women's contributions vary across studies, but most find that women spend at least 50 percent more time on household tasks (Bureau of Labor Statistics, May 8, 2008) and others report that women spend two to three times as much time on various household tasks as men (Hook 2004, 2006; Lee & Waite, 2005).

Women's work tends to be routine, which is usually nondiscretionary and repetitive. According to a study using the National Survey of Families and Households, based on a representative sample of Americans, the average married woman did about three times as much routine housework as the average married man (32 versus 10 hours per week). With respect to occasional labor, which includes those tasks that tend to be more time-flexible and discretionary, married men performed 10 hours of housework per week while women performed about six hours. In total, women performed about twice as much housework as did men, and other studies show an even greater imbalance (Coltrane, 2000). Moreover, the tasks that women do tend to be inflexible about their timing. For example, women are more likely to be responsible for changing the baby's diaper, which must be changed *now*, or for fixing dinner, which must be prepared in the next *hour*, whereas men are more likely

routine household labor: Non-discretionary, routine tasks that can be postponed, such as cooking, washing dishes, or cleaning.

occasional labor: Household tasks that are more time-flexible and more discretionary, such as household repairs, yard care, or paying bills.

> Men's share of housework is on the rise, but the tasks remain gendered. Women tend to do the "routine labor," which is repetitive and cannot be delayed, while men tend to do the "occasional labor," which has greater flexibility on when tasks can be done.

to do the yard work, which could be done any time this *week*. This difference alone can add to family stress.

The typical pattern in dual-earner families is presented in the book *The Second Shift*, by sociologist Arlie Hochschild (1989). In her sample of 50 dual-earner couples, 20 percent equally shared the housework. In 70 percent of families, men did somewhere between one-third and one-half of the housework, and in 10 percent of families, men did less than one-third. Hochschild found that at the end of a long workday, women returned to do their "second shift"—their second job of housework and childcare, which included arranging, supervising, and planning, in addition to accomplishing actual tasks. For the most part, men just returned home to "help." She found that women on average work an extra 15 hours per week compared to men.

Who Does What? Childcare

The research results of who does what with respect to childcare are not much different than who does the housework (Craig, 2006; U.S. Bureau of Labor Statistics, May 8, 2008). Regardless of the employment status of parents, mothers spend more time with their children than do fathers. One study of over 1,800 couples who completed time diaries revealed that when both partners are employed, 76 percent of the time spent on childcare is done by the mother. When the mother is not employed but the father is, she performs about 83 percent of childcare. If the father is not employed, but the mother is, she still continues to spend more time on childcare than does the father, accounting for 53 percent of parental time (Pailhe & Solaz, 2008).

What, specifically, are mothers doing with their children? One study compared the time that mothers and fathers spend on various childrearing tasks: giving spiritual, emotional, social, moral, and physical guidance; helping with homework; providing companionship, advice, and mentoring; sharing leisure and activities; fostering independence, intelligence, and responsibility; providing care, protection, and discipline; and providing income (Finley, Mira, & Schwartz, 2008). The researchers found that mothers are more involved than fathers in all domains studied, with the exception of providing income. Mothers were rated as 'often' or 'always' involved in each domain, whereas fathers were rated as 'sometimes involved' in each domain, except for providing income. Seven of the nine lowest-rated domains for fathers were in the expressive domain.

Fathers are willing to spend more time with their sons than their daughters, and fathers are even willing to reduce their own private leisure to spend time with their sons (Mammen, 2009). Boys get more of their father's time than do their sisters, or do girls in all-female families. Girls with brothers receive more of fathers' time than do girls in all-female families, but this time is primarily spent watching television together.

Renegotiating Family Work

Despite the imbalance in the division of housework and childcare, it does appear that many families are renegotiating how family labor is performed. Men's time spent in housework and childcare is on the rise, increasing by possibly 30 to 50 percent over the last generation (Galinsky, Aumann, & Bond, 2009; Sullivan & Coltrane, 2008). Nonetheless, despite these very real changes, family work is still not shared equally, as shown in Table 10.3. Although opinions differ significantly between husbands and wives, the table reveals that men's participation in childcare, cooking, and cleaning has increased, but still falls short of the amount of household labor performed by women. Consequently, fathers report having an extra hour or two of leisure per day as compared to mothers, as shown in Table 10.4.
👁️▶️ **Watch** on **myfamilylab.com**

Not surprisingly, with the lack of leisure and high demands of children, home, and work, mothers experience more stress and burnout than do their husbands in the work-family balancing act (Schor, 2002; Parker, 2009). This stress and burnout is significant because it can lead to depression and marital instability. In particular, when women value equality in the home but end up doing the majority of household labor, their sense of

👁️▶️ **Watch** the **Video**
*Core Concepts: Changing
Gender Roles at Home* on
myfamilylab.com

Table 10.3	Who Takes Most Responsibility For ...?		

Men's share of domestic work has increased, although women have most of the responsibility.

		1992	2008
Childcare			
Men	I do or share equally	41%	49%
	My spouse/partner does	58%	48%
	Others do	1%	4%
Women	I do	73%	67%
	My spouse/partner does or shares equally	21%	31%
	Others do	6%	3%
Cooking			
Men	I do or share equally	34%	56%
	My spouse/partner does	56%	38%
	Others do	9%	7%
Women	I do	75%	70%
	My spouse/partner does or shares equally	15%	25%
	Others do	9%	6%
Housecleaning			
Men	I do or share equally	40%	53%
	My spouse/partner does	51%	39%
	Others do	9%	8%
Women	I do	73%	73%
	My spouse/partner does or shares equally	18%	20%
	Others do	9%	7%

Note: Answer categories are different for men and women.
Source: Who takes most responsibility? from Families and Work Institute, National Study of the Changing Workforce, 1992, 2008.

fairness is violated and happiness with their marriage declines (Lavee & Katz, 2002). Men may compare how they contribute to household labor with how their fathers contributed, and believe that, *"Wow, I am doing a lot."* Whereas many women compare the household contributions of their partners to what they are doing and think, *"This isn't fair."*

Children's Labor in the Home

How much, and under what conditions, do sons and daughters provide housework or childcare? What impact does their labor have on themselves and their families? There are many reasons why children perform household labor. Some parents are attempting to socialize their children to future adult or parental roles—e.g., teaching a child how to use the vacuum or washing machine. Other parents simply need the extra assistance to keep up with housework and childcare demands—e.g., requiring a child to babysit a younger sibling after school.

Table 10.4	Leisure Time (in hours): Mothers and Fathers	

Fathers report an extra hour or two of leisure, compared to mothers.

	Married Mothers	Married Fathers
Employed Full-time	2.9	3.7
Not Employed	4.2	6.3
Mother Employed Part-time, Father Employed Full-time	3.4	3.6

Source: Bureau of Labor Statistics, May 2008.

Young children's housework is less gendered than that of adults or teens and may include picking up toys or making one's bed. Teenage girls do more housework than teenage boys on average. Girls tend to do more routine inside chores such as cleaning or cooking, or caring for siblings, whereas boys do occasional outside chores such as yard work (Antill, Goodnow, Russell, & Cotton, 1996). A longitudinal study that followed a group of boys through young adulthood found that boys who did more household chores as a child also did more of the routine housework as an adult (Anderson & Robson, 2006).

Children in two-parent, dual-earner families, and children of highly educated families tend to do less housework and childcare than do children in other family types. Lower-income families and single-parent families rely on children, especially daughters, to a considerable extent to help with numerous household tasks and to take care of younger siblings. These daughters have been nicknamed "mini-moms" (Dodson & Dickert, 2004).

Explanations for the Gendered Division of Labor

Several theories analyze the relationship between gender and the division of household labor, including (1) the time-availability perspective; (2) the relative resources perspective; and (3) the gender perspective.

Time-Availability Perspective

The **time-availability perspective** suggests that the division of labor is largely determined by (1) the need for household labor, such as the number of children in the home; and (2) each partner's availability to perform household tasks, such as the number of hours spent in paid work (Shelton, 1992). Both husband and wife are expected to perform domestic work to the extent that other demands in their lives allow them. The partner who has the most time available because of fewer other commitments will spend more time on housework. However, because gendered family decision-making often determines the amount of time that men and women spend in paid work, it is unclear whether women do the majority of the housework because they spend fewer hours in paid labor or whether they spend fewer hours in paid labor because they have to do the majority of the housework (Evertsson & Nermo, 2004).

Relative Resources Perspective

The theory behind the **relative resources perspective** is based on the premise of exchange theory (Blood & Wolfe, 1960; Becker, 1981). It posits that the greater the relative amount or value of resources contributed by a partner, the greater is his or her power within the relationship. This power can then be translated into bargaining to avoid tasks such as housework that offer no pay and minimal social prestige (Bittman, England, Sayer, Folbre, & Matheson, 2003). However, working-class partners often provide relatively similar resources to the family, yet their roles are often highly segregated (Rubin, 1976). Resources are usually defined as monetary ones, but they can take other forms as well, such as occupational prestige, education level, or even good looks or an exceptionally charismatic personality.

Gender Perspective ("Doing Gender")

The perspectives of time-availability and relative resources are largely gender-neutral. But some scholars suggest that gender itself is the ultimate explanatory variable, not how much time a partner has available or how many resources he or she brings to the relationship. "Doing gender," introduced in Chapter 6, suggests that housework is so ingrained as "women's work" that it functions as an area in which gender is symbolically created and reproduced (Fenstermaker Berk, 1985; West & Zimmerman, 1987). Wives do the majority of housework because it is expected of them as women and they have heard these messages since childhood. Likewise, men do less because housework is not a part of their gendered identity. This is likely why many men and women feel that the division of household labor is fair even when it is not split equally between partners. Gendered norms exert a powerful influence upon what we see as normative. When we remember the household tasks we may have done as children, most women will report that they were involved in "inside" domestic labor, such as helping with cooking, cleaning, or taking care of siblings, and men will remember that they were more involved in "outside" labor, such as mowing the lawn.

time-availability perspective: A perspective that suggests the division of labor is largely determined by (1) the need for household labor, such as the number of children in the home; and (2) each partner's availability to perform household tasks, such as the number of hours spent in paid work.

relative resources perspective: The greater the relative amount or value of resources contributed by a partner, the greater is his or her power within the relationship, which can then be translated into bargaining to avoid tasks such as housework that offer no pay and minimal social prestige.

Tying It All Together

Factors That Shape the Division of Household Labor

Families have a lot of work to do both inside and outside the home. How do they divide up household labor—both housework and childcare? There are many macro- and micro-level factors that influence how this work gets done.

Macro-level Factors

- Sex
- Cultural attitudes toward gender
- Cultural expectations for mothers and fathers
- Historical period
- Value attributed to specific resources, e.g., money
- Sex of children

Micro-level Factors

- Personal inclination
- Employment status and number of hours worked
- Presence and age of children
- Comparison to others, e.g., fathers

What Do You Think?

1. In looking back to how your parents negotiated the division of household labor, can you see any of these macro-level and micro-level factors in operation?
2. Do you think these macro-level and micro-level factors influence the division of household labor differently today than they did in your parents' generation? If you think they do operate differently, can you explain the difference and what caused it?

In other words, even girls do more routine labor, while boys do occasional labor. Moreover, which household task is more highly valued in our society? Typically, we pay more for someone to mow our lawn than to babysit our children. These gendered values are so ingrained that we rarely question this logic.

Clearly, who does what tasks in the home is usually not some random event. There are both micro-level and macro-level factors operating here, as shown in the feature box *Tying It All Together: Factors That Shape the Division of Household Labor*. Can you see how these factors operate in your own life?

You have learned that home and work were once considered "separate spheres" and were largely segregated by sex. Today, we recognize that work and family are not separate, but are highly interrelated with one another (Voydanoff, 2008; Whitehead, 2008). Family members have work to do both inside and outside the home. The next section explores the delicate art of juggling this household work among them.

What was the division of household labor when you were a child? If you were in a two-parent household, were housework and childcare divided along gendered lines? Which theoretical perspective is most useful for understanding the pattern of household labor? How do you think you and your partner will structure household labor?

:: Juggling Work and Family Life

We often hear parents, especially women, say that they can "have it all…" but combining work and family is not easy, as Lisa and Chris show us in the opening vignette (Bianchi & Milkie, 2010). If you know someone who is combining work and family, compare their situation with Lara, an American mother living in Hungary, described in the feature box *Diversity in Families: Why We Choose to Live in Hungary*. Their experiences are likely as different as night and day. Yet, the balance between a happy work life and a happy home life are what we all strive for. Let's look further to better understand the tension between work and family, and perhaps learn how to minimize this tension. As the example from Hungary shows—in a nation not nearly as wealthy as the United States—balancing work and family does not have to be so difficult.

Conflict, Overload, and Spillover

Researchers have been studying the mutual influences of work and family (Voydanoff 2008; Whitehead, 2008; Bass, Butler, Grzywacz, & Linney, 2009; Goodman, Crouter, & The Family

Diversity in Families

Why We Choose to Live in Hungary

I live in Hungary [a country in Eastern Europe], where the benefits for families surpass those of any other country I've heard about. Maternity leave is three years. Day care and preschool are free. Elementary school starts at 8 A.M. and runs until 2 P.M. with optional aftercare. Most schools also offer ballet, music lessons, computer clubs, and soccer in the afternoons.

We all receive a monthly family supplement grant, which increases with each child and lasts until the child turns 18. When the child hits school age, we get an additional lump sum at the beginning of each school year amounting to about $100 per child to cover school supplies.

All children have medical coverage through the age of 18—longer if they are in college—and pediatricians make house calls. If you have a child with a disability, you may stay home with the child for the rest of his or her life and receive the minimum wage.

There is no question that the United States needs more generous benefits for families. I am an American (my husband is Hungarian) and our choice to move to Hungary to have kids was a very conscious one. When I feel pangs of homesickness,

I think of my overworked, stressed-out friends with kids back home and think: No way. I feel like I've got a balance in my life I would have a difficult time achieving in the States. I wish that all American parents had the same opportunities we've got here in Hungary to make life easier for families.

—Lara

Source: Strong-Jekely, 2006.

What Do You Think?

1. Is Hungary a rich nation? Where does Hungary get the money to spend on these types of services? Why doesn't the United States have the money to spend this way, or does it?

2. Would you prefer the system of helping families in Hungary or the system in the United States? Defend your choice. What arguments would those people who feel differently make? How would you refute those arguments?

| Figure 10.4 | **Percentage of Fathers and Mothers in Dual-Earner Couples Reporting Work-Family Conflict (1977–2008)** |

Work-family conflict is common, and is reported more often by men than women.

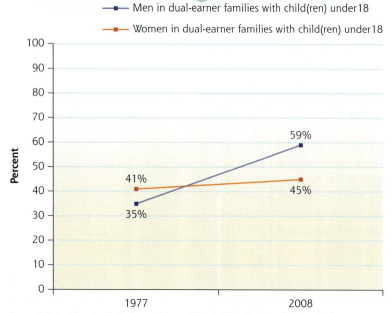

Source: Galinsky, Ellen, Kerstin Aumann, and James T. Bond. 2009. Times Are Changing: Gender and Generation at Work and at Home. New York: Families and Work Institute.

Life Project Key Investigators, 2009). From this research have come several important concepts that help us understand the reciprocal relationship between work and family life.

One such concept is **work-family conflict**, which is the tension people feel when the pressures from paid work and family roles are incompatible in some way (Nomaguchi, 2009). The conflict can go both ways: work is made more difficult by participation in family roles (e.g., it is difficult to work the expected overtime at your job because you need to pick up your children from day care), and participation in family roles is made more difficult by work (e.g., it is difficult to get to your son's soccer practice every Wednesday afternoon because it conflicts with the department meeting at work). People feel greater work-family conflict when (1) the demands of paid work and family responsibilities are higher; (2) the resources that help them manage those demands are fewer; or (3) the perceptions of demands that they feel they must fulfill are higher (Voydanoff, 2004). Work-family conflict has increased for both men and women over the past few decades (Nomaguchi, 2009; Winslow, 2005). In fact, now that men are doing more housework and childcare, they report even more work-family conflict than do women, as shown in Figure 10.4 (Galinsky, Aumann, & Bond, 2009).

Another concept is called **role overload**, which refers to feeling overwhelmed by many different commitments and not having enough time to meet each commitment effectively (Pearson, 2008; Duxbury, Lyons, & Higgins, 2008). Role overload can lead to stress and depression. A recent study of over 700 randomly selected mothers found that those who felt the most overload between their work, parent, and spouse roles had lower levels of mental well-being than did women who perceived less role overload. *Perception* of overload is the key here. Simply working more hours did not necessarily lead to more feelings of overload; in fact, women who worked *less than* 30 hours a week *or more than* 35 hours a week had the fewest feelings of role overload. What appears to make the difference in role overload is not how many hours are worked, but how much support is available. Mothers with higher incomes (who can, presumably, hire more help), higher marital quality, and higher-quality jobs were least likely to feel role overload (Glynn, Maclean, Forte, & Cohen, 2009).

Another related concept, **spillover**, refers to the negative (or sometimes positive) moods, experiences, and demands involved in one sphere that carry over, or "spill over," into the other sphere (Davis, Goodman, Pirretti, & Almeida, 2008). How do you purge the rushed and hectic mood at work when you now have to grocery shop with your toddler? How do you play with your children after work when your boss is still sending you e-mails in the evening? With the creation of computers, BlackBerries, cell phones, and other important technology, work increasingly encroaches upon family time (Conley, 2009). Other people may be required to travel for their jobs away from their homes and families for periods of time. These different work demands mean that families have trouble finding "quality time" together.

Likewise, family demands can "spill over" into employment. Who takes care of the children on teachers' workdays at school? How do you face the day's challenges at work when your child has a fever of 101 degrees? Even if you can arrange for childcare when your child is ill, the stress at home can affect your work performance.

Spillover could also be positive (Poelmans, Stepanova, & Masuda, 2008). One study measured positive family-to-work spillover by asking 156 couples to respond to statements such as "My family gives me ideas that can be used at work," or "My family helps me face challenges at work." The researchers found that in families with higher cohesion, such as feelings of togetherness and mutual support, both mothers and fathers expressed more positive family-to-work spillover. In particular, women who were satisfied with housework arrangements perceived more positive spillover, whereas satisfaction with their marital relationship increased men's positive spillover (Stevens, Minnotte, Mannon, & Kiger, 2007).

The relationship between work and family is gendered (Galinsky, Aumann, & Bond, 2009). Men receive pressure from their employers to fulfill work obligations and to ignore or minimize family obligations (Coltrane, 1997; Hertz & Marshall, 2001). The idea is to let someone else, presumably the wife, take time off from work when a child is sick or has to go to the dentist. Women get more pressure from home to fulfill home obligations at the cost of work obligations. Consequently, although men may miss more family functions (e.g., their child's violin recital or school play) men are not necessarily penalized at work for having children in the same way that women are penalized (Stone, 2008). In fact, many employers see men with children as more stable and hardworking, as the term "family man" implies. However, having children does not have this same effect for women. There is no equivalent "family woman" term.

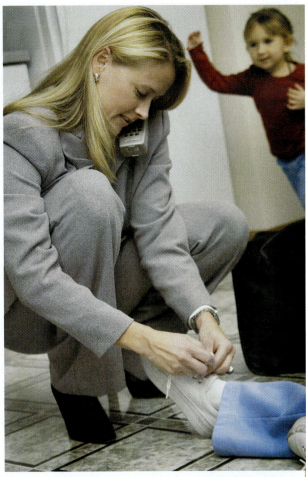

How do work and family influence one another? Social scientists talk about "work-family conflict," "role overload," and "spillover."

work-family conflict: A form of tension under which people feel that the pressures from paid work and family roles are incompatible in some way.

role overload: Feeling overwhelmed by many different commitments and not having enough time to meet each commitment effectively.

spillover: An occurrence caused by the demands involved in one sphere of work carrying over into work in another sphere.

Most of the research on the interface of work and family has been conducted in Western countries; however, a recent study using data from the IBM Corporation in 48 countries reveals that significant work-family conflicts are experienced throughout much of the world (Hill, Yang, Hawkins, & Ferris, 2004). In particular, the concern is usually on how the conflict affects family life, not necessarily how it affects work. In other words, work was thought to be more detrimental to family than family was thought to be detrimental to work. The research found that having a spouse or intimate partner contributed to a reduced conflict for women in developed countries, but not for women in developing countries. They also found that responsibility for children contributed more than twice as much to conflict for women as it did for men, likely due to the fact that women carry a larger share of childcare responsibilities.

What are the consequences of work-family conflict, role overload, and spillover? Stress is certainly one consequence (Bianchi & Milkie, 2010). Eighty-six percent of working mothers say that they sometimes or frequently experience stress in their lives, as compared to 44 percent of working fathers (Parker, 2009). Poor health is another consequence. In fact, only 28 percent of employees in 2008 said their health was excellent, compared to 34 percent in 2002 (Aumann & Galinsky, 2009). But much of this stress occurs because parents feel that there is not sufficient time to do it all, and do it well. In this next section, let's look at the time crunch that many parents experience.

The Time Crunch

What are the largest challenges that parents report facing today? Feeling rushed and not spending enough time with their children seems to be at the top of the list. One study that asked parents to rate a list of challenges found that 40 percent of full-time workers reported that balancing work and family is the biggest challenge they face as a parent, which is twice as many as who voiced the second concern of instilling moral values in their children (Rankin, 2002). Another recent study from the Pew Research Center, which conducts regular surveys on social and demographic trends, found that 40 percent of working moms (versus 25 percent of working dads, and 26 percent of stay-at-home moms) "always feel rushed" (Parker, 2009).

Finally, another study that used two different samples of adults in the United States found that nearly 50 percent of parents residing with their children feel that they spend too little time with them (Milkie, Mattingly, Nomaguchi, Bianchi, & Robinson, 2004). Parents find enjoyment in caring for their children, playing with them, and teaching them, and believe that spending time with their children is important for the child's sense of happiness and well-being (Kurz, 2002). Several factors are associated with experiencing time deficits with children. These include the amount of time in paid work, the age of the youngest child, and sex of the parent—parents who work longer hours, who have a younger child, and fathers are more likely to report feeling a time deficit. However, once the work hours are held constant, mothers actually feel more time deficits than fathers (Milkie, Mattingly, Nomaguchi, Bianchi, & Robinson, 2004).

Yet, despite their feelings to the contrary, parents actually spend *as much or even more time* with children than they did in the past (Bianchi, Robinson, & Milkie, 2006). Studies based on large and representative samples of parents in the United States find (1) the amount of time both mothers and fathers spend with children is on the rise, regardless of employment status; (2) mothers continue to spend significantly more time with their children than do fathers; and (3) unemployed mothers spend more time with their children than do employed mothers (Bianchi, Robinson, & Milkie, 2006; Kendig & Bianchi, 2008).

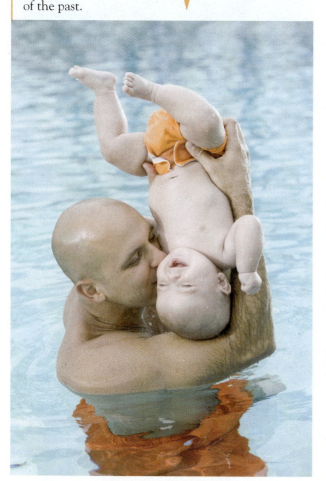

Parents feel a time crunch and report wanting to spend more time with their children. Yet, interestingly, parents today actually spend as much or more time with their children than parents of the past.

If parents spend more time with their children than they used to, why do parents report that they are not involved enough? One reason is that expectations for parenting have changed. Parents, especially mothers, are expected to be far more involved in their children's lives than they were in the past—a trend that some suggest is actually detrimental to children (Cline & Fay, 1990; Honore, 2008; Sayer, Gauthier, & Furstenberg, 2004). Parents hover over their children, paying extremely close attention to their children's experiences and trying to ward off any problems before they emerge. This constant vigilance has given rise to a new nickname—"helicopter parents." Parents drive their children from playdate to playdate; orchestrate their children's after-school activities; confront and blame teachers when their child performs poorly; and e-mail, text, or call their adult children daily when they are away at college. Some parents even run interference with their children's professors when they cannot enroll in a preferred class or if they received a lower grade than expected. The availability of technology is often to blame for the explosion in "helicopter parenting"—cell phones have been called the world's longest umbilical cord (Briggs, 2006).

Perhaps another reason why parents feel that they are not spending enough time with their children is because they are frustrated by their inability to respond spontaneously due to encroaching demands placed on them by their employers (Daly, 2001). As parents work more hours per week, and as work conditions and hours become less standardized, parents may find it difficult to meet their children's needs. They apparently continue to spend time with them, but it may be at greater personal cost, such as lack of leisure activities, exercise, or sleep (Nomaguchi & Bianchi, 2004; Pelham, 2010).

Consequently, a growing number of mothers report that they would prefer to work part-time or not at all, as shown in Table 10.5 (Pew Research Center, 2007). Among working mothers with minor children (age 17 and under), just one in five say full-time work is the ideal situation for them, down from one-third who felt this way in 1997, according to a Pew Research Center survey. Three in five (up from almost one-half in 1997) of today's working mothers say part-time work would be their ideal, and another one in five says she would prefer not working at all outside the home.

There is a similar shift in preferences among stay-at-home mothers. Today, nearly half of all stay-at-home moms now say that not working outside the home is the ideal situation for them, up from the 39 percent who felt that way in 1997. Just 16 percent of these mothers say their ideal situation would be to work full-time outside the home, down from the 24 percent who felt that way in 1997.

If mothers would prefer to stay at home or work part-time, then why do they work full-time? Some reasons are financial, others might be related to the fear they would be unable to enter the job market later or would reenter with a large disadvantage compared to other workers. The feature box *Policy and You: From Macro to Micro: Fixing Social INsecurity*, addresses some of these concerns and offers a proposal to help families have a parent at home. It is an innovative idea that would allow people to draw Social Security for a three-year period while raising children rather than having the funds unavailable to them until they are elderly.

Table 10.5	The Preferred Work Status of Mothers, 1997–2007 (Percent)			
Mothers nowadays seem to favor part-time over full-time work, and stay-at-home mothers are increasingly satisfied with their arrangement.				
	Working Mothers		**At-Home Mothers**	
	1997	**2007**	**1997**	**2007**
	n = 317	n = 259	n = 140	n = 153
Full-time work	32%	21%	24%	16%
Part-time work	48%	60%	37%	33%
Not working	20%	19%	39%	48%
Don't know	0%	0%	0%	3%

Note: Based on mothers with children under age 18.
Source: From 1997 to 2007, Full-Time Work Grows Less Attractive to Moms. Pew Research Center 2007.

Catch 22: Inflexible Full-Time Work or Part-Time Penalty

Part of the tension over balancing work and family is due to an ever-increasing workweek (Bunting, 2005; Morrissey, 2008) and a feeling that workers have little control or flexibility over their working conditions—when they work, how long of a day they work, whether they can miss a day to take care of children, or whether they can take extended time off and reenter without penalty (Kornbluh, Isaacs, & Waters Boots, 2004). For example, one

Policy and You: From Macro to Micro

Fixing Social *IN*security

Ask parents and many will tell you that they would like to take some time out from their jobs to devote more attention and energy to their young children. Parents, especially mothers, would like to work part-time, or stay home altogether. What is preventing them? One factor is the well-founded anxiety about the career setbacks that such an arrangement would cause. Mothers want the continued rewards of work, but with scaled-down hours. For many families, though, the biggest barrier is practical: they simply cannot afford to reduce their work hours.

Here is a proposal to help families. Why not allow working parents to draw Social Security benefits for up to three years during their prime child-rearing years? This would give them a choice about how much time to spend working and how much time to spend with their children. Those who elected to "borrow" on their Social Security would repay the system when they returned to work. For example, the government could increase the employee's share of the payroll taxes they pay when parents return to work, parents could defer their age of retirement with full Social Security benefits on a year-for-year basis, or parents could accept a reduced monthly benefit, as those who opt for early retirement do now.

How much of a difference would this make for parents trying to make ends meet? It would make a huge difference. Taxes and childcare costs take such a large portion out of parents' incomes that even modest Social Security benefits could largely replace the net income from an average job. For example, a parent earning a second salary of $30,000 (assuming the spouse also makes $30,000) would only net about $10,065 after taxes, childcare, and work expenses (see Table).

Among parents taking advantage of an early option to access Social Security, most would probably stay at home during their children's earliest years. But the needs of children continue after early childhood. A fifth grader struggling in school or a troubled teenager can also demand parental attention. This policy would let parents decide what makes sense for them and their families.

One issue that would need to be addressed is overcoming barriers to re-entering the workforce. Although common in other countries, it is probably unrealistic to ask employers to guarantee someone's job after a leave of a year or more. Continuation of health insurance would also need to be addressed. More fundamentally, we need to change the national mindset, so that nurturing children is seen as a respectable and worthwhile accomplishment that strengthens, rather than interferes, with the worker's attachment to employment.

Net Income after Taxes, Childcare, and Work Expenses

Example: A two-earner couple, where each parent makes	$30,000
The second salary:	$30,000
Subtract:	
Social Security and Medicare taxes	2,295
Additional state and local taxes	1,500
Estimated additional federal income tax	6,180
Additional childcare (estimated at $120/week)*	6,240
Commuting cost ($25/week times 50)	1,250
Cost of work clothing and dry cleaning	870
Cost of restaurant meals on work days ($25/week times 50)	1,250
Other (nonreimbursed expenses, paid help, meals out, etc.)	350
Net income	**$10,065**

The proposal offered here—allowing parents to draw Social Security at two points in their lives—could offer relief from the time crunch experienced by millions of Americans struggling to meet the dual demands of work and family. In the last century, we focused on meeting the needs of the elderly. Today, we recognize that compelling needs emerge earlier in our lives as we are raising our families. Yet, our policies have not adequately changed to compensate for the massive entry of women into paid employment. Our Social Security system has long been thought of as providing a measure of financial security in return for a lifetime of work. What could be a more vital contribution to the future of our country than raising children well?

Sources: Official Journal of the European Communities, 1998; Parker, 2009; Rankin 2002.

What Do You Think?

1. Do you think a program that would allow parents to draw upon Social Security as they raise their children would be popular among Americans? Why or why not? Would it be stigmatized as welfare?

2. What do you think might be some of the logistic barriers to adopting this type of program? Do you think the barriers (if any) are surmountable?

survey found that 43 percent of workers have no control over start and end times, and 54 percent of workers with children report that they have no time off to care for sick children without losing pay (Families and Work Institute, 2004). Meanwhile, work is demanding more time of its employees: the average American worked 48 more hours per year—six extra days or more than a work week—than did Americans a generation ago (Morrissey, 2008). ⊙─Watch on **myfamilylab.com**

Because of the inflexibility of many workplaces, some parents have opted to reduce their work hours to part-time, or wish that they could (Parker, 2009); however, they generally pay a steep price for this added flexibility. Workers who go part-time or a nonstandard (temporary, contract) route earn nearly $4.00 an hour less than regular full-time workers. Moreover, only 14 percent of part-time or nonstandard workers receive health insurance from their employers, compared to 69 percent of their counterparts working full-time in standard work arrangements, and only 16 percent receive a pension, compared with 66 percent of regular full-time workers (Wenger, 2003). Other than minimum wage laws, U.S. business law is entirely silent on the issue of part-time workers' compensation (Gornick, Heron, & Eisenbrey, 2007).

These drawbacks to part-time work are not found in many other countries. In 1997, the European Union (EU) drafted a Directive "to eliminate discrimination against part-time workers and improve the quality of part-time work" (Official Journal of the European Communities, 1998). The Directive prohibits employers from treating part-time workers less favorably than comparable full-time workers (unless they can demonstrate that the differential treatment is justified). It addresses issues of pay equity, Social Security, job benefits, training and promotion opportunities, and collective bargaining rights. How does this Directive actually work? Germany grants the right to work part-time in firms that have more than 15 workers; Belgium grants employees the right to work 80 percent time for five years; the UK allows employees the right to request flexible and part-time work to care for a child under the age of six or a disabled child under the age of 18, and Sweden allows parents to work six hours a day until their children turn eight (Gornick, Heron, & Eisenbrey, 2007).

Since the United States offers no options for part-time work, parents must scramble to find childcare for significant portions of each day. The next section examines childcare arrangements available in this country and some of the critical issues that affect the delicate balance of work and family life.

⊙─Watch the **Video**
Core Concepts: Working Women and Childcare on **myfamilylab.com**

If you plan to have children, what would be the preferred work schedule for you and your spouse or partner? Do you think it will be possible, or easy, to have this schedule? What would facilitate or interfere with your preferred schedule?

:: Who's Minding the Kids?

With increasing numbers of mothers turning to employment over the past several decades, many children are spending substantial amounts of time in the care of someone other than their parents (Capizzano & Main, 2005). Forty-two percent of children under the age of five with employed mothers spent at least 35 hours a week in childcare in 2002. Among families in which the mother works full-time, 50 percent of children are in full-time care. Given these figures, is the quality of childcare and its high costs a private matter or a public concern?

Childcare is a necessity for most families, but this necessity remains largely a private matter. Families are left on their own to find the highest-quality childcare that they can afford. However, quality controls are limited and vary by state. For example, most childcare facilities are not accredited (National Association of Child Care Resource & Referral Agencies, 2009). CPR and First Aid requirements vary substantially and are nonexistent in some states. Pay for childcare workers is low (median is around $10.00 per hour), few workers receive fringe benefits such as health insurance, sick pay, or vacation time, and turnover in these positions is high (Bureau of Labor Statistics, December 14, 2009).

Not all developed nations think of childcare as a private matter. Some see it as a public concern, and as a social good that can ultimately benefit everyone. What can other countries teach us about how to structure quality childcare and early education to the benefit of everyone? The feature box *Policy and You: From Macro to Micro: A Comparative Look at Early Childhood Education and Childcare Policies* shows what is possible.

Policy and You: From Macro to Micro

A Comparative Look at Early Childhood Education and Childcare Policies

early childhood education and care (ECEC) has become an important issue in many parts of the world because of the dramatic rise in labor force participation of mothers, the push for single mothers to work rather than receive public aid, and a growing interest in ensuring that all children begin elementary school with basic skills and are ready to learn. ECEC programs enhance and support children's cognitive, social, and emotional development. A review of a number of European countries show that the availability, quality, and affordability of ECEC programs far exceed what is found in the United States.

What is so different in these countries? In several countries, access to ECEC is a statutory right. Although compulsory school begins at age 6 or 7, ECEC availability begins at age one in Denmark, Finland, and Sweden (after generous maternity and family leave benefits are exhausted), two and a half in Belgium, three in Italy and Germany, and four in Britain. Most countries have full coverage of 3- to 6-year-olds.

In contrast, in the United States there is no statutory entitlement until ages 5–7, depending on the state. Access to publicly funded ECEC programs is generally restricted to "at risk" children, usually defined as poor or near-poor, (e.g., the Head Start Program). The demand for these programs among vulnerable groups far outstrips their availability. Only New York and Georgia have developed universal pre-kindergarten programs for all 4-year-olds regardless of family income.

In most countries reviewed, governments pay the largest share of the costs, with parents covering only 25–30 percent. Countries may also make arrangements for sliding scale payments for low-income families to help make programs affordable. Most countries require staff to complete at least three years of training at universities or other institutes of higher education. Their earnings are in accordance. In contrast, American parents pay an average of 70 percent of ECEC costs. Some of these costs can be recouped through tax benefits, but many low-income families find the tax system confusing and therefore, end up using informal or unregulated childcare. There is also no agreed-upon set of staff qualifications. Their status and pay are low and turnover is high.

In the U.S., families generally fend for themselves to find and pay for childcare. In other developed nations, high-quality childcare is readily available and the cost is subsidized by the government to make it more affordable to parents.

The United States is a national leader in research on child development, but has not developed the programs that research suggests are needed and which are increasingly available in other countries. In other words, the United States has not yet made the critical political commitment to early childhood education and care.

Source: The Clearinghouse on International Developments in Child, Youth, & Family Policies, 2001, 2007, 2008.

What Do You Think?

1. Why do you think the United States lags behind other European nations with respect to providing early childhood education and care? Is it related to cost, social views about working parents, stigma of ECEC, political issues, taxpayer revolts, or some other issue? Which groups might oppose ECEC, and why?

2. What will it take for our ECEC policies to become more responsive to working families?

Early Childhood Education and Care (ECEC): An international term for day care, preschool, and other programs to ensure that all children begin elementary school with basic skills and are ready to learn.

daycare centers: Nonresidential facilities that provide childcare.

family childcare providers: Private homes other than the child's home where childcare is provided.

nannies/babysitters: Non-relatives that provide childcare in the home.

Preschool-Age Children

According to the U.S. Census Bureau, 73 percent of children under the age of five with mothers who are employed full-time, and 66 percent of children with mothers who work part-time, spend time being cared for by a nonparent on a regular basis (U.S. Census Bureau, June 9, 2009). Some dual-earner families arrange working different shifts so that one parent can always be home with the children, and a few turn to relatives. However, most use more formal arrangements, such as **daycare centers**, where care is provided in nonresidential facilities, **family childcare providers**, where care is provided in a private home other than the child's home, or **nannies/babysitters**, where the child is cared for in the home by a non-relative. In fact, many parents, such as Lisa and Chris in the opening vignette, have multiple arrangements (e.g., with a grandparent on Tuesday and Thursday, and a daycare center on Monday, Wednesday, Friday) to ensure that their children are well cared for and to minimize costs.

There are some patterns of childcare use, as shown in Figure 10.5. For example, Black children are less likely than other groups to be cared for by a relative, and are more likely to be cared for in an organized daycare facility or school. In contrast, Asians are more likely than other groups to rely on relatives and are less likely to use organized daycare facilities or school-based activities (Laughlin & Rukus, 2009).

These differences reflect both culture and the costs of childcare. Relative care and care provided by other families are usually the least expensive childcare options. Full-day childcare costs in a daycare facility can cost over $10,000 a year *per child* (National Association of Child Care Resource & Referral Agencies, 2009), as shown in Table 10.6, which is higher than the costs of college tuition at public universities! Nannies and babysitters may cost even more. I perused the newspaper want ads and several nanny agencies in my hometown of Portland, Oregon and found that most adult nannies/babysitters charge $12–$18 per hour. However, even this may be more economical than a daycare center for families with two or more preschool-age children. Yet, more than one in four families with young children earns less than $25,000 per year (Children's Defense Fund Issue Basics, 2005); therefore, most forms of formal childcare remain out of their reach without public subsidy, or they are forced to compromise on quality.

School-Age Children

The costs of childcare may be reduced as children begin school, but parents who work full-time must look for childcare arrangements to supplement the school day. Most school-age children (6–12 years old) with employed parents are supervised before and after school. They are supervised by family, nanny/babysitters, or attend before- and after-school programs. However, largely because of cost, some school-age children are left virtually unsupervised, called **self-care**. According to U.S. Census reports, about 7 percent of elementary-school children ages 5–11, and 33 percent of middle-school children ages 12–14 take care of themselves after school on a regular basis, according to a nationwide survey of parents (Laughlin & Rukus, 2009; Johnson, 2005).

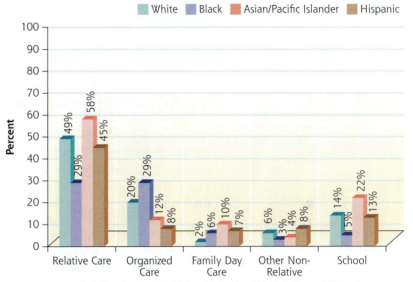

Figure 10.5 Childcare Arrangements of Preschoolers with Employed Mothers by Race/Ethnicity (Percent)

Relative and organized day care seem to be the most common ways that working parents arrange for childcare, but racial and ethnic groups appear to have different preferences.

Source: Laughlin, Lynda and Joseph Rukus. 2009. "Who's Minding the Kids in the Summer? Child Care Arrangements for Summer 2006." Presentation. Presented at the Annual Meeting of the Population Association of America, April 30–May 2, 2009, Detroit, MI.

Table 10.6 2008 Price of Childcare (Sample of States) per Child

Childcare is expensive, especially for an infant in a daycare center!

	Center Infant	Center 4-Year-Old	Family Home Infant	Family Home 4-Year-Old
California	$11,580	$8,234	$7,937	$7,180
Florida	$7,584	$6,033	$6,883	$5,835
Iowa	$8,273	$7,062	$6,266	$6,001
Massachusetts	$15,895	$11,678	$10,324	$9,805
Mississippi	$4,560	$4,056	$3,900	$3,380
New York	$13,630	$10,541	$9,737	$9,155
Oklahoma	$6,595	$4,881	$5,478	$4,873
Oregon	$9,936	$7,500	$5,700	$5,400
Wisconsin	$10,400	$8,424	$8,372	$7,384

Source: 2008 Price of Child Care (Sample of States) Per Child. NACCRRA, March 2009.

self-care: Children who are unsupervised and taking care of themselves.

While self-care is certainly not always harmful (e.g., it may make a child more independent), there are also potential problems with unsupervised children. However, most states do not have legal age limits for when it is appropriate to leave a child alone (U.S. Department of Health & Human Services, 2006). Other states may have *guidelines* that are distributed to child protective services, often suggesting that a child should be at least 10 or 12 before being left alone for even short times, but also recognizing that the maturity level of children can be different. Child welfare workers therefore have some degree of discretion, but can declare a parent unfit if the child is left alone when it is deemed inappropriate.

Effects of Childcare on Children's Well-Being

One research article headline reads, *"Study Finds that Child Care Does Impact Mother-Child Interaction"* (American Psychological Association, 1999b). Another headline reads, *"New Longitudinal Study Finds that Having a Working Mother Does No Significant Harm to Children"* (American Psychological Association, 1999a). Which headline is correct? Both articles are reporting findings from studies using large, longitudinal, nationally representative samples. The first article uses data from the National Institute of Child Health and Human Development (NICHD) Study of Early Child Care, a longitudinal study of approximately 1,300 children. The second uses data from the National Longitudinal Survey of Youth (NLSY), a survey of approximately 12,600 individuals. How can two good data sources yield opposite conclusions?

Ascertaining the effects of mothers' employment and childcare on the well-being of children is a complex task. It is made more difficult by the use of different measures of well-being, the different types of childcare settings and their quality, the different types of relationships that mothers and children have (regardless of employment or childcare), the role of the father and other family members in childcare, the mother's physical and emotional health, the child's temperament, the age of the child, the mother's hours of work and other working conditions, and many other factors not yet identified. Because of all the confounding factors, it is not surprising that some studies report a negative association between mother's employment and cognitive and social outcomes such as less attachment, or a child's greater level of aggression (Belsky, Weinraub, Owen, & Kelly, 2001), while others find positive outcomes such as children's higher language and other academic skills, especially among poor children (Loeb, Bridges, Bassok, Fuller, & Rumberger, 2007).

A study that garnered tremendous media attention was led by Jay Belsky, a family scientist at Penn State University (Belsky, Weinraub, Owen, & Kelly, 2001). The study team found that children who were in childcare for more than 30 hours per week during the first four years of life were somewhat more likely to behave aggressively as compared to those who had been in childcare for less than 10 hours a week. This finding received widespread attention because no

Table 10.7	**Location of Fatalities and Serious Injuries from Violence by Type of Childcare in the United States, 1985–2003 (Percent)**

Despite the stereotypes to the contrary, daycare centers are among the safest place for children's care.

	Fatalities, by Type of Care				Serious Injuries, by Type of Care			
Type of Incident	**Family Daycare**	**In-Home**	**Center**	**Total**	**Family Daycare**	**In-Home**	**Center**	**Total**
Violent assault	66%	32%	2%	255	61%	18%	21%	160
Shaking	84%	16%	0%	187	85%	12%	3%	168
Sexual assault	25%	75%	0%	16	47%	47%	5%	19
Total, N	330	123	5	458	249	59	39	347
(%)	(72%)	(27%)	(1%)	(100%)	(72%)	(17%)	(11%)	(100%)

Source: Wrigley, Julia and Joanna Dreby. 2005. "Fatalities in Child Care." CUNY Graduate School, November. Retrieved 9 March 2010 (www.gc.cuny.edu/press_information/current_releases/2005/November/Child_Care_Study.htm).

other issue is as fraught with worry as the choice of childcare. However, both groups of children exhibited levels of aggression that were well within the normal range. And, a follow-up study tracked the same children through early elementary school and found that by third grade, children who spent longer time in childcare had higher math and reading skills, and their greater likelihood of aggressive behavior had disappeared. But it also found that children with longer time in childcare had poorer work habits and social skills, although again the effects were very small and within the normal range (Lewin, 2005). One other little known area—safety— also seems to be on the side of childcare, especially childcare centers. The most dangerous place for children is in family day care, while the safest place is childcare centers, at least with respect to violence, sexual assault, or shakings that could result in serious injury or fatality, as shown in Table 10.7 on the facing page (Wrigley & Dreby, 2005).

It appears that the relationship between mother's employment and child well-being is somewhat mixed and contradictory because the results are small and dependent upon many other factors. Perhaps the most important factor is the quality of care that the child experiences (Perry-Jenkins, Repetti, & Crouter, 2000). Children in poor-quality childcare have been found to be delayed in language and reading skills, display more aggression, demonstrate lower mathematical ability, have poorer attention skills, and have more behavioral problems than children in higher-quality care (Children's Defense Fund, 2001).

Do you remember spending time in childcare or after-school care? What did you think of your experience? How might parents' views differ from the views of the child, and why?

Bringing It Full Circle

All families do meaningful work inside or outside the home, but the changing nature of the economy and the occupational structure has altered the context and meaning of work for many families. More women work outside the home for pay. Globalization and expanding technology has blurred the lines between work and family. The current recession has resulted in a rise in temporary employment, nonstandardized work schedules, and fewer union protections, e.g., fringe benefits such as health insurance. These changes have critical implications for how families combine work and family. Many families now need two paychecks to make ends meet. No longer are work and family domains separate; instead, they interact and influence each other. Issues such as work-family conflicts, spillover, feelings of time deficits with children, negotiations over the division of household labor, and struggles to find suitable childcare are among the issues that most employed families face today, as shown by Lisa and Chris in the opening vignette. Using the information you have learned in this chapter, let's return to Lisa and Chris's story (on page 271) and answer a few questions:

- Can you provide any examples of conflict, overload, and spillover in the story of Lisa and Chris?

- What differences might you see between a professional couple, such as Lisa and Chris, and a working-class couple in their division of household labor or in how they juggle work and family?

- Why do Lisa and Chris feel such a "time crunch" and what can be done about it? Can you think of both micro-level and macro-level causes and potential solutions?

For further review, turn to the Video Discussion Guide on page 449 to answer additional questions about how the chapter opening video relates to what you have learned in this chapter.

Chapter Review

10.1 What is the history of work in early America?

In early colonial America, most families worked closely with the land. By the 19th century, the U.S. economy was evolving from agriculture to industrialization. During this period work was done outside the home, and people were paid wages for their labor.

10.2 How has participation in the women's labor force changed in the last century?

For most of the 20th century, most married women with children did not work outside the home. However, by 1980 we began to see an important cultural shift: the majority of mothers, whether married, single, or divorced were now employed outside the home. This change likely reflected increasing job and educational opportunities for women, the acceptance of social and economic equality brought forth by the women's movement, and other changes in the economy.

10.3 How have increased technology and globalization contributed to a changing occupational structure?

First, the widespread use of technology such as personal computers, cell phones, fax machines, and pagers have changed both the way we do business and conduct our personal lives. Second, many jobs are being outsourced to other countries as companies search for less expensive labor and fewer governmental restrictions. Jobs in manufacturing, service, and sales are increasingly shipped to other countries.

10.4 How has the rise in unemployment affected families?

The U.S. unemployment rate was 9.6 percent in September 2010, and even higher for minority groups. Many people lost their jobs or had their income reduced, contributing to the rise in home foreclosures, bankruptcy, and the number of families who no longer have their health insurance.

10.5 How has the current recession contributed to unstable wages, working conditions, and a disposable workforce?

About 2.2 million hourly workers earned the minimum wage or even less in 2008. Half are adults age 25 or older, most of them women. There has been a large increase in the number of people with nonstandardized work schedules, meaning temporary work, weekend or evening shifts, or rotating schedules. This, along with low wages, makes family life difficult.

10.6 How serious a threat is losing health insurance?

Over 50 million Americans have no health insurance, a number that is rising quickly. Small firms are finding the cost of providing insurance to their workers prohibitive. Persons without insurance are more likely to delay or forgo needed health care because of the cost.

10.7 What does research have to say about who is doing the housework and childcare?

Regardless of how housework is defined or measured, research indicates that women do significantly more housework and childcare than do men. However, men and women are renegotiating household labor, and men's participation, especially in childcare, has increased significantly.

10.8 What are three common explanations for the gendered division of labor?

The time-availability perspective suggests that the division of labor is largely determined by the need for household labor, such as the number of children in the home, and each partner's availability to perform household tasks, such as the number of hours spent in paid work. The relative resources perspective suggests that the greater the relative amount or value of resources contributed by a partner, the

 **Key Terms**

daycare centers (p. 294)	household labor (p. 281)	nonstandard work schedules (p. 278)	routine household labor (p. 283)
"doing gender" (p. 286)	living wage (p. 277)	occasional labor (p. 283)	self-care (p. 295)
Early Childhood Education and Care (ECEC) (p. 294)	Medicaid (p. 281)	relative resources perspective (p. 286)	spillover (p. 289)
family childcare providers (p. 294)	Medicare (p. 281)	role overload (p. 289)	time-availability perspective (p. 286)
	nannies/babysitters (p. 294)		work-family conflict (p. 288)

greater is his or her power within the relationship to avoid tasks such as housework that offer no pay and minimal social prestige. "Doing gender" suggests that housework is ingrained as "women's work." Wives do the majority of housework because it is expected of them as women and they have heard these messages since childhood.

10.9 What are three important concepts that help explain the causes of stress for adults when they combine work and family?

First, work-family conflict is a form of tension where people feel that the pressures from paid work and family roles are incompatible in some way. Second, role overload refers to feeling overwhelmed by many different commitments and not having enough time to meet each commitment effectively. Third, spillover occurs when negative (or sometimes positive) moods, experiences, and demands involved in either the work or family domain carry over or "spill over" into the other domain. Families also experience a time crunch, and wish they had more time to spend with their children.

10.10 If balancing work and family can be stressful, why don't adults work part-time?

Most adults would like to, but there are limited part-time options and part-time workers generally are paid a lower wage for this added flexibility. This, however, is not the case in many European countries.

10.11 Who is taking care of preschool-age and school-age children while parents work?

About three-quarters of children under the age of five with mothers who are employed full-time, and 66 percent of children with mothers who work part-time, are cared for by a nonparent on a regular basis. Most families use formal arrangements, such as daycare centers, where care is provided in nonresidential facilities, family childcare providers, where care is provided in a private home other than the child's home, or by nannies or babysitters.

10.12 What are the effects of childcare on child well-being?

The relationship between childcare and child well-being is somewhat mixed and contradictory because the results are small and dependent upon many other factors, especially the quality of the childcare.

10.13 What could the United States learn from other countries about early childhood education and childcare policies?

The United States views childcare as a private matter left up to parents, but many other developed nations view childcare as a public concern. Because it is seen as a social good that can ultimately benefit everyone, childcare is more available, affordable, and of higher quality in these countries.

PEARSON
myfamilylab
www.myfamilylab.com

Experience, Discover, Observe, Evaluate

MyFamilyLab is designed just for you. Each chapter features a pre-test and post-test to help you learn and review key concepts and terms. Experience Marriage and Family in action with dynamic visual activities, videos, and readings to enhance your learning.

Here are a few activities you'll find for this chapter:

⊙ Watch **Core Concepts** video clips feature sociologists in action, exploring important concepts in the study of Marriage and the Family. Watch:

- Women in the Workplace
- Changing Gender Roles at Home
- Working Women and Childcare

✳ Explore **Social Explorer** is an interactive application that allows you to explore Census data through interactive maps. Explore the Social Explorer Map and Report:

- Unemployment Rates between 1980 and 2000

📖 Read **MySocLibrary** includes primary source readings from classic and contemporary sociologists. Read:

- Hochschild & Russell, "The Time Blend: When Work Becomes Home and Home Becomes Work"

11

Family Stress and Crisis: Violence among Intimates

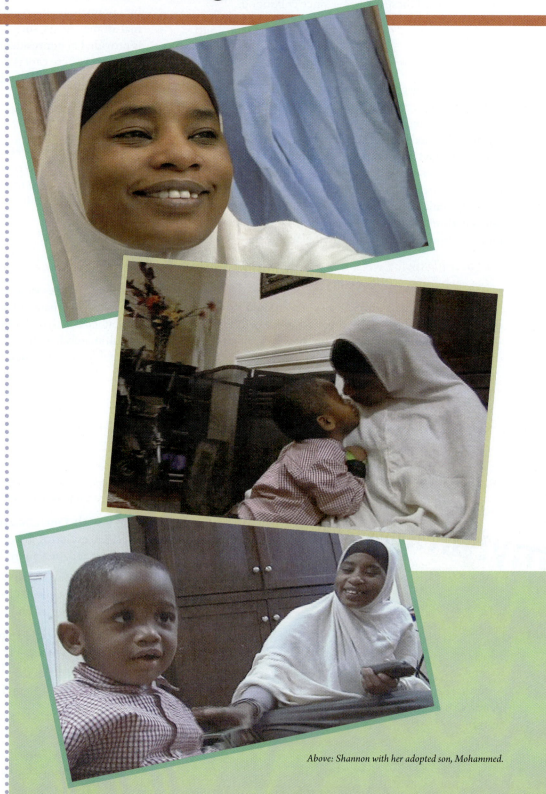

Above: Shannon with her adopted son, Mohammed.

Shannon's story began innocently enough, but quickly turned into a nightmare that would haunt her forever.

She was repeatedly beaten, abused, and threatened with death by a boyfriend who held her in captivity. One night, in the midst of the terror, she fought back. But the story does not end there.

As a young woman, a naïve Shannon agreed to go on a date with a man who had tirelessly pursued her. They went dancing and the date seemed to go well. Yet, as they drove home he viciously cursed at her, accusing her of staring at other men during their date. As she got out of the car he hit her hard, then ran after her, choking her, saying that she belonged to him. She could not believe what was happening; the violence was unprovoked and seemed to come from nowhere.

Later the young man repented, as batterers often do, and in an action that Shannon would forever regret, she went back to him. Eventually they moved in together. Immediately, his home became a prison in which she was locked inside. He controlled everything in the house, including her. The beatings began again. He hit her with bottles. He threw a pan of hot grease at her. He raped her. He pistol whipped her. He threatened to kill her. The few times she did escape he tracked her down and beat her even more.

One night, after a particularly violent episode of pistol-whipping and death threats, Shannon honestly believed he would kill her. He put his gun under the mattress, and told her to lie down. "I'm tired and can't go through this anymore," she told him. She grabbed the gun. He lunged after her and she shot him.

 Watch the **Video** *Intimate Partner Violence: Shannon* on **myfamilylab.com**

After the first shot, he laughed, and she shot again, hitting him in the head. Shannon remembers, "It was like a horror movie."

Covered in blood, Shannon blacked out, but came to after police arrived. During this period—the 1980s—there was little support for battered women. No one had ever heard of Battered Women's Syndrome, no one connected repeated violence to Post-Traumatic Stress Syndrome, or thought of her actions as self-defense. Shannon was alone, without the support of society or of social services.

Shannon was charged with murder. Her defense attorney believed in her innocence, but knowing that the odds were against her, he encouraged her to accept a plea bargain of 15 years to life. Shannon was sent to Framingham Prison in Massachusetts. There she met other battered women with stories similar to hers, all who had been sentenced to jail because they fought back against their attacker—an intimate partner.

These women, recognized as heroines by many today, are known as the "Framingham Eight." Together they petitioned the governor for early release, arguing that they all had acted in self-defense while fearing for their lives. Human rights organizations, such as Amnesty International, championed their rights. After

Questions That Matter

11.1 What is the difference between family stress and family crisis?

11.2 What are the ABC-X and Double ABC-X models of coping with a family crisis?

11.3 What is intimate partner violence?

11.4 What is the Conflict Tactics Scale?

11.5 What are the four different types of intimate partner violence?

11.6 Why do people stay in abusive relationships?

11.7 How does violence in gay and lesbian relationships compare to violence in heterosexual ones?

11.8 How common is rape and sexual assault?

11.9 What forms does child abuse take?

11.10 What are the consequences of child abuse?

11.11 What is trafficking and how common is it?

11.12 What are some types of elder abuse?

11.13 What theories do researchers use to explain violence?

11.14 How has the public responded to violence among intimates?

weighing the evidence, William Weld, the Massachusetts governor at the time, agreed and commuted the sentences of the "Framingham Eight." Still, by then Shannon had served eight years behind bars.

Because of the "Framingham Eight," people began to be aware of intimate partner violence.

The Massachusetts governor's ruling also opened doors for other governors to review cases. Today, the terms "Battered Women's Syndrome," "self-defense," and "post-traumatic stress syndrome" are part of our vocabulary, thanks in part to the efforts of Shannon.

Shannon's story reveals the darker side of family and intimate relationships. Her experience reminds us that for many people, families are not a haven of safety and security, but a place of pain and suffering. Fortunately, most families do not feel pain of this magnitude, but all families do experience some level of stress and face critical challenges. In this chapter, we will explore the nature of family stress and crises to better understand how families deal with or adapt to them. We will then look in depth at one crisis that is, unfortunately, all too common today: violence among intimates—including partners, children, and elderly parents. This chapter will illustrate that family stress and crises occur in a social context. To better understand the complex web of causes, consequences, and solutions, we need to look beyond individual personal experiences and see macro-level influences.

:: The Nature of Stress and Crisis

Family members usually fall into predictable and comfortable routines for everyday events like dividing household chores, taking vacations, and spending and saving money. A family crisis, whether positive or negative, can upset all of these routines. All families face a **crisis** at one time or another, which is a critical change or event that disrupts the functioning of the lives of one or more family members. An unexpected job loss drastically alters spending and saving. The accompanying loss of health insurance may prevent the family from getting necessary health care. Or, an arrival of new baby may quickly change the division of household labor that a couple has developed over the years. We tend to think of crises as negative turning points, such as the death of a child or a divorce. However, some crises are positive in nature.

Sometimes, a crisis occurs completely unexpectedly. A child is critically injured by a drunk driver; a wife tells her husband their marriage is over; a teenage girl learns she is pregnant. Other crises evolve more slowly from **family stress**, the tensions that occur either *within* the family (for example, violence or alcoholism) or *outside* the family (such as coping with a hurricane or other natural disaster). Family stress differs from other types of personal stress because events that affect one member, such as an illness, may ripple through the entire family, as systems theory from Chapter 1 shows us.

Stress can be normative, such as adjusting to the family changes brought on by the arrival of a new baby, or nonnormative, such as adjusting to the family changes brought on by caring for a child with a serious disability. Stresses may be **acute**, or short-term, such as cramming for an exam, planning a wedding, or having a disagreement with your partner. Or, stresses can be **chronic**, or long-term, such as Shannon's experience living with an abusive partner, challenges associated with combining work and family, or living with a chronic illness like diabetes.

What do you think are the most common family stressors? Take a guess, and then check your answers with Table 11.1.

crisis: A critical change of events that disrupts the functioning of a person's life.

family stress: Tensions that test a family's emotional resources.

acute stress: Short-term stress.

chronic stress: Long-term stress.

Responses to Stress

What are the stressors presently in your life? Managing your money? Studying for exams? Dealing with your parents? Combining school, work, and family? How do you cope with stress? Our bodies tend to have a fairly predictable pattern for coping with stress, including phases of alarm, resistance, and exhaustion known as **General Adaptation Syndrome (GAS)** (Selye, 1955, 1956):

- *Alarm Reaction:* In this first stage, the brain perceives a stressor and sends a message to the body, resulting in immediate changes in neurological and physiological states, so that the defensive forces of the body are mobilized for "fight or flight." Our normal state of balance is upset as the body responds to a perceived threat. Our metabolism increases (to give us increased energy), and hormone levels rise (giving us a feeling of anxiety).
- *Resistance:* In this second stage, the body continues to battle the stressor by maintaining its elevated state of alert. If the stress continues, it can wreak havoc on the immune system. It is no coincidence that you are often sick during or immediately after finals week—your body weakens as it tries to fight off the stress of taking exams.
- *Exhaustion:* Chronic stress over long periods can be dangerous and can lead to depression, fatigue, frequent headaches, panic attacks, insomnia, and eating disorders. It can also result in heart disease, ulcers, or diabetes. The stressful situation itself must be controlled or alleviated for health to improve.

Table 11.1	The Ten Most Common Family Stressors

Money is the number one cited family stressor.

1.	Finances and budgeting
2.	Children's behavior
3.	Insufficient time as a "couple"
4.	Lack of shared responsibility in family
5.	Communication with children
6.	Insufficient time for "me"
7.	Guilt for not accomplishing more
8.	Relationship with spouse
9.	Insufficient family "play time"
10.	Overscheduled family calendar

Source: Stress and the Healthy Family by D. Curran, Minneapolis, Minn.: Winston Press, 1985.

The Social Readjustment Rating Scale

Can we predict what types of stressors affect our health? Two physicians, Thomas Holmes and Richard Rahe, have quantified the impact of many life events on health and well-being (Holmes & Rahe, 1967). The result is known as the **Social Readjustment Rating Scale**, shown in the *Getting to Know Yourself* feature (page 304). It assigns a certain point value to stressful events that may have occurred over the past 12 months. For example, the death of a close friend is given a score of 37, while sex difficulties warrant a 39. The higher the total score, the greater the person's chance of becoming ill. As you can see, even positive events can be stressful and lead to illness because they too require a reorganization of life patterns and a change in daily routines.

How valid are these scales? Another study by Rahe and colleagues asked 2,500 U.S. sailors to rate scores of life events over the previous six months and recorded details of their health during the following six months (Rahe, Mahan, & Arthur, 1970). The relationship they found between stress scale scores and illness was small but statistically significant and supports the hypothesis that there is a link between life events and health.

Patterns of Family Crises

A family crisis often follows a reasonably predictable pattern with three distinct phases: (1) the *event* that causes the crisis; (2) the period of *disorganization* that follows; and (3) the *reorganization* that takes place afterwards. Family members may return to

General Adaptation Syndrome (GAS): The predictable pattern one's body follows when coping with stress, which includes the alarm reaction, resistance, and exhaustion.

Social Readjustment Rating Scale: A scale of major life events over the past year, each of which is assigned a point value. The higher the score, the greater the chance of having a serious medical event.

Getting to Know Yourself

The Holmes & Rahe Stress Scale–What is Your Stress Level?

In 1967, psychiatrists Thomas Holmes and Richard Rahe examined the medical records of over 5,000 people and asked them to tally the major events in their recent lives to see whether those who had experienced more stressful life events were more likely to have had a major medical event. Using the scale below, they did find a correlation—the higher the point level, the greater the chance of a major medical event. To find your stress level and your odds for a major illness, take the self-test below.

The Social Readjustment Rating Scale

INSTRUCTIONS: Write down the point value of each life event that has happened to you during the previous year.

Life Event	Mean Value	Life Event	Mean Value
1. Death of spouse	100	24. In-law troubles	29
2. Divorce	73	25. Outstanding personal achievement	28
3. Marital separation	65	26. Beginning or end of spouse's employment outside the home	26
4. Detention in jail or other institution	63	27. Beginning or end of formal schooling	26
5. Death of a close family member	63	28. Major change in living conditions (new home, remodeling, deterioration of neighborhood or home)	25
6. Major personal injury or illness	53		
7. Marriage	50	29. Change in personal habits (such as quitting smoking)	24
8. Loss of job by firing	47		
9. Marital reconciliation	45	30. Trouble with the boss	23
10. Retirement from work	45	31. Major change in working hours or conditions	20
11. Major change in the health or behavior of a family member	44		
		32. Change in residence	20
12. Pregnancy	40	33. Switch to a new school	20
13. Sexual difficulties	39	34. Major change in usual type and/or amount of recreation	19
14. Addition of a new family member (birth, adoption, older adult moving in)	39		
		35. Major change in amount of church activity	19
15. Major business readjustment	39	36. Major change in social activities (clubs, movies, visiting)	18
16. Major change in financial state, for better or worse	38		
		37. Acquisition of a loan (such as for a car)	17
17. Death of a close friend	37	38. Major change in sleeping habits	16
18. Change to a different line of work	36	39. Major change in number of family get-togethers	15
19. Major change in the number of arguments with spouse (whether more or fewer)	35		
		40. Major change in eating habits (such as eating much more or much less, or at unaccustomed places or times)	15
20. Acquisition of a mortgage for home or business	31		
21. Foreclosure on a mortgage or loan	30	41. Vacation	13
22. Major change in responsibilities at work, whether promotion or demotion	29	42. Major holidays	12
		43. Minor violations of the law (traffic tickets, jaywalking, disturbing the peace)	11
23. Departure from home of a child (through marriage, move to college, or military service)	29		

(Continued)

SCORING: Add up all your points.

- **150 points or less** means a relatively low amount of life change and a low susceptibility to stress-induced health breakdown.
- **150 to 300 points** implies about a 50% chance of a major health breakdown in the next two years.
- **300 points or more** raises the odds to about 80%, according to the Holmes-Rahe statistical prediction model.

Source: Adapted from Thomas Holmes and Richard Rahe. Holmes-Rahe Social Readjustment Rating Scale, *Journal of Psychosomatic Research*. Vol II, 1967.

What Do You Think?

1. This scale was developed over forty years ago. Do you think events should be assigned a substantially different point value, or even be excluded entirely? Should any new events be added?

2. Do you think the assigned point values of any items should differ for men and women? Across social classes? Across racial and ethnic groups? Why or why not? If so, which ones?

functioning at a level similar to where they were just before the crisis. They may also be strengthened and become more effective as a family, or they may be weakened by the crisis.

Family researchers Wesley Burr and Shirley Klein interviewed 51 families who had experienced a family crisis (1994). They asked the adults to draw a graph that illustrated how the crisis affected their overall family functioning over time, including such factors as marital satisfaction, communication, and family togetherness.

The results are shown in Figure 11.1. Only 15 percent said the family did not change. Fifty-one percent fell into a roller-coaster pattern, with a decline of family functioning during the crisis, but rebounding after time had passed. For example, the Nguyen family grieved when their eldest son, Quyet, left for college. The house felt empty with Quyet's absence, and his siblings and parents really missed him, especially at the dinner table when he would discuss the antics of his classmates during their high school senior year, or during high school baseball season when the family enjoyed watching Quyet play shortstop. It took the family many months to adjust to the loss of their cherished routines. However, in time they did adjust, and were able to return to their normal functioning.

Eighteen percent of families in the study claimed the crisis made the family stronger. For example, when one spouse has an extramarital sexual relationship, it can threaten the functioning of the entire family. Sometimes families are permanently injured; other times, however, families bounce back even stronger than before. Claire was devastated when she discovered that Peter had an affair with a colleague from work. She tried to ignore the signs, but finally confronted Peter and he confessed. He told Claire

Figure 11.1	**Five Patterns of the Effects of Stress/Crises on Family Functioning**

What happens after a family faces a stressful event or even a crisis? Five patterns have been identified; the most common is a roller coaster effect, with a decline in functioning, followed by an increase in functioning, and then, finally stabilizing.

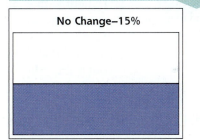
No Change–15%

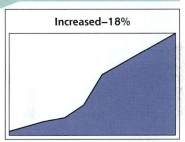
Increased–18%

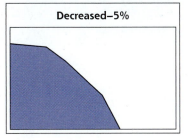
Decreased–5%

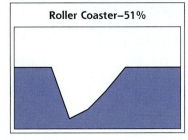
Roller Coaster–51%

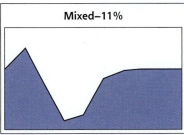
Mixed–11%

Percentage of families in the Burr and Klein (1994) study.

Source: Burr, Wesley R. and Shirley R. Klein. 1994. Reexamining Family Stress: New Theory And Research. Newbury Park, CA: Sage Publications.

A family crisis can stem from a positive event as well as a negative one. This family may face a period of disorganization and reorganization as their child finishes high school and moves away to college.

that he did not love his colleague and begged for her forgiveness. She did not forgive him easily, but together they went to marriage counseling to see if their marriage could be saved. They discovered that they still loved each other and wanted to remain together. With hard work, they learned more effective ways of communicating, of coping with stress, and of developing intimacy. Peter and Claire's relationship was not only able to endure, but to actually blossom after this crisis.

Only 5 percent of families in the study said family functioning declined permanently and that marital satisfaction, communication, and family togetherness were never the same. Marty was offered a generous promotion at his job, but it required that he and his family move out of state. It was a tough decision because his wife, Nikkonia, was very close with her mother who lived only a few miles away, and enjoyed visiting with her every week. Nikkonia also had a job that she enjoyed, although she was not the family breadwinner, so neither she or Marty felt that it was appropriate for him to turn down a "dream" promotion because of her job. Instead, Marty and Nikkonia sold their house which they had lived in for fourteen years, and bought a new one nearly 1,600 miles away where they had no family or friends, where the climate was considerably different, and where the subculture felt quite alienating. Marty worked very long hours, and Nikkonia was extremely lonely. She complained about the snobbery of the neighbors, the poorly funded schools for the children, the lack of fellowship at church, her own lack of job opportunities, and the fact that her mother was growing old without her. Marty either ignored her concerns or lashed out in anger when she voiced them. Their relationship grew very tense and fraught with conflict. "Doesn't she see what a good move this is for our family?" he asked himself. "Doesn't he see what a bad move this is for our family?" she wondered. The conflict reached a point where that Nikkonia decided that she and their children were better off in her hometown without Marty. She took the children and left.

For many other families in their research study, the outcome was not as clear. The remainder said their family's response was mixed. This may be due to the stress not yet being fully resolved.

Coping or Not: The ABC-X Models

Why are some families devastated by a crisis, while others bounce back stronger than before? Family scholar Reuben Hill proposed the **ABC-X model** to help us understand differences in family coping, as shown in Figure 11.2 (1958). A family crisis contains a number of elements, all of which affect how a family will fare. "A" factors are the *initial event* causing the crisis (e.g., graduation, extramarital affair, moving across the country). "B" factors are the *resources* a family has to meet the demands of the crisis (e.g., social support, money, religious faith, counseling). "C" factors are the *meanings families ascribe to the event* (e.g., human nature, a catastrophe, an opportunity, God's will). The outcome or "X" factors will depend upon the combination of ABC factors—the type of crisis itself, the resources of the family, and their perceptions of and meanings they associate with the crisis.

| **Figure 11.2** | **ABC-X Model of Family Stress and Crisis** |

The outcome of the crisis will depend on the combination of ABC factors—the type of crisis itself, the resources the family has to deal with it, and their perceptions of and meanings they associate with it.

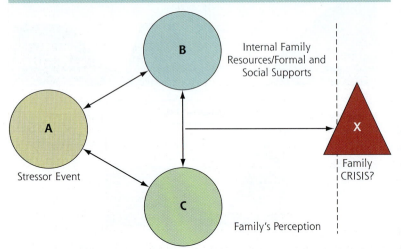

Source: Hill, Reuben. 1958. "Generic Features of Families Under Stress." Social Casework 49:139–50. (in Welch 2007).

Here's an example of the ABC-X model. Josie and Luis faced a crisis that no family should have to experience: their oldest daughter was killed in a car accident (Factor A). They are part of a large extended family, and their siblings and cousins rallied around them in the months afterwards, offering their love and support, and also provided instrumental care such as meals, childcare for their other children, and help running errands and general housekeeping (Factor B). How do you interpret or find meaning in a crisis of this magnitude? Armed with their Catholic faith, and with the help of their priest, Josie and Luis grew to believe that their daughter's life was not really cut short—she had actually accomplished all that God set out for her to do (Factor C). Together as a family they try to cope with their loss. While they miss her every day, as they nurture one another, this crisis has helped the family grow closer (Factor X).

Other researchers have expanded and built upon Hill's model (McCubbin & Patterson, 1982). For example, Figure 11.3 illustrates the **Double ABC-X model.** Do you ever notice that "when it rains it pours"—in other words, stresses may accumulate? A single event may cause multiple effects, or many stresses may happen all at once. The Double ABC-X model is designed to understand the effects of the accumulation of stresses and crises and how families adapt to them. The Double A Factor refers not only to the initial event, but also to *family life changes and transitions* that take place because of it. The Double B Factor includes both the *resources the family already has* and the *new coping resources* the family obtains because of the stress or crisis. The Double C factor takes into account not only the family's *perception of the stressor itself,* but also their *perceptions of the aftermath.* These two models reveal that it takes more than just events to devastate a family; the family's resources and perceptions are paramount.

In the next section, let's examine a particular type of crisis in depth—violence among intimates, which is violence that occurs among family members and intimate partners.

Figure 11.3	**Double ABC-X Model of Family Stress and Crisis: Pile-Up**

The Double ABC-X model is designed to understand the effects of the accumulation of stresses and crises and how families adapt to them.

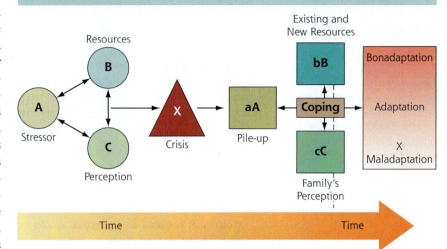

Source: McCubbin, Hamilton I. and Joan M. Patterson. 1982. "Family Adaptation to Crisis." In Family Stress, Coping, and Social Support, edited by H. I. McCubbin, A. E. Cauble and J. M. Patterson. 1983 Haworth Press. (in Welch 2007).

What types of family stresses or crises has your family faced? Can you identify the A, B, and C Factors? Which model in Figure 11.1 best reflects the way your family functioned before, during, and after the crisis?

ABC-X Model: A model designed to help us understand the variation in the ways that families cope with stress and crisis.

Double ABC-X Model: A model designed to help us understand the effects of the accumulation of stresses and crises and how families adapt to them.

📖 **Read the Document**
Through a Sociological Lens: Social Structure and Family Violence on **myfamilylab.com**

:: Violence among Intimates

What do former talk show host Oprah Winfrey, singer Rihanna, and actress Pamela Anderson have in common? In addition to being celebrities, they all have had the frightening experience of being abused within their families or close relationships. Rihanna and Pamela Anderson were victims of violence by their intimate partners. Oprah Winfrey revealed that several members of her extended family sexually abused her as a child. We find violence in families to be particularly abhorrent because we like to idealize families as safe havens. Yet, for many people, especially women and girls, this is not the case. 📖— **Read on myfamilylab.com**

Violence has touched the lives of millions of families, perhaps including your own family. There are many different types of violence among intimates, including intimate partner violence, child abuse, and elder abuse. As you will see, violence is more than simply a personal problem. It involves far more than "he just has a bad temper . . ." Violence among intimates is also a *social* problem. First, it affects large numbers of people.

Second, violence is not completely random—we can detect particular patterns and risk factors for both victims and perpetrators. Third, the causes, consequences, and solutions of violence must address its macro-level dimensions, including social, cultural, and economic factors.

:: Intimate Partner Violence

intimate partner violence: Violence between those who are physically and sexually intimate, such as spouses or partners. The violence can encompass physical, economic, sexual, or psychological abuse.

Conflict Tactics Scale: A scale based on how people deal with disagreements in relationships.

Intimate partner violence refers to violence between those who are physically and sexually intimate, such as spouses or partners. The violence can encompass physical, economic, sexual, or psychological abuse and many abusive situations include more than one type. You were introduced to Shannon and her story of intimate abuse in the opening vignette. Her story may seem extreme—she actually killed her partner—but the abuse she faced is all too common in our society.

How We Define and Measure Intimate Partner Violence?

Sociologist Murray Straus and his colleagues conducted some of the earliest nationwide studies of spousal and partner abuse in the United States. They faced some ridicule at first—how are you going to get people to talk about hitting, slapping, or biting their partner? However, in 1975 and 1985 they interviewed over 2,000 married or cohabiting adults with children ages 3–17, and from this information developed a conflict assessment tool that is still used today to measure intimate partner violence (Straus, Gelles, & Steinmetz, 1980). The **Conflict Tactics Scale (CTS)** asks people how they deal with disagreements in relationships:

Violence between those who are physically and sexually intimate is referred to as intimate partner violence. It can happen to any of us, even famous people. Chris Brown made headlines in 2009 for his brutal attack on his then-girlfriend, Rihanna.

Non-aggressive responses:

Discussed an issue calmly

Got information to back up your side of the issue

Brought in or tried to bring in someone to help settle the problem

Cried

Psychologically aggressive responses:

Insulted him/her or swore at him/her

Sulked or refused to talk about the issue

Stomped out of the room or house

Did or said something to spite him/her

Physically aggressive responses:

Threatened to hit him/her or throw something at him/her

Threw or smashed or hit or kicked something

Threw something at him/her

Pushed, grabbed, or shoved him/her

Slapped him/her

Kicked, bit, or hit him/her with a fist

Hit or tried to hit him/her with something

Beat him/her up

Choked him/her

Threatened him/her with a knife

Used a knife

Although the CTS is not without flaws, it remains an important assessment tool because it acknowledges different and multiple forms of violence. It allows us to make comparisons across groups, and over time; for example, do men and women engage in different types of violence? Do physically aggressive responses also include psychologically aggressive ones? Do types of violence differ across income or education levels?

Are Men or Women More Likely to Be Victims? Bias and the CTS Who do you think is more likely to be a victim of violence by an intimate partner, a man or a woman? Studies using the CTS have often found that *men* are more likely to be victims of physical aggression than are women (Felson, 2006; Sugarman & Hotaling, 1989). This research finding may surprise you. Upon closer scrutiny, the finding is misleading.

The CTS is certainly a better way of measuring violence than a single-item question such as, "Have you ever been hit?" However, it is also somewhat problematic for at least three reasons (DeKeseredy & Schwartz, 1998; Kishor, 2005; Fulfer, Tyler, Choi, Young, Verhulst, Kovach, & Dorsey, 2007). First, men are less likely than women to remember their own acts of violence, and they may not perceive their acts as abusive.

Second, CTS respondents are asked to tell the researcher how they *responded to* a situation of conflict or disagreement. Yet, violence and abuse can take place without a preceding disagreement, and therefore the CTS may again underreport some violence.

Third, women are more likely to experience the most extreme forms of violence, some of which the CTS does not list, including severe beatings and even murder. Finally, the CTS does not include acts of sexual violence or aggression, which are far more likely to be perpetrated by men.

Consequently, more recent studies show that women are far more likely to be victims of intimate-partner violence than are men. However, this does *not* mean that intimate partner violence against men is rare or inconsequential. Almost one-quarter of intimate partner homicides are committed against men, nearly 350 a year (U.S. Department of Justice, Bureau of Justice Statistics, 2007).

Frequency of Intimate Partner Violence

Until the 1970s, what we knew about spousal and partner abuse was based on small and nonrepresentative samples from the isolated case files of social workers, psychologists, and police. These data can be very biased because only certain types of abuse and abusers come to the attention of these professionals. However, since that time, family and social scientists have been using large and representative samples to understand how often spousal and partner violence occurs, who is likely to be a victim, and what are the causes and consequences.

Early surveys by Murray Straus and colleagues (Straus, Gelles, & Steinmetz, 1980) show an alarming rate of abuse in the United States, and this is confirmed in more recent studies. About 4.8 million incidents of intimate partner violence occur among women ages 18 and older each year (Centers for Disease Control and Prevention, 2009a). About 22 percent of women and 7 percent of men have been victims of intimate partner violence over the course of their lives (Tjaden & Thoennes, 2000, 2006). Most assaults consist of pushing, grabbing, shoving, slapping, and hitting, as shown in Table 11.2 on page 310 (Campbell, Glass, Sharps, Laughon, & Bloom, 2007).

Intimate partner violence also accounts for nearly 2 million injuries and 1,500 deaths in the United States every year (Centers for Disease Control and Prevention, 2008b). Differences between women's and men's rates become greater as the seriousness of the assault increases. For example, women were two to three times more likely than men to report that an intimate partner threw something at them, pushed, grabbed, or shoved them. However, women were 7 to 14 times more likely to report they had been beaten up, choked, tied down, threatened with a gun, or had a gun used on them.

Table 11.2	Percentage of Persons Raped and Physically Assaulted by an Intimate Partner in Lifetime, by Type of Assault and Sex of Victim		
Women are three times as likely as men to be assaulted by a intimate partner.			
Type of Assault		**Women (n = 8,000)**	**Men (n = 8,000)**
Threw something		8.1%	4.4%
Pushed, grabbed, shoved		18.1%	5.4%
Pulled hair		9.1%	2.3%
Slapped, hit		16.0%	5.5%
Kicked, bit		5.5%	2.6%
Choked, tried to drown		6.1%	0.5%
Hit with object		5.0%	3.2%
Beat up		8.5%	0.6%
Threatened with gun		3.5%	0.4%
Threatened with knife		2.8%	1.6%
Used gun		0.7%	0.1%
Used knife		0.9%	0.8%
Raped		7.7%	0.3%
Total physical assault by intimate partner		**22.1%**	**7.4%**

Source: Tjaden & Thoennes, 1998.

Figure 11.4	Women Raped or Physically Assaulted in Lifetime by Race/Ethnicity
Over half of women have been raped or physically assaulted, with American Indians/Alaska Natives reporting the highest rates.	

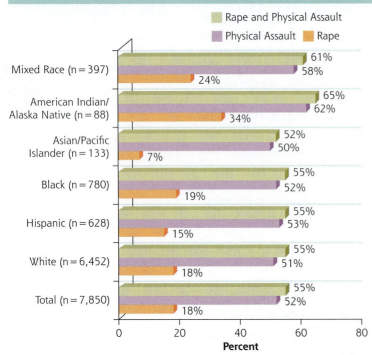

Source: Tjaden & Thoennes, 2000.

femicide: The killing of women.

Figure 11.4 reveals that differences across most racial or ethnic groups are relatively small. However, Native Americans and Alaska Natives are most likely to suffer abuse, including rape. Asian Americans are least likely to be raped; yet, their likelihood of other types of physical assault is close to that of other groups.

Women are particularly vulnerable when pregnant (Campbell, Glass, Sharps, Laughon, & Bloom, 2007; Datner, Wiebe, Brensinger, & Nelson, 2007; Samandari & Martin, 2010). A review of the literature reveals that intimate partners perpetrate one- to two-thirds of pregnancy-associated **femicides**, or killing of women, in the United States (Martin, Macy, Sullivan, & Magee, 2007).

Who is likely to be a victim? Who is likely to be a perpetrator? Several macro-level and micro-level characteristics increase the odds of being a victim or perpetrator, as shown in the *Tying it All Together* feature box. Keep in mind, however, that these are *risk* factors; these traits do *not* make violence inevitable (Crandall, Nathens, Kernic, Holt, & Rivara, 2004; Centers for Disease Control and Prevention, 2008a).

Types of Intimate Partner Violence

Relationship violence can take many forms. Family researcher and sociologist Michael Johnson has recently drawn attention to the importance of distinguishing among types of violence, motives of perpetrators, social characteristics of both partners, and the cultural context in which violence occurs. Johnson has identified four patterns of violence which have now become a common way to conceptualize intimate partner violence (2008, 2009).

- *Common couple violence* arises out of a specific argument in which at least one partner lashes out physically. It is less frequent than other types of abuse and less likely to escalate or cause severe injury. Yet, it is this type of violence that is usually captured in research studies.

- *Intimate terrorism* is physical, psychological, or sexual violence that is motivated by a desire to control the other partner. It is more likely than other types of violence to escalate over time and to cause serious injury and post-traumatic stress syndrome, as discussed in Shannon's story in the opening vignette. You can see that Shannon experienced intimate terrorism, which then turned into violent resistance, described next.

Tying It All Together

Factors that Shape Victimization and Perpetration of Intimate Partner Violence

A number of factors are associated with being a victim or a perpetrator of a crime. It is important to note that this does not mean that all of these factors are present; it simply means that they increase the likelihood of being a victim or a perpetrator. Some of these factors are micro-level factors that are experienced by the individual; others are macro-level factors that are embedded in our social structure. However, as you can see, these factors are interrelated.

Risk Factors for Victimization

Persons at risk of being victims of violence may have one or more of the following characteristics:

Micro-level Individual Factors

- Prior history of intimate partner violence
- Female sex
- Youth
- Heavy alcohol and drug use
- High-risk sexual behavior
- Experience of witnessing or suffering violence as a child
- Unemployment
- For women, being American Indian/Alaska Native or Black

Micro-level Relationship Factors

- Income, educational, or job status disparities between the partners
- Dominance and control of the relationship by the other partner
- Verbal abuse, jealousy, or possessiveness by the other partner

Macro-level Community Factors

- Poverty and associated factors such as overcrowding
- Low social capital—lack of institutions, relationships, and norms that shape the quality and quantity of a community's social interactions
- Weak community sanctions against intimate partner violence (such as police being unwilling to intervene)

Macro-level Societal Factors

- Traditional gender norms that suggest, for instance, women should be submissive or stay home and not enter workforce
- Power differentials

Risk Factors for Perpetration

Persons at risk of perpetrating violence may have one or more of the following characteristics:

Micro-level Individual Factors

- Low self-esteem
- Low income
- Low academic achievement
- Aggressive or delinquent behavior as a youth
- Heavy alcohol and drug use
- Depression
- Anger and hostility
- Personality disorders
- Prior history of being physically abusive
- Few friends and isolation from other people
- Unemployment
- Emotional dependence and insecurity
- Belief in strict gender roles including male dominance and aggression
- Desire for power and control in relationships
- Experience being a victim of physical or psychological abuse (consistently one of the strongest predictors of perpetration)

Micro-level Relationship Factors

- Marital conflict—fights, tension, and other struggles
- Marital instability—divorces and separations
- Dominance and control of the relationship by the male
- Economic stress
- Unhealthy family relationships and interactions

Macro-level Community Factors

- Poverty and associated factors such as overcrowding
- Low social capital—lack of institutions, relationships, and norms that shape the quality and quantity of a community's social interactions
- Weak community sanctions against intimate partner violence (such as unwillingness of neighbors to intervene when they witness violence)

Macro-level Societal Factors

- Traditional gender norms that suggest, for instance, women should be submissive or stay home and not enter the workforce

Source: Centers for Disease Control and Prevention, October 21, 2008

What Do You Think?

1. To what degree do the risk factors for victims and perpetrators differ, and why do they do so?
2. Do you think these risk factors differ among heterosexual and same-sex couples? Why or why not?

- *Violent resistance* is the non-legal term for self-defense. Research is scarce, but those who put up violent resistance are almost always women. It may indicate a woman will leave her abusive partner soon.
- *Mutual violent control* refers to a pattern of behavior in which both partners are controlling and violent and are battling for control.

This conceptualization reminds us that there are different motives, patterns, and consequences of intimate partner violence.

Stalking and Cyberstalking

As discussed in Chapter 4, stalking has received greater attention as a crime since California passed the first anti-stalking law in 1990. Stalking consists of obsessive contact or tracking of another person—attention that is unwanted and causes a reasonable person to be fearful. It touches the lives of 3.4 million adults annually (Baum, Catalano, Rand, & Rose, 2009). Stalking is a combination of many unwanted acts that, by themselves, are not abusive—such as sending flowers or gifts, calling on the telephone, or sending an e-mail—but when taken together, these acts constitute a form of mental abuse. Stalking exists on a continuum. It may be so subtle that the victim may not even be aware it is happening or, in contrast, the perpetrator may purposefully try to instill terror in the victim (Logan & Walker, 2009).

Given the importance of computers, cell phones, and e-mail in our lives, some stalkers harass or threaten their victims electronically, known as *cyberstalking*. Repeated unwanted attention could come in the form of e-mail, texts, bulletin boards, blogs, chat rooms, or other types of media (Stalking Resource Center, June 2009). One factor that distinguishes cyberstalking from other forms of stalking is ease; one can repeatedly threaten and harass a person by simply clicking a button on the computer. In fact, programs can be set up to send messages at random times when the sender is not even physically present at the computer. Although the contact may be indirect, it can be threatening nonetheless.

Consequences of Intimate Partner Violence

Intimate partner violence can have tragic results. In general, victims of repeated violence over time experience more serious consequences than victims of one-time incidents (Johnson & Leone, 2005). Minor forms of bruises, scratches, and welts are most common, but broken bones, severe bruising, or back pain are other consequences of violence.

Some consequences are not as visible, but just as real. The stress from intimate partner violence can wreak havoc on the immune and endocrine systems, causing conditions such as fibromyalgia, gynecological disorders, irritable bowel syndrome, or gastrointestinal problems (Centers for Disease Control and Prevention, 2009a; Leserman & Drossman, 2007). Because physical violence is typically accompanied by emotional or psychological abuse, many victims are depressed, have anxiety, have disturbed sleep, have low self-esteem, are socially isolated, and have thoughts of suicide (Afifi, MacMillan, Cox, Asmundson, Stein, & Sareen, 2009; Centers for Disease Control and Prevention, 2009a; Choudhary, Coben, & Bossarte, 2010). Victims of intimate partner violence are more likely to behave in unhealthy ways, such as engaging in high-risk sexual behavior (i.e., having unprotected sex or trading sex for food or money); using harmful substances (i.e., smoking cigarettes or using illicit drugs); or having unhealthy diet-related behaviors (i.e., binging and purging food).

Despite the clear need for mental health care, many women, especially minority women, often experience barriers to getting this care. Barriers include cultural or language differences, or lack of services and providers in poor or ethnic communities (Bryant-Davis, Chung, & Tillman, 2009; Rodriguez, Valentine, Son, & Muhammad, 2009; Weaver, 2009). Agencies specializing in the treatment of domestic violence and sexual assault victims face challenges that make it difficult to provide the full scope of services needed. They may have funding difficulties, tension between grassroots versus professional service providers, or a lack of comprehensive services (Macy, Giattina, Parish, & Crosby, 2010).

In addition to the consequences to the individual, there are also societal consequences. In other words, you and I are affected by intimate partner violence even if we do not know anyone who is a victim or perpetrator (which is highly unlikely). Victims lose nearly 8 million days of paid work a year, the equivalent of more than 32,000 full-time jobs. Costs affiliated with intimate partner violence exceed 8 billion dollars, most of which goes to medical and mental health care (Centers for Disease Control and Prevention, 2003; Max, Rice, Finkelstein, Bardwell, & Leadbetter, 2004).

Coping with Violence: Leaving and Staying

People often ask why some victims seem to stay in abusive situations. Most of the concern is aimed at women because they are generally thought to be more vulnerable than men: the violence is often more extreme, and they may be financially dependent or have children. Lenore Walker (1979, 1993) suggests that women stay in abusive relationships because of a condition called **learned helplessness**. Because of repeated verbal and physical assaults, these women have developed low self-esteem, and feel that they cannot control the abuse or the events around them. In essence, they have learned to feel helpless and they have difficulty envisioning a way out of their situation.

The truth is, however, that most women do not stay in abusive situations—at least not indefinitely. A longitudinal study conducted over two-and-a-half years revealed that three-quarters of battered women had left the relationship or the abuse in their relationships had ended (Campbell, Rose, Kub, & Nedd, 1998).

Leaving is often a *process* rather than a single event (Kim & Gray, 2008). It may be difficult for some women to gather the courage and resources to leave immediately. Recall the typology discussed by Johnson (Johnson, 2008, 2009). Men who engage in intimate terrorism use a wide range of control tactics that can cripple a victim's sense of command over her own life. What are some of these control tactics?

- *Blaming the victim:* "If you weren't so stupid, I wouldn't have to hit you." After hearing blaming comments often enough, some women begin to believe they must deserve the abuse and be unworthy of a positive, loving relationship.
- *Inducing shame:* Embarrassment and shame are common among abused women because they know many other women are not abused. They fear others will look down on them for provoking or tolerating abuse, or on their spouse/partner for being abusive. They may try to hide their bruises under makeup or clothing.
- *Lowering self-esteem:* "You're an idiot, and everybody thinks so. . . ." A victim's self-esteem can be eroded by repeated name calling, mind games, and emotional and physical bashing. She may begin to think of herself as not worthy of better treatment.
- *Creating financial dependency:* Some women are particularly vulnerable because they are financially dependent upon men. Perhaps they have children to support and lack specific job skills or recent employment experience. Some perpetrators foster this economic dependence by not allowing their partners to work, establish credit in their own name, or have their names on checking, savings, or other accounts.
- *Isolating the victim:* Whether initiated by the abuser as a control tactic or by the victim out of shame, isolation cuts off the abused from family and friends. The abused may cease going to church, work, or school, thereby without social support and no one to turn to for a "reality check."
- *Threatening retaliation:* Fear of retaliation keeps some victims in abusive relationships. The perpetrator may have threatened the woman, her children, or even her pets, and because he has been abusive before, the threats are real.
- *Exploiting love and hope:* Many abused women harbor fantasies that their abuser will miraculously change. They do not want the relationship to end, just the abuse. They

learned helplessness: The psychological condition of having low-self esteem, feeling helpless, and having no control that is caused by repeated abuse.

love their spouse/partner, and are told that if they just work harder in the relationship or external forces change, e.g., "If he can find a good job", the abuse will somehow stop.

- *Exploiting commitment to the relationship:* When we marry, we agree to take our partner "for better or worse, until death do us part." Although we take these vows seriously, most people would leave an out for domestic violence. Some people believe, however, that they must endure their marriage regardless of the costs. An abuser can exploit this commitment, e.g., "You can't leave; you promised you would stay."
- *Creating fear of abandonment:* Many people are afraid of being without a spouse or partner. They have low self-esteem, and are unsure whether they can live alone and take care of themselves. Women have been socialized to derive much of their social status through their affiliations with men.

These factors can contribute to **Battered Women's Syndrome,** a now recognized psychological condition to describe someone who has been the victim of consistent and/or severe domestic violence. It is often considered a subcategory of post-traumatic stress syndrome, and can be measured and treated by a trained mental health professional.

Violence in Gay and Lesbian Relationships

Until recently, we knew little about intimate partner violence among same-sex couples, probably for the same reason that we knew little about their relationships in general—the focus of study tends to be on majority groups, e.g., heterosexuals (Kaschak, 2002; Ristock, 2009). A book about intimate partner violence published as recently as 2001, *Couples in Conflict*, (Booth, Crouter, & Clements, 2001) includes 17 chapters on recognizing and responding to domestic violence, but does not include any chapters specifically on violence in same-sex couples. Despite this omission, the rate of abuse in gay and lesbian relationships is similar to or even higher than that in heterosexual relationships, around 25 to 30 percent (Aardvarc.org, 2008; Burke, Jordan, & Owen, 2002). Like heterosexual couples, violence is usually not a single event, but represents a pattern in the relationship. Same-sex couples are not immune to violence, abuse, jealousy, or struggles over power and control.

Some people may dismiss intimate partner violence among gay men or lesbians as less serious—"Come on, shouldn't men be able to defend themselves from one another?" "How much harm can two women do?" "Why doesn't he just leave—what's stopping him?" (Cruz, 2003; Ristock, 2009). However, the violence that same-sex couples inflict can be substantial and no less serious than the violence inflicted by abusive heterosexual men or women on their partners. One study found 79 percent of gay male victims had suffered some physical injury, with 60 percent reporting bruises, 23 percent reporting head injuries and concussions, 13 percent reporting forced sex with the intention to infect the victim with HIV, 12 percent reporting broken bones, and 10 percent reporting burns (Merrill & Wolfe, 2000). Thus, the issue of intimate partner violence deserves the same attention in same-sex relationships as it does in heterosexual ones.

Dating Violence

We think that forming relationships is about having fun, exploring your own identity, and getting to know someone else. At first glance, dating seems like the last place for violence to occur. Yet, young women ages 16–24 experience high rates of relationship violence (Manganello, 2008). One in five teenagers in a serious relationship reports having been hit, slapped, or pushed by a partner, with young women reporting these incidents ten times more often than young men (National Center for Victims of Crime,

Battered Women's Syndrome: A recognized psychological condition, often a subcategory of post-traumatic stress syndrome, used to describe someone who has been the victim of consistent and/or severe domestic violence.

Our culture fails to openly acknowledge the fact that young women between the ages of 16 and 24 face the highest rates of intimate partner violence.

My Family

"My Dating Violence Story"

In the following story, "Alicia" describes the pressure she felt to have a sexual relationship before she was ready. You will note that the ending could go a number of different ways.

We met in chemistry, 4th period. He was one of the cutest boys in school and a star on our soccer team. Although he seemed pretty shy to our classmates, he would talk hours on end to me. He made me feel special and I began to feel very strongly towards him. One night we were in my parents' basement watching his favorite television show. We started French kissing and I felt so pretty and wanted. He leaned me back on the couch and put his hand up my skirt. I wasn't too sure I wanted to go further since we had only been dating for two weeks. I told him I wasn't ready and he got up and stormed out.

I was concerned I had done something wrong so I called him on his cell phone a few moments later. He didn't pick up. Later that night my cell phone rang and I rushed to it, hoping it was him. It was. He said that I act like a baby and that real women have sex. He called me a tease and told me that if I wanted to be his girl that I would have to have sex with him. My eyes started to fill with tears. I knew I wasn't ready.

When I first started high school I made a vow to myself that I'd wait until I was in a long-term committed monogamous relationship with someone whom I loved before I started having sex. But now I'm starting to question myself, and it makes me feel confused. I tell him that I'm scared and he calls me a 'slut' for having him in my house when my parents weren't home. He says that I probably have all kinds of guys down there "just to tease them and kick them out." But I didn't kick him out, he just left! I'm starting to get really confused because just yesterday he was telling me how pretty and special I was. Now he's calling me names? What did I do to deserve this?

Maybe I should have just had sex with him. Maybe he is right. I tell him I have to go and I'll see him in school tomorrow. He asks me if he can come over again tomorrow and I say . . .

The story described above can end in many different ways depending upon whether or not this young woman knows she has a right to say and do what she wants.

He asks me if he can come over tomorrow and I say, "You said very nasty and untrue things about me because you were upset that I told you I wasn't ready. I do not want to be mistreated by someone I like and if you don't have enough respect for me to understand my decision to not have sex then I would rather we just be 'friends'." He hung up the phone and we never spoke again. But I was okay with that. Four months later I met a boy at summer camp, who is supportive and willing to wait until I am ready. I am glad I decided to do better for myself.

Source: Advocates for Youth. 2009. "The Facts: Adolescent Childbearing and Educational and Economic Attainment, 2009." Retrieved 1 December 2009. (www.advocatesforyouth. org/PUBLICATIONS/factsheet/fsadlchd.htm).

What Do You Think?

1. Have you, or someone you know well, been in a similar situation? Did that story end differently or in a similar fashion? How do you think most of these stories end?

2. Have the pressures put on women to be sexual changed over the last few generations? Do you think women in your parents' generation felt these same pressures? Why or why not?

2007). About one-third of unmarried adults under age 30 have experienced or used physical violence in a dating relationship in the past 12 months. Others are victims of sexual assault, or feel pushed into a sexual relationship before they are ready, as found in Alicia's dating violence story in the *My Family* feature box.

Many young women do not report violence to their parents, police, or other authority figures. They may be embarrassed, fear their parents' reaction, or worry that their partner will retaliate if they tell someone. Some women are overly dependent on their partners and fear they may never meet anyone else again (Few & Rosen, 2005).

Watch on **myfamilylab.com**

Watch the **Video**
Sexual Violence Billboards on
myfamilylab.com

Rape and Sexual Assault

Sexual assault is the type of intimate violence least likely to be reported; in fact, it is the most underreported violent crime in the United States (Tjaden & Thoennes, 2006). It is difficult to know precisely what percentage of rapes and sexual assaults go unreported to the police, but it has been estimated at about 60 percent (Rennison, 2003). A survey based on a nationally representative sample of nearly 10,000 adults found that 11 percent of women and 2 percent of men said that they had experienced forced sex at least once at some point in their lives (Basile, Chen, Lynberg, & Saltzman, 2007). Most victims knew their attackers. According to the women surveyed, 30 percent of perpetrators were intimate partners, 24 percent were family members, and 20 percent were acquaintances. Among the men surveyed, 32 percent of perpetrators were acquaintances, 18 percent were family members, 18 percent were friends, and 16 percent were intimate partners.

Rape on College Campuses   College students are particularly vulnerable to rape and sexual assault. A study by the U.S. Department of Justice reveals that 3 percent of college women are raped in a given 9-month academic year. While that might not sound like a lot of women when you first read the number, let's examine this figure. For a campus with 10,000 women, it means 350 rapes over the 9-month period, or about 500 per year. Over a typical 5-year college career, that equals 2,500 rapes for those 10,000 women (Fisher, Cullen, & Turner, 2000). Another way of presenting this statistic: between 20 and 25 percent of college women have been raped at least once while at college (Centers for Disease Control and Prevention, 2008b).

Who is being raped, and who is doing the raping? Among college students, about 80 percent of victims and perpetrators know each other; they are intimate partners, "friends," roommates, acquaintances, and classmates. Women are raped by their study partner on the way to the library, by the guy they just met at the party in the dorm, by their roommate's brother, or even by their partner.

The work of Mary Koss and her colleagues (Koss & Cook, 1993; Koss, Gidyzc, & Wisniewski, 1987) sheds interesting light on college-age perpetrators. In a survey of 32 college campuses, she found that while 12 percent of men had committed acts that would fit the legal definition of rape or attempted rape, only 1 percent thought their actions were criminal. Many made a distinction between "forcing a girl to have sex" and "rape," as though they are different, but the law, of course, makes no such distinction.

In another study, 521 college students completed a personality inventory and survey about sexual behavior, including whether they have committed rape or sexual assault (includes unwanted sexual behavior other than rape). The researchers found that those men who had committed sexual assault (but not rape) had remarkably comparable personality profiles to nonperpetrators (Voller & Long, 2010). There was little or no difference in personality traits like agreeableness, conscientiousness, extraversion, warmth, excitement-seeking, altruism, competence, tenderness or vulnerability. Men who rape, in contrast, had considerably different personality profiles in most of these areas. In other words, sexual assault perpetrators were more similar to nonperpetrators than to those who rape.

"Date Rape" Drugs   Alcohol or drugs are sometimes involved in a sexual assault (Roudsan, Leahy, & Walters, 2009). **Date rape drugs** such as gamma hydroxybutyrate (GHB), Rohypnol (popularly known as "roofies" or "roofenol"), or ketamine hydrochloride (Ketamine) can immobilize a person to facilitate an assault (U.S. Department of Health & Human Services, Office of Women's Health, 2008). The effects of these drugs cause people to be physically helpless, lose muscle control, feel very drunk, or lose consciousness. Victims of these drugs often cannot remember what happened. The drugs usually have no color, smell, or taste and can be easily

date rape drugs: Drugs such as gamma hydroxybutyrate (GHB), Rohypnol (popularly known as "roofies" or "roofenol"), or ketamine hydrochloride (Ketamine) that are used to immobilize a person to facilitate an assault.

So-called "date rape" drugs can immobilize a person by causing a lack of muscle control, a feeling of extreme intoxication, or a loss of consciousness.

added to flavored drinks without the victim's knowledge. How can you protect yourself from these drugs?

- Do not accept drinks from other people.
- Open containers yourself.
- Keep your drink with you at all times, even when you go to the bathroom.
- Do not share drinks.
- Do not drink from punch bowls or other large, common, open containers. They may already have drugs in them.
- Do not drink anything that tastes or smells strange. Sometimes GHB tastes salty.
- Have a non-drinking friend with you to make sure nothing happens.
- If you think that you have been drugged and raped:
  - Go to the police station or hospital right away.
  - Get a urine test as soon as possible. The drugs leave your system quickly. Rohypnol stays in the body for several hours and can be detected in the urine up to 72 hours after taking it. GHB leaves the body in 12 hours.
  - Do not urinate before getting help.
  - Do not douche, bathe, or change clothes before getting help. These things may give evidence of the rape.
  - Feelings of shame, guilt, fear, and shock are normal. You can call a crisis center or a hotline to talk with a counselor. One national hotline is the National Sexual Assault Hotline at 1-800-656-HOPE. (U.S. Department of Health & Human Services, Office of Women's Health, 2008).

What about a college environment makes rape and sexual assault so prevalent? What do you think is happening at your college? What can or should be done about it?

:: Child Abuse and Neglect

Child abuse is an attack on a child that results in an injury and violates our social norms. Nearly 800,000 children are determined to be victims of abuse or neglect each year (U.S. Department of Health & Human Services, Administration on Children, Youth, and Families, 2010). Tables 11.3 and 11.4 summarize information about these youngest victims of violence.

child abuse: An attack on a child that results in an injury and violates our social norms.

Table 11.3	The Most Common Types of Child Abuse (percent)
Neglect is by far the most common form of child abuse.	
Neglect	71%
Physical Abuse	16%
Sexual Abuse	9%
Other	9%
Psychological Maltreatment	7%
Medical Neglect	2%
Unknown or Missing	0%
Totals more than 100% because more than one category can be chosen.	

Source: U.S. Department of Health & Human Services, Administration on Children, Youth, & Families, 2010.

Table 11.4	Rate of Child Abuse by Race/Ethnicity per 1,000 Children
Black and American Indian children are most likely to be abused, whereas Asian American children are least likely.	
Black	16.6
American Indian/Alaska Native	13.9
Pacific Islander	11.6
Hispanic	9.8
White	8.6
Asian	2.4

Source: U.S. Department of Health & Human Services, Administration for Children & Families, 2010.

Children from birth to their first birthday have the highest rates of victimization: 22 per 1,000 children in that age group. Victims are slightly more likely to be female, and Blacks are overrepresented among abuse victims, given their size in the population. The most common type of maltreatment is neglect.

Over 1,700 children die as a result of abuse and neglect each year. More children under the age of four die from abuse and neglect than from falls, choking, drowning, fires, or motor vehicle accidents. Abuse occurs in all income, racial, religious, and ethnic groups, and in all types of communities (U.S. Department of Health & Human Services, Administration on Children, Youth and Families, 2010). ✳⊢**Explore** on **myfamilylab.com**

✳⊢**Explore** the **Concept**
Social Explorer Map: Adolescent Violence and Social Conditions on **myfamilylab.com**

Types of Child Abuse

There are several different types of child abuse, most commonly:

- *Neglect*, the failure to provide for the child's basic needs, is the most common form. Neglect can be physical, such as failing to provide adequate food, clothing, shelter, a safe environment, or medical care to a dependent child. Emotional or psychological neglect occurs when a parent (or caretaker) fails to meet a child's most basic need for love and affection, by being chronically cold and distant, or by allowing a child to witness spousal abuse or some other dysfunctional behavior in the family. An extreme form of neglect is outright abandonment.

- *Physical abuse* such as hitting, shaking, burning, or kicking inflicts physical injury and harm upon a child. Among substantiated child abuse cases, about one-quarter included physical abuse. The most extreme cases may result in the death of a child. One study of abused children admitted to a pediatric intensive care unit found the most common causes of death were skull fracture and internal bleeding (Irazuzta, McJunkin, Danadian, Arnold, & Zhang, 1997).

- *Sexual abuse* is inappropriate sexual behavior with a child for sexual gratification. It can include fondling a child's genitals, making the child fondle the perpetrator's genitals, and progressing to more intrusive sexual acts such as oral sex and vaginal or anal penetration. Sexual abuse also includes acts such as exhibition, Internet child pornography, or other ways of exploiting the child for sexual purposes.

- *Psychological or emotional maltreatment* can be verbal, mental, or psychological abuse that destroys a child's self-esteem. It often includes threatening, degrading, or humiliating the child and using extreme or bizarre forms of punishment, such as being confined to a dark room or tied to a chair for long periods of time. Emotional abuse probably occurs far more frequently than can be substantiated.

And as you might expect, often multiple forms of abuse occur simultaneously, as shown in Table 11.3.

Corporal Punishment

"I hit my 6-year-old daughter because she refused to eat her peas at dinner."

Is this child abuse? Does it matter whether the parent uses an open hand, a fist, or an object? Does it matter whether the blow leaves a welt? Does the reason for hitting the child make a difference? How about his or her age? Does it matter where the child was hit, or how often? What if we use the term "spank" instead of "hit"?

Not all forms of child abuse are clear-cut and obvious. For example, as discussed in Chapter 8, most adults believe it is appropriate to use corporal punishment on children. Surveys generally find about half to two-thirds of parents report having slapped or spanked a child, about a third have pushed, shoved, or grabbed a child, 10 percent have hit a child with an object, and 3 percent threw something at a child during the preceding 12 months (Straus & Donnelly, 2001; Vandivere, Tout, Capizzano, & Zaslow, 2003). Mothers are more likely to spank their children than are fathers, boys are more likely to be spanked than girls, and Black women are more likely to support spanking as a disciplinary technique than are White or Hispanic women.

Why Do Research?

What Do We Make of the Link Between Spanking and Children's IQ?

Family violence research pioneer Murray Straus is at it again. For over thirty years he has taught us about intimate partner violence and child abuse, and much of what we know today comes from his work. One of Dr. Straus's research interests is corporal punishment—spanking. He sees it as an insidious form of violence, one that most of us ignore, but that causes great harm to the spanked individual and the society at large that condones this type of violence. His continued research has unearthed a startling new discovery: children who are spanked have lower IQs than those who are not. Moreover, the difference is large enough to lower national IQ scores in countries where corporal punishment of children is routine.

This landmark study first examined the relationship between spanking and IQ in the United States, and then turned to see what the relationship looks like on a national basis. First, Dr. Straus and his colleague, Dr. Mallie Paschall, studied a nationally representative sample of 806 children in the United States ages 2 to 4 years, and a second representative sample of 704 children ages 5 to 9 years. Both groups were tested once and then retested four years later in a longitudinal research design. They found that the IQs of children ages 2 to 4 who were not spanked were five points higher four years later than the IQs of those children who were spanked. Likewise, the IQs of children ages 5 to 9 who were not spanked were nearly three points higher four years later than other children their age who were spanked. They also found that the more times a child was spanked, the more his or her IQ was affected. "How often parents spanked made a difference. The more spanking, the slower is the development of the child's mental ability. But even small amounts of spanking made a difference," Dr. Straus said.

Next, the researchers examined secondary data obtained from the International Dating Violence Study, which involved 17,404 college students at 68 universities in 32 countries. The study included two items about spanking, and respondents could "strongly disagree," "disagree," "agree," or "strongly agree" with each one:

- I was spanked or hit a lot by my parents before age 12.
- When I was a teenager, I was hit a lot by my mother or father.

The researchers used the percentage of students who "agreed" or "strongly agreed" to estimate the corporal punishment rate in each country. They then compared those rates to the national average IQ, while controlling for many important variables such as mother's education level or socioeconomic status. This statistical technique allows researchers to make sure that any differences are likely to be due to IQ, rather than the fact that some countries are poorer than others or that mothers in some countries may have lower educational levels than others.

The analysis showed that the countries with higher corporal punishment rates also had students with lower average IQs. The strongest association between spanking and IQ was found among those students whose parents continued to spank them into their teenage years. Why is this? First, Straus and Paschall speculate that corporal punishment is extremely stressful, even exhibiting similarities to post-traumatic stress symptoms, and these symptoms are associated with lower IQ. Second, a higher national level of economic development underlies both fewer parents using corporal punishment and a higher national IQ.

The researchers are glad to see a movement away from corporal punishment throughout the world, and hope that it may signal future gains in IQ scores. Twenty-four countries have banned corporal punishment, and there is evidence that attitudes favoring corporal punishment and actual use of corporal punishment have been declining even in nations that have not implemented the ban.

However, some researchers question the causal link that Straus and Paschall purport. For example, perhaps the relationship is spurious, meaning that there is another issue going on that may affect both corporal punishment and IQ. For example, average education levels are rising, and better-educated parents use less corporal punishment and are more likely to engage in activities to increase children's IQ, such as reading to them regularly.

At this point, we do not have all the answers, but Straus, once again, brings to light the downside of personal violence.

Sources: Kelly, 2009; Straus & Paschall, 2009.

What Do You Think?

1. Given what you have learned, what do you see as the pros and cons of spanking?
2. Why do you think that the United States is not among the countries that have banned spanking? What cultural norms are operating?

Figure 11.5 — Perpetrator's Relationship to the Victim

Parents are the most common abusers of children.

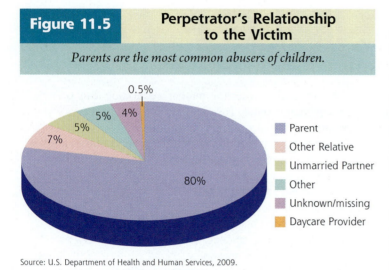

- Parent — 80%
- Other Relative — 7%
- Unmarried Partner — 5%
- Other — 5%
- Unknown/missing — 4%
- Daycare Provider — 0.5%

Source: U.S. Department of Health and Human Services, 2009.

Murray Straus, the pioneering domestic violence researcher introduced previously, argues that corporal punishment is detrimental to children, teaches them violent and abusive behavior, and legitimizes other forms of violence (Straus & Paschall, 2009; Straus, 2003). For example, being hit as a child is correlated with the frequency and intensity of their acting out (Polaha, Larzelere, Shapiro, & Pettit, 2004; Turner & Muller, 2004). Interestingly, it is also linked to a lower IQ in children, as shown in the feature box *Why Do Research? What Do We Make of the Link between Spanking and Children's IQ?*

Children who are spanked are also more likely to suffer from depression (Christie-Mizell, Pryor, & Grossman, 2008). Adults who were hit as adolescents are more likely to hit their spouses and physically assault someone outside the family (Busby, Holman, & Walker, 2008). Even Dr. Phil, the famous sex and family advisor, opposes spanking (Dr. Phil.com, 2009), but not all parents agree with him.

Who Would Abuse Children?

Neglect, physical abuse, and sexual abuse are more clear-cut. Most people who abuse children are not strangers, but are family members—80 percent as shown in Figure 11.5 (U.S. Department of Health & Human Services, Administration on Children, Youth and Families, 2009). Why would someone who supposedly loves a child abuse that child? It is easy to attribute child abuse to mental disorder, but fewer than 10 percent of abusers suffer from mental illness.

People of all ages can abuse children; however, young parents are more likely to engage in abusive behaviors, in part because they have less knowledge about child development, unrealistic expectations about parenthood, and little preparation for its demands. It is fairly easy to have unrealistic expectations about parenthood and children. Parenting is hard work!

Single parents are also more likely to abuse their children than are married parents. Blacks are more likely to abuse their children than are Whites, Hispanics, or Asians. Parents who earn less than $15,000 per year are 12–16 times more likely to physically abuse their children, 18 times more likely to sexually abuse them, and 44 times more likely to neglect them (Sedlak & Broadhurst, 1998; U.S. Department of Health & Human Services, Administration on Children, Youth and Families, 2010). The most common explanation is that low-income parents are under much stress and have lower levels of education, inadequate support systems, and higher rates of substance abuse. They are also more likely to be young and unmarried—other factors associated with child abuse.

Consequences of Child Abuse

Abuse leaves approximately 18,000 children permanently disabled each year. Health consequences that continue into adulthood for many victims include increased rates of gynecological problems, migraine headaches, digestive problems, asthma, and a host of other disorders (Child Welfare Information Gateway, 2004; Perry, 2002).

More insidious are the long-term emotional scars left behind (Walsh, Dawson, & Mattingly, 2010; Maas, Herrenkohl, & Sousa, 2008). Abuse is trauma. For example, physically abused children tend to be more aggressive, more likely to get involved in delinquent activities, have difficulty in school, be involved in early sexual activity, and be associated with teen pregnancy. This does not mean, however, that all physically abused children have these outcomes. One study reviewed the findings of 21 published reports on child abuse

Child abuse can take many forms: neglect, physical, sexual, psychological, and emotional abuse. Most abusers are family members.

to note any trends in children's behavior. They found that the number of abused children having difficulty in educational, behavioral, or emotional domains varied greatly, and a child may do poorly in one domain, but excel in another. About one in five abused children had difficulty and functioned poorly in all domains (Walsh, Dawson, & Mattingly, 2010). The emotional trauma can be long-lasting. Even as adults, children who have been abused are more likely to suffer nightmares, depression, panic disorders, and have suicidal thoughts (Hyman, 2000). It can also affect their relationship with their own children, increasing the likelihood of poor attachment, neglect, and abuse (Briere & Jordan, 2009).

Trafficking

Perhaps the most extreme form of child abuse is **trafficking**, which the United Nations defines as

> "the recruitment, transportation, transfer, harboring, or receipt of persons, by means of threat or use of force or other forms of coercion, of abduction, of fraud or deception, of the abuse of power or of a position of vulnerability or of the giving or receiving of payments to achieve the consent of a person having control over another person, for the purpose of exploitation. Exploitation includes, at the minimum, the exploitation or the prostitution of others or other forms of sexual exploitation, forced labor or services, slavery, servitude, or the removal of organs" (United Nations, April 2006; Seelke & Siskin, 2008).

Trafficking victims can be girls, boys, women, and men, who are forced to work as housekeepers, prostitutes, in the fields, forced into marriage, or recruited into arms groups (United Nations Children's Fund, November 2009). The United Nations estimates that there are at least 12 million adults and children in forced labor or sexual servitude at any given time (U.S. Department of State, 2009). The best-selling book by Ishmael Beah, *A Long Way Gone: Memoirs of a Boy Soldier* (2007), reveals the horrors of child soldiers in Africa and other places. Separated from his family by violence, Ishmael was forced at age 13 to fight in a civil war in Sierra Leone. Injected with drugs from the government's troops, he recalls killing too many people to even count. His story is about tragedy, survival, and forgiveness.

Sex Trafficking   Rania, in contrast, never wrote a book, but her story was discovered nonetheless. Years ago as a young Moroccan, she signed a contract that she could not read and set off to work as a cleaner in Cyprus. But when she arrived, a man told her that she was going to work in a cabaret, drink with the customers, and have sex with them when they wanted it. She refused and begged to be sent home, but she was told that she must repay her travel expenses. Rania was raped. She knew that if she returned home her strict Muslim brother would kill her for "having sex before marriage" and damaging her family's reputation. When she finally was able to flee, social workers took her to a government shelter for victims of sexual exploitation. While police investigated her case, she stayed in Cyprus and finally got her job as a cleaner (U.S. Department of State, 2009).

Sexual abuse is rapidly increasing in developing nations, and many girls and women (and sometimes boys as well) become victims of **sex trafficking** (Farr, 2005; Kristof & WuDunn, 2009). As many as 1.4 million a year are coerced, kidnapped, sold, or otherwise enslaved and trafficked across international borders for use as involuntary sex workers (U.S. Department of State, 2009).

The trafficking of children results from a broad range of factors. Increasing poverty, inequality, and economic crises of the last few decades in many countries have brought tremendous stress to families. When these stressors are coupled with patriarchal norms in which women and girls are disvalued, some families sell their daughters to traffickers or put them in vulnerable positions as domestic workers in far-off urban locations. Moreover, globalization has

trafficking: The recruitment, transportation, transfer, harboring, or receipt of persons, by means of threat or use of force or other forms of coercion, of abduction, of fraud or deception, of the abuse of power or of a position of vulnerability, or of the giving or receiving of payments to achieve the consent of a person having control over another person, for the purpose of exploitation.

sex trafficking: An industry in which children are coerced, kidnapped, sold, or deceived into sexual encounters.

As many as 1.4 million girls, women, and boys are bought and sold every year across international borders for sexual purposes. Some are sold into prostitution by their parents or other relatives; others are tricked into thinking that they are leaving home for a good job. Macro-level factors such as poverty, patriarchal norms, and economic opportunities (or the lack thereof) contribute to sex trafficking.

triggered an influx of money and goods, further aggravating disparities between rich and poor, and promoting new levels of consumerism. Around the world, girls are sought out in the mistaken belief that they are unlikely to be HIV-positive.

Children who are trafficked into prostitution face many dangers (U.S. Department of State, 2009). In addition to injuries and disease associated with multiple sexual encounters, they become dangerously attached to pimps and brothel operators and financially indebted to them. Moreover, they may become addicted to drugs given to subdue them. If the children do manage to escape and return to their families, they may be rejected because of the stigma associated with prostitution.

*H*ow do the theories introduced in Chapter 1 inform your thinking about sex trafficking? Compare and contrast these theoretical perspectives.

:: Elder Abuse

Abuse can happen at any age. Agnes, 85 years old, has arthritis and heart disease. When she lost her husband last year, she moved in with her 50-year-old daughter, Emily, and her family. The situation is difficult for all of them. Sometimes Emily feels at the end of her rope, caring for her mother, worrying about her college-age son, and fearing for her husband, who is about to be forced into early retirement. Emily has caught herself calling her mother names and accusing Agnes of ruining her life. Recently, she lost her temper and slapped her mother (American Psychological Association, 2010).

What constitutes **elder abuse**? Generally accepted definitions include (1) *physical abuse,* the willful infliction of physical pain or injury, such as slapping or bruising; (2) *sexual abuse,* the infliction of non-consensual sexual contact of any kind; (3) *psychological or emotional abuse,* the infliction of mental or emotional anguish such as humiliating, intimidating, or threatening; (4) *financial or material exploitation,* the improper use of an older person's resources without his or her consent for someone else's benefit; and (5) *caregiver neglect,* the failure of a caregiver to provide goods or services necessary to avoid harm or mental anguish, such as abandonment or delay or denial of food, water, or needed medical services (Hildreth, Burke, & Glass, 2009).

Given these various types of abuse, which is most common? A team of researchers set out to answer that question and compiled a representative sample of 5,777 elders across the country (Acierno, Hernandez, Amstadter, Resnick, Steve, Muzzy, & Kilpatrick, 2010). They found that the prevalence of abuse over the past year was 5.2 percent for financial abuse by a family member, 5.1 percent for neglect, 4.6 percent for emotional abuse, 1.6 percent for physical abuse, and 0.6 percent for sexual abuse. While these figures themselves are alarming, one in ten respondents reported emotional, physical, or sexual mistreatment or neglect in the past year. In other words, the data reveal that elder abuse is unfortunately quite common, and that financial abuse and neglect are the most common forms.

elder abuse: Abuse of an elderly person that can include physical abuse, sexual abuse, psychological abuse, financial or material exploitation, and neglect.

A survey of State Adult Protective Services (APS), which is a rigorous national data source, found 565,000 reported and substantiated cases of abuse among persons aged 60 and over (National Center on Elder Abuse, 2006). Ninety percent of these cases occurred in a domestic setting, not in an institution such as a nursing home or hospital. Reports of elder abuse to adult protective services are on the rise, climbing to 20 percent over recent years. Because only about one-quarter of abuse cases are reported and substantiated by adult protective service agencies, it is likely that the true extent of elders who are abused each year may even exceed 2 million (American Psychological Association, 2010).

*T*hinking about Agnes and her daughter Emily, discussed at the beginning of this section, would you say that this was an incident of elder abuse? If so, what type, and what should be done about it? Is this a personal problem or a social problem?

Many of these elders, like Agnes, are frail, vulnerable, and dependent upon others they trust for their physical and/or financial care (Centers for Disease Control and Prevention, 2009b). They may be physically limited or immobile, have mental or memory problems, or both. Abuse can also cause further health problems. One study of 842 women ages 60 and over who were capable of completing a telephone survey found abused women were significantly more likely to report more health conditions—including bone or joint problems, digestive problems, chronic pain, depression or anxiety, and high blood pressure—than women who had not been abused (Fisher & Regan, 2006).

As will be discussed more fully in Chapter 14, caring for an elderly person can be very difficult, particularly when he or she is mentally or physically impaired, when the caregiver is ill-prepared for the task, or when needed resources are lacking (Raschick & Ingersoll-Dayton, 2004; Lopez, Crespo, & Zarit, 2007). Caregiver stress and frustration sometimes lead to abuse or willful neglect. Abusers tend to have more personal problems than do non-abusers, such as mental and emotional disorders, alcoholism, drug addiction, and financial difficulty.

:: Explanations for Violence among Intimates

A quick survey of your classmates would probably indicate everyone abhors violence in family and intimate relationships. Then why is it so widespread in the United States and beyond? Two perspectives help us to explain violence among intimates. One focuses on micro-level individual causes, while the other examines macro-level societal and cultural factors that contribute to violence. In reality, both factors come into play to some degree.

Micro-Level Explanations

Focusing on the micro-level, two explanations for violence are often cited: (1) the intergenerational transmission of violence, and (2) the stress explanation.

intergenerational transmission of violence: A cycle of violence that is passed down to dependents.

The Intergenerational Transmission of Violence
The **intergenerational transmission of violence** perspective suggests that we learn norms and behaviors, including violence, by observing others. Our families of orientation are our primary source of early learning. Therefore, it makes sense that many adults who abuse their spouses, partners, or children learned this behavior in their own families. Perhaps they have witnessed abusive or violent behavior between their own parents, or perhaps they were abused as young children.

Researchers have found a tendency towards an intergenerational transmission of violence—that violence is a cycle *potentially* passed down to dependents (Busby, Holman, & Walker, 2008; Walker, Holman, & Busby, 2009; Briere & Jordan, 2009). For example, Heyman and Slep found that the frequency of violence experienced as a child in the home predicted adult abuse (2002). They also found that children who lived with two abusive adults were more likely to abuse than those who lived with only one.

Likewise, a study based on 45,000 responses to a web-based survey "Relationship Evaluation Questionnaire" (RELATE), found that 10 percent of couples without any reported violence in their family of orientation were violent in their current relationship, as compared to 32 percent of couples who reported that they had either witnessed or experienced violence in their home as children (Busby, Holman, & Walker, 2008). Although the sample is large, it is not based on a representative sample because people who completed RELATE may have been part of a class, workshop, or found the questionnaire on their own search of the Web. Nonetheless, it provides some degree of evidence of the intergenerational transmission of violence perspective.

However, it is also true that most people who witnessed or experienced abuse as children do *not* abuse others. An early study by Straus, Gelles, and Steinmetz reported a startling statistic—sons of the most violent parents are 1,000 times more likely to abuse their partners than the sons of nonviolent parents, but this also translates into a rate of 20 percent (Straus, Gelles, & Steinmetz, 1980). That means that 80 percent of those sons witnessing the most extreme forms of violence do *not* abuse their own wives and partners.

One micro-level explanation for violence among intimates suggests that we learn violent behavior by watching and imitating others, especially our families.

The RELATE study found that more than two-thirds of people who witnessed or experienced violence as children were not in an abusive relationship (Busby, Holman, & Walker, 2008). Therefore, it is very important to note that the intergenerational transmission of violence refers to a greater *likelihood* of engaging in violence, but not to determinism. Many persons who witnessed or experienced abuse as children grow up to be caring, supportive partners and parents without a hint of perpetuating domestic violence and abuse. Parents who are able to break the cycle of abuse realize that the abuse was wrong, perhaps through education, therapy, or a supportive partner, and they learn other ways to deal with their frustrations.

Stress Explanation   Violent families often contain inordinate amounts of stress or crises. These can include unemployment, poor health, or financial difficulties. Families that experience a great deal of stress are more likely to abuse their partners and their children. Early research by Murray Straus (1980) used the Holmes and Rahe stress scale with over 2,000 couples and assessed their level of violence using the Conflict Tactics Scale. He found that respondents who experienced none of the stresses in the Holmes and Rahe index had the lowest rate of violence. The likelihood of violence increased as the number of stresses experienced increased.

Alcohol and drug use can aggravate parental stress, decrease coping skills, and impair judgment. Sometimes specific traits of the child are associated with stress. For example, premature infants who require special care and who may cry harder and more frequently, have an increased risk of abuse.

Most often, families are expected to learn how to manage and effectively deal with the stressors on their own. Few families seek outside support such as counseling or working with community agencies in dealing with the problems they face. If a family cannot cope adequately with the stress or crisis, the tensions sometimes push them towards violence.

Macro-Level Explanations

The two theories just discussed—the intergenerational transmission of violence and the stress explanation—help us understand why some people are violent, but they do not place individual actions into their social context. Murray Straus, in his 1980 study just described, also said that stress by itself does not necessarily lead to violence. He suggested we need to look at social and cultural attitudes toward violence. Straus found that men who assaulted their partners were likely to believe that physical punishment of children and slapping a spouse were appropriate behaviors (Straus, 1980). Where do such attitudes come from?

At least three well-cited macro-level explanations are proposed for violence and abuse: (1) patriarchy; (2) cultural norms that support violence more generally; and (3) norms of family privacy.

Patriarchy   Violence is more likely to occur in cultures when men are considered dominant and have control over women and children. Anthropologist Peggy Sanday (1981) has written about sexual aggression around the world. She finds that rape is not universal and is absent in some cultures. Other cultures are more rape-prone, and they are ones in which women hold relatively low political and economic status, and that hold rigid gendered norms.

Can you think of examples of patriarchy in the United States that would condone and perpetuate intimate partner violence? Can you think of examples in developing countries that would condone and perpetuate violence? How are these examples similar or different?

In many cultures, violence against women actually has a wide degree of support. Using demographic and health surveys from seven countries—Armenia, Bangladesh, Cambodia, India, Kazakhstan, Nepal, and Turkey—one study estimated that the acceptance of "wife beating" ranged from a low of 29 percent in Nepal to a high of 57 percent in India (women only) and 56 percent in Turkey (men only) (Rani & Banu, 2009). In most of these countries, persons with lower incomes and education levels were more accepting of violence; however, so were younger persons. Many women supported "wife beating." The authors concluded that there is an intergenerational transmission of patriarchal norms that can influence both men and women's views (Rani & Banu, 2009).

Studies conducted in Palestine show similar results (Dhaher, Mikolajczyk, Maxwell, & Krämer, 2010; Haj-Yahia, 2010). One study interviewed 450 women living in three cities in the West Bank to assess their attitudes toward "wife beating." Overall, the women perceived violence against wives to be justified if a wife insults her husband (59 percent), if she disobeys her husband (49 percent), if she neglects her children (37 percent), if she goes out without telling her husband (25 percent), if she argues with her husband (11 percent), and if she burns the food (5 percent). Sixty-five percent of the women agreed with at least one reason for wife beating, and those with less education, who were employed, have more than one child, make few household decisions and were married less than ten years were most supportive overall (Dhaher, Mikolajczyk, Maxwell, & Krämer, 2010). Many Palestinian physicians also support moderate or severe violence against women, and one of the strongest predictors of their support of violence is their level of patriarchal attitudes (Haj-Yahia, 2010).

While Japan is a modern, developed nation, it is also one of the most patriarchal, and not surprisingly, also has high levels of violence against women (Nagae & Dancy, 2010). In-depth qualitative interviews with an admittedly small sample (11 women) indicate that physical, emotional, and even sexual abuse are systematic problems. Communication between spouses tended to be unilateral, with husbands dominating the conversation. The women identified the patriarchal society as a major contributor to violence (Nagae & Dancy, 2010).

One macro-level theory to explain violence among intimates examines a culture's tolerance for violence in general. Those cultures that promote and celebrate violence in sports may also have higher rates of violence among intimates.

But what is the prevalence of patriarchal attitudes in the United States? As you learned in Chapter 2, we also have vestiges of patriarchy. After all, not every American believes in equal rights, or that men and women should share the power and authority in intimate relationships or within society at large (Flood & Pease, 2009).

Cultural Norms Support Violence   A favorite American pastime is watching sports such as football, hockey, wrestling, or race car driving—all extremely violent activities, but considered fun and entertaining. If we shove, tackle, or drive fast in some contexts, we are applauded and may gain social prestige or financial rewards. In other contexts, however, we are punished if we act in any of these ways. Your professor cannot shove you because you failed to read the assigned material. You cannot drive 90 miles an hour down the street just because you may find it thrilling. The difficulty lies in the fact that sometimes the lines get blurred between what is and is not acceptable behavior. In the U.S. culture, some types of violence are extremely public, readily available on television, and are condoned by the culture.

Violence in the family is no exception because some dimensions of violence are also condoned by society. For example, most parents believe it is acceptable to hit their children when they are misbehaving, but where is the line between hitting and abuse? Not everyone agrees that a particular act is abusive. Because some forms of hitting are considered to be acceptable, it is unclear where the line is drawn. Therefore, it should not be surprising that some people, in the heat of passion, push the boundaries beyond "acceptable" limits. To avoid the distinction between acceptable and nonacceptable family violence, 19 countries fully prohibit hitting children, including countries as diverse as Sweden and Romania (Project NoSpank, 2007). The United Nations Committee on the Rights of Children has recommended that all countries prohibit spanking in the family and other social institutions (Vandivere, Tout, Capizzano, & Zaslow, 2003).

Norms of Family Privacy   We have all heard, "A man's home is his castle. . . ." "I didn't intervene because I knew they were married. . . ." "It's not really any of my business. . . ." suggesting that what goes on at home is a private affair. Families today are isolated like never before (Nock, 1998). Extended families are rare, and many families move hundreds or even thousands of miles away from their kin because of job or educational opportunities.

Figure 11.6	Power and Control Wheel

The Power and Control Wheel illustrates the methods by which batterers use power and control to abuse their victims.

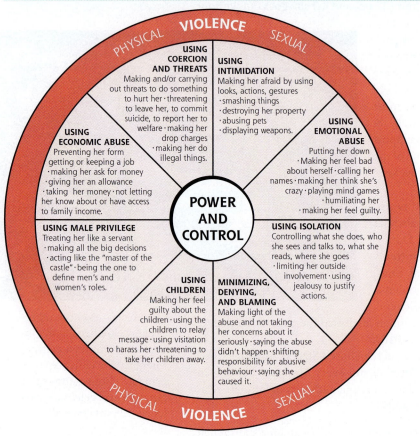

Source: Domestic Abuse Intervention Project, www.duluth-model.org.

We are not able to check in with one another as easily as we could have in the past.

Violence occurs in families that tend to be socially isolated (U.S. Department of Health & Human Services, Administration on Children, Youth and Families, 2009). Family members may have little contact with others, have few friends, and belong to few community organizations. Sometimes the isolation occurs first, and sometimes they isolate themselves afterwards to hide the abuse from others. These families lack social support to help them with their stress and anger and the challenges of raising children. Moreover, some people believe that violence is a private matter between family members, and are hesitant to intervene when they suspect violence. Who helped Shannon through her repeated ordeals with her boyfriend? Our norms regarding family privacy are very strong (Berardo, 1998).

A Synthesis: Power and Control

Although micro-level and macro-level explanations focus on different factors that contribute to violence, a focus on power and control synthesizes elements of both levels of analysis. This perspective, which admittedly describes perpetrators as men and victims as women, suggests that men who assault their partners are exerting their domination, power, and control over women (Vives-Cases, Gil-González, & Carasco-Portiño, 2009). Likewise, women who feel powerless within their relationships had higher rates of victimization (Filson, Ulloa, Runfola, & Hokoda, 2010). Batterers use threats and various forms of physical, sexual, and emotional abuse as a way to exert their dominance and gain control in a relationship, perhaps making up for inadequacies they feel in other domains. The "Power and Control Wheel" in Figure 11.6 depicts behaviors and privileges that batterers use to dominate and control their partners and/or children.

If you look closely at the Power and Control Wheel you can see a heterosexual bias—it reflects the power imbalances in male-female relationships, while ignoring the social and political context experienced by lesbians, gays, transgender persons, and bisexuals (LGTBs), such as homophobia or HIV-related abuse. Figure 11.7 illustrates a Power and Control Wheel that may more adequately reflect the realities for those who are not heterosexual (New York City Gay & Lesbian Anti-Violence Project, 2003).

:: The Public's Response

Longstanding cultural attitudes, inadequate enforcement by law enforcement officials, and traditional ideas about sex and gender contribute to the public's uncertainty as to the causes and consequences of violence, and what should be done about it (Mildorf, 2007). Let's look at a few public responses to violence.

Violence and the Law

Child advocates, feminists, family scholars, international human rights workers, and others have drawn attention to violence and abuse within families and intimate relationships.

| **Figure 11.7** | **Power and Control Wheel in Lesbian, Gay, Transgender, and Bisexual (LGTB) Relationships** |

Power and control may operate somewhat differently in LGTB couples; there are additional ways perpetrators may try to control and intimidate their victims.

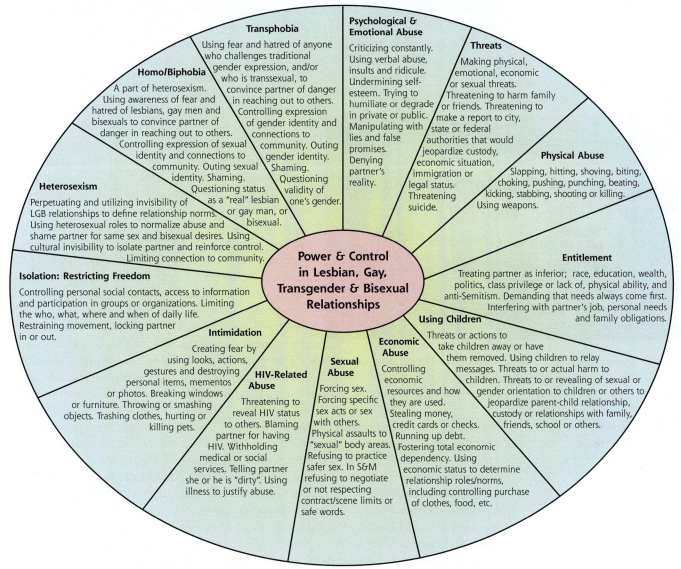

Power and Control Wheel in Lesbian, Gay, Transgender, and Bisexual (LGTB) Relationships from Building Safer Communities for Lesbian, Gay, Transgender, Bisexual and HIV-Affected New Yorkers, 2003 New York City Gay & Lesbian Anti-Violence Project.

They advocate for change, including stricter penalties for abusers. Violence was long ignored by legislators and law enforcement officers in the United States, as it continues to be in many parts of the world. For example, until the 1990s some states did not recognize spousal rape as a crime. Today, spousal rape is a crime in all fifty states and the District of Columbia, although differences in the treatment of spousal rape from that of non-spousal rape still remain, including more stringent reporting requirements or the requirement that the offender used force or threat of force.

There have been other recent legal gains as well, such as anti-stalking laws or the enforcement of restraining orders. Law enforcement officers now receive more training in how to deal with violence among intimates than they did in the past. They are trained to understand the law, but also to understand the dangers, family dynamics, the needs of victims, and resources in the community that could help.

Domestic Violence Shelters

When fleeing an abusive situation, where can an abused person go? Some people have family or friends who can provide emotional support and temporary shelter. Others do not; to whom can they turn?

Kate is one of the "lucky" victims of intimate violence, enduring "only" weekend battering for years. The final straw was when her boyfriend attempted to set her house on fire one night after a particularly brutal argument; Kate and her two children could have perished. Instead, they smelled smoke, got out of the house just in time, and fled to her sister's house. Kate has many siblings, all of whom live close by, and they are protective of her and her children. They saw to it that her family had a safe place to stay, food to eat, and the necessary things to leave her boyfriend once and for all (Seccombe, 2011).

Violence among intimates is against the law, and there are growing numbers of laws, policies, and programs to help victims and their families.

In contrast to Kate, Molly had no one to turn to in her time of need. She lived in an isolated, rural, mountainous area of West Virginia with her husband and three young sons, thirty miles from the nearest town. Molly's husband deliberately kept her isolated from family and friends. She could not work or leave the house without his permission, and he put a block on the telephone. He had been abusive to her for years, but when he began battering their oldest son who was only six years old, Molly knew she had to leave with her children.

But where could Molly and her sons go? She had heard about a domestic violence shelter in a distant community. One night, as her husband slept, Molly woke the boys, dressed them in multiple layers of clothing (since she knew that suitcases would be impossible to carry), and began the long trek down the mountain in the middle of the night. She rested briefly when her children were tired, then prodded them on again. Finally, she hitched a ride to the shelter from someone driving by in a pickup truck. The shelter was a lifesaver to Molly and her boys, but nonetheless, they lost everything they had ever owned (Seccombe, 2011).

A **domestic violence shelter**, sometimes called a "battered women's shelter," is a temporary safe house for women (with or without children) who are escaping an abusive relationship. Shelters began in the 1970s as a result of two critical forces: (1) the research pointing to the high numbers of women who were victims of violence and locked in relationships with their batterer, and (2) the resurgence of the women's movement that saw rape and battering as political and social issues. Shelter programs are premised on the idea that no one deserves to be beaten, and that battered women and their children need special resources to end the violence in their lives. They generally provide 24-hour hotlines, crisis intervention, and a place to stay on a temporary basis—a night, a week, or even months, depending on the demand for and supply of space. They may also offer legal advice, employment and job training assistance, and longer-term counseling. Unfortunately, shelters often face chronic funding challenges that limit their level of services (Macy, Giattina, Parish, & Crosby, 2010).

Treatment Programs for Abusers

Men and women who abuse others come from all walks of life. Intimate partner abusers tend to seek control of the thoughts, beliefs, and conduct of their partner, and punish their partner for resisting that control. They tend to minimize the seriousness of their violence, act impulsively, distrust others, control people and situations, and express feelings as anger. "If only you acted differently I wouldn't have had to hit you," "You made me do it," "I can't control it," "You just bruise easily," "I'll never do it again," the batterer might repeatedly say to his victim. Intervention and treatment must get to the root cause of the battering, rather than just the symptoms (Alabama Coalition Against Domestic Violence, 2008).

Abusers can enter a treatment program voluntarily or be court-ordered to do so. There is no guarantee that the program will be successful, but most programs generally try to teach the

domestic violence shelter: A temporary safe house for a woman (with or without children) who is escaping an abusive relationship.

abuser to be aware of his pattern of violence and to learn techniques for using nonviolent behavior such as relaxation techniques, exercise, or "time outs." One challenge of teaching anger management is that many abusers are actually quite good at managing their anger—they know not to explode in public, they know where not to leave bruises, and they know what to say afterwards so that their partner will not leave them. Treatment programs might also include issues such as education about domestic violence, changing attitudes and beliefs about using violence in a relationship, and achieving equality in relationships. However, this too can be challenging because long-held beliefs cannot be quickly or easily changed.

In the case of child abuse, intervention is first and foremost designed to protect the victims and then, to assist and strengthen families. Child welfare agencies, health care workers, counselors, educators, legal counsel, and other professionals may be called upon to provide counseling, temporary foster care, education programs, and family assessments. Children may be removed from the home and placed in temporary foster care. If a relative is available, the child may be released to their care.

Depending upon the severity of the abuse and the court's decision, the parent may be arrested, incarcerated, or asked to complete a parent education class. A parent may be allowed only supervised visits over a period of time, or none at all. Unfortunately, many government agencies who deal with child abuse are overburdened with high caseloads and few resources to adequately do their work. It is a difficult job, and given the concern that we express over child abuse, one cannot help but wonder why prevention, intervention, and treatment are not better funded.

Why do you think that domestic abuse shelters in the United States only serve women and their children, but not men?

Bringing It Full Circle

The focus on this chapter has been family stressors and crises, particularly highlighting the ways that they are rooted in macro-level social arrangements. To understand the causes and the consequences of these stressors, we must move beyond seeing them as only individual micro-level experiences. We need to see the connection between our personal experiences and the larger macro-level structural features of our society. In this chapter we have focused on one type of family crisis—violence among intimates, which is violence that occurs among family members and intimate partners—including spouses, nonmarital relationships, children, and the elderly. Shannon, from the opening vignette, experienced repeated intimate partner violence. As you recall, she eventually killed her attacker in self-defense. In reflecting upon what you have learned in this chapter, let's revisit Shannon's story to answer the following questions.

- In Shannon's situation, can you identify the A-factor—the event? The B-factor—the meaning assigned to the event? The C-factor—the resources available before, during, and after the event? What C-factors were absent?

- Of the four types of violence among intimates described in this chapter—common couple violence, intimate terrorism, violent resistance, and mutual violent control—which type do you think best describes Shannon's situation?

- What theory or theories do you think would be most helpful in explaining the violence that Shannon experienced?

For further review, turn to the Video Discussion Guide on page 449 to answer additional questions about how the chapter opening video relates to what you have learned in this chapter.

Chapter Review

11.1 What is the difference between family stress and family crisis?

Family stress includes tensions that test a family's emotional resources. They vary in type and degree, but are often a process rather than a single change of events. A crisis is a critical change of events that disrupts the functioning of a person's life. A crisis can be positive or negative, although we usually think of crises as negative.

11.2 What are the ABC-X and Double ABC-X models of coping with a family crisis?

The ABC-X model contains the stressor itself, resources available, and the perception of the stressors. The Double ABC-X model explains the effects of the accumulation of stresses and crises and how families adapt to them. The Double A Factor refers not only to the initial event, but also to family life changes and transitions that take place because of it. The Double B Factor includes both the resources the family already has and the new coping resources the family obtains because of the stress or crisis. The Double C factor takes into account the family's perception of the stressor itself, but also their perceptions of the aftermath.

11.3 What is intimate partner violence?

Intimate partner violence is the violence between those who are physically and sexually intimate, such as spouses or partners. The violence can encompass physical, economic, sexual, or psychological abuse. Many abusive situations include more than one type.

11.4 What is the Conflict Tactics Scale?

The Conflict Tactics Scale is an assessment tool that asks respondents how they deal with disagreements in intimate-partner relationships. It particularly focuses on violent behaviors.

11.5 What are the four different types of intimate partner violence?

To distinguish among types of violence, motives of perpetrators, social characteristics of both partners, and the cultural context in which violence occurs are considered. One typology describes common couple violence, intimate terrorism, violent resistance, and mutual violent control.

11.6 Why do people stay in abusive relationships?

Most do not stay in these relationships. Leaving is a process that does not occur all at once. It may be difficult for victims to find the courage or to orchestrate the logistics to leave the situation immediately.

11.7 How does violence in gay and lesbian relationships compare to violence in heterosexual ones?

There has been less attention paid to intimate partner violence among gay and lesbian couples, but the information we do have suggests that it is as common as, or more so, than among heterosexual couples.

11.8 How common is rape and sexual assault?

A national survey found that 11 percent of women and 2 percent of men said that they had experienced forced sex at least once at some point in their lives. Most victims knew their attackers. Rape and sexual assault are even more common among female college students.

11.9 What forms does child abuse take?

Child abuse is an attack on a child that results in an injury and violates our social norms. Child abuse takes many forms, including neglect, physical abuse, emotional maltreatment, and sexual abuse.

Key Terms

ABC-X Model (p. 306)
acute stress (p. 302)
Battered Women's
  Syndrome (p. 314)
child abuse (p. 317)
chronic stress (p. 302)
Conflict Tactics Scale (p. 308)

crisis (p. 302)
date rape drugs (p. 316)
domestic violence shelter (p. 328)
Double ABC-X Model (p. 307)
elder abuse (p. 322)
family stress (p. 302)
femicide (p. 310)

General Adaptation Syndrome
  (GAS) (p. 303)
intergenerational transmission
  of violence (p. 323)
intimate partner
  violence (p. 308)
learned helplessness (p. 313)

sex trafficking (p. 321)
Social Readjustment
  Rating Scale (p. 303)
trafficking (p. 321)

11.10 What are the consequences of child abuse?

Abuse leaves approximately 18,000 children permanently disabled each year. Health consequences that continue into adulthood for many victims can include increased rates of gynecological problems, migraine headaches, digestive problems, asthma, and a host of other disorders. Abuse is trauma, and can cause psychological and emotional problems as well, including aggression, delinquency, difficulty in school, and early sexual initiation.

11.11 What is trafficking and how common is it?

The United Nations defines trafficking as "the recruitment, transportation, transfer, harboring, or receipt of persons, by means of threat or use of force or other forms of coercion, of abduction, of fraud or deception, of the abuse of power or of a position of vulnerability or of the giving or receiving of payments to achieve the consent of a person having control over another person, for the purpose of exploitation. Exploitation includes, at the minimum, the exploitation or the prostitution of others or other forms of sexual exploitation, forced labor or services, slavery, servitude, or the removal of organs." The United Nations estimates that there are at least 12 million adults and children forced into labor or sexual servitude at any given time.

11.12 What are some types of elder abuse?

Elder abuse can include physical abuse, sexual abuse, psychological abuse, financial or material exploitation, or neglect, and affects the lives of about 2.1 million elderly each year.

11.13 What theories do researchers use to explain violence?

Researchers generally point to two lines of theoretical explanations. One focuses on macro-level factors, such as patriarchy, violent cultural norms, or norms of family privacy. Another explanation focuses on micro-level causes, including the intergenerational transmission of violence, or stress.

11.14 How has the public responded to violence among intimates?

In response to violence among intimates, new laws have been implemented, domestic violence shelters have been created, and treatment programs for abusers have been expanded to reduce violence.

PEARSON
myfamilylab
www.myfamilylab.com

Experience, Discover, Observe, Evaluate

MyFamilyLab is designed just for you. Each chapter features a pre-test and post-test to help you learn and review key concepts and terms. Experience Marriage and Family in action with dynamic visual activities, videos, and readings to enhance your learning experience.

Here are a few activities you will find for this chapter:

Explore Social Explorer is an interactive application that allows you to explore Census data through interactive maps. Explore the Social Explorer Map:

- Adolescent Violence and Social Conditions

Read MySocLibrary includes primary source readings from classic and contemporary sociologists. Read:

- Gelles, "Through a Sociological Lens: Social Structure and Family Violence"

Melanie visits her parents regularly, but her father will occasionally say unkind things about her mother, and visits with her mother can also be tense. For many years, Melanie's mantra was "I won't get divorced, I won't get divorced." Today she realizes that divorce sometimes happens, but she hopes that she will never put her own children through her experience.

If you are like many college students, you have seen divorce close up. Like Melanie, you may have watched your parents' marriage end, or perhaps you have experienced your own divorce or that of a sibling or friend. As family systems theory shows us, family relationships are interrelated, and therefore divorce requires that both children and adults in the family change their daily patterns, alter their dreams for the future, and start anew. When family relationships change, most people experience feelings of rejection, anger, hurt, betrayal, defeat, and fear. In this chapter, we will explore the process of divorce. Although a judge can grant a divorce decree in minutes, divorce is a long-term process that begins years before and often continues years after the official decree. ✳ Explore on **myfamilylab.com**

✳ **Explore** the **Concept**
Social Explorer Map: Divorce Rates Across the United States on
myfamilylab.com

:: Divorce in the United States

Divorce is a common occurrence in the United States. About one-third of people who have ever been married have also been divorced (Taylor, Funk, & Clark, 2007). In fact, the United States has one of the world's highest divorce rates—as Figure 12.1 shows, its rate is five times that of Mexico, twice that of China, and 40–50 percent higher than many other developed nations such as Japan or Germany. Only Russia's divorce rate is higher (United Nations Statistics Division, 2010).

Why do so many marriages in the United States end in divorce? This chapter will address this vital question. But first, let's see how social scientists measure divorce; some measurements are more useful than others.

How Common Is Divorce? It Depends on How We Measure It

We often hear that "half of all marriages end in divorce." But does this mean that half of all marriages that occurred last year ended in divorce? Of course not. Let's say that 100,000 couples married last year, and the courts granted 50,000 divorces. It appears like 50 percent of marriages ended in divorce. But this does not make sense because this percentage measures the number of weddings that took place in only one year, against the number of divorces among all weddings that have taken place over many years—10, 20, 30 years ago, or even longer.

What then is a better method of understanding the frequency of divorce? One method is to examine the rate of divorce per 1,000 people, which is called the **crude divorce rate**. In the United States in 2009, this rate was 3.4 divorces per 1,000 people, definitely not as sensational as the "50 percent" measure (Tejada-Vera & Sutton,

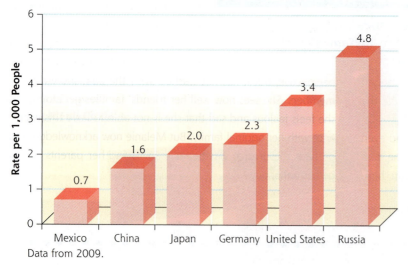

Figure 12.1 **Crude Divorce Rates per 1,000 Population for Selected Countries: 2007–2009**

The U.S. and Russia have the highest divorce rates in the world.

Country	Rate
Mexico	0.7
China	1.6
Japan	2.0
Germany	2.3
United States	3.4
Russia	4.8

Data from 2009.

Source: United Nations 2010.

crude divorce rate: The number of divorces per 1,000 people in the population.

2010). Since many different countries use this method, it makes international comparisons easier.

However, the crude divorce rate is problematic. Many people are not married, so why should they be included in a divorce statistic? In determining the divorce rate, it makes more sense to focus on how many *married* people get divorces. Therefore, another method of measuring the frequency of divorce is the **refined divorce rate**, or the number of divorces that occur per 1,000 married women ages 15 and older. (Note: the measure is computed using women but not men). The refined divorce rate was 16.9 divorces per 1,000 married women (The National Marriage Project, 2009), or fewer than 2 percent a year, a much less sensational number than the familiar "half of all marriages end in divorce," but considerably more accurate and useful.

The refined divorce rate provides a one-year snapshot of how many married women divorce. The other 983 out of 1,000 married women who did not divorce in that year *could* get a divorce the following year, or the year after that, or 10 years later, of course. So even though a married woman had less than a 2 percent chance of divorcing in one year, she has a far greater chance of divorcing over the course of her married life. What is unknown is just how high are her chances of a future divorce.

We do not know whether half of all current marriages will end in divorce because the divorce rate is always fluctuating. We do know, however, that the frequency of divorce is related to both micro-level choices and macro-level social factors, such as divorce laws, women's economic opportunities, and other norms. These factors have changed over time, as we will see in the next section.

Historical Trends

Some people believe that divorce in the United States is a relatively new phenomenon, but people throughout our history have found ways to terminate marriages (Degler, 1980). Although legal divorce was rare and difficult to obtain before 1850, married couples in troubled relationships separated or deserted one another. Women in colonial America had few legal rights and their ability to initiate divorce was limited. Husbands were the head of the household, and they generally controlled the labor of children as well as that of their wives. An early study of marriage and divorce conducted in the mid-1800s examined 29 cases of divorce granted on the grounds of "cruelty" (Wright, 1889). In almost every case the wife committed the "cruelty" by attempting to break out of her traditional subordinate role in one way or another. In half of these cases, the wife had refused to do domestic chores, such as keeping her husband's clothes in repair or cooking his meals.

Early feminists such as Susan B. Anthony, Elizabeth Cady Stanton, and Amelia Bloomer spoke out in favor of making divorce more available to women as a way of improving their rights and their position in marriage (Degler, 1980). By the mid-19th century, the divorce rate began to rise as it became easier for women to initiate and obtain a divorce. During the five years from 1872 to 1876, 63 percent of all divorces initiated and granted to women were on grounds such as cruelty, desertion, drunkenness, and neglect to provide for the family—each demonstrating failure on the husband's part to fulfill his role (Degler, 1980).

In the late 19th and early 20th centuries the divorce rate rose; more women began filing for divorce because of their spouse's drinking, infidelity, or failure to support the family.

refined divorce rate: A measure of divorce based on the number of divorces that occur out of every 1,000 married women.

Figure 12.2

Crude and Refined Divorce Rates: 1940–2009

The divorce rate peaked in the late 1940s after World War II, and peaked again in 1980. Divorce has declined significantly since then.

Sources: National Marriage Project, 2009, Tejada-Vera & Sutton, March 2010.

D*o you think the divorce rate in the United States will stabilize, fall, or rise over the next decade? How will our changing demographic structure (e.g., an increase in the Hispanic population, delayed marriage, and childbearing) and social trends (e.g., economic recession, greater equality between men and women) influence the divorce rate?*

The divorce rate rose steadily between 1860 and 1940, though it dropped somewhat during the Great Depression of the 1930s. It is unlikely that marriages were happier during this extremely difficult period when as many as one in four workers lost their jobs. Instead, many unhappily married couples probably could not afford to divorce or they needed to keep the family together simply to survive.

After the Depression and World War II the divorce rate rose quickly, and by 1946 it peaked at nearly 18 divorces per 1,000 married women, higher than today's rate. Why the surge in divorce? There are many reasons, including high rates of marriage during the 1940s, some of which may have been impulsive; stressors of war and reunification upon relationships; increasing urbanization and geographic mobility that broke down traditional ties; and women's greater economic opportunities that allowed them to be more self-supporting.

Figure 12.2 illustrates the trends in the divorce rate between 1940 and 2009 (Hamilton, Martin, & Ventura, 2010; Tejada-Vera & Sutton, 2010). After the rush of divorces following World War II, the divorce rate dropped considerably to around nine per 1,000 married women during the 1950s. Why was there a decline at this time? Domesticity was the cultural norm: women married younger, had more children than in previous decades, and were less likely to divorce. But in the late 1960s and 1970s, the divorce rate began to rise again, peaking at nearly 23 divorces per 1,000 married women around 1980. Since then, however, the divorce rate has declined sharply to less than 17 per 1,000 married women in 2009. Thus, despite all the attention divorce receives in the media, married couples are much less likely to get divorced today than they were 30 years ago.

:: Why Do People Divorce?

If we were to ask a number of couples why they divorced, we would receive many different answers: "We fell out of love. . .," "We grew apart. . .," "We are just too different. . .," "She met someone new. . .," "He doesn't listen to me. . .," "We disagree about how to spend money. . . ." The explanations that people offer tend to focus on individual micro-level issues. Family scientists, however, try to look at the *patterns* associated with divorce to see the big picture. These patterns reveal that marriages end not only for individual reasons; something more is at work than simple incompatibility (Hewitt, Baxter, & Western, 2005). Let's look at examples of critical micro-level and macro-level factors that influence the odds of divorce. ⊙ Watch on **myfamilylab.com**

⊙ **Watch** the **Video**
Core Concepts: Infidelity on
myfamilylab.com

Micro-Level Factors

If we look at patterns of divorce, we can see that certain risk factors make divorce more likely (Amato, 2010). Naturally, this does not mean that all people with these risk factors will divorce; it just means that they have a greater chance of doing so.

intergenerational transmission of divorce: A pattern noted by researchers that people whose parents divorced are also more likely to divorce.

Parental Divorce   People whose parents have divorced are also more likely to divorce themselves (Amato & Hohmann-Marriott, 2007; Sassler, Cunningham, & Lichter, 2009). This pattern is known as the **intergenerational transmission of divorce**. Parents serve as role models for their children; parents who remain married impart to their children a greater commitment to marriage (Amato & Deboer, 2001). Adult children model their own parents' behaviors, including problematic traits such as poor communication skills. Children with divorced parents sometimes experience negative long-term consequences that continue into their own adulthood and can harm their marriages, such as emotional problems, anxiety, and depression (Cartwright, 2005). Children whose parents divorced tend to marry younger, have lower incomes, are more likely to be involved in a nonmarital pregnancy, and are less likely to go to college, which puts them in several higher risk categories for divorcing (McLanahan & Sandefur, 1994). Certainly not all children of divorced parents experience divorce themselves, but they do have a greater chance.

One study looked at the quality of a *parent's remarriage* in predicting divorce (Yu & Adler-Baeder, 2007). Over 500 young adults completed a questionnaire regarding the quality of their parents' marital relationships and various aspects of their own committed relationships. Children whose parents had a higher-quality remarriage were less likely to divorce.

Age at Marriage   Couples who marry at a young age are in one of the highest risk categories for divorce (Lowenstein, 2005). Teenagers who marry are at particularly high risk because they tend to be poorly prepared for marriage and its responsibilities. Generally, teens are not as mature as people in their twenties or thirties—they do not yet know what kind of adult they will be, or with what type of spouse they will be most compatible. Moreover, teen marriages are often precipitated by a premarital pregnancy, which increases the likelihood that the marriage will fail. Practically speaking, a teenage couple is also likely to struggle with a low income and an interrupted education, which also puts them in a higher risk category.

Parental Status   Couples who have children—particularly young children—or who have many children are less likely to divorce (Bramlett & Mosher, 2002; Hewitt, 2009). This, of course, says nothing about the quality of these marriages—a couple may stay in an unfulfilling marriage because they feel it is the appropriate thing to do for their children's sake. But regardless of marital quality, the fact remains that childfree married couples are more likely to divorce than couples with children because fewer barriers prevent them from leaving an unhappy marriage.

One of the factors that predict divorce is the sex of the children. Parents who have sons are less likely to divorce than are parents who have only daughters. Fathers tend to be more engaged with their children if they have sons.

Nonmarital Childbearing   Couples that bear or conceive children prior to marriage have higher divorce rates than do other couples. Pregnancy may encourage people to marry when they may not otherwise have chosen to do so. It may also cause them to marry before they are financially or emotionally ready. Pregnancy, caring for a newborn, and raising a child put additional stresses on a relationship. Couples who have not had the opportunity to know themselves and their partner as a couple may have a difficult time making the transition to their roles as parents.

Sex of Children   Couples who have sons are less likely to divorce than are couples who have daughters (Dahl & Moretti, 2003). Couples with sons are at lower risk for divorce because fathers in these families are more engaged with their children, and therefore mothers perceive the relationship as more equitable and stable (Mammen, 2009).

Race and Ethnicity   Different racial or ethnic groups vary in their tendency to divorce, with Hispanic and Asian groups least likely to divorce and Blacks most likely to do so (Clarkwest, 2007). Social scientists generally offer a cultural explanation for this variation, focusing on the primacy of the family in Hispanic and Asian

cultures, where the needs of the group outweigh the needs of the individual. Catholicism, which does not legally recognize divorce, is also a factor in Hispanic families. The higher divorce rate among Blacks may be related to the lack of jobs for urban Black males and high rates of unemployment or poverty.

Education   On average, people with lower levels of education are more likely to divorce than those with higher levels of education (Heaton, 2002; Jalovaara, 2003; Cohn, 2009). However, the educational relationship is less clear for women than it is for men. Women with very high levels of education are also more likely to divorce, especially later in the marriage, because an advanced degree contributes to their ability to be economically independent and therefore, leave an unhappy marriage.

Income   Divorce is more common among people with lower incomes than among those with higher incomes (National Marriage Project, 2009; Taylor, Funk, & Clark, 2007). Financial and job-related stresses can contribute to marital problems. While not all wealthy couples have happy marriages and not all couples with lower incomes are doomed to an unhappy or unstable union, unemployment, poverty, and financial strains decrease displays of affection, cause marital conflict, and even increase the likelihood of family violence and disruption.

Degree of Similarity between Spouses   Spouses are less likely to divorce when they share characteristics such as age, religion, race, or ethnic group and are more likely to divorce when these characteristics differ (Bratter & King, 2008; Vaaler, Ellison, & Powers, 2009; Zhang & Van Hook, 2009). For example, a large study of over 23,000 married couples found that interracial marriages faced a higher risk of divorce, especially marriages involving a Black husband and a White wife, or a Hispanic husband and a White wife (Zhang & Van Hook, 2009). Couples who differ from each other in some of these important ways may have different values, norms, or experiences. They may encounter additional stress from outsiders who disapprove of their marriage, which could lead to greater conflict and less social support.

The Couple's Ages   The likelihood of a couple divorcing rises during adulthood and then declines as the couple ages (Taylor, Funk, & Clark, 2007; U.S. Census Bureau, 2007). This decline may happen because unhappy couples divorce long before reaching middle or old age. Or, drawing upon exchange theory, divorce may decline with age because unhappy older couples decide it is better to remain married than to divorce later in life. Dividing many years worth of joint assets such as a home, retirement accounts, and savings can be problematic, and perhaps older couples see that the financial or emotional costs of divorce would outweigh its benefits.

While individual micro-level reasons help us to understand why people divorce, they do not provide a complete picture because they miss the broad social context in which divorce occurs.

Macro-Structural Factors

Why did the divorce rate increase in the 1960s and 1970s? And why is the divorce rate declining today? Is it because married couples love each other more today? Probably not. Why is divorce in the United States still so common, but so rare in the Middle East? Do married couples there love each other more than we do? Divorce may have very little to do with micro-level issues such as "We fell out of love," or "We have irreconcilable differences." Many people stay in loveless marriages and consider irreconcilable differences irrelevant.

If we want to know why divorce occurs, instead of looking only at micro-level factors of the individual, we should also pay attention to cultural macro-level factors such as (1) the level of socioeconomic development; (2) the dominant religion practiced; (3) the divorce laws; (4) the status of women, including their employment situation; and (5) the general attitudes toward divorce.

Level of Socioeconomic Development   Generally, less developed countries in Africa, Asia, Central and South America, and the Middle East have significantly lower divorce rates than do developed countries in North America and Europe (United Nations Statistics Division, 2010). Most people cannot support themselves on their own in less developed countries, and families are of the utmost importance. Religious and cultural customs reinforce the family as the primary social institution. China, which has undergone rapid socioeconomic development over the past 20 years, has also seen a tremendous surge in its divorce rate, increasing about 50 percent since 2000 (United Nations Statistics Division, 2010).

Religion   A second factor that influences the rate of divorce in a country is the level of religiosity and the most widely practiced religion of its citizens (Trent & South, 1989). Much of Central and South America is dominated by Roman Catholicism, which forbids divorce in all but the most extreme circumstances. In Italy and Ireland, the Catholic Church was influential in prohibiting divorce until anti-abortion laws were also overturned in the 1980s and 1990s, respectively. In the United States, divorce rates rose accordingly as the influence of religion waned and the culture became more secular.

Divorce Laws   Divorce laws certainly help predict the likelihood of divorce, and they are quite different throughout the world (Kneip & Bauer, 2009). In many parts of the Middle East, men can divorce their wives for almost any reason, often by simply declaring "I divorce thee" (Human Rights Watch, 2004a). Women do not have the same prerogative. Only recently have Egyptian women been allowed to initiate divorce at all and the process remains highly discriminatory, as shown in the feature box *Diversity in Families: Patriarchy and Divorce in Egypt* on page 340.

   While U.S. divorce laws may seem simple in comparison, it was not long ago that one of the marriage partners had to be the one "at fault" in a divorce proceeding. Common grounds for divorce included mental cruelty, adultery, or desertion. Beginning in the 1960s, states slowly began to amend their laws to reflect the concept of **no-fault divorce**. Now, a couple can go before a judge without the need to blame each other; instead, they can claim irreconcilable differences and state that they both wish to divorce. A no-fault law was first passed in Oklahoma in 1953 and then in Alaska in 1962, and no-fault divorce laws spread through the 50 states during the 1970s. By 1987, the final holdout state, Utah, enacted no-fault divorce legislation (Vlosky & Monroe, 2002).

   A high number of divorces were granted during the period after the states' legislation was passed (Rodgers, Nakonezny, & Shull, 1997). This increase may indicate that there was a backlog of unhappy couples waiting until the legislation went into effect. Today, states vary somewhat in the details of their divorce laws (for example, some states require waiting periods), but no-fault divorce is now available in all 50 states.

Women's Status and Employment   Divorce laws tend to be more restrictive in patriarchal societies where women have fewer legal rights or economic opportunities (Amato, 1994; Greenstein & Davis, 2006). In many countries, laws regarding child custody and spousal support are designed to perpetuate patriarchy. In Iran, for example, wives are entitled to spousal support for only three months, despite the very limited economic opportunities available to women. Therefore, most divorced women in Iran return to their birth families, often in shame. In India, a divorced woman rarely receives any of the assets that she and her former husband have accumulated, for these are assumed to belong to her husband and his family. As these examples illustrate, in patriarchal societies divorce puts women at such an economic disadvantage that they often do not ask for a divorce.

   Even in the United States, women have been economically dependent on men to support them for much of the country's history. This changed briefly during World War II when many middle-class married women secured paid employment. Women's employment declined after the war, but began to rise again by the 1970s, when a large number of married women with children joined the workforce. This change in women's employment patterns enabled women to support themselves more easily and therefore, end unhappy

no-fault divorce: A type of divorce, now prevalent in all fifty states, in which a divorcing couple can go before a judge without one party having to blame the other.

Diversity in Families

Patriarchy and Divorce in Egypt

"The question of settling divorce should be in the hands of the wiser party, and that is men. Men are wise, which is why they do not have to go to court. Islamic law would consider the wise wife an exception, and you cannot generalize an exception."

—Ayman Amin Shash, chief judge, technical bureau of the National Center for Judicial Studies, Cairo; July 7, 2004

Egyptian men have a unilateral and unconditional right to divorce without resort to legal proceedings. They only need to renounce their wives, repeating three times that they are now divorced and registering the divorce within 30 days with a religious notary to make it official. A repudiated woman then has to observe a waiting period of up to one year in which she cannot marry another man just in case her former husband changes his mind. She will receive some compensation called "maintenance" during the waiting period, with consideration for the husband's means, the circumstances of the divorce, and the length of marriage.

In contrast to men, women have a much more difficult time initiating a divorce. To begin *fault-based* divorce proceedings, women, unlike men, must obtain legal counsel, provide evidence of harm, often through eyewitness testimony, and submit to compulsory mediation. There are only four grounds that a woman can use: (1) husband's illness, including mental illness, venereal disease, and impotence; (2) non-provision of maintenance or financial support; (3) absence or imprisonment; and (4) "injury," which includes a variety of forms of physical and mental harm.

Judges do not grant women fault-based divorce easily, and they often require substantial evidence of "harm." Judges tend to require a higher threshold of harm for poor or illiterate rural women on the assumption that physical abuse or polygyny, for example, is a natural part of their lives and does not necessarily warrant a divorce. Egypt's chief judicial inspector admitted, *"What is harm for some women isn't harm for another. Some women accept beatings and insults as a joke, while others do not."*

Beginning in 2000, Egyptian women were given a second option—the right to file for a no-fault divorce on the basis of "incompatibility." However, this requires that a woman forfeit her rights to alimony and she must repay her dowry. Given women's limited work experience and earning potential, the meager safety net provided by social services, and the high degree of patriarchy woven into Egypt's laws and policies, divorced women face very dim prospects. Therefore, this option is only available to women with significant financial resources or those who are most desperate for a divorce. As one man told his wife who wanted a "no-fault" divorce: *"Leave the house if you want a divorce. Give up the house, the*

Only recently have women in Egypt been allowed to file for divorce, and the grounds for divorce remain strict compared to men who initiate divorce.

children, the furniture, and the clothing that you're wearing. . . I will not give you anything. . . You will go to your family's house and they'll bring you back to lick my shoes."

Source: Human Rights Watch. 2004b. "Domestic Violence." Retrieved 19 July 2005 (hrw.org/women/domesticviolence.html).

What Do You Think?

1. How do divorce laws reflect patriarchy? Do you think that Egypt is unique in its approach to divorce for women? Why or why not?

2. Do you think the changes made in 2000 to the divorce law help Egyptian women? Why or why not?

marriages. Women who are more self-sufficient, such as with above-average incomes or who earn more than half the household income, are more likely to divorce than are those who are economically dependent (Rogers, 2004).

Attitudes toward Divorce   In many parts of the world today, women who divorce are stigmatized. Until recently in the United States, in fact, the term "divorcée," which applied to women only, had sexually suggestive connotations. Fifty years ago a person who was known to have divorced—man or woman—would probably not have been elected to a major political office. Yet, by 1980 the fact that Ronald Reagan had a divorce in his past did not prevent him from being elected President of the United States (Rothstein, 2001). By the 1992 presidential election, candidate Bob Dole's divorce was barely mentioned. Societal attitudes towards divorce changed as it became more common—both a cause and a consequence of an increasing divorce rate.

As divorce became less stigmatized, unhappy couples considered it an appropriate way to end their relationship. Moreover, couples that contemplate marriage may have begun to see marriage as only semi-permanent, noting that they could "opt out" if it did not work. One study based on a nationally representative sample of high school seniors found that only 57 percent of adolescent boys and 63 percent of adolescent girls claim, "It is 'very likely' that I will stay married to the same person for life" (National Marriage Project, 2009). Defining marriage as a less than permanent relationship supports a self-fulfilling prophecy; if partners enter marriage with the idea that it could easily be terminated, it is more likely that it will.

This attitude towards marriage does not necessarily mean that people take the events of marriage and divorce lightly. In fact, more people now oppose divorce and believe that it should be more difficult to obtain than people of a generation ago, as shown in Table 12.1. Likewise, the Pew Research Center's 2007 study with a representative sample of adults across the United States found that 45 percent of adults ages 18–29 believe that divorce "should be avoided except in extreme situations," compared to only 32 percent of adults ages 65 and over (Pew Research Center, 2007). To repeat, it is *younger* adults, not older adults, who want divorce to be more restrictive, perhaps because many of them experienced divorce as children.

The researchers also found that Blacks were more likely than Whites or Hispanics to favor a more restrictive divorce, as shown in Figure 12.3. In fact, a fear of divorce keeps many low-income mothers from marrying in the first place (Edin & Kefalas, 2005). It thus appears that those people who are at a higher risk for divorce would like the divorce process to be more difficult.

Table 12.1	Should Divorce Be Easier or More Difficult to Obtain?		
	Easier	More Difficult	Stay Same
1974	34%	45%	22%
2006	25%	47%	29%

Americans have come full circle on divorce. Today, people are likely to say either make it harder or keep it the same; fewer want divorce made easier.

Source: General Social Surveys, 1972–2006.

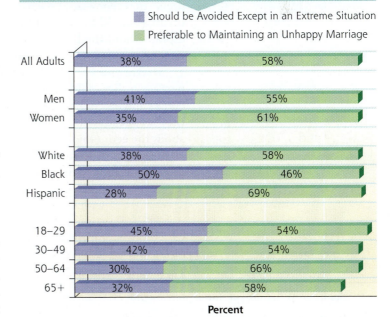

Figure 12.3	Views about Divorce, by Sex, Race/Ethnicity, and Age (Percent) "Which statement comes closer to your views about divorce?"

Many people believe that divorce should be avoided except in extreme circumstances, and it is younger adults who want divorce to be more restrictive. Also, Blacks are more likely than Whites or Hispanics to want divorce to be more restrictive.

Should be Avoided Except in an Extreme Situation
Preferable to Maintaining an Unhappy Marriage

	Avoided Except in Extreme Situation	Preferable to Unhappy Marriage
All Adults	38%	58%
Men	41%	55%
Women	35%	61%
White	38%	58%
Black	50%	46%
Hispanic	28%	69%
18–29	45%	54%
30–49	42%	54%
50–64	30%	66%
65+	32%	58%

Percent

Note: Whites include only non-Hispanic whites. Blacks include non-Hispanic Blacks. Hispanics are of any race. Don't know responses are not shown.

Source: Pew Research Center, July 1, 2007.

Tying It All Together

Factors That Affect the Frequency of Divorce

Why do people divorce? Many macro-level factors influence the individual micro-level behaviors and choices we make. For example, the level of socioeconomic development is likely to affect the age at which people marry, the number of children they have, and the couple's level of personal resources.

Micro-level Factors Associated with Divorce

- Parental divorce
- Age at marriage
- Absence of children
- Nonmarital childbearing
- Sex of children
- Race and ethnicity
- Education
- Income
- Degree of similarity
- The couple's ages

Macro-level Factors Associated with Divorce

- Level of socioeconomic development
- Religion
- Divorce laws
- Women's status and employment
- Attitudes toward divorce

What Do You Think?

1. Identify a few different countries, and reflect upon their macro-level factors associated with divorce. How do they differ from the United States?
2. Do you think that any micro-level factors associated with divorce operate differently across racial or ethnic groups?

Researchers Martin and Parashar (2006) compared data from the period 1974–2002 and also found that people have come to support more restrictive divorce laws in recent years. In particular, an intriguing change has occurred in attitudes towards divorce among *women*. In the past, researchers found that the more education women had, the more likely they were to support easier access to divorce. Attending college was thought to broaden women's perceptions and make them more open to lifestyles other than "married with children." In recent years, however, women with college degrees are the most likely to say that divorce should be more difficult to obtain, while women with less than a high school diploma hold the least restrictive views about divorce. What might explain this trend referred to as "the education crossover"?

Martin and Parashar (2006) suggest that women's attitudes are related to the expected "utility of divorce." Women with less education (and who likely have lower incomes and less prestigious jobs) want to marry to increase their financial prospects, but they are faced with a pool of potentially risky marriage partners. If women are unsure about the economic prospects of their partners, they will probably want to keep divorce as an option. In contrast, women who have more education (and presumably higher incomes and jobs with more prestige) can be more selective about whom they marry.

Let's consider your odds for divorce. Are they high or low? For example, did your parents divorce? Do you plan to have children? What do you think your income will be when you are finished with school? What are your attitudes toward divorce? What type of culture do you live in?

They can wait until they are confident they have found a relationship with long-term stability and are less likely to anticipate divorce. In other words, the researchers suggest that women who feel their options are more limited may want to keep divorce as a viable option, whereas women with greater earning potential are less likely to foresee the need for a divorce, and therefore think divorce should be more difficult to obtain.

As this research shows us, individual reasons are important in the decision to seek a divorce, but they can be greatly influenced by macro-level factors. Taken together, as shown in the *Tying It All Together* feature box, both micro-individual factors and macro-structural factors can provide us with a clearer picture of why people divorce.

:: Experiencing Divorce

My parents just divorced last year, but they've had a crummy marriage for years. I honestly don't know what took them so long to finally do it, to get a divorce. I've always hated it when they fought. Little things would set one of them off, and then they would both go ballistic. They would often pull me in the middle: "Matt, what do you think?" they would ask. Just leave me out of it.

—Matt, Age 20

Divorce is a *process*; it is rarely quick or easy (Amato, 2007; Wallerstein, 2007; Cartwright & McDowell, 2008; Gregson & Ceynar, 2009). Although a judge may grant the divorce decree in a matter of minutes, most couples have gone through a period of many years in which they have analyzed, redefined, and reorganized not only their relationship, but also nearly every aspect of their lives (Willén & Montgomery, 2006). This process may include a separation to provide the emotional distance needed to work on resolving marital problems—sometimes followed by reconciliation, but perhaps finally ending in a divorce. In a study involving a national sample of over 1,000 people interviewed several times between 1980 and 1992 (Amato & Rogers, 1997), researchers reported that marital problems identified in the first interview in 1980 predicted divorce up to 12 years later. In other words, couples who divorce tend to report problems in the marriage as early as 9 to 12 years before the actual divorce occurs.

Women and men often provide different reasons for a divorce and experience the process and its aftermath differently. Although each may have difficult feelings including guilt, depression, embarrassment, failure, or low self-esteem, women and men experience divorce differently because of the different opportunities and constraints that society presents to each sex.

These differences are apparent even in the first stage in the process of divorce—voicing marital problems. Women report more marital problems than do their husbands, although interestingly, women tend to blame themselves for many of these problems (Amato & Rogers, 1997). This tendency may reflect women's subordinate position in many marriages; as a result, wives monitor and interpret their marriages more often than do husbands. Some of the biggest concerns between husbands and wives (and acknowledged by both) include the husband not spending enough time at home, his irritating habits, his use of alcohol or drugs, and his foolish spending of money. For wives, both acknowledged that her feelings are easily hurt. There were smaller perceived differences between the two sexes in who gets angry or jealous or who is domineering, critical, moody, and untalkative (Amato & Rogers, 1997). Nonetheless, despite the fact that women report more marital problems, they may not be more likely to initiate divorce (Hewitt, 2009).

The Phases of Separation

In the first phase of a marital separation, *preseparation*, one or both partners begin to think about the benefits of a separation. They may first fantasize about leaving and being free of the responsibilities associated with marriage. But when they think about the logistics, people considering separation commonly experience anxiety, sadness, fear, anger, and loneliness at the same time. Couples in this stage may not fully reveal their intention to separate to friends and family. They may continue to attend family functions together or they may concoct a story to explain a partner's absence from events.

During the *early separation phase*, couples face a series of issues as they separate. Who will be the one to move out? How shall we work out financial matters, such as the house

Divorce is usually a long process. Sometimes couples separate, reconcile, then separate again before they ultimately divorce.

payment, the car payment, and other bills? How do we explain this decision to our children? How should parental responsibilities be divided? Should family, friends, and teachers be told of our intent, and if so, how? Couples may have conflicting feelings about both the separation and the possibility of divorce looming over the horizon.

In the *mid-separation phase*, the realities of daily living set in, such as maintaining two households, arranging visitation for the children, and living on a reduced income. Sometimes couples reconcile simply to avoid these pressures whether or not they have resolved the problems in the relationship. Unresolved problems may then resurface, causing another separation or leading directly to a divorce.

Finally, during the *late separation phase*, a couple must learn to live as two single people. They also must decide on their next step. Not all separated couples divorce; many continue to work on the problems they faced as a married couple and then successfully reconcile. Others remain separated indefinitely but do not divorce because of financial reasons or religious objections. They may file for a **legal separation**, a binding agreement signed by both spouses that provides details about child support. Others may decide that their marital problems cannot be solved, and they therefore seek a divorce.

The Stations of Divorce

Divorce does not end a relationship between two people alone; it alters or even severs many personal and legal ties. Your divorce may signal the end of your relationships with other family members; with friends who find themselves taking sides; with neighbors whom you will rarely see now that you have moved away; with community groups of which you are no longer a member or can no longer afford to join; or even with your children whom you may see infrequently. Bohannan (1971) refers to the emotional, legal, economic, co-parental, community, and psychic dimensions of divorce as the **stations of divorce**. They are interrelated, and taken together they are an attempt to capture the complexity of the divorce experience. We will discuss several of these dimensions below.

The Emotional Divorce   Ending a marriage is extremely stressful (Blekesaune, 2008). Divorced individuals, compared with those who are married, have more health problems, experience more depression and anxiety, and have a greater risk of mortality (Hughes & Waite, 2009; Lorenz, Wickrama, Conger, & Elder, 2006; Waite, Luo, & Lewin, 2009).

The emotional aspects of divorce begin long before any legal steps are taken, and may end long afterward. One or both partners may feel angry, resentful, sad, or rejected. Generally one spouse initiates the breakup of the marriage (Hewitt, Western, & Baxter, 2006). Symbolic interaction theory reminds us here of how the interpretation we attach to events affects its meaning. Initiators have the advantage of preparing emotionally for the separation. A common pattern is that an initiator expresses general discontent at first, but without attributing it to the marriage *per se*. They may try to alter the relationship or their spouse's behavior by suggesting such remedies as a new job, having a baby, or some other substantial change to the nature of the relationship. They may even use the threat of leaving as a way to demand change. The other spouse's reaction—anger, resentment, sadness, resolve, or rejection—shapes his or her emotional response.

However, the labels of "initiator" versus "noninitiator" may really be accidental and random (Hopper, 1993). In fact, divorcing spouses sometimes disagree as to who the initiator actually was (Hewitt, Western, & Baxter, 2006; Sweeney, 2002). Hopper found that both

legal separation: A binding agreement signed by both spouses that provides details about child support.

stations of divorce: The interrelated emotional, legal, economic, co-parental, community, and psychic dimensions of divorce, which together attempt to capture the complexity of the divorce experience.

spouses were generally aware that they had multiple marital problems, experienced discontent and contemplated divorce or separation, and were ambivalent about the best way to resolve their marital problems (1993).

Many factors influence how men and women experience a divorce, such as the degree of unhappiness and conflict they experience in the marriage, whether they have young children, their ages, and the amount of time they have been married. Men and women often have different emotional challenges following divorce (Blekesaune, 2008). As feminist theory reminds us, society offers men and women different opportunities and constraints that help explain our gendered experiences. For example, women are more likely than men to have financial problems after a divorce, as discussed below (Grall, 2009). In contrast, men often have a more difficult time emotionally after a divorce, and in some cases, this stress is so extreme that it can lead to increased illness or an early death. One reason for this emotional difficulty is that men tend to have a weaker network of supportive relationships (Chu, 2005). Men are also more dependent upon marriage, and those who have been in more traditional marriages may find routine household tasks such as cooking, cleaning, and shopping to be daunting. Finally, most men lose custody of their children, and for many fathers this loss in itself is a depressing proposition (Bokker, Farley, & Bailey, 2006; Hawthorne & Lennings, 2008).

Legal Divorce

A **legal divorce** terminates the marriage contract by a court order of the state. Partners are then legally free to conduct separate lives and to remarry. Although the legal proceedings themselves are very businesslike and may take only a few minutes to conduct, they mask the adversarial nature of most divorces. The couple must divide their assets and property, including their home, cars, savings, and retirement accounts. They must also divide their debts, including credit card debt or loans. If they have children, they must decide whom the children should live with, and how often the children should visit the noncustodial parent. They will also need a child support agreement.

Few couples can make these decisions easily, and therefore they turn to lawyers to help them. Hiring lawyers to oversee the division of assets and child visitation can cost an average of over $15,000 (Kallen, 2008). Because a lawyer represents only his or her client's interests, which are not necessarily in the interests of all parties, both sides usually hire their own representation, increasing the drain on the couple's assets.

Some assets are difficult to divide easily. For example, suppose one spouse has earned a college degree while the other has worked full-time at a low-wage job to put his or her partner through school. How can the couple, or the court, divide this asset—the college degree—which translates into real future earning power? A court in Kentucky in 1979 had such a case before it: Inman v. Inman. The couple met while they were university undergraduates, and both had intended to go to medical school. Mr. Inman attended medical school first while Ms. Inman supported him with the understanding that after he received his medical degree, it would be her turn to attend medical school. Instead, the couple separated a year after Mr. Inman finished his studies. In court, Ms. Inman asked that she be awarded compensation for her husband's medical degree, arguing that she had paid for it in the anticipation of joint benefits, but because of the divorce only Mr. Inman would reap the benefits. After hearing her argument, the court ordered the husband to reimburse her for the costs of his medical school, plus inflation and interest (Weitzman, 1985).

Economic Divorce

In one common stereotype of divorce, a wife runs off with most of the marital assets and takes her ex-husband "to the cleaners." What really happens to the financial well-being of men, women, and children after a divorce? 📖▶ Read on **myfamilylab.com**

The economic fallout after a divorce is actually less painful to men than for women and children (Gadalla, 2009; DeNavas-Walt, Proctor, & Smith, 2010). A study using a large and nationally representative sample compared men and women's incomes for up to five years during and after divorce or separation (Gadalla, 2008). It found a dramatic decline in women's income and a slight decline in men's income during the divorce year. One in five women

📖▶ **Read the Document**
Characteristics of Women with Children Who Divorce in Midlife Compared to Those Who Remain Married on **myfamilylab.com**

legal divorce: The termination of the marriage contract by a state court order.

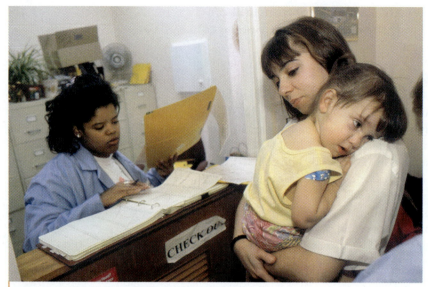

What happens to a family's standard of living after a divorce? During the divorce year women and children's income declines significantly, whereas men experience only slight declines, on average. One in five women become impoverished, as compared to only 1 in 13 men.

became impoverished, as compared to only one in 13 men. One year later, women's average income was 80 percent of men's, although women remained twice as likely as men to be impoverished. Four years after divorce, women's average income reached 85 percent of men's (Gadalla, 2008; 2009).

The U.S. Census Bureau reports similar findings, as shown in Table 12.2. An average married couple has an annual income of around $72,000, compared to $48,000 for a single male-headed family (no wife present) and less than $33,000 for a single female-headed family (no husband present). Female-headed families are more than twice as likely as male-headed families, and five times as likely as married-couple families to live in poverty (DeNavas-Walt, Proctor, & Smith, 2010).

Why is there such a large income difference after a divorce? After a divorce, fathers become *single*, and mothers become *single parents* (Weitzman, 1985). A woman's employment opportunities may be more restricted than those of her ex-husband because the demands of raising children may force her to alter her work schedule; reduce her ability to work overtime; and limit opportunities for the travel, relocation, and further training needed for advancement.

These constraints are further aggravated by the fact that many women have intermittent work histories because they may have decided—by mutual agreement—that the husband would support the family while the wife stayed at home to care for their children. In her book, *Opting Out: Why Women Really Quit Careers and Head Home* (2007), author Pamela Stone found that even high-achieving and well-educated women have difficulty balancing work and family because of uncompromising workplaces with excessive hours and unrelenting demands. Women felt pushed out of their jobs by workplaces inhospitable to families.

Yet, after several years of unemployment, some women cannot easily re-enter the labor force. Their skills might be outdated and they cannot command high salaries. Still, the law expects both parents to support their children, and mothers must become self-supporting relatively quickly. Some spouses may request **alimony**, a (generally temporary) payment by one partner to the other, usually a husband to a wife (Shehan, Berardo, Owens, & Berardo, 2002). Alimony is designed to support the more dependent spouse for a period of time (Ho & Sussman, 2008). The courts recognize that some people may need some short-term financial assistance, especially if they have been out of the labor market for a period of time while raising children. However, alimony is not commonly awarded.

Consequently, female-headed households in the United States are often on the economic margins (DeNavas-Walt, Proctor, & Smith, 2010). They would fare quite differently in many other developed nations, including most of Western Europe, where the government intervenes and assists divorced families to a greater extent than in the United States (Warner, 2005).

Co-Parental Divorce   When the divorcing couple has children, they must try to design and agree upon parenting strategies. One crucial issue is the matter of custody. Who will have the right to make important decisions about the children's lives, and where will the children live?

The person who has **legal custody** of the children has the legal authority to make important decisions concerning their welfare, such as where they will go to school, in what

Table 12.2	Median Income and Percent in Poverty by Family Type, 2009		

Married couple households are least likely to be in poverty, whereas single-parent households, especially single-mother households, have higher rates of poverty.

	Median Income	Percent in Poverty
Married couple families	$71,830	5.8%
Male householder, no wife present	$48,084	16.9%
Female householder, no husband present	$32,597	29.9%

Source: DeNavas-Walt, Proctor, & Smith, 2010.

alimony: Payment by one partner to the other to support the more dependent spouse for a period of time.

legal custody: A custody agreement where one parent has the legal authority to make important decisions concerning the children after a divorce, such as where they will go to school, in what community or state they will reside, or who will be notified in case of a health emergency or school problem.

community or state they will reside, and who will be notified in case of a health emergency or school problem. Legal custody may have nothing to do with a child's living arrangement.

In the past, courts usually gave **sole legal custody** to the parent with whom the child lived. But this trend is changing. Under **joint legal custody,** non-custodial parents (usually fathers) retain their legal rights with respect to their children. One multi-year study of custody issues among 378 divorcing families (Wilcox, Wolchik, & Braver, 1998) found that mothers were more likely to prefer joint legal custody, as opposed to sole maternal custody, when they were:

- experiencing low levels of conflict with their ex-husband;
- experiencing low levels of anger/hurt over the divorce;
- experiencing fewer visitation problems;
- perceiving the ex-husband as more competent as a parent;
- experiencing little psychological distress; and/or
- receiving social support to maintain the father-child relationship.

Fathers with joint legal custody pay more child support, spend more time with their children, and have more overnight visits with them (Seltzer, 1998).

Physical custody refers to the place where the children actually reside. Courts maintain that decisions about living arrangements should be based on the best interests of the child. Theoretically, these decisions should not discriminate against men or women in any systematic way. In over 80 percent of divorces, however, mothers have **sole physical custody**, meaning that the child legally lives with one parent, and only "visits" the other (Grall, 2009).

Noncustodial fathers often have a poorer and more marginalized relationship with their children than do custodial fathers and their children face added risks (Carlson, 2006; Hawthorne & Lennings, 2008; Peters & Ehrenberg, 2008; Swiss & Le Bourdais, 2009). First, this may be the result of a selection effect: single fathers with custody (or married fathers) may value their relationship with their children more, which is why they sought custody (or remained married) in the first place. Second, the presence of children in the home allows the father a greater sense of control over the children's lives. Third, co-residence may also free the father from the aggravation associated with negotiating future visits. Fourth, living together may encourage fathers to become more involved in their children's lives. For example, a father is available to take his son or daughter to soccer practice and even coach the team.

Today, some families and courts are choosing **joint physical custody**, in which children spend a substantial portion of time in the homes of both parents, perhaps alternating weeks or days within a week (Lyster, 2007; Spruijt & Duindam, 2010). Because this arrangement requires a tremendous amount of cooperation, it tends to work best when both parents want it and are willing to work with one another to provide smooth transitions for the children. It generally does not work well when the parents are in conflict, or when one parent feels that the arrangement was foisted upon him or her.

Joint physical custody is controversial. Critics suggest that it disrupts children's routines and school schedules. They claim that it can exacerbate conflict between parents because no two parenting strategies are identical, and that it creates conflicting loyalties within children. On the other hand, supporters suggest that it lightens the economic and emotional responsibilities of single parenthood and that it provides men with the opportunity to care for and nurture their children on a routine basis, which is in the child's best interest.

One review of 33 different studies that compared children living in sole custody or joint custody two-parent families found that children in joint custody arrangements had less behavior and emotional problems, higher self-esteem, and better family relations and school performance than children in sole custody arrangements (Bauserman, 2002). Moreover, these children were as well-adjusted as children in two-parent families. Other studies echo these conclusions and find that joint physical custody has somewhat positive effects (Spruijt & Duindam, 2010). However, again this may be due to a selection effort. That is, couples with more amicable divorces and less overt conflict are more likely to choose joint physical custody.

sole legal custody: A child custody arrangement in which legal custody is granted solely to the parent with whom the child lives.

joint legal custody: A custody agreement in which noncustodial parents (usually fathers) retain their legal rights with respect to their children.

physical custody: A child custody arrangement that decides where the child will reside.

sole physical custody: A child custody arrangement in which the child legally lives with one parent and "visits" the other parent.

joint physical custody: A custody agreement in which children spend a substantial portion of time in the homes of both parents, perhaps alternating weeks or days within a week.

More than 200 children a day are kidnapped by a non-custodial parent, often for revenge or other self-serving reasons.

Some custody situations are contentious. Perhaps one of the most difficult situations to arise from this conflict has to do with a parent abducting a child. According to the U.S. Department of State, **child snatching** is an epidemic, with well more than 200 children a day kidnapped by a noncustodial parent (Rigler & Wieder, 2007). Most of these children are under age three since they are easy to transport, and are less able to complain or report the kidnapping to others.

When a parent kidnaps a child, the parent usually claims that he or she is acting in the best interest of the child; however, few cases actually involve saving the child from a harmful custodial parent. Far more often, child snatching is done for revenge or other self-serving reasons. Most cases of child snatching occur prior to the final court decree that outlines the economic and custody arrangements, and the children are held as pawns. "Searching parents worry and wonder, constantly tormented by this act. It is a revenge far sweeter and longer lived then a beating or even murder, for it never ends" (Rigler & Wieder, 2007).

The Community Divorce Marriage joins families and friendship networks. Divorce breaks them apart, sometimes in a confusing or bitter fashion. Relationships between former in-laws or friends that the couple shared can deteriorate or vanish altogether. Divorced people may feel uncomfortable with their old friends because they are uncertain of their allegiances. Also, their married friends may become reluctant to remain friends with a divorced person because he or she is seen as a threat to their own marriage. Community ties to teachers, neighbors, religious organizations, and children's recreation groups and sports teams can also sever if a parent and children move to a different, perhaps more affordable, neighborhood or school (Braver, Ellman, & Fabricius, 2003).

Divorce can also affect the extended family. One group that has sought legal protection and captured media attention in their quest to maintain ties with children is grandparents (Giles-Sims & Lockhart, 2005). Grandparents are important kin who provide unique benefits to children. Sometimes, grandchild/grandparent relationships are strengthened, as divorcing adults look to their own parents for financial help or childcare. However, in some divorces, the parent may choose to deny even visitation to former in-laws, their children's grandparents. A retired couple, Lola and Bill, lost touch for seven years with their two grandchildren after their daughter divorced her husband and he got custody. "When they came back to us, we had to mourn the children that we lost and we had to start from scratch," Lola said (Navarro, 2007). In her grief-filled years, Lola helped to organize the National Committee of Grandparents for Children's Rights, an organization that lobbies for laws to protect children's rights to have contact with their grandparents following a divorce. The organization has had some success and grandparents can pursue visitation rights in some cases. However, most grandparents are still at the mercy of the custodial parent, and some of the gains grandparents have made have been eroded in state courts on the grounds that grandparental rights' statutes violate parental rights.

The Psychic Divorce As time moves on most people adjust to the separation and divorce (Gregson & Ceynar, 2009; Thomas & Ryan, 2008). There is no specific time frame for this adjustment, as some people take many months, while others take many years. The psychic divorce refers to the process of regaining psychological autonomy and beginning to feel whole and complete again as a single person. As people experience this phase of the divorce, ex-wives and ex-husbands must learn to distance themselves from the still-loved and still-hated aspects of the ex-spouse. Forgiveness is an important predictor of well-being (Bonach, Sales, & Koeske, 2005), but it often takes years to achieve (Yaben, 2009). The feature box *My Family: A Poppy in the Rain* examines one woman's "letting go" ceremony. It gave her the finality she needed to say goodbye to her ex-spouse.

child snatching: The act of a noncustodial parent kidnapping his or her child.

My Family

A Poppy in the Rain

Seven years ago in a light summer rain I got married in a meadow of wildflowers. The morning of the wedding, my soon-to-be husband and I went running with our friends, and called it the Dowry Dash. We talked about wearing our running shoes to the wedding, but our friends decided it wouldn't be a good idea, as it would be too easy to run away if one of us got the jitters.

People said rain at a wedding brings lasting happiness. They must be right, because I still feel happy. Today it's cool, gray and raining—just like our wedding day—with the tall grass and willows in the field behind our house generously soaked from the morning's shower.

Things change in seven years. Today I performed a ceremony to say good-bye to my soon-to-be ex-husband, to symbolically put the marriage behind me so I can start my new life. I found a tape of the music played during the wedding. I sat down on the floor and sorted through old photos from races and good times my husband and I had shared with our running friends.

Then I removed the photograph of my husband from the leather frame my sister gave me and replaced it with one of my dog, Joanie, sitting alone, looking windblown and happy. I called Joanie over to show her the picture that will now sit on my desk, and through tears, explained why this was so.

Afterwards I took her for a run in the rain, down to the field on a narrow path, through thick weeds and tiny yellow wildflowers, both of us getting wet from the light drizzle. We stopped momentarily by a ditch, watching the muddy water flow downstream. I imagined the water carrying away my pain, flushing me clean.

Rounding the curve, my eyes caught sight of a beautiful white poppy in the field, several yards off the path. It was the only flower out there in acres of high, green vegetation, and its white color stood out like a single cloud in a clear blue sky.

I ran over to it through the dripping grass, jumping over tall weeds, then bent down to take a closer look. I separated the delicate wet petals with my fingers.

The poppy reminded me of the calla lilies I carried in my wedding; still, it was different. This flower had a genuine, thorny, wild look—the way I've heard people describe me. A bright yellow display of anthers surrounded a five-sided centerpiece of deep maroon. It had a rough, spiky stem and leaves. The livery hairs on the stem gave it a mature, stalwart look.

Standing alone in the rain-soaked meadow, the poppy had been strong enough to weather the morning's downpour; its petal hadn't collapsed. As we ran further away, I could still see it, a brilliant white dot in the carpeted shades of green and yellow framed by cottonwood and willow trees. Standing out there in the drenched field, the poppy looked happy—soft yet tough, determined to live among the thick stalks and grasses.

"The psychic divorce" is the process of regaining autonomy, feeling whole again, and letting go.

Later, when Joanie and I arrived home, I was still thinking about the flower. I stood on the back doorstep, watching the sun begin to break through the clouds. In the meadow 400 yards away, I could see the poppy, distinct and proud. It was looking upward at the broken sky, its arms outstretched in the rain, smiling confidently, happy to be alive.

Source: Nitzky, Alene. 1998. "A Poppy in the Rain." Runner's World, 9 April, pp. 22–23.

What Do You Think?

1. Why are ceremonies and rituals so important?

2. What life changes tend to have rituals associated with them, and which ones do not? Why is that?

A Helping Hand: Divorce Mediation

Given that divorce touches so many aspects of our lives, how can a divorcing couple sort through all the decisions they must make? Many divorce settlements are reached through informal negotiation rather than through the courts (Lowenstein, 2009). **Divorce mediation** is a non-adversarial means of resolution in which the divorcing couple, along with a third party, such as a therapist or trained mediator, negotiate the terms of their financial, custody, and visitation settlement (Katz, 2007). When couples decide to mediate, they choose to work as a team to resolve all of their divorce issues, avoiding the expensive and demoralizing court process that can exacerbate differences between the divorcing parties.

The couple and the mediator meet in a series of sessions, usually lasting one to two hours. In the first session, the couple and the mediator identify the issues that need to be discussed, the order in which they will be addressed, and what information should be gathered and shared. Further meetings revolve around how to compromise on the various issues that were identified to best meet the needs of both parties and their children (Law and Mediation Offices of David L. Price, 2000).

How long mediation lasts really depends on how contentious the divorce is, whether the couple has children, and the size of their assets. Couples can be in mediation for a few weeks or even a few years. Once an agreement is reached by a mediating couple and filed with the court, it has the same force and effect as an order made by the court. Either party can go to the court and ask for its help in enforcing the agreement. An alternative option would be to return to mediation. Sometimes an amendment to the agreement, acceptable to both parties, solves the problem (Thomas, 2008).

Although mediation is a relatively new process that emerged only in the last few decades, couples who go through mediation are more likely to be happy with the process and results (Thomas, 2008), although men are more likely to experience initial reluctance than are women (Przybyla-Basista, 2008).

divorce mediation: A non-adversarial means of resolution, in which the divorcing couple, along with a third party, such as a therapist or trained mediator, negotiate the terms of their financial, custody, and visitation settlement.

child support order: A legal document delineating the amount and circumstances surrounding the financial support of noncustodial children.

O f all the dimensions of divorce—emotional, legal, economic, co-parental, community, and psychic—which do you think are most challenging to adults, and why? Which are most challenging to children, and why? Are these dimensions different?

:: Divorce and Children: Child Support

Non-custodial parents have a legal responsibility to support their children. For much of U.S. history, these payments were arranged privately between former spouses; the noncustodial parent (usually the father) negotiated a **child support order** with the mother, a legal document delineating the amount and circumstances of the financial support of noncustodial children. Not surprisingly, the amount of these awards varied widely, even among similar types of families. In the past, the administrative authority for child support was left to the local courts, and an individual judge had the power to decide whether the noncustodial father should be required to pay and the amount of the payment. Enforcement was minimal; usually the burden of attempting to collect overdue payments was left to the mother.

Since then, the federal government has stepped up its efforts to improve the collection of child support payments. Congress passed laws to increase the proportion of children who were eligible for child support, to increase and standardize child support orders, and to improve collection rates (Garfinkel, Meyer, & McLanahan, 1998). Furthermore, strong child support enforcement increases fathers' involvement with their children (Nepomnyaschy & Garfinkel, 2007).

How successful have these governmental efforts been? Unfortunately, overall trends in child support have not improved much, as shown in Table 12.3. According to the U.S. Census

Table 12.3	Child Support Receipt for Custodial Parents: 1993 and 2007	

Child support receipt has improved, but still over half of families do not receive the full amount owed to them on a regular basis.

	1993	2007
Received Any Child Support	76%	76%
Received Full Amount	37%	47%
Received Partial Payment	39%	30%
Average Child Support Due	$4,490	$5,350
Average Child Support Received	$2,920	$3,350

Source: Grall, 2009.

Bureau, only about 54 percent of custodial parents have some type of agreement or court award to receive child support from the noncustodial parent (Grall, 2009). Of these custodial parents, only about three-quarters receive any child support at all, and less than half of custodial parents received the full amount. In 2007, the average amount of child support due was $5,350, but the average amount received was $3,350. Custodial parents who received the full payments due were likely to be older, highly educated, and divorced (rather than never married) (Grall, 2009).

Fewer than half of children who are owed child support receive the full amount from their noncustodial parent. What, if anything, should the government do about fathers and mothers who do not pay their child support? How can the courts encourage them to make their payment, and what should be the consequences if they fail to pay?

:: What Are the Effects of Divorce on Children?

About half of all divorce cases occur in families with children. While at least one spouse *chose* to divorce, the children probably did not have any choice in the matter, as Melanie revealed in the opening vignette. These children must live with their parents' decision. Very few children want their parents to separate and divorce (Hetherington & Kelly, 2003). What can they tell us about their experiences? It is difficult to interview children because of a fear that an interview will have harmful effects. Perhaps some of the most interesting research takes place in therapists' offices around the country. Although their samples are not representative, therapists, family counselors, and social workers may be able to offer a deeper look into the minds and hearts of children during their parents' divorce. What do their stories reveal? The feature box *Why Do Research? Divorce through the Eyes of Children* on page 352 describes through pictures how children feel about their parents' divorce.

Some people try to brush off the effects of their parents' divorce (*"Hey, I turned out just fine...."*) but the truth is that many are deeply affected, and remain so for many years (Amato, 2007; Ahrons, 2007; Dennison & Koerner, 2008; Cartwright & McDowell, 2008). Some factors that influence the consequences of divorce on children are micro-level ones, such as personal coping skills, or their relationship with their (usually) noncustodial father. Others are more macro in nature, such as their mother's economic situation. Because the interweaving of factors is complex, it may be helpful to distinguish between short-term and long-term effects.

Short-Term Effects

The first year or two after a divorce can be particularly difficult for both adults and children because of grief and the numerous transitions they face (Ricci, 2007). During this highly stressful time, parents may be distracted and preoccupied with their own grief and distress, thereby making it more difficult to be an effective parent (Taylor & Andrews, 2009). While in the midst of this crisis period, parents may not be able to offer the support, nurturing, and discipline that their children need. Some, in fact, turn to their children for comfort and support (Afifi, Afifi, & Coho, 2009; Koerner, Jacobs, & Raymond, 2004). While providing this kind of support can, at times, lead to closer and more intimate relationships between parents and their children, sometimes it involves putting a child into an adult role that may be well beyond his or her years. The healthiest children were those with at least one parent who practiced an authoritative parenting style (Campana, Henderson, Stolberg, & Schum, 2008).

Sometimes these problems occur before as well as after the divorce. In one study that was based on a large and nationally representative sample, researchers examined children's academic performance and psychological well-being before and after their parents' divorce, and compared these results with their peers in families whose parents did not divorce (Sun & Li, 2002). On average, children whose parents divorced had poorer academic performance and lower levels of psychological well-being both before and after the divorce as compared to the other children.

Why Do Research?

Divorce through the Eyes of Children

Research is clear about the effects of divorce on children. Survey data tell us that for many children divorce can be very unsettling. But what do children tell us about their experiences? It is difficult to interview children—human subjects committees closely safeguard children, worried that interviews may have harmful effects. Perhaps some of the most interesting research is done in the office of therapists around the country. Although a far cry from representative samples, therapists and family counselors may be able to offer a deeper look into the minds and hearts of children during their parents' divorce. How do children really feel about their parents' divorce? These pictures represent a sample of the thousands of stories children "tell" to their therapists.

During this time, children are also grieving the loss of their intact family and dealing with new feelings and fears (Ricci, 2007). Young children in particular are egocentric, and may feel that they are responsible for their parents' conflict and divorce—that if they had just behaved better, their parents would not have felt the need to separate. They may not have the maturity to describe the guilt and sadness they feel.

In the crisis period, children generally face a number of situations that they must learn to cope with, like Melanie, in the chapter opening vignette. These may include (1) parental conflict; (2) the loss of a parent; (3) living with a reduced standard of living; and (4) adjusting to many transitions, possibly including a new home and a new school, or even a new stepfamily. If your parents divorced, consider how you experienced these issues and how you dealt with them.

Parental Conflict   Sometimes parents involve children in their disputes by trying to use them as a weapon to hurt the ex-spouse, getting them to take sides in a dispute, or using them as a way to find out information. Parents may communicate their anger and hostility towards one another to their children, demeaning and ridiculing their ex-spouse. These situations cause children tremendous stress (Michael, Torres, & Seemann, 2007). During and after a break-up, children have fewer health, emotional, and behavioral problems if their parents can cooperate or at least minimize overt conflict in front of them (Ahrons, 2005; Bing, Nelson, & Wesolowski, 2009).

Loss of a Parent   During a separation and after a divorce, children most often live with their mothers and many children see their fathers only sporadically, if at all. Somewhere between 15 and 40 percent of children have not seen their noncustodial parent over the course of a year; the figure is highest for children whose parents have never married, and somewhat lower for children whose parents have divorced (Koball & Principe, 2002). Yet the research continues to show that fathers are extremely important to their children's lives (Booth, Scott, & King, 2010; Hawkins, Amato, & King, 2007; Lundberg, McLanahan, & Rose, 2007). Children whose fathers are more involved in their lives are less likely to have behavioral problems, including delinquency and depression (Carlson, 2006). Fathers provide important social capital, in addition to love and material support. Moreover, noncustodial fathers who have frequent contact with their children during their younger years often have closer relationships with them as they mature into adulthood as well (Aquilino, 2006).

Why do so many noncustodial fathers fail to see their children regularly? The issue is more complex than you might think. Certainly many fathers *choose* to ignore their children, but the residential parent (generally the mother) is a gatekeeper (Trinder, 2008), and she may also interfere with the relationship between father and children in different ways:

- not supporting access;
- not cooperating in arranging visits;
- being inflexible about altering visitation schedules; and
- discouraging children from visiting (Pearson & Thoennes, 1998).

A Reduced Standard of Living   As we have discussed, the standard of living for mothers and their children often declines considerably after a divorce. Everyone in the family must adjust to a lower income. Certain types of clothing, outings, vacations, or other aspects of a family's lifestyle that were the norm before the divorce may no longer be possible. Given the severely limited budgets of most divorced families, consumption patterns must change drastically. Teenagers may need to work at after-school jobs to provide basic necessities for the family.

Adjusting to Transitions   After a divorce, both children and adults must go through many transitions (Kelly, 2007; Sun & Li, 2009). The departure of one parent is likely to be only the first of many transitions to come. If the legal settlement requires that assets

A divorce brings many transitions into the lives of children and their parents. Sometimes the family home is sold, which may require moving to a new neighborhood, attending a new school, and making new friends, leaving the familiar behind.

be divided, then the family's home may have to be sold, necessitating a move to a new house or apartment. For children this may mean adjusting to new schools, new neighborhoods, and new friends, while leaving behind all that was familiar. Children must also adapt to a visitation schedule with the noncustodial parent and adjust to seeing that parent in unfamiliar surroundings. A study of college students found that about half of the students saw their parents' divorce coming, but for others it came as a shock. They reported that the divorce caused them particular difficulty over the holidays (Bulduc, Caron, & Logue, 2006).

Over time, both parents are likely to resume dating, and children will meet their parents' new partners. Cohabitation is increasingly common, so many children must also adapt to other adults moving in (and out) of the household (Xu, Hudspeth, & Bartkowski, 2006). Finally, since most single parents eventually remarry, children will likely experience stepparent relationships. These issues are discussed more fully in Chapter 13.

Longer-Term Effects

Often, children continue to feel the effects of their parents' divorce for years after the actual divorce. While most children adjust adequately over time to the transitions in their lives, some are plagued by depression or other behavioral problems. In the 1970s and early 1980s, Wallerstein and colleagues conducted a longitudinal study of 60 families in the San Francisco area who had experienced a divorce, interviewing them in depth, and following them over a period of 25 years (Wallerstein, 1983; Wallerstein & Blakeslee, 1989). This is a small and nonrepresentative sample, and we should therefore be careful about interpreting and generalizing the results. However, it is one of the few studies that followed people over many years and obtained detailed accounts of their experiences. Their findings are thought-provoking, if not definitive, and have set the stage for later research. The researchers found that many years following a divorce, over one-third of the (now adult) children were still depressed and suffering from a number of behavioral problems related to the divorce.

Since the results of the Wallerstein study were published, other researchers have also found that parental divorce often has long-term effects for many children (El-Sheikh, Buckhalt, Keller, Cummings, & Acebo, 2007; Whitton, Rhoades, Stanley, & Markman, 2008; Sun & Li, 2008a; Ängarne-Lindberg, Wadsby, & Berterö, 2009). Children whose parents divorce are more likely to become pregnant or impregnate others prior to marriage, drop out of school, use alcohol or drugs, and be idle or unemployed. They are more likely to have behavioral problems, experience depression, and have overall poorer health. They also express some degree of anxiety about their own future marriages (Dennison & Koerner, 2008).

For example, one study based on representative samples containing over 35,000 adults, compared outcomes of children who grew up in single-mother families because of divorce or widowhood to children in families with two biological parents (Biblarz & Gottainer, 2000). They found that—even controlling for important background factors such as race, sex, mother's level of education, year, and age—children from single-mother homes produced by parental divorce were significantly less likely than those from families with two biological parents to complete high school, attend college (given high school completion), or graduate from college (given college entry). They also held occupations that are generally lower in status, and they had a lower level of psychological well-being. In contrast, children from widowed single-mother homes did not differ significantly from families with two biological parents on any of these variables, except having slightly lower odds of completing high school.

More recently, another study of about 9,000 teens followed for twelve years into adulthood, assessed the impact of their parents' divorce on their income and earnings (Sun & Li, 2008). Like others, this study also found that children whose parents divorced achieved, on average, lower educational credentials and lower incomes. Some of this difference may be explained by their own parents' lower levels of education and income as compared to others, but some difference remains, which the researchers attribute to divorce. In particular, they found that those children who were in unstable living situations after the divorce (e.g., first a single-parent household, then a stepparent household) seemed to fare worse than those children whose lives were more stable after the divorce.

Age and Sex of the Child   The ages of children at the time of their parents' divorce and their sex seem to be important factors in understanding their adjustment. Divorce may be most difficult for school-age children, who may experience a greater number of transitions with school and friendships during their parents' changes from marriage to separation, divorce, cohabitation, and remarriage (Cavanagh & Huston, 2008). Boys may experience more difficulty than girls; they are more likely to do poorly in school, and are more likely to be aggressive, anxious, lonely and easily distracted in the classroom, particularly if they have little contact with their fathers (Cavanagh & Huston, 2008; UNH Cooperative Extension, 2006).

Others have found that the effects of divorce are not very different for boys and girls (Schoppe-Sullivan, Schermerhorn, & Cummings, 2007). There might be a "sleeper effect" among girls, meaning that their behavioral problems are simply delayed until adolescence or adulthood. Some girls and young women whose parents had divorced seemed to have a lingering sadness about the divorce, and were hesitant and fearful of making a commitment themselves.

A Word of Caution   We should be aware of two points, however. First, these findings certainly do not mean that *all* children from divorced households experience these outcomes. Many children whose parents have divorced lead happy, well-adjusted, and successful lives (Harvey & Fine, 2004). You know many of these people; you may even *be* one of these people. The research only indicates that there is a correlation: children whose parents have divorced are more likely to have these problems than are children from families in which parents have not divorced. In fact, many of these negative outcomes are related to the higher rates of poverty among children growing up in divorced households and are far less apt to occur if the family has adequate financial resources.

The second point we should keep in mind is that it may be the transitions associated with divorce, rather than divorce itself, that are problematic for children (Amato, 2005; Cavanagh & Huston, 2008; Teachman, 2008). Changes associated with separation, divorce, cohabitation, and remarriage—such as moving, going to a new school, making new friends, losing pets, and having people move out of and into the household—can be stressful to children and weaken their sense of security.

If you had children and then later got divorced, how would you minimize the impact of divorce on your children? Think about both short-term and long-term effects.

Which Is Worse for Children, Divorce or Marital Conflict?

At this point in life, I'm almost positive that I'll never get married. . . I'm just so disillusioned by the whole concept. I don't think my parents' divorce has affected me negatively that much. Their marriage, however, has screwed me up more than I'll probably ever know (Harvey & Fine, 2004).

People wonder whether it is better for children if unhappy parents stay married or get divorced. Much of the answer depends on how much conflict there is in the home.

The question that people want the answer to is, "Are children better off when their parents remain unhappily married, or are they better off when their parents divorce?" The answer is not simple because it depends on many things, especially the *severity of the conflict* in the marriage.

Children do not fare well when there is tremendous conflict in their parents' marriage (Cummings, Schermerhorn, Goeke-Morey, & Cummings, 2006; Kaczynski, Lindahl, Malik, & Laurenceau, 2006; Michael, Torres, & Seemann, 2007). This is true regardless of whether parents divorce or remain married. In fact, many researchers suggest that it is the amount and intensity of conflict (e.g., violence, verbal abuse, spiteful behaviors) rather than a divorce *per se* that causes the most harm to children. For example, a longitudinal study, based on telephone and in-person interviews conducted in 1980 and then again in 1992, found that children in families with high marital conflict in 1980 actually were doing *better* in 1992 if their parents had divorced than if they had stayed together (Amato & Booth, 1997). They also found that children from low-conflict families were *worse* off if their parents had divorced. These findings suggest that the worst situations for children are to be in either (1) a high-conflict marriage that does not end in divorce or (2) a low-conflict marriage that does end in divorce.

However, it is important to note that most couples who divorce do not experience extreme forms of conflict. Only one-quarter of parents in the study who divorced between 1980 and 1992 reported any sort of domestic violence or reported that they disagreed "often" or "very often" with their spouse. In fact, only 30 percent reported at least two serious quarrels during the previous month. Consequently, the researchers concluded that the majority of children whose parents divorced probably experienced relatively low conflict and therefore would have been better off if their parents had stayed together (Amato & Booth, 1997).

:: Should Divorce Be More Difficult to Obtain?

Some people believe that divorce should be more difficult to obtain (Kapinus & Flowers, 2008; Martin & Parashar, 2006). What do you think about divorce? Take a look at the self-quiz in the *Getting to Know Yourself* feature box and compare your answers to those of your friends or partner.

"Would I Be Happier?"

People who divorce do so because they believe they will be happier afterward. But this belief is not necessarily valid. A research team headed by Linda Waite of the University of Chicago used data collected by the National Survey of Families and Households (NSFH), based on a large nationally representative sample of adults in the United States (Waite & Gallagher, 2000). Out of more than 5,000 married adults, 645 reported being unhappily married. Waite's research focused on these unhappily married people, who were interviewed again five years later. By then, some had divorced. The researchers used detailed measures of psychological well-being to compare those who had stayed married to those who had divorced. Were the divorced people happier?

The study found that, on average, the people in the divorced group were no happier than those who remained married. First, divorce did not reduce or eliminate feelings of depression,

Getting to Know Yourself

My Attitudes toward Divorce

The self-quiz below assesses your opinions about divorce, and the difficulty or ease by which you believe it should be obtained. Please answer T if you think the statement is mostly true or if you mostly agree with it, and F if you think the statement is mostly false or if you mostly disagree with it. You may want to compare your answers to those of your partner, family members, friends, or classmates.

1. Marriage is forever and the bonds should never be broken.　　T　F

2. I think no-fault divorce has been a good thing for our society because people should be allowed to get divorced if they are not happy.　　T　F

3. I think divorce is harmful to many children.　　T　F

4. My religion considers divorce to be a sin.　　T　F

5. I think people who want a divorce should be required to see a counselor for several sessions before the divorce is granted.　　T　F

6. Divorce should be more difficult to obtain if you have children.　　T　F

7. I think divorce should be available to anyone based on irreconcilable differences.　　T　F

8. I cannot imagine ever getting divorced.　　T　F

9. Single parents can do just as good a job of raising children as can two-parent families.　　T　F

10. Divorce is detrimental to our society.　　T　F

Scoring: Give yourself 1 point for every T for questions 1, 3, 4, 5, 6, 8, and 10. Give yourself 1 point for every F for questions 2, 7, and 9. Add up your points. The higher your score, the more likely you think that divorce should be more difficult to obtain.

What Do You Think?

1. Can you identify any micro-level and macro-level factors that have influenced your opinions?

2. How do your answers compare to others? Are you surprised by the differences or similarities? Why or why not?

---

raise self-esteem, or increase a sense of mastery. This was the case regardless of income, race, sex, or age. Second, the researchers also found that two-thirds of those who stayed married over the five years reported that their marriages had improved. Interestingly, those who were in the least happy marriages at the time of the first interview reported the most dramatic turnaround.

Why didn't divorce make people happier? The study authors suggest that while divorce eliminates some stresses, it creates new ones as well that can have negative consequences. These include the reactions of children; potential disappointments and aggravations in custody, child support, and visitation orders; new financial stresses; or health problems.

To follow up on the finding that two-thirds of unhappy marriages had become happier five years later, the researchers also conducted focus group interviews with 55 formerly unhappy spouses who had turned their marriages around (Waite & Gallagher, 2000). Many of these couples had experienced periods of serious family problems in their marriage, including alcoholism, infidelity, verbal abuse, neglect, depression, illness, or work problems. Most of these couples did not see divorce as a quick fix to their problems and they had family and friends who encouraged them to stay married. Because of this, they invested great effort in overcoming or enduring problems in their relationships. Their stories fell into three broad types:

- *The marital endurance ethic:* Most commonly, couples reported that their marriages got happier not just because partners resolved problems but because they stubbornly outlasted them. Over time, many of the sources of conflict ceased.

- *The marital work ethic:* Some spouses actively worked to solve problems, change their behavior, and improve their communication. They enlisted help or advice from others, including counselors or clergy. They may have rearranged their work or family schedules to attack the problem and to spend more time together.
- *The personal happiness ethic:* For these persons, the marriage problems did not diminish appreciably; however, they found alternative ways to improve their own happiness. They built a happy life despite an unhappy marriage.

Covenant Marriage

As you learned in Chapter 7, there is a growing marriage movement designed to promote and protect traditional marriage. Although much of this movement is rooted in religious communities, it has also produced political change (Maher, 2006). For example, Georgia now allows no-fault divorce only if both parties agree to the divorce and if no children are involved. Oklahoma spent $10 million on an initiative to reduce divorce by 30 percent by 2010. In three states—Arizona, Arkansas, and Louisiana—a covenant marriage is now legal. This type of marriage demands premarital counseling, and an oath of lifelong commitment, and makes divorce more difficult to obtain by requiring counseling and offering only limited grounds for divorce, such as adultery, addiction, or imprisonment.

Professor Waite's research found that some people stay married despite being in an unhappy marriage because they find alternative ways to be happy; they build a happy life despite an unhappy marriage. What do you think of this approach? Could you ever see yourself in this situation? Why or why not?

Many people support each of these ideals in principle. Nine in ten adults surveyed believe that partners should agree to seek counseling if they are unable to resolve problems. However, taken together, less than half of adults support covenant marriage. Moreover, only about 2 percent of new marriages in Louisiana, and even fewer in Arizona and Arkansas, are covenant marriages (Stritof & Stritof, 2006).

:: The "Good Divorce"

My parents got divorced when I was twelve and my brother was eight. I felt sad at first, and a little embarrassed because my friends' parents all seemed happily married. But, you know, it was okay. We technically lived with my mom, but my dad was always there for us. We stayed with him a lot, whenever we wanted to. He still took my brother and me to our ball games and celebrated our birthdays at the house. I never heard my mom complain about child support, so I guess he paid everything he was supposed to. I don't really know; they didn't involve me in those kinds of things. I think he and my mom really tried hard to get along for our sake. And it seemed to work most of the time. My brother and I always felt loved and cared for.

—Krish, Age 29

Have you ever known anyone who had a "good divorce"? What factors made this resolution possible for them? What factors seem to prevent other divorcing couples from having a "good divorce"?

Some couples part with respect and dignity, and work cooperatively to raise their children. For them divorce represents a major change in family functioning, but not a devastating one (Ängarne-Lindberg, Wadsby, & Berterö, 2009). Family scholar Constance Ahrons, for her book, *The Good Divorce* (1994), interviewed nearly 100 divorcing couples over a five-year period in one region of Wisconsin to determine the ways in which they functioned after the divorce. She found that about half of the couples had a "good divorce," meaning they remained amicable toward one another, avoided serious conflict, and worked diligently to preserve family ties. They remained committed to their children and continued to be responsible for their children's emotional, economic, and physical well-being.

Some even celebrated holidays together or went together on outings with their children. Ahrons used the term **binuclear families** to describe divorced parents who live in two households, but remain one family in spirit because of their children. Her respondents did not always find it easy to remain on good terms, however, partly because there are so few role models of good behavior, as you will read about in Chapter 13.

Years later, Ahrons interviewed the children of her divorced respondents to see how they fared (Ahrons, 2005). She was able to locate about 90 percent of the children, who were then in their 30s. About three-quarters of these adult children believed their parents' divorce was a good idea, and felt that they and their parents were better off for it. In particular, parents who made the effort to have a "good divorce" and maintain family bonds had children who felt stronger and more secure in their lives. Her results remind us that divorce does not have to be a devastating event for children.

A "good divorce" may not always be possible, but research suggests that it should be the model to strive for because children fare better after divorce when both parents remain involved in and committed to their lives (Gasper, Stolberg, Macie, & Williams, 2008).

Some couples have what has been nicknamed a "good divorce," meaning they remain amicable, avoid serious conflict, work diligently to preserve family ties, and remain committed to their children's happiness and well-being.

Bringing It Full Circle

Divorce is common in American society, although the divorce rate has declined significantly over the past several decades. The fluctuating divorce rate has many macro-level and micro-level explanations, which are interrelated because macro-level factors shape our personal experiences and choices. As we saw in the opening vignette, conflict and divorce affect many relationships within the family, and families must sort through the emotional, legal, economic, co-parental, community, and psychic dimensions of separation and divorce. Children like Melanie are particularly affected by conflict and divorce, and they are more likely than other children to experience social and emotional challenges. Programs like mediation can offer a helping hand as couples move through the process of divorce. But, as we will see in the next chapter, sometimes divorce does not just end a relationship. With high rates of remarriage, it can also mean the beginning of a new family unit. Let's return a moment to Melanie's experience with her parents' divorce in the opening vignette. With the information you have learned in this chapter, consider the following questions:

- How would you describe Melanie's experiences with the different stations of her parents' divorce: emotional, legal, economic, co-parental, community, and psychic?

- Since the research shows that children do better if they remain in close contact with their noncustodial parents, should children like Melanie be required to stay with their fathers even if they do not really want to?

- Do you think that Melanie's family had a "good divorce"? Explain your answer.

- If you or someone close to you divorced, how would you explain it to your child? Would you focus only on micro-level issues, or would any macro-level issues be relevant?

For further review, turn to the Video Discussion Guide on page 449 to answer additional questions about how the chapter opening video relates to what you have learned in this chapter.

binuclear family: A type of family consisting of divorced parents living in two separate households but remaining one family in spirit for the sake of the children.

Chapter Review

12.1 What is the best way to calculate the divorce rate?

Many different methods are used to calculate the divorce rate. Some of them are misleading. The two best methods are the crude and refined divorce rates.

12.2 Is the rate of divorce in the United States currently increasing?

No. Although the rate of divorce in the United States has varied over the years, it has been declining since 1980.

12.3 What kinds of micro-level factors influence divorce?

Micro-level factors associated with divorce include whether or not one's parents had divorced, age at marriage, the presence of children, nonmarital childbearing, the sex of children, race and ethnic background, education, income, degree of similarity between spouses, and the age of the couple.

12.4 What kinds of macro-level factors influence divorce?

Macro-level factors associated with divorce include a country's level of socioeconomic development, the most widely practiced religion, divorce laws, the status of women, and the general attitudes toward divorce.

12.5 What are the phases of a separation?

In the first phase of a marital separation, *preseparation*, one or both partners begin to think about the benefits of a separation. During the *early separation phase*, couples face a series of issues as they separate. Who will be the one to move out? How shall we work out financial matters, such as the house payment, the car payment, and other bills? In the *mid-separation phase*, the realities of daily living set in, such as maintaining two households, arranging visitation for the children, and living on a reduced income.

12.6 How is divorce experienced differently by women and men?

The different opportunities and constraints for men and women that are embedded in our culture can result in different experiences for men and women during a divorce. For example, women are more likely to report marital problems. They are also more likely to be impoverished after a divorce.

12.7 What are the stations of divorce?

These describe six important components of the divorce experience: the emotional, legal, economic, co-parental, community, and psychic divorce.

12.8 What is divorce mediation?

Divorce mediation is a non-adversarial means of resolution in which the divorcing couple, along with a third party, such as a therapist or trained mediator, negotiate the terms of their financial, custody, and visitation settlement. When couples decide to mediate, they choose to work as a team to resolve their divorce issues, avoiding the lengthy and often adversarial court process.

12.9 How common is child support and alimony?

Most divorcing couples with children have a child support order that outlines the amount of monthly support, its duration, and other specific features of the arrangement. However, despite the order, many noncustodial parents fail to maintain their full payment on a regular basis. Alimony is a payment to the spouse. It is awarded with far less frequency.

Key Terms

alimony (p. 346)
binuclear family (p. 359)
child snatching (p. 348)
child support order (p. 350)
crude divorce rate (p. 334)
divorce mediation (p. 350)

intergenerational transmission of divorce (p. 336)
joint legal custody (p. 347)
joint physical custody (p. 347)
legal custody (p. 346)
legal divorce (p. 345)

legal separation (p. 344)
no-fault divorce (p. 339)
physical custody (p. 347)
refined divorce rate (p. 335)
sole legal custody (p. 347)

sole physical custody (p. 347)
stations of divorce (p. 344)

12.10 What are the short-term and long-term consequences of divorce for children?

A growing number of research studies suggest that divorce can be more harmful for children than previously thought. In the short term, children must learn to deal with parental conflict; the loss of a parent; a reduced standard of living; and adjusting to many transitions. Over the long term, many, but not all, children suffer emotionally, socially, and academically when their parents divorce.

12.11 Is it better for children if their parents stay in an unhappy marriage or get a divorce?

In marriages with a high degree of conflict, children may be better off if their parents divorce. In marriages with less conflict between spouses, which comprise the majority of divorce situations, it may be better for the children if their parents stay married.

12.12 Are people happier when they divorce?

One large study of unhappily married people followed them over five years and found that those who divorced were no happier than those who remained married. For example, divorce did not reduce or eliminate feelings of depression, raise self-esteem, or increase a sense of mastery. This was the case regardless of income, race, sex, or age. Second, the researchers also found that two-thirds of those who stayed married over the five years reported that their marriages had improved. Interestingly, those who were in the least happy marriages at the time of the first interview reported the most dramatic turnaround.

12.13 What is meant by a "good divorce"?

Not all divorces represent the same degree of crisis and disorganization. For example, when both parents make a concerted effort to get along and co-parent, the negative effects of divorce can be reduced considerably or even eliminated.

PEARSON
myfamilylab®
www.myfamilylab.com

Experience, Discover, Observe, Evaluate

MyFamilyLab is designed just for you. Each chapter features a pretest and post-test to help you learn and review key concepts and terms. Experience Marriage and Family in action with dynamic visual activities, videos, and readings to enhance your learning experience.

Here are a few activities you will find for this chapter:

Watch Core Concepts video clips feature sociologists in action, exploring important concepts in the study of Marriage and the Family. Watch:
- Infidelity

Explore Social Explorer is an interactive application that allows you to explore Census data through interactive maps. Explore the Social Explorer Map:
- Divorce Rates Across the United States

Read MySocLibrary includes primary source readings from classic and contemporary sociologists. Read:
- Hilton & Anderson, "Characteristics of Women with Children Who Divorce in Midlife Compared to Those Who Remain Married"

13 Family Life, Partnering, and Remarriage after Divorce

Top: Daneen and Jim; Middle: Connor, Jim, Daneen, Jamie, Kate, and Lindsay; Bottom: Kate, Lindsay, Connor, and Jamie.

We hear a lot about the negative aspects of "broken homes" or "wicked stepmothers."

But can't good things come of divorce, repartnering, and blending families?

Daneen and Jim show us what is possible after a divorce. They met, fell in love, and gave careful consideration to what the future could hold in store. Both had a son and daughter from a previous marriage. They wanted the best for their children and for themselves. After much thought, Jim and Daneen decided to marry. Daneen's children, Connor and Kate, were 10 and 8 years old, while Jim's children, Lindsay and Jamie, were 14 and 10 at the time. Five years later Daneen and Jim, as well as their four children, believe they have successfully blended their families. Both Daneen and Jim consider all the children to be "their own."

Their path to success wasn't completely smooth, however. For both families it was a big adjustment. For example, Jamie worried that this new woman and her family would take away his time with his father. His dad was his rock, especially because he rarely saw his own mother who lives in another state. Jamie was very cautious, not ready to trust Daneen. It took some time, but the barriers are down now, and Daneen and Jamie are very close. She has become the mother that he never really had. Meanwhile Daneen's own son Connor, whose father lives nearby, also had some difficulty adjusting to their blended family. He

Daneen and Jim both had 2 children from previous marriages when they married.

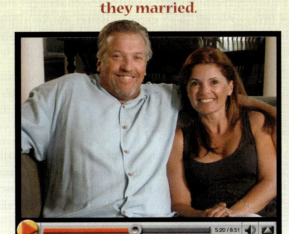

👁 ━ **Watch** the **Video** *Remarriage and Blending Families: Daneen and Jim* on **myfamilylab.com**

worried about his father's feelings, fearing that his father would be upset by his ex-wife getting remarried, but they too have worked through these concerns.

As a stepmom, Daneen feels that she always tries to treat the kids equally. Although Jamie and Lindsay sometimes tease her about being "stepmonster," Jamie maintains that Daneen is always fair. Daneen worried at first about how she would manage with a teenage stepdaughter, but she feels that she and Lindsay have really connected. And Kate, the youngest of the four children, adores her older stepsister. Kate is still working through some conflicted feelings for her stepfather Jim, however. Because she spent her early years without a father in the home, she can still put up a "wall" at times with Jim.

Despite some initial tensions, the four children have been able to bond. Being fairly close in age helps; in fact, Jamie's and Connor's birthdays are only two weeks apart. They share academic and athletic interests, although they have distinctive personalities. An important way that the children have bonded is through helping one another cope with some of the disappointments they each face with their noncustodial parents.

Q **UESTIONS** *That Matter* •

13.1 What are some common feelings experienced by adults after a divorce?

13.2 What is the biggest issue facing women after a divorce?

13.3 What are some issues facing fathers after a divorce?

13.4 How common is cohabitation among divorced people?

13.5 Which groups in the United States are more likely to remarry?

13.6 Why do men and women remarry at different rates?

13.7 How strong and stable are remarried relationships?

13.8 What are some common stereotypes of stepfamilies?

13.9 How do stepfamilies differ from biological families?

13.10 How do children fare in stepfamilies?

13.11 How do adults fare in stepfamilies?

13.12 How can stepfamilies be strengthened?

Divorce can be very difficult for children, but one of the upsides is that children and their custodial parent (usually a mother) often become closer as a result of the divorce.

✳ Explore the Concept
Social Explorer Map: The Increase of Single Women with Children on **myfamilylab.com**

it is also true that many children lead happy, well-adjusted lives. They continue to have warm relationships with one or both of their parents—more often with the custodial parent—and with their siblings (Frank, 2008).

In fact, it is these positive relationships that help beat the odds against negative outcomes, such as dropping out of school or teen pregnancy. A primary factor in children's short-term and long-term adjustment to divorce is how effectively the custodial parent—usually the mother—functions as a parent (Hutchinson, Afifi, & Krause, 2007; Luedemann, Ehrenberg, & Hunter, 2006). The feature box *Why Do Research? When Is a Correlation Only a Correlation?* on the previous page focuses on successful men raised by divorced mothers who have beaten the odds, including President Barack Obama. In other words, there may be a correlation between divorce and negative child outcomes, but we should not overstate this correlation. A correlation does not imply that all children from divorced families will experience negative outcomes, nor does it imply that divorce alone is the cause of any problems that do occur.

Oddly, however, the positive side of parent-child relationships after a divorce has rarely been studied. Instead, most researchers begin with a deficit model—that a home without two parents is somehow a "broken home."

Issues for Custodial Mothers: Downward Mobility

Often the first months or years after divorce are difficult because of a multitude of conflicting emotions: elation, anger, depression, and sadness. These emotions can be heightened by the significant financial losses that many families face. We have seen in Chapter 12 that divorce can often alter a family's standard of living, especially for mothers. Nearly one-third of custodial mothers receive some sort of public assistance (Grall, 2009), food stamps in particular. ✳ Explore on **myfamilylab.com**

Most women are aware that their standard of living is likely to drop significantly after a divorce (Poortman & Seltzer, 2007). Using data on over 5,000 parents collected for the National Survey of Families and Households, researchers found that 72 percent of mothers assumed that their standard of living would be worse or much worse after divorce, compared to 54 percent of fathers who thought their standard of living would be worse. Substantial differences were also found *within the same family*; more than twice as many mothers as fathers from the same family expected their standard of living to be worse (Poortman & Seltzer, 2007). Women in their twenties and thirties are more confident that they can maintain employment to provide sufficient income for their families, while older women are less confident about their earning capabilities (Arendell, 1986).

How do newly single mothers manage? Most drastically cut their expenses or move to cheaper housing so they can pay their monthly bills. Terry Arendell's qualitative study found that few women she interviewed had extra money left at the end of the month after paying for the minimum necessities (1986). Women of all ages and all income levels talked about the anxiety, depression, and despair associated with their financial difficulties after a divorce:

I've been living hand to mouth all these years, ever since the divorce. I have no savings account. The notion of having one is [as] foreign to me as insurance—there's no way I can afford insurance. I have an old pickup that I don't drive very often. In the summertime I don't wear pantyhose to work because I can cut costs there. Together the kids

" In the summertime I don't wear pantyhose to work because I can cut costs there."

and I have had to struggle and struggle. Supposedly struggle builds character. Well, some things are not character building. There have been times when we've scoured the shag rug to see if we could find a coin to come up with enough to buy milk so we could have cold cereal for dinner. That's not character building.

Custodial Fathers: A Growing Group

I thought, 'Hey, she'll go in [into drug rehabilitation center], get cleaned up, and come and get these kids.' But, no! [laughing] It did not happen that way at all. These kids have been living with me; they are my pride and joy and have been since '94, that's when they came to live with Daddy. But in the beginning I tell you, I did not want any part of it and they [Child Service Workers] had to practically threaten me to do it—they made me realize there was no other place for my kids to go, and my kids had been through a lot of bad things with their mother. I didn't know the extent of it until they was living with me. (Hamer & Marchioro, 2002:121).

After a divorce, most children reside with their mother. About 83 percent of custodial parents are mothers. However, this also means that some custodial parents are fathers—totaling about 2.3 million (Grall, 2009; Hook & Chalasani, 2008). Men account for one in every six custodial parents, up from one in ten in 1980. Forty percent of custodial fathers live with only their children; the remaining live with a cohabiting partner or other adults, including family members or friends (U.S. Census Bureau, July 1, 2007). The vast majority of custodial fathers are White (83 percent) and another 13 percent are Black or Hispanic. Their average age is 38; only one in nine custodial fathers is under the age of 25 (Grall, 2009).

In the past, fathers usually could not obtain custody of their children unless the mother was proved to be unfit, did not want the children, or there were other extenuating circumstances. Today, fathers may seek and gain custody for a wide variety of reasons, often through mutual agreement with the mother. Fathers may also step in because the mother is physically, emotionally, or financially unable to care for the children, or because they want to be the primary caretakers of their children. Moreover, fathers may seek and obtain custody at the request of their children.

Compared to two-parent families, single-father families have lower incomes; are twice as likely to be impoverished; have less education; and are more likely to live in rental housing than own their home. While these households are more vulnerable than two-parent families, at least financially, they do have higher incomes than those headed by single mothers (Grall, 2009).

A study based on a representative sample of nearly 17,000 parents compared the amount of time that single and married parents spend caring for their children (Hook & Chalasani, 2008). They analyzed the total amount that parents spend caring for or interacting with children in a 24-hour period, and classified the care into one of three categories: (1) physical care and planning (e.g., organizing, looking after, waiting for, helping, teaching not related to education, traveling); (2) play and companionship (e.g., reading to or with, playing, talking and listening, attending events); and (3) achievement-related activities (e.g., doing homework, attending school conferences, contacting with teachers, waiting associated with education). The results are found in Table 13.1. Several

| Table 13.1 | Minutes Spent Caring For Children |

First, single fathers spend more time than married fathers, but less time than single or married mothers, caring for very young children. Second, as children age, the amount of time single fathers spend with children, as compared to married or single mothers, is more comparable. Third, single fathers spend more time in direct physical care than do married fathers, but less time than single or married mothers.

Youngest Child, ages 0–5	Total	Physical	Play	Achievement
Single Fathers	127	78	45	4
Single Mothers	142	102	34	6
Married Fathers	106	59	43	4
Married Mothers	150	101	44	5
Youngest Child, ages 6–11				
Single Fathers	73	47	15	11
Single Mothers	80	53	14	13
Married Fathers	54	29	16	9
Married Mothers	72	49	12	12
Youngest Child, ages 12–14				
Single Fathers	43	23	10	10
Single Mothers	46	29	10	7
Married Fathers	24	15	5	4
Married Mothers	35	22	6	7

Source: Hook, Jennifer L. & Chalasani, Satvika. 2008. "Gendered Expectations? Reconsidering Single Fathers' Child-Care Time." Journal of Marriage and the Family 70(4):978–90.

Diversity in Families

"I'm Turning Out to be a Darn Good Dad..."

A growing number of fathers are asking for and being awarded custody of their children in the United States. Nick is one of these custodial fathers. Here is what he had to say about the situation:

It wasn't supposed to be this way, you know. Leah and I married right out of college, and we both assumed things would be great between us and that we would never have any major problems. It's not always easy to explain it to outsiders, but sometimes the best-laid plans just go up in smoke. Problems in our marriage began to surface within a couple of years, and we thought that maybe if we had a baby, things would be better. Clearly, having a baby is not the answer to marital problems! Don't get me wrong, I absolutely love my daughter, but she was not the glue to hold together an unhappy marriage. After seven years of marriage, when little Sabrina was four, Leah and I separated.

During the separation, we shared custody of Sabrina. She spent Sunday through Wednesday with me, and Thursday through Saturday with Leah. I rented a two-bedroom apartment and tried to fix Sabrina's room up like her old room, but most of her bedroom things were new and unfamiliar to her because Leah kept our condo. I have always been a pretty hands-on dad, but taking care of Sabrina full-time, for even four days a week, was definitely a new and often difficult experience. Waking her up in the morning, fixing her breakfast, helping her dress, taking her to preschool, picking her up at 5:00, cooking, cleaning, entertaining, teaching... it's hard. The handing-off process was usually awkward; Sabrina would cry for the parent she was saying goodbye to, and Leah and I would often argue about something.

After a year of separation, about the time Sabrina was ready to begin kindergarten, Leah and I decided to divorce. Leah told me that she didn't want custody. She said it was too tough, her job too demanding, and mothering was just too stressful. She asked for traditional visitation, which included every Wednesday after school, every other weekend, and four weeks in the summer. I have to say I was shocked. Full custody isn't what I was envisioning, but I immediately said, "deal." I cannot envision arguing about who has to take our daughter. I know we both love her, so I said "Yes, I will have custody."

Leah gave us the condo, and through a mediator we worked out other aspects of the divorce agreement, including child support. That was a tough one—Leah didn't think she should pay anything because I earn a little more than she does, but the mediator really insisted. So, now she pays $400 a month, which I need because of afterschool care costs, health insurance, and a million and one other things that pop up monthly. Leah pays her child support every month, although not necessarily on time, which can irk me, and has been the cause of some big arguments. However, she has never missed any of her visitations, and from what I can tell, seems to be a good noncustodial mom to Sabrina.

I'm turning out to be a darn good dad, although I'm still not very good at fixing hair, buying "girlie" clothes or other things like that. Sabrina is almost nine now, and I'm hoping her mother will step in a little more, especially around adolescence. But, I've learned to be a great cook, an active soccer coach, and a happy PTA member. Who would have thought? It all comes down to this: I love that little girl. Being a single dad to Sabrina is definitely not easy, but I'm doing the best that I can.

—Nick, Age 34

What Do You Think?

1. How do you think single fathering compares to single mothering? Are the issues faced by single mothers and fathers similar or different?

2. Why do you think the number of single-father families is on the rise? What micro-level and macro-level factors might explain the increase?

findings are apparent: first, single fathers spend more time than married fathers, but far less time than single or married mothers caring for very young children. Second, as children age, the amount of time single fathers spend with children is more comparable to mothers. Third, the types of activities in which parents engage with their children varies, with single fathers generally spending more time in direct physical care than do married fathers, but less time than single or married mothers.

In the feature box *Diversity in Families: "I'm Turning Out to be a Darn Good Dad ..."* meet Nick, a single father raising a daughter after his divorce.

Most studies of custodial fathers focus on the experience of White fathers who obtain custody following a divorce. One study by Hamer and Marchioro (2002) describes the circumstances in which low-income and working-class Black men come to gain custody of their children, how they transition to a full-time parent role, and what types of social support networks they use in parenting.

The researchers interviewed 24 men from an impoverished Midwestern urban area. They found the subjects generally became full-time fathers by default, often without any explicit discussion with the mother. Some mothers gradually withdrew from parenting by leaving their children progressively more with the father. Other mothers abruptly disengaged themselves from their children. Most fathers were reluctant to accept their children, but did so because of pressure or because they assumed the situation would be only temporary.

The fathers' transition to full-time parenting was difficult for several reasons. First, they lacked confidence in their parenting abilities. Second, they had little money and found it difficult to provide for their children. Third, they had to make drastic changes in their lifestyle and give up a degree of freedom.

Extended family members may ease these difficulties. Eight of the 24 fathers lived with other family members, usually parents or siblings. These fathers, along with those who lived independently, relied upon family to help with babysitting, preparing children's meals, doing the laundry, and a multitude of parenting tasks. "If it weren't for my family, times would be very, very rough," says one dad (Hamer & Marchioro, 2002:124). Custodial fathers tend to have closer ties with their parents than custodial mothers have with their parents, and they have more frequent contact with their parents (Hilton & Kopera-Frye, 2007). Custodial fathers also receive a broader range of support from extended kin than do custodial mothers. This help is likely related to their closer and more frequent contact, but it also may be related to a gender bias—people assume men need more help than women do with respect to parenting and other domestic tasks, and therefore are more likely to offer it.

Over 2 million fathers have custody of their children, sometimes by default, but increasingly by choice.

W*hy do single fathers have closer ties and receive more assistance from their extended families than do single mothers? Are single fathers more likely to ask for help? Are family members more likely to offer help to single fathers than to single mothers? Why or why not?*

:: Repartnering after a Divorce

There are many paths after a divorce. Some adults, feeling angry or betrayed, swear they will never marry again while others desperately look for mates to ward off loneliness or financial difficulties. Generally, finding a new partner after a divorce, or **repartnering**, is the most important factor in improving life satisfaction for both men and women (Shapiro, 1996). Women, in particular, gain financially from repartnering. In fact, on average the financial gains women make from repartnering outweigh the benefits of reentering the labor force after divorce or increasing their working hours (Jansen, Mortelmans, & Snoeckx, 2009).

Dating Again

If the divorcing partners are young and were married only a short time, it may not be very difficult for them to begin dating. There are likely many single people in their "pool of eligibles," and many of their friends are probably single and can introduce them to potential partners.

repartnering: The act of entering into a relationship after a divorce, which may lead to cohabitation or marriage.

In contrast, dating and courtship may be more difficult or awkward for people who are older and who have been married a long time because they may be unaware of changing dating norms (Remarriage.com, 2008). Their concerns may include questions such as, is it okay for a woman to initiate a date? Should we meet at the restaurant or should one person pick up the other at home? Who pays for dinner? Who pays for the babysitter? What sexual expectations will there be? Am I supposed to like her children right away? Are my children supposed to like him right away?

Many older people complain that it is not as easy to find dating partners as when they were younger. Older women often find it difficult to meet men their age because men tend to date younger women (Ahrons, 2007; Calistanti & Kiecolt, 2007; Sassler, 2010).

As shown in Chapter 3, the most common way to meet partners is through friends, but as we age, fewer of our friends are single or know others who are single. Consequently, on-line dating is popular. There are approximately 1,400 online dating sites, the largest being eHarmony.com with over 20 million users and Match.com with 15 million users (Scott, 2009). Nearly half of adults (49 percent) know at least one person who has dated someone they met online (Greenberg, 2009), and most have relatively positive things to say about the experience. 📖—|**Read** on **myfamilylab.com**

📖—|**Read** the **Document**
Transitions in Parental Repart-nering after Divorce on **myfamilylab.com**

Cohabitation after a Divorce

As we have learned in Chapter 3, most people today live with a partner before marriage (Kennedy & Bumpass, 2008). Cohabitation is not just for the young; it is also becoming common among previously married and middle-aged adults (Kreider, 2008; Teachman, 2008; U.S. Census Bureau, January 14, 2010; Xu, Hudspeth, & Bartkowski, 2006) and children are present in about half of these relationships. In fact, the number of people ages 45–54 who are cohabiting (and presumably have been previously married) is close to the number of people ages 15–24 who are cohabiting (and presumably have never been married) (Fields, 2004).

Divorced people who cohabit may view the arrangement as an extension of serious dating rather than an alternative to marriage *per se*. Cohabitation may or may not lead to marriage with that particular partner. About two-thirds of remarrying women under age 45 have cohabited with a partner between their first and second marriages (Teachman, 2008). The longer the time since a divorce, the more likely people are to cohabit, as shown in Figure 13.1 (Bramlett & Mosher, 2002). Bulcroft & Bulcroft (1991) found that, among single persons over age 55 who date, cohabitation is favored almost as much as marriage; others report that cohabiters have, on average, a significantly longer time between divorce and remarriage (Bulcroft & Bulcroft, 1991; Xu, Hudspeth, & Bartkowski, 2006). Thus, it seems that for other divorced persons, cohabitation may not simply be a precursor to marriage, but may replace it altogether. This is why some researchers interested in relationships after divorce prefer to focus on "repartnering" rather than "remarriage" *per se*. However, as Figure 13.1 also shows, rates of cohabitation do vary across racial and ethnic groups. Whites are most likely to cohabit after a divorce, and Blacks are least likely to cohabit regardless of how much time has passed since the separation or divorce.

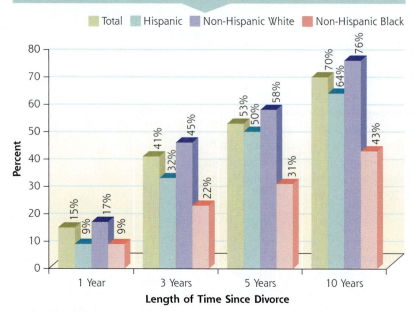

| **Figure 13.1** | **Likelihood of Cohabitation by Length of Time Since Divorce, Women Ages 15–44** |

The longer the time since a divorce, the more likely people are to cohabit.

Legend: Total, Hispanic, Non-Hispanic White, Non-Hispanic Black

1 Year: 15%, 9%, 17%, 9%
3 Years: 41%, 32%, 45%, 22%
5 Years: 53%, 50%, 58%, 31%
10 Years: 70%, 64%, 76%, 43%

Percent (y-axis), Length of Time Since Divorce (x-axis)

Source: Bramlett & Mosher, 2002.

When a couple decides to cohabit or remarry, the decision often occurs quickly after the relationship begins, unlike first marriages in which the partners may have dated for years before making a commitment to marry (Wu & Schimmele, 2005). The relationship may progress quickly because divorced men and women feel they do not need as much time to get to know one another. They believe they have learned from past relationship mistakes, are more focused about what they are looking for in a partner, or are a better judge of character. Yet, Ganong and Coleman (1989) found that many couples preparing for remarriage fail to address critical issues: fewer than 25 percent discussed financial matters with their partner, and 13 percent did not discuss any substantive issues at all.

How do you think divorced parents with children should handle dating? What are some dilemmas you would face if in this situation, and how would you handle them? Do you think dating issues are different between mothers and fathers?

:: Remarriage

About 21 percent of all currently married men and women have been married at least twice. Of these, about 4 percent have been married three or more times. As shown in Figure 13.2, among all people ages 25 and over who have previously divorced, 52 percent of men and 44 percent of women have remarried (U.S. Census Bureau, August 27, 2008). Others who do not remarry remain single for different reasons; perhaps they prefer a single lifestyle or have not met the "right" person. Older persons may avoid marriage because of the potential loss of Social Security benefits, the challenges posed by merging households, or the lack of support of older children (Mahay & Lewin, 2007).

We often talk as though remarriage, and the new family structures it creates, were a modern invention. However, remarriage has always been a common feature of family life in the United States (Phillips, 1997). In early American history, life expectancy was considerably lower than it is today. Since it was difficult to maintain a household as a widow or widower, quick remarriage was common. If children were present, the remarriage substituted a new parent for the old one.

Nonetheless, it took until the 1970s for family scientists to begin to take a real interest in the subject of remarriage as a research topic. Today, most remarriages take place after divorce rather than widowhood. With divorce, the ex-spouse is still alive, perhaps living within the vicinity and exercising his or her parental rights. This provides many new situations that families did not face in the past when remarriage involved a widow or a widower.

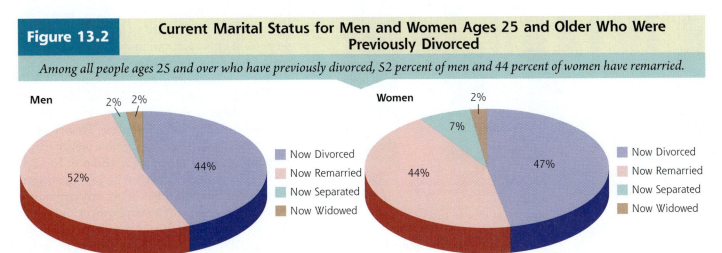

Figure 13.2 — **Current Marital Status for Men and Women Ages 25 and Older Who Were Previously Divorced**

Among all people ages 25 and over who have previously divorced, 52 percent of men and 44 percent of women have remarried.

Men: Now Divorced 44%, Now Remarried 52%, Now Separated 2%, Now Widowed 2%
Women: Now Divorced 47%, Now Remarried 44%, Now Separated 7%, Now Widowed 2%

Source: U.S. Census Bureau, August 27, 2008.

Table 13.2	Probability of Remarriage by Duration of Divorce, Women Ages 15–44			
The majority of divorced women remarry within five years. Younger women, high school graduates, and women with higher incomes are most likely to remarry.				
	1 year	**3 years**	**5 years**	**10 years**
Total	15%	39%	54%	75%
Age at divorce				
Less than 25	17%	41%	57%	81%
25 and over	14%	37%	51%	68%
Education				
Less than high school	17%	37%	50%	74%
High school	17%	41%	56%	78%
More than high school	13%	36%	53%	71%
Income				
Less than $25,000	14%	30%	42%	62%
$25,000–$49,999	16%	40%	54%	73%
$50,000 or more	17%	46%	65%	87%

Source: Bramlett & Mosher, 2002.

Figure 13.3	Probability of Remarriage by Duration of Divorce by Race/Ethnicity, Women Ages 15–44

Whites are more likely than Blacks or Hispanics to remarry after a divorce.

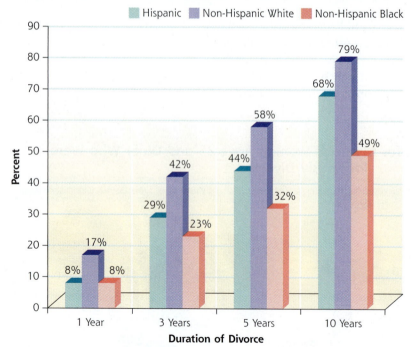

Source: Bramlett & Mosher, 2002.

U.S. Demographic Trends: Who Remarries, and When?

Most men and women remarry, often relatively quickly. As shown in Table 13.2, 39 percent of women remarry within three years after a divorce and 54 percent are remarried after five years. By ten years after a divorce, three-quarters of women have remarried (Bramlett & Mosher, 2002). Younger women and higher-earning women are more likely to marry than are older women or those with lower incomes, although the effects of education levels are somewhat mixed.

Self-help books tend to advise people not to rush into a new relationship after one has ended, fearing that a relationship on the rebound will not be very stable. Although this sounds like common sense, it really is an empirical question, and research can help sort fact from fiction. One study (Wolfinger, 2006) decided to test the rebound effect, that is, the study asked whether relationships that began quickly after a divorce were more likely to break up than those that began at a later date. Using a large and nationally representative sample from the National Survey of Families and Households, Wolfinger measured the time between divorce and remarriage, then examined whether the length of this time period predicted a subsequent divorce. He found no evidence of a rebound effect; those who remarried quickly were no more likely to divorce than were those who remarried after a longer period of time (Wolfinger, 2006).

Racial/Ethnic Differences in Remarriage

Whites are more likely to remarry than are other racial or ethnic groups, and they remarry more quickly, as shown in Figure 13.3 (Bramlett & Mosher, 2002). By five years after a divorce, more than half of White women have remarried compared to only a third of Black women, and 44 percent of Hispanic women. These differences remain ten years post-divorce.

Why are minority groups, particularly Blacks, less likely to remarry than are Whites? The answer may be related to the reason minority groups are less likely to marry in the first place. There is often a shortage of available marriageable men, particularly in inner-city urban areas (Edin & Kafalas, 2005; Wilson, 1987, 1993). With jobs moving to the suburbs from the urban areas, urban minority males face high rates of unemployment. Suburban jobs are often difficult to get to because public transportation is limited. Together with racism and discrimination, many minority males living in the inner cities experience poverty, and Harvard sociologist William Julius Wilson (1987) suggests these conditions significantly reduce the pool of men eligible for marriage.

Sex Differences in Remarriage   Men are more likely to remarry than are women, and they do so more quickly (Ahrons, 2007; Bramlett & Mosher, 2002; Goodwin, Mosher, & Chandra, 2010; Wu & Schimmele, 2005). Men remarry on average within three years, compared to five years for women. But sex alone does not predict when or whether a person will remarry. For women, the likelihood of remarrying decreases substantially with age, especially if divorced when in their 40s or 50s. In contrast, age at divorce makes little difference for men. For example, James, who divorced when he was 30, is only slightly more likely to remarry within five years than is Lawrence, who divorced when he was 55. However, Karla, who also divorced at 30, is at least six times more likely to remarry than Renée, who divorced at 55. In fact, fewer than 7 percent of women who divorced between the ages of 50 and 59 remarry within five years, compared to 46 percent of men in that age group (Lampard & Peggs, 1999).

The reasons for these sex differences include both micro-level and macro-level factors. First, there is choice; some women do not want to remarry (Mahay & Lewis, 2007). If they can support themselves and their families easily enough, they might not feel the need to remarry. But for many other women who would like to remarry, cultural norms make it more difficult for them to find available spouses than men.

Why Do Men and Women Remarry at Different Rates?   A number of reasons help to explain why men are more likely to remarry, and to do so more quickly than women:

- *Men tend to have more experience initiating contacts.* Men have a lifetime of socialization experiences that encourage them to be the initiator in personal relationships. Many women, particularly older women, have never asked a man out on a date. When they were younger, to do so was considered improper. Even today, many women are more comfortable in being "chosen" rather than doing the choosing themselves. In addition, men often have a larger circle of casual friends and acquaintances than do women, and they can draw upon this circle to meet potential partners. Men are also more likely to have worked outside the home for a longer period of time, perhaps in managerial or professional positions that require skills in initiating and directing conversation. Moreover, because their incomes are considerably higher than those of most women, men typically have more money to treat someone to a dinner, movie, or some other type of date.

- *There is a double standard of aging.* People make different evaluations of the attractiveness of older men and older women. When men age they are considered to be "distinguished." Their graying hair, facial wrinkles, and weight gain is offset by their increased occupational prestige or financial assets. However, when women age they are typically considered less attractive and therefore, less desirable. For example, a study asked both elderly persons and college students to rate photographs of men and women at three different ages. Although both men and women were perceived to diminish in attractiveness as they aged, the decline for women was greater than that for men. Moreover, ratings of women's femininity decreased with age, whereas evaluations of men's masculinity were unaffected (Deuisch, Zelenski, & Clark, 1986). Susan Sontag labeled this concept the **double standard of aging** (1979).

- *The pool of eligible partners is larger for men than it is for women because of cultural norms.* Women generally marry men who are older, or at least the same age. When a female is 23 and a male is 25, their age difference is not problematic because there are a near equal number of partners available to each of them. But imagine this same

Men are more likely to remarry after a divorce, and they do so more quickly. There are several reasons for this, including the cultural norm that allows men a wider range of dating partners. Older men can date women their own age, or much younger, like Jay and Gloria in the sitcom, *Modern Family*. Generally, the same latitude is not given to older women.

double standard of aging: The view that women's attractiveness and femininity decline with age, but men's attractiveness and masculinity do not decline.

Do you think the stigma surrounding older women dating younger men has changed in recent years? What evidence do you have to support your opinion?

couple thirty years later. The female is now 53, and the male 55. Cultural norms allow men to choose partners from a wide age group, including women much younger than themselves. A 55-year-old man marrying a 35-year-old woman would generate little concern. However, although theoretically a 55-year-old woman could also marry a 35-year-old man, it would likely draw attention. In fact, many people would wonder what he sees in such an "old woman," or why she is "robbing the cradle."

- *Women are more likely to have children living with them.* Women who have custody of children are less likely to remarry than women who do not have children or do not have custody. One reason is that women may not have the time or financial resources to date. A second reason is that some men are hesitant to take on the financial and emotional responsibilities that come with a "ready-made" family. A third reason is that stepfamilies have a unique set of issues that can strain a relationship, as discussed in the next section. Some women may be hesitant or very cautious about remarrying and bringing a new person into these established family relationships. Finally, children may try to sabotage their mother's relationships out of fear or jealousy.

Power and Equity between Spouses

Remarried couples tend to perceive their new relationships as more equitable than their first marriages (Pyke, 1994; Pyke & Coltrane, 1996). Women often believe they have more power and autonomy regarding financial and other decisions. One study compared data from 111 remarried and first-married spouses and found that remarried spouses endorsed more autonomous standards in childrearing, friendships, and finances (Allen, Baucom, Burnett, Epstein, & Rankin-Esquer, 2001). Different reasons have been offered for this increased feeling of autonomy, power, and equity:

- women have greater levels of financial resources in their second marriages than in their first;
- women seek more power because of specific experiences in their prior marriages;
- men concede more during marital conflicts than they did in their first marriages; and
- both remarried men and women have expanded their ideas about their roles in marriage (Coleman, Ganong, & Fine, 2000).

One area of interest is the division of household labor among remarried couples. One study analyzed a study sample of 215 men and women who were in second marriages following a divorce and residing in Southern California (Pyke & Coltrane, 1996). The researchers used both interview and survey data to examine the marital processes underlying the division of household labor—to examine how the meanings associated with housework, paid work, and earnings affect the allocation of domestic labor. They suggest that not everyone values the equal sharing of tasks or women's financial contributions to the family in the same way. For example, in some families men may view these contributions as threats rather than assets. Researchers Pyke and Coltrane found many people used housework experiences in their previous marriages as a point of reference for their new situation. For many women, this comparison tempered the feeling that housework should be shared and instead made them grateful that "he helps. . . ." Even an unequal division of domestic labor was at least less unequal than in the previous marriage.

One surprising finding, also related to using the previous marriage as a reference point, was that husbands who had extramarital affairs in their first marriage were less likely to share housework. Many used their fidelity in their second marriages to excuse them from participation in what they saw as mundane tasks. One male participant justified doing little housework in his remarriage this way: *"I'm home and I'm not drinking or doing drugs. I should be considered a good guy"* (Pyke & Coltrane, 1996).

Satisfaction and Stability of Remarriages

Reflecting upon happiness in remarriage, we find second (and third) marriages are more likely to end in divorce (Barna, 2008; Xu, Hudspeth, & Bartkowski, 2006). This may indicate a selection bias—people who have divorced obviously consider divorce as an option to end an unhappy relationship. They also tend to more openly express criticism and anger than do couples in first marriages (although this is not always a negative trait). They are also more prone to disagreements, in part because of tension between stepchildren and stepparents, or between stepparents on issues related to childrearing or discipline (Brown & Booth, 1996; Kurdek, 1999). In fact, both remarried men and women are more likely to be depressed than are first-married men and women (LaPierre, 2009).

Figure 13.4 reports the percentage of women who get divorced again after a remarriage, across racial and ethnic groups over time. At one year of remarriage, the divorce rates of Whites, Blacks, and Hispanics are roughly the same. But over time, Blacks have the highest rate of re-divorce followed by Whites, while Hispanics have the lowest rate of re-divorce. After ten years of remarriage, 48 percent of Blacks, 39 percent of Whites, and 29 percent of Hispanics have divorced again (Bramlett & Mosher, 2002).

A second divorce is also more common among younger persons, those earning less income, and those who are not working. In addition, a second divorce is more common among persons with children from a previous relationship. Ten years into the second marriage, 43 percent of women who had two or more children at the time of the remarriage divorced again, as compared to 32 percent of women who were childfree.

The instability and fragile quality of a remarriage may reflect a problem in one or more of four areas critical to marital success (Ihinger-Tallman & Pasley, 1987):

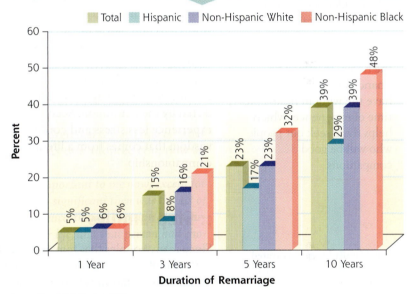

Figure 13.4 Probability of Second Marriage Disruption by Duration of Remarriage, Women Ages 15–44

Blacks are most likely to have second marriages end in divorce; Hispanics are least likely, and Whites are somewhere in the middle.

Source: Bramlett & Mosher, 2002.

- *Individuals may fail to make a real commitment to remarriage.* Having lived through at least one divorce, people may see that divorce is a remedy for an unhappy or unfulfilling marriage. Instead of making the necessary effort to resolve problems, they use divorce as the "easy way out" of what they perceive as a difficult situation.

- *The couple may fail to become a cohesive unit.* Developing bonds between adults with separate life histories and including other families may be difficult. Couples must learn to think of themselves as a "we," not simply an "I." There is bound to be conflict and confusion over new rules, new norms, and new ways of allocating assets. Children may wittingly or unwittingly pit one parent against the other: "But mom said I could!" To avoid this dilemma, the new couple must make a concerted effort to work together to develop a unified set of household rules.

- *Individuals may fail to communicate appropriately with one another.* Poor communication is a common problem, perhaps exacerbated by a previous marriage in which communication patterns were problematic. Learning how to communicate more effectively is difficult and time-consuming, but it is critical to break destructive old habits that interfere with the development of a strong family.

wife may have been considerably younger than the man she married, perhaps by as much as twenty years. Indeed, she could be the same age as some of his older children. The second wife was treated as a child rather than a spouse, given her age and the patriarchal norms of the time. She had little power in the relationship and little authority over children in the household despite having to cook for them, clean up after them, and raise them. To gain some power, the stepmother would have a child or two of her own. Not surprisingly, she might favor her own biological children, further exacerbating strained stepfamily relationships and contributing to the stereotype of the "evil stepmother" (Mitterauer & Sieder, 1982).

The Unique Features of Stepfamilies

Stepfamilies are common, yet the expectations, obligations, and rules within them are ambiguous (Mahoney, 2006; Stewart, 2007). Over a third of children born in the United States today will be in a stepfamily before reaching age 18 (Parke, 2007) and half will have a stepparent at some point in their lifetime (Stewart, 2007). Yet, no socially prescribed script explains how family members are expected to relate to one another. What names do children use for their stepparent? To what extent can stepparents discipline their stepchildren? How are stepparents and stepchildren supposed to feel about one another? Do stepparents and their stepchildren even count one another as part of their "family"? For example, your father's new wife is technically your stepparent, but what if you are grown and out of the house? Do you refer to her as "my dad's new wife," or as "my stepmother"?

Stepfamilies have unique features compared to families in which both biological parents reside (Stewart, 2007; National Stepfamily Resource Center, 2008; Allan, Crow, & Hawker, 2010). These features include:

- *Stepfamilies come about because of a loss through death or divorce.* Children grieve over the loss of a parent, including the loss of stability; the loss of their fantasy about how they want life to be; and the loss of their old home, school, neighborhood, or friends. Adults grieve over similar things: the loss of a partner; the loss of their dreams about the way they thought marriage would be; and the losses that come with change.
- *The parent/child relationship has a longer history than the new couple's relationship.* This can make it challenging for the adults to see their relationship as a primary, long-term one. A new spouse can feel like an outsider. Sometimes the close relationships that develop between divorced parents and their children contribute to the difficulty the new spouse has in joining the family. This new person has not been a part of funny or tragic family memories, or a part of developing sentimental traditions. *"Why do her children expect to open their gifts on Christmas Eve instead of Christmas Day?"* the new stepfather may ask himself. *"Don't his children know the value of saying grace before meals?"* the stepmother may wonder about her stepchildren who visit every other weekend. Remarried families have different histories, which accentuate the need for them to tolerate differences. In time, the family can develop meaningful and shared experiences and rituals.

One of the tasks of a new stepfamily is to establish their own shared experiences, rituals, and traditions.

- *A biological parent lives elsewhere.* Children usually continue to love their noncustodial parents and often long for their return. Children who do best after a divorce are those who have access to both parents. But how is that access facilitated? Can it be maintained? Even when fathers have no contact with children after a divorce or after an ex-spouse remarries, children hold on to their memories. Meanwhile, there is a new adult in the household. *"Is he supposed to be my 'new dad'? I already have one,"* a child might wonder.
- *Children in stepfamilies hold membership in two households.* Living in two households can be an enriching experience. Theoretically, it can provide twice the love, twice the material goods, twice the

number of family vacations, and twice the parental involvement in the child's schooling or other activities. However, it can also create confusion and conflict, including playing one parent off against another. *"But dad lets me stay up until 9:00 at his house, so why do I have to go to bed at 8:30 here?",* a child might complain to her mother. Two households can also create loyalty conflicts. For example, suppose a son feels close and loving towards his new stepmother, but at the same time learns his biological mother does not like her. The child may feel pulled in two directions. To please mom requires rebuffing the stepmother, but that would displease his father. It helps to have flexible family boundaries in stepfamilies so that children can more easily move from one household situation to another.

- *The model for stepparenting is ambiguous and poorly defined.* How do you stepparent? What authority does a stepparent have over his or her stepchildren? Biological parents have the opportunity to grow into parenting roles as their children grow; however, stepparents are often expected to adjust quickly (Chedekel & O'Connell, 2002). Biological parents have bonded with their children and are often more tolerant of their children's personalities and behaviors than someone who does not know them as well or have a sense of history with them. The reverse is also true: children are bonded to (and thus often more tolerant of) their biological parents than they are of their stepparents. But roles and emotional bonds take time to develop. Stepfathers seem to be more satisfied with their family life if they adopt a father-like role (Marsiglio, 1992), whereas stepmothers are less likely to assume a mother-like role and instead act more like a friend (Church, 1999).

- *No legal relationship exists between stepparents and stepchildren.* The legal status of stepparents and the rights of parents are remarkably different. Legally, stepparents are largely invisible (Gately, Pike, & Murphy, 2005; Gold, 2009; Mason, Harrison-Jay, Svare, & Wolfinger, 2002). For example, biological parents have child support obligations, custody rights, and inheritance rights regardless of the social and emotional bonds between parent and child. In contrast, stepparents in most states have no obligation during the marriage to support their stepchildren. Without written authority, a stepparent cannot access school records or authorize emergency medical care. Stepparents also do not have any legal right to custody or even visitation if the marriage terminates through divorce or death. Moreover, in the case of divorce, they have no obligation to pay child support, regardless of whether their stepchildren have long depended on their income.

- *The children in stepfamilies have additional sets of relatives.* Living in a stepfamily offers the chance for many additional relationships, possibly including an extra set (or two) of grandparents, aunts and uncles, and cousins. The ties between these relatives can range from extremely close to none at all. The outcome of these relationships depends largely on the investment the "steprelatives" make (Cherlin & Furstenberg, 1994). The possibilities represent one of the exciting by-products of stepfamilies.

Multiple Relationships and Dynamics

Remarriage may add new family members in all three generations: parents, children, and grandparents. Let's take a look at one example of multiple family relationships. Nancy and Jim recently divorced after many years of marriage. They had two children together, Ella and David, who were ages eight and ten, respectively, at the time of the divorce. Both children continued to live with Nancy, spending every other weekend, six weeks in the summer, and some holidays with their father. Two years after the divorce Jim married Elaine, the custodial parent of a six-year-old daughter, Jamie. The next year Nancy remarried Craig, who had also been divorced and who has joint custody of two daughters, ages six and eleven. Within the next four years, Jim and Elaine had two children of their own, a son and a daughter.

When Ella and David, the two biological children of our original couple, Nancy and Jim, are 15 and 17, their family will look like this: They will have two biological parents, two stepparents, three stepsisters, a half-brother, and a half-sister. The extended family will also have grown to include two sets of stepgrandparents, two sets of biological grandparents, and an expanded network of aunts, uncles, and cousins.

Several components of these stepfamily relationships make them complex (Ahrons & Rodgers, 1987):

1. *Former spouse subsystem.* This relationship becomes more complicated as former spouses remarry or become involved in significant relationships. Tensions are more likely to arise if one of the former spouses marries quickly before other family relationships have been reorganized and stabilized. For the spouse who remains single, the remarriage may bring to light jealousy, old romantic feelings, or animosity. With respect to Jim's remarriage to Elaine, Nancy said:

   "When Jim told me he was getting married, I reacted with a cutting comment, saying that I hoped she was better prepared for long evenings alone than I was. But what I was really scared about was that he would be different with her than he was with me. What if he had really changed? I realized that I wanted his marriage to fail. Then I would know that I was right in divorcing him."

   Jim's remarriage initiated a critical set of changes for all participants. Even though Nancy and Jim had been divorced for two years, Jim's remarriage caused their relationship to change even further. Jim experienced many conflicts:

   "When Elaine and I decided to get married I felt guilty and like I needed to tell Nancy immediately. I dreaded telling her. When I did tell her she didn't say much, but I knew she was feeling upset. I wanted the kids to be part of the wedding and I knew Nancy was going to feel jealous and left out. I'd feel much better if she had someone else in her life. Elaine's relationship with her ex-husband is nothing like my relationship with Nancy and she didn't understand my wanting to ease Nancy's pain by not flaunting my new life at her."

   Because of the children they had together, Nancy and Jim's lives are intertwined, yet Nancy faces a new set of loyalties—Jim's attachment to his new life with Elaine. It is difficult for Nancy to see that Elaine's needs are important, or that Elaine is a significant person to the children or to Jim. Six months after Jim's remarriage, Nancy summarized the new situation in this way:

   "Things have changed a lot since Jim remarried. He's less willing to accommodate when I need to change plans around the kids. He always has to check with Elaine first. I really resent that—the kids should come first. I invited Jim to Ella's birthday party but he couldn't come because of plans he had made with Elaine and her child. And I feel uncomfortable calling him at home about anything. Elaine usually answers the phone and I feel like she's listening the whole time. Jim has asked to take the kids on a week's vacation to visit Elaine's parents over Easter. I know it's his time with the kids but I think he should give them some special time and not make them spend it with Elaine's family."

   Researchers find a pattern of deteriorating co-parental relations after remarriage, particularly if the ex-husband remarries and the ex-wife does not. The number and frequency of shared childrearing activities like birthday parties are highest when both partners are single and lowest when only the husband has remarried. Conversely, conflict is highest when only the husband has remarried, and lowest when both are single.

2. *Remarried Couple Subsystem.* Second, Ahrens and Rodgers discuss the remarried couple subsystem (1987). Remarried couples overwhelmingly report being unprepared for remarried life, including the exchange of children, money, and decision-making.

When Jim and Elaine married, they fantasized about their plans for blending their families, minimizing problems, and remaining optimistic they could cope because of the love they share. But many problems created more stress than they had imagined. As Elaine describes:

> "When Jim and I decided to get married, I was surprised by his feelings about Nancy. I didn't have any of those feelings about my ex, Tom. When Tom remarried last year it didn't make much difference in my life. He hadn't seen much of Jamie [their daughter] anyway and he just saw her less after he remarried. It was a relief not to have much to do with him. So, after living alone with Jamie for three years, I was really excited to have a family again and give Jamie more of a dad.
>
> But it's not working out that way. Jamie is angry a lot about not having time alone with me, which ends up with Jim and me fighting a lot. Jim feels badly about not spending enough time with his kids, and when the kids are together, it just seems to be everyone fighting over Jim. And I feel resentful at not having enough time alone with Jim. Between every other weekend with his kids and the long hours we both work, we never seem to have time alone together. Last Friday we were finally spending an evening all alone and, just as I was putting dinner on the table, Nancy called. Jim and I spent the next two hours talking about Nancy. It ended up spoiling our whole evening."

Elaine's concerns are not unusual. Remarriage when children are present requires reorganization and realignment, and these are rarely simple or quick.

3. *Sibling Subsystem.* A third subsystem discussed by Ahrons and Rodgers is the sibling subsystem (1987). The typically competitive struggles among siblings can become more heated in remarried families, as children must learn to share parental time, household space, and parental affection. Research suggests the transition to remarriage may, in fact, be more stressful to children than the transition to divorce. The reason is that the newly married parent is preoccupied with his or her new mate and children may feel neglected in the transition (Stewart, 2005).

How Similar Are the Expectations of Stepparents, Parents, and Stepchildren?

Do all members of a stepfamily see the role of the stepparent in the same way? To answer this question, family researchers Mark Fine, Larry Ganong, and Marilyn Coleman conducted a study of 40 families that surveyed each stepparent, biological parent, and one child between 10 and 19. One question asked respondents to describe the "ideal way" the stepparent should relate to stepchildren. Possible responses included "distant relative," "teacher," "friend," "stepparent," "acquaintance," "advisor," "boss," "parent," "uncle/aunt," and "enemy." Parents and stepparents were in general agreement—they most commonly identified "parent" as the ideal way stepparents should relate to stepchildren. The stepchildren, however, felt differently; they believed the role of "friend" was most appropriate.

Stepfamilies are complex entities and face many unique challenges compared to other families, as shown in the movie *Step Brothers*. Reflecting on systems theory, we can see many interrelated layers, including the former spouse subsystem, the remarried couple subsystem, and the sibling subsystem.

These different views can create tension in the home if clear expectations are not communicated between parents, stepparents, and stepchildren (Fine, Ganong, & Coleman, 1997).

You have learned that stepfamilies can be quite complex entities. To better understand why they are different and how to best live within them, we should be mindful of both the associated macro-level and micro-level factors. Yes, stepfamilies do comprise a set of personal relationships, but they are highly influenced by social norms, or in some ways, by

Tying It All Together

Factors that Influence Stepfamilies

Why are stepfamilies so complex? Although some stepfamilies are characterized by loving relationships, others face many challenges as they try to define themselves and negotiate relationships. Many micro-level factors contribute to their complexity, owing to the personal nature of the relationships. However, macro-level social factors also shape stepfamily dynamics because societal norms and expectations are vague and inconsistent. Do we, as a society, define stepfamilies as true families?

Micro-level Factors

- Multiple relationships and multiple dynamics are often conflicting
- Some stepfamily members may live with the new family while others do not
- Stepfamilies may be created from some type of loss
- Children may belong to two households
- New family members feel different degrees of affection and love toward each other
- Parents may not be equally committed to placing child(ren)'s needs first

Macro-level Factors

- Expectations, obligations, and rules for stepfamily members are vague and confusing
- Stereotypes are negative, such as the "evil stepmother"
- Stepfamily members may each have different expectations
- Relationships between stepfamily members have little or no legal standing

What Do You Think?

1. How does American culture uniquely influence these macro- and micro-level factors associated with stepfamilies? How might these factors be different in developing nations, or are they different?
2. Why is the "evil stepmother" such a prevalent stereotype, when there is no real equivalent for stepfathers, or is there?

Have you, or someone close to you, lived in a stepfamily? What were some of the specific micro-level factors and macro-level factors that shaped this experience? From your experience or from the experiences of someone close to you, what do you think are some of the biggest difficulties in living with a stepfamily? What are the best ways to help stepfamilies?

the lack of social norms. The feature box *Tying It All Together* summarizes the micro-level and macro-level factors that shape stepfamily relationships in the United States today.

:: Surviving and Thriving in Stepfamilies

With so many different relationships, and with little guidance, many stepfamilies struggle to move beyond the obstacles. They usually make their way on their own, but sometimes stepfamilies seek outside help (Higgenbotham, Skogrand, & Torres, 2010). Let's look at how children and adults fare in stepfamilies. We will first turn to the example of children in stepfamilies.

How Do Children Fare in Stepfamilies?

As described in Chapter 12, we have learned that children from single-parent households face an increased chance of certain negative outcomes, but what about *after* their parents remarry? While a few studies show that some aspects of children's circumstances improve in stepfamilies (Sweeney, Wang, & Videon, 2009; Wen, 2008), most find that many children in stepfamilies continue to have social, emotional, and behavioral difficulties (Brown, 2006; McLanahan & Sandefur, 1994).

Certainly not all stepchildren experience problems. Many stepchildren grow up feeling secure in happy homes made possible by their parent's remarriage. Among some minority groups, living in a stepfamily is often reported to have significantly positive effects on a child's well-being through increased income, for example. Furthermore, high-quality relationships with stepfathers may have a positive effect on internalized problems, such as depression and low self-esteem, and on externalized problems, such as impulsivity and restlessness (White & Gilbreth, 2001).

Yet children living in stepfamilies, like children from single-parent homes, still tend to earn lower grades in school, complete fewer grades, and score lower on achievement tests as compared to children of two-parent biological families (Carlson, 2006; Ganong & Coleman, 2004). Stepchildren also have higher rates of depression and emotional problems, particularly when there is conflict between the two households. They are more likely to exhibit behavioral problems, such as alcohol and drug abuse, teenage pregnancy or impregnating others, idleness, and arrest. Differences may not be large, but on average, many children in stepfamilies do face potential disadvantages.

Explanations for Added Risk   Let's again be clear: most stepchildren do well in school and do not have emotional, behavioral, or delinquency problems; what we are discussing here is an increased chance of negative outcomes. One explanation points to *stress and instability*, suggesting repartnering and remarriage create many stressful transitions and potential conflicts for both adults (Cooper, McLanahan, Meadows, & Brooks-Gunn, 2009) and their children (Magnuson & Berger, 2009). Moving to a new residence, adapting to a parent's new partner, living with new family members, and settling into new routines could all contribute to poorer school performance, depression, early romance, and behavioral problems (Cavanagh, Crissey, & Raley, 2008; Cavanagh & Huston, 2006; Sweeney, 2010).

A second explanation focuses primarily on *social capital deprivation* (Shriner, Mullis, & Schlee, 2009). This perspective suggests children living in stepfamilies are disadvantaged because of their reduced levels of social capital (connections to other adults or institutions in the community) related to the divorce. Remarriage does not repair these deficits completely, perhaps because stepparents are expending resources on their own biological children from a prior union or because they are not fully invested in their stepchildren (McLanahan & Sandefur, 1994; Schwartz & Finley, 2006).

A third explanation suggests that *parenting quality* may be compromised as parents invest time and energy in their new relationships rather than in childrearing. For example, parents may not spend as much time talking with their children, helping them with their homework, or monitoring their friends and activities as they did prior to the remarriage because they are preoccupied with their new partner (Pong, 1997; Stoll, Armaut, Fromme, & Felker-Thayer, 2006).

Children in stepfamilies also face added risk for academic, social, and emotional difficulties. Possible reasons include the many transitions the child has made, the reduced level of social capital the child has, and a compromised parent quality the child experiences—the parents may be so involved in their new relationships that they do not pay full attention to the needs of the child.

How Do Adults Fare in Stepfamilies?

Being in a new loving relationship can be exciting, but if there are children involved, both men and women may need to make significant adjustments. For example, the privacy that newly partnered couples crave can be non-existent—married life might begin with a group of teenagers living with you! For noncustodial stepparents, the stepchildren may visit on a part-time basis—perhaps every other weekend and several weeks or months at a time in the summer. The presence of stepchildren invariably brings an ex-spouse into the picture. What potential tensions can arise with an "ex" or with your spouse's "ex"? The feature box *My Family: Journey to Healing* on page 384 offers one woman's account of living in a stepfamily.

The situations of stepmothers and stepfathers are somewhat distinct from each other, and therefore, stepmothers and stepfathers face different issues with their stepchildren.

Same-sex couples are not allowed to marry in most states, and are therefore disadvantaged with respect to Social Security, pension policies, and medical issues.

- Married couples are eligible for Social Security spousal benefits, which can allow them to earn half their spouse's Social Security benefit if it is larger than their own. Unmarried partners in lifelong relationships are not eligible for spousal benefits.
- Medicaid regulations protect the assets and homes of married spouses when the other spouse enters a nursing home or long-term care facility; no such protections are offered to same-sex partners.
- Tax laws and other regulations of 401(k)s and pensions discriminate against same-sex partners, costing the surviving partner in a same-sex relationship tens of thousands of dollars a year, and possibly more than $1 million over a lifetime. For example, if a person with a 401(k) pension plan dies, the money rolls over to a *legal spouse* without any tax penalty. However, since gays and lesbians cannot legally marry in most states, the surviving partner would have to pay a 20 percent federal tax.

The effect of this unequal treatment is striking. Assume Deborah dies at age 60 with $100,000 in her 401(k) account, which she leaves to her life partner, Ruth, also age 60. Ruth will receive the sum less taxes (at least $20,000), for a total of no more than $80,000. Ruth cannot roll the sum over into a tax-free IRA. If Ruth were a man—let's call him Rubin—as Deborah's widower, Rubin would receive the full $100,000 and be able to shield it from taxes until age 70½. In other words, the survivor of the legally married couple has a nest egg to invest that is roughly 20% larger than that of the surviving spouse in the same-sex couple. The nest egg can grow in a tax-deferred account until the maximum age of disbursement for the surviving spouse in a legally married couple. The surviving spouse of the same-sex couple, however, cannot roll the initial disbursement into an IRA (Cahill, South, & Spade, 2000).

Even basic rights such as hospital visitation or the right to die in the same nursing home as one's partner are regularly denied to same-sex couples. U.S. government policies affecting the aging population assume heterosexuality, close relationships with children, and extended families to provide basic needs as we age. These policies produce social, economic, and health consequences for LGBT elders (Grant, 2009; Hu, 2005). They may hide their sexual orientation from their health care and social service providers out of fear, further compromising their ability to get needed care and assistance. Several studies document widespread homophobia among those entrusted with the care of the elderly in the United States. Therefore, many LGBT seniors remain hidden, reinforcing isolation and forgoing services they may truly need. One study indicates that only 35 percent of older lesbian, bisexual, or transgender women are "out" to all of their healthcare providers, and 12 percent have no confidence that they will receive appropriate and unbiased treatment from medical personnel (MetLife, 2006).

Childfree Older Families

As you learned in Chapter 8, the number of couples without children is on the rise. About 10 percent of elders today do not have children (Kinsella & He, 2009), but 20 percent of women ages 40–44 are childfree. What implications does this have for an aging population? One of the many benefits we assume will accrue from having children is that we will be happier in old age because children will provide social support, caregiving when we are frail, or financial help if we need it. But how do older childfree couples really fare?

Are your parents still married to one another? If so, what types of transitions have they endured together? Have these transitions been smooth or difficult, and why?

Couples without children are as well-adjusted in later life as those with children, and rely upon their spouses, friends, and other kin for social support. Their finances are generally better (Plotnick, 2009), and they report being happy (or unhappy) as frequently as do those couples with children (Koropeckyj-Cox, 2008; Koropeckyj-Cox & Call, 2007; Koropeckyj-Cox, Pienta, & Brown, 2007). However, the childfree are more likely than other older adults to go to a nursing facility when their health deteriorates and they are unable to take care of themselves.

:: Widowhood

The death of a spouse stands as one of life's most stressful events (Holmes & Rahe, 1967). It means the loss of a companion and friend, perhaps the loss of income, and the ending of a familiar way of life. Many widowed men and women experience extreme sadness, weight loss, loneliness, insomnia, and depression. Widowhood can occur at any point in the life cycle, but because it is most likely to occur among the elderly, research tends to focus on that age group. Nonetheless, when people become widowed at a younger age, their difficulties may be exacerbated because death during young adulthood and middle age is so unexpected. Few of their friends are likely to be widowed, and they may stand alone from their peer group in an important way, as shown in the feature box *My Family: My Experience with Widowhood* on page 404.

Over 14 million persons are classified as "widowed" in the United States, and about three-quarters of widows are women (U.S. Census Bureau, January 14, 2010). The number of persons who have *experienced* widowhood, however, is much larger as many widowed people have remarried, and are therefore no longer classified as widows or widowers.

There are three primary reasons for the significantly higher rates of widowhood among women than men. First, mortality rates among females are lower than for males; therefore, they live to older ages. The life expectancy of females at age 65 exceeds that of males by nearly seven years. Second, wives are typically a few years younger than their husbands and consequently, have a greater chance of outliving them. Third, widowed women are less likely to remarry than are widowed men. As we learned in Chapter 13, there is a lack of eligible men because our cultural norms encourage older men to date and marry younger women, but not the reverse (Berardo & Berardo, 2000).

We have all heard statements suggesting that an elderly person often dies soon after his or her spouse dies: *"He just gave up. . ."*; *"She died of sadness. . ."*; *"He saw no reason to go on after Rose died. . . ."* Is there really an increased probability of death among new widows and widowers? Two Harvard sociology professors decided to answer this question by following nearly 4,500 U.S. couples ages 67 and older for five years (Elwert & Christakis, 2006). They found that there seems to be some truth to the "widow effect" as there is an increase in the likelihood of death after a spouse dies. The "widow effect," however, does not occur equally among racial and ethnic groups. White men were 18 percent more likely to die shortly after their wives' deaths, and White women were 16 percent more likely to die shortly after their husbands' deaths. But among Blacks, a spouse's death had no effect on the mortality of the survivor.

Why would widowhood contribute to an early death for Whites, but not for Blacks? Upon marrying, Blacks and Whites appear to receive many of the same health, financial, and social benefits such as emotional support, caretaking when ill, and enhanced social support, so what could account for the "widow effect"? We do know that Blacks are almost twice as likely to live with other relatives (Pew Research Center, March 18, 2010), are more active in religious groups, and when married are less likely to adhere to a traditional gendered division of labor, which may reduce dependence on a spouse. It seems that Blacks may somehow manage to extend the benefits of marriage into widowhood, and are therefore less likely than Whites to die soon after their spouse (Elwert & Christakis, 2006).

The Process of Grief and Bereavement

People handle their grief over the death of a loved one in a variety of ways. Some try to remain stoic, others cry out in despair. Some people fear death, while others, perhaps because of a strong religious faith, see death as part of a larger "master plan." The *Getting to Know Yourself* feature box on page 406 offers the opportunity to assess your own attitudes toward death and offers some insights into your possible grieving process.

One of the more popular perspectives on death and dying is based on the work of Elizabeth Kubler-Ross (1969). Her work with 200 primarily middle-aged cancer patients suggested five somewhat distinct stages that dying people and their loved ones experience.

Getting To Know Yourself

Death and Grief Assessment

Answer the questions below as either true (T) or false (F) as they pertain to your life experiences. Keep in mind that there are no "right" or "wrong" answers. Wait until you have completed the assessment before you read the key.

1. T F Death scares me.
2. T F I rarely think about death.
3. T F I am afraid of dying in a painful manner.
4. T F I am troubled about the idea of life, death, and their overall purpose and meaning.
5. T F I rarely go to funerals, even if it is someone close to me who has died.
6. T F I am concerned about a nuclear holocaust.
7. T F We do not talk about death in my family.
8. T F I hate to look at either pictures of dead bodies or real dead bodies.
9. T F When people talk about death, I get real nervous.
10. T F I am concerned with how fast my life appears to be going.
11. T F I am horrified to fly in an airplane because of the possibility of a crash.
12. T F Life is too short.
13. T F I am afraid of contracting AIDS or some other disease.
14. T F Hospital treatments such as operations scare me.
15. T F Hearing about cancer, heart attacks, and strokes makes me feel uneasy.
16. T F In my family, we experience grief and deep feelings of loss when someone dies.
17. T F Grief can be felt in death and in other life events.
18. T F Each person grieves in his or her own way.
19. T F Children are capable of grieving.
20. T F The amount of time required for grieving varies from person to person.
21. T F Keeping busy is not the cure for grief.
22. T F Sometimes people grieve even if death has not occurred.

23. T F It is not very wise to tell a grieving person that you know how he or she feels.
24. T F Listening to a grieving person is a healthy form of support.
25. T F Unresolved childhood grieving may resurface later in life.
26. T F When others grieve, it is helpful to provide support in and around the house.
27. T F Religion and culture strongly influence how we grieve.
28. T F Shock and numbness are normal responses to grievers.
29. T F If you feel sad, it is okay to express it to those who are grieving.
30. T F Avoiding the grieving person is not a healthy approach.

Key: Give yourself 1 point for each False answer in items 1–15. Also give yourself 1 point for each True answer to items 16–30. The highest score you can earn is 30 points. The higher your score, the healthier and more knowledgeable you are about death, dying, and grief.

What Do You Think?

1. Do the findings from this assessment accurately reflect you, your expectations, and your life experience? Why or why not?

2. What have been your experiences with grief? How are they similar to or different from other people your age?

Source: Hammond, Ron J. and Barbara Bearnson. 2003a. "Death and Grief Assessment." pp. 125–26 in The Marriages and Families Activities Workbook. Wadsworth.

Second, widows may face the daunting practical problems of maintaining a house alone. A study of 201 widows drawn from public death records in a Midwestern metropolitan area found that their financial problems were not a primary cause of stress (although they were a major cause of stress for women getting divorced) (Miller, Smerglia, Gaudet, & Kitson, 1998). The researchers found that the lack of practical support such as help with home repairs significantly increased widows' stress.

Most of these studies, however, are cross-sectional research rather than longitudinal studies that follow people over time. Lee and DeMaris (2007) used longitudinal data from the National Survey of Families and Households to examine sex differences in psychological well-being before and after widowhood. They found that men whose wives died during the course of the study were already highly depressed at the first interview, even before their wives died. Apparently the anticipation of their wife's death was depressing in and of itself. However, they found no such anticipatory effect of depression for wives.

:: Grandparents and Their Grandchildren

What are some rituals that Americans use to mourn the dead? How might these be similar to or different from those used in other developed or developing countries?

Almost all parents eventually become grandparents. On average, first grandchildren are born when grandparents are in their late forties or early fifties, although the age is increasing as young couples wait longer to have children. Some people may not become grandparents until their seventies. Compared with children in the past, children today are more likely to have all four grandparents alive when they are born, and most will continue to have at least two grandparents alive when they reach adulthood.

The role of grandparent has changed over the past century in several ways (Cherlin & Furstenberg, 1986; Kemp, 2007):

- Grandparenting has become a role distinct from parenting because grandparents are now less likely to have their own children still living in the home (except, of course, for the "boomerangers").

- Grandparents are healthier and better educated, and have greater economic security, than in the past (Kinsella & He, 2009).

- Grandparents, and grandfathers in particular, are now more likely to recognize the importance of having direct emotional involvement with young children. Grandfathers have opportunities to participate in nurturing children that seemed unavailable to them as fathers or to grandfathers in the past (Cunningham-Burley, 2001).

- Grandparents and their grandchildren can more easily travel long distances and communicate by telephone or computer.

Families are now able to construct their own conception of what it means to be a grandparent (Kemp, 2007; Walker, Manoogian-O'Dell, McGraw, & White, 2001). Relationships between grandparents and their grandchildren can take many forms, as shown in Table 14.4.

Most grandparents report that their relationships with their grandchildren are meaningful, fun, and pleasurable (AARP, September 2007; Reitzes, 2004). In a national study of grandparents, Cherlin and Furstenberg (1986) found that over half of grandparents reported a **companionate** relationship with their grandchildren, enjoying fun recreational activities, occasional overnight stays, and even babysitting. Grandparents reported that they enjoy spending time with their grandchildren, but they "are ready to leave the tough work of parenting to the parents" (Cherlin & Furstenberg, 1986). As one grandmother confided,

Afterwards the grandchildren go back home where, of course, they find the routine, the direction of their parents. I get the good part, because I can play, enjoy myself; that is, I have no direct responsibility. . . . . I enjoy being a grandmother. . . I chose to be a grandmother such that when she arrives it's great fun (Gattai & Musatti, 1999).

Meanwhile, nearly one-third of grandparents had **remote**, or emotionally distant, relationships with their grandchildren, usually because they lived far away and did not, or could not, keep in regular touch. Another 15 percent of grandparents were highly **involved**,

companionate grandparenting: A type of grandparenting where the grandparents and grandchildren enjoy recreational activities, occasional overnight stays, and even babysitting with an emphasis on fun and enjoyment.

remote grandparenting: A type of grandparenting in which the grandparents and grandchildren are emotionally or physically distant.

involved grandparenting: A type of grandparenting in which the grandparents and grandchildren have frequent interaction or possibly even live together.

Table 14.4	Types of Grandparent-Grandchild Relationships
Family researchers classify grandparent-grandchild relationships into three broad types.	
Companionate	Grandparents and grandchildren have fun together, enjoy recreation together on a regular basis, and are important to one another's lives.
Remote	The grandparent-grandchild relationship is emotionally distant. Visits may be infrequent. Grandparents are only minimally involved in their grandchildren's lives.
Involved	Grandparents are highly involved in their grandchildren's lives. They may take care of their grandchildren on a regular basis, and perhaps even live together.

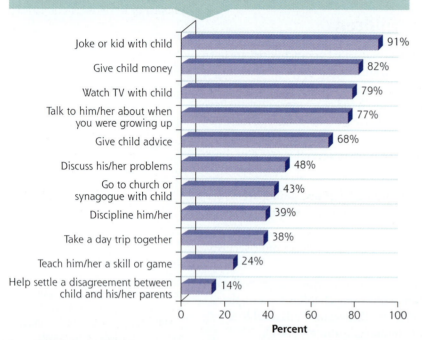

| Figure 14.3 | Percentage of Grandparents Engaging in Activities with Grandchild over Past 12 Months |

Most grandparents have companionate relationships with their grandchildren and engage in a variety of fun and intimate activities.

- Joke or kid with child — 91%
- Give child money — 82%
- Watch TV with child — 79%
- Talk to him/her about when you were growing up — 77%
- Give child advice — 68%
- Discuss his/her problems — 48%
- Go to church or synagogue with child — 43%
- Discipline him/her — 39%
- Take a day trip together — 38%
- Teach him/her a skill or game — 24%
- Help settle a disagreement between child and his/her parents — 14%

Percent (0, 20, 40, 60, 80, 100)

Source: Cherlin, Andrew J. and Frank F. Furstenberg. 1986. *The New American Grandparent: A Place In the Family, A Life Apart.* New York: Basic Books.

with more frequent interaction, and sometimes even living together. Figure 14.3 shows the percentage of grandparents engaging in various activities with their children during the previous 12 months (Cherlin & Furstenberg, 1986).

Researchers also point to the changing relationship between grandparents and grandchildren. Cherlin and Furstenberg (1986) found a marked shift in the balance between respect and affection. They asked all respondents in a national survey, "Are you and the [study child] more friendly, less friendly, or about the same as your grandparents were with you?" Forty-eight percent reported that they were "more friendly," while only 9 percent said "less friendly." Similarly, 55 percent claimed that their relationship with the child was "closer" than their own relationship with their grandparents, and only 10 percent said that it was "not as close." When respondents were asked about respect, most reported no difference. However, 22 percent said they were more respectful of their grandparents, whereas only 2 percent believed their grandchildren showed them greater respect (Cherlin & Furstenberg, 1986).

Grandmothers and Grandfathers: Same or Different?

Grandmothers and grandfathers have different parenting styles, and perhaps you noticed these differences when you were very young. Grandmothers are more likely to plan and orchestrate family activities, nurture their grandchildren, and assume caregiving responsibilities (Walker, Manoogian-O'Dell, McGraw, & White, 2001). This is consistent with their role at all ages of being the family "kinkeeper" and maintaining family contact (Fingerman, 2004). For example, it is usually the women in the family who are responsible for sending greeting cards on holidays and birthdays. **Kinkeeping**, the maintaining of ties among family members, carries over into the grandmother role as well.

In contrast, grandfathers are more likely to focus on practical issues, and spend more time exchanging help and services with their grandsons than with their granddaughters. One consequence of this difference in style is that family members generally feel more obligation to and are closer to their grandmothers than to their grandfathers (Monserud, 2008). This may be the reason why grandmothers report greater satisfaction and overall meaning in grandparenthood than do grandfathers (Somary & Stricker, 1998). Another consequence is that children tend to feel closer to their grandparents (grandmother *and* grandfather) on their mother's side, rather than their father's side, especially when the mother reports having good relationships with her aging parents.

Racial and Ethnic Differences in Grandparenting Styles

We can observe different styles of grandparenting across racial and ethnic groups. For example, in minority families grandparents are more likely to live with their grandchildren, and play a valued role in child rearing, often mimicking parent-like behavior, than are grandparents in White families (Uttal, 1999; Dilworth-Anderson, 2001; Pew Research Center, February 24, 2010, March 18, 2010).

A study by psychologist Andrea Hunter (1997) examined Black mothers' and fathers' reliance upon grandmothers for parenting support. She used a sample of 487 parents ages 18–34 from the National Survey of Black Americans, and examined their responses to the

kinkeeping: Maintaining ties among family members.

following questions: (a) "Do you have anyone who gives you advice about child rearing or helps you with problems having to do with children? If yes, what is this advisor's relationship to you?"; and (b) "Do you have someone to count on to take care of the children? If yes, what is this person's relationship to you?" Hunter found that 57 percent of the mothers and 56 percent of the fathers reported relying upon grandmothers for parenting support more often than upon anyone else. Most people said they receive both advice and childcare from the grandmother.

Another study of Apache grandmothers shows how the roles of grandparents are socially constructed and can vary dramatically from one culture to another. The author noted four key differences between Apache and "Anglo-American" grandparenting styles (Bahr, 1994):

In many minority groups grandparents play a prominent role within families. They are often a "third parent."

- *Obligation and responsibility:* An Anglo-American grandparent is a "spoiler" of grandchildren who may interact or give gifts, but who can also have meaningful relationships with grandchildren with only minimal obligation and responsibility. Among the Apache, particularly among grandmothers, grandparenting means heavy obligation and responsibility. The grandmother's role is that of a parent substitute within the family. There is virtually no such thing as minimal involvement and responsibility.

- *Gender differences in grandparental role behavior:* In Anglo-American society, grandmothers are somewhat more important than grandfathers because they tend to have warmer and closer relationships with their own children as well as with their grandchildren. Among the Apache, the importance of grandmothers far exceeds the importance of grandfathers. Although Apache and Anglo-American patterns are similar, the magnitude of the difference between grandmothers and grandfathers is striking. This is not only a function of grandmothers' greater longevity, but also of the cultural norm of their greater affinity with and responsibility to children.

- *Grandparents as part of a viable, functioning family network:* In Anglo-American families, kinship ties between parents, adult children, and grandchildren are valued, but households tend to be independent. They rarely share their homes and finances. In Apache families, not only are kinship ties valued, but households are likely to be extended and often include cross-generational members like grandparents, aunts, uncles, or cousins. Family households have loose, permeable boundaries, and families are highly interdependent upon other family members. This dependence is seen as a strength rather than a weakness on the part of family members.

- *Economic security and economic responsibility:* Among Anglo Americans, grandparenthood and retirement are times of fairly secure economic status. Grandparents are likely to own their own homes and have accumulated savings. They generally are not responsible for rearing or educating their grandchildren or for providing long-term support for their adult children. In contrast, in Apache families being an elder and a grandparent is a time of heavy economic demand. Grandparents, including grandmothers, may be economically responsible for the support of their adult children and grandchildren. They may continue to work in the formal or informal sector of the economy so they can provide some or all the assistance to their often multigenerational family. Apache grandparents remain active and influential participants in community life.

Three theories explain why racial and ethnic minority families are more likely than White families to rely upon grandparents (and other kin) to provide childcare for their grandchildren. The *cultural* explanation suggests that these practices are the product of different cultural experiences and adaptations (Uttal, 1999). The *structural* explanation conceives of childcare arrangements as an adaptation to structural constraints, such as racism or poverty (Goodman & Silverstein, 2002). The *integrative* explanation combines the other two explanations and suggests these arrangements are due to the intersection of cultural values with structural constraints, operating alongside gendered expectations (Minkler & Fuller-Thomson, 2005).

Through in-depth interviews with seven Black mothers, seven Mexican-American mothers, and 17 Anglo-American mothers, Lynet Uttal found that the major difference among the groups was how the mothers *felt* about using kin for care (1999). Anglo-American mothers tended to feel that relying upon grandparents and other kin was in some way inappropriate or problematic, whereas Black and Mexican-American mothers willingly accepted this help because they felt it was appropriate and acceptable (even if not necessarily ideal). Unlike the other groups, the Anglo-American mothers in Uttal's study were particularly concerned about being a burden or imposing, as indicated by this quote:

I don't think I'd want to be that owing to her. In debt to your mommy! I just don't like it when someone does a favor for you. There's an implied obligation that if someone does something for you, you should do something for them. I think it's better to pay for someone's services, and get it over with. I'd feel this big obligation.

Grandchildren and Grandparents Living Together

About 6 million grandchildren live with their grandparents (Kreider, 2008). Blacks and Asians are most likely to co-reside, and Whites are least likely, as shown in Table 14.5.

Table 14.5	**Number and Percentage of Children Who Live with At Least One Grandparent**	
White children are least likely to live with a grandparent.		
	Number	**Percentage**
White, Not Hispanic	2,592,000	6%
Black	1,590,000	14%
Asian	301,000	13%
Hispanic (any race)	1,643,000	12%

Source: Kreider, 2008.

We used to think of these as three-generational families—perhaps the adult child and grandchildren needed some financial help, or perhaps an elder was too frail to live independently, and therefore moved in with their adult child and grandchildren. However, another trend in co-residence has caught our attention: now almost a third of these grandchildren live with their grandparent *without their parents present in the household* (Kreider, 2008).

Mothers and fathers are absent due to death, desertion, incarceration, drug problems, physical or mental illnesses, unemployment, HIV/AIDS, or child abuse, among other reasons (Goyer, 2006). One study of 129 grandparents raising their grandchildren examined the situations that precipitated this relationship (Sands & Goldberg-Glen, 2000). They found multiple problems in the homes of the grandchildren's parents that led the grandparents to take over the care of their grandchildren. The most commonly reported problem was substance abuse, but the parents' inability to care for the child, neglect, and psychological and financial problems were also cited as factors. Many of these problems are long-term issues for families. When the grandparents in this study first began to take care of their grandchildren, only one-third expected to be the caregiver until the grandchild came of age. But at the time of the interview, over three-quarters of grandparents reported this expectation.

What are some characteristics of these intergenerational families maintained by the grandparents?

*H*ow have your grandparents' social or cultural backgrounds affected their grandparenting? Can you pinpoint specific instances in which their social class, race, or ethnic background, for example, had an impact on their roles, values, or grandparenting style?

• They are usually headed by both grandparents or by only grandmothers —rarely are they headed by only grandfathers. The reason may be that

women live longer and are more likely than men to assume a caregiving role.

- Most grandparents raising their grandchildren are
younger than 65. Only one in five is 65 or older.
- Children in grandparent-maintained families are
more likely to be Black, younger, and living in the
South than are children in intergenerational families
headed by their parents.
- Children in grandparent-maintained families are less
likely than children in single-parent families to be
poor (Fields, 2003; Kreider, 2008).

Grandparent caregivers face a number of problems
(Smith & Palmieri, 2007; MacNeil, Kosberg, Durkin,
Dooley, DeCoster, & Williamson, 2010). Most are not
particularly eager to take on the care of their grandchildren,
but feel it is a "last resort" decision over which they have little
choice. In addition to financial difficulties, grandparents may
experience poor health, depression, and decreased life satisfaction (Cooney & Shin An, 2006; Leder, Grinstead, & Torres, 2007; Smith & Palmieri, 2007). Sometimes, they must
seek legal authority to make decisions on behalf of their children regarding the grandchildren's medical care, school en-
rollment, immunizations, and public assistance and other
support services (Robinson-Dooley & Kropf, 2006). Yet
they step in because they know that their grandchild needs
help and that they may be the best able to provide it.

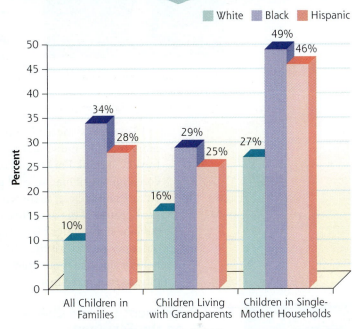

Figure 14.4

Percent of Children Below the Poverty Line for All Children in Families, Children Living with Grandparents, and Children in Single-Mother Households

Many children who live with their grandparents are better off financially than if they lived with a single parent, but poverty rates remain high.

Source: Kreider, 2008, DeNavas-Walt, Proctor, & Smith, 2010.

:: Retirement

Work provides us with income, but for many of us, work is also an important part of our identity. "I *am* a professor. . ." "I *am* a firefighter. . ." "I *am* a doctor. . ." is how we describe our work:
we *are* the occupation. Consequently, retirement is an important transition not only because
it reduces our income, but also because it alters a major part of the way we see ourselves
(Ekerdt, 2009).

Still, many people eagerly await this change and see retirement as a legitimate, earned privilege. The median age at
retirement fell from 69 years in 1950 to 64 in 2008, during a
time when life expectancy has increased (Social Security
Administration, 2009). However, the current recession has
many older persons working longer as shown in Table 14.6.
Likewise, many older workers are now retiring in stages, rather
than all at once (Calvo, Haverstick, & Sass, 2009). This trend
too has been exacerbated by the recession; over a third of
surveyed adults ages 62 and over (who have not retired) say
they have delayed or will delay retirement due to the recession
(Taylor, Kochhar, Morin, Wang, Dockterman, & Medina,
2009).

Table 14.6	Labor Force Participation among the Elderly, 1995–2009		
The current recession has many older persons working longer.			
	1995	2000	2009
Age 55—64	57%	59%	65%
Age 65 +	12%	13%	17%

Source: Pew Research Center, September 3, 2009.

The Social Construction of Retirement

The notion of ending work at a specific age—retirement—is a social construction. Most
people in the world today have to work to support themselves (and sometimes other family
members) and would never think to retire twenty or thirty years before they expected to die.

Americans think of 65 as the golden retirement age, but many cultures know no such thing as retirement. Individuals must work until they are no longer physically able.

Americans' ideas of retirement, and the decline in the average retirement age, reflect more than just individual micro-level explanations such as, "I'm tired of my job," "I want to travel," "I think I'm too old to work," or even "I've saved enough money." It also reflects a convergence of macro-level public and private employment policies, and other aspects of culture and society, as shown in the *Tying It All Together* feature box. People now retire earlier because of the existence of the Social Security program, because employer-sponsored pensions or savings plans are more common, and because many employers are enticing older persons to exit the labor force.

For significant numbers of elderly to be able to withdraw from the labor force, four conditions must exist in a society (Morgan & Kunkel, 1998). First, a society must produce an economic surplus large enough to support its nonemployed members. Second, a mechanism must be in place to divert some of that surplus to the nonemployed members, such as through a pension or government transfer program. Third, nonemployed members should be viewed positively by the rest of society, and their activities or leisure must be seen as legitimate. And finally, nonemployed members must have accumulated an acceptable number of years of productivity to warrant this support by the other members of society. These four conditions materialized in the United States after industrialization during the late 19th and 20th centuries.

However, these four conditions are now under threat. The cost of caring for the elderly—Social Security, health care programs, and even private retirement plans—are consuming a greater share of our country's gross domestic product (GDP), as shown in Figure 14.5. People are rightly concerned that these programs as configured are not sustainable as baby boomers age (Schieber, 2008). Furthermore, these programs for the elderly compete with funding for other groups; programs for children, for example, have received a declining proportion of federal spending (Uhlenberg, 2009).

Figure 14.5

Total Retirement Income Claims on the Economy

The cost of caring for the elderly—Social Security, healthcare programs, and even private retirement plans—are consuming an increasing share of our country's gross domestic product (GDP).

Legend: Private Retirement Plans / Medicaid / Medicare / Social Security

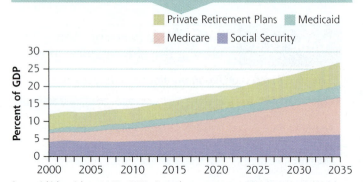

Percent of GDP — years 2000 to 2035

Source: Schieber, Sylvester J. May 2008. Beyond the Golden Age of Retirement. University of Michigan Retirement Research Center Policy Brief. http://www.mrrc.isr.umich.edu/publications/policy/pdf/Schieber.pdf.

Men, Women, and Retirement

Traditionally, retirement was seen as a transition important primarily to men because they were the primary breadwinners and were thought to derive more status and identity from their jobs than did women. Nonetheless, as more women enter the labor force, we must rethink our old conceptions. Today, with almost half the workforce consisting of women, and with the majority of men married to employed women, couples are forging new retirement

Tying It All Together

Factors that Shape Retirement

Work is a big part of our lives, yet the age at which we retire has been declining. What would motivate someone to retire?

A host of personal, micro-level reasons affect your ability to retire, such as whether you have enough money to retire or are tired of your job or career. But these reasons do not make up the whole picture. Many macro-level factors often influence the micro-level factors. For example, the creation of Social Security has given many elders the economic security to retire. Likewise, our culture's current view that elders deserve leisure has made it legitimate to simply be "tired of working."

Micro-Level Factors

- Tired of the job
- A desire to travel
- Feeling too old to work
- Feeling financially secure that one has enough money

Macro-Level Factors

- Society has an economic surplus that can support the nonemployed
- Pensions or government transfer programs are in place to divert the surplus to the unemployed members of society
- Other members of society believe elders' activities or leisure are legitimate
- Elders are seen as having earned the right to leisure

What Do You Think?

1. How might these micro- and macro-level factors operate differently for women and men?
2. What changes in these macro-level factors do you foresee in the near future?

paths. They not only face two retirements, but they must also coordinate their retirements and address whether to take up other paid work after they retire.

Researchers at Cornell University conducted a five-year study of retirement with 762 men and women between the ages of 50 and 72 selected from six large employers in New York. Respondents were interviewed three separate times. The key questions were: (1) How do sex and career pathways influence the planning and timing of retirement?; and (2) How do the timing of retirement, stresses of the retirement transition, and re-employment decisions affect marital quality and retirement satisfaction for both women and men? (Cornell Gerontology Research Institute, 2000)

The researchers noted a tremendous difference in retirement ages, ranging from the 40s to "never." The men in the sample began to plan for retirement earlier than did the women (at ages 49 and 54, respectively), although they retired at similar ages (Han & Moen, 1999). The researchers also found that the process of retiring was associated with a decrease in marital quality for both men and women (Moen, Kim, & Hofmeister, 2001). Newly retired men and women both reported more conflict in their relationship than couples who had not retired or who had already retired. Conflicts arose more often when one spouse, particularly the wife, was still employed while the other spouse began to retire. This escalated conflict may be due to their difference in role status and power; men in this cohort were happier when their wives conformed to more traditional gender norms.

Given the differences in men's and women's employment experiences over the life course in terms of continuity, occupations, pay, and expectations, it is likely they would have different experiences associated with retirement as well. The researchers found that overall, men are more satisfied with retirement than are women. Seventy-one percent of men and 56 percent of women report they are better off in their retirement than in the five years just before (Quick & Moen, 1998).

While good health and a comfortable postretirement income are some of the most important predictors of happiness, there are some interesting differences among men and women as well. For example, part-time employment is linked to retirement satisfaction among men, but not among women. The researchers speculate that women are more likely to be busy with volunteer work or other family activities and are less interested in part-time employment after retirement.

How do you plan to save for your retirement years? Specifically, what do you need to do now (or soon) to retire "in the manner to which you would like to become accustomed"?

Women who had more year-long employment gaps during their working years are more likely to be satisfied in retirement, perhaps because retirement is a less dramatic transition for them.

:: Health

Most elderly persons report their health is good or excellent. There is no denying, however, that as we age our health is likely to decline in a number of ways. We are more likely to lose some of our vision and hearing, develop chronic conditions such as arthritis, heart disease, or diabetes, and suffer severe memory impairment (National Center for Health Statistics, 2010). We may need someone to help us with many things we used to do for ourselves: cooking, cleaning, home repairs, and perhaps even personal care. The health status of older adults is a result of many factors, including diet, exercise, and heredity, and structural factors such as socioeconomic status, racism, and access to health care. 👁️ Watch on **myfamilylab.com**

👁️ Watch the Video *Core Concepts: Physical Challenges of Living Longer* on **myfamilylab.com**

Activities of Daily Living

Gerontologists—researchers studying the elderly—have measured the degree of physical impairment by using a common set of **Activities of Daily Living (ADLs)** such as bathing, dressing, eating, getting into and out of bed, walking indoors, and using the toilet (Hooyman & Kiyak, 2010). By using a common set of measures, gerontologists can track the degree of impairment of elders and make some comparisons across different samples. Millions of elderly persons cannot perform at least one ADL by themselves. Millions more have trouble with most or all of them. Gerontologists estimate that the number of older persons needing significant care may increase dramatically over the next 50 years as the size of the "oldest-old" cohort increases: 14 million elders may need significant care by 2020, and 24 million by 2060.

Severe Memory Loss

I think there comes a point in everyone's life when we pause to reflect on the past, realize the present and look to the future. That happened for me at the age of 46. In the fall of that year I started to become forgetful—which was not like me at all. I had a very stressful job and worked long hours, so I blamed that for my forgetfulness. I couldn't remember things like my home phone number, my associates' names or on bad days, how to get home. I remember that many times I would stop at a gas station, and after filling my tank, not knowing whether I was going to work or coming home from work. I tried desperately to hide it and became pretty good at it! But one day in December, my husband and I were out shopping, and he went to a different department in the store. The next thing

" I would stop at a gas station, and after filling my tank, not knowing whether I was going to work or coming home from work. "

I knew is that I couldn't remember where I was or how I had gotten there. It was time to fess up. I sought medical attention and after eight long months of testing, including all of the alphabet soup tests (EEG, EKG, MRI, etc.), blood work, spinal taps, B12 shots and neuropsychological testing, I was diagnosed with Alzheimer's disease. It was a relief to me because there was a name to it. Although it is an incurable disease, at least I knew what I was dealing with. My family, however, took a dimmer view. My husband likened it to the Titanic—that the ship was sinking, and he and my son were going to survive and I wasn't. My son reflected that it was like his mother was on death row, but innocent of the crime (Alzheimer's Association, 2010b).

gerontologists: Researchers studying issues affecting the elderly.

Activities of Daily Living (ADLs): General day-to-day activities such as cooking, cleaning, bathing, and home repair.

Perhaps one of the most difficult disabilities facing elders, and those who care for them, is severe memory loss, known as **dementia**. Dementia includes a decline in memory and at least one of the following cognitive abilities, severe enough to interfere with daily life (Alzheimer's Association, 2010a):

- Ability to generate coherent speech and understand spoken or written language;
- Ability to recognize or identify objects, assuming intact sensory function;
- Ability to execute motor activities, assuming intact motor abilities, sensory function and comprehension of the required task; and
- Ability to think abstractly, make sound judgments and plan and carry out complex tasks.

The late U.S. President Ronald Reagan and British Prime Minister Margaret Thatcher are just two examples among the millions of elders who experience dementia, the most common of which is Alzheimer's Disease.

Alzheimer's disease is by far the most common form of dementia, affecting about 5.3 million persons, and is the fifth leading cause of death among persons ages 65 and over (Alzheimer's Association, 2010a). The disease starts subtly—a person may have difficulty remembering names or recent events. It progresses over the course of years, and later symptoms include impaired judgment, disorientation, confusion, behavior changes, lack of recognition of loved ones, and eventually, the inability to walk, speak, and even swallow. Alzheimer's disease is ultimately fatal. Given the changing demographics of our country, and the increase in the size of the "oldest-old" cohort, we are likely to see a large increase in the number of people with Alzheimer's—10 million baby boomers are expected to eventually develop the disease.

Unfortunately, no treatment is yet available to fully stop the deterioration of brain cells in Alzheimer's disease. The U.S. Food and Drug Administration has approved five drugs that temporarily slow the worsening of symptoms for six to 12 months, on average, for about half the individuals who take them. Given that the direct and indirect costs of Alzheimer's and other dementias are estimated at $148 billion each year, not to mention the cost in terms of families' heartache and despair, it is no wonder researchers are vigorously pursuing an agenda of prevention, treatment, and cure (Alzheimer's Association, 2010a).

Long-Term Care and Caregiving

It is clear that many elders are going to need long-term care for their chronic physical or mental conditions. Some will live for a decade or more without being able to perform any of their ADLs. How do we care for the growing numbers of elderly who can no longer care for themselves?

Formal Care   Some elderly persons rely upon **formal care** provided by social service agencies on a paid or volunteer basis. This term includes a variety of types of care: paid visiting nurses, meals or housecleaning programs, a paid personal attendant, assisted living facilities, and nursing home care. Assisted living facilities vary in their scope: some are little more than apartments for seniors with optional food and housekeeping services, while others provide more skilled nursing care. The price varies by what is included, but averages somewhere around $30,000 to $40,000 per year (Assisted Senior Living, 2009; MetLife Mature Market Institute, 2009). Assisted living facilities are a booming business, with about 33,000 such facilities operating in 2009 (Helpguide.org, 2010).

In contrast, nursing homes provide the most intensive level of care, at an average cost of almost $75,000 per year (Assisted Senior Living, 2009; MetLife Mature Market Institute, 2009). They are for people who cannot be cared for at home, and who have likely moved beyond what most assisted living centers can provide, but do not need the services of a hospital. Few elderly persons actually live in nursing homes, although that number rises with age. Most people do not need the intense level of care, cannot afford such care, and would rather be cared for at home. More than 70 percent of nursing home residents are women, and the average age at admission is 80 years (Houser, 2007).

dementia: The loss of mental functions such as thinking, memory, and reasoning.

Alzheimer's disease: The most common form of dementia; at present, it is incurable.

formal care: Care provided by social service agencies on a paid or volunteer basis.

Informal care refers to unpaid care that is provided by someone close to the recipient, such as a family member. If a spouse is unavailable, usually daughters or daughter-in-laws step in to provide care.

Informal Care In contrast to formal care, most elders rely primarily on **informal care**, unpaid care by someone close to the care recipient, usually a wife, daughter, husband, or son (National Alliance for Caregiving and AARP, 2009). Other relatives, such as nieces, siblings, and grandchildren, or even friends or neighbors, also sometime serve as informal caregivers. About 66 million people (29 percent of the population) care for an aging adult, averaging nearly 20 hours per week. They provide a wide variety of hands-on care and continue to do so even after an elder is institutionalized.

A spouse is generally the first person in line to provide care if she or he is able. When a spouse is unavailable or unable to provide this level of care, adult children, usually daughters, daughters-in-law, or even granddaughters will step in. The "typical" caregiving situation is a 49-year-old woman caring for her 69-year-old widowed mother for an average of four to five years (Houser, 2007; National Alliance for Caregiving and AARP, 2009). Some of these caregivers also have children to care for, as does Amy in the opening vignette. These caregivers are nicknamed the "**sandwich generation**" because they are members of the middle generation providing care to both a younger and an older generation. One study of 273 married respondents who provided care found that having children, particularly daughters, seems to increase, rather than decrease, the amount of time people spent in caregiving to frail relatives. The researchers found that children are more likely to connect the generations, rather than constrain the help that both mothers and fathers provide (Gallagher & Gerstel, 2001).

Caring for elderly parents or a spouse can be a labor of love, but it is also time intensive, potentially expensive, and often stressful (National Alliance for Caregiving and AARP, 2009; National Family Caregivers Association, 2008). Most caregivers provide assistance seven days a week with little help from formal services, as does Amy, introduced in the opening vignette. A recent national survey of more than 1,200 caregivers found that more than a third of caregivers provided all the help to the person they care for during the past 12 months and received no help from anyone else. Among caregivers who did receive some assistance, one-third said they provided most of the unpaid care (National Alliance for Caregiving and AARP, 2009). Because most female caregivers are employed, they have to make sacrifices at work to accommodate caregiving, including arriving late or leaving early, working fewer hours, taking a leave of absence, turning down a promotion, choosing early retirement, or giving up work completely—sacrifices that cost an average of $240,000 in lost wages over a lifetime (Houser, 2007; National Alliance for Caregiving and AARP, 2009).

Table 14.7	Strain and Stress of Caregiving		
Many people find caregiving to be highly stressful or a financial hardship, although not all caregivers feel this way.			
Health			
Excellent or very good			57%
Average			26%
Fair or poor			17%
Impact of caregiving on health			
Made it better			8%
No impact			74%
Made it worse			17%
Emotional Stress	**Scale**		
Very stressful	5		17%
	4		14%
Somewhat stressful	3		22%
	2		22%
Not at all stressful	1		25%
Financial hardship			
Great deal	5		9%
	4		6%
	3		15%
	2		19%
No hardship	1		51%

Source: National Alliance for Caregiving and AARP. 2009 November. Caregiving in the U.S.: Executive Summary.

Caregivers often spend their own money to provide medicines, groceries, or other supplies to the person they are caring for. Over a third of Blacks report in the national survey that they spend between $101 and $500 of their own money every month to provide care, as compared to less than one-quarter of Whites. Not surprisingly, Blacks are more likely than Whites to say that caregiving creates a financial hardship for them (National Alliance for Caregiving and AARP, 2009).

Given these challenges, many people find caregiving to be highly stressful, as shown in Table 14.7. Thirty-one percent report that they find caregiving highly stressful, and another 22 percent report that it is moderately stressful. Likewise, 15 percent report experiencing a great deal of financial hardship, and another 15 percent report moderate hardship. Many caregivers say that caregiving has been hard on their health and emotional well-being, and decreases their time spent with friends or other family members (National Alliance for Caregiving and AARP, 2009). It is labor, but often a labor of love.

informal care: Unpaid care by someone close to the care recipient.

"sandwich generation": A generation of people who are in the middle of two living generations providing care to members of cohorts on both sides of them, parents and children.

How would you cope if you realized, at around age 60, that you were becoming forgetful and were losing your memory? How would you react? What would you do?

Bringing It Full Circle

Our population is aging rapidly, with the number of elders increasing almost four times as fast as the population as a whole. Persons ages 85 and over—referred to as the "oldest old"—represent the fastest-growing cohort in the United States. These demographic changes will have far-reaching consequences for family life in the future. For example, large numbers of elderly persons, especially women, are widowed; other women, such as Amy in the opening vignette, serve as family caregivers to frail parents or grandparents. How will our lives change as the number of elders grows? We will likely see these types of issues take center stage, and our social and health policies will need to take our changing demographics and family structures into account. With the information that you have learned from this chapter, let's reflect back upon the opening vignette—the story of Amy who is caring for both a frail parent and her own young child.

- What stresses or strains are associated with caregiving, and how might these be affected by race, ethnicity, social class, and sex?
- What options does Amy have for reducing some of the stress in her life? What types of formal supports should be available to her? Why are they not available now, or are they?
- Reflecting upon Amy's experience, how will you care for an aging parent who needs assistance? How will their needs, and your potential response to their needs, affect your work, family, and other dimensions of your life?

For further review, turn to the Video Discussion Guide on page 449 to answer additional questions about how the chapter opening video relates to what you have learned in this chapter.

Chapter Review

14.1 What is a "demographic revolution"?

The *demographic revolution* refers to how the aging population is rapidly increasing today, and will continue to increase into the 21st century. Only a century ago very few people—one in 25—were ages 65 or older. Many younger people rarely met an elderly person. But the elderly population has been increasing almost four times as fast as the population as a whole, and seniors now constitute one of every eight people. In 2030, one in five Americans could be age 65 or older as the baby boom generation ages.

14.2 Which group of elders is increasing most rapidly?

Persons ages 85 and over—referred to as the "oldest-old"—are the fastest-growing cohort in the United States. In 2010 they number nearly 6 million, or 14 percent of all elders; however, they will increase to about 19 million in 2050. That would make the "oldest-old" about 25 percent of all elders and about 6 percent of the total population. And it is estimated that there may be a million persons ages 100 and over. The "oldest-old" group is more likely to have health problems and to need assistance; these individuals are also more likely to be female, widowed, live alone, and have financial difficulties.

14.3 In the past, were the elderly treated differently than they are today?

The "good old days" of the past are largely a myth. Rich, White, property-owning elderly men were generally treated with respect. However, poor or minority elders were often treated as outcasts. Industrialization decreased elders' status further because it was difficult for them to work in physically taxing and dangerous factories, yet most worked as long as they could because there were no pensions or Social Security.

14.4 Why was Social Security created?

With industrialization increasing, poverty was becoming more conspicuous. Elders were particularly vulnerable because few were covered by employer pensions, and they had a difficult time competing with younger men and women for jobs. During the Great Depression, many elders lost their jobs, and Social Security was created in 1935 to provide some degree of financial support upon turning age 65.

14.5 What patterns are associated with adult children leaving their parents' home?

Adult children used to leave home primarily for marriage or to join the military. Now, they leave home for college or to take a job. These types of transitions are less "final" than those of the past, and therefore, children today are more likely to return to their parents' home for a period of time. The recession also has caused many adult children to move back home with their parents, often repeatedly, and they have been given the nickname "boomerangers."

14.6 What type of relationships do parents have with their adult children after they finally leave home for good?

Most adult children receive substantial help from their older parents, with school, childcare, and mortgage assistance, until their parents are very old and frail. Most aging parents give far more assistance to their children then they receive from them.

14.7 Are the elderly satisfied with their marriages?

Most researchers have found that marriage begins with a high level of satisfaction, but the satisfaction begins to decline as couples have children, and then rises again when the children leave home. However, at least one researcher has found no evidence of the upturn; he suggested instead that variation in marital quality may simply be due to cohort differences—people of different cohorts, or ages, have different expectations about marriage.

14.8 What unique issues do LGBT elders face?

While lesbian, gay, bisexual, or transgender (LGBT) elders face many of the same issues that other elders face, such as health problems or the need for reliable transportation or housing assistance, they also have many unique concerns. Most federal programs and laws treat same-sex couples differently from married heterosexual couples, including Social Security, which pays survivor benefits to widows and widowers, but not to the surviving same-sex life partner of someone who dies; Medicaid, which protects the assets and homes of married spouses when the other spouse enters a nursing

Key Terms

Activities of Daily Living (ADLs) (p. 414)

Alzheimer's disease (p. 415)

baby boom generation (p. 392)

centenarian (p. 393)

companionate grandparenting (p. 407)

dementia (p. 415)

formal care (p. 415)

gerontologists (p. 414)

informal care (p. 417)

involved grandparenting (p. 407)

kinkeeping (p. 408)

life-course perspective (p. 396)

life expectancy (p. 392)

life-stage perspective (p. 395)

life-span perspective (p. 396)

remote grandparenting (p. 407)

"sandwich generation" (p. 416)

Social Security (p. 395)

home or long-term care facility, but offers no such protections to same-sex partners; or pensions, in which legal spouses avoid a tax penalty that same-sex partners must pay.

14.9 Do men and women experience widowhood differently?

Generally speaking, yes. Most widowers are females: they have longer life expectancies, they are generally several years younger than their husbands, and they are less likely to remarry. They are also more likely than widowed men to live in poverty. Consequently, because of their greater number there may be more avenues for social support.

14.10 What type of relationship do grandparents typically have with their grandchildren?

Most report a companionate relationship, meaning that they enjoy recreational activities, occasional overnight stays, and have fun together. A growing number of grandparents are raising their grandchildren because of the parent's absence or unsuitability for parenthood.

14.11 How is retirement a "social construction"?

Historically, and in many societies today, retirement as a concept has not existed. People had to work to support themselves and they were not exempt because of their age. Retirement is a relatively recent phenomenon. It is found in societies that have an economic surplus, pensions,

and/or government transfer; a belief that elders' activities or leisure are legitimate, and that they have an earned right to leisure. Moreover, retirement is seen and experienced differently by different groups in our society, e.g., men and women.

14.12 What is "caregiving"?

The term "caregiving" is often used to refer to caring for a frail elderly person, although technically speaking, it can be done with any age group. In this chapter, caregiving refers primarily to "informal care", which is unpaid care by someone close to the care recipient, usually a wife, daughter, husband, or son.

14.13 What type of stresses do caregivers experience?

Caring for elderly parents or a spouse can be a labor of love, but it is also time intensive, potentially expensive, and often stressful. Most caregivers provide assistance seven days a week with little help from formal services. Because most female caregivers are employed, they have to make sacrifices at work to accommodate caregiving, including arriving late or leaving early, working fewer hours, taking a leave of absence, turning down a promotion, choosing early retirement, or giving up work completely. Many caregivers are also taking care of their own children, and are therefore nicknamed the "sandwich generation."

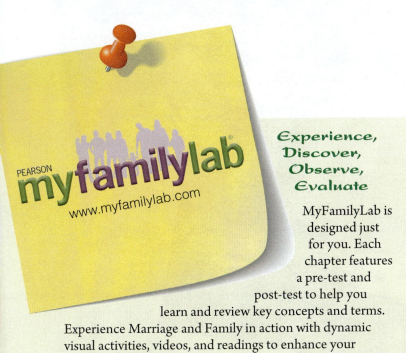

PEARSON myfamilylab
www.myfamilylab.com

Experience, Discover, Observe, Evaluate

MyFamilyLab is designed just for you. Each chapter features a pre-test and post-test to help you learn and review key concepts and terms. Experience Marriage and Family in action with dynamic visual activities, videos, and readings to enhance your learning experience.

Here are a few activities you will find for this chapter:

👁 **Watch Core Concepts** video clips feature sociologists in action, exploring important concepts in the study of Marriage and the Family. Watch:

- The Longevity Revolution
- Physical Challenges of Living Longer

✳ **Explore Social Explorer** is an interactive application that allows you to explore Census data through interactive maps. Explore the Social Explorer Report:

- Where are the Elderly?

📖 **Read MySocLibrary** includes primary source readings from classic and contemporary sociologists. Read:

- Newman, "Men and Women: Together and Apart in Later Years"

15

Looking Ahead: Helping Families Flourish

Top: Noe and Sophie; Middle: Sophie, Noe, Hugo, and Alain; Bottom: Hugo and Alain.

It's easy to be ethnocentric—to assume that your culture's way of doing things is the right way.

Yet, if we step back for a moment we can see that other cultures have some pretty good ideas too.

The United States and France are two highly developed countries, but their governments' approaches to family policies are strikingly different. Sophie and Alain are teachers currently living in the U.S., but who originally hail from France. As the parents of two young boys, they are in a unique position to compare the effects of social policies in each country on family life.

In France, Sophie tells us a woman is given sixteen weeks of fully paid maternity leave, including six weeks prior to the child's birth and ten weeks after. She was relieved to be able to stop teaching during her pregnancy; it reduced her stress, allowed her to rest, and helped her to prepare mentally for the baby. She notices that American women have no such luxury.

In addition to the maternity leave, either parent can take up to three years leave from their job. Granted, they tell us, this is not on full salary, but a stipend is paid from the government each month. There is no such equivalent in the U.S. Instead, Sophie and Alain see their American colleagues returning very soon after a baby is born because the family cannot afford to take unpaid leave or they fear that their jobs will be lost.

Even more incredible to Sophie and Alain is the high cost of childcare in the U.S., which they say costs nearly a full teacher's salary. In France, State daycare is available and far less expensive.

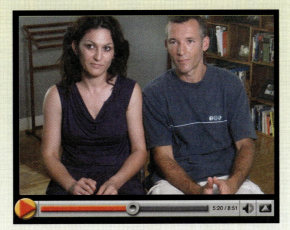

👁 **Watch** the **Video** *A Comparison of Family Policies: France and the United States: Sophie and Alain* on **myfamilylab.com**

Most of their friends back in France use the State daycare. In fact, the demand is so high that in the larger cities you must put your name on a waiting list when you learn you are pregnant.

Sophie and Alain also describe the monthly stipend for each child that the French government pays. It is a valuable benefit because children are expensive. Meanwhile, most of their American colleagues are bewildered at the thought of the government paying parents to take care of their children.

They are also perplexed by our health care system, which they say is expensive and quite uncoordinated. For example, Sophie has an eye condition requiring medication that is free in France, but costs them $50 every three weeks in the U.S.

Information like this can leave us wondering whether they see any benefits from living in the U.S. However, there is one issue in particular in which the U.S. shines, they say. They have been extremely impressed with the special education program for their youngest son, who was recently diagnosed with autism. They refer to France as being in the "Stone Age" with respect to special education, early intervention, or general assistance to the disabled or those with special needs. They feel their son is reaping benefits in the U.S.

QUESTIONS *That Matter* •

15.1 What is family resilience?

15.2 What are the components of family resilience?

15.3 What is missing from models of resilience?

15.4 What is the difference between universal and selective approaches to family policies and programs?

15.5 How does family policy in the United States compare to other countries?

15.6 What are some examples of policies or programs in the United States that help to support families?

15.7 What are some examples of policies or programs in the United States that help to improve children's lives?

15.8 What are some examples of policies or programs in the United States that help the elderly?

15.9 What are some examples of family policies or programs that are still needed to support families?

15.10 What are the three themes of this text?

Families are of interest to just about everyone. Look no further than our popular culture represented in movies, television, or music, and you will see that families and their relationships take center stage. Yet, in many ways, what could be more mundane—getting up in the morning, having breakfast, walking the kids to the school bus, going to work, making dinner, helping with homework, and putting the kids to bed at the end of a long day? Families can offer us the best times of our lives: falling in love, getting married, or the birth or adoption of a baby. Families can also offer us some of the worst times: conflict, betrayal, violence, and divorce. As you have learned in previous chapters, relationships take place in a social context. This allows us to ask, what kind of world do we *want* for our children? This chapter looks to the future by examining the macro-level social policies and programs that can create a more compassionate environment for our families. What is it that families need to really flourish? Let's take a creative look at the many options and opportunities that could improve the health, security, and well-being of families, drawing from other countries as well as our own, as shown in the opening vignette with Alain and Sophie.

:: What Do Families Need to Flourish?

Many aspects of family life, from communication to divorce, derive from macro-level changes in family demographics, needs, and functions. For example, as more women join the labor market, family members must find ways to meet both work and family demands. What resources are available to help them accomplish this balancing act? Or, as our country's demographics change, who will help care for a growing number of frail elders? Questions like these raise two interrelated points. First, *what do healthy families need to thrive*? Second, recognizing that many families face particular challenges—poverty, abuse, or neglect, for example—*what do challenged families need to become resilient*? As we will see in this chapter, families have surprisingly similar needs.

resilience: A multi-faceted ability to thrive despite adversity.

Family Resilience

Many adults and children do not have "picture-perfect" family lives (Miley, O'Melia, & DuBois, 2011). We have seen in earlier chapters that many people experience racism or sexism, grow up in impoverished environments, are torn by divorce, or are victims of intimate partner violence or child abuse. Yet, despite the toll these events can take, many adults and children overcome adversity and lead successful and well-adjusted lives. These individuals show **resilience**. The term "resilience" is derived from Latin roots meaning "to jump or bounce back" (Silliman, 1994). It is the capacity to rebound from adversity, misfortune, trauma, or other transitional crises strengthened and more resourceful (Walsh, 2006); it is a multi-faceted ability to thrive despite adversity (Benard & Truebridge, 2009; Pransky & McMillen, 2009).

Some people, like Jim Carrey, are born into poverty, but become very successful despite the odds. What contributes to this resiliency?

The Kauai Longitudinal Study (Werner, 1994, 1995; Werner & Smith, 1989, 1992), based upon 698 children born in 1955 on the island of Kauai in Hawai'i, examined the long-term effects of growing up in high-risk environments. Most of these children were born to unskilled sugar plantation workers of Japanese, Filipino, Hawaiian, Portuguese, Polynesian, and mixed racial descent. Fifty-four percent of them lived in poverty. Approximately one-third (210) were considered "high risk" because of exposure to a combination of at least four individual, parental, or household risk factors, such as having a serious health problem, familial alcoholism, violence, divorce, or mental illness in the family. The children were assessed from birth to ages 1, 2, 10, 18, and 32 years.

Two-thirds of those children who experienced four or more risk factors by age 2 developed learning or behavior problems by age 18. However, these children went on to become stable, confident, and productive adults, as rated on a variety of measures. In a later follow-up at age 40, all but two of the study participants were still successful. In fact, many had outperformed the children from low-risk families.

A key insight of this research is that we can develop resilience at any point in the life course. Among the two-thirds of high-risk children who had learning or behavioral problems at age 18, 50 percent of them did not exhibit these problems at age 30. Instead, they had satisfying jobs and stable marriages, and in other measures were deemed successful by the research team. The researchers also noted that teenage delinquency is not automatically a precursor to a life of crime. Meanwhile, a few individuals identified as resilient at age 18 in this study had developed significant problems by age 30.

The evidence shows us that many adults and children reared in poverty or with other disadvantages do overcome their adversities. What factors produce this resilience?

Individual, Family, and Community Factors

Individuals do not operate in isolation, but rather, our lives are embedded within larger social systems (Bronfenbrenner, 1979). To understand resiliency we must consider factors at a number of levels, including (Benard & Truebridge, 2009; Walsh, 2006):

- Individual-level protective factors
- Family protective and recovery factors
- Community strengths

Individual-level protective factors include such micro-level traits as a positive self-concept, sociability, intelligence and scholastic competence, autonomy, high self-esteem, creativity, independence, good communication and problem-solving skills, humor, and good mental and physical health. For example, the resilient high-risk adolescents in the Kauai Longitudinal Study had developed a sense that obstacles were not insurmountable, and they believed they had control over their fate. They had a high degree of self-esteem and self-efficacy, and many developed a special skill or hobby that was a source of pride.

Kurt Hummel's character in the television show Glee, reminds us of the importance of family protective and recovery factors for building resilience. Here Kurt received the support of his father after "coming out."

Family protective factors are those micro-level characteristics or dynamics that shape the family's ability to endure in the face of risk factors; they protect a family from crises. These can include such family characteristics as warmth, affection, cohesion, and traditions. **Family recovery factors** assist families in "bouncing back" from a crisis situation (McCubbin, McCubbin, Thompson, Han, & Allen, 1997). These types of factors include commitment, communication, and emotional support for each other. However, if parents cannot provide a nurturing environment, other family members such as siblings, grandparents, or aunts and uncles, may step in. Resilient families generally have reasonable and clear-cut expectations for their children. They participate in family celebrations, share spiritual connections, and have specific traditions and predictable routines. Moreover, resilient families generally share core values for financial management and the use of leisure time, even when money and time are in short supply. The *Getting to Know Yourself* feature box asks you to evaluate your family. Do you believe that you have a strong family that offers protective and recovery factors?

Macro-level **community factors**, such as social networks and religious and faith-based fellowships, also affect resilience (Silliman, 1998; Miller, 2000). Community institutions are important means of developing resilient youth and fostering resilience among adults. Researchers indicate several key community strengths (Blyth & Roelkepartian, 1993). First, a strong community has opportunities for participation in community life; extracurricular activities in school, religious youth groups, or other activities help to bond youth

individual-level protective factors: Traits including a positive self-concept, sociability, intelligence and scholastic competence, autonomy, self-esteem, androgyny, good communication and problem-solving skills, humor, and good mental and physical health.

family protective factors: Family characteristics or dynamics that shape the family's ability to endure in the face of risk factors.

family recovery factors: Family characteristics or dynamics that assist families in bouncing back from a crisis situation.

community factors: Community features that help promote resilience, such as social networks and religious and faith-based fellowships.

Getting to Know Yourself

Do You Have a Strong Family?

Answer the following questions as accurately as possible. You may do this for your family of origin or from your marriage or partnership.

1. I feel that my family is the best that it can be. Do you agree or disagree? (Circle one.)

1	2	3	4	5
Strongly Disagree	Disagree	Don't Know	Agree	Strongly Agree

2. T F My family often spends time together having fun.
3. T F My family often takes part in traditions.
4. T F My family members communicate well. We can talk about most things openly.
5. T F My family members express their feelings often.
6. T F My family members respect each other's feelings.
7. T F My family values working together and we often do.
8. T F My family shares the experience of religion and spirituality.
9. T F My family members enjoy each other's company.
10. T F Each member of my family is valued and important to other members.
11. T F When serious problems develop in my family we work them out eventually.
12. T F My family allows for each of us to be unique.
13. T F Every member of my family is committed to its well-being and success.
14. T F We often express appropriate physical affection in my family (hugs, kisses, etc.)
15. T F We can turn to one another when things get tough in my family.
16. T F We often express verbal affection in my family (love, praise, acceptance, etc.).
17. T F We often spend time together just taking it easy.
18. T F Each person in my family is allowed to suffer the consequences of his or her own actions.
19. T F In my family we have favorite foods that we usually eat on holidays.
20. T F In my family if things get too bad we will seek outside help.
21. T F In my family we respect and maintain each other's boundaries.
22. T F In my family everyone's input is considered when major decisions are made.
23. T F In my family parents are clearly the leaders.
24. T F In my family we give each other space when it is needed.
25. T F In my family we have healthy relationships with extended family members.
26. T F In my family adult children are allowed to make their own decisions.
27. T F In my family everyone is supported in his or her interests.
28. T F In my family we forgive each other when mistakes are made.
29. T F In my family members will listen to each other and are supportive.

Scoring: First, give yourself the number of points that corresponds to the answer you put for question 1 (i.e., if you put "4" for number 1 you get 4 points). Second, give yourself 1 point for each True answer in questions 2–29 (0 points for those questions you answered False). Third, add your points together. Scores can range from low of 1 to a high of 34. The higher your score, the stronger your family is, and the more likely your family is to have protective and recovery factors.

What Do You Think?

1. If you answered "False" to any of these questions, what, if anything, could be done to improve that area?
2. Are strong families perfect families? Might a strong family also have some weaknesses?

Source: Hammond, Ron J. and Barbara Bearnson. 2003b. The Marriages and Families Activities Workbook. Belmont, CA: Wadsworth/Cengage Learning.

Tying It All Together:

Factors That Influence Family Resilience

What factors are important for building strong families? Strong families do not happen by accident. Their relative strength depends upon what individuals bring to them, as well as the traits of the family as a whole. Macro-level factors in the social environment are also critical to building strong families, as families are embedded in broader social networks. Below are some of the micro-level and macro-level factors that work together to build family resilience.

Micro-level Factors

- Individual-level protective factors include personality traits and disposition, such as self-confidence.
- Family protective factors, such as family warmth, include characteristics or dynamics that shape the family's ability to endure in the face of risk factors.

- Family recovery factors such as religious beliefs that assist families in "bouncing back" from a crisis.

Macro-level Factors

- Community factors include adequate schools.
- Family policies and programs, such as Social Security or maternity leaves, offer assistance to help families thrive.

What Do You Think?

1. Can you identify the micro-level factors that you have, and those that you do not have that promote resilience?
2. What community factors are present and/or missing in your neighborhood that could help with resilience?

to their schools, churches, or communities. In these settings, they can learn important skills, such as teamwork, group pride, or leadership. Adults also need opportunities to hone these skills. Second, a strong community should provide ways for members to contribute to the welfare of others (Blyth & Roelkepartian, 1993). Helping others can foster a sense of inner strength and self-esteem. Third, a strong community provides opportunities to connect with peers and other adults. Resilience is more likely when there is access to a role model, a friend, or a confidant. For youth, teachers may play a critical role in providing this type of social support. Finally, healthy communities have community facilities and events for youth. Education and youth activities should receive high priority in the community's budget, with a functioning committee focusing on youth issues.

What Is Missing? Macro-Level Factors

Strengthening families requires individuals, families, and communities to work together. But broader macro-level factors must also play a part—notably national and state policies (Seccombe, 2002). For example, how do we best help a woman who is battered by her husband or partner? Should we focus on getting her into therapy so that she can improve her self-esteem, which will eventually allow her to end the abusive relationship? This may be an important component of resilience, but it is not enough. Most battered women do not seek therapy because they do not have the time, money, or trust in therapists. Even when therapy is helpful, it occurs *after the fact* when the psychological, physical, and emotional damage has already been done. Therefore, we must focus on the macro-level structural changes that could prevent violence in the first place, or at least minimize its chance of recurrence. These changes include passing and enforcing laws to prevent and protect women from violence, providing safe houses for their escape, and changing a culture that tolerates violence.

Sound economic and social policies and programs that are designed to strengthen all types of families, healthy as well as vulnerable, such as national health insurance, livable wages, and maternity leaves, can provide families and youth with the necessary tools to master resilience. They add an important level of strength above and beyond individual, family, and community factors. These micro-level and macro-level factors are summarized in the *Tying It All Together* feature box above.

Strong community programs such as clubs and organizations can help children connect with peers and mentors to bolster self-esteem.

What type of micro-level individual or family resilience traits do you possess? How are these different from those you see in a close friend or partner? What avenues for resilience does your community offer you?

Let's return to the question: What do families need to thrive? Policy decisions—particularly at the national level—have the potential to significantly improve our lives.

:: Family Policy

The government regulates many aspects of families. For example, the government prohibits certain people from marrying each other, requires people who intend to marry to have a blood test, and requires two witnesses for a legal wedding ceremony. The government also touches the lives of families by an *absence* of certain policies. For example, U.S. adults have no guaranteed maternity leave, national health insurance, or subsidized childcare. These family policies reflect historical, cultural, political, and social factors in the United States, including norms that favor personal over collective responsibility. The United States has little in the way of a comprehensive, collective vision for families, unlike other developed nations (Warner, 2005; Zimmerman, 2001). The policies in place are selective in nature and are available only for a few, rather than being universal policies available to all citizens.

A "Selective" Approach to Family Benefits

The United States has a long history of rugged individualism and a general distrust of both government and governmental programs. U.S. policies reflect and promote the concept of self-sufficiency. Our culture expects people to be in charge of their own destinies and shows little tolerance for those who seem unwilling or unable to support themselves (Axinn & Stern, 2008; Day, 2009). Borrowing from early English poor laws, our policies evolved over the 17th and 18th centuries to make clear distinctions between "worthy" needy people who cannot support themselves through no fault of their own, and "unworthy" people.

Not surprisingly then, the United States has embraced a laissez-faire approach in which families are largely left to fend for themselves. Many of our social policies and programs tend to be **selective programs**, meaning that only certain people are eligible for government services. For example, only the elderly or certain categories of poor people qualify for governmental health insurance; it is not available to all citizens. Likewise, only low-income parents receive assistance with their childcare costs, rather than all parents regardless of income. Many policies and programs are **means-tested programs**, meaning that persons need to meet an income requirement to qualify for benefits. These income thresholds are kept relatively low to limit the number of program users and thus control costs. On the other hand, police and fire protection and public education are available to all persons, regardless of income.

A "Universal" Approach to Family Benefits

When we compare U.S. social philosophy to that of most of Europe, Canada, and other developed nations, we see vastly different approaches as Sophie and Alain explain in the opening vignette. Most developed nations take a universal approach consisting of an interrelated, coordinated set of proactive economic and social programs and policies to help strengthen all families. **Universal programs** are not means-tested; rather, they are available to everyone. For example, as shown in Table 15.1, in a recent review of 23 developed nations, the United States was the only country without universal health insurance coverage, paid maternal/parental leave at childbirth, or family allowance/child dependency grant, which offsets some of the costs of raising children (Social Security Administration, 2010). [●—**Read** on **myfamilylab.com**

While the United States thinks of health care and childcare in individualistic terms and expects parents to "figure them out" on their own, other countries have specific policies to ensure that all citizens receive these benefits. Yet, how do you arrange for a paid maternal leave after the birth of your child when an employer tells you that you will be fired if you do not return to work quickly? How do you go about finding a family allowance, when most people in the United States have never even heard of such a program? How do you secure comprehensive

selective programs: Programs for which only a select group of people is eligible.

means-tested programs: Programs for which beneficiaries need to meet some eligibility requirement to qualify.

universal programs: Programs to help strengthen all families without any eligibility requirement.

[●—**Read** the **Document**
Caring for Our Young: Child Care in Europe and the United States on **myfamilylab.com**

Table 15.1	Child Policies in 23 Developed Countries Compared with the United States		
	The U.S. is the only developed country without universal health insurance/ health care, paid maternal/paternal leave at childbirth, or a family allowance/ child dependency grant for families.		
Country	Universal Health Insurance/Health Care	Paid Maternal/Parental Leave at Childbirth	Family Allowance/Child Dependency Grant
Australia	Yes	Yes	Yes
Austria	Yes	Yes	Yes
Belgium	Yes	Yes	Yes
Canada	Yes	Yes	Yes
Czech Republic	Yes	Yes	Yes
Denmark	Yes	Yes	Yes
Finland	Yes	Yes	Yes
France	Yes	Yes	Yes
Germany	Yes	Yes	Yes
Hungary	Yes	Yes	Yes
Iceland	Yes	Yes	Yes
Italy	Yes	Yes	Yes
Japan	Yes	Yes	Yes
Luxembourg	Yes	Yes	Yes
Netherlands	Yes	Yes	Yes
New Zealand	Yes	Yes	Yes
Norway	Yes	Yes	Yes
Poland	Yes	Yes	Yes
Portugal	Yes	Yes	Yes
Spain	Yes	Yes	Yes
Sweden	Yes	Yes	Yes
Switzerland	Yes	Yes	Yes
United Kingdom	Yes	Yes	Yes
United States	**No**	**No**	**No**

Source: Office of Research, Evaluation and Statistics, Social Security Administration, Social Security Programs throughout the World, April 2010.

health insurance when your employer does not offer this option and the cost of purchasing health insurance yourself exceeds your budget? President Obama asked this question, and has attempted to answer it through the passage of health care reform legislation.

Other countries have adopted programs of universal health care and childcare because their citizens believe poverty and inequality are caused by the structure of society, and therefore they look for structural, rather than individual, solutions. They fund safety net programs through **progressive taxation**—those who earn more pay a higher percentage of their income in taxes. U.S. citizens are more likely to equate poverty and its consequences with individual failure, immorality, lack of thrift, or laziness. For example, when asked "Why are there people in this country who live in need?," 39 percent of U.S. adults blamed personal laziness, compared to only 16 percent of Swedes and 15 percent of the French (Larsen, 2006). The Swedes, French, and many other people around the world believe families should not be left to fend for themselves because they are the collective responsibility of all citizens. Therefore, they are willing to pay higher taxes than U.S. adults to ensure that all citizens are well cared for in their countries. How does this form of governmental policy work? In the feature box, *My Family: What a Difference Location Can Make!*, the author describes the assistance available to her as a new mother living in France. Compare her story to that of a new mother living in the United States.

progressive taxation: A tax system under which those who earn more pay a higher percentage of their income in taxes than those who earn less.

Do you think that a more universal approach to social and health benefits will encourage people in the United States to become lazy and dependent upon the government for help? Why or why not? Can you identify the factors that have shaped your values? Do you know of people who have very different values? Can you guess why they see the world as they do?

Maternity and Family Leaves

Another critically important way to invest in families is by providing paid **maternity** (or **family**) **leaves** at times of need, such as after the birth of a child. These are often called maternity leaves, but they could include paternity leaves as well.

Why are these leaves so important? Lengthy maternity leaves are associated with better maternal and child health, and lower family stress. Moreover, with extended leave benefits women are likely to breastfeed for longer periods, which improves children's immunity and reduces their later risk of obesity. The benefit of longer parental leaves also extends to employers. Women are more likely to return to work after childbirth in those countries that have longer leaves. It is more cost-effective for a company to develop a well-planned parental leave policy than it is to rehire and retrain new employees.

The United States is the only developed country that does not offer paid maternity leaves. Other countries know that maternity leaves are associated with better health and well-being.

Even fathers now want time off to help bond with and care for a newborn. One-third of fathers stay home more than two weeks, but generally they work in professional jobs with a higher degree of flexibility, and must use their vacation time or take unpaid leave (Oppenheimer, June 15, 2008). For example, Erich and Anna's daughter was born on Valentine's Day: *"It was all the things they say: all the excitement, all the fear, all the anxiousness, and all the joy,"* says Erich, age 32 (Oppenheimer, June 15, 2008: A9). He used a week and a half of sick and vacation time from his job. Staying home any longer was not financially feasible, but he wanted to be involved. He scaled back his work to four days a week; Anna works three days as a community health nurse. *"We're a little tighter financially than some parents, but the trade-offs are worth it,"* Eric says (Oppenheimer, June 15, 2008: A9). Erich and Anna are unique in that their employers offer the opportunity to work part-time; most U.S. employers do not provide this flexibility.

The United States has, by far, the least generous family leave policy of any nation, including poor and developing nations, as shown in Table 15.3. The Family Medical Leave Act of 1993, signed by President Clinton, requires employers with over 50 employees to offer 12 weeks of *unpaid* leave for maternity or to care for a sick family member. Employers in small firms are not required to offer even unpaid leaves. Therefore, many women take only a brief leave from work after having a baby because they cannot afford unpaid leave. They return to work soon after exhausting their short-term disability, vacation, or sick pay. Among women who worked during their pregnancy, 58 percent returned to work within three months after giving birth and 72 percent within six months (Johnson, 2008). While some women may have returned to work quickly because they enjoyed their jobs, it is likely that finances were a primary reason for a quick return. Only one-third receive any paid leave from an employer, usually of short duration.

By way of contrast:

- Denmark offers 52 weeks of paid maternity leave to women at 100 percent of their salary.
- In the Netherlands, women receive 16 weeks of paid maternity leave at 100 percent. They may also take unpaid leave for six months or reduce their working hours by half for up to six months, while they receive 75 percent of their salary for those leave hours.
- Spain offers women 16 weeks of leave at 100 percent of their salary.
- The United Kingdom allows maternity pay at 90 percent for six weeks, and a flat rate after that for up to a year.
- Canada provides up to 15–18 weeks of maternity benefits, depending upon the province, paid at 55 percent of average earnings up to a ceiling (United Nations Statistics Division, 2010).

maternity (or **family**) **leave:** A paid and guaranteed leave from work to care for children, including after the birth of a child.

Many countries around the world have been increasing the length of paid maternity leave over the past five years to give parents even more time with their babies (United Nations Statistics Division, 2010).

Table 15.3	A Comparison of Maternity Leave Benefits in Developing and Developed Nations	
Compare the United States with every other country listed. How do we compare?		
	Length of Maternity Leave	**Percentage of Wages Paid in Covered Period**
Developing Nations		
Afghanistan	90 days	100%
Bangladesh	16 weeks	100%
Cuba	18 weeks	100%
Egypt	90 days	100%
Guatemala	84 days	100%
India	12 weeks	100%
Kenya	3 months	100%
Mozambique	60 days	100%
Republic of Korea	60 days	100%
Developed Nations		
Canada	17–18 weeks	55% for 15 weeks
Denmark	52 weeks	100%
Finland	105 days	80%
Ireland	28 weeks	80% or fixed rate
Italy	5 months	80%
Japan	14 weeks	67%
Netherlands	16 weeks	100%
Spain	16 weeks	100%
Sweden	480 days	80% for 390 days; flat rate afterwards
Switzerland	98 days	80%
United Kingdom	52 weeks	90% for 6 weeks; flat rate afterwards
United States	**12 weeks(a)**	**0**

(a) Applies only to workers in companies with 50 or more workers.

Source: Adapted from United Nations Statistics Division, 2010.

Leave is also far more generous in many poor or developing nations than it is in the United States. Even in Afghanistan, one of the poorest nations on Earth, the law entitles women in qualifying jobs up to 90 days of maternity leave paid at 100 percent. Of course, not all Afghan women receive this pay, as many of them work in the underground economy, but at least the law offers an element of protection for some that most American women can only dream about.

Flexible Time and Place of Employment

The adoption of more flexible work environments could do much to enhance family life. Many parents report a high degree of tension in trying to balance work and family demands, including marital conflict, shorter periods spent breastfeeding infants, less involvement with their older children, and depression (Parker-Pope, 2007). Flexibility in daily work hours, known as **flextime**, and in the location of work, **flexplace**, is high on the agenda of families and family scientists. One IBM study of over 6,000 employees found job flexibility improved the precarious work-family balance many face, even after

flextime: Flexibility in the daily hours of work.

flexplace: Flexibility in the location of work, including working from home.

Many parents appreciate flexible schedules and flexible workplaces so they can more easily combine work and family.

accounting for other factors like number of hours worked, hours spent in domestic labor, marital status, occupation, and gender (Hill, Hawkins, Ferris, & Weitzman, 2001). Another study of 3,200 workers at a major pharmaceutical company found that those with job flexibility were more likely to engage in healthful behaviors. They exercised more and attended more employer-sponsored health classes. They reported getting more sleep, and were more likely to describe themselves as living a healthful lifestyle (Parker-Pope, 2007).

About half of companies now offer flextime, according to a national study of nearly 3,000 employees, although only about one-quarter allow it on a daily basis (Bond, Galinsky, & Hill, 2004). Given the current recession, many employees feel it is not available without repercussions for their careers (Blake, 2010; Clark, 2010). Corporate norms seem to dictate working longer hours than ever before, even for those employees with family responsibilities.

Flexplace, more often now referred to as **telecommuting**, involves maintaining a virtual office or working from home. Telecommuting is rising in popularity because of a growing concern about the automobile's effect on global warming, the rising price of gasoline, and the increasing numbers of parents combining work and family. There are an estimated 45 million telecommuters, up 10 percent in just over three years (Gajendran & Harrison, 2007). However, most telecommuters also maintain an on-site office. Among the nearly 13,000 employees studied by Bond, Galinsky, and Hill, only 2 percent worked primarily at home, and 9 percent spent a portion of their work week working at home (2004).

More flexible work environments could benefit working parents by decreasing commuting time and the stresses associated with negotiating rush-hour traffic, and allowing them to synchronize work schedules with their children's activities and other family responsibilities. Flexible work environments may be ideal for the worker, but are they ideal for business? The analysis of over 46 telecommuting studies published in the past 20 years involving 12,833 employees, reveals its overall beneficial effect because the arrangement provides employees with more control, and thus satisfaction with their work. Employees who were allowed to telecommute some or part of the time had less desire to leave the company and were given higher performance ratings by supervisors (Gajendran & Harrison, 2007). Nonetheless, given the current economic conditions, many workers are skittish about telecommuting, fearing that if they are out of sight, they may also be out of the boss's mind (Blake, 2010; Clark, 2010).

Living Wage

The federal minimum wage was increased in 2007 after being stagnant at $5.15 per hour for over a decade. The increase took place in three increments: $5.85 in 2007; $6.55 in 2008; and $7.25 per hour in 2009. Minimum wage rates are important, as shown in Table 15.4, because 76 percent of those directly affected by the 2009 minimum wage increase were ages 20 and over, and 25 percent were parents. The average minimum-wage worker brings home over half (48 percent) of his or her family's weekly earnings

Table 15.4	Characteristics of Workers Benefitted by Minimum Wage Increase to $7.25 in 2009
Minimum wage rates are important because 71 percent of those directly affected by the 2009 minimum wage increase were ages 20 and over and 25 percent were parents.	

Number of workers	5.3 million
Gender	
Male	39%
Female	61%
Family Status	
Parent	25%
Married Parent	15%
Unmarried Parent	9%
Age	
16–19	30%
20 and over	71%
Work Hours	
1–19	22%
20–34	36%
Full time (35 and over)	43%

Source: Filion, Kai. 2009. "Fact Sheet for 2009 Minimum Wage Increase—Minimum Wage Issue Guide." Retrieved 3 May 2010. Economic Policy Institute (www.epi.org/publications/entry/mwig_fact_sheet/).

(Filion, 2009). Yet, the minimum wage remains inadequate to support a family. Many families earning the minimum wage are living below the poverty line and need programs such as food stamps, reduced-fee school lunch programs, and other benefits to make ends meet. A worker earning $7.25 per hour earns $290 a week, or $15,080 per year, a few thousand dollars below the poverty line for a family of three, as described in Chapter 2 (DeNavas-Walt, Proctor, & Smith, 2010).

In response to this concern, the living wage movement has gained a significant foothold in at least 60 local governments, including New York City, Baltimore, Portland (Oregon), Chicago, Minneapolis, and many other cities (Fairris & Reich, 2005; Freeman, 2005; Thompson & Chapman, 2006). Recall from Chapter 10 that a living wage is pay that is above federal or state minimum wage levels. Living wage proponents argue that (1) wages should be high enough to allow workers to meet basic needs, and (2) municipal governments should encourage or require living wages for their employees and contractors, rather than exacerbate the problems low-wage workers face by using public money to create jobs that keep people poor (Thompson & Chapman, 2006). A typical living wage ordinance requires contractors and businesses receiving governmental financial assistance to pay what is deemed a "livable wage" in that community, one that will ultimately decrease the number of people dependent on social programs. Usually these wages range from 150 percent to 225 percent of the current federal minimum wage. For example, effective July 1, 2009, the City of Los Angeles pays $10.30 per hour to those workers in covered contracts if they also receive health insurance, and $11.55 per hour to those workers who do not (City of Los Angeles, 2010). Living wage movements have expanded their goals to include vacation days and health and other benefits.

Critics of living wage legislation claim these laws actually harm those they are intended to help by reducing their work opportunities. As the price of labor increases, they say, a loss of jobs will result, and these workers will be even worse off. Consequently, wage subsidies are usually administered as federal tax credits. These credits shift much of the financial burden from the local governments to the federal government, which is better-equipped to absorb these costs. An example of a wage subsidy, or tax credit for low-income persons, is the Earned Income Tax Credit (EITC).

Earned Income Tax Credit (EITC)

The **Earned Income Tax Credit** (EITC) is a refundable federal tax credit for low-income working families that can reduce the amount of taxes owed and result in a tax refund for those who qualify. To qualify, a family (married and filing taxes jointly) must have adjusted gross income in 2010 of less than $45,373 with two children, $40,545 with one child and $18,470 with no children (Internal Revenue Service, 2009).

The EITC lifts millions of families out of poverty each year and is one of the country's largest sources of assistance for poor and low-income working families. Enacted in 1975 and expanded in the 1990s, it helped 6.5 million Americans avoid poverty last year (Sherman, 2009), and helps millions of other low-income families at a cost of about $54 billion in 2010 (Williams & Johnson, 2009). The EITC encourages employment because it offers a real supplement to wages for qualifying low-income workers. The EITC makes it easier for families to transition from welfare into work. The boost in income provides a critical element of security for poor families. It can contribute to basic necessities, enable families to make special needed purchases, or build a savings cushion to offset a future job loss, illness, or another situation that can leave families vulnerable. Without the EITC, poverty rates among children would be about one-third higher than they are now.

The EITC receives enthusiastic bipartisan support because it encourages work and gives a helping hand to the lowest-income families. Yet at the same time, this benefit has had less impact than it could in the United States. The EITC is a once-a-year tax credit, unlike family allowances, which provide monthly support. Furthermore, the EITC offsets only *some* of the taxes the worker would pay and does not really augment wages.

telecommuting: Flexibility in the location of work, including working from home.

Earned Income Tax Credit: A refundable federal tax credit for low-income working families that reduces the amount of taxes owed.

Welfare: Temporary Assistance for Needy Families (TANF)

Welfare has been one of the most vexing social policy concerns in the United States. Its principal cash program, **Temporary Assistance for Needy Families (TANF)**, formerly called Aid to Families with Dependent Children (AFDC), has been accused of fostering long-term dependency, family breakups, and illegitimacy (Murray, 1988). Welfare recipients are stigmatized as lazy and unmotivated, looking for a free ride at the expense of the taxpayer (Seccombe, 2011). ✳ Explore on **myfamilylab.com**

✳ Explore the Concept
Social Explorer Report: Welfare Recipients on **myfamilylab.com**

Both Republicans and Democrats have tried to reconstruct welfare or end it completely. President Bill Clinton signed sweeping welfare reform legislation, which became federal law on July 1, 1997. Many details of welfare law were turned over to states, which set lifetime welfare payments at a maximum of five years and required the majority of adult recipients to work after two years. Since the passage of welfare reform, many people have left welfare, usually for low-wage work. From 1994 to 2009, national caseloads fell by two-thirds, declining from 5 million to around 1.7 million families (Administration for Children & Families, 2010).

Although declining caseload numbers are often seen as a sign of success, families leaving welfare for work are not necessarily better off financially (Seccombe & Hoffman, 2007; Loprest & Zedlewski, 2006; Moffitt, 2008). The results of a nationwide study found their median wage to be $7.75 per hour, and 60 percent of these families continue to live in poverty (Loprest & Zedlewski, 2006). More than half could not pay their rent or utilities during the past year, half experienced two or more bouts of food insecurity (i.e., they did not have money to purchase food for their family), over a quarter used a food bank, and one-third did not have a car, making it more difficult to work or take children to school.

Statewide studies of families leaving welfare support national reports. For example, a study in Oregon, which followed 552 former welfare recipients until 18 months after leaving TANF, found that recipients' average income hovered near the poverty line, but their income rendered them ineligible for a number of important services (Seccombe & Hoffman, 2007). Forty percent had no health insurance and 21 percent had at least one child uninsured. Thirty-two percent had cut or skipped meals entirely because of a lack of money and 8 percent had cut or skipped their children's meals. Most reported outstanding debt, including 54 percent who had a medical debt averaging nearly $2,500, a sum nearly impossible to repay given their inadequate incomes.

The study included women like "Molly" who suffered a tubal pregnancy, yet tried to avoid seeking medical care because she had no insurance and no way to pay the medical bill. Finally, after enduring pain for nearly two weeks, she went to the emergency room of her local hospital and was immediately taken to surgery. Her fallopian tube was removed at a cost of $14,000. She discusses her debt:

There's all these doctor's offices that I owe money to, and I had to set up payment plans with all of them. But, you know, it's like paying as much as rent every month to each doctor's office. I'm never going to come up with the money. I mean, I can try to make my payments, but it's never going to happen. I make eleven bucks an hour. I have to pay rent, gas, utilities, groceries, diapers, and, you know, daycare is way expensive. That's like 400 bucks a month, and now they want me to pay 400 bucks a month to different offices. And I'm like, dude, I'm not made of money. The next time something like that happens, I'm just going to dig a grave in the backyard. Fourteen grand's not worth it.

"it's like paying as much as rent every month to each doctor's office."

—Molly
(Seccombe & Hoffman, 2007) [4].

Temporary Assistance to Needy Families (TANF): The principal cash welfare program in the United States.

Other countries have a different approach to helping poor families, as we saw in the opening vignette. For example, in her book *Saving Our Children from Poverty* (1996), economist

Why Do Research?

Surviving Welfare and Low-wage Work

How do single mothers in the United States survive with meager welfare benefits and low-wage work? It is not easy, as a study of nearly 400 poor and low-income single mothers revealed. Researchers used both quantitative data, such as filling out budgets, and qualitative data based on in-depth interviews to determine how families on welfare and those who work in low-wage jobs make ends meet. Using multiple methods is rarely done because of the cost, time involved, and the fact that many researchers are experienced with only a single strategy for collecting data. Yet, using multiple methods allows us to obtain a better understanding of how poor and low-income families make ends meet. Here are a few excerpts that describe some of the strategies that low-income families use.

1. Contributions from family, friends, boyfriends:

"The kids give me a headache about clothes. Usually my mom, brother, or sister-in-law gives me money to buy them clothes. I can't afford it. I get clothes at church and other charitable clothes giveaways, or at garage sales."

"He [baby's father] sometimes gives me money. When I send her up there to his mother's house, he buys her Pampers and baby food, but all he puts into my hand is a $20 bill. I mean, what does he expect me to buy with $20? I can't even buy but two boxes of Pampers with $20. He's coming over here tonight to bring her back, and I said I needed $40 'cause she needs so many things right now. But I don't think he gonna bring it."

2. Reported work:

"Working overtime if I have to, anything to get a few extra dollars. I try to get to work one-half hour early, and leave one-half hour late, that's an extra five hours worth of pay each week! It comes in handy."

2. Unreported side jobs:

"I collect junk, trash pick—I'm the ultimate trash picker—and I go to garage sales. I have my friends picking up stuff in alleys and at garage sales for me too. They're all like, 'Oh, let's grab this for her!' whenever they see some old crap. Then on weekends, I'll get this friend of mine to help me load his pickup and we get a table at the flea market for about $50. Some weekends I'll make $200 or $300 on old junk I might have paid $20 total for, but that's not all the time."

3. Underground work:

"Some of our friends will sell drugs. I know some of my friends who have turned tricks. Usually, some people do it for their family, and some people do it for drugs. At one point I did sell drugs in order to keep my family [together]. When my husband left, and I had to make sure I could pay my bills. That's what I did."

4. Agency-based strategies:

"This morning I went to Catholic Charities and got a $20 voucher for the Market Basket [grocery store]. You can only go once a year. They're cutting back a lot of programs: no more emergency assistance, no more back payments in rent, no more rent assistance. These cuts will affect me a lot. I will have to dig deep. I don't know what I am going to do."

Source: Edin, Kathryn and Laura Lein. 1997. Making Ends Meet: How Single Mothers Survive Welfare and Low-wage Work. New York: Russell Sage Foundation.

What Do You Think?

1. What might be some of the ethical issues involved in doing qualitative and quantitative research on poor and low-income families?

2. Did any of these survival strategies bother you personally? If so, why?

Barbara Bergmann states that only one-quarter of single mothers in France receive welfare-type benefits, compared to two-thirds of single mothers in the United States. The reason is not that France is stingy towards its citizens. In contrast, France has made a successful commitment to enhancing low-tier jobs so they pay a living wage, and the government does not automatically eliminate an array of benefits vital to a family's well-being. A single mother in France who moves from welfare to work retains approximately $6,000 in government cash and housing grants. She continues to receive health insurance and pays only a small amount for childcare, as do all French citizens. Therefore, even though France has an unemployment rate 50 percent higher than that in the United States, its poverty rate is considerably lower. In contrast, in the *Why Do Research? Surviving Welfare and Low-wage Work* feature box, researchers Katherine Edin and Laura Lein show us how nearly 400 low-income or welfare-reliant single mothers try to survive.

Do you think the current economic recession has changed these policies and programs for families? For example, are any expanding or retracting? Why might this be the case?

Watch the **Video**
Core Concepts: Government, Business, and Family Policy on
myfamilylab.com

:: Specific Policies and Programs for Children

Children depend on others to meet their basic needs of food, shelter, clothing, and love. What can we do to improve their circumstances, and therefore, improve their resilience and chance for a good and productive life? **Watch** on **myfamilylab.com**

Early Childhood Interventions

Early childhood interventions attempt to improve the quality of lives of children. While most of the care young children receive comes from families, early childhood interventions are formal supports designed to augment this care. They can include (Children's Defense Fund, 2008):

- Public health and social welfare programs that provide prenatal care, immunizations, or food and nutritional supplements, including the feeding program Women, Infants, and Children (WIC);
- Childcare programs designed to ensure high-quality care, or to provide financial assistance to families needing childcare;
- Programs to promote early childhood development, such as parenting classes, Head Start, preschool, and kindergarten; and
- Income or other safety-net programs.

Researchers from RAND, a prominent research institute in California, conducted a project to determine whether early childhood intervention programs offer lasting success (Karoly, Kilburn, & Cannon, 2005). They examined 20 programs that provided three types of child development services from the prenatal period to kindergarten: (1) parental education and home visiting; (2) early childhood education combined with parent education; and (3) early childhood education only. Of these 20 programs, 19 demonstrated favorable effects on child outcomes in at least one of the following domains: cognitive and academic achievement; behavioral and emotional competencies; educational progression and attainment; child maltreatment; health; delinquency and crime; social welfare program use; and labor market success. In other words, early childhood intervention programs *do* work. Moreover, many benefits can be translated into dollar figures and compared with program costs. For example, if children do better in school, less money will be spent on remedial or special education classes. Cost-benefit analyses estimate that for every dollar invested, the returns to society range from $1.80 to $7.07. In other words, early childhood education is cost-effective and pays important dividends for years to come (Karoly, Kilburn, & Cannon, 2005).

The *Policy and You: From Macro to Micro: Head Start Programs* feature box describes one well-known intervention program that combines early childhood education with parent education—Head Start. This program is designed to improve school readiness and basic cognitive skills for low-income preschool-aged children, working with both the child and his or her family. This program currently serves over 900,000 children at an average cost of $7,326, yet funding falls far short and cannot cover all who qualify (Administration for Children and Families, Office of Head Start, 2009).

State Children's Health Insurance Program (SCHIP)

Children are especially vulnerable to poor health and in need of preventive care; therefore, the State Children's Health Insurance Program (SCHIP) was created in the 1990s to insure children in working families with incomes too high to qualify for Medicaid, but too low to afford private family coverage (Ross, Horn, & Marks, 2008). (Note: The program is sometimes referred to as Children's Health Insurance Program or CHIP.) Congress created SCHIP as a federal/state partnership similar to Medicaid, with the goal of expanding health insurance to children. It is the single largest expansion of health insurance coverage for children since the initiation of Medicaid in the mid-1960s. While eligibility criteria differ by

early childhood intervention:
Attempts to maintain or improve the quality of life for young children.

Policy and You: From Macro to Micro

Head Start Programs

Head Start began in 1965 as part of the War on Poverty program launched by President Lyndon B. Johnson. Nearly half the nation's poor people were children under age 12, and Head Start was developed to respond to the needs of poor children as early as possible. Research showed that early intervention through high-quality programs enhances children's physical, social, emotional, and cognitive development; enables parents to be better caregivers and teachers to their children; and helps parents meet their own goals, including economic independence.

Head Start was envisioned as a comprehensive program that would provide health and nutritional services to poor children, while developing their cognitive skills and engaging parents as well. To improve school readiness, children may be taught the alphabet, numbers, colors, and shapes. They are monitored to keep them up to date on immunizations; testing is also available for hearing and vision. Many programs are integrated to include children with special physical or cognitive needs. Class size is limited to 17 to 20 children, with two teachers. Parents are encouraged to work as teacher's aides, so they understand what their children are learning and help carry on that learning at home.

Head Start began by primarily serving four-year-olds, who attend for one year before starting kindergarten. However, with the reauthorization of the program in 1994, Congress established a new program for pregnant women and low-income families with infants and toddlers called Early Head Start. Today 46 percent of children attending Head Start are age three or younger. The Early Head Start program provides resources to community programs to address the needs of younger children and their families. Its goals are similar to those of Head Start—to demonstrate the impact of early, continuous, intensive, and comprehensive services to pregnant women and very young children and their families.

Measuring the program's actual success is not a simple matter. Head Start is said to save taxpayers' money because attendees are more likely to graduate from high school and get a job than their peers. However, its precise long-term benefits are difficult to gauge, and researchers disagree even about the short-term benefits. Nevertheless, one government publication states that, in the long term, $6 are saved for every $1 invested in the Head Start program. Other studies find that Head Start graduates are more likely than their peers to stay in the proper grade level for their age in elementary school. The price tag? Nearly $7 billion.

Source: Adapted from U.S. Department of Health and Human Services, Administration for Children and Families, Office of Head Start, 2009.

What Do You Think?

1. Draft an argument in favor of Head Start programs; then draft an argument against them. Be sure to include the bottom line: does it work? Is Head Start worth the money?

2. Why do you think so many poor children have deficits in their early education? Try to offer both micro-level and macro-level explanations.

state, 43 states and the District of Columbia now cover children living in households with incomes up to twice the poverty line (around $34,000 for a family of three) (Kaiser Family Foundation, October 2010). Despite this program, millions of needy families remain ineligible, are not aware of SCHIP, or otherwise do not or cannot enroll in this program. Ten percent of all children, and 15 percent of children from poor households, are uninsured, as shown in Figure 15.1 on page 438 (DeNavas-Walt, Proctor, & Smith, 2010).

If low-income and poor children are eligible for SCHIP, then why are they not covered? First, it is possible that some families do not know of the program or cannot access it for some reason—perhaps there are distance, language, or cultural reasons. Second, the program is underfunded and cannot cover all eligible children. For example, eligibility changes in Texas resulted in more than 180,000 children being dropped in just one year (Children's Defense Fund, 2007). Third, applications are subject to bureaucratic rules such as 90-day waiting periods, strict asset limits, or other regulations that limit their coverage. The result can be very disturbing, as shown in the Johnson household:

Thirteen-year-old Devante Johnson, of Houston, Texas, had advanced kidney cancer and could not afford to be without health care coverage. But last year, that is exactly what happened when Devante spent four desperate months uninsured while his mother tried to renew his Medicaid coverage. For years Devante and his two younger brothers were covered by Medicaid. Texas families who qualify for Medicaid or the Children's Health Insurance Program (CHIP) are required to renew their coverage every six months, and Devante's mother, Tamika, had tried to get a head start by sending in her paperwork two months before Medicaid was set to expire. The application sat for six weeks until it was processed and then transferred to CHIP because an employee believed their family no longer qualified for Medicaid. At that point, the

"I did everything I possibly could,"

paperwork got lost in the system. Tamika grew more and more desperate as she watched her son get worse. "I did everything I possibly could," Tamika said. "I would literally get off the phone in tears, crying because they [CHIP employees] frustrated me so much." For four months Devante went without health insurance as employees attempted to reinstate his coverage. As a result he could no longer receive regular treatment and had to rely on clinical trials for care. Meanwhile, his tumors grew. Time was running out. It wasn't until a state representative intervened that Devante's coverage was immediately reinstated. Two days later, Devante was able to start a promising new treatment. But it was too late. Devante Johnson died at the age of 14, from complications of the disease (Children's Defense Fund, 2007) [13].

| **Figure 15.1** | **Uninsured Children by Poverty Status, Age, and Race, and Hispanic Origin: 2009 (Percent)** |

Despite programs to help uninsured children, many remain uninsured, creating the need for health care reform.

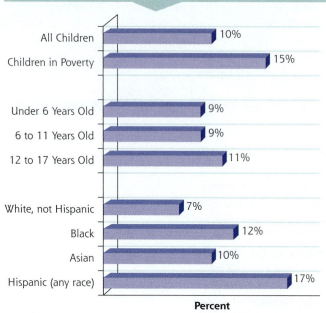

Source: DeNavas-Walt, Proctor, & Smith, 2010.

Child Support

The parents of nearly 22 million children under age 21 live apart (Grall, 2009). Inadequate child support payments from the noncustodial parent have hurt many families. As we learned in Chapter 12, less than half of custodial parents receive the full amount of their court-ordered child support payment, and about a third receive only a partial or sporadic payment. Nearly one-quarter receive nothing at all from their noncustodial parents. While the average child support payment due is $5,300 per year, only $3,300 is actually received, shortchanging children out of $2,000 a year (Grall, 2009).

Parents who fail to make payments are more likely to be under 30, Black, never married, and have less education than most people their age. Moreover, nearly 6 million noncustodial parents and their children are not protected by *any* child support agreement at all, because they did not have the need to make child support legal, did not feel the other parent could pay, or did not want any contact with the other parent, as shown in Figure 15.2 (Grall, 2009). A national policy to bolster child support enforcement could help millions of families escape poverty and obtain economic security, and thus, improve family outcomes.

Since 1988, the government has made greater efforts to secure child support from the absent parent with passage of the Family Support Act. The Act includes withholding child support from fathers' wages; requiring states to adopt uniform standards for setting child support awards; and implementing computerized systems for locating delinquent parents. Some states take additional steps, such as intercepting tax returns, withdrawing funds from bank accounts, suspending drivers' licenses, or even sending nonpaying parents to jail. Despite these state efforts, compliance is still woefully inadequate. Consequently, child support enforcement was an important component of the welfare reform changes of 1996, and states must now comply with more rigorous federal guidelines to secure child support.

Will further enforcing child support orders really help children? For the 4 million custodial parents who fail to receive the full amount of child support, and the nearly 6 million who do not have a child support agreement, rigorous collection could add several thousand dollars a year to their family income. Although this additional money would not bestow great wealth upon these families, it would nonetheless make their lives far more comfortable and secure (especially given that child support payments are not taxed). About one-quarter of all custodial single parents live in poverty (Grall, 2009), and the addition of several thousand dollars a year could provide a possible financial safety net for their families.

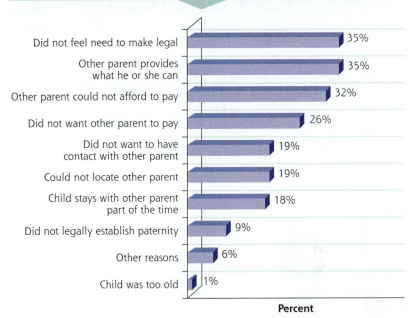

Figure 15.2 Reasons No Legal Agreement Established for Custodial Parents: 2008 (Percent)

Nearly 6 million custodial parents have no childcare agreement. The reasons are listed here.

Source: U.S. Census Bureau, Current Population Survey, April 2008.

Childcare Policies

As we discussed in Chapter 10, childcare is expensive for families in the United States. Costs for full-time care can easily reach $10,000 a year or more per child (National Association of Child Care Resource & Referral Agencies, 2009). Given that most families have more than one child, often spaced only a few years apart, childcare bills can easily amount to $20,000 per year. These costs are out of reach of many families. While some subsidies are available to families leaving TANF for work, for example, most people pay the cost of childcare themselves. This imposes a considerable hardship on many families.

Families can offset some of the costs of childcare in two ways (Internal Revenue Service, 2009). One option is a childcare tax credit on the family's income tax form. Under current law, the Child and Dependent Care tax credit can cover between 20 and 35 percent of expenses to care for children younger than 13, depending upon family income. The lower the family's income, the higher the allowable percentage. There is a dollar limit on the expenses toward which you can apply the credit: $3,000 for the care of one child, $6,000 for two or more. While this represents a real savings to families at tax time, it does not come close to covering the full costs of care.

As a second option, available only if provided by an employer, a family can set aside up to $5,000 in pre-tax dollars in a flexible spending plan for childcare (Internal Revenue Service, 2009). The family does not pay taxes on this set-aside amount, so in a 25 percent tax bracket, the family receives a 25 percent "bonus" ($1,250), which can be a real boon to many families. However, there are two problems with the flexible spending plan. First, given that most childcare costs far exceed $5,000, these savings, while helpful, are

Canada's Universal Child Care plan
Choice. Support. Spaces.

For each child under six, you will receive $100 per month.

But you may need to apply.

The Government of Canada's **Universal Child Care Benefit** came into effect on July 1, 2006. It provides Canadian families with $100 per month for each child under six.

If you already receive the Canada Child Tax Benefit (CCTB), you will automatically receive the Universal Child Care Benefit. If you are one of the ten percent of families who do not receive the CCTB, you need to complete the CCTB form.

It's simple to apply

Log on to www.universalchildcare.ca and click on the application links. It's that easy. Or, visit your local Service Canada Centre to obtain the form in person. You can also call 1 800 959-2221.

You can apply anytime

The first benefit cheques have been mailed. You can apply anytime and receive payments retroactively up to 11 months from your date of application.

This initiative is part of Canada's Universal Child Care Plan which will also support the creation of thousands of real child care spaces through the **Child Care Spaces Initiative**.

For more information, visit the website at www.universalchildcare.ca

 Government   Gouvernement
of Canada   du Canada

Canada

Other developed nations have a more proactive approach to helping families. For example, this ad was posted in Canadian newspapers reminding all families with young children to apply for benefits. No stigma is attached to receiving help with childcare.

inadequate to meet the needs of most families. For example, if the real cost of childcare is $10,000, and by law the 25 percent tax benefit can be taken on only half that amount—$5,000—the real tax saving is reduced to 12.5 percent (half of 25 percent). Second, wealthier families in a higher tax bracket save more money than lower-income families in a lower income tax bracket. Therefore, this program is highly regressive: the wealthier end up getting a higher benefit than those families who need it the most.

How do other countries handle childcare issues, and what can the United States learn from them? In most of Europe, publicly funded childcare is readily available to everyone, often on a sliding scale based on income. In the United States, only 1 percent of children ages 2 and under, and 14 percent of children ages 3 to school-age, are in publicly funded childcare programs. Compare these statistics with Denmark, where 48 percent of children up to age 2, and 85 percent of children ages 3 to school-age, are in publicly funded childcare. Or, compare them with those of France and Belgium, where 20 percent of children to age 2 and 95 percent of children ages 3 and older are in publicly funded childcare. In the United States, parents bear most of the costs of childcare themselves. Quality care is seen as a private good rather than a public one, even though as a society we benefit from having educated children who are well cared for.

France provides an example of what is possible (Bergmann, 1996; Warner, 2005). French parents at all income levels receive government assistance with childcare. Daycare centers for young children or smaller family childcare units are readily available, staffed by an educated and valued work force that is well paid and which receives full benefits. Free public nursery schools are available for children ages $2\frac{1}{2}$ to 6, and by the time they are 3 years old, virtually all French children attend them. There is also a well-coordinated before-school and after-school care program for a nominal fee. Because these programs are universal and available to all French citizens regardless of income, there is no stigma attached to using them. They are considered programs that all families may need, rich, poor, or in-between.

:: Specific Policies and Programs for the Elderly

As we saw in Chapter 14, both the number and the proportion of elderly persons are increasing substantially in the United States. We face new challenges in learning how best to deal with our changing demographic structure and care for the frailest members of our society. In the next section, we will look at several policies related to the economic well-being and health of the elderly, while comparing U.S. policies to those of other nations.

Social Security and Economic Well-Being

Less than 9 percent of elders live in poverty, the lowest proportion of any age group (DeNavas-Walt, Proctor, & Smith, 2010). Yet to truly understand the economic well-being of the elderly, we must examine more than just the poverty line because many elderly live only slightly above it. They are not represented in the poverty statistics, but they are vulnerable nonetheless.

Moreover, subgroups of elderly differ substantially in their level of income and assets. Chances are an 80-year-old Black female who lives alone is significantly worse off than a 66-year-old married White male. Sex, race, ethnicity, and age interact to influence an individual's median income and likelihood of living in poverty. Sociologists refer to the notions of **cumulative advantage** and **cumulative disadvantage** to describe how early life choices influence status in later life. Individuals such as White males who have greater opportunities for financial success can build upon their successes to perpetuate their advantages into older age. Meanwhile, those who have faced early disadvantages carry these over into old age, often resulting in poverty or near-poverty.

Ideally, elders in the United States receive income from three primary sources: (1) retirement benefits from Social Security; (2) payments from private pensions; and (3) income from assets and personal savings. The Social Security Administration refers to these sources as a "three-legged stool"—all three "legs" are needed to provide support.

The United States is one of over 150 countries that have some sort of financial program for elders, known here as Social Security and discussed in Chapter 14. Each program operates somewhat differently but provides at least a minimal financial benefit for this group. Some serve virtually everyone above a certain age threshold, such as in the United States and United Kingdom, while others serve only people who meet an eligibility requirement. For example, in China, less than one-quarter of elders are covered, while in Mexico about one-third are covered (Social Security Administration, 2010).

The amount of money provided to the elderly also varies, and programs provide greater coverage to married couples than to singles. The difference in benefit size between married couples and singles is particularly acute in the United States, where elderly women who live alone are among the poorest in all developed countries; only in Australia are single elderly women worse off than in the United States. It appears that our "three-legged stool" may be adequate for married couples, but the cumulative disadvantage for single women, especially minority women, results in lower pay, less in savings and assets, and reduced Social Security benefits.

Health Policy

Health care is a rapidly growing segment of the U.S. economy, and the elderly use a sizable portion of healthcare services. Since most no longer work, how do they get their health insurance? Medicare, introduced in Chapter 10, is a federal health insurance program for people ages 65 and older (and some people with certain disabilities under age 65) (Medicare.gov, January 2010). It was created in 1965 and today is virtually universal among the elderly in the United States. However, elders still pay a significant amount of money for health care; Medicare is *not* free health care.

Medicare really is made up of several distinct programs. Part A is "hospital insurance." Most people receive Part A automatically when they turn 65 and do not have to pay any monthly premiums. It covers overnight stays in hospitals, about three months in a skilled nursing facility, hospice care, and some home health care. The yearly *deductible* (the amount the recipient must pay before Medicare chips in) was $1,100 in 2010 (Medicare.gov, April 2010).

Part B is sometimes called "supplemental insurance." It is optional and for most people requires a $96 monthly premium (in 2010). Part B covers 80 percent of costs such as doctors' fees, outpatient hospital treatment, and lab services. The other 20 percent, referred to as a *co-payment*, is the part the elderly pay themselves. In addition to the monthly premium and co-payments, there is a yearly deductible (an initial uncovered outlay) of $155 (Medicare.gov, April 2010). Part C includes care in health maintenance organizations, and Part D, created in 2006, covers some prescription drug costs.

Have you, or someone close to you, used any of the programs or policies introduced in this chapter so far? Did the program(s) help, and if so how? If not, do you have any idea why not? What suggestions do you have to change the direction of our country's family policies? Can the efforts of one person affect social change?

cumulative advantage and disadvantage: Early life chances that influence status in later life.

relationships are structured quite differently today than they were a generation ago. We have seen that dating is far more informal than in the past, nonmarital sex is more common, people marry at older ages, more men and women are voluntarily childfree, family size is considerably smaller, more women work outside the home, and the division of household labor is more equitable. People may ask, "Are these societal changes good or bad?" There is no easy answer because they reflect larger changes in our social structure, *and we could not return to the "good old days" even if we really wanted to.* For example, with our current economic recession, more women *need* to work outside the home simply to make ends meet. The need to work, along with the increased levels of education required for that work, leads people to marry later (which, in turn, leads to increased nonmarital sex), smaller family size, more women remaining childfree, and more egalitarian relationships.

Social Science Theory and Research: Can It Tell Me Right from Wrong?

A third theme of this text has been to show what roles theory and research can play in helping us understand families and relationships. Rather than relying upon generalizations or inaccurate observations, social science research can provide a clearer picture of families and the relationships of their members. For example, we cannot assume that the poor routinely buy steak with food stamps just because we have always heard it is so, and we cannot assume all partners have an equitable division of household labor just because our parents might have. Instead of relying upon personal experience or what seems like common sense—often based on stereotypes or other fallacies—theory and observed data together can help us understand and interpret the occurrence of specific events, the conditions under which they occur, and the meanings people assign to them.

Social science research answers questions empirically. This information can then be used to guide our personal choices as well as public policy.

Information gleaned from social science research can be very liberating and can guide the way to understanding our "common-sense" world. Isn't it better to form opinions, have preferences, and meet our challenges head-on, armed with information obtained scientifically? *Nonetheless, despite our enthusiasm for empiricism, generally speaking, research cannot always tell us what is right or wrong.* For example, researchers cannot tell us whether abortion should be legal, nor under what conditions it should be illegal. However, findings from research can provide us with other important information that may help us answer these vexing questions. It can tell us how many abortions occurred last year, among what age groups, the percentage of unmarried women who had abortions, the level of support from their partner or parents, the percentage who would reportedly seek an illegal abortion if a legal abortion were unavailable, and the reported range of feelings from regret to relief that women feel after having an abortion. Data collected to address these types of questions can help guide discussions of abortion, inform personal choices, influence our values, and shape public policy.

*R*eflect upon the information about families that you have learned in previous chapters of this text. Can you think of specific examples that represent each of these three themes? Which theme resonates with you the most, and why?

Bringing It Full Circle

What kind of family life do we want in the 21st century? How do we make our choices with our families? Families are not socially isolated entities that can survive solely by their own effort; they are woven into a larger network that is part of a broader social system. Families can become resilient and flourish only when we provide the micro-level and macro-level support they need. While micro-level individual and family strengths are invaluable and can help us make sound choices, and community support is paramount, broad social and economic policies designed to help us care for one another must also be available. Our opening vignette with Alain and Sophie reveals the importance of these policies for building strong families. Let's review what you have learned in this chapter to answer the following questions:

- How do family policies and programs, or their absence, reflect social values? How do American values differ from those of France?

- Many Americans believe that strong family policies will actually weaken families by making members lazy and dependent on government programs or handouts. How do you think Sophie and Alain would respond to this argument?

- Of all the different programs and policies discussed in this chapter, which do you think would be most effective in helping to build stronger families?

For further review, turn to the Video Discussion Guide on page 449 to answer additional questions about how the chapter opening video relates to what you have learned in this chapter.

Chapter Review

15.1 What is family resilience?

Family resilience is the multi-faceted ability of a family to thrive despite adversity. It is the capacity to rebound from misfortune, trauma, or other transitional crises to become strengthened and more resourceful.

15.2 What are the components of family resilience?

Discussions of family resilience usually focus on (1) individual protective factors, which include micro-level traits, such as a positive self-concept, sociability, intelligence and scholastic competence, autonomy, self-esteem, creativity, independence, good communication and problem-solving skills, humor, and good mental and physical health; (2) family protective factors such as warmth, affection, and cohesion; (3) family recovery factors including commitment, communication, and emotional support; and (4) community institutions like religious fellowships, clubs, and organizations.

15.3 What is missing from models of resilience?

Further consideration should be given to the importance of macro-level policies and programs to helping families flourish. Sound economic and social policies and programs that strengthen all families—healthy as well as vulnerable—can provide families and children with the necessary tools to increase resilience. They add an important level of strength above and beyond individual, family, and community factors.

15.4 What is the difference between universal and selective approaches to family policies and programs?

Most developed nations have an interrelated, coordinated set of proactive economic and social programs and policies to help strengthen all families, which is called a universal approach. These programs are available to everyone, regardless of income. In the United States in contrast, many policies and programs are selective, meaning that only certain people are eligible for government services, usually poor or low-income persons.

15.5 How does family policy in the United States compare to other countries?

Compared to many other countries, the United States lags behind in formulating a comprehensive family policy. For example, we are the only developed country without paid maternity leaves, family allowances, or national health insurance. Many other less developed nations have these benefits as well.

15.6 What are some examples of policies or programs in the United States that help to support families?

The United States, while lacking the depth of family policy found in many developed nations, offers a number of programs that have been helpful to many, including the Earned Income Tax Credit (EITC), Temporary Assistance for Needy Families (TANF), living wages, and flexible time and place of employment.

Key Terms

community factors (p. 423)

cumulative advantage and disadvantage (p. 441)

early childhood interventions (p. 436)

Earned Income Tax Credit (p. 433)

family protective factors (p. 423)

family recovery factors (p. 423)

flexplace (p. 431)

flextime (p. 431)

individual-level protective factors (p. 423)

maternity (or family) leave (p. 430)

means-tested programs (p. 426)

national health insurance (p. 429)

progressive taxation (p. 427)

resilience (p. 422)

selective programs (p. 426)

telecommuting (p. 433)

Temporary Assistance to Needy Families (TANF) (p. 434)

universal programs (p. 426)

15.7 What are some examples of policies or programs in the United States that help to improve children's lives?

Examples of programs and policies designed to help children include early child intervention, the State Children's Health Insurance Program (SCHIP), child support enforcement, and childcare policies.

15.8 What are some examples of policies or programs that help the elderly?

Social Security has improved the economic well-being of elders, and Medicare has helped elders obtain health care.

15.9 What are some examples of policies or programs that are still needed to support families?

Examples include national health insurance, guaranteed and paid maternity leaves, living wages, further child support, and childcare assistance.

15.10 What are the three themes of this text?

First, micro-level and macro-level perspectives are linked and together provide the best appreciation of family and intimate relationships and the choices and constraints we face; second, families are not static but are always changing and adapting to micro-level and macro-level forces; and third, social science theory and research can help us better understand families and intimate relationships.

PEARSON
myfamilylab
www.myfamilylab.com

Experience, Discover, Observe, Evaluate

MyFamilyLab is designed just for you. Each chapter features a pre-test and post-test to help you learn and review key concepts and terms. Experience Marriage and Family in action with dynamic visual activities, videos, and readings to enhance your learning experience.

Here are a few activities you will find for this chapter:

Watch Core Concepts video clips feature sociologists in action, exploring important concepts in the study of Marriage and the Family. Watch:

- Health Care Outside of the United States
- Government, Buisness, and Family Policy

Explore Social Explorer is an interactive application that allows you to explore Census data through interactive maps. Explore the Social Explorer Report:

- Welfare Recipients

Read MySocLibrary includes primary source readings from classic and contemporary sociologists. Read:

- Clawson & Gerstel, "Caring for Our Young: Child Care in Europe and the United States"

c. Social mobility is impossible in a democracy.

d. Another term for social mobility is "poverty guidelines."

e. Institutional discrimination improves the chances of upward social mobility.

3. Which of the following best describes Becca's situation?

    a. She was raised by parents who were illegal immigrants, even though she was born in the United States.

b. She was born into the upper middle class, but her parents lost their fortune in gambling.

c. She had limited social capital.

d. She was homeless due to her mental illness.

e. She was lazy and afraid of hard work.

Answers: 1. d; 2. b; 3. c

Chapter 3: Building Relationships

Exploring Families Video: Cohabitation: Meghan and Jono

Jono and Meghan are a happy couple living together and unmarried. They represent a new and growing trend: Instead of marrying first and then going to college, getting a job, saving money, buying a house, or having a baby, couples now expect to do many, or even all of these things, before marriage.

Discussion Questions:

1. Are Jono and Meghan "single"? What is problematic about the definition of single?

2. Not all singles are the same. Which type are Jono and Meghan?

3. What are some common ways that people meet potential partners? Have these changed over the past generation? How did Meghan and Jono meet?

4. Who cohabits, and why do they do so? Are Jono and Meghan reflective of national trends?

5. Debate the following statement: Cohabitation is a good test for marriage.

Multiple Choice Questions:

1. Meghan and Jono provide an example of

    a. voluntary stable singles.

    b. a spurious relationship.

    c. cohabitation.

    d. cross-sex friendship.

    e. calling.

2. People who cohabit are more likely to divorce. This represents:

    a. a spurious relationship.

    b. calling.

    c. an homogamous relationship.

    d. propinquity.

    e. a dating script.

3. Which of the following is TRUE with respect to cohabitation?

    a. Cohabitation didn't occur in the U.S. until the 1960s.

    b. Today nearly 2 million households are maintained by cohabiting couples.

    c. Most Americans see cohabitation as "a good thing for society."

    d. The majority of married couples began their union by cohabiting.

    e. Compared to their married counterparts, cohabiting couples tend to have higher levels of education.

Answers: 1. c; 2. a; 3. d

Chapter 4: Love and Loving Relationships

Exploring Families Video: Arranged Marriage: Rati and Subas

Rati and Subas, both from Nepal, have an arranged marriage. The concept of love as a prerequisite for marriage has a very different meaning in Nepal than it does in the U.S.

Discussion Questions:

1. What are the pros and cons of an arranged marriage?

2. What are the pros and cons of using romantic love as the basis for marriage?

3. How do micro- and macro-level perspectives on love help us understand the relationship between Rati and Subas?

4. Why do you think most Americans are strongly opposed to arranged marriages?

5. In the story of Rati and Subas, do you feel that either one was exploited, devalued, or mistreated?

Multiple Choice Questions:

1. The marriage between Rati and Subas is an example of:
   a. companionate love.
   b. the principle of least interest.
   c. Reiss' wheel theory of love.
   d. the triangular theory of love.
   e. attachment theory.

2. In contrast to Subas and Rati, most Americans try to control and channel love using what mechanism?
   a. kinship rules
   b. formally free
   c. close supervision
   d. avoidant attachment
   e. principle of least interest

3. Which of Lee's styles of love best describes the relationship of Subas and Rati?
   a. storge
   b. agape
   c. biochemical
   d. mania
   e. eros

Chapter 5: Sexual Identity, Behavior, and Relationships

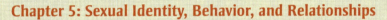

Exploring Families Video: Perspectives on Sexual Identity and Behavior: Kayla and Chris

Kayla and Chris discuss sexual relationships among young adults. We have the opportunity to hear about the double standard from both a male and a female perspective.

Discussion Questions:

1. Drawing upon Kayla and Chris's discussion of sexual relationships among young adults, what examples can you provide to show that sex occurs in a social context?

2. How do men and women's sexual scripts differ, and did you see any evidence of this difference in their discussion?

3. What were Chris's and Kayla's opinions of the double standard? Did they agree with one another? What is your opinion?

4. Describe premarital trends and attitudes toward it. What do you think about premarital sex?

5. Kayla and Chris speak of casual sexual "hook ups." Do you think this is a common practice among college students, or is its frequency exaggerated?

Multiple Choice Questions:

1. The norms or rules surrounding sexual behavior are called:
   a. intersexed.
   b. sexology.
   c. double standard.
   d. sexual scripts.
   e. epidemiology.

2. Chris thinks that a/an _____ still exists: females who have many sexual partners are treated more harshly than are men.
   a. menarche
   b. epidemiology
   c. double standard
   d. sexual orientation
   e. double prejudice

3. Which of the following is true regarding premarital sex?
   a. Fifty-nine percent of adults reported that premarital sex is "only sometimes or not at all wrong."
   b. By age 25, 98 percent of women and 99 percent of men have engaged in premarital sex.
   c. Studies show that about 1 college student in 10 has engaged in "hooking up."
   d. Teenage pregnancy has been rising over the past three decades.
   e. Children are not sexual beings until they hit adolescence.

Chapter 6: Communication

Exploring Families Video: Communication in Relationships

Do men and women communicate differently? Our families share their opinions on this issue.

Discussion Questions:

1. How important is communication in relationships, according to our respondents?

2. Do the people in the video believe that men and women communicate differently? What evidence do they provide?

3. Communication exists in a cultural context. Did the couples in the video offer any evidence of this?

4. What examples do the respondents provide of the different types of communication?

5. What are your views of men, women, and communication? Do you think the respondents in our vignettes are exaggerating the communication differences between men and women?

Multiple Choice Questions:

1. Which of the following were shown in the vignette and best reveal that communication occurs in a cultural context:
    a. the French often speak loudly and with their hands, and others assume incorrectly that they are arguing.
    b. the Hispanic gay couple fear homophobia.
    c. cohabitation brings better communication.
    d. ego conflict occurs among Blacks more than Hispanics.
    e. nonverbal communication is the same everywhere.

2. The couples in the vignette seem to have _____ relationships.
    a. non-regulated
    b. intimate partner power
    c. ego conflict
    d. relative love and need theory
    e. regulated

3. The respondents are listening to their partner with good eye contact and body language, and encouraging the other person to continue talking. This characterizes:
    a. nonverbal communication.
    b. active listening.
    c. pseudoconflict.
    d. relative love and need theory.
    e. the Sapir-Whorf hypothesis.

Answers: 1. a; 2. e; 3. b

Chapter 7: Marriage

Exploring Families Video: Marriage: Scherazade and Roderick

Scherazade and Roderick, married for 13 years, show us that a good marriage is the result of shared values, commitment, and communication.

Discussion Questions:

1. How is Scherazade and Roderick's marriage different from and/or similar to marriages in the past?

2. Do you think Scherazade and Roderick best illustrate the marital decline perspective or the marriage resilience perspective? Defend your answer.

3. Of the six marriage types identified by Cuber and Haroff, which one best describes the marriage of Scherazade and Roderick?

4. Describe the factors associated with happy and successful marriages. Which of these factors do you see in Scherazade and Roderick's relationship?

5. What is a "peer" marriage? Would you say that Scherazade and Roderick have a peer marriage? Why or why not?

Multiple Choice Questions:

1. Roderick and Scherazade illustrate:
    a. an arranged marriage.
    b. a peer marriage.
    c. that cohabitation is replacing marriage.
    d. a covenant marriage.
    e. a devitalized marriage.

2. Scherazade and Roderick's lives are intertwined, although they work in different fields. Both physical and emotional intimacies are important to them, and they work hard at communication and compromise so that their relationship continues to be satisfying and enjoyable. This exemplifies what type of marriage?
    a. vital marriage
    b. open marriage
    c. passive-congenial marriage
    d. conflict-habituated marriage
    e. covenant marriage

3. Reflecting on Scherazade and Roderick, what is the "marriage premium"?
   a. A type of marriage in which spouses do not share certain social characteristics such as race, ethnicity, religion, education, age, and social class.
   b. A trend for women and men to marry at a later age.
   c. Laws forbidding interracial marriage, which existed at the state level until 1967.
   d. A term developed by Jessie Bernard to describe the different ways wives and husbands experience marriage and its benefits.
   e. The concept that married people are happier, healthier, and financially better off than those who are not married.

Chapter 8: Thinking About Parenthood

Exploring Families Video: Adoption: Tracey and Juan

After experiencing infertility, Tracey and Juan adopted two children from Colombia.

Discussion Questions:

1. How serious a problem is infertility? Are Juan and Tracey unique in their difficulties getting pregnant?
2. What treatments or alternatives are available for infertility?
3. What are the trends in international adoption? Why do people, including Juan and Tracey, choose to adopt internationally?
4. Are the adoptions of Juan and Tracey's children considered "open" or "closed"? Are they "private" or "public"?
5. Do you think the transition to parenthood is the same for biological and adoptive parents, or are there differences?

Multiple Choice Questions:

1. Juan and Tracey represent the _____ percent of adults of childbearing age who suffer from infertility.
   a. 2
   b. 5
   c. 12
   d. 20
   e. 29

2. Why did Juan and Tracey decide to adopt their children from Colombia?
   a. Tracey visited Colombia when she was in college.
   b. They decided on Colombia for humanitarian reasons.
   c. Juan was born in Colombia and continues to have family there.
   d. The waiting time was shorter than an adoption from the U.S.
   e. They actually planned to adopt from Guatemala, but there was a mistake in the paperwork.

3. Adoption:
   a. touches the lives of nearly one in ten people in some way, either through a friend, family member, or personal experience.
   b. is increasingly well-covered in college family textbooks.
   c. in the past was usually "open," but today is likely to be "closed."
   d. from China and Guatemala is on the decline.
   e. was not a good choice for Juan and Tracey.

Chapter 9: Raising Children

Exploring Families Video: Same-Sex Parents Raising Children: Karen and Betsy

Karen and Betsy are a married lesbian couple raising their two young children.

Discussion Questions:

1. Identify the ways in which Karen and Betsy's family is similar to other parenting contexts.

2. Identify the ways in which Karen and Betsy's family is different from other parenting contexts.

3. How is "mothering" as an identity and an activity in Karen and Betsy's household similar to and/or different from those found in heterosexual two-parent families? Are there any "fathering" identities or activities in their household?

4. Do you anticipate that agents of socialization will operate differently for Karen and Betsy's family, compared to heterosexual two-parent families? Why or why not?

5. Should same-sex couples be allowed to marry and/or raise children?

Multiple Choice Questions:

1. Which statement best describes Karen and Betsy's family situation?
   a. They have two children, a son and a daughter.
   b. They have one daughter who was adopted from China.
   c. They would like to have children someday.
   d. Karen wants to have children, but Betsy does not.
   e. Karen has three children from a previous marriage, and Betsy is helping her raise them.

2. Betsy and Karen explain that there is sometimes awkwardness surrounding:
   a. role-taking.
   b. the id.
   c. father's and mother's day.
   d. visitation during the holidays.
   e. their children's biological fathers.

3. Karen and Betsy:
   a. display a permissive parenting style.
   b. believe in formal operative thought.
   c. explained to their son that he is likely gay.
   d. have sensorimotor intelligence which they share with their children.
   e. are proud to live in a state that legally recognizes their family.

Answers: 1. a; 2. c; 3. e

Chapter 10: Families and the Work They Do

Exploring Families Video: Balancing Work and Family Life: Lisa and Chris

Lisa and Chris are a dual-earner couple with one young son. They both have demanding jobs, and struggle to combine work and family.

Discussion Questions:

1. How does the situation of Lisa and Chris differ from that of earlier generations? What is different about their story compared to forty or fifty years ago?

2. If Lisa and Chris are representative of other dual-earner couples, how do you think they divide up the household labor and childcare?

3. Work-family conflict, role overload, and spillover are useful concepts to our understanding of how work and family affect each other. Can you spot examples of these three concepts in the interview with Lisa and Chris?

4. The time crunch is one of the largest challenges that parents report today. How do Chris and Lisa experience the time crunch?

5. What are some options for childcare in the United States, and what type(s) have Lisa and Chris selected for their son? What are some issues they face with childcare?

Multiple Choice Questions:

1. Chris works at a full-time job that sometimes demands that he work at night and on weekends. This type of job has a/an:
   a. minimum wage.
   b. nonstandard work schedule.
   c. time availability perspective.
   d. secondary schedule.
   e. occasional labor.

2. Lisa and Chris feel overwhelmed by many different commitments and feel that they do not have enough time to meet each commitment effectively. This is the definition of:
   a. role overload.
   b. time crunch.
   c. doing gender.
   d. spillover.
   e. self-care.

3. Chris and Lisa both work outside the home full-time and their son goes to childcare. What is the effect on child well-being of having both parents working?
   a. The effects are usually found to be quite positive.
   b. The effects are usually found to be quite negative.
   c. The effects are usually mixed and contradictory because researchers only report what supports their opinion.
   d. It largely depends on the quality of the childcare program.
   e. The effects on boys are usually found to be negative, but the effects on girls are usually positive.

Answers: 1. b; 2. a; 3. d

Chapter 11: Family Stress and Crisis: Violence among Intimates

Exploring Families Video: Intimate Partner Violence: Shannon

Shannon, a victim of extreme violence by her intimate partner, eventually shot and killed her attacker. She was sent to prison, and there, met others who were imprisoned simply because they too fought back. Together they joined forces, "The Framingham Eight," and are credited with increasing our understanding of the legal and emotional plight of battered women.

Discussion Questions:

1. Can you identify the three stages of the General Adaptation Syndrome (GAS) in Shannon's story? Do you think that all victims experience these three stages?

2. What are the four types of intimate-partner violence identified by Johnson, and which best describes Shannon's experience?

3. What are some consequences of intimate partner violence that you observed in Shannon's story?

4. Why didn't Shannon leave her abuser?

5. What theoretical explanations for violence are most useful in explaining Shannon's situation?

Multiple Choice Questions:

1. Shannon represents the _____ percent of women who have been victims of intimate-partner violence over the course of their lives.
   a. 3
   b. 11
   c. 14
   d. 22
   e. 50

2. Which type of violence did Shannon experience, using the typology developed by Johnson?
   a. common couple violence
   b. femicide
   c. double ABC-X Model
   d. trafficking
   e. intimate terrorism

3. Which theory used to explain Shannon's intimate-partner violence integrates both micro-level and macro-level perspectives?
   a. norms of family privacy
   b. power and control
   c. stress
   d. the intergenerational transmission of violence
   e. patriarchy

Answers: 1. d; 2. e; 3. b

Chapter 12: The Process of Divorce

Exploring Families Video: A Child's View of Divorce: Melanie

Melanie's parents divorced when she was a child. She talks about this experience and her parents' remarriages.

Discussion Questions:

1. How common is divorce? What are the pros and cons of the different ways to measure the divorce rate?
2. Do you think Melanie's experience is typical or atypical of a child's experience as her parents divorce?
3. What stations of divorce can you identify in Melanie's story?
4. What are some of the short- and long-term effects of divorce on children? Did Melanie experience these effects?
5. Do you think it would have been better for Melanie if her parents stayed married? What does the research suggest?

Multiple Choice Questions:

1. The refined divorce rate clarifies how common divorce, and Melanie's experience, really is. Which of the following represents the refined divorce rate?
   a. the number of divorces per 1,000 married women
   b. the number of divorces per 1,000 married couples
   c. the number of divorces per people over age 16
   d. the number of divorces in a year as compared to the number of marriages in a year
   e. the number of divorces per 1,000 people

2. Which of the following statements about Melanie's experience is TRUE?
   a. Her parents had joint physical custody.
   b. She was upset when her parents remarried.
   c. Her father had sole physical custody.
   d. She experienced some negative short-term effects of the divorce, but they have long since been resolved.
   e. She was relieved when her parents told her that they were getting divorced.

3. Which tends to be worse for children like Melanie: experiencing their parents' divorce or experiencing their marital conflict?
   a. It depends on the severity of the conflict.
   b. Boys are worse off with a divorce, but there is no real difference among girls.
   c. Divorce is worse for children.
   d. It depends on who has custody.
   e. It depends on whether alimony is awarded.

Answers: 1. a; 2. b; 3. a

Chapter 13: Family Life, Partnering, and Remarriage after Divorce

Exploring Families Video: Remarriage and Blending Families: Daneen and Jim

Jim and Daneen married after being divorced for many years. Each has two children from a previous marriage, and they are now trying to build a strong blended stepfamily.

Discussion Questions:

1. Both Jim and Daneen spent years as single parents before meeting. What are some issues that single parents face? Are any of these evident in their story?
2. Jim was a custodial father before he married Daneen. What do you know about this small but growing group?
3. What type of stepfamily configuration does their family represent? Do you think this configuration is harder or easier than other configurations?
4. What are some of the challenges that stepfamilies face, and how are Daneen and Jim working to overcome them?
5. Drawing upon the example of Jim and Daneen, how can stepfamilies achieve greater success for parents and children? Are the factors needed for success always the same for parents and children?

Multiple Choice Questions:

1. Like Jim and Daneen, about _____ percent of American adults have been married at least twice.
   a. 9
   b. 14
   c. 21
   d. 30
   e. 45

2. Jim and Daneen's children are examples of:
   a. mutual children.
   b. half-siblings.
   c. nonresidential children.
   d. stepsiblings.
   e. repartnering.
3. Which statement best describes Jim and Daneen's family?
   a. After an initial adjustment, the family seems to be doing well.
   b. The girls are struggling emotionally, but the boys seem to be doing well.

c. Jim and Daneen, like many remarried families, are now contemplating divorce.
d. Jim's children only live with them every other weekend, and this causes jealousy among the children.
e. There is tremendous conflict between stepparent and stepchildren.

Answers: 1. c; 2. d; 3. a

Chapter 14: Family Life, Partnering, and Remarriage after Divorce

Exploring Families Video: The Sandwich Generation: Amy

Amy is a member of the so-called "sandwich generation"—she takes care of her young son and her aging mother.

Discussion Questions:

1. Reflecting on Amy's situation, describe the demographic revolution, including among the oldest-old cohort.
2. Amy's mother is widowed. What are the circumstances of many widowed women?
3. What are the two types of caregiving? Which type does Amy represent?
4. What are some of the challenges associated with caregiving? Do you observe any of these challenges in Amy's story?
5. Reflecting on Amy's experience, what are your plans for your mother or father's care when they are no longer able to care for themselves?

Multiple Choice Questions:

1. Like many other women, Amy cares for her child and her parent at the same time. Amy is a member of the so-called _____.
   a. life-span perspective
   b. kinkeeping association
   c. formal care network
   d. remote caregiving group
   e. sandwich generation

2. Gerontologists measure the degree of an elder's impairment by using a set of measures called:
   a. dementia scale (DS).
   b. activities of daily living (ADL).
   c. life expectancy (LE).
   d. life stage perspective (LSP).
   e. mobility grade (MG).
3. Which statement is TRUE of caregivers like Amy?
   a. More than a third of caregivers provided all the help to the person they care for during the past 12 months and received no help from anyone else.
   b. A spouse is usually the caregiver, but if a spouse is unavailable the adult son is likely to provide care.
   c. About 85 percent of caregivers report that providing care is highly stressful.
   d. About 50 percent of caregivers report a great deal of financial hardship associated with caregiving.
   e. Almost 10 million people are caring for an aging adult.

Answers: 1. e; 2. b; 3. a

Chapter 15: Looking Ahead: Helping Families Flourish

Exploring Families Video: A Comparison of Family Policies: France and the United States: Sophie and Alain

Sophie and Alain are French citizens working in the United States. They share some interesting contrasts in family policy between the two countries.

Discussion Questions:

1. Describe the differences in family policy between the U.S. and France, according to Sophie and Alain.

2. Why do you think the U.S. family policies are so limited, compared to France?

3. How does health insurance policy and childcare differ between the two countries?

4. Sophie and Alain's son is autistic. Describe the differences in policy for children with special needs.

5. Do you think that strong family policies will make people lazy and come to expect government handouts?

Multiple Choice Questions:

1. France's strong set of family policies are examples of what mechanisms to build family resilience?
   a. individual-level protective factors
   b. community strengths
   c. macro-level policies
   d. family recovery factors
   e. means-tested programs

2. Family policies and programs in France tend to be _____, whereas they tend to be _____ in the U.S.
   a. open; closed
   b. mean-tested; simple
   c. universal; selective
   d. resilient; expensive
   e. cumulative advantaged; cumulative disadvantaged

3. Which of the following benefits does the U.S. government offer?
   a. national health insurance
   b. paid maternity leave for 6 weeks
   c. unpaid maternity leave for up to 1 year
   d. special education in schools for qualifying children
   e. a family allowance grant from the government

Answers: 1. c; 2. c; 3. d

Glossary

ABC-X Model   A model designed to help us understand the variation in the ways that families cope with stress and crisis.

active listening   Extremely attentive listening, where the listener has good eye contact and body language, and encourages the other person to continue talking.

Activities of Daily Living (ADLs)   General day-to-day activities such as cooking, cleaning, bathing, and home repair.

acute stress   Short-term stress.

adolescence   The period of life that occurs between childhood and adulthood.

agents of socialization   The primary groups responsible for gender socialization.

alimony   Payment by one partner to the other to support the more dependent spouse for a period of time.

Alzheimer's disease   The most common form of dementia; at present, it is incurable.

androgyny   Possessing both masculine and feminine traits in near equal proportion.

antimiscegenation laws   Laws forbidding interracial marriage, which existed at the state level until 1967.

anxious/ambivalent attachment   An attachment type where infants become nervous when their parent leaves the room and can show rejection when the parent returns.

assisted reproductive technology (ART)   All fertility treatments in which either egg or sperm (or both) are handled.

attachment theory   A theory postulating that the way in which infants form attachments early in life will affect relationships throughout later life.

authoritarian parenting style   A parenting style that is strict, punitive, and not very warm.

authoritative parenting style   A parenting style that is demanding and maintains high levels of control over the children, but is also warm and receptive.

avoidant attachment   An attachment type where infants show little attachment to their primary parent.

baby boom generation   People born in the years after World War II through the early 1960s.

Battered Women's Syndrome   A recognized psychological condition, often a subcategory of post-traumatic stress syndrome, used to describe someone who has been the victim of consistent and/or severe domestic violence.

bilateral   Descent that can be traced through both male and female sides of the family.

binuclear family   A type of family consisting of divorced parents living in two separate households but remaining one family in spirit for the sake of the children.

biochemical perspective of love   Theories that suggest humans are attracted to certain types of people, at which point the brain releases natural chemicals that give us a rush we experience as sexual attraction.

birth centers   Freestanding facilities (usually with close access to, but not affiliated with, a hospital) where childbirth is approached as a normal, healthy process.

bisexual   An orientation in which a person is attracted to both males and females.

blended (or reconstituted) family   Another term for step-family; a family that may consist of stepparents, stepsiblings, or half-siblings.

calling   A dating practice of the 18th and 19th centuries in which a young man would visit a young woman in her parents' home.

centenarian   A person who lives to be at least 100 years old.

child abuse   An attack on a child that results in an injury and violates our social norms.

child snatching   The act of a noncustodial parent kidnapping his or her child.

child support order   A legal document delineating the amount and circumstances surrounding the financial support of noncustodial children.

chronic stress   Long-term stress.

civil union   A public policy designed to extend some benefits to partners who are not legally married.

closed adoption   An adoption where identifying information is sealed and unavailable to all parties.

cohabitation   An arrangement in which two people live together without being married.

communication   An interactive process that uses symbols like words and gestures to both send and receive messages.

community factors   Community features that help promote resilience, such as social networks and religious and faith-based fellowships.

companionate family   A marriage based on mutual affection, sexual attraction, compatibility, and personal happiness.

companionate grandparenting A type of grandparenting where the grandparents and grandchildren enjoy recreational activities, occasional overnight stays, and even babysitting with an emphasis on fun and enjoyment.

companionate love A type of love that grows over time, based on strong commitment, friendship, and trust.

concrete operational thought Piaget's third stage of cognitive development, which occurs between the ages of 7 and 12, when children begin to see the causal connections in their surroundings, and can manipulate categories, classification systems, and hierarchies in groups.

Conflict Tactics Scale A scale based on how people deal with disagreements in relationships.

conflict Disagreements over decision making, problem solving, or achieving goals, which can result from differences between group members in personality, perception, information, tolerance for risk, and power or influence.

conflict theory A theory that emphasizes issues surrounding social inequality, power, conflict, and social change.

conflict-habituated marriage A type of marriage that includes frequent conflict, although it may be enduring.

content analysis A research method that systematically examines the content of materials.

content conflict A type of conflict where individuals disagree about information.

controlling the development of love A macro-level perspective on love suggesting that all societies control or channel love.

courtly love A poetic style of the Middle Ages when poets or troubadours would write songs of unrequited love and present them at the court of their aristocratic/royal masters.

covenant marriage A type of marriage available in three states that restricts access to divorce, requires premarital counseling, and imposes other rules and regulations.

crisis A critical change of events that disrupts the functioning of a person's life.

cross-sex friendship A friendship between a man and a woman that is strictly platonic.

crude divorce rate The number of divorces per 1,000 people in the population.

cumulative advantage and disadvantage Early life chances that influence status in later life.

cunnilingus The oral stimulation of the woman's genitals by her partner.

cyberstalking (or electronic monitoring) Stalking contact using electronic technology.

date rape drugs Drugs such as gamma hydroxybutyrate (GHB), Rohypnol (popularly known as "roofies" or "roofenol"), or ketamine hydrochloride (Ketamine) that are used to immobilize a person to facilitate an assault.

dating script A set of expectations around dating that are somewhat different for men and women.

daycare centers Nonresidential facilities that provide child care.

dementia The loss of mental functions such as thinking, memory, and reasoning.

developmental theory A theory that suggests families, and individual family members, go through distinct stages over time, with each stage having its own set of tasks, roles, and responsibilities.

devitalized marriage An enduring marriage that exists without much passion.

direct financial costs Out-of-pocket expenses for things such as food, clothing, housing, and education.

discrimination Behaviors, actions, or practices based on racial or ethnic preferences that have harmful impacts.

divorce mediation A non-adversarial means of resolution, in which the divorcing couple, along with a third party, such as a therapist or trained mediator, negotiate the terms of their financial, custody, and visitation settlement.

"doing gender" A theory of power that suggests that we take power differentials among men and women for granted and continue to reproduce them; for example, housework is so ingrained as "women's work" that it functions as an area in which gender is symbolically created and reproduced.

domestic violence shelter A temporary safe house for a woman (with or without children) who is escaping an abusive relationship.

Double ABC-X Model A model designed to help us understand the effects of the accumulation of stresses and crises and how families adapt to them.

double standard The idea that men have been allowed far more permissiveness in sexual behavior than women.

double standard of aging The view that women's attractiveness and femininity decline with age, but men's attractiveness and masculinity do not decline.

dowry A financial gift given to a woman's prospective in-laws by her parents.

Early Childhood Education and Care (ECEC) An international term for day care, preschool, and other programs to ensure that all children begin elementary school with basic skills and are ready to learn.

early childhood intervention Attempts to maintain or improve the quality of life for young children.

Earned Income Tax Credit A refundable federal tax credit for low-income working families that reduces the amount of taxes owed.

egalitarian The expectation that power and authority are vested in both men and women, equally.

ego According to Freud, the rational component of personality that attempts to balance the need for immediate gratification with the demands of society.

ego conflict   A type of conflict where individuals believe they must win at all costs to save face.

elder abuse   Abuse of an elderly person that can include physical abuse, sexual abuse, psychological abuse, financial or material exploitation, and neglect.

empirical approach   An approach that answers questions through a systematic collection and analysis of data.

ethnic group   A group of people who share specific cultural features.

ethnicity   Shared cultural characteristics, such as language, place of origin, dress, food, religion, and other values.

experiment   A controlled method for determining cause and effect.

extended family   A family comprised of parents, children, and other relatives such as grandparents.

extramarital sex   Sex, while married, with someone other than your spouse.

family   A relationship by blood, marriage, or affection, in which members may cooperate economically, may care for children, and may consider their identity to be intimately connected to the larger group.

family allowance (or child allowance)   A cash benefit to families provided by the government to help offset the costs of raising children.

family childcare providers   Private homes other than the child's home where child care is provided.

Family Medical Leave Act (FMLA)   An act that requires employers with over 50 employees to provide 12 weeks of *unpaid* leave to eligible employees (both men and women) to care for themselves or their immediate families with specified medical conditions.

family of orientation   The family that you are born into.

family of procreation   The family you make through marriage, partnering, and/or parenthood.

family protective factors   Family characteristics or dynamics that shape the family's ability to endure in the face of risk factors.

family recovery factors   Family characteristics or dynamics that assist families in bouncing back from a crisis situation.

family stress   Tensions that test a family's emotional resources.

fellatio   The oral stimulation of the man's genitals by his partner.

femicide   The killing of women.

feminist theory   A theory in which gender is seen as the central concept for explaining family structure and family dynamics.

feminization of love   The process beginning in the 19th century in which love became associated with the private work of women in the home, namely, nurturing and caring for family members.

fertility rate   A measure reported as: (1) average number of children born to a woman during her lifetime; (2) number of children born per 1,000 women ages 15–44 (some other countries use 49 as the cut-off age); or (3) number of children born per 1,000 population.

fictive kin   Nonrelatives whose bonds are strong and intimate.

flexplace   Flexibility in the location of work, including working from home.

flextime   Flexibility in the daily hours of work.

focus group   A small group interview of people who are brought together to discuss a particular topic.

food insecurity   A lack of available nourishing food on a regular basis.

formal care   Care provided by social service agencies on a paid or volunteer basis.

formal operational thought   Piaget's fourth stage of cognitive development, beginning at adolescence and continuing through adulthood, in which children develop capacities for abstract thought and can conceptualize more complex issues or rules that can be used for problem solving.

gender   Culturally and socially constructed differences between males and females found in the meanings, beliefs, and practices associated with "femininity" and "masculinity."

gender socialization   Teaching the cultural norms associated with being male or female.

General Adaptation Syndrome (GAS)   The predictable pattern one's body follows when coping with stress, which includes the alarm reaction, resistance, and exhaustion.

gerontologists   Researchers studying issues affecting the elderly.

gestational surrogacy   A type of surrogacy where the intended mother's egg is combined with the man's sperm and implanted in the surrogate through in vitro fertilization.

half-sibling   A child who shares one biological parent with another child.

heterogamous marriage   A type of marriage in which spouses do not share certain social characteristics such as race, ethnicity, religion, education, age, and social class.

heterosexual   Having an attraction and preference for developing romantic and sexual relationships with the opposite sex.

hidden curriculum   Gender socialization which is taught informally in school.

homogamous marriage   A type of marriage in which spouses share certain social characteristics such as race, ethnicity, religion, education, age, and social class.

homogamous relationships　Relationships in which we spend most of our time with people who are very similar to ourselves.

homophobia (or anti-gay prejudice)　Having very strong negative feelings toward homosexuality.

homosexual　Having an attraction and preference for relationships with members of one's own sex.

hooking up　Sexual interactions without commitment or even affection for one another.

household labor　In general, the unpaid work done to maintain family members and/or a home.

human agency　The ability of human beings to create viable lives even when they are constrained or limited by social forces.

id　According to Freud, the part of the personality that includes biological drives and needs for immediate gratification.

in-depth interview　A research method that allows an interviewer to obtain detailed responses to questions.

individual discrimination　One person exhibiting a negative behavior towards another person.

individual-level protective factors　Traits including a positive self-concept, sociability, intelligence and scholastic competence, autonomy, self-esteem, androgyny, good communication and problem-solving skills, humor, and good mental and physical health.

informal care　Unpaid care by someone close to the care recipient.

institutional discrimination　Social institutions such as the government, religion, and education create policies and practices that are systematically disadvantageous to certain groups.

interethnic marriage　A type of marriage in which spouses come from different countries or have different cultural, religious, or ethnic backgrounds.

intergenerational transmission of divorce　A pattern noted by researchers that people whose parents divorced are also more likely to divorce.

intergenerational transmission of violence　A cycle of violence that is passed down to dependents.

interracial marriage　A type of marriage in which spouses come from different racial groups.

intersexed　Those born with genitalia that do not clearly identify them as unambiguously male or female.

intimate partner power　A type of power that involves decision making among intimate partners, their division of labor, and their sense of entitlement.

intimate partner violence　Violence between those who are physically and sexually intimate, such as spouses or partners. The violence can encompass physical, economic, sexual, or psychological abuse.

involuntary stable singles　Unmarried adults who can expect to be single for life even though they may not want to be.

involuntary temporary singles　Singles actively searching for a mate but unable to find a suitable one.

involved grandparenting　A type of grandparenting in which the grandparents and grandchildren have frequent interaction or possibly even live together.

joint legal custody　A custody agreement in which noncustodial parents (usually fathers) retain their legal rights with respect to their children.

joint physical custody　A custody agreement in which children spend a substantial portion of time in the homes of both parents, perhaps alternating weeks or days within a week.

kinkeeping　Maintaining ties among family members.

learned helplessness　The psychological condition of having low-self esteem, feeling helpless, and having no control that is caused by repeated abuse.

Lee's styles of love　A categorization of six types of love that describe how couples are attracted to one another.

legal custody　A custody agreement where one parent has the legal authority to make important decisions concerning the children after a divorce, such as where they will go to school, in what community or state they will reside, or who will be notified in case of a health emergency or school problem.

legal divorce　The termination of the marriage contract by a state court order.

legal separation　A binding agreement signed by both spouses that provides details about child support.

life expectancy　The amount of time (in years) a person can expect to live from birth.

life-course perspective　A perspective that sees age-related transitions as socially produced, socially recognized, and shared—a product of social structure, historical forces, and culture.

life-span perspective　A perspective that claims development is a lifelong process, is multidirectional, and consists of both positive and negative changes involving gains and losses.

life-stage perspective　A perspective that claims development proceeds through a fairly set pattern of sequential stages that most people experience.

listening　The process of giving thoughtful attention to what we hear.

living wage　Wages that are above federal or state minimum wage levels, usually ranging from 100 to 130 percent of the poverty line.

looking-glass self　Cooley's suggestion that we come to see ourselves as others perceive and respond to us.

love   A strong affection for one another arising out of kinship or personal ties; attraction based on sexual desire; and affection based on admiration, benevolence, or common interests.

macro-level   Focus on the interconnectedness of marriage, families, and intimate relationships with the rest of society.

marital decline perspective   The view that the institution of marriage is increasingly being threatened by hedonistic pursuits of personal happiness at the expense of long-term commitment.

marital resilience perspective   The view that overall, marriage is no weaker than in the past, but that all families need an increase in structural supports to thrive.

marriage   An institutional arrangement between persons to publicly recognize social and intimate bonds.

marriage movement   The activities of a group of some religious leaders, marriage and family therapists, and government leaders who hope to influence public policy to promote and strengthen traditional marriage.

marriage premium   The concept that married people are happier, healthier, and financially better off than those who are not married.

master status   The major defining status or statuses that a person occupies.

masturbation   Sexually stimulating one's own body.

maternity (or family) leave   A paid and guaranteed leave from work to care for children, including after the birth of a child.

matriarchy   A form of social organization in which the norm or expectation is that the power and authority in society would be vested in women.

matrilineal   A descent pattern where lineage is traced exclusively or primarily within women's families.

matrilocal   The expectation that a newly married couple will live with the family of the wife.

means-tested programs   Programs for which beneficiaries need to meet some eligibility requirement to qualify.

Medicaid   The federal-state healthcare program for eligible poor of all ages.

medicalization of childbirth   The belief that childbirth is a medical event in need of drugs and technological intervention.

Medicare   A federal health insurance program for people aged 65 and older (and some people with disabilities under age 65).

menarche   A woman's first menstrual period.

micro-level   Focus on the individual and his or her interactions in specific settings.

minority group   A category of people who have less power than the dominant group, and who are subject to unequal treatment.

monogamy   Marriage between one man and one woman.

mortality rate (or death rate)   A measure of the number of deaths in a population.

mutual child(ren)   The child (or children) born to a couple that has remarried.

nannies/babysitters   Non-relatives that provide childcare in the home.

national health insurance   A healthcare system for all citizens that considers health care a public right.

neolocal   The expectation that a newly married couple establishes a residence and lives there independently.

no-fault divorce   A type of divorce, now prevalent in all fifty states, in which a divorcing couple can go before a judge without one party having to blame the other.

nonregulated couples   Couples who have many negative communication exchanges.

nonresidential child(ren)   A child (or children) living in the household of a divorced parent less than half of the time.

nonstandard work schedules   Job schedules that are part-time, sub-contracted, temporary in nature, occur at night, or offer irregular work schedules.

nonverbal communication   Communicating without words, by using gestures, expressions, and body language.

nuclear family   A family comprised of adults and their children.

observational study   A research method that goes into the natural setting and observes people in action.

occasional labor   Household tasks that are more time-flexible and more discretionary, such as household repairs, yard care, or paying bills.

open adoption   A type of adoption that involves direct contact between the biological and adoptive parents.

opportunity costs   Lost opportunities for income by working only part-time or not at all because of children.

oral sex   Oral stimulation of the genitals.

passive-congenial marriage   An enduring marriage that includes little conflict but also little excitement.

patriarchy   A form of social organization in which the norm or expectation is that men have a natural right to be in positions of authority over women.

patrilineal   A descent pattern where lineage is traced exclusively (or at least primarily) through the man's family line.

patrilocal   The expectation that a newly married couple will live with the husband's family.

peer marriage   A type of marriage in which couples consider themselves to have equal status or standing in the relationship.

permissive parenting style   A parenting style that places few controls or demands on the child.

personal power   The degree of autonomy a person has to exercise his or her will.

physical custody   A child custody arrangement that decides where the child will reside.

polyandry   The marriage pattern in which wives are allowed to have more than one husband.

polygamy   A system that allows for more than one spouse at a time (gender unspecified).

polygyny   The marriage pattern in which husbands can have more than one wife.

pool of eligibles   The group from which we are likely to choose our mates.

poverty guidelines   Guidelines established in 1964 as a way to measure the number of people living in poverty; based on a thrifty food budget, multiplied by three (sometimes called the "poverty line").

power   The ability to exercise your will.

prejudice   A negative attitude about members of selected racial and ethnic groups.

preoperational thought   Piaget's second stage of cognitive development, occurring from ages 2 through 7, as the child learns language, symbolic play, and symbolic drawing, but does not grasp abstract concepts.

primary labor market   Jobs that are characterized by having relatively high pay, benefits, and job security.

principle of least interest   The idea that unequal emotional involvement between romantic partners has implications for the quality and stability of relationships.

private adoption   An adoption arranged directly between adoptive parents and the biological birth mother, usually with the assistance of an attorney.

progressive taxation   A tax system under which those who earn more pay a higher percentage of their income in taxes than those who earn less.

pronatalism   A cultural value that encourages childbearing.

propinquity   Geographical closeness.

pseudoconflict   Falsely perceiving that our partner is interfering with our goals or has incompatible goals.

public adoption   An adoption that occurs through licensed public agencies.

qualitative research   Narrative description with words rather than numbers to analyze patterns and their underlying meanings.

quantitative research   Research that focuses on data that can be measured numerically.

race   A category describing people who share real or perceived physical straits that society deems socially significant, such as skin color.

racial (or ethnic) socialization   Teaching minority children about prejudice, discrimination, and the coping skills necessary to develop and maintain a strong and healthy self-image.

random sample   A sample in which every "person of interest" has an equal chance of being selected into your research study.

refined divorce rate   A measure of divorce based on the number of divorces that occur out of every 1,000 married women.

regulating couples   Couples who use communication to promote closeness and intimacy.

Reiss's wheel theory of love   A developmental theory that shows relationships moving from the establishment of rapport, to self-revelation, mutual dependence, and finally, need fulfillment.

relative love and need theory   A theory of power that looks at the way that love itself is feminized, defined, and interpreted.

relative resources perspective   The greater the relative amount or value of resources contributed by a partner, the greater is his or her power within the relationship, which can then be translated into bargaining to avoid tasks such as housework that offer no pay and minimal social prestige.

remote grandparenting   A type of grandparenting in which the grandparents and grandchildren are emotionally or physically distant.

repartnering   The act of entering into a relationship after a divorce, which may lead to cohabitation or marriage.

residential stepchild(ren)   A child (or children) living in the household with a remarried couple more than half of the time.

resilience   A multi-faceted ability to thrive despite adversity.

resource theory   A theory of power that suggests that the spouse with the more prestigious or higher paying job can use that advantage to generate more power in the relationship and thereby influence decision making.

role overload   Feeling overwhelmed by many different commitments and not having enough time to meet each commitment effectively.

role taking   According to Mead, the process of mentally assuming the role of another person to understand the world from their point of view and to anticipate their response to us.

romantic love   A type of love that is characterized by passion, melodrama, and excitement, and which receives a lot of media attention.

routine household labor   Nondiscretionary, routine tasks that can be postponed, such as cooking, washing dishes, or cleaning.

"sandwich generation" A generation of people who are in the middle of two living generations providing care to members of cohorts on both sides of them, parents and children.

Sapir-Whorf hypothesis The concept that language shapes our culture, and at the same time, our culture shapes our language.

secondary analysis A research method in which the data were collected for some other purpose but still are useful to the researcher.

secure attachment An attachment type where infants feel safe when their mothers are out of sight.

selection effect (for cohabitation) An explanation for the fact that people who cohabit tend to be the same ones who later divorce.

selection effect (for marriage) The hypothesis that people who marry may be different from those who do not marry; for example, they may be happier, healthier, and have more money.

selective programs Programs for which only a select group of people are eligible.

self-care Children who are unsupervised and taking care of themselves.

self-disclosure Telling a person something private about yourself that he or she would not otherwise know.

sensorimotor stage Piaget's first stage of cognitive development (from birth to age 2) in which infants and toddlers understand the world primarily through touch, sucking, listening, and looking.

sex Biological differences between men and women, and their role in reproduction.

sex trafficking An industry in which children are coerced, kidnapped, sold, or deceived into sexual encounters.

sexology A field comprised of a multidisciplinary group of clinicians, researchers, and educators who study sexuality.

sexual orientation The sexual and romantic pattern of partners of choice.

sexual scripts The norms or rules regarding sexual behavior.

siblings Children who share both biological parents.

social capital The goods and services that are by-products of social relationships, including connections, social support, information, or financial help.

social class A social position based primarily on income and wealth, but occupational prestige and educational level may be relevant as well.

social exchange theory A theory that draws upon a model of human behavior used by many economists. It assumes that individuals are rational beings, and their behavior reflects decisions evaluated on the basis of costs—both direct and opportunity costs—and benefits.

social institution A major sphere of social life, with a set of beliefs and rules that is organized to meet basic human needs.

social learning theory Developed by Alfred Bandura, the theory that behavior is learned through modeling and reinforcement.

social mobility Movement from one social class to another.

social power The ability to exercise your will over another person.

Social Readjustment Rating Scale A scale of major life events over the past year, each of which is assigned a point value. The higher the score, the greater the chance of having a serious medical event.

Social Security A federal government-sponsored cash assistance program for seniors (and survivors).

social stratification The hierarchical ranking of categories of people within society.

social structure A stable framework of social relationships that guides our interactions with others.

socialization The lifelong process by which we learn the cultural values, rules, expectations, and skills needed to function as human beings and participate in society.

sociobiology An evolutionary theory that all humans have an instinctive impulse to pass on their genetic material.

socioeconomic status (SES) Some combination of education, occupation, and income.

sociological imagination The recognition that our personal experiences are, in large part, shaped by forces within the larger society.

sole legal custody A child custody arrangement in which legal custody is granted solely to the parent with whom the child lives.

sole physical custody A child custody arrangement in which the child legally lives with one parent and "visits" the other parent.

spillover An occurrence caused by the demands involved in one sphere of work carrying over into work in another sphere.

spurious When a relationship between two variables is actually caused by a third variable.

stalking Conduct directed at a specific person that would cause a reasonable person to be fearful.

stations of divorce The interrelated emotional, legal, economic, co-parental, community, and psychic dimensions of divorce, which together attempt to capture the complexity of the divorce experience.

status The social position that a person occupies.

stepsiblings Children not biologically related but whose parents are married to one another.

stereotypes   Oversimplified sets of beliefs about a group of people.

Sternberg's triangular theory of love   A theory that sees love as having three elements: intimacy, passion, and commitment.

structural functionalism theory   A theory that attempts to determine the structure, systems, functions, and equilibrium of social institutions.

superego   According to Freud, this is our conscience, which draws upon our cultural values and norms to help us understand why we cannot have everything we want.

surrogacy   The act of giving birth to a child for another person or a couple who then adopts or takes legal custody of the child.

survey   A form of research that gathers information about attitudes or behaviors through the answers that people give to questions.

symbolic interaction theory   A theory that emphasizes the symbols we use in everyday interaction—words, gestures, appearances—and how these are interpreted.

systems theory   A theory that proposes that a family system—the family members and the roles that they play—is larger than the sum of its individual members.

telecommuting   Flexibility in the location of work, including working from home.

Temporary Assistance to Needy Families (TANF)   The principal cash welfare program in the United States.

theory   A general framework, explanation, or tool used to understand and describe the real world.

time-availability perspective   A perspective that suggests the division of labor is largely determined by (1) the need for household labor, such as the number of children in the home; and (2) each partner's availability to perform household tasks, such as the number of hours spent in paid work.

total marriage   A type of marriage in which spouses share many facets of their lives such as a business they own, friends, or hobbies with few independent interests.

traditional surrogacy   A type of surrogacy where the man's sperm is implanted in the surrogate through artificial insemination.

trafficking   The recruitment, transportation, transfer, harboring, or receipt of persons, by means of threat or use of force or other forms of coercion, of abduction, of fraud or deception, of the abuse of power or of a position of vulnerability, or of the giving or receiving of payments to achieve the consent of a person having control over another person, for the purpose of exploitation.

transgender   When a person feels as comfortable, if not more so, in expressing gendered traits that are associated with the other sex.

transsexual   An individual who undergoes sex reassignment surgery and hormone treatments.

universal programs   Programs to help strengthen all families without any eligibility requirement.

unrequited love   When one person's feelings are not reciprocated by the other person in the relationship.

value conflict   A type of conflict that results from differing opinions on subjects that relate to personal values and issues of right or wrong.

verbal communication   The spoken exchange of thoughts, feelings, or other messages.

vital marriage   A type of marriage in which the lives of partners are intertwined; physical and emotional intimacy are important, and both work hard at communication and compromise so their relationship continues to be satisfying and enjoyable.

voluntary stable singles   Unmarried adults desiring a single (unmarried) lifestyle.

voluntary temporary singles   Unmarried adults who may be delaying marriage while pursuing education or establishing a career.

wage premium   Generally, married men earn more than their unmarried counterparts, particularly married men with stay-at-home wives.

work-family conflict   A form of tension under which people feel that the pressures from paid work and family roles are incompatible in some way.

References

Aardvarc.org. 2008. "Domestic Violence in Gay and Lesbian Relationships." Retrieved 25 March 2010 (www.aardvarc.org/dv/gay.shtml).

AARP. 2005 May. *Sexuality At Midlife and Beyond: 2004 Update of Attitudes and Behaviors*. Washington, DC.

—. 2007. "Grandparents Devoted To Grandchildren, But Their Support Constrained By Concerns About Their Financial Futures, Questions About Grandkids' Money Values." Retrieved 26 April 2010 (www.aarpfinancial.com/content/AboutUs/news_template.cfm?).

abcnews.go.com. 2009. "Pros and Cons: Elective C-Section."

Abramovitz, Mimi. 1996a. *Regulating the Lives of Women: Social Welfare Policy From Colonial Times to the Present (Revised Edition)*. Boston, MA: South End Press.

Acevedo, Bianca P. and Arthur Aron. 2009. "Does a Long-Term Relationship Kill Romantic Love?" *Review of General Psychology* 13(1): 59–65.

Acierno, Ron, Melba A. Hernandez, Amanda B. Amstadter, Heidi S. Resnick, Kenneth Steve, Wendy Muzzy, and Dean G. Kilpatrick. 2010. "Prevalence and Correlates of Emotional, Physical, Sexual, and Financial Abuse and Potential Neglect in the United States: The National Elder Mistreatment Study." *American Journal of Public Health* 100(2): 292–97.

Adams, Bert N. 2004. "Families and Family Study in International Perspective." *Journal of Marriage and Family* 66 (December): 1076–88.

Adams, Bert N. and Jan Trost. (Eds.) 2004. *Handbook of World Families*. Thousand Oaks, CA: Sage.

Adams, Brooke. 2005. "Fundamentalists: Most Espouse Polygamy as a Tenet, but Fewer Actually Practice It as Their Lifestyle." *Salt Lake Tribune*, 11 August.

Administration for Children & Families. 2010. "TANF: Total Number of Families (Fiscal Year 2009)." Retrieved 3 May 2010. U.S. Department of Health and Human Services (www.acf.hhs.gov/programs/ofa/data-reports/caseload/2009/2009_family_tan.htm).

Administration for Children & Families, Office of Head Start. 2009. "Head Start Program Fact Sheet." Retrieved 3 May 2010. U.S. Department of Health and Human Services (www.acf.hhs.gov/programs/ohs/About/ fy2008.html).

Administration for Children & Families, U.S. Department of Health and Human Services. 2009. "Office of Family Assistance (OFA)." Retrieved 17 June 2009 (www.acf.hhs.gov/opa/fact_sheets/tanf_factsheet.html).

Administration on Aging. 2009. "Fact for Features From the Census Bureau." Retrieved 23 April 2010 (www.aoa.gov/AoAroot/Aging_Statistics/Census_Population/Population/2001/factsforfeatures2001.aspx).

—. 2010. "A Profile of Older Americans: 2009." Retrieved 23 April 2010 (www.aoa.gov/AoAroot/Aging_Statistics/Profile/2009/4.aspx).

Advocates for Youth. 2009. "The Facts: Adolescent Childbearing and Educational and Economic Attainment, 2009." Retrieved 1 December 2009 (www.advocatesforyouth.org/PUBLICATIONS/factsheet/fsadlchd.htm).

Afifi, Tracie O., Harriet MacMillan, Brian J. Cox, Gordon J.G. Asmundson, Murray B. Stein, and Jitender Sareen 2009. Mental Health Correlates of Intimate Partner Violence in Marital Relationships in a Nationally Representative Sample of Males and Females. pp. 1398–1417.

Afifi, Tamara D., Walid A. Afifi, and Amanda Coho. 2009. "Adolescents' Physiological Reactions to Their Parents' Negative Disclosures About the Other Parent in Divorced and Nondivorced Families." *Journal of Divorce & Remarriage* 50(8, November): 517–40.

Ahmed, Sania Sultan and Sally Bould. 2004. "One Able Daughter is Worth 10 Illiterate Sons: Reframing the Patriarchal Family." *Journal of Marriage and Family* 66(5, December): 1332–41.

Ahrons, Constance R. 1994. *The Good Divorce: Keeping Your Family Together When Your Marriage Comes Apart*. New York: HarperCollins.

Ahrons, Constance R. 2005. *We're Still Family: What Grown Children Say About Their Parents' Divorce*. New York: HarperCollins.

—. 2007. "Introduction to the Special Issue on Divorce and Its Aftermath." *Family Process* 46(1): 3–6.

Ahrons, Constance R. and Roy H. Rodgers. 1987. *Divorced Families: A Multidisciplinary Development View*. New York: Norton.

Ainsworth, Mary D. Salter, Mary C. Blehar, Everett Waters, and Sally Wall. 1978. *Patterns of Attachment: A Psychological Study of the Strange Situation*. Hillsdale, NJ: Lawrence Erlbaum.

Alabama Coalition Against Domestic Violence. 2008. "Why Do Abusers Batter?" Retrieved 12 May 2008 (www.acadv.org/abusers.html).

Alchin, Linda K. No date. "Courtly Love." The Middle Ages. Retrieved 24 January 2010 (www.middle-ages.org.uk/courtly-love.htm).

Ali, Lorraine. 2008. "True or False: Having Kids Makes You Happy." Retrieved 6 March 2010. Newsweek.com (www.newsweek.com/id/143792).

Ali, Lorraine and Raina Kelley. 2008. "The Curious Lives of Surrogates." Retrieved 15 December 2009. Newsweek.com (www.newsweek.com/id/129594).

Allan, Graham, Graham Crow, and Sheila Hawker. 2010. *Stepfamilies: A Sociological Review*. New York: Palgrave Macmillan.

Allen, Brenda J. 2004. *Differences Matter: Communicating Social Identity*. Long Grove, IL: Waveland Press.

Allen, Elizabeth Sandin, Donald H. Baucom, Charles K. Burnett, Norman Epstein, and Lynn Rankin-Esquer. 2001. "Decision-Making Power, Autonomy, and Communication in Remarried Spouses Compared With First-Married Spouses." *Family Relations* 50: 326–34.

Allen, Katherine. 1997. "Lesbian and Gay Families." In *Contemporary Parenting*, edited by T. Arendell. Thousand Oaks, CA: Sage Publications.

Altman, Irwin and Joseph Ginat. 1996. *Polygamous Families in Contemporary Society*. Cambridge, England: Cambridge University Press.

Alzheimer's Association. 2010a. *Alzheimer's Disease: Facts and Figures*. Chicago.

—. 2010b. "Kris's Story." Retrieved 2 May 2010 (www.alz.org/living_With_alzheimers_8810.asp).

Amato, Paul R. 1994. "The Impact of Divorce on Men and Women in India and the United States." *Journal of Comparative Family Studies* 25: 207–21.

—. 2004. "Tension between Institutional and Individual Views of Marriage." *Journal of Marriage and Family* 66 (November): 959–65.

—. 2005. "The Impact of Family Formation Change on the Cognitive, Social, and Emotional Well-being of the Next Generation."*Marriage and Child Well-being: The Future of Children* 15: 75–96.

—. 2007. "Divorce and the Wellbeing of Adults and Children." *National Council on Family Relations Report* 52(4, December): F3–F4, F18.

Amato, Paul. 2010. "Research on Divorce: Continuing Trends and New Developments." *Journal of Marriage and Family* 72: 650–666.

Amato, Paul R. and Alan Booth. 1997. *A Generation at Risk: Growing up in an Era of Family Upheaval*. Cambridge, MA: Harvard University Press.

Amato, Paul R. and Danelle B. Deboer. 2001. "The Transmission of Marital Instability Across Generations: Relationship Skills or Commitment to Marriage?" *Journal of Marriage and Family* 63: 1038–51.

Amato, Paul R. and Bryndl Hohmann-Marriott. 2007. "A Comparison of High and Low-Distress Marriages That End in Divorce." *Journal of Marriage and Family* 69: 621–38.

Amato, Paul R. and Stacy J. Rogers. 1997. "A Longitudinal Study of Marital Problems and Subsequent Divorce." *Journal of Marriage and the Family* 59: 612-24.

Amato, Paul, Alan Booth, David Johnson, and Stacy Rogers. 2007. *Alone Together: How Marriage in America is Changing*. Cambridge, MA: Harvard University Press.

Ambert, Anne-Marie. 2005. "Same-Sex Couples and Same-Sex-Parent Families: Relationships, Parenting, and Issues of Marriage." Retrieved 14 March 2010. Ottawa, CA/ Vanier Institute of the Family (www.vifamily.ca/library/cft/samesex_05.html).

American Psychological Association Online. 2009. "Answers to Your Questions About Transgender Individuals and Gender Identity." Retrieved 14 August 2009 (www.apa.org/topics/transgender.html).

American Psychological Association. 1999a. "New Longitudinal Study Finds That Having a Working Mother Does No Significant Harm To Children." In *Press Release for "Short-Term and Long-Term Effects of Early Parental Employment on Children of the National Longitudinal Survey of Youth," Developmental Psychology, Vol. 35, No. 2.* Retrieved 27 July 2003.

—. 1999b. "Study Finds That Child Care Does Impact Mother-Child Interaction" (Press Release for "Child Care and Mother-Child Interaction in the First 3 Years of Life," NICHD Early Child Care Research Network, *Developmental Psychology*, Vol. 35, No. 6.). Retrieved 27 July 2003.

—. 2004. "APA Policy Statement: Sexual Orientation, Parents, & Children." In *APA Online: Public Interest*. Retrieved 3 December 2009 (www.apa.org/pi/lgbc/policy/parents.html).

—. 2005. "Controlling Anger—Before It Controls You." Retrieved 6 May 2008 (www.apa.org/pubinfo/anger.html).

—. 2009. "Answers to Your Questions For a Better Understanding of Sexual Orientation and Homosexuality." APA Public Interest (www.apa.org/topics/sorientation. html).

—. 2010a. "Elder Abuse and Neglect: In Search of Solutions." Washington, D.C. (www.apa.org/pi/aging/resources/guides/elder-abuse.aspx).

American Society for Reproductive Medicine. 2009. "Frequently Asked Questions About Infertility." Retrieved 15 December 2009 (www.asrm.org/Patients/faqs.html).

American Society of Plastic Surgeons. 2009a. "2000/2007/2008 National Plastic Surgery Statistics: Cosmetic and Reconstructive Procedure Trends." Retrieved 20 January 2010 (www.plasticsurgery.org/Media/stats/2008-cosmetic-reconstructive-plastic-surgery-minimally-invasive-statistics.pdf).

—. 2009b. "2008 Quick Facts: Percentage Change 2008 Vs. 2007." Retrieved 20 January 2010 (www.plasticsurgery.org/Media/stats/2008-quick-facts-cosmetic-surgery-minimally-invasive-statistics.pdf).

—. 2009c. "National Clearinghouse of Plastic Surgery Statistics." Retrieved 19 January 2010 (www.plasticsurgery.org/Media/Statistics.html).

Amnesty International. 2004. "What is Female Genital Mutilation? Section One." In *Female Genital Mutilation—A Human Rights Information Pack*. Retrieved 5 November 2003 (www.amnesty.org/ailib/intcam/femgen/fgm1.htm).

Anderson, Gillian and Karen Robson. 2006. "Male Adolescents' Contributions to Household Labor as Predictors of Later-Life Participation in Housework." *The Journal of Men's Studies* 14(1, Winter): 1060–65.

Anderson, Margaret and Patricia Hill Collins. 1995. *Race, Class and Gender: An Anthology*. Belmont, CA: Wadsworth Publishing Company.

Angel, Jacqueline, Maren A. Jimenez, and Ronald J. Angel. 2007. "The Economic Consequences of Widowhood for Older Minority Women." *The Gerontologist* 47: 224–34.

Antill, John K., Jacqueline Jarrett Goodnow, Graeme Russell, and Sandra Cotton. 1996. "The Influence of Parents and Family Context on Children's Involvement in Household Tasks." *Sex Roles* 34(3/4): 215–36.

APA Task Force on Gender Identity and Gender Variance. 2008. *Report of the Task Force on Gender Identity and Gender Variance*. Washington DC: American Psychological Association.

Aquilino, William S. 2006. "The Noncustodial Father-Child Relationship From Adolescence Into Young Adulthood." *Journal of Marriage and Family* 68(4): 929–46.

Arditti, Joyce A. and Debra A. Madden-Derdich. 1997. "Joint and Sole Custody Mothers—Implications for Research and Practice." *Families in Society: The Journal of Contemporary Human Services* 78(1): 36–45.

Arendell, Terry. 1986. *Mothers and Divorce: Legal, Economic, and Social Dilemmas*. Berkeley, CA: University of California Press.

Arendell, Terry. 2000. "Conceiving and Investigating Motherhood: The Decade's Scholarship." *Journal of Marriage and the Family* 62(4, November): 1193–207.

Arliss, Laurie P. 1991. Gender Communication. Englewood Cliffs, NJ: Prentice Hall.

Aronson, Elliot, Timothy D. Wilson, and Robin M. Ackert. 2010. *Social Psychology, 5th Ed.* Upper Saddle River, NJ: Prentice Hall.

Asante, Molefi K., Yoshitaka Miike, and Jing Yin. 2007. *The Global Intercultural Reader*. New York: Routledge.

Ashford, Lori and Donna Clifton. February 2005. *Women of Our World*. Population Reference Bureau: Available online: www.prb.org/pdf05/womenofourworld2005.pdf.

Assisted Senior Living. 2009. "The Cost of Assisted Living." Retrieved 26 April 2010 (www.assistedseniorliving.net/ba/facilty-costs.cfm/).

Aubrey, Jennifer Stevens and Kristin Harrison. 2004. "The Gender-Role Content of Children's Favorite Television Programs and Its Link to Their Gender-Related Perceptions." *Media Psychology* 6(2): 111–46.

Aubry, Tim, Bruce Tefft, and Nancy Kingsbury. 2006. "Behavioral and Psychological Consequences of Unemployment in Blue-Collar Couples." *Journal of Community Psychology* 18(2, February): 99–109.

Aumann, Kerstin and Ellen Galinsky. 2009. *The State of Health in the American Workforce: Does Having an Effective Workplace Matter?* 2008 National Study of the Changing Workforce. New York: Families and Work Institute.

Avellar, Sarah and Pamela J. Smock. 2005. "The Economic Consequences of the Dissolution of Cohabiting Unions." *Journal of Marriage and Family* 67 (May): 315–27.

AVERT.ORG. 2010. "How Many Gay People Are There?" Retrieved 14 February 2010 (www.avert.org/gay-people.htm).

Axinn, June and Mark J. Stern. 2008. *Social Welfare: A History of the American Response to Need, 7th Ed.* Boston: Allyn & Bacon.

Axinn, William G. and Arland Thornton. 2000. "The Transformation in the Meaning of Marriage." pp. 147–65 in *The Ties That Bind: Perspectives on Marriage and Cohabitation*, edited by L. J. Waite, C. Bachrach, M. J. Hindin, L. Thompson and A. Thornton. New York: Aldine de Gruyter.

Ängarne-Lindberg, Teresia, Marie Wadsby, and Carina Berterö. 2009. "Young Adults With Childhood Experience of Divorce: Disappointment and Contentment." *Journal of Divorce & Remarriage* 50(3, April): 172-84.

Baca Zinn, Maxine, D. Stanley Eitzen, and Barbara Wells. 2008. *Diversity in Families, 8th Ed.* Boston, MA: Allyn & Bacon.

Bachman, Jerald G., Lloyd D. Johnston, and Patrick M. O'Malley. 1993. *Monitoring the Future: Questionnaire Responses From the Nation's High School Seniors, 1991*. Ann Arbor, MI: Institute for Social Research.

—. 2001. *Monitoring the Future: Questionnaire Responses From the Nation's High School Seniors, 2000*. Ann Arbor, MI: Institute for Social Research.

—. 2009. *Monitoring the Future: Questionnaire Responses From the Nation's High School Seniors, 2008*. Ann Arbor, MI: Institute for Social Research.

Bahr, Kathleen S. 1994. "The Strengths of Apache Grandmothers: Observations on Commitment, Culture and Caretaking." *Journal of Comparative Family Studies* 25: 233–48.

Bailey, Eric J. 2008. *Black America, Body Beautiful*. Westport, CT: Praeger Publishers.

Bailey, J. Michael, David Bobrow, Marilyn Wolfe, and Sarah Mikach. 1995. "Sexual Orientation of Adult Sons of Gay Fathers."*Developmental Psychology* 31: 124–29.

Bailey, J. Michael and Richard C. Pillard. 1991. "A Genetic Study of Male Sexual Orientation." *Archives of General Psychiatry* 48: 1089–96.

Bailey, J. Michael, Richard C. Pillard, Michael C. Neale, and Yvonne Agyei. 1993. "Heritable Factors Influence Sexual Orientation in Women." *Archives of General Psychiatry* 50: 217–23.

Bakanic, Von. 2008. *Prejudice: Attitudes aAbout Race, Class, and Gender.* Upper Saddle River, NJ: Prentice Hall.

Baker, Kaysee and Arthur A. Raney. 2007. "Equally Super? Gender-Role Stereotyping of Superheroes in Children's Animated Programs."*Mass Communication & Society* 10(1): 25–41.

Baker, Maureen. 2006. *Restructuring Family Policies: Convergences and Divergences.* Toronto: University of Toronto Press.

Bandura, Alfred. 1973. *Aggression: A Social Learning Analysis.* Englewood Cliffs, NJ: Prentice Hall.

Bandura, Alfred. 1977. *Social Learning Theory.* New York: General Learning Press.

—. 1997. *Self-Efficacy: The Exercise of Control.* New York: W.H. Freeman.

Banister, Judith. 2009. "Son Preference in Asia—Report of a Symposium." Retrieved 4 March 2010. U.S. Census Bureau (www.census.gov/ipc/www/ebspr96a.html).

Barna, George. 2008 March. "New Marriage and Divorce Statistics." Retrieved 26 April 2010. The Barna Group, Ltd. (www.barna.org).

Barnett, Rosalind C. and Caryl Rivers. 2004. "Men Are From Earth, and So Are Women. It's Faulty Research That Sets Them Apart."*Chronicle of Higher Education* 51(2): B11.

Baron, Naomi S. 2008. *Always On: Language in an Online and Mobile World.* New York: Oxford University Press.

Baron-Cohen, Simon. 2003. *The Essential Difference: The Truth About the Male and the Female Brain.* New York: Basic Books.

Barr, Simone C. and Helen A. Neville. 2008. "Examination of the Link Between Parental Racial Socialization Messages and Racial Ideology Among Black College Students." *Journal of Black Psychology* 34(2): 131–55.

Basile, Kathleen C., Jieru Chen, Michele C. Lynberg, and Linda Saltzman. 2007. "Prevalence and Characteristics of Sexual Violence Victimization." *Violence and Victims* 22(4): 437–48.

Bass, Brenda L., Adam B. Butler, Joseph G. Grzywacz, and Kirsten D. Linney. 2009. "Do Job Demands Undermine Parenting? A Daily Analysis of Spillover and Crossover Effects." *Family Relations* 58(2, April): 201–15.

Baucom, Donald H., Douglas K. Snyder, and Kristina Coop Gordon. 2009. *Helping Couples Get Past the Affair.* New York: Guilford Press.

Baum, Katrina, Shannan Catalano, Michael Rand, and Kristina Rose. 2009 January. *Stalking Victimization in the United States.* Bureau of Justice Statistics No. NCJ 224527. Washington, DC: U.S. Department of Justice.

Baumrind, Diana. 1966. "Effects of Authoritative Parental Control on Child Behavior." *Child Development* 37(4): 887–907.

—. 1968. "Authoritarian versus Authoritative Parental Control." *Adolescence* 3: 255–72.

Bauserman, Robert. 2002. "Child Adjustment in Joint-Custody versus Sole-Custody Arrangements: A Meta-Analytic Review." *Journal of Family Psychology* 16(1): 91–102.

Beah, Ismael. 2007. *A Long Way Gone.* New York: Sarah Crichton Books.

Bearak, Barry. 2010. "Malawi: Prosecutors State Case Against Gay Couple." Retrieved 21 February 2010. New York Times (www.nytimes.com/2010/02/19/world/ africa/19briefs-Malawi.html).

Becker, Gary S. 1981. *A Treatise on the Family.* Cambridge, MA: Harvard University Press.

Becker, Jill B., Karen J. Berkley, Nori Geary, Elizabeth Hampson, James P. Herman, and Elizabeth A. Young, eds. 2008. *Sex Differences in the Brain: From Genes to Behavior.* New York: Oxford University Press.

Beebe, Steven A., Susan J. Beebe, and Mark V. Redmond. 2011. *Interpersonal Communication Relating to Others, 6th Ed.* Boston, MA: Allyn & Bacon.

Beebe, Steven A. and John T. Masterson. 2006. *Communicating in Small Groups: Principles and Practices, 8th Ed.* Boston: Allyn & Bacon.

Belsky, Jay and Michael Rovine. 1990. "Patterns of Marital Change Across the Transition to Parenthood: Pregnancy to Three Years Postpartum." *Journal of Marriage and the Family* 52: 5–19.

Belsky, Jay, Martha Weinraub, Margaret Owen, and Jean F. Kelly. 2001. "Quantity of Child Care and Problem Behavior." Presented at the Biennial Meeting of the Society for Research on Child Development, Minneapolis, MN.

Benard, Bonnie and Sara L. Truebridge. 2009. "A Shift in Thinking: Influencing Social Workers' Beliefs About Individual and Family Resilience in an Effort to Enhance Well-Being and Success for All." P. Chapter 11 in *The Strengths Perspective in Social Work Practice, 5th Ed.,* edited by Dennis Saleebey. Boston: Allyn & Bacon.

Bentley, Keisha C., Valerie N. Adams, and Howard C. Stevenson. 2009. "Racial Socialization: Roots, Processes, & Outcomes." In *Handbook of African American Psychology,* edited by Helen A. Neville, Brendesha M. Tynes and Shawn O. Utsey. Thousand Oaks, CA: Sage Publications.

Berardo, Felix M. 1998. "Family Privacy: Issues and Concepts." *Journal of Family Issues* 19(1): 4–19.

Berardo, Felix M. and Donna H. Berardo. 2000. Widowhood. pp. 3255–61 in *Encyclopedia of Sociology, 2nd Ed.* Edited by E. F. Borgatta and R. J. Montgomery. New York: Macmillion.

Bergmann, Barbara R. 1996. *Saving Our Children From Poverty: What the United States Can Learn From France.* New York: Russell Sage Foundation.

Berke, Melvin R. and Joanne B. Grant. 1981. *Games Divorced People Play.* Englewood Cliffs, NJ: Prentice Hall.

Berlin, Lisa J., Jean M. Ispa, Mark A. Fine, Patrick S. Malone, Jeanne Brooks-Gunn, Christy Brady-Smith, Catherine Ayoub, and Yu Bai. 2009. "Correlates and Consequences of Spanking and Verbal Punishment for Low-Income White, African American, and Mexican American Toddlers." *Child Development* 80(5): 1403–20.

Bernard, Jessie. 1972. *The Future of Marriage.* New York: World Pub.

—. 1973. *The Future of Marriage.* New York: Bantam.

Berns, Roberta M. 2001. *Child, Family, School, Community: Socialization and Support, 5th Ed.* New York: Thomson Learning.

Bernstein, Amy B., Robin A. Cohen, Kate M. Brett, and Mary Ann Bush. 2008. "Marital Status is Associated With Health Insurance Coverage for Working-Age Women at All Income Levels" (NCHS Data Brief, No.11). Retrieved 21 February 2010. National Center for Health Statistics (www.cdc.gov/nchs/data/databriefs/db11.htm).

Bernstein, Basil. 1960. "Language and Social Class: A Research Note." *British Journal of Sociology (London)* 11(3): 271–76.

—. 1973. *Class, Codes, and Control, Vol. 1.* London: Routledge & Kegan Paul.

Bernstein, Jared. 2007. "Viewpoints: Tax Incentives for Businesses in Response to a Minimum Wage Increase." Retrieved 4 March 2008. Washington, DC: Economic Policy Institute (www.epi.org/content.cfm/webfeatures_viewpoints_minwage_tax_incentives_testimony_01102007).

Bernstein, Robert and Tom Edwards. 2008. "An Older and More Diverse Nation by Midcentury" (Press Release). Retrieved 22 August 2008. U.S. Census Bureau (www.census.gov/Press-Release/www/releases/archives/population/012496.html).

Bertrand, Marianne and Sendhil Mullainathan. 2004. "Are Emily and Greg More Employable Than Lakisha and Jamal? A Field Experiment on Labor Market Discrimination." *American Economic Review* 94 (September): 991–1013.

Berzon, Betty. 2004. *Permanent Partners: Building Gay & Lesbian Relationships That Last.* New York: Plume Publishing.

Beverly, Brenda, Teena M. McGuinness, and Debra J. Blanton. 2008. "Communication Challenges for Children Adopted From the Former Soviet Union." *Language, Speech, and Hearing Services in Schools* 39: 1–11.

Bianchi, Suzanne, John P. Robinson, and Melissa A. Milkie. 2006. *Changing Rhythms of American Family Life.* New York: Russell Sage Foundation.

Biblarz, Timothy J. and Greg Gottainer. 2000. "Family Structure and Children's Success: A Comparison of Widowed and Divorced Single-Mother Families." *Journal of Marriage and the Family* 62: 533–48.

Biblarz, Timothy J. and Evren Savci. Lesbian, Gay, Bisexual, and Transgender Families. *Journal of Marriage and Family.* 72(3):480–497.

Biblarz, Timothy J. and Judith Stacey. 2010. "How Does the Gender of Parents Matter?" *Journal of Marriage and Family* 72(1, February): 3–22.

Bing, Nicole M., W.M. Nelson, III, and Kelly L. Wesolowski. 2009. "Comparing the Effects of Amount of Conflict on Children's Adjustment Following Parental Divorce." *Journal of Divorce & Remarriage* 50(3, April): 159–71.

Bittman, Michael, Paula England, Liana Sayer, Nancy Folbre, and George Matheson. 2003. "When Does Gender Trump Money? Bargaining and Time in Household Work." *American Journal of Sociology* 109: 186–214.

Blaauw, Eric, Frans W. Winkel, Ella Arensman, Lorraine Sheridan, and Adrienne Freeve. 2002. "The Toll of Stalking: The Relationship Between Features of Stalking and Psychopathology of Victims." *Journal of Interpersonal Violence* 17(1, January): 50–63.

Blackwell, Debra L. and Daniel T. Lichter. 2004. "Homogamy Among Dating, Cohabiting, and Married Couples." *The Sociological Quarterly* 45: 719–737.

Blake, John. 2010. "More Workers Are Choosing Fear Over Flex Time, Experts Say." Retrieved 3 May 2010. CNN.com (www.cnn.com/2010/LIVING/worklife/03/29/flex.time/index.html).

Blekesaune, Morten. 2008. "Partnership Transitions and Mental Distress: Investigating Temporal Order." *Journal of Marriage and Family* 70(4, October): 879–90.

Bleske-Rechek, April. 2008. "Attraction in Young Adults' and Middle-Aged Adults' Cross-Sex Friendships." Presented at the 80th Annual Midwestern Psychological Association Conference, May 1-3, Chicago, IL.

Block, Jennifer. 2008. *Pushed: The Painful Truth About Childbirth and Modern Maternity Care.* Cambridge, MA: Da Capo Press.

Blood, Robert O. and Donald M. Wolfe. 1960. *Husbands and Wives: The Dynamics of Married Living.* New York: Free Press.

Blumenthal, David. 2006. "Employer-Sponsored Health Insurance in the United States—Origins and Implications." *New England Journal of Medicine* 355(1, 6 July): 82–88.

Blumstein, Phillip and Pepper Schwartz. 1983. *American Couples: Money, Work, Sex*. New York: William Morrow.

Blyth, Dale A. and Eugene C. Roelkepartian. 1993. *Healthy Communities, Healthy Youth*. Minneapolis: Search Institute.

Bogle, Kathleen A. 2008. *Hooking Up: Sex, Dating, and Relationships on Campus*. New York: NYU Press.

Bohannan, Paul. 1971. "The Six Stations of Divorce." pp. 33–62 in *Divorce and After: An Analysis of the Emotional and Social Problems of Divorce*, edited by P. Bohannan. New York: Doubleday.

Bokker, Lon Paul, Roy C. Farley, and William Bailey. 2006. "The Relationship Between Custodial Status and Emotional Well-Being Among Recently Divorced Fathers." *Journal of Divorce and Remarriage* 44(3/4): 83–98 (DOI: 10.1300/J087vol44n03_06).

Bonach, Kathryn, Esther Sales, and Gary Koeske. 2005. "Gender Differences in Perceptions of Coparenting Quality Among Expartners." *Journal of Divorce and Remarriage* 43(1/2): 1–28.

Bond, James T., Ellen Galinsky, and E. Jeffrey Hill. 2004. *When Work Works: Summary of Families and Work Institute Research Findings*. Families and Work Institute and IBM.

Booth, Alan, Ann C. Crouter, and Mari Clements. 2001. *Couples In Conflict*. Mahwah, NJ: Lawrence Erlbaum Associates.

Booth, Alan, Mindy E. Scott, and Valarie King. 2010. "Father Residence and Adolescent Problem Behavior: Are Youth Always Better Off in Two-Parent Families?" *Journal of Family Issues* 31(5): 585–605.

Bornstein, Marc H. 2002. *Handbook of Parenting Vol. 4*. Philadelphia, PA: Lawrence Erlbaum Associates.

Bouchard, Geneviéve. 2006. "Cohabitation Versus Marriage: The Role of Dyadic Adjustment in Relationship Dissolution." *Journal of Divorce & Remarriage* 46(1-2, August): 107–17.

Boucher, Debora, Catherine Bennett, Barbara McFarlin, and Rixa Freeze. 2009. "Staying Home to Give Birth: Why Women in the United States Choose Home Birth." *Journal of Midwifery & Women's Health* 54(2, March-April): 119–26.

Bowlby, John. 1969. *Attachment and Loss*. New York: Basic Books.

Bradley, Nicki. 2006. "Authoritative Parenting: An Overview." In *Parenting Advice*. Retrieved 29 November 2009. Families.com (Parenting.families.com/blog/authoritative-parenting-an-overview).

Bradshaw, Carolyn, Arnold S. Kahn, and Bryan K. Saville. 2010. To Hook Up or Date: Which Gender Benefits? Sex Roles 62(9–10 May): 661–669.

Bramlett, Matthew D. and William D. Mosher. 2002. "Cohabitation, Remarriage, Divorce, and Remarriage in the United States." National Center for Health Statistics. *Vital Health Statistics* 23(22).

Branden, Nathaniel. 2008. *The Psychology of Romantic Love: Romantic Love in an Anti-Romantic Age*. New York: Tarcher Press.

Bratter, Jenifer L. and Rosalind B. King. 2008. "'But Will It Last?': Marital Instability Among Interracial and Same-Race Couples." *Family Relations* 57(2): 160–71.

Braver, Sanford L., Ira M. Ellman, and William V. Fabricius. 2003. "Relocation of Children After Divorce and Children's Best Interests: New Evidence and Legal Considerations." *Journal of Family Psychology* 17.

Bremner, Jason, Carl Haub, Marlene Lee, Mark Mather, and Eric Zuehlke. 2009 September. *World Population Highlights Key Findings From PRB's 2009 World Population Data Sheet*. Population Bulletin No. 64 (3). Washington, DC: Population Reference Bureau.

Breslau, Naomi, Nigel S. Paneth, and Victoria C. Lucia. 2004. "The Lingering Academic Deficits of Low Birth Weight Children." *Pediatrics* 114(4, October): 1035–40.

Briere, John and Carol E. Jordan. 2009. "Childhood Maltreatment, Intervening Variables, and Adult Psychological Difficulties in Women." *Trauma, Violence, & Abuse* 10(4): 375–88.

Briggs, Sarah. 2006. "Confessions of a 'Helicopter Parent.'" Retrieved 5 January 2010. Experience.com (www.experience.com/alumnus/channel?channel_id=parents_survival_guide&page_id=helicopter_parents).

Brink, Susan. 2008. 21 January. Modern Puberty. Los Angeles Times. Retrieved 22 March 2008. articles.latimes.com/2008/jan/21/health/he-puberty21

Brisch, Karl Heinz. 2004. Treating Attachment Disorders: From Theory to Therapy. New York: Guilford Press.

Brizendine, Louann. 2006. The Female Brain. New York: Broadway.

Broderick, Carlfred and James Smith. 1979. "The General Systems Approach to the Family." pp. Vol. 2, pp. 112–29 in *Contemporary Theories About the Family*, edited by Wesley Burr, Reuben Hill, F. Ivan Nye and Ira Reiss. Englewood Cliffs, N.J.: Prentice Hall.

Bronfenbrenner, Urie. 1979. *The Ecology of Human Development*. Cambridge, MA: Harvard University Press.

Bronte-Tinkew, Jacinta, Jennifer Carrano, Allison Horowitz, and Akemi Kinukawa. 2008. "Involvement mong Resident Fathers and Links to Infant Cognitive Outcomes." *Journal of Family Issues* 29: 1211–44.

Brooks-Gunn, Jeanne and Elisabeth Hirschhorn Donahue. 2008. "Introducing the Issue." In *Children and Electronic Media*. 3–10. Retrieved 22 November 2009. The Future of Children/Princeton-Brookings (www.futureofchildren. org).

Brooks-Gunn, Jeanne and Lisa B. Markman. 2005. "The Contribution of Parenting to Ethnic and Racial Gaps in School Readiness." *The Future of Children* 15(1): 138–67.

Brown, Edna, Terri L. Orbuch, and Jose A. Bauermeister. 2008. "Religiosity and Marital Stability Among Black American and White American Couples." *Family Relations* 57: 186–97.

Brown, Heidi. 2009. "U.S. Maternity Leave Benefits Are Still Dismal." Retrieved 16 December 2009. Forbes.com (www. forbes.com/2009/05/04/maternity-leave-laws-forbes-woman-wellbeing-pregnancy.html?feed=rss_news).

Brown, Judith K. 1975. "Iroquois Women: An Ethnohistoric Note." pp. 235–51 in *Toward an Anthropology of Women*, edited by Rayna R. Reiter. New York: Monthly Review Press.

Brown, Mackenzie. 2008. "The State of Our Unions." Retrieved 22 February 2010. Redbook (www.redbookmag. com/love-sex/advice/types-of-marriages?click=main_sr).

Brown, Susan L. and Alan Booth. 1996. "Cohabitation Versus Marriage: A Comparison of Relationship Quality." *Journal of Marriage and the Family* 58: 668–78.

Browne, Joy. 2006. *Dating for Dummies, 2nd Ed.* Hoboken, NJ: Wiley.

Bryant, Chalandra M., Robert Joseph Taylor, Karen D. Lincoln, Linda M. Chatters, and James S. Jackson. 2008. "Marital Satisfaction Among African Americans and Black Caribbeans: Findings From the National Survey of American Life." *Family Relations* 57: 239–53.

Bryant-Davis, Thema, Haewoon Chung, and Shaquila Tillman. 2009. "From the Margins to the Center." *Trauma, Violence, & Abuse* 10(4): 330–57.

Bucx, Freek, Frits van Wel, Trudie Knun, and Louk Hagendoorn. 2008. "Intergenerational Contact and the Life Course Status of Young Adult Children." *Journal of Marriage and Family* 70(1): 144–56.

Bulanda, Ronald E. 2004. "Paternal Involvement With Children: The Influence of Gender Ideologies." *Journal of Marriage and the Family* 66: 40–45.

Bulcroft, Kris A. and Richard A. Bulcroft. 1991. "The Nature and Functions of Dating in Later Life." *Research on Aging* 13: 244–60.

Bulcroft, Richard A. and Kris A. Bulcroft. 1993. "Race Differences in Attitudinal and Motivational Factors in the Decision to Marry." *Journal of Marriage and the Family* 55: 338–55.

Bulduc, Jessica L., Sandra L. Caron, and Mary Ellen Logue. 2006. "The Effects of Parental Divorce on College Students." *Journal of Divorce and Remarriage* 46(3/4): 83–104 (DOI: 10.1300/J087vol46n03_06).

Bullough, Vern L. 1976. *Sexual Variance in Society and History*. New York: John Wiley & Sons.

Bumiller, Elisabeth. 1990. *May You Be The Mother of a Hundred Sons*. New York: Fawcett Columbine.

Bunting, Madeleine. 2005. *Willing Slaves: How the Overwork Culture is Ruling Our Lives*. New York: HarperCollins.

Bureau of Justice Statistics. 2009. 8 December. "Prisoners in 2008." Retrieved 21 February 2010. bjs.ojp.usdoj.gov/ index.cfm?ty=pbdetail&iid=17653.

Bureau of Labor Statistics. 2008. "Married Parents' Use of Time Summary." Retrieved 31 December 2009 (www.bls. gov/news.release/atus2.nr0.htm).

—. 2009a. "Child Care Workers." In *Occupational Outlook Handbook, 2010-2011 Edition*. Retrieved 9 March 2010 (www.bls.gov/oco/ocos170.htm).

—. 2009b. "Economic News Release: Employment Situation Summary." Retrieved 9 November 2009 (www.bls.gov/ news.release/empsit.nr0.htm).

—. 2009c. "The Employment Situation: June 2009" (Press Release). Retrieved 3 August 2009. U.S. Department of Labor (www.bls.gov/news.release/pdf/empsit.pdf).

—. 2009d. "Quarterly Census of Employment and Wages." Retrieved 9 November 2009 (www.bls.gov/cew).

—. 2009e. "Women in the Labor Force: A Databook (2009 Edition)." Retrieved 28 December 2009. U.S. Department of Labor (www.bls.gov/cps/ wlf-databook2009.htm).

—. 2010a. "Employment Situation Archived News Release." Retrieved 9 March 2010 (www.bls.gov/schedule/ archives/empsit_nr.htm).

—. 2010b. "Employment Situation News Release." Retrieved 5 March 2010. Washington, D.C./U.S. Department of Labor (www.bls.gov/news.release/empsit.htm).

Bures, Regina M., Tanya Koropeckyj-Cox, and Michael Loree. 2009. "Childlessness, Parenthood, and Depressive Symptoms Among Middle-Aged and Older Adults." *Journal of Family Issues* 30(5): 670–87.

Burke, Tod, Michael L. Jordan, and Stephen S. Owen. 2002. "A Cross-National Comparison of Gay and Lesbian Domestic Violence." *Journal of Contemporary Criminal Justice* 18(3, August): 231–57.

Burns, John. 1998, 11 May. "Though Illegal, Child Marriage is Popular in Parts of India." In *Global Studies: India & South Asia, 4th Ed.*, edited by J. 1. New York Times Reprinted in Norton. Guilford, CT: Pushkin.

Burr, Wesley R. and Shirley R. Klein. 1994. *Reexamining Family Stress: New Theory And Research*. Newbury Park, CA: Sage Publications.

Busby, Dean M., Thomas B. Holman, and Eric Walker. 2008. "Pathways to Relationship Aggression Between Adult Partners." *Family Relations* 57 (January): 72–83.

Buss, David M. 1989. "Sex Differences in Human Mate Preferences: Evolutionary Hypotheses Tested in 37 Cultures." *Behavioral and Brain Sciences* 12: 1–49.

—. 2009. "The Great Struggles of Life: Darwin and the Emergence of Evolutionary Psychology." *American Psychologist* 64(140–148).

Buss, David M. and Joshua D. Duntley. 2008. "Adaptations for Exploitation." *Group Dynamics: Theory, Research, and Practice* 12: 53–62.

Butzer, Bethany and Lorne Campbell. 2008. "Adult Attachment, Sexual Satisfaction, and Relationship Satisfaction: A Study of Married Couples." *Personal Relationships* 15(1): 141–54.

Buunk, Abraham P., Karlijn Massar, and Pieternel Dijkstra. 2007.

Byers, E. Sandra. 2005. "Relationship Satisfaction and Sexual Satisfaction: A Longitudinal Study of Individuals in Long-Term Relationships." *The Journal of Sex Research* 42: 113–18.

Cahill, Sean, Ken South, and Jane Spade. 2000. *Outing Age: Public Policy Issues Affecting Gay, Lesbian, Bisexual, and Transgender Elders.* The Policy Institute of the National Gay and Lesbian Task Force Foundation.

Caine, Barbara. 2010. *Friendship: A History (Critical Histories of Subjectivity and Culture).* London: Equinox Publishing.

Calvert, Sandra L. 2008. "Children as Consumers: Advertising and Marketing." In *Children and Electronic Media.* 205–34. Retrieved 22 November 2009. The Future of Children/Princeton-Brookings (www.futureofchildren. org).

Calasanti Toni and K. Jill Kiecolt. 2007. "Diversity among Late-life Couples." *Generations* 31: 10–17.

Calvo, Esteban, Kelly Haverstick, and Steven A. Sass. 2009. "Gradual Retirement, Sense of Control, and Retirees' Happiness."*Research on Aging* 31(1): 112–35.

Cameron, Deborah. 1998. "Gender, Language, and Discourse: A Review Essay." *Signs* 23(4): 945.

Campana, Kathryn L., Sandra Henderson, Arnold L. Stolberg, and Lisa Schum. 2008. "Paired Maternal and Paternal Parenting Styles, Child Custody, and Children's Emotional Adjustment to Divorce." *Journal of Divorce and Remarriage* 48(3/4): 1–20.

Campbell, Jacquelyn C., Nancy Glass, Phyllis W. Sharps, Kathryn Laughon, and Tina Bloom. 2007. "Intimate Partner Homicide."*Trauma, Violence, & Abuse* 8(3): 246–69.

Campbell, Jacquelyn C., Linda Rose, Joan Kub, and Daphne Nedd. 1998. "Voices of Strength and Resistance: A Contextual and Longitudinal Analysis of Women's Responses to Battering." *Journal of Interpersonal Violence* 13: 743–62.

Cancian, Francesca M. 1987. *Love in America: Gender and Self-Development.* New York: Cambridge University Press.

Capizzano, Jeffrey and Regan Main. 2005. "Many Young Children Spend Long Hours in Child Care." In *No. 22 in "Snapshots of America's Families III."* Retrieved 11 July 2005. Urban Institute (Available online: www.urban.org/urlprint.cfm?ID=9232).

Carlson, Marcia J. 2006. "Family Structure, Father Involvement, and Adolescent Behavioral Outcomes." *Journal of Marriage and Family* 68(1): 137–54.

Carroll, Joseph. 2007. "Most Americans Approve of Interracial Marriages." Retrieved 21 February 2010. Gallup Poll (www.gallup.com/search/default.aspx?q=interracial+marriage&s=p=1).

Carter, Wendy Y. 2006. "Attitudes Toward Pre-Marital Sex, Non-Marital Childbearing, Cohabitation, and Marriage Among Blacks and Whites" (NSFH Working Paper No. 61). Retrieved 8 July 2006. Center for Demography and Ecology, University of Wisconsin-Madison (www.ssc.wisc.edu/cdc/nsfhwp/nsfh61.pdf).

Cartwright, Claire. 2005. "You Want to Know How It Affected Me? Young Adults' Perceptions of the Impact of Parental Divorce."*Journal of Divorce and Remarriage* DOI: 10.1300/J087v44n03_08: 125–43.

Cartwright, Claire and Heather McDowell. 2008. "Young Women's Life Stories and Accounts of Parental Divorce." *Journal of Divorce & Remarriage* 49(1-2, June): 56–77.

Cassidy, Jude. 2000. "Adult Romantic Attachments: A Developmental Perspective on Individual Differences." *Review of General Psychology* 4: 111–31.

Cassidy, Tina. 2007. *Birth: The Surprising History of How We Are Born.* New York: Grove Press.

Cavanagh, Shannon E., Crissey, Sarah R., & Raley, R. Kelly. (2008). Family structure history and adolescent romantic relationships. *Journal of Marriage and Family* 70: 698–714.

Cavanagh, Shannon E. and Aletha C. Huston. 2008. "The Timing of Family Instability and Children's Social Development." *Journal of Marriage and Family* 70(5, December): 1258–69.

CensusScope. 2008. "Social Science Data Analysis Network, University of Michigan." Retrieved 20 August 2008 (www.ssdan.net).

Center for Nutrition Policy and Promotion. 2009. "USDA Food Plans: Cost of Food." Retrieved 21 January 2010. U.S. Department of Agriculture (www.cnpp.usda.gov/USDAFoodPlansCostofFood.htm).

Centers for Disease Control and Prevention. 2003. *Costs of Intimate Partner Violence Against Women in the United States.* Atlanta, GA: CDC, National Center for Injury Prevention and Control.

—. 2007. "A Glance at the HIV Epidemic." Retrieved 25 June 2007 (www.cdc.gov/hiv/resources/factsheets/At-A-Glance.htm).

—. 2008a. "Fact Sheet: HIV/AIDS Among African Americans." Retrieved 14 August 2009 (www.cdc.gov/hiv/topics/aa/resources/factsheets/aa.htm).

—. 2008b. "Intimate Partner Violence: Risk and Protective Factors." Retrieved 12 July 2009 (www.cdc.gov/ViolencePrevention/intimatepartnerviolence/riskprotectivefactors.html).

—. 2008c. "Sexual Violence: Facts at a Glance." Retrieved 26 March 2010 (www.cdc.gov/ViolencePrevention/pdf/sv-datasheet-a.pdf).

—. 2009 November. *Sexually Transmitted Disease Surveillance, 2008*. Atlanta, GA: U.S. Department of Health & Human Services.

—. 2009a. "Assisted Reproductive Technology (ART) Report: National Summary." Retrieved 15 December 2009 (apps.nccd.cdc.gov/ART/NSR.aspx?SelectedYear=2007).

—. 2009b. "Deaths Among Persons With AIDS Through December 2006." Retrieved 21 February 2010 (www.cdc.gov/hiv/topics/surveillance/resources/reports/2009supp_vol14no3/default.htm).

—. 2009c. "HIV/AIDS in the United States: Fact Sheet." Retrieved 18 February 2010 (www.cdc.gov/hiv/resources/factsheets/us.htm).

—. 2009d. "Intimate Partner Violence: Consequences." Retrieved 25 March 2010 (www.cdc.gov/ViolencePrevention/intimatepartnerviolence/consequences.html).

—. 2009e. *Understanding Elder Mistreatment: Fact Sheet*. www.cdc.gov/violenceprevention/pub/EM_factsheet.html.

Central Intelligence Agency. 2009 November. "Country Comparison: Infant Mortality Rate." Retrieved 5 November 2009 (www.cia.gov/library/publications/the-world-factbook/rankorder/2091rank.html).

—. 2010. "The World Factbook." Retrieved 23 April 2010 (www.cia.gov/library/publications/the-world-factbook/geos/us.html).

Chambers, Wendy C. 2007. "Oral Sex: Varied Behaviors and Perceptions in a College Population." *Journal of Sex Research* 44(1): 28–42.

Chancer, Lynn S. 2006. Gender, Race, and Class. Boston: Blackwell Publishing.

Cheah, Charissa S. L, Christy Y. Y. Leung, Madiha Tahseen, and David Schultz. 2009. "Authoritative Parenting Among Immigrant Chinese Mothers of Preschoolers." *Journal of Family Psychology* 23(3): 311–320.

Chedekel, David S. and Karen O'Connell. 2002. *The Blended Family Sourcebook: A Guide to Negotiating Change*. New York: McGraw-Hill.

Cherlin, Andrew J. and Frank F. Furstenberg. 1986. *The New American Grandparent: A Place in the Family, A Life Apart*. New York: Basic Books.

—. 1994. "Stepfamilies in the United States: A Reconsideration." *Annual Review of Sociology* 20: 359–81.

Cherney, Isabelle D. and Kamala London. 2006. "Gender-Linked Differences in the Toys, Television Shows, Computer Games, and Outdoor Activities of 5- to 13-Year-Old Children." *Sex Roles: A Journal of Research* 54(9-10, May): 717–26.

Child Labor Public Education Project. "Child Labor in U.S. History." Retrieved 17 July 2006 (www.continuetolearn.uiowa.edu/laborctr/child_labor/About/us_history.html).

Child Welfare Information Gateway. 2004. "Stepparent Adoption: Factsheet for Families." Retrieved 28 September 2007 (www.childwelfare.gov/pubs/f_step.cfm).

—. 2008. "Stepparent Adoption: Factsheet for Families." Retrieved 13 April 2010 (www.childwelfare.gov/pubs/f_step.cfm).

Children's Defense Fund Issue Basics. 2005 April. *Child Care Basics*.

Children's Defense Fund. 2001. "The State of America's Children: Yearbook 2001."

—. 2005. "Defining Poverty and Why It Matters for Children" (Available online: www.childrensdefensefund.org).

—. 2007. *2006 Annual Report*. Washington, D.C.

—. 2008. *The State of America's Children 2008*. Washington, DC.

—. 2009. "Moments in America for Children." Retrieved 3 May 2010 (www.childrensdefense.org/child-research-data-pulbications/moments-in-america-for-children.html).

Choudhary, Ekta, Jeffrey Coben, and Robert M. Bossarte. 2010. Adverse Health Outcomes, Perpetrator Characteristics, and Sexual Violence Victimization Among U.S. Adult Males. *Journal of Interpersonal Violence* 25: 1523–1541.

Christie, Les. 2009. "Foreclosures: 'April Was a Shocker'." *CNNMoney.Com*, 13 May. Retrieved 9 November 2009 (money.cnn.com/2009/05/13/real_estate/April_foreclosure_stats/).

Christie-Mizell, C. André, Erin M. Pryor, and Elizabeth Grossman, R.B. 2008. "Child Depressive Symptoms, Spanking, and Emotional Support: Differences Between African American and European American Youth." *Family Relations* 57 (July): 335–50.

Christopher, F. Scott and Susan Sprecher. 2000. "Sexuality in Marriage, Dating, and Other Relationships: A Decade Review." *Journal of Marriage and the Family* 62(4): 999–1017.

—. 2001. "Sexuality in Marriage, Dating, and Other Relationships: A Decade Review." In *Understanding Families in the New Millennium: A Decade in Review*, edited by Robert M. Milardo. Minneapolis, MN: National Council on Family Relations.

Chu, Judy. 2005. "Adolescent Boys' Friendships and Peer Group Culture." *New Directions for Child and Adolescent Development* 2005(107): 7–22.

Church, Elizabeth. 1999. "Who Are the People in Your Family? Stepmothers' Diverse Notions of Kinship." *Journal of Divorce and Remarriage* 31: 83–105.

City of Los Angeles, Department of Public Works. 2010. "Living Wage Ordinance: Notice to Employees." Retrieved 3 May 2010 (Bca.lacity.org/site/pdf/lwo/living%20wage%20poster.pdf).

Clark, Josh. 2010. "Employees With Flex Time Put in More Hours." Retrieved 3 May 2010. Discovery News (News.discovery.com/human/telecommuting-productivity-flex-time.html).

Clarke, Cheril N. 2010. *Love and Marriage: The Gay and Lesbian Guide to Dating and Romance.* Dodi Press.

Clarkwest, Andrew. 2007. "Spousal Dissimilarity, Race, and Marital Dissolution." *Journal of Marriage and Family* 69(3, August): 639–53.

Cline, Foster W. and Jim Fay. 1990. *Parenting With Love and Logic: Teaching Children Responsibility.* Colorado Springs, CO: Pinon Press.

Clopper, Cynthia G. and David B. Pisoni. 2004. "Some Acoustic Cues for the Perceptual Categorization of American English Regional Dialects." *Journal of Phonetics* 32: 111–40.

Cloud, John. 2009. "Kids Who Get Spanked May Have Lower IQs." *Time Magazine,* 26 September. Retrieved 4 March 2010 (www.time.com/time/printout/0,8816,1926222,00.html).

Cockerham, William C. 1997. *This Aging Society.* Upper Saddle River, NJ: Prentice Hall.

Cockrell, Stacie, Cathy O'Neill, and Julia Stone. 2008. *Babyproofing Your Marriage: How to Laugh More and Argue Less As Your Family Grows.* New York: HarperCollins.

Cohen, Elizabeth. 2009. "Mom Won't Be Forced to Have C-Section." Retrieved www.cnn.com/2009/HEALTH/10/15/hospitals.ban.vbacs/index.html. CNNhealth.com (2 March 2010).

Cohen, Theodore and John C. Durst. 2001. "Leaving Work and Staying Home: The Impact on Men of Terminating the Male Economic Provider Role." In *Men and Masculinity: A Text-Reader,* edited by T. Cohen. Belmont, CA: Wadsworth Publishing Co.

Cohn, D'Vera. 2009. "The States of Marriage and Divorce: Lots of Ex's Live in Texas." Retrieved 5 April 2010. Pew Research Center (pewresearch.org/pubs/1380/marriage-and-divorce-by-state).

Coleman, Marilyn, Lawrence H. Ganong, and Mark Fine. 2000. "Reinvestigating Remarriage: Another Decade of Progress." *Journal of Marriage and the Family* 62: 1288–307.

CollegeBoard. 2009. "2009-10 College Prices." Retrieved 14 December 2009 (www.collegeboard.com/student/pay/add-it-up/4494.html).

Collins, Randall. 1986. "Courtly Politics and the Status of Women, Ch. 12." pp. 297–322 in *Weberian Sociological Theory.* New York: Cambridge University Press.

Coltrane, Scott. 1997. *Family Man: Fatherhood, Housework, and Gender Equity.* New York: Oxford University Press.

—. 2000. "Research on Household Labor: Modeling and Measuring the Social Embeddedness of Routine Family Work." *Journal of Marriage and the Family* 62 (November): 1208–33.

Commonwealth Fund Commission on a High Performance Health System. 2009 February. *The Path to a High Performance U.S. Health System: A 2020 Vision and the Policies to Pave the Way.* New York: Commonwealth Fund.

Conger, John J. 1975. "Proceedings of the American Psychological Association, Incorporated, for the Year 1974: Minutes of the Annual Meeting of the Council of Representatives." *American Psychologist* 30: 620–51.

Conger, Rand D. and Katherine J. Conger. 2008. "Understanding the Processes Through Which Economic Hardship Influences Families and Children." pp. 64–81 in *Handbook of Families and Poverty,* edited by D. R. Crane and T. B. Heaton. Thousand Oaks, CA: Sage Publications.

Conley, Dalton. 2009. *Elsewhere, U.S.A.: How We Got From the Company Man, Family Dinners, and the Affluent Society to the Home Office, BlackBerry Moms, and Economic Anxiety.* New York: Pantheon.

Cooney, Teresa M. and Jeong Shin An. 2006. "Women in the Middle Generational Position and Grandmothers' Adjustment to Raising Grandchildren." *Journal of Women & Aging* 18(2): 3–24.

Coontz, Stephanie. 1992. *The Way We Never Were: American Families and the Nostalgia Trap.* New York: Basic Books.

—. 1997. *The Way We Really Are: Coming to Terms With America's Changing Families.* New York: Basic Books.

—. 2000. *The Way We Never Were: American Families and the Nostalgia Trap.* New York: Basic Books.

—. 2005. "Fact Sheet on Polygamy." Retrieved 26 October 2008. Polygamy.com (www.polygamy.com/articles/templates/?a=171&z=3).

—. 2006. "Three 'Rules' That Don't Apply." *Newsweek,* 5 June, p. 49.

—. 2007. "The Paradoxical Origins of Modern Divorce." *Family Process* 46 (March): 7–16.

Cooper, Carey E., Sara S. McLanahan, Sarah O. Meadows, and Jeanne Brooks-Gunn. 2009. "Family Structure Transitions and Maternal Parenting Stress." *Journal of Marriage and Family* 71(3, August): 558–74.

Cooper, M. Lynne, Mark Pioli, Ash Levitt, Amelia E. Talley, Lada Micheas, and Nancy L. Collins. 2006. "Attachment Styles, Sex Motives, and Sexual Behavior: Evidence for

Gender-Specific Expressions of Attachment Dynamics." pp. 243–74 in *Dynamics of Romantic Love: Attachment, Caregiving, and Sex*, edited by M. Mikulincer and G. S. Goodman. New York: Guilford Press.

Cornell Gerontology Research Institute. 2000. "His and Her Retirement? The Role of Gender and Marriage in the Retirement Process." Issue Brief. *The Edward R. Roybal Centers for Research on Applied Gerontology*, Fall.

Corsaro, William A. 1997. *A Sociology of Childhood*. Thousand Oaks, CA: Pine Forge Press.

Cosentino, Barbra Williams. 2006. "Elective Cesarean: Is It For You?" Retrieved 16 December 2009. Babycenter (www.babycenter.com/0_elective-cesarean-is-it-for-you_1498696.bc).

Costanzo, Erin S., Susan K. Lutgendorf, Anil K. Sood, Barrie Anderson, Joel Sorosky, and David M. Lubaroff. 2005. "Psychosocial Factors and Interleukin-6 Among Women With Advanced Ovarian Cancer." *Cancer* 104(22 15 July): 305–313.

Cott, Nancy F. 1978. "Passionlessness: An Interpretation of Victorian Sexual Ideology, 1790–1850." *Signs* 4: 219–36.

—. 2000. *Public Vows: A History of Marriage and the Nation*. Cambridge, MA: Harvard University Press.

Covel, Simona. 2003. "The Heart Never Forgets." *American Demographics*, July 1.

Covenant Marriage Movement. 2008. "Home Page." Retrieved 22 February 2010 (www.covenantmarriage.com/index.php).

Cowan, Philip A., Carolyn P. Cowan, Marsha K. Pruett, Kyle D. Pruett, and Jessie J. Wong. 2009. "Promoting Fathers' Engagement With Children: Preventive Interventions for Low-Income Families." *Journal of Marriage and Family* 71(3rd edition): 663–79.

Cox, Martha J., Blair Paley, Margaret Burchinal, and C. Chris Payne. 1999. "Marital Perceptions and Interactions Across the Transition to Parenthood." *Journal of Marriage and the Family* 61: 611–25.

Craig, Lyn. 2006. "Does Father Care Mean Fathers Share?" *Gender & Society* 20(2): 259–81.

Crandall, Marie L., Avery B. Nathens, Mary A. Kernic, Victoria L. Holt, and Frederick P. Rivara. 2004. "Predicting Future Injury Among Women in Abusive Relationships." *Trauma-Injury Infection and Critical Care* 56(4): 906–12.

Crissey, Sarah R. 2005. "Race/Ethnic Differences in the Marital Expectations of Adolescents: The Role of Romantic Relationships."*Journal of Marriage and Family* 67(3): 697–709.

—. 2009 January. *Educational Attainment in the United States: 2007*. Current Population Reports No. P20-560. Washington, DC: U.S. Census Bureau.

Crohn, Helen M. 2006. "Five Styles of Positive Stepmothering From the Perspective of Young Adult Stepdaughters." *Journal of Divorce and Remarriage* 46(1): 119–34.

Crompton, Rosemary. 2006. "Class and Family." *Sociological Review* 54(4): 658–77.

Crowl, Alicia, Soyeon Ahn, and Jean Baker. 2008. "A Meta-Analysis of Developmental Outcomes for Children of Same-Sex and Heterosexual Parents." *Journal of GLBT Family Studies* 4(3): 385–407.

Cruz, J. Michael. 2003. "'Why Doesn't He Just Leave?': Gay Male Domestic Violence and the Reasons Victims Stay." *The Journal of Men's Studies* 11(3): 309–23.

Cuber, John F. and Peggy B. Haroff. 1965. *Sex and the Significant Americans*. Baltimore, MD: Penguin.

Cui, Ming, M. Brent Donnellan, and Rand D. Conger. 2007. "Reciprocal Influences Between Parents' Marital Problems and Adolescent Internalizing and Externalizing Behavior." *Developmental Psychology* 43(6): 1544–52.

Cummings, E. Mark, Alice C. Schermerhorn, Davies, Marcie C. Goeke-Morey, and Jennifer S. Cummings. 2006. "Interparental Discord and Child Adjustment: Prospective Investigations of Emotional Security as an Explanatory Mechanism." *Child Development* 77(1): 132–52.

Cunningham, Mick & Thornton, Arland. 2007. "Direct and Indirect Influences of Parents' Marital Instability on Childrens' Attitudes Toward Cohabitation in Young Adulthood." *Journal of Divorce and Remarriage* 46(3): 125–43.

Cunningham, Mick and Arland Thornton. 2005. "The Influence of Union Transitions on White Adults' Attitudes Toward Cohabitation."*Journal of Marriage and Family* 67(3, August): 710–20.

Cunningham-Burley, Sarah. 2001. "The Experience of Grandfatherhood." pp. 92–96 in *Later Life: Connections and Transitions*, edited by Alexis J. Walker, Margaret Manoogian-O'Dell, Lori McGraw and Diana L. White. Thousand Oaks, CA: Pine Forge Press.

Curran, Dolores. 1985. Stress and the Healthy Family: How Healthy Families Handle the 10 Most Common Stresses. New York, NY: Harper Collins.

Curtis, Kristen T. and Christopher G. Ellison. 2002. "Religious Heterogamy and Marital Conflict: Findings From the National Survey of Families and Households." *Journal of Family Issues* 23: 551–76.

D'Emilio, John and Estelle B. Freedman. 1998. *Intimate Matters: A History of Sexuality in America*. New York: Harper & Row.

Dahl, Gordon and Enrico Moretti. 2003. "The Demand for Sons: Evidence From Divorce, Fertility, and Shotgun Marriage," National Bureau of Economic Research, September. Unpublished draft.

—. 2008. "The Demand for Sons." *Review of Economic Studies* 75(4, October): 1085–120.

Dailey, Rene M., Kelly R. Rossetto, Abigail Pfiester, and Catherine A. Surra. 2009. "A Qualitative Analysis of On-Again/Off-Again Romantic Relationships: 'It's Up and Down, All Around'." *Journal of Social and Personal Relationships* 26(4): 443–66.

Daly, Kerry J. 2001. "Deconstructing Family Time: From Ideology to Lived Experience." *Journal of Marriage and Family* 63: 283–94.

Datner, Elizabeth M. Douglas J. Wiebe, Colleen M. Brensinger, and Deborah B. Nelson. 2007. "Identifying Pregnant Women Experiencing Domestic Violence in an Urban Emergency Department." *Journal of Interpersonal Violence* 12(1): 124–35.

Davidson, Michele R. 2002. Outcomes of High-Risk Women Cared For by Certified Nurse-Midwives. *Journal of Midwifery & Women's Health* 47(1 January–February): 46–49.

Davis, Kelly D., W. Benjamin Goodman, Amy E. Pirretti, and David M. Almeida. 2008. "Nonstandard Work Schedules, Perceived Family Well-Being, and Daily Stressors." *Journal of Marriage and Family* 70 (November): 991–1003.

Davis, Kingsley. 1940. "Extreme Social Isolation of a Child." *American Journal of Sociology* 45: 554–65.

—. 1947. "Final Note on a Case of Extreme Isolation." *American Journal of Sociology* 52: 432–37.

Dawley, Katy. 2003. "Origins of Nurse-Midwifery in the United States and Its Expansion in the 1940s." *Journal of Midwifery & Women's Health* 48(2, March/April): 86–95.

Day, Phyllis J. 2009. *A New History of Social Welfare, 6th Ed.* Boston: Allyn & Bacon.

de Jonge, Ank, Birgit van der Goes, Anita Ravelli, Marianne Amelink-Verburg, Ben Mol, Jan Nijhuis, Jack Bennebroek Gravenhorst, and Simone Buitendijk. 2009. "Perinatal Mortality and Morbidity in a Nationwide Cohort of 529688 Low-Risk Planned Home and Hospital Births." *BCOG: An International Journal of Obstetrics & Gynaecology* 116(9): 1177–84.

De Lew, Nancy, George Greenbery, and Kraig Kinchen. 1992. A Layman's Guide to the U.S. Health Care System. Health Care Financing Review 14: 151–165.

DeNavas-Walt, Carmen, Bernadette D. Proctor, and Jessica C. Smith, U.S. Census Bureau, Current Population Reports, P60-238, Income, Poverty, and Health Insurance Coverage in the United States: 2009, U.S. Government Printing Office, Washington, DC, 2010.

de Rougemont, Denis. 1956. *Love in the Western World.* New York: Pantheon.

Deal, Ron L. and Laura Petherbridge. 2009. *The Smart Stepmom: Practical Steps to Help You Thrive.* Ada, MI: Bethany House.

Degler, Carl N. 1980. *At Odds: Women and the Family in America From the Revolution to the Present.* New York: Oxford University Press.

DeKeseredy, Walter S. and Martin D. Schwartz. 1998. *Woman Abuse on Campus: Results From the Canadian National Survey.* Thousand Oaks, CA: Sage Publications.

DeLamater, John J. and Morgan Sill. 2010. "Sexual Desire in Later Life." P. in Chapter 6: Sexual Practices in *Sex Matters: The Sexuality and Society Reader, 3rd Ed.*, edited by Mindy Stombler, Dawn M. Baunach, Elisabeth O. Burgess, Denise Donnelly, Wendy Simonds and Elroi J. Windsor, eds. Boston: Pearson Education Inc.

DeLeire, Thomas and Ariel Kalil. 2005. "How Do Cohabiting Couples With Children Spend Their Money?" *Journal of Marriage and Family* 67 (May): 286–95.

Demo, David H. and Katherine R. Allen. 1996. "Diversity Within Lesbian and Gay Families: Challenges and Implications for Family Theory and Research." *Journal of Social and Personal Relationships* 13(3): 415–34.

Demos, John. 1970. *A Little Commonwealth: Family Life in Plymouth Colony.* New York: Oxford University Press.

—. 1986. "The Rise and Fall of Adolescence." In *Past, Present, and Personal.* New York: Oxford University Press.

DeNavas-Walt, Carmen, Bernadette D. Proctor, and Jessica D. Smith. 2008. September. Income, *Poverty, and Health Insurance Coverage in the United States: 2007.* Technical Report No. P60–235. Washington, DC: U.S. Census Bureau.

—. 2009. September. *Income, Poverty, and Health Insurance Coverage in the United States: 2008.* Technical Report No. P60–236(RV). Washington, DC: U.S. Census Bureau.

Dennison, Renee Peltz and Susan Silverberg Koerner. 2008. "A Look at Hopes and Worries About Marriage: The Views of Adolescents Following a Parental Divorce." *Journal of Divorce and Remarriage* 48(3/4): 91–107.

DePaulo, Bella. 2006. *Singled Out: How Singles Are Stereotyped, Stigmatized, and Ignored, and Still Live Happily Ever After.* New York: St. Martin's Press.

DePaulo, Bella M., and Wendy L. Morris. 2005. Singles in Society and in Science. *Psychological Inquiry* 16(2-3): 57–83.

Derne, Steve. 2003. "Arnold Schwarzenegger, Ally McBeal, and Arranged Marriages: Globalization's Effect on Ordinary People in India." *Contexts* 2(1): 12-18. Reprinted. pp. 146–153 in *Globalization: The Transformation of Social Worlds*, edited by D. S. Eitzen and M. Baca Zinn. Belmont, CA: Wadsworth Publishing Co., 2006.

Desmond, Katherine A. and Thomas Rice. 2007 September. *The Burden of Out-of-Pocket Health Spending Among Older Versus Younger Adults: Analysis From the Consumer Expenditure Survey, 1998-2003.* Medicare Issue Brief. Menlo Park, CA: The Henry J. Kaiser Family Foundation.

Deuisch, Francine M., Carla M. Zelenski, and Mary E. Clark. 1986. "Is There a Double Standard of Aging?" *Journal of Applied Social Psychology* 16(9): 771–85.

DeVito, Joseph A. 2011a. *Essentials of Human Communication, 7th Ed.* Boston: Allyn & Bacon.

—. 2011b. *Interpersonal Messages; Communication and Relationship Skills, 2nd Ed.* Boston: Allyn & Bacon.

Dewar, Gwen. 2009. "How to Help Kids Make Friends: Evidence-Based Tips." *Parenting Science.* Retrieved 21 October 2009. www.parentingscience.com/kids-make-friends.html.

DeWolfe, Chris and Tom Anderson, 3 February. 2009. "Founders of MySpace, Interviewed by Charlie Rose." The Charlie Rose Show, PBS.

Dhaher, Enas A., Rafael T. Mikolaczyk, Annette E. Maxwell, and Alexander Krämer. 2010. "Attitudes Toward Wife Beating Among Palestinian Women of Reproductive Age From Three Cities in West Bank." *Journal of Interpersonal Violence* 25(3): 518–37.

Dickens, A.G. 1977. *The Courts of Europe: Politics, Patronage, and Royalty, 1400-1800.* New York: McGraw-Hill.

Didion, Joan. 2006. *The Year of Magical Thinking.* New York: Vintage Books.

Diekman, Amanda B. & Murnen, Sarah K. 2004. "Learning to Be Little Women and Little Men: The Inequitable Gender Equality of Nonsexist Children's Literature." *Sex Roles: A Journal of Research,* March.

Dill, Bonnie Thornton and Ruth Enid Zambrana. 2009. *Emerging Intersections: Race, Class, and Gender in Theory, Policy, and Practice.* New Brunswick, NJ: Rutgers University Press.

Dilworth-Anderson, Peggye. 2001. "Extended Kin Networks in Black Families." pp. 104–06 in *Families in Later Life: Connections and Transitions,* edited by Alexis J. Walker, Margaret Manoogian-O'Dell, Lori A. McGraw and Diana L. White. Thousand Oaks: Pine.

Dodson, Lisa and Jillian Dickert. 2004. "Girls' Family Labor in Low-Income Households: A Decade of Qualitative Research."*Journal of Marriage and Family* 66: 318–32.

Domhoff, G. William. 2005. *Who Rules America: Power, Politics, and Social Change.* New York: McGraw-Hill.

Domingue, Rachel and Debra Mollen. 2009. "Attachment and Conflict Communication in Adult Romantic Relationships." *Journal of Social and Personal Relationships* 26(5): 678–96.

Doss, Brian D., Galena K. Rhoades, Scott M. Stanley, and Howard J. Markham. 2009. "The Effect of the Transition to Parenthood on Relationship Quality: An Eight-Year Prospective Study." *Journal of Personality and Social Psychology* 96: 601–19.

Dover, Kenneth J. 1978. *Greek Homosexuality.* Cambridge, MA: Harvard University Press.

Downs, Barbara. 2003 October. *Fertility of American Women: June 2002.* Current Population Reports No. P20-548. Washington DC: US Census Bureau.

Dr. Phil.com. 2009 November. "Advice-Spanking Research." Retrieved 26 March 2010 (www.drphil.com/articles/article/256).

Drago, Robert. 2009. "The Parenting of Infants: A Time-Use Study." *Monthly Labor Review* 132(10, October): 33–43.

Dubowitz, Howard, Susan Feigelman, Donna Harrington, Raymond Starr, Susan Zuravin, and Richard Sawyer. 1994. "Children in Kinship Care: How Do They Fare?" *Children and Youth Services Review* 16(1-2): 85–106.

Dumas, Tara M., Heather Lawford, Thanh-Thanh Tieu, and Michael W. Pratt. 2009. "Positive Parenting in Adolescence and Its Relation to Low Point Narration and Identity Status in Emerging Adulthood: A Longitudinal Analysis." *Developmental Psychology* 45(6, November): 1531–44.

Duncan, Greg J., Bessie Wilkerson, and Paula England. 2006. "Cleaning Up Their Act: The Effects of Marriage and Cohabitation on Licit and Illicit Drug Use." *Demography* 43(4, November): 691–710.

Dunn, Daniel M. and Lisa J. Goodnight. 2011. *Communication: Embracing Difference.* Boston: Allyn & Bacon.

Duntley, Joshua D. and David M. Buss. 2008. "Evolutionary Psychology is a Meta-Theory for Psychology." *Psychological Inquiry* 19: 30–34.

Dupuis, Sara B. 2007. "Examining Remarriage: A Look at Issues Affecting Remarried Couples and the Implications Towards Therapeutic Techniques." *Journal of Divorce & Remarriage* 48(1-2, December): 91–104.

Duvall, Evelyn. 1977. *Marriage and Family Development.* Philadelphia: Lippincott.

Duvall, Evelyn and Brent Miller. 1985. *Marriage and Family Development (6th Ed.).* New York: Harper and Row.

Duxbury, Linda, Sean Lyons, and Christopher Higgins. 2008. "Too Much to Do, and Not Enough Time: An Examination of Role Overload." pp. 125–40 in *Handbook of Work-Family Integration: Research, Theory, and Best Practices,* edited by Karen Korabik, Donna S. Lero and Denise L. Whitehead. Amsterdam: Elsevier.

Dwyer, Kathleen M., Bridget K. Fredstrom, Kenneth H. Rubin, Cathryn Booth-LaForce, Linda Rose-Krasnor, and Kim B. Burgess. 2010. "Attachment, Social Information Processing, and Friendship Quality of Early Adolescent Girls and Boys." *Journal of Social and Personal Relationships* 27(1): 91–116.

Dye, Jane Lawler. May 2008. *Participation of Mothers in Government Assistance Programs: 2004.* Current Population Reports No. pp. 70–116. Washington, DC: U.S. Census Bureau.

Dykstra, Pearl A. and Aafke E. Komter. 2006. "Structural Characteristics of Dutch Kin Networks." pp. 21–43 in *Family Solidarity in the Netherlands,* edited by Pearl A. Dykstra, Matthijs Kalmijn, Trudee C. Knijn, Aafke E. Komter, Aart C. Liefbloer and Clara H. Mulder. Amsterdam: Dutch University Press.

Eastwick, Paul W. and Eli J. Finkel. 2008. "Sex Differences in Mate Preferences Revisited: Do People Know What They Initially Desire in a Romantic Partner?" *Journal of Personality and Social Psychology* 94(2, February): 245–64.

Eaton, Daince K., Laura Kann, Steve Kinchen, Shari Shanklin, James Ross, Joseph Hawkins, William A. Harris, Richard Lowry, Tim McManus, David Chyen, Connie Lim, Nancy D. Brener, and Howell Wechsler. 2008 August 8. *Youth Risk Behavior Surveillance—United States, 2007.* Technical Report No. Morbidity and Mortality Weekly Report, v. 57, no. SS-4. Atlanta, GA: Centers for Disease Control and Prevention.

Economist.com. 2004. "Ever Higher Society, Ever Harder to Ascend." Retrieved 24 June 2006 (www.economist.com/world/na/PrinterFriendly.cfm?story_id=3518560).

Edin, Kathryn and Maria Kefalas. 2005. *Promises I Can Keep: Why Poor Women Put Motherhood Before Marriage.* Chicago, IL: University of Chicago Press.

Edin, Kathryn and Laura Lein. 1997. *Making Ends Meet: How Single Mothers Survive Welfare and Low-Wage Work.* New York: Russell Sage Foundation.

Edin, Kathryn, and Rebecca Joyce Kissane. 2010. Poverty and the American Family: A Decade in Review. *Journal of Marriage and Family* 72(3 June): 460–479.

Edwards, Renee and Mark A. Hamilton. 2004. "You Need to Understand My Gender Role: An Empirical Test of Tannen's Model of Gender and Communication." *Sex Roles* 50(7/8): 491–504.

Eggebeen, David J. 2005. "Cohabitation and Exchanges of Support." *Social Forces* 83(3): 1097–110.

Ehrenreich, Barbara. 2001. *Nickel and Dimed: On (Not) Getting By in America.* New York: Henry Holt and Co.

Ehrenreich, Barbara and Deirdre English. 1989. *For Her Own Good: 150 Years of Experts' Advice to Women.* New York: Anchor Books/Doubleday.

Einstein, Elizabeth and Linda Albert. 2005. *Strengthening Your Stepfamily.* Atascadero, CA: Impact Publishers.

Eitzen, D. Stanley and Kelly Eitzen Smith. 2009 http: //www.census.gov/Press-Release/www/releases/archives/facts_for_features_special_editions/014346.html. *Experiencing Poverty: Voices From the Bottom.* Upper Saddle River, NJ: Prentice Hall.

Ekerdt, David J. 2009. "Frontiers of Research on Work and Retirement." *The Journals of Gerontology: Series B* 65B(1): 69–80.

El-Sheikh, Mona, Joseph A. Buckhalt, Peggy S. Keller, E. Mark Cummings, and Christine Acebo. 2007. "Child Emotional Insecurity and Academic Achievement: The Role of Sleep Disruptions." *Journal of Family Psychology* 21(1): 29–38.

Elder Jr., Glen H. 1998. "The Life Course and Human Development." pp. 939–91 in *Handbook of Child Psychology,* vol. Vol. 1, 5th ed., edited by Richard M. Lerner. Theoretical Models of Human Development. New York: Wiley.

Elder, Jr., Glen H. 1999. *Children of the Great Depression: Social Change in Life Experience. 25th Anniversary Edition.* Boulder, CO: Westview Press (Originally published in 1974, University of Chicago Press).

Elliott, Leland, Cynthia Brantley, and Cynthia Johnson. 1997. *Sex on Campus: The Naked Truth aAbout the Real Sex Lives Of College Students.* New York: Random House.

Elwert, Felix and Nicholas A. Christakis. 2006. "Widowhood and Race." *American Sociological Review* 71(1): 16–41.

Embassy of France. 2006. "Childcare." Retrieved 15 January 2006. Embassy of France in the United States (www.ambafrance-us.org/atoz/childcare.asp).

Employee Benefit Research Institute. 2009. "Domestic Partner Benefits: Facts and Background." Retrieved 26 October 2009 (www.ebri.org/pdf/publications/facts/0209fact.pdf).

Encyclopedia of Surgery. 2009. "Sex Reassignment Surgery." Retrieved 21 February 2010 (www.surgeryencyclopedia.com/Pa-St/Sex-Reassignment-Surgery.html).

Engels, Friedrich. 1902, original 1884. *The Origin of the Family.* Chicago: Charles H. Kerr and Co.

England, Paula and Reuben Thomas. 2007. "The Decline of the Date and the Rise of the College Hook Up." In *Family in Transition,* edited by A. S. Skolnick and J. H. Skolnick. Boston: Allyn & Bacon.

Entertainment Software Association. 2010. "Industry Facts." Retrieved 16 April 2010 (www.theesa.com/facts/index.asp).

Epstein, Marina, Jerel P. Calzo, Andrew P. Smiler, and L. Monique Ward. 2009. "'Anything From Making Out to Having Sex': Men's Negotiations of Hooking Up and Friends With Benefits Scripts." *Journal of Sex Research* 46(5, September-October): 414–24.

Erens, Bob, Sally McManus, Alison Prescott, and Julia Field. 2003 April. *National Survey of Sexual Attitudes and Lifestyles II: Reference Tables and Summary Report.* London: National Centre for Social Research.

Eskridge, Jr., WIlliam N. and Darren R. Spedale. 2006. *Gay Marriage: For Better or for Worse?* New York: Oxford University Press.

Etaugh, Claire. 2003. "Witches, Mothers, & Others: Females in Children's Books." *Bradley University Hilltopics* (Peoria, IL), Winter, pp. 10–13.

Evans, Gary W., Carrie Gonnella, Lyscha A. Marcynyszyn, L. Gentile, and N. Salpekar. 2005. "The Role of Chaos in Poverty and Children's Socioemotional Adjustment." *Psychological Science* 16(7, July): 560–65.

Evenson, Ranae J. and Robin W. Simon. 2006. "Clarifying the Relationship Between Parenthood and Depression." *Journal of Health and Social Behavior* 46: 341–58.

Evertsson, Marie and Magnus Nermo. 2004. "Dependence Within Families and the Division of Labor: Comparing Sweden and the United States." *Journal of Marriage and Family* 66 (December): 1272–86.

Fagan, Jay. 2009. "Relationship Quality and Changes in Depressive Symptoms Among Urban, Married African Americans, Hispanics, and Whites." *Family Relations* 58(3, July): 259–74.

Fairris, David and Michael Reich. 2005. "The Impacts of Living Wage Policies: Introduction to the Special Issue." *Industrial Relations* 44(1): 1–13.

Families and Work Institute. 2004. *Workplace Flexibility: What Is It? Who Has It? Who Wants It? Does It Make a Difference?* New York: Families and Work Institute.

Family Focus. 2008. "Same-Sex 'Marriage' and Civil Unions." Retrieved 25 June 2008 (www.family.org/socialissues/A000000464.cfm).

Farley, John E. 2010. *Majority-Minority Relations, 6th Ed.* Upper Saddle River, NJ: Prentice Hall.

Farr, Kathryn. 2005. *Sex Trafficking: The Global Market in Women and Children*. New York: Worth Publishers.

Farrell, Betty G. 1999. *Family: The Making of an Idea, an Institution, and a Controversy in American Culture.* Boulder, CO: Westview Press.

Federal Interagency Forum on Aging Related Statistics. 2008 March. *Older Americans 2008: Key Indicators of Well-Being.*

Federal Interagency Forum on Child and Family Statistics. 2009. *America's Children: Key National Indicators of Well-Being, 2009.*

Feeney, Judith A. and Patricia Noller. 2004. "Attachment and Sexuality in Close Relationships." In *Handbook of Sexuality in Close Relationships*. Mahwah, NJ: Lawrence Erlbaum.

Fehr, Beverly. 1988. "Prototype Analysis of the Concepts of Love and Commitment." *Journal of Personality and Social Psychology* 55(4): 557–79.

—. 1993. "How Do I Love Thee? Let Me Consult My Prototype." pp. 87–120 in *Individuals in Relationships*, edited by Stephen Duck. Thousand Oaks, CA: Sage Publications.

Fehr, Beverly, Susan Sprecher, and Lynn G. Underwood. 2009. *The Science of Compassionate Love: Research, Theory, and Practice.* Malden, MA: Wiley-Blackwell.

Feiring, Candice. 2002. "Learning the Ways of Romance." In *Readings on Adolescence and Emerging Adulthood.* Jeffrey J. Arnett, ed. pp. 173–182. Upper Saddle River, NJ: Prentice Hall.

Feldman, Robert S. 2010. *Child Development, 5th Ed.* Upper Saddle River, NJ: Prentice Hall.

Felmlee, Diane H. 2001. "From Appealing to Appalling: Disenchantment With a Romantic Partner." *Sociological Perspectives* 44(3): 263–80.

Felmlee, Diane H. and Anna Muraco. 2009. "Gender and Friendship Norms Among Other Adults." *Research on Aging* 31(3, 1 May): 318–44.

Felmlee, Diane H. and Susan Sprecher. 2006. "Love: Psychological and Sociological Perspectives." pp. 389–409 in *Handbook of Sociology of Emotions*, edited by J. E. Stets and J. H. Turner.

Felson, Richard B. 2006. "Is Violence Against Women About Women or About Violence?" *Contexts* 5(2): 21–25.

Fenigstein, Allan and Matthew Preston. 2007. "The Desired Number of Sexual Partners as a Function of Gender, Sexual Risks, and the Meaning of 'Ideal'." *Journal of Sex Research* 44(1): 89–95.

Fenstermaker Berk, S. 1985. *The Gender Factory: The Apportionment of Work in American Households.* New York: Plenum Press.

Fetto, John. 2003. "Love Stinks." *American Demographics* 25: 10–11.

Few, April L. and Karen H. Rosen. 2005. "Victims of Chronic Dating Violence: How Women's Vulnerabilities Link to Their Decisions to Stay." *Family Relations* 54 (April): 265–79.

Fields, Jason. 2003. "Children's Living Arrangements and Characteristics: March 2002." In *Current Population Reports, P20-547.* U.S. Census Bureau, U.S. Department of Commerce.

—. 2004. *America's Families and Living Arrangements: 2003.* Technical Report No. P20-553. Washington, D.C.: U.S. Census Bureau, November.

Fields, Jason and Lynne M. Casper. 2001. "America's Families and Living Arrangements: March 2000." In *Current Population Reports, P20-537.* Washington D.C.: U.S. Census Bureau.

Filion, Kai. 2009. "Fact Sheet for 2009 Minimum Wage Increase—Minimum Wage Issue Guide." Retrieved 3 May 2010. Economic Policy Institute (www.epi.org/publications/entry/mwig_fact_sheet/).

Filson, Jennifer, Emilio Ulloa, Cristin Runfola, and Audrey Hokoda. 2010. "Does Powerlessness Explain the Relationship Between Intimate Partner Violence and Depression?" *Journal of Interpersonal Violence* 25(3): 400–15.

Fine, Mark, Lawrence H. Ganong, and Marilyn Coleman. 1997. "Consistency in Perceptions of the Step-Parent Role Among Step-Parents, Parents, and Stepchildren." *Journal of Social and Personal Relationships* 15: 810–28.

Finer, Lawrence B. 2007. "Trends in Premarital Sex in the United States, 1954-2003." *Public Health Reports* 122 (January-February): 73–78.

Fingerman, Karen L. 2004. "The Role of Offspring and In-Laws in Grandparents' Ties to Their Grandchildren." *Journal of Family Issues* 25: 1026–49.

Finlay, Barbara. 2007. *Before the Second Wave: Gender in the Sociological Tradition*. New York: Prentice Hall.

Finley, Gordon E., Sandra D. Mira, and Seth J. Schwartz. 2008. "Perceived Paternal and Maternal Involvement: Factor Structures, Mean Differences, and Paternal Roles." *Fathering* 6(1, Winter): 62–82.

Firestone, Robert W., Lisa A. Firestone, and Joyce Catlett. 2008. *Sex and Love in Intimate Relationships*. Washington, DC: APA Press.

Fisher, Allen P. 2003. "A Critique of the Portrayal of Adoption in College Textbooks and Readers on Families, 1998-2001."*Family Relations* 52: 154–60.

Fisher, Bonnie S., Francis T. Cullen, and Michael G. Turner. 2000. *The Sexual Victimization of College Women*. Technical Report No. NCJ 182369. Washington, DC: U.S. Department of Justice, National Institute of Justice.

Fisher, Bonnie S. and Saundra L. Regan. 2006. "The Extent and Frequency of Abuse in the Lives of Older Women and Their Relationship With Health Outcomes." *The Gerontologist* 46: 200–09.

Fisher, Helen E. 2000. *The First Sex: The Natural Talents of Women and How They Are Changing the World*. New York: Ballantine Books.

Fisher, Helen. 2004. *Why We Love: The Nature and Chemistry of Romantic Love*. New York, NY: Owl Books.

—. 2009. "Jealousy—The Monster." *O, The Oprah Magazine*, September.

—. 2010. *Why Him? Why Her?: How to Find and Keep Lasting Love*. New York: Henry Holt and Company.

Fisher, Helen, Arthur Aron, and Lucy L. Brown. 2006. "Romantic Love: A Mammalian Brain System for Mate Choice." *Philosophical Transactions of the Royal Society* 361: 2173–86.

Fisher, Helen and Jr. Thomson, J. Anderson. 2007. "Lust, Romance, Attraction, Attachment: Do the Side-Effects of Serotonin-Enhancing Antidepressants Jeopardize Romantic Love, Marriage and Fertility?" pp. 245–83 in *Evolutionary Cognitive Neuroscience*, edited by Steven M. Platek, Julian P. Keenan and Todd K. Shakelford. Cambridge, MA: MIT Press.

Fisher, Kimberley, Muriel Egerton, Jonathan I. Gershuny, and John P. Robinson. 2006. Gender Convergence in the American Heritage Time Use Study (AHTUS). *Social Indicators Research* 82(1): 1–33.

Fitzgerald, F. Scott. 1925 (Reprinted 1999). *The Great Gatsby*. New York: Scribner.

Fitzpatrick, Laura. 2009. "A Brief History of China's One Child Policy." *Time*, 27 July. Retrieved 9 November 2009 (www.time.com/time/world/article/0,8599,1912861,00.html).

Fleck, Carole. 2009. "Grandparents Help Out." Retrieved 4 December 2009. AARP Bulletin Today (bulletin.aarp.org/yourmoney/personalfinance/articles/more_grandparents_giving_money_to_kids_.html).

Fletcher-Janzen, Elaine. 2009. "Intelligent Testing: Bridging the Gap Between Classical and Romantic Science in Assessment." pp. 15–29 in *Intelligent Testing: Integrating Psychological Theory and Clinical Practice*, edited by J. C. Kaufman. New York: Cambridge University Press.

Flood, Michael. 2008. "Men, Sex, and Homosociality: How Bonds Between Men Shape Their Sexual Relations With Women." *Men and Masculinities* 10(1): 339–359.

Flood, Michael and Bob Pease. 2009. "Factors Influencing Attitudes to Violence Against Women." *Trauma, Violence, & Abuse* 10(2): 125–42.

Foucault, Michel. 1978. *The History of Sexuality: An Introduction (R. Hurley Translation)*. Harmondsworth: Penguin.

Fox, Greer L., Carol Bruce, and Terri. Combs-Orme. 2000. "Parenting Expectations and Concerns of Fathers and Mothers of Newborn Infants." *Family Relations* 49(2): 123–31.

Fraley, R. Chris and Phillip R. Shaver. 2000. "Adult Romantic Attachment: Theoretical Developments, Emerging Controversies and Unanswered Questions." *Review of General Psychology* 4(2): 132–54.

Frank, Hallie. 2008. "The Influence of Divorce on the Relationship Between Adult Parent-Child and Adult Sibling Relationships."*Journal of Divorce & Remarriage* 48(3–4, February): 21–32.

Franklin II, Clyde W. 1992. "'Hey, Home—Yo, Bro.' Friendship Among Black Men." In *Men's Friendships*. Peter M. Nardi, ed. pp. 201–214. Newbury Park, CA: Sage Publications.

Frech, Adrianne and Kristi Williams. 2007. "Depression and the Psychological Benefits of Entering Marriage." *Journal of Health and Social Behavior* 48(2): 149–63.

Fredrix, Emily. 2008. "Not-Such-Baby 'Boomerangs' Adults Returning to Nest Often Deplete." *Oakland Tribune* (Oakland, CA), 22 March.

Freeman, Richard. 2005. "Fighting for Other Folks' Wages: The Logic and Illogic of Living Wage Campaigns." *Industrial Relations* 44(1): 14–31.

Friedan, Betty. 1963. *The Feminine Mystique*. New York: Dell.

Fry, Richard and D'Vera Cohn. 2010. "New Economics of Marriage: The Rise of Wives." Retrieved 20 January 2010 (pewresearch.org/pubs/1466/economics-marriage-rise-of-wives).

Fry, Richard and Jeffrey S. Passel. 2009. "Latino Children: A Majority Are U.S.-Born Offspring of Immigrants." Retrieved 20 January 2010. Pew Hispanic Center (pewhispanic.org/reports/report.php?ReportID=110).

Fryar, Cheryl D., Rosemarie Hirsch, Kathryn S. Porter, Benny Kottiri, Debra J. Brody, and Tatiana Louis. 2007.

"Drug Use and Sexual Behaviors Reported by Adults: United States, 1999-2002." Centers for Disease Control and Prevention, 384. Hyattsville, MD: National Center for Health Statistics, 28 June.

Fulfer, Jamie L., Jillian J. Tyler, Natalie Choi, J.S., Jill A. Young, Steven J. Verhulst, Regina Kovach, and J. Kevin Dorsey. 2007. "Using Indirect Questions to Detect Intimate Partner Violence." *Journal of Interpersonal Violence* 22(2): 238–49.

Furman, Wyndol. 2002. "The Emerging Field of Adolescent Romantic Relationships." *Current Directions in Psychological Science* 11(5): 177–181.

Furman, Jason and Sharon Parrott. 2007. "A $7.25 Minimum Wage Would Be a Useful Step in Helping Working Families Escape Poverty." Retrieved 1 October 2007. Center on Budget and Policy Priorities (www.cbpp.org/1-5-07mw.htm).

Furstenberg, Frank F., Jr. 2007. "Should Government Promote Marriage?" *Journal of Policy Analysis and Management* 26(4): 956–60.

Gadalla, Tahany M. 2008. "Gender Differences in Poverty Rates After Marital Dissolution: A Longitudinal Study." *Journal of Divorce and Remarriage* 49(3/4): 225–38.

—. 2009. "Impact of Marital Dissolution on Men's and Women's Incomes: A Longitudinal Study." *Journal of Divorce & Remarriage* 50(1, January): 55–65.

Gajendran, Ravi and David Harrison. 2007. "The Good, the Bad, and the Unknown About Telecommuting: Meta-Analysis of Psychological Mediators and Individual Consequences." *Journal of Applied Psychology* 92(639-650): 1524–41.

Galinsky, Ellen, Kerstin Aumann, and James T. Bond. 2009. *Times Are Changing: Gender and Generation at Work and at Home.* New York: Families and Work Institute.

Galinsky, Ellen, James T. Bond, and Kelly Sakai. 2008. *2008 National Study of Employers.* New York: Families and Work Institute.

Gallagher, Sally K. 1994. "Doing Their Share: Comparing Patterns of Help Given by Older and Younger Adults." *Journal of Marriage and the Family* 56: 567–78.

Gallagher, Sally K. and Naomi Gerstel. 2001. "Connections and Constraints: The Effects of Children on Caregiving." *Journal of Marriage and the Family* 63: 265–75.

Gallup News Service. 2007. "Whites, Blacks, Hispanics Assess Race Relations in the U.S." Retrieved 7 April 2008 (www.gallup.com/poll/28312/Whites-Blacks-Hispanics-Assess-Race-Relations-US.aspx).

Gallup.com. 2008. "Homosexual Relations." Retrieved 19 September 2008 (www.gallup.com/poll/1651/Homosexual-Relations.aspx).

Galvin, Kathleen M., Carma L. Bylund, and Bernard J. Brommel. 2008. *Family Communication: Cohesion and Change, 7th Ed.* Boston: Allyn & Bacon.

Ganong, Lawrence H. and Marilyn Coleman. 1989. "Preparing for Remarriage: Anticipating the Issues, Seeking Solutions." *Family Relations* 38: 28–33.

—. 1997. "How Society Views Stepfamilies." *Marriage and Family Review* 26: 85–106.

—. 2004. *Stepfamily Relationships: Development, Dynamics, and Interventions.* New York: Kluwer Academic.

Gantert, Tom. 2008. "Having a Husband Adds Work, Study Says." *The Sunday Oregonian,* 6 April, p. A8.

Gardner, Margo, Jodie Roth, and Jeanne Brooks-Gunn. 2008. "Adolescents' Participation in Organized Activities and Developmental Success Two and Eight Years After High School: Do Sponsorship, Duration, and Intensity Matter?" *Developmental Psychology* 44(3): 814–30.

Garfinkel, Irwin, Daniel R. Meyer, and Sara S. McLanahan. 1998. "A Brief History of Child Support Policies in the United States." pp. 14–30 in *Fathers Under Fire: The Revolution in Child Support Enforcement,* edited by Irwin Garfinkel, Sara S. McLanahan, Daniel R. Meyer and Judith A. Seltzer. New York: Russell Sage Foundation.

Garner, Abigail. 2005. *Families Like Mine: Children of Gay Parents Tell It Like It Is.* New York: Harper Paperbacks.

Gartstein, Masha and Mary K. Rothbart. 2009. "Temperament." In *Encyclopedia of Infant and Early Childhood Development,* edited by Marshall Haith and Janette Benson. Elsevier Ltd.

Gasper, Jill A.F., Arnold L. Stolberg, Katherine M. Macie, and Larry J. Williams. 2008. "Coparenting in Intact and Divorced Families: Its Impact on Young Adult Adjustment." *Journal of Divorce & Remarriage* 49(3-4, September): 272–90.

Gately, Natalie J., Lisbeth T. Pike, and Paul T. Murphy. 2005. "An Exploration of the Impact of the Family Court Process on 'Invisible' Stepparents." *Journal of Divorce and Remarriage* DOI: 10.1300/J087v44n03_03: 31–52.

Gates, Gary J. 2006 October. *Same-Sex Couples and the Gay, Lesbian, Bisexual Population: New Estimates From the American Community Survey.* Los Angeles, CA: The Williams Institute.

Gattai, Flavia Budini and Tullia Musatti. 1999. "Grandmothers' Involvement in Grandchildren's Care: Attitudes, Feelings, and Emotions." *Family Relations* 48: 35–42.

Gay & Lesbian Advocates & Defenders. 2008. "Gina and Heidi Nortonsmith." Retrieved 3 July 2008 (www.glad.org/marriage/Goodridge/Gina&Heidi.shtml).

General Social Survey. 2009. *Dataset: General Social Surveys, 1972-2006 [Cumulative File] Characteristics Ascribed to Blacks* [MRDF]. www.norc.org/GSS+Website/Browse+GSS+Variables/Subject+Index/ [producer].

Gentleman, Amelia. 2008. "India Nurtures Business of Surrogate Motherhood." Retrieved 20 December 2009.

New York Times (travel.nytimes.com/2008/03/10/world/asia/10surrogate.html?sq=women&st=nyt&scp=19&pagewanted=all).

Gerson, Kathleen. 2001. "Dilemmas of Involved Fatherhood." pp. 324–39 in *Shifting the Center: Understanding Contemporary Families*, edited by Susan J. Ferguson. Mountain View, CA: Mayfield Publishing Company.

Gerson, Michael. 2009. "Today's Singles, Lost Without a Courtship Narrative." Retrieved 4 February 2010. washingtonpost.com (www.washingtonpost.com/wp-dyn/content/article/2009/09/15/AR2009091502981.html).

Gettleman, Jeffrey. 2010. "Kenyan Police Disperse Gay Wedding." Retrieved 21 February 2010. New York Times (www.nytimes.com/2010/02/13/world/africa/13kenya.html).

Gibb, Jack R. 1961. "Defensive Communication." *Journal of Communication* 11: 141–48.

Gibson-Davis, Christine M., Kathryn Edin, and Sara McLanahan. 2005. "High Hopes but Even Higher Expectations: The Retreat From Marriage Among Low-Income Couples." *Journal of Marriage and Family* 67: 1301–12.

Gierveld, Jenny de Jong, Marjolein Broese van Groenou, Adriaan W. Hoogendoorn, and Johannes H. Smit. 2008. "Quality of Marriages in Later Life and Emotional and Social Loneliness." *The Journals of Gerontology: Series B* 64B(4): 497–506.

Gilbert, Dennis and Joseph A. Kahl. 1993. *The American Class Structure: A New Synthesis, 4th Ed.* Belmont, CA: Wadsworth.

Giles-Sims, Jean and Charles Lockhart. 2005. "Grandparents' Visitation Rights Using Culture to Explain Cross-State Variation." *Journal of Divorce and Remarriage* 44(3/4): 1–16 (DOI: 10.1300/J087vol44n03_01).

Girschick, Lori B. 2008. *Transgender Voices: Beyond Women and Men.* Lebanon, NH: University Press of New England.

Glenn, Norval D. 1998. "The Course of Marital Success and Failure in Five American 10-Year Marriage Cohorts." *Journal of Marriage and the Family* 60: 569–76.

Glick, Jennifer E. and Jennifer Van Hook. 2002. "Parent's Coresidence With Adult Children: Can Immigration Explain Race and Ethnic Variation?" *Journal of Marriage and the Family* 64: 240–53.

Glynn, Keva, Heather Maclean, Tonia Forte, and Marsha Cohen. 2009. "The Association between Role Overload and Women's Mental Health." *Journal of Women's Health (Larchmont)* 18(2, February): 217–23.

Gold, Joshua M. 2009. "Stepparents and the Law: Knowledge for Counselors, Guidelines for Family Members." *The Family Journal* 17(3, 1 July): 272–76.

Gold, Mitchell and Mindy Drucker. 2008. *Crisis: 40 Stories Revealing the Personal, Social, and Religious Pain and Trauma of Growing Up Gay in America.* Austin, TX: Greenleaf Book Group, LLC.

Goldberg, Abbie E. and Maureen Perry-Jenkins. 2007. "The Division of Labor and Perceptions of Parental Roles: Lesbian Couples Across the Transition to Parenthood." *Journal of Social and Personal Relationships* 24: 297–318.

Gona, Roopa, and Stephanie Merry. 2007. "Can't Buy Me Love?" *The Columbia Journalist.* www.nyc24.org/2007/issue2/story2/.

Gonzales, Felisa. 2008. *Hispanic Women in the United States, 2007 (Fact Sheet).* Washington, DC: Pew Hispanic Center.

Goode, William J. 1959. "The Theoretical Importance of Love." *American Sociological Review* 24: 38–47.

Goodman, Catherine Chase and Merril Silverstein. 2002. "Grandmothers Raising Grandchildren: Family Structure and Well-Being in Culturally Diverse Families." *The Gerontologist* 42(5): 676–89.

Goodman, W. Benjamin, Ann C. Crouter, and The Family Life Project Key Investigators. 2009. "Longitudinal Associations Between Maternal Work Stress, Negative Work-Family Spillover, and Depressive Symptoms." *Family Relations* 58 (July): 245–58.

Goodwin, Paula Y., William D. Mosher, and Anjani Chandra. 2010. *Marriage and Cohabitation in the United States: A Statistical Portrait Based on Cycle 6 (2002) of the National Survey of Family Growth.* Technical Report No. Vital Health Stat 23 (28). National Center for Health Statistics.

Goodwin, Robin. 2009. *Changing Relations: Achieving Intimacy in a Time of Social Transition.* New York: Cambridge University Press.

Gorchoff, Sara M., Oliver P. John, and Ravenna Helson. 2008. "Contextualing Change in Marital Satisfaction During Middle Age: An 18-Year Longitudinal Study." *Psychological Science* 19(11): 1194–200.

Gordon, Linda. 1979. "The Struggle for Reproductive Freedom: Three Stages of Feminism." pp. 107–36 in *Capitalist Patriarchy and the Case for Socialist Feminism*, edited by Z. Eisenstein. New York: Monthly Review Press.

Gordon-Reed, Annette. 2008. *The Hemingses of Monticello: An American Family.* New York: Norton.

Gorer, Geoffrey. 1977. *Death, Grief, and Mourning.* New York: Beaufort Books.

Gornick, Janet C., Presser and Caroline Ratzdorf. 2009. "Outside the 9-to-5." *The American Prospect* 20(5): 21–24.

Gornick, Janet C., Alexandra Heron, and Ross Eisenbrey. 24 May 2007. *The Work-Family Balance: An Analysis of European, Japanese, and U.S Work-Time Policies.* Technical Report No. Briefing Paper #189. Washington, DC: Economic Policy Institute.

Gosselin, Julie. 2010. "Individual and Family Factors Related to Psychosocial Adjustment in Stepmother Families With Adolescents." *Journal of Divorce & Remarriage* 51(2, February): 108–23.

Gosselin, Julie and Hélène David. 2007. "Risk and Resilience Factors Linked With the Psychosocial Adjustment of Adolescents, Stepparents and Biological Parents." *Journal of Divorce & Remarriage* 48(1-2, December): 29–53.

Gottman, John M., James Coan, Sybil Carrere, and Catherine Swanson. 1998. "Predicting Marital Happiness and Stability From Newlywed Interactions."*Journal of Marriage and the Family* 60: 5–22.

Gottman, John M. 1994. *Why Marriages Succeed or Fail.* New York: Simon & Schuster.

Gottman, John and Julie Schwartz Gottman. 2008. *And Baby Makes Three: The Six-Step Plan for Preserving Marital Intimacy and Rekindling Romance After Baby Arrives.* New York: Three Rivers Press.

Goyer, Amy. 2006. "Intergenerational Relationships: Grandparents Raising Grandchildren." Retrieved 29 October 2007. AARP.org (www.aarp.org/research/international/perspectives/nov_05_grandparents.html).

Grall, Timothy S. 2009 November. *Custodial Mothers and Fathers and Their Child Support: 2007.* Current Population Reports No. P60-237. Washington, D.C.: U.S. Census Bureau.

Grant, Jaime M. 2009. *Outing Age: Public Policy Issues Affecting Gay, Lesbian, Bisexual, and Transgender Elders.* National Gay and Lesbian Task Force Policy Institute.

Gray, John. 1992. *Men Are From Mars, Women Are From Venus: A Practical Guide for Improving Communication and Getting What You Want in Your Relationships.* New York: Thorsons.

Gray, Ronald F., Alka Indurkhya, and Marie C. McCormick. 2004. "Prevalence, Stability, and Predictors of Clinically Significant Behavior Problems in Low Birth Weight Children at 3, 5, and 8 Years of Age." *Pediatrics* 114(3, September): 736–43.

Grabill, Wilson H., Clyde V. Kiser, and Pascal K. Whelpton. 1958. *The Fertility of American Women.* New York: Wiley & Sons.

Greenberg, Kenneth. 2009. "Half of Americans Know Someone Who Has Dated a Person They Met Online, According to New Study From People Media." Retrieved 22 January 2010. PRWeb.com (www.prweb.com/printer/2758114.htm).

Greenfield, Emily A. and Nadine F. Marks. 2004. *Linked Lives: Adult Children's Distress and Their Parents' Well-Being.* Center for Democracy and Ecology No. CDF Working Paper No. 2004-27. Madison, WI: University of Wisconsin-Madison.

Greenstein, Theodore N. and Shannon N. Davis. 2006. "Cross-National Variations in Divorce: Effects of Women's Power, Prestige and Dependence." *Journal of Comparative Family Studies* 37: 253–73.

Gregson, Joanna and Michelle L. Ceynar. 2009. "Finding 'Me' Again: Women's Postdivorce Identity Shifts." *Journal of Divorce & Remarriage* 50(8, November): 564–82.

Grello, Catherine M., Deborah P. Welsh, and Melinda S. Harper. 2006. "No Strings Attached: The Nature of Casual Sex in College Students." *The Journal of Sex Research* 43(3, August): 255–67.

Greven, Philip. 1970. *Four Generations: Population, Land, and Family in Colonial Andover, Massachusetts.* Ithaca: Cornell University Press.

Griffith, Wendy. 2006. "A Look at India's Arranged Marriages." Retrieved 24 July 2006. CBN.com (www.cbn.com/cbnnews/news/050323c.aspx).

Grogger, Jeffrey. 2009. "Speech Patterns and Racial Wage Inequality." Working Paper Series 08.13, Harris School of Public Policy, University of Chicago, September.

Groothof, Hinke A.K., Pieternel Dijkstra, and Dick P.H. Barelds. 2010. "Sex Differences in Jealousy: The Case of Internet Infidelity." *Journal of Social and Personal Relationships* 26(8): 1119–29.

Grossman, Arnold H. and Anthony R. D'Augelli. 2006. "Transgender Youth: Invisible and Vulnerable." *Journal of Homosexuality* 51(1): 111–28.

Guerrero, Laura K. and Alana M. Chavez. 2005. "Relational Maintenance in Cross-Sex Friendships Characterized by Different Types of Romantic Intent: An Exploratory Study." *Western Journal of Communication* 69(4): 339–359.

Gutman, Herbert. 1976. *The Black Family in Slavery and Freedom, 1750-1925.* New York: Pantheon.

Guttman, Joseph, Amnon Lazar, and Moran Karni. 2008. "Teachers' and School Children's Stereotypic Perception of the Child of Divorce: 20 Years Later." *Journal of Divorce and Remarriage* 49(1): 131–41.

Haas, Kate. 2010. "Who Will Make Room for the Intersexed?" In *Sex Matters: The Sexuality and Society Reader, 3rd Ed.,* edited by M. Stombler, D. M. Baunach, E. O. Burgess, D. Donnelly, W. Simonds and E. J. Windsor, eds. New York: Prentice Hall.

Haber, Carole. 1983. *Beyond Sixty-Five: The Dilemma of Old Age in America's Past.* Cambridge: Cambridge University Press.

Hadley, Jack. 2007. "Insurance Coverage, Medical Care Use, and Short-Term Health Changes Following an Unintentional Injury or the Onset of a Chronic Condition." *Journal of the American Medical Association* 297(10, 14 March): 1073–84.

Haj-Yahia, Muhammad M. 2010. "Palestinian Physicians' Misconceptions aAbout and Approval of Wife Abuse." *Journal of Interpersonal Violence* 25(3): 416–42.

Hall, Carl T. 2002. "Pediatricians Endorse Gay, Lesbian Adoption 'Children Deserve to Know Their Relationships With Both Parents Are Stable, Legally Recognized'."

Retrieved 13 July 2006. San Francisco Chronicle (www.sfgate.com/cgi-bin/article.cgi?file=/chronicle/archive/2002/02/04/MN227427).

Hall, Edward T. 1966. *The Hidden Dimension.* Garden City, NY: Anchor Books/Doubleday.

—. 1976. *Beyond Culture.* Garden City, NY: Doubleday.

Hall, Mark A., Mary Anne Bobinski, and David Orentlicher. 2008. *Health Care Law and Ethics, 7th Ed.* New York: Aspen.

Haller, Jr., John S. 1972. "From Maidenhood to Menopause: Sex Education for Women in Victorian America." *Journal of Popular Culture* 6(1): 46–69.

Halpern-Felsher, Bonnie L., Jodi L. Cornell, Rhonda Y. Kropp, and Jeanne M. Tschann. 2005. "Oral Versus Vaginal Sex Among Adolescents: Perceptions, Attitudes, and Behavior." *Pediatrics* 115: 845–51.

Hamer, Dean and Peter Copeland. 1994. *The Science of Desire.* New York: Simon and Schuster.

Hamer, Jennifer and Kathleen Marchioro. 2002. "Becoming Custodial Dads: Exploring Parenting Among Low-Income and Working-Class African American Fathers." *Journal of Marriage and the Family* 64: 116–29.

Hamilton, Brady E., Joyce A. Martin, and Stephanie J. Ventura. 2009. "Births: Preliminary Data for 2007." Vol. 57, No. 12. Retrieved 18 August 2009. Hyattsville, MD/National Center for Health Statistics (www.cdc.gov/nchs/data/nvsr/nvsr57/nvsr57_12.pdf).

Hamilton, Brady E., Stephanie J. Ventura, Joyce A. Martin, and Paul D. Sutton. 2006. "Final Births for 2004." Retrieved 13 July 2006. Hyattsville, MD/National Center for Health Statistics (www.cdc.gov/nchs/products/pubs/pubd/hestats/finalbirths04/finalbirths04.htm).

Hammond, Ron J. and Barbara Bearnson. 2003a. "Death and Grief Assessment." pp. 125–26 in *The Marriages and Families Activities Workbook.* Wadsworth.

—. 2003b. *The Marriages and Families Activities Workbook.* Belmont, CA: Wadsworth/Cengage Learning.

Han, Shin-Kap and Phyllis Moen. 1999. "Work and Family Over Time: A Life Course Approach." *The Annals of the American Academy of Political and Social Sciences* 562: 98–110.

Han, Wen-Jui. 2005. "Maternal Nonstandard Work Schedules and Child Cognitive Outcomes." *Child Development* 76: 137–54.

Han, Wen-Jui, Christopher Ruhm, J., and Jane Waldfogel. 2009. "Parental Leave Policies and Parents' Employment and Leave-Taking."*Journal of Policy Analysis and Management* 28(1): 29–54.

Han, Wen-Jui, Christopher Ruhm, Jane Waldfogel, and Elizabeth Washbrook. 2009. Public Policies and Women's Employment After Childbearing. Electronic document. National Bureau of Economic Research Working Paper No. 14660. www.nber.org/papers/w14660 Cambridge, MA.

Handel, Gerald, Spencer E. Cahill, and Frederick Elkin. 2007. *Children and Society: The Sociology of Children and Childhood Socialization.* New York: Oxford University Press.

Hanson, Barbara and Carol Knopes. 1993. "Prime Time Tuning Out Varied Cultures." *USA Today,* 6 July.

Hardy, Melissa A. and Kim Shuey. 2000. "Retirement." pp. 2401–10 in *Encyclopedia of Sociology,* 2d ed., edited by Edgar F. Borgatta and Rhonda J. Montgomery. New York: Macmillan.

Hareven, Tamara K. 1977. "The Historical Study of the Family in Urban Society." In *Family and Kin in American Urban Communities, 1780-1940,* edited by T. K. Hareven. New York: Franklin and Watts.

—. 2000. *Families, History, and Social Change: Life Course; Cross-Cultural Perspectives.* Westview Press: Boulder, CO.

Harvey, John H. and Mark Fine. 2004. *Children of Divorce: Stories of Loss and Growth.* Mahwah, NJ: Lawrence Erlbaum Associates.

Harvey, John H., Amy Wenzel, and Susan Sprecher. 2004. *The Handbook of Sexuality in Close Relationships.* Oxford, England: Taylor & Francis.

Harvey, Vickie. 2003. "'We're Just Friends': Myth Construction As A Communication Strategy In Maintaining Cross-Sex Friendships."*The Qualitative Report* 8: 314–332.

Hatfield, Elaine. 1988. "Passionate and Companionate Love." In *The Psychology of Love,* edited by Robert J. Sternberg and Michael L. Barnes. New Haven, CT: Yale University Press.

Hawkins, Alan J., Kimberly R. Lovejoy, Erin K Holmes, Victoria L. Blanchard, and Elizabeth B. Fawcett. 2008. "Increasing Fathers' Involvement in Child Care With a Couple-Focused Intervention During the Transition to Parenthood." *Family Relations* 57(1): 49–59.

Hawkins, Alan J., Steven L. Nock, Julia C. Wilson, Laura Sanchez, and James D. Wright. 2002. "Attitudes About Covenant Marriage and Divorce: Policy Implications From a Three-Stage Comparison." *Family Relations* 51: 166–75.

Hawkins, Daniel N., Paul R. Amato, and Valarie King. 2007. "Nonresident Father Involvement and Adolescent Well-Being: Father Effects or Child Effects?" *American Sociological Review* 72(6, December): 990–1010.

Hawthorne, Bruce and C.J. Lennings. 2008. "The Marginalization of Nonresident Fathers: Their Postdivorce Roles." *Journal of Divorce and Remarriage* 49(3/4): 191–209.

Hayashi, Aiko. 2004. Japanese Women Shun the Pill. Electronic document.

Hays, Sharon. 2001. "The Mommy Wars: Ambivalence, Ideological Work, and the Cultural Contradictions of Motherhood." pp. 305–23 in *Shifting the Center: Understanding Contemporary Families, 2nd Ed.,* edited by Susan J. Ferguson. Mountain View, CA: Mayfield Publishing Company.

He, Wan, Manisha Sengupta, Victoria A. Velkoff, and Kimberly A. DeBarros. 2005 December. *65+ in the United States: 2005.* Current Population Reports: Special Studies, P23-209. Washington, D.C.: U.S. Census Bureau.

Health Behavior News Service. 2007. "Depressed People Gain More From Being Married." In *Center for the Advancement of Health. Medical News Today,* 9 June. Retrieved 25 June 2008. Washington, D.C. (www.medicalnewstoday.com/articles/73661.php).

Heaton, Tim B. 2002. "Factors Contributing to Increasing Marital Stability in the United States." *Journal of Family Issues* 23-3 (April): 392–409.

Hefling, Kimberly. 2004. "Benefits Cited as More US Women Over 40 Give Birth." The Associated Press. *The Oregonian,* 27 November, pp. A-2.

Helms, Heather M., Christine M. Proulx, Mary Maguire Klute, Susan M. McHale, and Ann M. Crouter. 2006. "Spouses' Gender-Typed Attributes and Their Links With Marital Quality: A Pattern-Analytic Approach." *Journal of Social and Personal Relationships* 23 (December): 843–64.

Helpguide.org. 2010. "Assisted Living Facilities for Seniors: Exploring Services and Options." Retrieved 26 April 2010 (Helpguide.org/elder/assisted_living_facilities.htm).

Hendrick, Susan S. and Clyde Hendrick. 1992. *Romantic Love.* Newbury Park, CA: Sage Publicatons.

Henry, Pamela J. and James McCue. 2009. "The Experience of Nonresidential Stepmothers." *Journal of Divorce & Remarriage* 50(3, April): 185–205.

Herbenick, Debby. 2009. "Unrequited Love and Lust: When The One You Want Doesn't Want You Back." Retrieved 8 February 2010. Psychology Today (www.psychologytoday.com/blog/the-pleasures-sex/200911/unrequited-love-and-lust-when-the-one-you-want-doesn-t-want-you-back).

Hertz, Rosanna and Nancy L. Marshall. 2001. *Working Families: The Transformation of the American Home.* Berkeley, CA: University of California Press.

Hetherington, E. Mavis and John Kelly. 2003. *For Better or Worse: Divorce Reconsidered.* New York: W.W. Norton and Co.

Hewitt, Belinda. 2009. "Which Spouse Initiates Marital Separation When There Are Children Involved?" *Journal of Marriage and Family* 71(2): 362–72.

Hewitt, Belinda, Janeen Baxter, and Mark Western. 2005. "Marriage Breakdown in Australia: The Social Correlates of Separation and Divorce." *Journal of Sociology* 41(2): 163–83.

Hewitt, Belinda, Mark Western, and Janeen Baxter. 2006. "Who Decides? The Social Characteristics of Who Initiates Marital Separation." *Journal of Marriage and Family* 68: 1165–77.

Heyman, Richard E. and Amy M. Smith Slep. 2002. "Do Child Abuse and Interparental Violence Lead to Adulthood Family Violence?" *Journal of Marriage and Family* 64: 864–70.

Higgenbotham, Brian, Linda Skogrand, and Eliza Torres. 2010. "Stepfamily Education: Perceived Benefits for Children." *Journal of Divorce & Remarriage* 51(1, January): 36–49.

Higgins, Louise T., Mo Zheng, Yali Liu, and Chun Hui Sun. 2002. "Attitudes to Marriage and Sexual Behaviors: A Survey of Gender and Culture Differences in China and United Kingdom." *Sex Roles* 46: 75–89.

Hildreth, Carolyn J., Alison E. Burke, and Richard M. Glass. 2009. "Elder Abuse." *Journal of the American Medical Association* 302(5): 588.

Hill, E. Jeffrey, Alan J. Hawkins, Maria Ferris, and Michelle Weitzman. 2001. "Finding an Extra Day a Week: The Positive Influence of Perceived Job Flexibility on Work and Family Life Balance." *Family Relations* 50: 49–58.

Hill, E. Jeffrey, Chongming Yang, Alan J. Hawkins, and Maria Ferris. 2004. "A Cross-Cultural Test of the Work/Family Interface in 48 Countries." *Journal of Marriage and Family* 17: 1300–16.

Hill, Michael. 2006. *Social Policy in the Modern World.* Boston: Blackwell Publishing.

Hill, Reuben. 1958. "Generic Features of Families Under Stress." *Social Casework* 49: 139–50.

Hill, Shirley A. 2005. *Black Intimacies.* Lanham, MD: AltaMira Press.

Hill, Shirley. 2002. "Teaching and Doing Gender in African American Families." *Sex Roles* 47(11/12): 493–506.

Hilton, Jeanne M. and Karen Kopera-Frye. 2007. "Differences in Resources Provided by Grandparents in Single and Married Parent Families." *Journal of Divorce and Remarriage* DOI: 10.1300/J087v47n01_03: 33–54.

Hines, Melissa. 2005. *Brain Gender.* New York, NY: Oxford University Press.

Hirsch, Jennifer S. 2003. *A Courtship After Marriage: Sexuality and Love in Mexican Transnational Families.* Berkeley, CA: University of California Press.

Hite, Shere. 1977. *The Hite Report.* New York: Dell.

Ho, Victoria M. and Stephanie A. Sussman. 2008. "Appellate Court Trends in Permanent Alimony for 'Gray Area' Divorces: 1997-2007." *Florida Bar Journal* 82(4, April): 45.

Hochschild, Arlie. 1989. *The Second Shift: Working Parents and the Revolution at Home.* New York: Viking.

Hoefer, Michael, Nancy Rytina, and Brian C. Baker. 2010. Estimates of the Unauthorized Immigrant Population Residing in the United States: January 2009. Electronic document. *In:* Population Estimates. www.dhs.gov/xlibrary/assets/statistics/publications/ois_ill_pe_2009.pdf.

Hofferth, Sandra L. and Kermyt G. Anderson. 2003. "Are All Dads Equal? Biology Versus Marriage as a Basis or Parental Investment."*Journal of Marriage and Family* 65: 213–32.

Hoffnung, Michele. 2006. "What's in a Name? Marital Name Choice Revisited." *Sex Roles: A Journal of Research* 55(11-12, December): 817–25.

Hofstede, Geert and Gert-Jan Hofstede. 2004. *Cultures and Organizations: Software of the Mind*. New York: McGraw-Hill.

Hohmann-Marriott, Bryndl E. 2006. "Shared Beliefs and the Union Stability of Married and Cohabiting Couples." *Journal of Marriage and Family* 68: 1015–28.

Holcombe, Emily, Kristin Peterson, and Jennifer Manlove. 2009. *Ten Reasons to Still Keep the Focus on Teen Childbearing*. Child Trends Research Brief, March.

Hollist, Cody S. & Miller, Richard B. 2005. "Perceptions of Attachment Style and Marital Quality in Midlife Marriage." *Family Relations* 54(1): 46–57.

Holmberg, Diane, Karen L. Blair, and Maggie Phillips. 2010. "Women's Sexual Satisfaction as a Predictor of Well-Being in Same-Sex Versus Mixed-Sex Relationships." *Journal of Sex Research* 47(1, January): 1–11.

Holmes, Thomas H. and Richard H. Rahe. 1967. "The Social Readjustment Rating Scale." *Journal of Psychosomatic Research* 11: 213–18.

Honore, Carl. 2008. *Under Pressure: Rescuing Our Children From the Culture of Hyperparenting*. London: Orion Publishing.

Hook, Jennifer L. & Chalasani, Satvika. 2008. "Gendered Expectations? Reconsidering Single Fathers' Child-Care Time." *Journal of Marriage and the Family* 70(4): 978–90.

Hook, Jennifer L. 2004. "Reconsidering the Division of Household Labor: Incorporating Volunteer Work and Informal Support."*Journal of Marriage and Family* 66 (February): 101–17.

—. 2006. "Care in Context: Men's Unpaid Work in 20 Countries, 1965-2003." *American Sociological Review* 71(4, August): 639–60.

Hooyman, Nancy and H. Asuman Kiyak. 2010. *Social Gerontology: A Multidisciplinary Perspective, 9th Ed.* Boston: Pearson Education Inc.

Hopper, Joseph. 1993. "The Rhetoric of Motives in Divorce." *Journal of Marriage and the Family* 55: 801–13.

Horn, Wade F. and Tom Sylvester. 2006. "Father Facts: Research Notes." Retrieved 16 July 2006. National Fatherhood Initiative, Fatherhood Online (www.fatherhood.org/fatherfacts_rsh.asp).

Houseknecht, Sharon K. and Jaya Sastry. 1996. "Family 'Decline' and Child Well-Being: A Comparative Assessment." *Journal of Marriage and the Family* 58: 726–39.

Houser, Ari N. 2007. "Long-Term Care Trends: Women & Long-Term Care Research Report." Retrieved 19 March 2008 (www.aarp.org/research/longtermcare/trends/fs77r_ltc.html).

Hu, Mandy. 2005. *Selling Us Short: How Social Security Privatization Will Affect Lesbian, Gay, Bisexual, and Transgender Americans*. Washington, DC: National Gay and Lesbian Task Force Policy Institute.

Huang, Grace S. 2002. "TANF Reauthorization and Its Effects on Asian and Pacific Islander Families" (Policy Paper). *Asian & Pacific Islander Institute on Domestic Violence*, October. Retrieved 28 August 2008. San Francisco (www.apiahf.org/apidvinstitute/ResearchAndPolicy/Policypaper.htm).

Huffstutter, P.J. 2007. "Experts: Elders Need Some Sex Education, Too." *Los Angeles Times*, 15 December.

Huggins, Sharon L. 1989. "A Comparative Study of Self-Esteem of Adolescent Children of Divorced Lesbian Mothers and Divorced Heterosexual Mothers." *Journal of Homosexuality* 18(1/2): 123–35.

Hughes, Diane and Deborah Johnson. 2001. "Correlates in Children's Experiences of Parents' Racial Socialization Behaviors."*Journal of Marriage and Family* 63(4, November): 981–95.

Hughes, Diane, James Rodriguez, Emilie P. Smith, Deborah J. Johnson, Howard C. Stevenson, and Paul Spicer. 2006. "Parents' Ethnic-Racial Socialization Practices: A Review of Research and Directions for Future Study." *Developmental Psychology* 42(5, September): 747–70.

Hughes, Mary Elizabeth, and Linda J. Waite. 2009. Marital Biography and Health at Mid-Life. *Journal of Health and Social Behavior* 50(3): 344–358.

Human Rights Campaign. 2008a. "Domestic Partner Benefits." Retrieved 26 October 2008 (www.hrc.org/issues/workplace/benefits/4814.htm).

—. 2009a. "Parenting Laws: Joint Adoption." Retrieved 2 March 2010 (www.hrc.org/state_laws).

—. 2009b. "Parenting Laws: Second Parent Adoption." Retrieved 2 March 2010 (www.hrc.org/state_laws).

Human Rights Watch. 2004a. "Divorced From Justice: Women's Unequal Access to Divorce in Egypt." Retrieved 8 April 2010 (hrw.org/reports/2004/egypt1204/index.htm).

—. 2004b. "Domestic Violence." Retrieved 19 July 2005 (hrw.org/women/domesticviolence.html).

Hunter, Andrea G. 1997. "Counting on Grandmothers: Black Mothers' and Fathers' Reliance on Grandmothers for Parenting Support."*Journal of Family Issues* 18: 251–69.

Hurst, Charles. 2010. *Social Inequality: Forms, Causes, and Consequences, 7th Ed.* Upper Saddle River, NJ: Prentice Hall.

Hutchinson, Susan L., Tamara Afifi, and Stephanie & Krause. 2007. "The Family That Plays Together Fares Better." *Journal of Divorce and Remarriage* 46(3): 21–48.

Hyman, Batya. 2000. "The Economic Consequences of Child Sexual Abuse for Adult Lesbian Women." *Journal of Marriage and the Family* 62: 199–211.

Ihinger-Tallman, Marilyn and Kay Pasley. 1987. *Remarriage.* Newbury Park, CA: Sage Publications.

Ingoldsby, Bron, Suzanne Smith, and J. Elizabeth Miller. 2003. *Exploring Family Theories.* Los Angeles, CA: Roxbury Press.

Ingraham, Chrys. 1999. *White Weddings: Romancing Heterosexuality in Popular Culture.* New York: Routledge.

Internal Revenue Service. 2009. "EITC Thresholds and Tax Law Updates." Retrieved 4 December 2009 (www.irs.gov/indivduals/article/0,id=150513,00.html).

Intersex Society of North America. 2008. "How Common is Intersex?" Retrieved 14 August 2009 (www.isna.org/faq/frequency).

Irazuzta, Jose E, James E McJunkin, Kapriel Danadian, Forest Arnold, and Jianliang Zhang. 1997. "Outcome and Cost of Child Abuse." *Child Abuse and Neglect* 21: 751–57.

Ishii-Kuntz, Masako. 2003. "Balancing Fatherhood and Work: Emergence of Diverse Masculinities in Contemporary Japan." pp. 198–216 in *Men and Masculinities in Contemporary Japan: Dislocating the Salaryman Doxa*, edited by J. Roberson and N. Suzuki. New York: Routledge.

—. 2008, 19 September. *Sharing of Housework and Childcare in Contemporary Japan.* Division for the Advancement of Women. New York: United Nations.

Ishii-Kuntz, Masako, Katsuko Makino, Kuniko Kato, and Michiko Tsuchiya. 2004. "Japanese Fathers of Preschoolers and Their Involvement in Child Care." *Journal of Marriage and Family* 66 (August): 779–91.

Ispa, Jean M., Mark A. Fine, Linda C. Halgunseth, Scott Harper, JoAnn Robinson, Lisa Boyce, Jeanne Brooks-Gunn, and Christy Brady-Smith. 2004. "Maternal Intrusiveness, Maternal Warmth, and Mother-Toddler Relationship Outcomes: Variations Across Low-Income Ethnic and Acculturation Groups." *Child Development* 75(6, December): 1613–31.

Ivy, Diana K. and Phil Backlund. 2008. *Genderspeak: Personal Effectiveness in Gender Communication, 4th Ed.* Boston: Pearson/Allyn & Bacon.

Jacobs, Julie N. and Michelle L. Kelley. 2006. "Predictors of Paternal Involvement in Childcare in Dual-Earner Families With Young Children." *Fathering* 4(1): 23–47.

Jalovaara, Marika. 2003. "The Joint Effects of Marriage Partners' Socioeconomic Positions on the Risk of Divorce." *Demography* 40(1, February): 67–81.

Jansen, Mieke, Dimitri Mortelmans, and Laurent Snoeckx. 2009. "Repartnering And (Re)Employment: Strategies to Cope With the Economic Consequences of Partnership Dissolutions." *Journal of Marriage and Family* 71 (5, December): 1271–93.

Jasinski, Jana L., Jennifer K. Wesely, James D. Wright, and Elizabeth E. Mustaine. 2010. *Hard Lives, Mean Streets: Violence in the Lives of Homeless Women.* Boston: Northeastern.

Jayson, Sharon. 2005. "Hyphenated Names Less-and-Less Used." *USA Today* (www.usatoday.com/life/2005-05-30-name-change_x.htm), 30 May.

—. 2008. "Single Moms' Sons Can Succeed, New Research Shows." *USA Today*, 29 August. Retrieved 18 April 2010. Indiana Mothers for Custodial Justice (imfcj.blogspot.com/2008/08/single-moms-sons-can-succeed-new.html).

Jenny, Carole, Thomas A. Roesler, and Kimberly L. Poyer. 1994. "Are Children at Risk for Sexual Abuse by Homosexuals?" *Pediatrics* 94(1 July): 41–44.

Johnson, Christine A., Scott M. Stanley, Norval D. Glenn, Paul R. Amato, Steve L. Nock, Howard J. Markman, and M. Robin Dion. 2002. *Marriage in Oklahoma: 2001 Baseline Statewide Survey on Marriage and Divorce.* Bureau for Social Research. Stillwater, OK: Oklahoma State University.

Johnson, Dana. 2009. "Adopting an Institutionalized Child: What Are the Risks?" Retrieved 16 December 2009. Association for Research in International Adoption (www.adoption-research.org/risks.htm).

Johnson, Julia Overturf. 2005 October. *Who's Minding the Kids? Child Care Arrangements: Winter 2002.* Current Population Reports No. P70-101. Washington, D.C.: U.S. Census Bureau.

Johnson, Michael P. 2008. *A Typology of Domestic Violence: Intimate Terrorism, Violent Resistance, and Situational Couple Violence.* Boston: Northeastern University Press.

—. 2009. "Differentiating Among Types of Domestic Violence: Implications for Healthy Marriages." pp. 281–97 in *Marriage and Families: Complexities and Perspectives*, edited by H. Elizabeth Peters and Claire Kamp Dush. New York: Columbia University Press.

Johnson, Michael P. and Janel M. Leone. 2005. "The Differential Effects of Intimate Terrorism and Situational Couple Violence." *Journal of Family Issues* 26(3): 322–49.

Johnson, H. Durell. 2004. Summer. *Gender, Grade, and Relationship Differences in Emotional Closeness Within Adolescent Friendships.* Adolescence San Diego. Retrieved 25 September 2008. Findarticles.com/p/articles/mi_m2248/is_154_39/ai_n6364174/print?tag=artBody; col1.

Johnson, Tallese D. 2008 February. *Maternity Leave and Employment Patterns of First-Time Mothers: 1961–2003.* Current Population Reports No. P70-113. Washington, D.C.: U.S. Census Bureau.

Johnston, Lloyd D., Patrick M. O'Malley, Jerald G. Bachman, and John E. Schulenberg. 2009. *Monitoring the Future National Survey Results on Drug Use: 1975-2008.* Technical Report No. Volume I: Secondary School Students

Kontula, Osmo and Elina Haavio-Mannila. 2009. "The Impact of Aging on Human Sexual Activity and Sexual Desire." *Journal of Sex Research* 46(1, January): 46–56.

Kopecky, Courtney C. and William G. Powers. 2002. "Relational Development and Self-Image Communication Accuracy." *Communication Research Reports* 19(3, Summer): 283–90.

Korn, Peter. 2010. "Natural Birth? Nope, C-Section Rates on Rise." Retrieved 2 March 2010 (www.portlandtribune. com/news/story.php?story_id=126644252863826200).

Kornbluh, Karen, Katelin Isaacs, and Shelley Waters Boots. 2004 May. *Workplace Flexibility: A Policy Problem.* Work & Family Program: Issue Brief #1.

Koropeckyj-Cox, Tanya. 2002. "Beyond Parental Status: Psychological Well-Being in Middle & Old Age." *Journal of Marriage and Family* 64: 957–71.

—. 2005. "Singles, Society, and Science: Sociological Perspectives." *Psychological Inquiry* 16(2-3): 91–97.

—. 2008. "Loneliness in Later Life." pp. 229–32 in *Encyclopedia of the Life Course and Human Development,* edited by D. S. Carr and A. Pienta. Farmington Hills, MI: Thomson/Gale.

Koropeckyj-Cox, Tanya and Vaughn Call. 2007. "Characteristics of Childless Older Persons and Parents: Cross-National Comparisons." *Journal of Family Issues* 28: 1362–414.

Koropeckyj-Cox, Tanya and Gretchen Pendell. 2007a. "Attitudes About Childlessness in the United States." *Journal of Family Issues* 28(8): 1054–82.

—. 2007b. "The Gender Gap in Attitudes About Childlessness in the United States." *Journal of Marriage and Family* 69(4): 899–915.

Koropeckyj-Cox, Tanya, Amy Mehraban Pienta, and Tyson H. Brown. 2007. Women of the 1950s and the "Normative" Life Course: The Implications of Childlessness, Fertility Timing, and Marital Status for Psychosocial Well-Being in Late Midlife. *International Journal of Aging and Human Development* 64: 299–330.

Koropeckyj-Cox, Tanya, Victor Romano, and Amanda Moras. 2007. "Through the Lenses of Gender, Race, and Class: Students' Perceptions of Childless/Childfree Individuals and Couples." *Sex Roles* 56(7–8): 415–28.

Koss, Mary P. and Sarah L. Cook. 1993. "Facing the Facts: Date and Acquaintance Rape Are Significant Problems for Women." In *Current Controversies in Family Violence,* edited by R. Gelles and D. Loseke. Newbury Park, CA: Sage Publications.

Koss, Mary P., Christine Gidyzc, and Nadine Wisniewski. 1987. "The Scope of Rape: Incidence and Prevalence in a National Sample of Higher Education Students." *Journal of Consulting and Clinical Psychology* 55: 162–70.

Kramer, Laura. 2007. *The Sociology of Gender: A Brief Introduction, 2nd Ed.* New York: Oxford University Press.

Kreider, Rose M. 2008. February. *Living Arrangements of Children: 2004.* Technical Report No. P70-114. Washington, DC: U.S. Census Bureau.

Kreider, Rose M. and Diana B. Elliott. 2009. "America's Families and Living Arrangements: 2007." In *Current Population Reports, P20-561. U.S. Census Bureau,* September. Washington, DC.

Kristof, Nicholas D. and Sheryl WuDunn. 2009. *Half the Sky: Turning Oppression into Opportunity for Women Worldwide.* New York: Knopf.

Kroska, Amy. 2003. "Investigating Gender Differences in the Meaning of Household Chores and Child Care." *Journal of Marriage and Family* 65: 456–73.

Kubler-Ross, Elisabeth. 1969. *On Death and Dying.* New York, NY: Macmillan.

Kurchinka, Mary Sheedy. 1998. *Raising Your Spirited Child.* New York: Harper Perennial.

Kurdek, Lawrence A. 1994. "Areas of Conflict for Gay, Lesbian, and Heterosexual Couples: What Couples Argue About Influences Relationship Satisfaction." *Journal of Marriage and the Family* 56: 923–34.

—. 1999. "The Nature and Predictions of the Trajectory of Change and Marital Quality for Husbands and Wives Over the First 10 Years of Marriage." *Developmental Psychology* 35: 1283–96.

—. 2003. "Differences Between Gay and Lesbian Cohabiting Couples." *Journal of Social Personal Relationships* 20: 411–36.

—. 2004. "Are Gay and Lesbian Cohabiting Couples Really Different From Heterosexual Married Couples?" *Journal of Marriage and the Family* 6(4): 880–900.

—. 2006. "Differences Between Partners From Heterosexual, Gay, and Lesbian Cohabiting Couples." *Journal of Marriage and Family* 68(2): 509–28.

—. 2007. "Avoidance Motivation and Relationship Commitment in Heterosexual, Gay Male, and Lesbian Partners." *Personal Relationships* 13: 521–35.

—. 2008. "Change in Relationship Quality for Partners From Lesbian, Gay Male, and Heterosexual Couples." *Journal of Family Psychology* 22(5): 701–11.

—. 2009. "Assessing the Health of a Dyadic Relationship in Heterosexual and Same-Sex Partners." *Personal Relationships* 16: 117–27.

Kurlansky, Judith. 2004. *The Complete Idiot's Guide to Dating, 3rd Ed.* New York: Alpha Books.

Kurz, Demie. 2002. "Caring for Teenage Children." *Journal of Family Issues* 23: 748–67.

La Leche League International. 2004. *The Womanly Art of Breastfeeding: 7th Revised Edition.* New York: Plume Publishing.

Labov, William. 1966. *The Social Stratification of English in New York City.* Washington, D.C.: Center for Applied Linguistics.

Lachance-Grzela, Mylene & Bouchard, Amanda G. 2010. "Why do women do the lions share of the housework? A decade of research." Sex Roles Doi 10.1007/11197-010-9797-z

—. 1972. *Language in the Inner City*. Philadelphia: University of Pennsylvania Press.

Lakoff, Robin Talmach. 2000. *The Language War*. Berkeley, CA: University of California Press.

Lamb, Kathleen A. 2007. "'I Want to Be Just Like Their Real Dad'." *Journal of Family Issues* 28(9): 1162–88.

Lamb, Kathleen A., Gary R. Lee, and Alfred DeMaris. 2003. "Union Formation and Depression: Selection and Relationship Effects." *Journal of Marriage and Family* 65: 953–62.

Lamb, Sharon and Lyn Mikel Brown. 2006. *Packaging Girlhood: Rescuing Our Daughters From Marketers' Schemes*. New York: St. Martins Press.

Lampard, Richard and Kay Peggs. 1999. "Repartnering: The Relevance of Parenthood and Gender to Cohabitation and Remarriage Among the Formerly Married." *The British Journal of Sociology* 50: 443–65.

Lane, Shelley D. 2010. *Interpersonal Communication: Competence and Contexts*. Boston: Allyn & Bacon.

Langer, Gary, Cheryl Arnedt, and Dalia Sussman. 2004. "Primetime Live Poll: American Sex Survey." Retrieved 9 June 2007 (abcnews.go.com/print?id=156921).

Lantz, Herman, Jane Keyes, and Martin Schultz. 1975. "The Family in the Preindustrial Period: From Base Lines in History to Change." *American Sociological Review* 40(February): 21–36.

LaPierre, Tracey A. 2009. "Marital Status and Depressive Symptoms Over Time: Age and Gender Variations." *Family Relations* 58(4, October): 404–16.

Lareau, Annette. 2003. *Unequal Childhoods: Class, Race, and Family Life*. Berkeley: University of California Press.

Lareau, Annette and Dalton Conley, eds. 2008. *Social Class: How Does It Work?* New York: Sage Publications.

Larsen, Christian Albrekt. 2006. *The Institutional Logic of Welfare Attitudes: How Welfare Regimes Influence Public Support*. Hampshire, UK: Ashgate Publishing, Ltd.

Laslett, Peter. 1971. *The World We Have Lost*. New York, NY: Charles Scribner's Sons.

Laughlin, Lynda and Joseph Rukus. 2009. "Who's Minding the Kids in the Summer? Child Care Arrangements for Summer 2006." Presentation. Presented at the Annual Meeting of the Population Association of America, April 30-May 2, 2009, Detroit, MI.

Laumann, Edward O., John H. Gagnon, Robert T. Michael, and Stuart Michaels. 1994. *The Social Organization of Sexuality: Sexual Practices in the United States*. Chicago, IL: University of Chicago Press.

Lavee, Yoav and Ruth Katz. 2002. "Division of Labor, Perceived Fairness, and Marital Quality: The Effect of Gender Ideology." *Journal of Marriage and Family* 64: 27–39.

Law and Mediation Offices of David L. Price. 2000. "Frequently Asked Questions About Divorce Mediation." Retrieved 10 April 2010 (library.findlaw.com/2000/Aug/1/129039.html).

Le Mare, Lucy, Karyn Audet, and Karen Kurytnik. 2007. "A Longitudinal Study of Service Use in Families of Children Adopted From Romanian Orphanages." *International Journal of Behavioral Development* 31: 242–51.

Leaper, Campbell and Carly K. Friedman. 2006. "The Socialization of Gender." pp. 561–87 in *The Handbook of Socialization: Theory and Research*, edited by J. E. Grusec and P. D. Hastings. New York: Guilford Press.

Leder, Sharon, Linda Nicholson Grinstead, and Elisa Torres. 2007. "Grandparents Raising Grandchildren." *Journal of Family Nursing* 13(3): 333–52.

Lee, Gary R., Marion C. Willets, and Karen Seccombe. 1998. "Widowhood and Depression: Gender Differences." *Research on Aging* 20: 611–30.

Lee, Gary R. and Alfred DeMaris. 2007. "Widowhood, Gender, and Depression." *Research on Aging* 29(1): 56–72.

Lee, John A. 1973. *The Colors of Love: An Exploration of the Ways of Loving*. Don Mills, Ontario: New Press.

—. 1988. "Love-Styles." pp. 38–67 in *The Psychology of Love*, edited by Robert J. Sternberg and Michael L. Barnes. New Haven, CT: Yale University Press.

Lee, John A. 1974. "The Styles of Loving." *Psychology Today*, October, pp. 46–51.

Lee, Mei-Yin, Yueh-Chih Chen, Huei-Shyong Wang, and Duan-Rung Chen. 2007. "Parenting Stress and Related Factors in Parents of Children With Tourette Syndrome." *Journal of Nursing Research* 15(3): 165–74.

Lee, Sharon M. and Barry Edmonston. 2005. June. "New Marriages, New Families: U.S. Racial and Hispanic Intermarriage." *Population Bulletin*.

Lee, Vicki L. 2003. Human Agency. Electronic document. www.actusinfo.org/pre-07/human-agency.html.

Lee, Yun-Suk and Linda J Waite. 2005. "Husbands' and Wives' Time Spent on Housework: A Comparison of Measures." *Journal of Marriage and Family* 67 (May): 328–36.

Leeder, Elaine. 2004. *The Family in Global Perspective: A Gendered Perspective*. Thousand Oaks, CA: Sage Publications.

Leman, Kevin. 2007. *Step-Parenting 101*. Nashville, TN: Thomas Nelson.

Leonhardt, David. 2007. "He's Happier, She's Less So." In *Nytimes.Com. New York Times*, 26 September. Retrieved 27 September 2007 (www.nytimes.com/2007/09/26/business/26leonhardt.html).

Leserman, Jane and Douglas A. Drossman. 2007. "Relationship of Abuse History to Functional Gastrointestinal Disorders and Symptoms." *Trauma, Violence, & Abuse* 8(3): 331–43.

LeVay, Simon. 1991. "A Difference in Hypothlamic Structure Between Heterosexual and Homosexual Men." *Science* 253: 1034–37.

Levin, Diane E. and Jean Kilbourne. 2008. *So Sexy So Soon: The New Sexualized Childhood and What Parents Can Do To Protect Their Kids*. New York: Ballantine Books.

Levine, Judith A., Clifton R. Emery, and Harold A. Pollack. 2007. "The Well-Being of Children Born to Teen Mothers." *Journal of Marriage and the Family* 69(1): 105–22.

Lewandowski, Gary, Arthur Aron, Sharon Bassis, and Johnna Kunak. 2006. "Losing a Self-Expanding Relationship: Implications for the Self-Concept." *Personal Relationships* 13(3): 317–31.

Lewin, Tamar. 2005. "3 New Studies Assess Effects of Child Care." Retrieved 5 January 2010. NYTimes.com (www.nytimes.com/2005/11/01/national/01child.html?_r=1&pagewanted=print).

Lewontin, R.C. 2006. "Confusion About Human Races" (Web Forum Organized by the Social Science Research Council). Retrieved 18 August 2008 (Raceandgenomics.ssrc.org/Lewontin/printable.html).

Lichter, Daniel T. and Zhenchao Qian. 2008. "Serial Cohabitation and the Marital Life Course." *Journal of Marriage and Family* 70(4, November): 861–78.

Liebow, Elliot. 1995. *Tell Them Who I Am: The Lives of Homeless Women*. New York: Penguin.

Lin, I-Fen. 2008. "Consequences of Parental Divorce for Adult Children's Support of Their Frail Parents." *Journal of Marriage and Family* 70(1): 113–28.

Lindau, Stacy T., L. Philip Schumm, Edward O. Laumann, Wendy Levinson, Colm A. O'Muircheartaigh, and Linda J. Waite. 2007. "A Study of Sexuality and Health Among Older Adults in the United States." *New England Journal of Medicine* 357 (23 August): 762–74.

Linden, Michael. 2009. "Turning Point: The Long Term Effects of Recession-Induced Child Poverty." Retrieved 21 January 2010. First Focus Campaign for Children (www.firstfocus.net/Download/TurningPoint.pdf).

Lindsey, Eric W., Penny R. Cremeens, and Yvonne M. Caldera. 2010. Gender Differences in Mother-Toddler and Father-Toddler Verbal Initiations and Responses During a Caregiving and Play Context. Sex Roles:DOI 10.1007/s11199-010-9803-5.

Lindsey, Linda. 1997. *Gender Roles: A Sociological Perspective, 3rd Ed.* Upper Saddle River, NJ: Prentice Hall.

—. 2011. *Gender Roles: A Sociological Perspective, 5th Ed.* Upper Saddle River, NJ: Prentice Hall.

Lino, Mark and Andrea Carlson. 2009. *Expenditures on Children in Families, 2008*. Washington, D.C.: U.S. Department of Agriculture, Center for Nutrition Policy & Promotion, Publication No. 1528-2008.

Livingston, Gretchen, Susan Minushkin, and D'Vera Cohn. 2008. "Hispanics and Health Care in the United States: Access, Information and Knowledge." In *Pew Hispanic Center*. Retrieved 22 August 2008. Washington, D.C. (pewhispanic.org/reports/report. php?ReportID=91).

Lloyd, Sally A. 1987. "Conflict in Premarital Relationships: Differential Perceptions of Males and Females." *Family Relations* 36(3, July): 290–94.

Lloyd, Sally A., April L. Few, and Katherine R. Allen. 2009. Handbook of Feminist Family Studies. Thousand Oaks, CA: Sage Publications.

Lobo, Susan, Steve Talbot, and Traci L. Morris. 2010. *Native American Voices, 3rd Ed.* Upper Saddle River, NJ: Prentice Hall.

Loeb, Susanna, Margaret Bridges, Daphna Bassok, Bruce Fuller, and Russell W. Rumberger. 2007. "How Much is Too Much? The Influence of Preschool Centers on Children's Social and Cognitive Development." *Economics of Education Review* 26(1, February): 52–66.

Loeffler, William. 2008. Different Cultures Have a Different Rite of Passage. Pittsburgh Tribune-Review, 13 July.

Lofas, Jeannette. 2005. "Classic Complaints: Normal for the Stepfamily." Retrieved 17 April 2010. The Stepfamily Foundation, Inc. (www.winningstepfamilies.com/ClassicStepfamilyComplaints.html).

Logan, Cassandra, Emily Holcombe, Suzanne Ryan, Jennifer Manlove, and Kristin Moore. 2007. "Childhood Sexual Abuse and Teen Pregnancy: A White Paper." Retrieved 1 December 2009. Child Trends (www.thenationalcampaign.org/resources/pdf/childhood.pdf).

Logan, T.K. and Robert Walker. 2009. "Partner Stalking." *Trauma, Violence, & Abuse* 10(3): 247–70.

Lopez, Javier, Maria Crespo, and Steven H. Zarit. 2007. "Assessment of the Efficacy of a Stress Management Program for Informal Caregivers of Dependent Older Adults." *The Gerontologist* 47: 205–14.

Loprest, Pamela and Sheila Zedlewski. August 30, 2006. *The Changing Role of Welfare in the Lives of Low-Income Families With Children*. Technical Report No. Occasional Paper No. 73. Washington, D.C.: The Urban Institute.

Lorenz, Frederick O., K.A.S. Wickrama, Rand D. Conger, and Jr. Elder, Glen H. 2006. The Short-Term and Decade-Long Effects of Divorce on Women's Midlife Health. *Journal of Health and Social Behavior* 47: 111–125.

Lovell, Philip and Julia B. Isaacs. 2010. *Families of the Recession: Unemployed Parents & Their Children*. Washington, DC: First Focus Campaign for Children.

Lowenstein, Ludwig F. 2005. "Causes and Associated Features of Divorce as Seen by Recent Research." *Journal of Divorce and Remarriage* 42(3/4): 153–71 (DOI: 10.1300/J087vol42n03_09).

—. 2009. "Mediation With Separated Parents: Recent Research 2002-2007." *Journal of Divorce & Remarriage* 50(4, May): 233–47.

Luedemann, Marei B., Marion F. Ehrenberg, and Michael A. Hunter. 2006. "Mothers' Discussions With Daughters Following Divorce."*Journal of Divorce and Remarriage* 46(1): 29–55.

Luft, Joe. 1969. "Of Human Interaction." In *Palo Alto*. Retrieved 30 June 2008. Cited by Tim Borchers, 1999, Allyn & Bacon (www.abacon.com/commstudies/interpersonal/indisclosure.html).

Lundberg, Shelly, Sara McLanahan, and Elaina Rose. 2007. "Child Gender and Father Involvement in Fragile Families." *Demography* 44(118): 79–92.

Luo, Michael. 2009. "Job Woes Exacting a Toll on Family Life." *The New York Times*, 12 November. Retrieved 30 December 2009. NYTimes.com (www,nytimes.com/2009/11/12/us/12families.html?_r=1&pagewanted=print).

Lustig, Myron W. and Jolene Koester. 2010. *Intercultural Competence: Interpersonal Communication Across Culture, 6th Ed.* Boston: Allyn & Bacon.

Lyster, Mimi E. 2007. *Building A Parental Agreement That Works.* Berkeley, CA: Nolo Publishers.

Maas, Carl, Todd I. Herrenkohl, and Cynthia Sousa. 2008. "Review of Research On Child Maltreatment and Violence in Youth."*Trauma, Violence, & Abuse* 9(1): 56–67.

Macaulay, Ronald K.S. 2005. *Talk That Counts: Age, Gender, and Social Class Differences in Discourse.* New York: Oxford University Press.

Maccoby, Eleanor E. 2007. "Historical Overview of Socialization Research and Theory." pp. 13–41 in *Handbook of Socialization: Theory and Research*, edited by Joan E. Grusec and Paul D. Hastings. New York: The Guilford Press.

Maccoby, Eleanor E. 1998. *The Two Sexes: Growing up Apart, Coming Together.* Cambridge, MA: Harvard University Press.

Macionis, John. 2011. *Sociology, 14th Ed.* Upper Saddle River, NJ: Prentice Hall.

MacNeil, Gordon, Jordan I. Kosberg, Daniel W. Durkin, W. Keith Dooley, Jamie DeCoster, and Gail M. Williamson. 2010. "Caregiver Mental Health and Potentially Harmful Caregiving Behavior: The Central Role of Caregiver Anger." *The Gerontologist* 50(1): 76–86.

MacPhee, David, Janet Fritz, and Jan Miller-Heyl. 1996. "Ethnic Variations in Personal Social Networks and Parenting." *Child Development* 67: 3278–95.

Macy, Rebecca J., Mary C. Giattina, Susan L. Parish, and Carmen Crosby. 2010. Domestic Violence and Sexual Assault Services: Historical Concerns and Contemporary Challenges. *Journal of Interpersonal Violence* 25: 3–32.

Madden, Mary and Amanda Lenhart. 5 March 2006. *Online Dating: Americans Who Are Seeking Romance Use the Internet to Help Them in Their Search, But There is Still Widespread Public Concern About the Safety of Online Dating.* Washington D.C.: Pew Internet & American Life Project.

Madden, Mary and Lee Rainie. 2006. *Not Looking for Love: The State of Romance in America.* Pew Internet & American Life Project.

Magnuson, Katherine and Lawrence M. Berger. 2009. "Family Structure States and Transitions: Associations With Children's Well-Being During Middle Childhood." *Journal of Marriage and Family* 71(3, August): 575–91.

Mahay, Jenna, and Alisa C. Lewin. 2007. Age and the Desire to Marry. *Journal of Family Issues* 28(5): 706–723.

Maher, Bridget E. 2006. "Why Marriage Should Be Privileged in Public Policy." Retrieved 6 June 2006. Family Research Council (www.frc.org/index.cfm?i=IS03D1).

Maier, Thomas. 2009. *Masters of Sex: The Life and Times of William Masters and Virginia Johnson, the Couple Who Taught America to Love.* New York: Basic Books.

Malernee, Jamie. 2006. "Twenty-Somethings' View on Marriage, Family." *Connecticut Post*, 29 October, pp. C1, C6.

Mallinson, Christine and Robin Dodsworth. 2009. "Revisiting the Need for New Approaches to Social Class in Variationist Sociolinguistics."*Sociolinguistic Studies* 3(2): 253–78.

Mammen, Kristin. 2009. "Fathers' Time Investments in Children: Do Sons Get More?" *Journal of Population Economics*, 10.1007/s00148-009-0272-5.

Manganello, Jennifer A. 2008. "Teens, Dating Violence, and Media Use." *Trauma, Violence, & Abuse* 9(1):3–18.

Manning, Wendy and Susan Brown. 2006. "Children's Economic Well-Being in Married and Cohabiting Parent Families." *Journal of Marriage and the Family* 68(2): 345–62.

Manning, Wendy D., Monica A. Longmore, and Peggy C. Giordano. 2007. "The Changing Institution of Marriage: Adolescents' Expectations to Cohabit and to Marry." *Journal of Marriage and Family* 69(3, August): 559–75.

Manpower Inc. 2009. "About Manpower." Retrieved 4 August 2009 (www.manpower.com/About/About.cfm).

Manzoli, Lamberto, Paolo Villari, Giovanni M. Pirone, and Antonio Boccia. 2007. "Marital Status and Mortality in the Elderly: A Systematic Review and Meta-Analysis." *Social Science and Medicine* 64: 77–94.

Markey, Charlotte N. and Patrick M. Markey. 2009. "Correlates of Young Women's Interest in Obtaining Cosmetic Surgery." *Sex Roles* 61(3-4, August): 158–66.

Marsiglio, William. 1992. "Stepfathers With Minor Children Living at Home: Parenting Perceptions and Relationship Quality." *Journal of Family Issues* 13: 195–214.

Marsiglio, William and Joseph H. Pleck. 2005. "Fatherhood and Masculinities." pp. 249–69 in *The Handbook of Studies on Men and Masculinities*, edited by Robert W. Connell, Jeff Hearn and Michael S. Kimmel. Thousand Oaks, CA: Sage Publications.

Marsiglio, William, Kevin Roy, and Greer Litton Fox, eds. 2005. *Situated Fathering: A Focus on Physical and Social Spaces*. Lanham, MD: Rowman and Littlefield Publishers.

Martin, Joyce A., Brady E. Hamilton, Paul D. Sutton, Stephanie J. Ventura, Fay Menacker, and Martha L. Munson. 8 September 2005. *Births: Final Data for 2003*. Technical Report No. 54 (2). Centers for Disease Control and Prevention.

Martin, Sandra L., Rebecca J. Macy, Kristen Sullivan, and Melissa L. Magee. 2007. "Pregnancy-Associated Violent Deaths." *Trauma, Violence, & Abuse* 8(2): 135–48.

Martin, Steven P. and Sangeeta Parashar. 2006. "Women's Changing Attitudes Toward Divorce, 1974-2002: Evidence for an Educational Crossover." *Journal of Marriage and Family* 68(1, February): 29.

Marx, Karl and Friedrich Engels. 1971, original 1867. *Manifesto of the Communist Party*. New York: International Publishers (Original work published 1867).

Mason, Mary Ann, Sydney Harrison-Jay, Gloria Messick Svare, and Nicholas H. Wolfinger. 2002. "Stepparents." *Journal of Family Issues* 23(4): 507–22.

Massey, Douglas S. and Nancy A. Denton. 1993. *American Apartheid: Segregation and the Making of the Underclass*. Cambridge, MA: Harvard University Press.

Massey, Douglas S. and Garvey Lundy. 2001. "Use of Black English and Racial Discrimination in Housing Markets." *Urban Affairs Review* 36(4): 452–69.

Masters, William H. and Virginia E. Johnson. 1966. *Human Sexual Response*. Boston, MA: Little, Brown and Company.

Masuda, Masahiro. 2003. "Meta-Analyses of Love Scales: Do Various Love Scales Measure the Same Psychological Constructs?" *Japanese Psychological Research* 45: 25–37.

Mathews, T.J. and Brady E. Hamilton. 2009. *Delayed Childbearing: More Women Are Having Their First Child Later in Life*. Technical Report No. NCHS Data Brief, no. 21. Hyattsville, MD: National Center for Health Statistics.

Max, Wendy, Dorothy P. Rice, Eric Finkelstein, Robert A. Bardwell, and Steven Leadbetter. 2004. "The Economic Toll of Intimate Partner Violence Against Women in the United States." *Violence and Victims* 19(3): 259–72.

McAdoo, Harriette Pipes. 2006. *Black Families, 4th Ed.* Newbury Park, CA: Sage Publications.

McCool, W.F. and S.A. Simeone. 2002. "Birth in the United States: An Overview of Trends Past and Present." *Nursing Clinics of North America* 37(4, December): 735–46.

McCubbin, Hamilton I., Marilyn A. McCubbin, Anne I. Thompson, Sae-Young Han, and Chad T. Allen. 1997. "Families Under Stress: What Makes Them Resilient." Commemorative Lecture. Washington, DC: AAFCS, 22 June.

McCubbin, Hamilton I. and Joan M. Patterson. 1982. "Family Adaptation to Crisis." In *Family Stress, Coping, and Social Support*, edited by Hamilton I. McCubbin, A. Elizabeth Cauble and Joan M. Patterson. Springfield, IL: Thomas.

McDonald, Steve, Nan Lin, and Dan Ao. 2009. "Networks of Opportunity: Gender, Race, and Job Leads." *Social Problems* 56(3, August): 385–402.

McDowell Group. 2003. "Areas of Expertise." Retrieved 19 March 2006 (www.mcdowellgroup.net/pages/areaexpert/aknative.html).

McLanahan, Sara and Gary Sandefur. 1994. *Growing up With a Single Parent: What Hurts, What Helps*. Cambridge, MA: Harvard University Press.

McLoyd, Vonnie C., Ana Mari Cauce, David Takeuchi, and Leon Wilson. 2000. "Marital Processes and Parental Socialization in Families of Color: A Decade Review of Research." *Journal of Marriage and the Family* 62(4, November): 1070–93.

Mead, Margaret. 1935. *Sex and Temperament in Three Primitive Societies*. New York: Morrow.

Media Awareness Network. 2008. "Video Games—Gender Stereotyping." Retrieved 22 August 2008 (www.media-awareness.ca/english/parents/video_games/concerns/gender_videogames).

Medicare.gov. 2010. "Medicare & You." Retrieved 3 May 2010 (www.medicare.gov/Library/PDFNavigation/PDFInterim.asp?Language=English&Type.html).

Medora, Nilufer P. 2003. "Mate Selection in Contemporary India." pp. 209–30 in *Mate Selection Across Cultures*, edited by R. R. Hamon and B. B. Ingoldsby. Thousand Oaks, CA: Sage Publications.

Mehl, Matthias R., Simine Vazire, Nairan Ramirez-Esparza, Richard B. Slatcher, and James W. Pennebaker. 2007. Are Women Really More Talkative Than Men? Science 317(5834 July): 82.

Mercer, Jean. 2006. *Understanding Attachment: Parenting, Child Care, and Emotional Development*. Westport, CT: Praeger.

Merriam-Webster Online. 2010. "Love." Retrieved 22 January 2010 (www.merriam-webster.com/dictionary/love).

Merrill, Gary S. and Valerie A. Wolfe. 2000. "Battered Gay Men: An Exploration of Abuse, Help Seeking, and Why They Stay." *Journal of Homosexuality* 39(2): 1–30.

MetLife Mature Market Institute. 2009 October. *Market Survey of Long-Term Care Costs: The 2009 MetLife Market Survey of Nursing Home, Assisted Living, Adult Day Services, and Home Care Costs.*

MetLife. 2006. "Out and Aging: The MetLife Study of Lesbian and Gay Baby Boomers." *MetLife Mature Market Institute*, November. Westport, CT (www.metlife.com/WPSAssets/15374435731164722885V1FOutandAging.pdf).

Miall, Charlene E., and Karen March. 2005. Open Adoption as a Family Form: Community Assessments and Social Support. *Journal of Family Issues* 26: 380–410.

Michael, Kerry C., Aurora Torres, and Eric A. Seemann. 2007. "Adolescents' Health Habits, Coping Styles and Self-Concept Are Predicted by Exposure to Interparental Conflict." *Journal of Divorce & Remarriage* 48(1-2, December): 155–74.

Michael, Robert T., John. Gagnon, Edward O. Laumann, and Gina Kolata. 1994. *Sex in America: A Definitive Survey*. New York: Little, Brown and Company.

Mikulincer, Mario and Philip R. Shaver. 2007. *Attachment in Adulthood: Structure, Dynamics, and Change*. New York: Guilford Press.

Mildorf, Jarmila. 2007. *Storying Domestic Violence: Constructions and Stereotypes of Abuse in the Discourse of General Practitioners*. Lincoln, NE: University of Nebraska Press.

Miley, Karla Krogsrud, Michael W. O'Melia, and Brenda L. DuBois. 2011. *Generalist Social Work Practice: An Empowering Approach, 6th Ed.* Boston: Allyn & Bacon.

Milkie, Melissa A., Marybeth J. Mattingly, Kei M. Nomaguchi, Suzanne M. Bianchi, and John P. Robinson. 2004. "The Time Squeeze: Parental Statuses and Feelings About Time With Children." *Journal of Marriage and Family* 66 (August): 739–61.

Miller, Gerald R. and Mark Steinberg. 1975. *Between People: A New Analysis of Interpersonal Communication*. Chicago: Science Research Associates.

Miller, J. Elizabeth. 2000. "Religion and Families Over the Life Course." In *Families Across Time: A Life Course Perspective*, edited by S. Price, S. McKenry and M. Murphy. Los Angeles, CA: Roxbury.

Miller, Nancy B., Virginia L. Smerglia, D. Scott Gaudet, and Gay C. Kitson. 1998. "Stressful Life Events, Social Support, and the Distress of Widowed and Divorced Women." *Journal of Family Issues* 19: 181–203.

Mills, C. Wright. 1959. *The Sociological Imagination*. New York: Oxford University Press.

Mincy, Ronald, Jennifer Hill, and Marilyn Sinkewicz. 2009. "Marriage: Cause or Mere Indicator of Future Earnings Growth." *Journal of Policy Analysis and Management* 28(3, 9 June): 417–39.

Minkler, Meredith and Esme Fuller-Thomson. 2005. "African American Grandparents Raising Grandchildren: A National Study Using the Census 2000 American Community Survey." *Journal of Gerontology* 60B(2): S82–92.

Mintz, Steven. 2003. "Introduction: The Contemporary Crisis of the Family." Retrieved 5 July 2005. Council on Contemporary Families (www.contemporaryfamilies.org/public/fact1.php).

—. 2004. *Huck's Raft: A History of American Childhood.* Cambridge, MA: Belknap Press.

Mintz, Steven and Susan Kellogg. 1989. *Domestic Revolution: A Social History of Family Life*. New York: Free Press.

Miranda, Carolina A. 2004. Fifteen Candles. *Time Magazine*, 19 July: 6.

Mitchell, Katherine Stamps, Alan Booth, and Valarie King. 2009. "Adolescents With Nonresident Fathers: Are Daughters More Disadvantaged Than Sons?" *Journal of Marriage and Family* 71(3, August): 650–62.

Mitterauer, Michael and Reinhard Sieder. 1982. *The European Family: Patriarchy to Partnership From the Middle Ages to Present*. Chicago, IL: University of Chicago Press.

Moen, Phyllis, Jungmeen Kim, and Heather Hofmeister. 2001. "Couples' Work/Retirement Transitions, Gender, and Marital Quality." *Social Psychology Quarterly* 64: 55–71.

Moffitt, Robert. 2008 February. *Welfare Reform: The U.S. Experience*. Technical Report No. 1334-08. Madison, WI: Institute for Research on Poverty.

Monger, George. 2004. *Marriage Customs of the World: From Henna to Honeymoons*. Santa Barbara, CA: ABC-CLIO.

Monserud, Maria A. 2008. "Intergenerational Relationships and Affectual Solidarity Between Grandparents and Young Adults." *Journal of Marriage and Family* 70(1): 182–95.

Monsour, Michael. 2002. *Women and Men as Friends: Relationships Across the Life Span in the 21st Century*. Mahwah, NJ: Lawrence Erlbaum.

Mooney, Carol Garhart. 2009. *Theories of Attachment: An Introduction to Bowlby, Ainsworth, Gerber, Brazelton, Kennell, and Klaus*. St. Paul, MN: Redleaf Press.

Moore, Mignon R. 2004. "Who Wears the Pants? Sources of Power and Conflict in Black and Latina Lesbian Families." Presented at the Annual Meeting of the American Sociological Association, 14 August, San Francisco, CA.

Morgan, Leslie and Suzanne Kunkel. 1998. *Aging: The Social Context*. Thousand Oaks, CA: Pine Forge Press.

Morin, Rich and Paul Taylor. 2008. "Revisiting the Mommy Wars: Politics, Gender and Parenthood." Retrieved 9 March 2010. Pew Research Center (pewsocialtrends.org/pubs/709/politics-gender-parenthood).

Morrissey, Taryn W. 2008. "Familial Factors Associated With the Use of Multiple Child-Care Arrangements." *Journal of Marriage and the Family* 70 (May): 549–63.

Mossaad, Nadwa. 2010. "The Impact of the Recession on Older Americans." Retrieved 23 April 2010. Population Reference Bureau (www.prb.org/Articles/2010/recessionolderamericans.aspx).

Muehlenhard, Charlene L. and Sheena K. Shippee. 2009. "Men's and Women's Reports of Pretending Orgasm." *Journal of Sex Research* 25 (August): 1–16.

Mulsow, Miriam, Yvonne M. Caldera, Marta Pursley, Alan Reifman, and Aletha C. Huston. 2002. "Multilevel Factors Influencing Maternal Stress During the First Three Years." *Journal of Marriage and Family* 64 (November): 944–56.

Muraco, Anna. 2006. "Intentional Families: Fictive Kin Ties Between Cross-Gender, Different Sexual Orientation Friends." *Journal of Marriage and Family* 68 (December): 1313–25.

Murdoch, Stephen. 2007. *IQ: A Smart History of a Failed Idea*. Hoboken, NJ: John Wiley & Sons.

Murkoff, Heidi and Sharon Mazel. 2008. *What to Expect When You're Expecting, 4th Ed.* New York: Workman Publishing.

Murray, Charles. 1988. *In Pursuit of Happiness and Good Government*. New York, NY: Simon and Schuster.

Myers, Scott M. 2006. "Religious Homogamy and Marital Quality: Historical and Generational Patterns, 1980–1997." *Journal of Marriage and Family* 68(2): 292–304.

Nadig, Larry A. 2006b. "How to Express Difficult Feelings." Retrieved 29 September 2008 (www.drnadig.com/feelings.htm).

Nagae, Miyoko and Barbara L. Dancy. 2010. "Japanese Women's Perceptions of Intimate Partner Violence (IPV)." *Journal of Interpersonal Violence* 25(4): 753–66.

National Adoption Information Clearinghouse. 2002. "Single Parent Adoption: What You Need to Know." Retrieved 11 June 2003. U.S. Department of Health & Human Services: Administration for Children & Families (http://www.calib.com/naic/pubs/factsheets.cfm).

National Alliance for Caregiving and AARP. 2009 November. *Caregiving in the U.S.: Executive Summary*.

National Association of Child Care Resource & Referral Agencies. 2009a. "Parent's Perception of Child Care in the United States: NACCRRA's National Parent Poll, January 2009."

—. 2009b. "What Child Care Providers Earn." Retrieved 23 December 2009 (www.naccrra.org/randd/child-care-workforce/what-providers-earn).

National Association of Realtors. 2009. "Metropolitan Median Prices." Retrieved 9 November 2009 (www.realtor.org/Research/research/metroprice).

National Campaign to Prevent Teen and Unplanned Pregnancy. 2009. "National Campaign Analysis: Preliminary 2007 Teen Birth Data." Retrieved 1 December 2009 (www.thenationalcampaign.org/resources/birthdata/analysis.aspx).

National Center for Education Statistics. 2009. "Status Dropout Rates by Race/Ethnicity." In *Student Effort and Educational Progress: Elementary/Secondary Persistence and Progress*. Retrieved 20 February 2010 (nces.ed.gov/programs/coe/2009/section3/indicator20.asp).

National Center for Health Statistics. 2004. "Married Adults Are the Healthiest, New CDC Report Shows." *Centers for Disease Control and Prevention*, 15 December. Retrieved 21 February 2010 (www.cdc.gov/nchs/pressroom/04facts/marriedadults.htm).

—. 2009. *Health, United States, 2008 With Chartbook*. Hyattsville, MD.

—. 2010. *Health, United States, 2009: With Special Feature on Medical Technology*. Hyattsville, MD.

National Center for Victims of Crime. 2007. *Teen Dating Violence Fact Sheet*.

National Coalition Against Domestic Violence. 2009. "Domestic Violence Facts." Retrieved 23 September 2009 (www.ncadv.org/files/DomesticViolenceFactSheet(National).pdf).

National Coalition for the Homeless. 2009. "How Many People Experience Homelessness?" Retrieved 9 November 2009 (www.nationalhomeless.org/factsheets/How_Many.html).

National Conference of State Legislatures. 2010. "Same Sex Marriage, Civil Unions and Domestic Partnerships." Retrieved 20 February 2010 (www.ncsl.org/IssuesResearch/HumanServices/SameSexMarriage/tabid/16430/Default.aspx).

National Family Caregivers Association. 2008a. "Caregiving Depression-Symptoms and Hope." Retrieved 20 March 2008 (www.nfcares.org/improving_caregiving/depression.cfm).

National Heart Lung and Blood Institute. 2008. "What is Asthma?" In *Diseases and Conditions Index*. Retrieved 5 December 2009 (www.nhlbi.nih.gov/health/dci/Diseases/Asthma/Asthma_WhatIs.html).

National Institute of Mental Health. 2009. "Eating Disorders." Retrieved 21 November 2009 (ww.nimh.nih.gov/health/topics/eating-disorders/index.html).

National Institute on Media and the Family. 2009. "Fact Sheet: Media's Effect On Girls: Body Image And Gender Identity." Retrieved 16 April 2010 (www.mediafamily.org/facts/facts_mediaeffect.shtml).

National Marriage Project. 2007. "State of Our Union 2007." Retrieved 6 September 2007. Rutgers University Press (marriage.rutgers.edu/Publications/SOOU/TEXTSOOU2007.htm).

National Stepfamily Resource Center. 2007. "Frequently Asked Questions." Retrieved 28 September 2007 (www.stepfamiles.info/faqs/faqs.php).

——. 2008. "Home Page." Retrieved 4 September 2008 (www.stepfamilies.info/index.php).

Navarro, Mireya. 2007. "My Child's Divorce Is My Pain." *The New York Times*, 2 September.

NBC News/People Magazine. 2005. "National Survey of Young Teens' Sexual Attitudes and Behaviors." Retrieved 21 June 2007 (www.msnbc.msn.com/id/6839072).

Nepomnyaschy, Lenna and Irwin Garfinkel. 2007. "Child Support, Fatherhood, and Marriage: Findings From the First Five Years of the Fragile Families and Child Wellbeing Study." *Asian Social Work and Policy Review* 1(1): 1–20.

Neuman, Lawrence W. 2009. *Understanding Research.* Boston: Pearson.

New York City Gay & Lesbian Anti-Violence Project. 2003. "Building Safer Communities for Lesbian, Gay, Transgender, Bisexual and HIV-Affected New Yorkers."

New York Times. 2005. *Class Matters.* New York: Times Books.

Newport, Frank. 2009. "Extramarital Affairs, Like Sanford's, Morally Taboo." Retrieved 16 November 2009. Gallup Poll (www.gallup.com/poll/121253/extramarital-affairs-sanford-morally-taboo.aspx).

NHS Knowledge Service. 2009. "Home Birth 'Safe as in Hospital'." Retrieved 16 December 2009 (www.nhs.uk/news/2009/04April/Pages/HomeBirthSafe.aspx).

NICHD Early Child Care Research Network. 2005. "Duration and Developmental Timing of Poverty and Children's Cognitive and Social Development From Birth Through Third Grade." *Child Development* 76(4, July): 795–810.

Nitzky, Alene. 1998. "A Poppy in the Rain." *Runner's World*, 9 April, pp. 22–23.

Nock, Steven L. 1998. *Marriage in Men's Lives.* New York: Oxford University Press.

Nock, Steven L., James D. Wright, and Laura A. Sanchez. 1999. "America's Divorce Problem." *Society* 36: 43–52.

Nokoff, Natalie and Anne Fausto-Sterling. 2008. "Raising Gender." Retrieved 5 December 2009. National Sexuality Resource Center (Nsrc.sfsu.edu/article/raising_gender).

Nomaguchi, Kei M. 2009. "Change in Work-Family Conflict Among Employed Parents Between 1977 and 1997." *Journal of Marriage and Family* 71 (February): 15–32.

Nomaguchi, Kei M. and Suzanne M. Bianchi. 2004. "Exercise Time: Gender Differences in the Effects of Marriage, Parenthood, and Employment." *Journal of Marriage and Family* 66 (May): 413–30.

Nomaguchi, Kei M. and Melissa A. Milkie. 2003. "Costs and Rewards of Children: The Effects of Becoming a Parent on Adults' Lives." *Journal of Marriage and Family* 65: 356–74.

Nord, Mark, Margaret Andrews, and Steven Carlson. 2009 November. *Household Food Security in the United States, 2008.* Technical Report No. Economic Research Service, Economic Research Report 83. Washington, DC: U.S. Department of Agriculture.

Nye, F. Ivan. 1979. "Choice, Exchange, and the Family." pp. Vol. 2., pp. 1–41 in *Contemporary Theories About the Family*, edited by Wesley Burr, Reuben Hill, F. Ivan Nye and Ira Reiss. New York: Free Press.

O'Hare, William P. 1995. "3.9 Million U.S. Children in Distressed Neighborhoods." *Population Today* 22: 4–5.

Obama, Barack. 2007. *The Audacity of Hope: Thoughts on Reclaiming the American Dream.* New York: Vintage Books.

Obegi, Joseph H. and Ety Berant, eds. 2009. *Attachment Theory and Research in Clinical Work With Adults.* New York: Guilford Press.

Official Journal of the European Communities. 1998. "Council Directive 97/81/EC of 15 December 1997 Concerning the Framework Agreement on Part-Time Work Concluded by UNICE, CEEP and the ETUC." Retrieved 5 January 2010. Eur-Lex (eur-lex.europa.eu/LexUriServ/LexUriServ.do?uri=CELEX: 31997L0081: EN: HTML).

Ogunwole, Stella U. 2006 February. *We the People: American Indians and Alaska Natives in the United States.* Technical Report No. CENSR-28. Washington DC: US Census Bureau.

Okun, Barbara F. 2002. *Effective Helping: Interviewing and Counseling Techniques, 6th Ed.* Monterey, CA: Brooks/Cole.

Olsen, Charlotte. 1996. "African American Adolescent Women. Perceptions of Gender, Race, and Class." *Marriage and Family Review* 24(1-2, Summer): 107–15.

Omariba, D. Walter Rasugu and Michael H. Boyle. 2007. "Family Structure and Child Mortality in Sub-Saharan Africa: Cross-National Effects of Polygyny." *Journal of Marriage and Family* 69 (May): 528–43.

Onion, Amanda. 2005. "Scientists Find Sex Differences in Brain." *ABC News: Technology & Science*, 19 January. Retrieved 23 June 2006 (abcnews.go.com/Technology/Health/story?id=424260&page=1).

Oppenheimer, Laura. 2008. "Dads Get Off-The-Job Training." *The Oregonian* (Portland, OR), 15 June, p. A1; A9.

Orenstein, Peggy. 1994. *School Girls.* New York, NY: Anchor Books.

Orshansky, Mollie. 1965. "Counting the Poor: Another Look at Poverty." *Social Security Bulletin* 28: 3–29.

Osborne, Cynthia. 2005. "Marriage Following the Birth of a Child Among Cohabiting and Visiting Parents." *Journal of Marriage and Family* 67(1, February): 14–26.

Osborne, Cynthia, Wendy D. Manning, and Pamela J. Smock. 2007. "Married and Cohabiting Parents' Relationship Stability: A Focus on Race and Ethnicity." *Journal of Marriage and Family* 69: 1345–66.

Osmond, Marie and Barrie Thorne. 1993. "Feminist Theories: The Construction of Gender in Families and Society." pp. 591–622 in *Sourcebook of Family Theories and Methods: A Contextual Approach*, edited by Pauline Boss, William Doherty, Ralph LaRossa, Walter Schumm and Suzanne Steinmetz. New York: Plenum.

Oswald, Ramona Faith and Linda S. Culton. 2003. "Under the Rainbow; Rural Gay Life and Its Relevance for Family Providers." *Family Relations* 52(1, January): 72–81.

Oxfam International. 2006 November. *Free, Quality Education for Every Afghan Child.*

Pai, Manacy and Anne E. Barrett. 2007. "Long-Term Payoffs of Work? Women's Past Involvement in Paid Work and Mental Health in Widowhood." *Research on Aging* 29(5): 436–56.

Pailhe, Ariane and Anne Solaz. 2008. "Time With Children: Do Fathers and Mothers Replace Each Other When One Parent Is Unemployed?" *European Journal of Population* 24(2): 211–36.

Palfrey, Dale Hoyt. 1997. La Quinceañera: An Hispanic Celebration of Budding Womanhood. Electronic document. www.mexconnect.com/mex_/travel/dpalfrey/dpquince.html.

Pande, Rohini P. and Nan Marie Astone. 2007. "Explaining Son Preference in Rural India: The Independent Role of Structural Versus Individual Factors." *Population Research and Policy Review* 26(3, June).

Pande, Rohini P. and Anju Malhotra. 2006. *Son Preference and Daughter Neglect in India: What Happens to Living Girls?* Washington, DC: International Center for Research on Women.

Pardo, Tamara. 2008. "Growing up Transgender: Research and Theory." In *Research Facts and Findings*. Retrieved 14 August 2009. ACT for Youth Center of Excellence (www.actforyouth.net/documents/GrowingUpTransPt1_March08.pdf).

Parke, Mary. 2007. "Are Married Parents Really Better for Children? What Research Says About the Effects of Family Structure on Child Well-Being." In *Couples and Married Research and Policy Brief (May 2003)*. Retrieved 14 April 2010. Center for Law and Social Policy (www.clasp.org/admin/site/publications_states/files/0086.pdf).

Parker, Ginny. 1999. Japan Approves Birth Control Pill. Electronic document. Associated Press. http://www.yorkweekly.com/1999news/6_2_w2.htm.

Parker, Kim. 2009. "The Harried Life of the Working Mother." Retrieved 25 October 2009. Pew Research Center (pewsocialtrends.org/pubs/745/the-harried-life-of-the-working-mother).

Parker-Pope, Tara. 2007. "Does Flex Time Lead to Better Health?" *New York Times Online*, 13 December (Well.blogs.nytimes.com/2007/12/13/does-flex-time-lead-to-better-health/).

Parrillo, Vincent N. 2008. *Strangers to These Shores: Race and Ethnic Relations in the United States, 9th Ed.* Boston: Allyn & Bacon.

Parrott, Sharon and Liz Schott. 2009. "Overview of the TANF Provisions in the Economic Recovery Act." Retrieved 23 June 2009. Washington, D.C.: Center on Budget and Policy Priorities (www.cbpp.org/cms/index.cfm?fa=view&id=2693).

Parsons, Talcott. 1937. *The Structure of Social Action.* New York: McGraw-Hill.

Parsons, Talcott and Robert F. Bales. 1955. *Family, Socialization, and the Interactions Process.* New York: Free Press.

Partenheimer, David. 2003. "Race Has Powerful Effects on Children's Perceptions of Occupations, Study Finds" (Press Release). Retrieved 6 January 2004. American Psychological Association (www.apa.org/releases/race_jobs.html).

—. 2005. "Do Opposites Attract or Do Birds of a Feather Flock Together?" (Press Release). Retrieved 21 June 2005. American Psychological Association (www.apa.org/releases/attraction.html).

Pascoe, C.J. 2007. *Dude, You're a Fag: Masculinity and Sexuality in High School.* Berkeley, CA: University of California Press.

Patterson, Charlotte J. and Paul D. Hastings. 2007. "Socialization in the Context of Family Diversity." pp. 328–51 in *Handbook of Socialization: Theory and Research*, edited by Joan E. Grusec and Paul D. Hastings. New York: The Guilford Press.

Paul, Annie Murphy. 2006. "The Real Marriage Penalty." *New York Times Magazine*, 19 November, pp. 22–23.

Pawelski, James G., Ellen C. Perrin, Jane M. Foy, Carole E. Allen, James E. Crawford, Mark Del Monte, Miriam Kaufman, Jonathan D. Klein, Karen Smith, Sarah Springer, J. Lane Tanner, and Dennis L. Vickers. 2006. "The Effects of Marriage, Civil Union, and Domestic Partnership Laws on the Health and Well-Being of Children." *Pediatrics*, 118: 349–64.

Pearson, Jessica and Nancy Thoennes. 1998. "Programs to Increase Fathers' Access to Their Children." pp. 220–52 in *Fathers Under Fire*, edited by Irwin Garfinkel, Sara S. McLanahan, Daniel R. Meyer and Judith A. Seltzer. New York, NY: Russell Sage Foundation.

Pearson, Quinn M. 2008. "Role Overload, Job Satisfaction, Leisure Satisfaction, and Psychological Health Among Employed Women."*Journal of Counseling & Development* 86(1): 57–63.

Pedersen, Willy and Hans W. Kristiansen. 2008. "Homosexual Experience, Desire and Identity Among Young Adults." *Journal of Homosexuality* 54(1-2): 68–102.

Pelham, Brett W. 2010. "Rest Eludes Nearly 30% of Americans." Retrieved 2 March 2010. Gallup Poll (www.gallup.com/poll/125471/rest-eludes-nearly-americans.aspx?version=print).

Peplau, Letitia A. and Kristin P. Beals. 2004. "The Family Lives of Lesbians and Gay Men." pp. 233–48 in *Handbook of Family Communication*, edited by Anita Vangelisti. Mahwah, NJ: Lawrence Erlbaum Associates.

Perillous, Carin and David M. Buss. 2008. "Breaking Up Romantic Relationships: Costs Experienced and Coping Strategies Deployed."*Evolutionary Psychology* 6(164–181).

Perkins, Daniel F. and Kate Fogarty. 2005. "Active Listening: A Communication Tool." In *FCS2151, One of a Series of the Family, Youth, and Community Sciences Department, Florida Cooperative Extension Service, Institute of Food and Agricultural Sciences, University of Florida.* Retrieved 29 September 2008 (Edis.ifas.ufl.edu/he361).

Perry, Bruce D. 2002. "Childhood Experience and the Expression of Genetic Potential: What Childhood Neglect Tells Us About Nature and Nurture." *Brain and Mind* 3(1): 79–100.

Perry-Jenkins, Maureen, Abbie E. Goldberg, Courtney P. Pierce, and Aline G. Sayer. 2007. Shift Work, Role Overload, and the Transition to Parenthood. *Journal of Marriage and the Family* 69: 123–138.

Perry-Jenkins, Maureen, Rena L. Repetti, and Ann C. Crouter. 2000. "Work and Family in the 1990s." *Journal of Marriage and the Family* 62(4, November): 981–98.

Peter, Jennifer. 2004. "Gay Marriage in MA." *Nitecrawler*, 4 February. Retrieved 9 March 2004 (donfox.blogdns.org/archives/000531.html).

Peters, Brad and Marion F. Ehrenberg. 2008. "The Influence of Parental Separation and Divorce on Father-Child Relationships."*Journal of Divorce & Remarriage* 49(1-2, June): 78–109.

Pew Center on the States. 2009. March. *One in 31: The Long Reach of American Corrections.* Washington, DC: The Pew Charitable Trusts.

Pew Hispanic Center. 2006a. *From 200 Million to 300 Million: The Numbers Behind the Population Growth (Fact Sheet).* Washington, D.C.

—. 2008. "Gay Marriage Is Back On The Radar For Republicans, Evangelicals." Retrieved 25 June 2008 (pewresearch.org/pubs/868/gay-marriage).

Pew Research Center for the People & the Press. 2009. "Majority Continues to Support Civil Unions." Retrieved 20 February 2010 (people-press.org/report/553/same-sex-marriage).

Pew Research Center. 2007a. "As Marriage and Parenthood Drift Apart, Public is Concerned About Social Impact: Generation Gap in Values, Behaviors" (pewresearch.org/pubs/526/marriage-parenthood).

—. 2007b. "Motherhood Today: Tougher Challenges, Less Success." Retrieved 7 March 2010 (pewresearch.org/pubs/468/motherhood).

—. 2008a. "Perpetual Minors: Human Rights Abuses Stemming From Male Guardianship and Sex Segregation in Saudi Arabia." In *Human Rights Watch.* Retrieved 5 May 2008 (www.hrw.org).

—. 2008b. "Religion in America: Non-Dogmatic, Diverse, and Politically Relevant." Retrieved 24 June 2008 (pewresearch.org/pubs/876/religion-america-part-two).

—. 2009. Retrieved 24 June 2009. PollingReport.com (www.pollingreport.com/prioriti.htm).

—. 2010a. "Millennials: Confident, Connected, Open to Change."

—. 2010b. "The Return of the Multi-Generational Family Household." Retrieved 4 April 2010 (pewresearch.orgs/pubs/1528/multi-generational-family-household).

Pfeffer, Carla A. 2010. ""Women's Work?" Women Partners of Transgender Men Doing Housework and Emotion Work." *Journal of Marriage and Family* 72(1, February): 165–83.

PFLAG. 2009. "Get Support: Welcome to TNET!" Retrieved 14 February 2010 (Community.pflag.org/Page.aspx?pid=380).

Phillips, Julie A. and Megan M. Sweeney. 2005. "Premarital Cohabitation and Marital Disruption Among White, Black, and Mexican American Women." *Journal of Marriage and Family* 67 (May): 296–314.

Phillips, R. 1997. "Stepfamilies From a Historical Perspective." pp. 5–18 in *Stepfamilies: History, Research and Policy*, edited by Ira Levin and Marvin Sussman. New York: Haworth.

Pifer-Bexler, Jennifer. 2009. "Study: 86.7 Million Americans Uninsured Over Last Two Years." Retrieved 5 March 2010. CNNhealth.com (www.cnn.com/2009/HEALTH/03/04/uninsured.epidemic.obama/).

Pineo, Peter. 1961. "Disenchantment in the Later Years of Marriage." *Marriage and Family Living* 23: 3–11.

Pinquart, Martin, and Daniela Teubert. 2010. A Meta-Analytic Study of Couple Interventions During the Transition to Parenthood. Family Relations 59(3 July): 221–231.

Legislation on Divorce Rates: A Response to a Reconsideration." *Journal of Marriage and the Family* 59: 1026–30.

Rodgers, Roy H. and James M. White. 1993. "Family Development Theory." pp. 225–54 in *Sourcebook of Family Theories and Methods: A Contextual Approach*, edited by Pauline G. Boss, William J. Doherty, Ralph LaRossa, Walter R. Schumm and Suzanne K. Steinmetz. New York: Plenum Press.

Rodriguez, Michael, Jeanette M. Valentine, John B. Son, and Marjani Muhammad. 2009. "Intimate Partner Violence and Barriers to Mental Health Care for Ethnically Diverse Populations of Women." *Trauma, Violence, & Abuse* 10(4): 358–74.

Roebuck Bulanda, J. and Susan Brown. 2007. "Race-Ethnic Differences in Marital Quality and Divorce." *Social Service Review* 36: 945–67.

Roer-Strier, Dorit and Dina Ben Ezra. 2006. "Intermarriages Between Western Women and Palestinian Men: Multidirectional Adaptation Processes." *Journal of Marriage and Family* 68(1): 41–55.

Rogers, Stacy J. 2004. "Dollars, Dependency, and Divorce: Four Perspectives on the Role of Wives' Income." *Journal of Marriage and Family* 66 (February): 59–74.

Rohall, David E., Melissa A. Milkie, and Jeffrey W. Lucas. 2007. *Social Psychology: Sociological Perspectives*. Boston: Allyn & Bacon.

Rohner, Ronald P. and Robert A. Veneziano. 2001. "The Importance of Father Love: History and Contemporary Evidence." *Review of General Psychology* 5(4, December): 382–405.

Rooks, Judith. 1997. *Midwifery and Childbirth in America*. Philadelphia: Temple University Press.

Rosenberg, Matt. 2009. "China's One Child Policy." Retrieved 9 November 2009. About.com (geography. About.com/od/populationgeography/a/onechild.htm).

Rosenfeld, Michael J. 2008. *The Age of Independence: Interracial Unions, Same-Sex Unions and the Changing American Family*. Cambridge, MA: Harvard University Press.

Rosin, Mark Bruce. 2009. *Stepfathering*. New York: Simon and Schuster.

Ross, Catherine E. and Marieke Van Willigen. 1996. "Gender, Parenthood, and Anger." *Journal of Marriage and the Family* 58: 572–84.

Ross, Donna Cohen, Aleya Horn, and Caryn Marks. 2008. "Health Coverage for Children and Families in Medicaid and SCHIP: State Efforts Face New Hurdles: Executive Summary." Retrieved 15 July 2008. Kaiser Commission on Medicaid and the Uninsured (www.kff.org/medicaid/upload/7740_ES.pdf).

Rossi, Alice S. 1968. "Transition to Motherhood." *Journal of Marriage and the Family* 30: 26–39.

Rothbart, Mary K. and Brad Sheese. 2007. "Temperament and Emotion Regulation." pp. 331–50 in *Handbook of Emotion Regulation*, edited by J. Gross. New York: Guilford Press.

Rothman, Barbara Katz. 1991. *In Labor: Women and Power in the Birthplace*. New York, NY: W.W. Norton and Co.

Rothstein, Donna S. 2001. "Youth Employment in the United States." *Monthly Labor Review* 124: 6–17.

Roudsan, Bahman S., Matthew M. Leahy, and Scott T. Walters. 2009. "Correlates of Dating Violence Among Male and Female Heavy-Drinking College Students." *Journal of Interpersonal Violence* 24(11): 1892–905.

Rubin, Lillian B. 1976. *Worlds of Pain*. New York: Basic Books.

Rutley, Daniel. 2001. *Escaping Emotional Entrapment: Freedom From Negative Thinking and Unhealthy Emotions*. Lakeland, FL: Pax Publishing.

Saad, Lydia. 2008. "By Age 24, Marriage Wins Out" (http://www.gallup.com/poll/109402/Age-24-Marriage-Wins.aspx).

Saad, Lydia. 2004. "Romance to Break Out Nationwide This Weekend." Retrieved 25 September 2008. Gallup Poll (www.gallup.com/poll/10609/Romance-Break-Nationwide-Weekend.aspx).

—. 2009. "Republicans Move to the Right on Several Moral Issues." Retrieved 14 February 2010. Gallup Poll (www.gallup.com/poll/118546/republicans-veer-right-several-moral-issues.aspx).

Sabol, William J., Heather C. West, and Matthew Cooper. 2009. "Prisoners in 2008." Retrieved 21 February 2010. Bureau of Justice Statistics, U.S. Department of Justice (bjs.ojp.usdoj.gov/content/pub/pdf/p08.pdf).

Salkind, Neil J. 2009. *Exploring Research, 7th Ed.* Boston: Pearson.

Samandari, Ghazeleh and Sandra L. Martin. 2010. "Homicide Among Pregnant and Postpartum Women in the United States: A Review of the Literature." *Trauma, Violence, & Abuse* 11(1): 42–54.

Sample, Neal. 1999. "What I Felt Like Being Adopted" (http: //www.stepfamilynetwork.net/Adoption.htm).

Sanday, Peggy Reeves. 1981. "The Socio-Cultural Context of Rape: A Cross-Cultural Study." *Journal of Social Issues* 37: 5–27.

Sandberg, John F. and Sandra L. Hofferth. 2001. "Changes in Children's Time With Parents: United States." *Demography* 38: 423–36.

Sands, Roberta G. and Robin S. Goldberg-Glen. 2000. "Factors Associated With Stress Among Grandparents Raising Their Grandchildren." *Family Relations* 49: 97–105.

Santelli, John S., Mark Orr, Laura D. Lindberg, and Daniela C. Diaz. 2009. "Changing Behavioral Risk for Pregnancy

Among High School Students in the United States: 1991-2007." *Journal of Adolescent Health* 44(7): 25–32.

Sapir, Edward. 1949. *Selected Writings of Edward Sapir in Language, Culture, and Personality, David G. Mandelbaum, Ed.* Berkeley, CA: University of California Press.

Sarkadi, Anna, Robert Kristiansson, Frank Oberklaid, and Sven Bremberg. 2008. "Fathers' Involvement and Children's Developmental Outcomes: A Review of Longitudinal Studies." *Acta Paediatrica* 97: 153–58.

Sassler, Sharon, Anna Cunningham, and Daniel T. Lichter. 2009. "Intergenerational Patterns of Union Formation and Relationship Quality." *Journal of Family Issues* 30(6): 757–86.

Saul, Stephanie. 2009. "Building a Baby, With Few Ground Rules." Retrieved 20 December 2009. New York Times (www.nytimes.com/2009/12/13/us/13surrogacy.html?_r=1&pagewanted=print).

Sax, Leonard. 2005. *Why Gender Matters: What Parents and Teachers Need to Know About the Emerging Science of Sex Differences?* New York: Doubleday.

—. 2006. *Why Gender Matters: What Parents and Teachers Need to Know About the Emerging Science of Sex Differences.* New York: Doubleday.

Sayer, Liana C., Anne H. Gauthier, and Frank F. Furstenberg, Jr. 2004. Educational Differences in Parents' Time with Children: Cross-National Variations. *Journal of Marriage and Family* 66: 1152–1169.

Sbarra, David A. 2006. "Predicting the Onset of Emotional Recovery Following Nonmarital Relationship Dissolution: Survival Analyses of Sadness and Anger." *Personality and Social Psychology Bulletin* 32(3): 298–312.

Scanzoni, John. 2004. "Household Diversity: The Starting Point for Healthy Families in the New Century." pp. 3–22 in *Handbook of Contemporary Families*, edited by M. Coleman and L. H. Ganong. Thousand Oaks, CA: Sage Publications.

Scaramella, Laura V., Tricia K. Neppl, Lenna L. Ontai, and Rand D. Conger. 2008. "Consequences of Socioeconomic Disadvantage Across Three Generations." *Journal of Family Psychology* 22(5): 725–33.

Scarcella, Cynthia Andrews, Jennifer Ehrle Macomber, and Rob Geen. 2003. Identifying and Addressing the Needs of Children in Grandparent Care. Electronic document. *In:* No. B-55 in Series, "New Federalism: National Survey of America's Families". www.urban.org/publications/310842.html.

Schaefer, Richard T. 2011. *Racial and Ethnic Groups, Census Update, 12th Ed.* Upper Saddle River, NJ: Prentice Hall.

Schaie, K. Warner and Glen H. Elder, Jr. 2005. *Historical Influences on Lives and Aging.* New York, NY: Springer Publishing Co.

Schieber, Sylvester J. 2008 May. *Beyond the Golden Age of Retirement.* University of Michigan Retirement Research Center Policy Brief No. 6.

Schiebinger, Londa, and Shannon K. Gilmartin. 2010. Housework is an Academic Issue. Electronic document. *In:* Academe Online. www.aaup.org/AAUP/pubsres/academe/2010/JF/feat/schlie.htm.

Schilt, Kristen. 2006. "Just One of the Guys? How Transmen Make Gender Visible at Work." *Gender & Society* 20(4, August): 465–90.

Schmid, Randolph E. 2005. "Scent Studies Find Gay, Straight Divide." *The Oregonian* (Portland, OR), 10 May, A, p. 3.

—. 2007. "Elderly Health Care Costs Growing Slowly." Retrieved 3 May 2010. BlueCross BlueShield Association (www.bcbs.com/news/national/elderly-health-costs-growing-slowly.html).

Schoen, Cathy, Robin Osborn, Michelle M. Doty, Meghan Bishop, Jordon Peugh, and Nandita Murukutla. 2007. "Toward Higher-Performance Health Systems: Adults' Health Care Experiences in Seven Countries, 2007." *Health Affairs* 26(6, November/December): w717–34.

Schoenborn, Charlotte A., and Patricia F. Adams. 2010. Health Behaviors of Adults: United States, 2005–2007. National Center for Health Statistics. Vital Health Statistics 10(245).

Schoppe-Sullivan, Sarah J., Alice C. Schermerhorn, and E. Mark Cummings. 2007. "Marital Conflict and Children's Adjustment: Evaluation of the Parenting Process Model." *Journal of Marriage and Family* 69(5, December): 1118–34.

Schor, Juliet B. 2002. "Time Crunch Among American Parents." pp. 83–102 in *Taking Parenting Public*, edited by S. A. Hewlett, N. Rankin and C. West. Lanham, Maryland: Rowman & Littlefield.

Schwartz, Karyn. 2007. "Spotlight on Uninsured Parents: How a Lack of Coverage Affects Parents and Their Families" (Kaiser Low-Income Coverage and Access Survey). *The Kaiser Commission on Medicaid and the Uninsured*, June. Menlo Park, CA/The Henry J. Kaiser Family Foundation.

Schwartz, Pepper. 1994. *Love Between Equals: How Peer Marriage Really Works.* New York: Free Press.

—. 2001. "Peer Marriage: What Does It Take to Create a Truly Egalitarian Relationship?" pp. 182–89 in *Families in Transition, 11th Ed.*, edited by Arlene S. Skolnick and Jerome H. Skolnick. Boston: Allyn & Bacon.

—. 2007. *Sexual Satisfaction in Committed Relationships.* Allentown, PA: The Society for the Scientific Study of Sexuality.

Schwartz, Seth J. and Gordon E. Finley. 2006. "Father Involvement, Nurturant Fathering, and Young Adult

Psychosocial Functioning."*Journal of Family Issues* 27(5): 712–31.

Schweitzer, Ivy. 2006. *Perfecting Friendship: Politics and Affiliation in Early American Literature*. Chapel Hill: University of North Carolina Press.

Science Daily. 2006. "Transgender Experience Led Stanford Scientist to Critique Gender Difference." Retrieved 21 November 2006 (www.sciencedaily.com/releases/2006/07/060714174545.htm).

Scott, Megan K. 2009. "Multitaskers Say One Online Dating Site Won't Do." Retrieved 22 January 2010. Fall River, MA: The Herald News (www.heraldnews.com/lifestyle/x545172880/Multitaskers-say-one-online-dating-site-wont-do).

Searle, Eleanor. 1988. *Predatory Kinship and the Creation of Norman Power, 840-1066*. Berkeley, CA: University of California Press.

Sears, William and Martha Sears. 2001. *The Attachment Parenting Book: A Commonsense Guide to Understanding and Nurturing Your Baby*. New York: Little, Brown.

Seccombe, Karen. 1991. "Assessing the Costs and Benefits of Children: Gender Comparisons Among Childfree Husbands and Wives."*Journal of Marriage and the Family* 53: 191–202.

—. 2002. "'Beating the Odds' Versus 'Changing the Odds': Poverty, Resilience, and Family Policy." *Journal of Marriage and Family* 64: 384–94.

—. 2007. *Families in Poverty*. Boston: Allyn & Bacon.

—. 2011. *So You Think I Drive a Cadillac?: Welfare Recipients' Perspectives on the System and Its Reform*. Needham Heights, N.J.: Allyn & Bacon.

Seccombe, Karen and Kim A. Hoffman. 2007. *Just Don't Get Sick: Access to Health Care in the Aftermath of Welfare Reform*. Piscataway, NJ: Rutgers University Press.

Sedlak, Andrea J. and Diane D. Broadhurst. 1998. "Executive Summary of the Third National Incidence Study of Child Abuse and Neglect" (www.casanet.org/library/abuse/stabuse.htm).

Seelke, Clare Ribando and Alison Siskin. 2008. "Trafficking in Persons: U.S. Policy and Issues for Congress" (CRS Report for Congress). Retrieved 26 March 2010 (fpc.state.gov/documents/organization/109559.pdf).

Segal, Marcia Texler and Theresa A. Martinez, eds. 2007. *Intersections of Gender, Race, and Class: Readings for a Changing Landscape*. New York: Oxford University Press.

Seiffge-Krenke, Inge. 2006. "Coping With Relationship Stressors: The Impact of Different Working Models of Attachment and Links to Adaptation." *Journal of Youth and Adolescence* 35(1, February): 24–38.

Seiler, William J. and Melissa L. Beall. 2011. *Communication: Making Connection, 8th Ed*. Boston: Allyn & Bacon.

Seltzer, Judith A. 1998. "Fathers by Law: Effects of Joint Legal Custody on Nonresidental Fathers' Involvement With Children."*Demography* 35: 135–46.

—. 2004. "Cohabitation and Family Change." pp. 57–78 in *Handbook of Contemporary Families*, edited by M. Coleman and L. H. Ganong. Thousand Oaks, CA: Sage Publications, Inc.

Selye, Hans. 1955. "Stress and Disease." *Scientific American* 122 (7 October): 625–31.

—. 1956. *The Stress of Life*. New York: McGaw-Hill.

Shackleford, Todd K., Martin Voracek, David P. Schmitt, David M. Buss, Viviana A. Weekes-Shackleford, and Richard L. Michalski. 2004. "Romantic Jealousy in Early Adulthood and in Later Life." *Human Nature* 15: 283–300.

Shanhong, Luo and Eva C. Klohnen. 2005. "Assortative Mating and Marital Quality in Newlyweds: A Couple-Centered Approach."*Journal of Personality and Social Psychology* 88: 304–26.

Shapiro, Adam D. 1996. "Explaining Psychological Distress in a Sample of Remarried and Divorced Persons: The Influence of Economic Distress." *Journal of Family Issues* 17: 186–203.

Shaver, Philip R. and Mario Mikulincer. 2009. "Attachment Theory and Attachment Styles." pp. 62–81 in *Handbook of Individual Differences*, edited by M. R. Leary and R. H. Hoyle. New York: Guilford Press.

Shehan, Constance L., Felix M. Berardo, Erica Owens, and Donna H. Berardo. 2002. "Alimony: An Anomaly in Family Social Science."*Family Relations* 51: 308–16.

Shelton, Beth Anne. 1992. *Women, Men and Time: Gender Differences in Paid Work, Housework, and Leisure*. Westport, CT: Greenwood.

Shepard, Judy. 2009. *The Meaning of Matthew: My Son's Murder in Laramie, and a World Transformed*. New York: Hudson Street Press.

Sherman, Arloc. 2009. "Income Gaps Hit Record Levels in 2006, New Data Show Rich-Poor Gap Tripled Between 1979 and 2006." Retrieved 9 November 2009. Washington, DC: Center for Budget and Policy Priorities (www.cbpp.org/cms/index.cfm?fa=view&id=2789).

Sherman, Arloc and Aviva Aron-Dine. 2007. "New CBO Data Show Income Inequality Continues to Widen: After-Tax Income for Top 1 Percent Rose by $146,000 in 2004." Retrieved 1 October 2007. Center on Budget and Policy Priorities (www.cbpp.org/1-23-07inc.htm).

Sherman, Aurora M., Jennifer E. Lansford, and Brenda L. Volling. 2006. "Sibling Relationships and Best Friendships in Young Adulthood: Warmth, Conflict, and Well-Being." *Personal Relationships* 13(2): 151–165.

Shilts, Randy. 1987. *And The Band Played On: Politics, People, and the AIDS Epidemic*. New York, NY: St. Martins Press.

Shipler, David K. 2004. *The Working Poor: Invisible in America.* New York: Vintage Books.

Shriner, Michael, Ronald L. Mullis, and Bethanne M. Schlee. 2009. "The Usefulness of Social Capital Theory for Understanding the Academic Improvement of Young Children in Stepfamilies Over Two Points in Time." *Journal of Divorce & Remarriage* 50(7, October): 445–58.

Shulman, Shmuel, Sophie D. Walsh, Osnat Weisman, and Michal Schelyer. 2009. "Romantic Contexts, Sexual Behavior, and Depressive Symptoms Among Adolescent Males and Females." *Sex Roles* 61(11-12, December): 850–63.

Silliman, Ben. 1994. "1994 Resiliency Research Review: Conceptual & Research Foundations." Retrieved 16 June 2001 (http://www.cyfernet.org/research/resilreview.html).

—. 1998. "The Resiliency Paradigm: A Critical Tool for Practitioners." *Human Development and Family Life Bulletin* (Ohio State University, College of Human Ecology), Spring.

Simmons, Tavia and Jane Lawler Dye. 2003 October. *Grandparents Living With Grandchildren: 2000.* Census 2000 Brief No. C2KBR-31. Washington, DC: U.S. Census Bureau.

Simon, Rita J. and Howard Alstein. 2000. *Adoption Across Borders: Serving the Children in Transracial and Intercountry Adoptions.* Lanham, MD: Rowman & Littlefield.

Simon, Rita J. and Rhonda M. Roorda. 2000. *In Their Own Voices: Transracial Adoptees Tell Their Stories.* New York: Columbia University Press.

—. 2009. *In Their Siblings' Voices: White Non-Adopted Siblings Talk About Their Experiences Being Raised With Black and Biracial Brothers and Sisters.* New York: Columbia University Press.

Simons, Ronald L., Leslie G. Simons, Callie H. Burt, Holli Drummund, Eric Stewart, Gene H. Brody, Frederick X. Gibbons, and Carolyn Cutrona. 2006. "Supportive Parenting Moderates the Effect of Discrimination Upon Anger, Hostile View of Relationships, and Violence Among African American Boys." *Journal of Health and Social Behavior* 47(December): 373–89.

Simpson, George Eaton and J. Milton Yinger. 1985. *Racial and Cultural Minorities: An Analysis of Prejudice and Discrimination, 5th Ed.* New York: Plenum.

Simpson, Jeffry A., W. Steven Rholes, Lorne Campbell, Sisi Tran, and Carol L. Wilson. 2003. Adult Attachment, the Transition to Parenthood, and Depressive Symptoms. *Journal of Personality and Social Psychology* 84: 1172–1187.

Slotter, Erica B., Wendi L. Gardner, and Eli J. Finkel. 2010. "Who Am I Without You? The Influence of Romantic Breakup on the Self-Concept." *Personality and Social Psychology Bulletin* 36(2): 147–60.

Small, Wolf Joanne. 2007. *The Adoption Mystique: A Hard-Hitting Exposé of the Powerful Negative Social Stigma That Permeates Child Adoption in the United States.* Bloomington, IN: Authorhouse.

Smit, Laura. 2005. *Loves Me, Loves Me Not.* Ada, MI: Baker Academic.

Smith, Alison J. 2004. "Who Cares? Fathers and the Time They Spend Looking After Children" (Sociology Working Paper No. 2004-05).*Department of Sociology, University of Oxford.* Oxford, England (www.nuff.ox.ac.uk/users/smith/2004-05).

Smith, Earl, and Angela Hattery. 2009. Interracial Relationships in the 21st Century. Durham, NC: Carolina Academic Press.

Smith, Gregory C. and Patrick A. Palmieri. 2007. "Risk of Psychosocial Difficulties Among Children Raised by Custodial Grandparents."*Psychiatric Services* 58 (October): 1303–10.

Smith, Lynne, Patrick C.L. Heaven, and Joseph Ciarrochi. 2008. "Trait Emotional Intelligence, Conflict Communication Patterns, and Relationship Satisfaction." *Personality and Individual Differences* 44(6, April): 1314–25.

Smith, Sandi W. and Steven Wilson. 2009. *New Directions in Interpersonal Communication Research.* Newbury Park, CA: Sage Publications.

Smith, Suzanne R., Raeann R. Hamon, J. Elizabeth Miller, and Bron B. Ingoldsby. 2009. Exploring Family Theories, 2nd Ed. New York: Oxford University Press.

Smith, Tom W. 2006. March. *American Sexual Behavior: Trends, Socio-Demographic Differences, and Risk Behavior.* National Opinion Research Center No. General Social Survey Topical Report No. 25. University of Chicago.

Smith-Rosenberg, Carol. 1975. "The Female World of Love and Ritual: Relations Between Women in Nineteenth-Century America."*Signs: A Journal of Women in Culture and Society* 1: 1–29.

Sneed, Joel, Fumiaki Hamagami, John McArdle, Patricia Cohen, and Henian Chen. 2007. "The Dynamic Interdependence of Developmental Domains Across Emerging Adulthood." *Journal of Youth and Adolescence* 36(3): 351–362.

Snow, Judith. 2004. *How It Feels to Have a Gay or Lesbian Parent: A Book by Kids for Kids of All Ages.* New York: Routledge.

Social Security Administration. 2010. "Social Security Programs Throughout the World." Retrieved 3 May 2010 (www.ssa.gov/policy/docs/progdesc/ssptw).

Society for Research in Child Development. 2008. *Improving After-School Programs in a Climate of Accountability.* Social Policy Report Brief No. 22 (2).

Solarz, Andrea, ed. 2008. *Lesbian Health: Current Assessments and Directions for the Future.* Washington, DC: National Academies Press.

Somary, Karen and George Stricker. 1998. "Becoming a Grandparent: A Longitudinal Study of Expectations and Early Experiences as a Function of Sex and Lineage." *The Gerontologist* 38: 53–61.

Sontag, Susan. 1979. "The Double Standard of Aging." In *Psychology of Women: Selected Readings,* edited by J. H. Williams. New York: Norton.

Sorgen, Carol. 2008. "Seeing Green: All About Jealousy." Retrieved 10 November 2008. WebMD (www.wewbmd.com/sex-relationships/guide/seeing-green-all-About-jealousy).

Soto, Mauricio. 2009. "How Is the Financial Crisis Affecting Retirement Savings?" Retrieved www.urban.org/publicaions/901206.html. Washington, D.C./Urban Institute.

Spenser, Colin. 1995. *Homosexuality in History.* New York: Harcourt Brace & Company.

Spock, Benjamin, Dr. 2004. "Gay and Lesbian Parents" (Webpage). In *Dr. Spock.* Retrieved 25 May 2006 (www.drspock.com/article/0,1510,4028,00.html).

Sprecher, Susan. 2002. "Sexual Satisfaction in Premarital Relationships: Associations With Satisfaction, Love, Commitment, and Stability." *The Journal of Sex Research* 39(13): 190–97.

Sprecher, Susan, Diane Felmlee, Maria Schmeeckle, and Xiaoling Shu. 2006. "No Breakup Occurs on an Island: Social Networks and Relationship Dissolution." pp. 457–78 in *Handbook of Divorce and Relationship Dissolution,* edited by Mark A. Fine and John H. Harvey. Mahwah, NJ: Lawrence Erlbaum.

Sprecher, Susan, F. Scott Christopher, and Rodney Cate. 2006. Sexuality in Close Relationships. *In* Handbook on Personal Relationships. Anita L. Vangelisti and Daniel Perlman, eds. pp. 462–482. New York: Cambridge University Press.

Spruijt, Ed and Vincent Duindam. 2010. "Joint Physical Custody in The Netherlands and the Well-Being of Children." *Journal of Divorce & Remarriage* 51(1, January): 65–82.

Stacey, Judith and Timothy J. Biblarz. 2001. "How Does the Sexual Orientation of Parents Matter?" *American Sociological Review* 66: 159–83.

Stalking Resource Center. 2009 June. *Stalking Fact Sheet.* Washington, DC: National Center for Victims of Crime.

Stanton, Glenn T. 2005. "How Is Marriage Dying in Our Culture?" In *CitizenLink.* Retrieved 30 June 2005. Focus on the Family (www.family.org/cforum/fosi/marriage/facts/a0028319.cfm).

Stein, Peter J. 1976. *Single.* Englewood Cliffs, NY: Prentice Hall.

—. 1981. "Understanding Single Adulthood." pp. 9–20 in *Single Life: Unmarried Adults in Social Contexts,* edited by P. Stein. New York: St. Martin's Press.

Steinbeck, John. 1939 (Reprinted 2002). *The Grapes of Wrath.* New York: Penguin.

Steinberg, Stephen. 1981. *The Ethnic Myth: Race, Ethnicity, and Class in America.* Boston, MA: Beacon Press.

Steinhauser, Paul. 2009. "CNN Poll: Generations Disagree on Same-Sex Marriage." *CNN.Com/US,* 4 May. Retrieved 14 February 2010 (www.cnn.com/2009/US/05/04/samesex.marriage.poll/index.html).

Steinmayr, Ricarda and Birgit Spinath. 2009. "What Explains Boys' Stronger Confidence in Their Intelligence?" *Sex Roles* 61(9-10): 736–49.

Stepfamily Foundation. 2005. "Classic Complaints in Stepfamilies." Retrieved 28 September 2007 (www.stepfamily.org/classic_complaints_in_stepfamilies.htm).

—. 2007. "Statistics on Stepfamilies in the United States." Retrieved 28 September 2007 (www.stepfamily.org/statistics.html).

Stephens, William N. 1963. *The Family in Cross-Cultural Perspective.* New York: Holt, Rinehart, and Winston.

Sterk-Elifson, C. 1994. "Sexuality Among African American Women." pp. 99–127 in *Sexuality Across the Life Course,* edited by A. Rossi. University of Chicago Press.

Sternberg, Robert J. 1986. "A Triangular Theory of Love." *Psychological Review* 93(2): 119–35.

—. 1988. *The Triangle of Love.* New York: Basic Books.

Sternberg, Robert J. and Karen Sternberg, eds. 2008. *The New Psychology of Love.* New Haven, CT: Yale University Press.

Stevens, Daphne Pedersen, Krista Lynn Minnotte, Susan E. Mannon, and Gary Kiger. 2007. "Examining the 'Neglected Side of the Work-Family Interface'." *Journal of Family Issues* 28(2): 242–62.

Stevenson, Betsey and Justin Wolfers. 2007. "The Paradox of Declining Female Happiness." bpp.wharton.upenn.edu/betseys/papers/Paradox%20of%20declining%20female%20happiness.pdf.

Stewart, Susan D. 2005. "How the Birth of a Child Affects Involvement With Stepchildren." *Journal of Marriage and Family* 67(2, May): 461.

—. 2007. *Brave New Stepfamilies.* Thousand Oaks, CA: Sage Publications.

Stoll, Barre M., Genevieve L. Arnaut, Donald K. Fromme, and Jennifer A. Felker-Thayer. 2006. "Adolescents in Stepfamilies." *Journal of Divorce and Remarriage* 44(1): 177–89.

Stombler, Mindy, Dawn M. Baunach, Elisabeth O. Burgess, Denise Donnelly, Wendy Simonds, and Elroi J. Windsor, eds. 2010. *Sex Matters: The Sexuality and Society Reader, 3rd Ed.* New York: Prentice Hall.

Stone, Linda. 2006. *Kinship and Gender, 3rd Ed.* Boulder, CO: Westview Press.

Stone, Pamela. 2007a. *Opting Out? Why Women Really Quit Careers and Head Home.* Berkeley, CA: University of California Press.

—. 2007b. *Opting Out? Why Women Really Quit Careers and Head Home.* Berkeley, CA: University of California Press.

—. 2008. *Opting Out? Why Women Really Quit Careers and Head Home.* Berkeley, CA: University of California Press.

Straus, Murray A. 1980. "Social Stress and Marital Violence in a National Sample of American Families." *Annals of the New York Academy of Sciences* 347: 229–50.

—. 2003. *The Primordial Violence: Corporal Punishment by Parents, Cognitive Development, and Crime.* Walnut Creek, CA: AltaMira Press.

Straus, Murray A. and Denise A. Donnelly. 2001. *Beating the Devil Out of Them: Corporal Punishment in American Families and Its Effects on Children, 2nd Ed.* New Brunswick, NJ: Transaction Publishers.

Straus, Murray A. and Mallie J. Paschall. 2009. "Corporal Punishment by Mothers and Development of Children's Cognitive Ability: A Longitudinal Study of Two Nationally Representative Age Cohorts." *Journal of Aggression, Maltreatment & Trauma* 48: 459–83.

Straus, Murray A., Richard J. Gelles, and Suzanne K. Steinmetz. 1980. *Behind Closed Doors: Violence in the American Family.* New York: Anchor Books.

Strazdins, Lyndall, Mark S. Clements, Rosemary J. Korda, Dorothy H. Broom, and Rennie M. D'Souza 2006. "Unsociable Work? Nonstandard Work Schedules, Family Relationships and Children's Well-Being." *Journal of Marriage and the Family* 68(2): 394–410.

Stritof, Sheri and Bob Stritof. 2006. "Covenant Marriage Statistics." Retrieved 6 June 2006. About.com (marriage.About.com/cs/covenantmarriage/a/covenant_3.htm).

Strong, Bryan, Christine DeVault, Barbara W. Sayad, and William L. Yarber. 2002. *Human Sexuality: Diversity in Contemporary America.* 4th Ed. Boston, MA: McGraw Hill.

Sudarkasa, Niara. 1999. "Interpreting the African Heritage in Afro-American Family Organization." pp. 59–73 in *American Families: A Multicultural Reader*, edited by S. Coontz, M. Parson and G. Raley. New York: Routledge.

Sugarman, David B. and Gerald T. Hotaling. 1989. "Dating Violence: Prevalence, Context, and Risk Markers." pp. 3–32 in *Violence in Dating Relationships: Emerging Social Issues*, edited by Maureen A. Pirog-Good and Jan E. Stets. New York: Praeger.

Sukel, Kayt. 2008. "The Unexpected Dependent: When Retirement Is Not for You Alone." Retrieved 4 December 2009. AARP Bulletin Today (Bulletin.aarp.org/yourworld/family/articles/the_unexpected_dependent,html).

Sullivan, Deborah A. and Rose Weitz. 1988. *Labor Pains: Modern Midwives and Home Birth.* New Haven, CT: Yale University Press.

Sullivan, Oriel and Scott Coltrane. 2008. "Men's Changing Contribution to Housework and Child Care" (Discussion Paper Prepared for 11th Annual Conference of the Council on Contemporary Families, April 25-26, 2008). Retrieved 31 December 2009 (www.contemporaryfamilies.org/subtemplate.php?t=briefingPapers&ext=menshousework).

Sun, Yongmin and Yuanzhang Li. 2002. "Child Well-Being During Parents' Marital Disruption Process: A Pooled Time-Series Analysis." *Journal of Marriage and the Family* 64: 472–88.

—. 2008a. "Stable Postdivorce Family Structures During Late Adolescence and Socioeconomic Consequences in Adulthood." *Journal of Marriage and Family* 69(742–762).

—. 2009. "Postdivorce Family Stability and Changes in Adolescents' Academic Performance." *Journal of Family Issues* 30(11): 1527–55.

Suro, Roberto. 2006. "A Developing Identity: Hispanics in the United States." In *Carnegie Reporter. Carnegie Foundation*, Spring. New York.

Sutton, Paul D. 2008. *Births, Marriages, Divorces, and Deaths: Provisional Data for September 2007.* National Vital Statistics Report No. V. 56, No. 18. Hyattsville, MD: National Center for Health Statistics.

Sweeney, Megan M. 2002. "Remarriage and the Nature of Divorce." *Journal of Family Issues* 23(3): 410–40.

Sweeney, Megan M., Hongbo Wang, and Tami Videon. 2009. "Reconsidering the Association between Stepfamilies and Adolescent Well-Being." In H.E. Peters and C. M. Kamp Dush (Eds.), Marriage and Family: Perspectives and Complexities (pp. 177–225). New York: Columbia University Press.

Swiss, Liam and Céline Le Bourdais. 2009. "Father-Child Contact After Separation." *Journal of Family Issues* 30(5): 623–52.

Szinovacz, Maximiliane E. 2000. "Changes in Housework After Retirement: A Panel Analysis." *Journal of Marriage and the Family* 62: 78–92.

Tach, Laura and Sarah Halpern-Meekin. 2009. "How Does Premarital Cohabitation Affect Trajectories of Marital Quality?" *Journal of Marriage and Family* 71(2, May): 298–317.

Tamis-LeMonda, Catherine S., Niobe Way, Diane Hughes, Hiro Yoshikawa, Ronit Kahana Kalman, and Erika Y. Niwa. 2008. "Parents' Goals for Children: The Dynamic Co-Existence of Individualism and Collectivism in Cultures and Individuals." *Social Development* 17: 183–209.

Tan, Tony Xing and Yi Yang. 2005. "Language Development of Chinese Adoptees 18-35 Months Old." *Early Childhood Research Quarterly* 20: 57–68.

Tannen, Deborah. 1990. *You Just Don't Understand: Women and Men in Conversation*. New York: Morrow.

—. 1994. *Gender and Discourse*. New York: Oxford University Press.

Tanner, James Mourilyan. 1978. *Foetus Into Man: Physical Growth From Conception to Maturity*. Cambridge, England: Harvard University Press.

Tarmann, Allison. 2003. "International Adoption Rate in U.S. Doubled in the U.S." Retrieved 14 April 2003. Population Reference Bureau (www.prb.org/Template.cfm?Section=PRB&template=/ContentManagement/Content.).

Taylor, Paul, Cary Funk, and April Clark. 2007. *Generation Gap in Values, Behaviors: As Marriage and Parenthood Drift Apart, Public is Concerned About Social Impact*. Pew Research Center No. 1 July. Washington, D.C.: Pew Research Center.

Taylor, Paul, Cary Funk, and Peyton Craighill. 2006. *Are We Happy Yet?* Technical Report No. 13 February. Washington, D.C.: Pew Research Center.

Taylor, Paul, Jeffrey Passel, Richard Fry, Richard Morin, Wendy Wang, Gabriel Velasco, and Daniel Dockterman. 2010. The Return of the Multi-Generational Family Household. Electronic document. pewresearch.orgs/pubs/1528/multi-generational-family-household.

Taylor, Paul, Rakesh Kochhar, Rich Morin, Wendy Wang, Daniel Dockterman, and Jennifer Medina. 2009, September 3. *America's Changing Workforce: Recession Turns a Graying Office Grayer*. Washington, D.C.: Pew Research Center.

Taylor, Paul, Rich Morin, D'Vera Cohn, Richard Fry, Rakesh Kochhar, and April Clark. 2008. 9 April. *Inside the Middle Class: Bad Times Hit the Good Life*. Washington, DC: Pew Research Center.

Taylor, Raymond and Beth Andrews. 2009. "Parental Depression in the Context of Divorce and the Impact of Children." *Journal of Divorce & Remarriage* 50(7, October): 472–80.

Teachman, Jay D. 2002. "Childhood Living Arrangements and the Intergenerational Transmission of Divorce." *Journal of Marriage & Family* 64: 717–29.

—. 2004. "The Childhood Living Arrangements of Children and the Characteristics of Their Marriages." *Journal of Family Issues* 25-1: 86–111.

—. 2008. "The Living Arrangements of Children and Their Educational Well-Being." *Journal of Family Issues* 29(6): 734–61.

Tejada-Vera, Betzaida and Paul D. Sutton. 2009. *Births, Marriages, Divorces, and Deaths: Provisional Data for May 2009*. Technical Report No. National Vital Statistics Reports, Vol. 58, No. 12. Hyattsville, MD: National Center for Health Statistics.

Temperament.com. 2009. "Temperament and Parenting: Temperament FAQs." Retrieved 5 December 2009 (www.temperament.com/temperament.comfaqs.html).

Tennov, Dorothy. 1999. *Love and Limerence: The Experience of Being in Love*. New York: Scarborough Place.

The Annie E. Casey Foundation. 2009. *KIDS COUNT Indicator Brief: Reducing the Teen Birth Rate*. Baltimore, MD: The Annie E. Casey Foundation, July.

The Gottman Institute. 2004. "What We've Learned: What Makes Same-Sex Relationships Succeed or Fail?" Retrieved 14 March 2010 (www.gottman.com/research/gaylesbian/self_help/).

The Marriage Movement. 2004. "Can Government Strengthen Marriage? Evidence From the Social Sciences." Retrieved 5 July 2005. National Fatherhood Initiative, Institute for Marriage and Public Policy, and Institute for American Values (www.marriagemovement.org/gov/gov_print.htm).

The National Gay and Lesbian Taskforce. 2007. "Lesbian, Bisexual, and Transgender Female Elders—Women's History Month 2007 Fact Sheet." Retrieved 2 May 2010 (www.thetaskforce.org/downloads/misc/LBTFemaleEldersFactSheet.pdf).

The National Marriage Project. 2009. *The State of Our Unions: Marriage in America 2009*. Charlottesville, VA: University of Virginia.

The Wedding Report, Inc. 2010. "Cost of Wedding." Retrieved 21 February 2010 (Costofwedding.com).

The White House. 2004. "President Calls for Constitutional Amendment Protecting Marriage" (Press Release). Retrieved 7 October 2005 (http://www.whitehouse.gov/news/releases/2004/02/20040224-2.html).

Thigpen, Jeffry W. 2009. "Early Sexual Behavior in a Sample of Low-Income, African American Children." *Journal of Sex Research* 46(1, January): 67–79.

Thomas, Alexander and Stella Chess. 1957. "An Approach to the Study of Sources of Individual Difference in Child Behavior." *Journal of Clinical and Experimental Psychopathology* 18: 347–57.

Thomas, Cindy and Marilyn Ryan. 2008. "Women's Perception of the Divorce Experience: A Qualitative Study." *Journal of Divorce & Remarriage* 49(3-4, September): 210–24.

Thomas, Erik R. and Jeffrey Reaser. 2004. "Delimiting Perceptual Cues Used for the Ethnic Labeling of African American and European American Voices." *Journal of Sociolinguistics* 8(1): 54–87.

Thomas, Joan C. 2008. "Divorce Mediation: Frequently Asked Questions." Retrieved 10 March 2008. DivorceMag.com (www.divorcemag.com/articles/Mediation/mediation_faq.html).

Thompson, Jeff and Jeff Chapman. 2006. "The Economic Impact of Local Living Wages." Retrieved 8 September 2008. Economic Policy Institute (www.epi.org/content.cfm/bp170).

Thompson, Linda and Alexis J. Walker. 1989. "Gender in Families: Women and Men in Marriage, Work, and Parenthood." *Journal of Marriage and the Family* 51: 845–71.

Thornhill, Randy and Steven W. Gangestad. 2008. *The Evolutionary Biology of Human Female Sexuality*. New York: Oxford University Press.

Tierney, John. 2003. "Iraqi Marriage Bedevils Americans." New York Times News Service. *The Oregonian*, 28 September, p. A-2.

Tita, Alan T.N., Mark B. Landon, Catherine Y. Spong, Yinglei Lai, Kenneth J. Leveno, Michael W. Varner, Atef H. Moawad, Steve N. Caritis, Paul J. Meis, Ronald J. Wapner, Yoram Sorokin, Menachem Miodovnik, Marshall Carpenter, Alan M. Peaceman, Mary J. O'Sullivan, Baha H. Sibai, Oded Langer, John M. Thorp, Susan M. Ramin, and Brian M. for the Eunice Shriver NICHD Maternal-Fetal Medicine Units Network Mercer. 2009. "Timing of Elective Repeat Cesarean Delivery at Term and Neonatal Outcomes." *New England Journal of Medicine* 360(2, 8 January): 111–20.

Tjaden, Patricia and Nancy Thoennes. 2000 November. *Full Report of the Prevalence, Incidence, and Consequences of Violence Against Women: Findings From the National Violence Against Women Survey*. Washington, D.C.: National Institute of Justice and Centers for Disease Control and Prevention.

—. 2006. "Extent, Nature, and Consequences of Rape Victimization: Findings From the National Violence Against Women Survey" (Report NCJ 210346). *National Institute of Justice*. Washington, D.C. (www.ncjrs.gov/pdffiles1/nij/210346.pdf).

Todd, Peter. 2007. "Choosing A Mate: What We Really Want" (Indiana University Press Release). Retrieved 23 September 2008 (www.eurekalert.org/pub_releases/2007-09/iu-cam083007.php).

Tolman, Deborah L. 2005. *Dilemmas of Desire: Teenage Girls Talk About Sexuality*. Cambridge, MA: Harvard University Press.

Trask, Bahira Sherif, and Raeann R. Hamon. 2007. Cultural Diversity and Families. Thousand Oaks, CA: Sage Publications.

Trenholm, S. 2008. *Thinking Through Communication*. Boston: Allyn and Bacon.

Trent, Katherine and Scott J. South. 1989. "Structural Determinants of the Divorce Rate: A Cross-Societal Analysis." *Journal of Marriage and the Family* 51: 391–404.

Trinder, Liz. 2008. "Maternal Gate Closing and Gate Opening in Postdivorce Families." *Journal of Family Issues* 29(10): 1298–324.

Troy, Adam B., Jamie Lewis-Smith, and Jean-Philippe Laurenceau. 2006. "Interracial and Intraracial Romantic Relationships: The Search for Satisfaction, Conflict, and Attachment Style." *Journal of Social and Personal Relationships* 23 (February): 65–80.

Tubbs, Stewart L. and Sylvia Moss. 2008. *Human Communication: Principles and Contexts, 11th Ed*. New York: McGraw-Hill.

Tucker, M. Belinda. 2000. "Marital Values and Expectations in Context: Results From a 21-City Survey." pp. 166–87 in *The Ties That Bind: Perspectives on Marriage and Cohabiation*, edited by Linda J. Waite, Christine Bachrach, Michell J. Hindin, Elizabeth Thomson and Arland Thornton. New York: Aldine de Gruyter.

Turner, Heather A. and Paul A. Muller. 2004. "Long-Term Effects of Child Corporal Punishment on Depressive Symptoms in Young Adults." *Journal of Family Issues* 25: 761–82.

U.S. Census Bureau. 2006. "Current Population Survey, March and Annual Social and Economic Supplements, 2005 and Earlier, Table UC-1" (http://www.census.gov/population/socdemo/hh-fam/uc1.pdf).

—. 2007. "Families and Living Arrangements" (http://www.census.gov/population/www/socdemo/hh-fam/cps2007.html).

—. 2008 August. *American Community Survey: California S1002.Grandparents*.

—. 2008a. "Marital Status of the Population 15 Years Old and Over by Sex and Race: 1950 to Present" (http://www.www.census.gov/population/www/socdemo/hh-fam/ms1.csv).

—. 2008b. "Table SF1. Percent Childless and Births Per 1,000 Women in the Last Year: Selected Years, 1976 to 2006." In *Fertility of American Women*. Retrieved 7 March 2010 (www.census.gov/population/www/socdemo/fertility.html).

—. 2009 January. *Table MS-2. Estimated Median Age at First Marriage, by Sex: 1890 to the Present*. Technical Report No. Current Population Survey, March and Annual Social and Economic Supplements, 2009 and earlier. Washington, DC.

—. 2009a. "Age and Sex in the United States: 2008." Retrieved 12 April 2010 (www.census.gov/population/www/socdemo/age/age_sex_2008.html).

—. 2009b. "The Older Population in the United States: 2008." Retrieved 23 April 2010 (www.census.gov/population/www/socdemo/age/older_2008.html).

—. 2009c. "America's Families and Living Arrangements: 2008." Retrieved 12 April 2010. www.census.gov/population/www/socdemo/hh-fam/cps2008.html.

—. 2009ab. "American Indian and Alaska Native Heritage Month: November 2009" (Press Release). Retrieved 20

January 2010 (www.census.gov/Press-Release/www/releases/archives/facts_for_features_special_editions/014346.html).

—. 2010a. "America's Families and Living Arrangements: 2009." Retrieved 21 February 2010 (www.census.gov/population/www/socdemo/hh-fam/cps2009.html).

—. 2010b. "Labor Force, Employment, & Earnings: Labor Force Status." In *2010 Statistical Abstract*. Washington, DC.

U.S. Conference of Mayors. 2008 December. *A Status Report on Hunger and Homelessness in America's Cities: A 25-City Survey*. Washington, DC.

U.S. Department of Agriculture Economic Research Service. 2009. "Food Security in the United States: Definitions of Hunger and Food Security." In *Briefing Rooms*. Retrieved 8 December 2009 (www.ers.usda.gov/Briefing/FoodSecurity/labels.htm).

U.S. Department of Health and Human Services. 2007. "Caseload Data." Retrieved 14 April 2008 (www.acf.hhs.gov/programs/ofa/caseload/2007/tanf_family.htm).

—. 2009. "The 2009 HHS Poverty Guidelines." Retrieved 21 January 2010 (aspe.hhs.gov./poverty/09poverty.shtml).

U.S. Department of Health and Human Services, Administration For Children and Families. 2006. "Children Home Alone and Babysitter Age Guidelines." Retrieved 17 July 2006 (www.nccic.org/poptopics/homealone.html).

U.S. Department of Health and Human Services, Administration on Children, Youth and Families. 2008. "Child Maltreatment 2006."

U.S. Department of Health and Human Services, Administration on Children, Youth. 2009. "Child Maltreatment 2007." Retrieved 26 March 2010. Washington, DC: Government Printing Office (www.acf.hhs.gov/programs/cb/pubs/cm07/cm07/pdf).

U.S. Department of Health and Human Services, Office of Women's Health. 2008. "Date Rape Drugs: Frequently Asked Questions." Retrieved 28 March 2010 (www.womenshealth.gov/faq/date-rape-drugs.cfm).

U.S. Department of Housing and Urban Development. 2010. "Final FY 2010 Fair Market Rent Documentation System." Retrieved 21 January 2010 (www.huduser.org/portal/datasets/fmr/fmrs/docsys.html&data=fmr10).

U.S. Department of Justice. 2009. "Incidents and Offenses." Retrieved 14 February 2010 (www.fbi.gov/ucr/hc2008/incidents.html).

U.S. Department of Justice, Bureau of Justice Statistics. 2007. "Homicide Trends in the U.S.: Intimate Homicide." Retrieved 10 October 2008 (www.ojp.usdoj.gov/bjs/homicide/intimates.htm).

U.S. Department of Labor, Bureau of Labor Statistics, October 22, 2010, Economic News Release: Regional and State Employment and Unemployment Summary. Available online: http://data.bls.gov/cgi-bin/print.pl/news.release/laus.nr0.htm

U.S. Department of State. 2009a. "Total Adoptions to the United States." Retrieved 9 November 2009 (Adoption.state.gov/news/total_chart.html?css=print).

—. 2009b. "Trafficking in Persons Report 2009." Retrieved 25 March 2010 (www.state.gov/g/tip/rls/tiprpt/2009/).

U.S. Equal Employment Opportunity Commission. 2010a. "Charges of Discrimination FY1997-FY2009." Retrieved 18 January 2010 (www1.eeoc.gov//eeoc/statistics/enforcement/sex.cfm?renderforprint=1).

—. 2010b. "Race-Based Charges FY1997-FY2009." Retrieved 18 January 2010 (www1.eeoc.gov//eeoc/statistics/enforcement/race.cfm?renderforprint=1).

Uebelacker, Lisa A., Emily S. Courtnage, and Mark A. Whisman. 2003. "Correlates of Depression and Marital Dissatisfaction: Perceptions of Marital Communication Style." *Journal of Social and Personal Relationships* 20 (December): 757–69.

Uhlenberg, Peter. 2009. "Children in an Aging Society." *The Journals of Gerontology: Series B* 64B(4): 489–96.

Umana-Taylor, Adriana J., Edna C. Alfaro, Mayra Y. Bamaca, and Amy B. Guimond. 2009. "The Central Role of Familial Ethnic Socialization in Latino Adolescents' Cultural Orientation." *Journal of Marriage and Family* 71(1): 46–60.

Umberson, Debra and Walter Gove. 1989. "Parenthood and Psychological Well-Being: Theory, Measurement, and Stage in the Family Life Course." *Journal of Family Issues* 10: 440–62.

Umberson, Debra. 2006. "Parents, Adult Children, and Immortality." *Contexts* 5(4, Fall): 48–53.

Umberson, Debra, Tetyana Pudrovska, and Corinne Reczek. 2010, forthcoming. "Parenthood and Well-Being Over the Life Course." *Journal of Marriage and Family*.

United Nations Children's Fund. 2009 November. *The State of the World's Children: Special Edition*.

United Nations Statistics Division. 2005. "Table 5c—Maternity Leave Benefits." In *Statistics and Indicators on Women and Men*. Retrieved 14 January 2006 (unstats.un.org/unsd/demographic/products/indwm/ww2005/tab5c.htm).

—. 2010. "Statistics and Indicators on Women and Men: Table 5g. Maternity Leave Benefits." Retrieved 3 May 2010 (unstats.un.org/unsd/demographic/poducts/indwm/tab5g.htm).

United Nations, Office on Drugs and Crime (UNODC). 2006 April. *Trafficking in Persons: Global Patterns*.

University of New Hampshire Cooperative Extension. 2006. *The Effects of Divorce on Children*.

USA.gov. 2010. "Grandparents Raising Grandchildren" (www.usa.gov/Topics/Grandparents.shtml).

Uttal, Lynet. 1999. "Using Kin for Child Care: Embedment in the Socioeconomic Networks of Extended Families." *Journal of Marriage and the Family* 61: 845–57.

Vaaler, Margaret L., Christopher G. Ellison, and Daniel A. Powers. 2009. "Religious Influences on the Risk of Marital Dissolution." *Journal of Marriage and Family* 71(4, October): 917–34.

Valeo, Tom. 2007. January. "Good Friends Are Good For You." *WebMD*. Retrieved 23 September 2008. www. webmd.com/balance/features/good-friends-are-good-for-you?page=3.

van Teijlingen, Edwin, George Louis, Peter McCaffery, and Maureen Porter, eds. 2004. *Midwifery and the Medicalization of Childbirth: Comparative Perspectives*. Hauppage, NY: Nova Science Publisher.

Vanden Boogart, Matthew R. 2006. "Discovering the Social Impacts of Facebook on a College Campus." M.Sc. Thesis, As cited in Baron, Always On, p. 97, Kansas State University. Master's Thesis.

Vandivere, Sharon, Kathryn Tout, Jeffrey Capizzano, and Martha Zaslow. 2003. "Left Unsupervised: A Look at the Most Vulnerable Children." In *Child Trends Research Brief*. Retrieved 27 July 2003 (www.childtrends.org).

VanLaningham, Jody, David R. Johnson, and Paul R. Amato. 2001. "Marital Happiness, Marital Duration, and the U-Shaped Curve: Evidence From a Five-Wave Panel Study." *Social Forces* 78: 1313–41.

Vedantam, Shankar. 2006. "Male Scientist Writes of Life as Female Scientist." Retrieved 21 November 2006. washingtonpost.com (/www.washingtonpost.com/wp-dyn/content/article/2006/07/12/AR2006071201883.html).

Ventura, Stephanie J. 2009. *Changing Patterns of Nonmarital Childbearing in the United States*. Technical Report No. NCHS Data Brief, no. 18. Hyattsville, MD: National Center for Health Statistics.

Verbrugge, Lois M. 1979. "Marital Status and Health." *Journal of Health and Social Behavior* 24: 16–30.

—. 1979b. "Marital Status and Health." *Journal of Marriage and Family* 41(2): 267–85.

Vienna Institute of Demography. 2008. "European Demographic Data Sheet 2008." Retrieved 16 December 2009 (www.oeaw.ac.at/vid/datasheet/download/sources_notes_datasheet2008.pdf).

Vincent, Wilson, John L. Peterson, and Dominic J. Parrott. 2009. "Differences in African American and White Women's Attitudes Towards Lesbians and Gay Men." *Sex Roles* 61(9-10, November): 599–606.

Vives-Cases, Carmen, Diana Gil-González, and Mercedes Carasco-Portiño. 2009. "Verbal Marital Conflict and Male Domination in the Family as Risk Factors of Intimate Partner Violence." *Trauma, Violence, & Abuse* 10(2): 171–80.

Vlosky, Denise Ashbaugh and Pamela A. Monroe. 2002. "The Effective Dates of No-Fault Divorce Laws in the 50 States." *Family Relations* 51: 317–24.

Voller, Emily K., and Patricia J. Long. 2010. Sexual Assault and Rape Perpetration by College Men: The Role of the Big Five Personality Traits. *Journal of Interpersonal Violence* 25: 457–480.

Voorpostel, Marieke and Rosemary Bleiszner. 2008. "Intergenerational Solidarity and Support Between Adult Siblings." *Journal of Marriage and Family* 70(1): 157–67.

Voydanoff, Patricia. 2004. "Community as a Context for the Work-Family Interface." *Organizational Management Journal* 1(1): 49–54.

—. 2008. "A Conceptual Model of Work-Family Interface." pp. 37–56 in *Handbook of Work-Family Integration: Research, Theory, and Best Practices*, edited by Karen Korabik, Donna S. Lero and Denise L. Whitehead. Burlington, MA: Elsevier.

Vrangalova, Zhana and Ritch C. Savin-Williams. 2010. "Correlates of Same-Sex Sexuality in Heterosexually Identified Young Adults." *Journal of Sex Research* 47(1, January): 92–102.

Wage and Hour Division, U.S. Department of Labor. 2010. "Minimum Wage Laws in the States—January 1, 2010." Retrieved 6 March 2010 (www.dol.gov/whd/minwage/america.htm).

Wagner, Marsden. 2008. *Born in the USA: How a Broken Maternity System Must Be Fixed to Put Women and Children First*. Berkeley, CA: University of California Press.

Waite, Linda J. and Maggie Gallagher. 2000. *The Case for Marriage: Why Married People Are Happier, Healthier, and Better Off Financially*. New York: Doubleday.

Waite, Linda J., Ye Luo, and Alise C. Lewin. 2009. Marital Happiness and Marital Stability: Consequences for Psychological Well-Being. *Social Science Research* 38: 201–212.

Waldfogel, Jane. 2006. *What Children Need*. Cambridge, MA: Harvard University Press.

Walker, Alexis J. 1999. "Gender and Family Relationships." In *Handbook of Marriage and the Family*. Marvin B. Sussman, Susan K. Steinmetz and Gary W. Peterson, eds. pp. 439–474. New York: Plenum.

Walker, Alexis J., Margaret Manoogian-O'Dell, Lori A. McGraw, and Diana L.G. White. 2001. *Families in Later Life: Connections and Transitions*. Thousand Oaks, CA: Pine Forge Press.

Walker, Eric C., Thomas B. Holman, and Dean M. Busby. 2009. "Childhood Sexual Abuse, Other Childhood Factors, and Pathways to Survivors' Adult Relationship Quality." *Journal of Family Violence* 24(6, August): 397–406.

Walker, Lenore. 1979. *The Battered Woman Syndrome*. New York: Harper Colophon.

—. 1993. "The Battered Woman Syndrome Is a Psychological Consequence of Abuse." In *Current Controversies in Family Violence*, edited by Richard J. Gelles and Dorileen R. Loseke. Newbury Park, CA: Sage Publications.

Wallace, Danielle M. 2007. "'It's A M-A-N Thang': Black Male Gender Role Socialization and the Performance of Masculinity in Love Relationships." *The Journal of Pan African Studies* 1(7, March): 11–22.

Waller, Maureen and Sara McLanahan. 2005. "'His' and 'Her' Marriage Expectations: Determinants and Consequences." *Journal of Marriage and Family* 67: 53–67.

Waller, Willard. 1937. "The Rating and Dating Complex." *American Sociological Review* 2: 727–34.

Wallerstein, Judith S. 1983. "Children of Divorce: The Psychological Tasks of the Child." *American Journal of Orthopsychiatry* 53: 230–43.

—. 2007. "Adult Children of Divorce Speak Out." *National Council on Family Relations Report* 52(4, December): F12–F13; F19.

Wallerstein, Judith S. and Sandra Blakeslee. 1989. *Second Chances: Men, Women and Children a Decade After Divorce*. New York: Ticknor & Fields.

Walsh, Froma. 2006. *Strengthening Family Resilience, Second Edition (Guilford Family Therapy Series)*. New York: Guilford Press.

Walsh, Wendy A., Jean Dawson, and Marybeth J. Mattingly. 2010. "How Are We Measuring Resilience Following Childhood Maltreatment? Is the Research Adequate and Consistent? What is the Impact on Research, Practice, and Policy?" *Trauma, Violence, & Abuse* 11(1): 27–41.

Walzer, Susan. 1998. *Thinking About the Baby: Gender and Transitions Into Parenthood*. Philadelphia: Temple University Press.

Wang, Bo and Pamela Davidson. 2006. "Sex, Lies, and Videos in Rural China: A Qualitative Study of Women's Sexual Debut and Risky Sexual Behavior." *The Journal of Sex Research* 43(3, August): 227–35.

Wang, Wendy and Rich Morin. 2009. "Recession Brings Many Young Adults Back to the Nest." Retrieved 4 April 2010. Pew Research Center (pewsocialtrends.org/pubs/748/recession-brings-many-young-adults-back-to-the-nest).

Ward, Jane. 2010. "Straight Dude Seeks Same: Mapping the Relationship Between Sexual Identities, Practices, and Cultures." In *Sex Matters: The Sexuality and Society Reader, 3rd Ed.*, edited by Mindy Stombler, Dawn M. Baunach, Elisabeth O. Burgess, Denise Donnelly, Wendy Simonds and Elroi J. Windsor, eds. New York: Prentice Hall.

Ward, Russell and Glenna Spitze. 2007. "Nestleaving and Coresidence by Young Adult Children." *Research on Aging* 29(3): 257–77.

Wardhaugh, Ronald. 2010. *An Introduction to Sociolinguistics*. New York: Wiley-Blackwell.

Wardrip, Keith E., Danilo Pelletiere, and Sheila Crowley. 2009. *Out of Reach 2009: Persistent Problems, New Challenges for Renters*. Washington, DC: National Low Income Housing Coalition.

Warner, Judith. 2005. *Perfect Madness: Motherhood in the Age of Anxiety*. New York: Penguin Group USA.

Warner, Rebecca L. 2006. "Being a Good Parent." pp. 65–83 in *Couples, Kids and Family Life: Social Worlds From the Inside Out*, edited by Jaber F. Gubrium and James A. Holstein. New York: Oxford University Press.

Weaver, Hilary N. 2009. "The Colonial Context of Violence." *Journal of Interpersonal Violence* 24(9): 1552–63.

Weigel, Daniel J. 2007. "Parental Divorce and the Types of Commitment-Related Messages People Gain From Their Families of Origin." *Journal of Divorce and Remarriage* DOI: 10.1300/J087v47n01_02: 15–32.

Weigel, Daniel J., Bennett. 2006. "Roles and Influence in Marriage: Both Spouses Perceptions Contribute to Marital Commitment." *Family and Consumer Sciences Research Journal* 35: 74–92.

Weininger, Elliot B. and Annette Lareau. 2009. "Paradoxical Pathways: An Ethnographic Extension of Kohn's Findings on Class and Childrearing." *Journal of Marriage and Family* 71(3, August): 680–95.

Weis, David L. 1998. "Basic Sexological Premises." In *Sexuality in America: Understanding Our Sexual Values and Behavior*, edited by Robert T. Francoeur, Patricia Barthalow and David L. Weis. New York: Continuum.

Weiss, R. 2002. LA Times-Washington Post News Service. *The Oregonian*, 13 November, pp. A-10.

Weitzman, Lenore J. 1985. *The Divorce Revolution: The Unexpected Consequences for Women and Their Children in America*. New York: Free Press.

Welch, Charles E., III and Paul C. Glick. 1981. "The Incidence of Polygamy in Contemporary Africa: A Research Note." *Journal of Marriage and the Family*, 191–93.

Welch, Kelly J. 2010. *Family Life Now: A Conversation About Marriage, Families, and Relationships, 2nd Ed.* Boston: Pearson Education Inc.

Wellner, Alison Stein. 2005. "U.S. Attitudes Towards Interracial Dating Are Liberalizing." Population Reference Bureau. Retrieved 2 October 2008. www.prb.org/Articles/2005/USAttitudesTowardInterracialDatingAreLiberalizing.aspx.

Wen, Ming. 2008. "Family Structure and Children's Health and Behavior." *Journal of Family Issues* 29(11): 1492–519.

Wenck, Stan and Connie J. Hansen. 2009. *Love Him, Love His Kids: The Stepmother's Guide to Surviving and Thriving in a Blended Family*. Cincinnati, OH: Adams Media.

Wenger, Jeffrey. 2003. *Share of Workers in "Nonstandard" Jobs Declines*. Washington, D.C.: Economic Policy Institute.

Werner, Emmy E. 1994. "Overcoming the Odds." *Developmental and Behavioral Pediatrics* 15: 131–36.

—. 1995. "Resilience in Development." *American Psychological Society* 4: 81–85.

Werner, Emmy E. and Ruth S. Smith. 1989. *Vulnerable but Invincible: A Longitudinal Study of Resilient Children and Youth.* New York: Adams, Bannister, Cox.

—. 1992. *Overcoming the Odds.* Ithaca, NY: Cornell University Press.

West, Candace and Don H. Zimmerman. 1987. "Doing Gender." *Gender and Society* 1: 125–31.

West, Candace and Don H. Zimmerman. 1983. "Small Insults: A Study of Interruptions in Cross-Sex Conversations Between Unacquainted Persons." In *Language, Gender and Society*, edited by B. Thorne, C. Kramarae and N. Henley. Cambridge House: Newbury House.

West, Richard and Lynn Turner. 2006. *Introducing Communication Theory: Analysis and Application With PowerWeb.* New York: McGraw-Hill.

Westoff, Charlies F. 2003. *Trends in Marriage and Early Childbearing in Developing Countries.* Technical Report No. DHS Comparative Reports # 5. Cavelton, MD: ORC Macro.

White, James M. 2008. *Family Theories, 3rd Ed.* Thousand Oaks, CA: Sage Publications.

White, Lynn and Joan G. Gilbreth. 2001. "When Children Have Two Fathers: Effects of Relationships With Stepfathers and Noncustodial Fathers on Adolescent Outcomes." *Journal of Marriage and the Family* 63: 155–67.

White, Lynn and Stacy J. Rogers. 2000. "Economic Circumstances and Family Outcomes: A Review of 1990's." *Journal of Marriage and Family* 62: 1035–51.

Whitehead, Barbara Dafoe and David Popenoe. 2002. "Why Men Won't Commit." In *The State of Our Unions: The Social Health of Marriage in America.* The National Marriage Project.

Whitehead, Denise L. 2008. "Historical Trends in Work-Family: The Evolution of Earning and Caring." pp. 13–36 in *Handbook of Work-Family Integration: Research, Theory, and Best Practices*, edited by Karen Korabik, Donna S. Lero and Denise L. Whitehead. Burlington, MA: Elsevier.

Whiting, Jason B., Donna R. Smith, Tammy Barnett, and Erika L. Grafsky. 2007. "Overcoming the Cinderella Myth: A Mixed Methods Study of Successful Stepmothers." *Journal of Divorce and Remarriage* DOI: 10.1300/J087v47n01_06: 95–109.

Whitton, Sarah W., Galena K. Rhoades, Scott M. Stanley, and Howard J. Markman. 2008. "Effects of Parental Divorce on Marital Commitment and Confidence." *Journal of Family Psychology* 22(5, October): 789–93.

Whoriskey, Peter. 2009. "GM To Build More Cars Overseas." Retrieved 9 March 2010 (extracted From cbsnews.com).

www.washingtonpost.com (www.cbsnews.com/stories/2009/05/08/politics/washingtonpost/main5001058.shtml).

Wilcox, Kathryn, L., Sharlene A. Wolchik, and Sanford L. Braver. 1998. "Of Maternal Preference for Joint or Sole Legal Custody." *Family Relations* 47: 93–101.

Wilcox, W. Bradford and Nicholas Wolfinger. 2007. "Then Comes Marriage? Religion, Race, and Marriage in Urban America." *Social Science Research* 36: 569–89.

Wilkenfeld, Britt, Kristin Anderson Moore, and Laura Lippman. 2008. "Neighborhood Support and Children's Connectedness" (Child Trends Fact Sheet). The Annie E. Casey Foundation.

Wilkinson, Doris Y. 1997. "American Families of African Descent." In *Families in Cultural Context: Strength and Challenges in Diversity*, edited by Mary Kay DeGenova. Mountain View, CA: Mayfield Publishing Company.

Willén, Helena and Henry Montgomery. 2006. "From Marital Distress to Divorce: The Creation of New Identities for the Spouses." *Journal of Divorce and Remarriage* 45(1/2): 125–47 (DOI: 10.1300/J087vol45n01_07).

Williams, Erica and Nicholas Johnson. 2009. "How Much Would a State Earned Income Tax Credit Cost in 2010?" Retrieved 3 May 2010. Center on Budget and Policy Priorities (www.cbpp.org/cms/index.cfm?fa=view&id=2992).

Williams, Juanita H. 1993. "Sexuality in Marriage." pp. 93–122 in *Handbook of Human Sexuality*, edited by B. B. Wolman and J. Money. Northvale, NJ: Jason Aronson.

Wilson, Scott. 2009. "Culture Wars: Obama Makes Explicit His Objection to DOMA." Retrieved 24 November 2009. washingtonpost.com (voices.washingtonpost.com/44/2009/08/17/obama_makes_explicit_his_objec.html).

Wilson, Stephan M., Lucy W. Ngige, and Linda J. Trollinger. 2003. "Connecting Generations: Kamba and Maasai Paths to Marriage in Kenya." pp. 95–118 in *Male Selection Across Cultures*, edited by Raeann R. Hamon and Bron B. Ingoldsby. Thousand Oaks, CA: Sage Publications, Inc.

Wilson, William J. 1987. *The Truly Disadvantaged: The Inner City, the Underclass, and Public Policy.* Chicago, IL: University of Chicago Press.

Wilson, William J. 1993. *The New Urban Poverty and the Problem of Race.* Ann Arbor, MI: University of Michigan.

Wilson, William J. 1996. *When Work Disappears: The World of the New Urban Poor.* New York, NY: Alfred A. Knopf.

Winslow, Sarah. 2005. "Work-Family Conflict, Gender, and Parenthood, 1977-1997." *Journal of Family Issues* 26(6): 727–55.

Wissink, Inge B., Maja Dekovic, and Anne Marie Mejier. 2009. "Adolescent Friendship Relations and

Developmental Outcomes." *The Journal of Early Adolescence* 29(3): 405–425.

Wittstein, Ilan S., David R. Thiemann, Joao A.C. Lima, Kenneth L. Baughman, Steven P. Schulman, Gary Gerstenblith, Katherine C. Wu, Jeffrey J. Rade, Trinity J. Bivalacqua, and Hunter C. Champion. 2005. Neurohumoral Features of Myocardial Stunning Due to Sudden Emotional Stress. *New England Journal of Medicine* 352(6–10 February): 539–548.

Wolfinger, Nichohengas H. 2006. *Understanding the Divorce Cycle: The Children of Divorce in Their Own Marriages.* New York: Cambridge University Press.

Wong, Grace. 2005. "Ka-Ching! Wedding Price Tag Nears $30K." In *CNNMoney.Com.* Retrieved 25 June 2008 (money.cnn.com/2005/05/20/pf/weddings/).

Wood, Julia T. 2002. "A Critical Response to John Gray's Mars and Venus Portrayals of Men and Women." *The Southern Communications Journal* 67(2): 201–11.

—. 2009. *Gendered Lives: Communication, Gender, and Culture, 8th Ed.* Boston: Wadsworth/Cengage Learning.

World Health Organization. 2009. "Gender, Women, and Health: Sexual Violence." Retrieved 18 August 2009 (www.who.int/gender/violence/sexual_violence/en/index.html).

WorldNetDaily. 2003. "'Gay Marriage Ban Struck Down in Massachusetts; Landmark Ruling Could Pave Way for Legalization Throughout U.S." Retrieved 3 October 2008 (Worldnetdaily.com/news/article.asp?ARTICLE_ID=35673).

Wright, Carroll. 1889. *A Report on Marriage and Divorce in the United States 1867-1886.* Washington DC: Bureau of Labor.

Wrigley, Julia and Joanna Dreby. 2005. "Fatalities in Child Care." *CUNY Graduate School*, November. Retrieved 9 March 2010 (www.gc.cuny.edu/press_information/current_releases/2005/November/Child_Care_Study.htm).

Wu, Zheng and Christopher M. Schimmele. 2005. "Repartnering After First Union Disruption." *Journal of Marriage and Family* 67 (February): 27–36.

Xu, Xiaohe, Clark D. Hudspeth, and John P. Bartkowski. 2006. "The Role of Cohabitation in Remarriage." *Journal of Marriage and Family* 68(2): 261–74.

Xu, Xiaohe and Martin King Whyte. 1990. "Love Matches and Arranged Marriages: A Chinese Replication." *Journal of Marriage and the Family* 52: 709–22.

Yaben, Sagrario Yarnoz. 2009. "Forgiveness, Attachment, and Divorce." *Journal of Divorce & Remarriage* 50(4, May): 282–94.

Yanowitz, Karen L. & Weathers, Kevin J. 2004. "Do Boys and Girls Act Differently in the Classroom? A Content Analysis of Student Characters in Educational Psychology Textbooks." *Sex Roles: A Journal of Research* 51 (July).

Yates, Michael D. 2009. *In and Out of the Working Class.* Winnipeg, MB: Arbeiter Ring.

Yeung, Wei-jun Jean, Miriam R. Linver, and Jeanne Brooks-Gunn. 2002. "How Money Matters for Young Children's Development: Parental Investment and Family Processes." *Child Development* 73: 1861–79.

Yount, Kathryn M. 2002. "Like Mother, Like Daughter? Female Genital Cutting in Minia, Egypt." *Journal of Health and Social Behavior* 43 (September): 336–58.

Yu, Tianyi and Francesca Adler-Baeder. 2007. "The Intergenerational Transmission of Relationship Quality: The Effects of Parental Remarriage Quality on Young Adults' Relationships." *Journal of Divorce and Remarriage* 47(3/4): 87–102 (DOI: 10.1300/J087vol47n03_05).

Zhang, Yuanting and Jennifer Van Hook. 2009. "Marital Dissolution Among Interracial Couples." *Journal of Marriage and Family* 71(1, January): 95–107.

Zhang, Zhenmei and Mark D. Hayward. 2001. "Childlessness and the Psychological Well-Being of Older Persons." *Journals of Gerontology: Social Sciences* 56B: S311–20.

Zhou, Min and III Bankston, Carl L. 2006. "Delinquency and Acculturation in the Twenty-First Century: A Decade's Change in a Vietnamese American Community." pp. 117–39 in *Immigration and Crime: Ethnicity, Race, and Violence*, edited by J. Martinez, Ramiro and J. Valenzuela, Abel. New York: New York University Press.

Zhu, Wei Xing, Li Lu, and Therese Hesketh. 2009. "China's Excess Males, Sex Selective Abortion, and One Child Policy: Analysis of Data From 2005 National Intercensus Survey." *British Medical Journal* 338 (9 April): b1211.

Zimmerman, Shirley L. 2001. *Family Policy: Constructed Solutions to Family Problems.* Thousand Oaks, CA: Sage.

Zinczenko, David. 2007. "Who Handles Break-Ups Better?" In *Dave Zinczenko's Mysteries of the Sexes Explained.* Retrieved 25 September 2008. Yahoo! Health (Health.yahoo.com/experts/menlovesex/29235/who-handles-break-ups-better).

Zuckerman, Miron, Bella M. DePaulo, and Robert Rosenthal. 1981. "Verbal and Nonverbal Communication of Deception." *Advances in Experimental Social Psychology* 14: 1–59.

Name Index

Subject Index

Photo Credits

Chapter 1: pp. 2, 3, and 34 top left: Shutterstock; p. 6 left: RoxyFer/Shutterstock; p. 6 right: Doug Berry/Photodisc/Getty Images Royalty Free; p. 8: Andrew Holbrooke/Corbis; p. 9: Supplied by Karen Seccombe; p. 12: AP Images/Tom Green Defense Team; p. 14: Shutterstock; p. 15: Alain Le Garsmeur/Impact/HIP/The Image Works; p. 18: Library of Congress #LC-DIG-nclc-01293; p. 19: Jeff Greenberg/The Image Works; p. 20: Shutterstock; p. 21: Andy Dean Photography/Shutterstock; p. 22: Patrick Olear/PhotoEdit Inc.; p. 26: Shutterstock; p. 31: Golden Pixels LLC/Alamy; p. 32: Shutterstock

Chapter 2: pp. 36, 37, and 66 top left: Shutterstock: 44 left: Beau Lark/Corbis Royalty Free; p. 44 right: STEVE LINDRIDGE/Alamy Royalty Free; p. 47 top left: Larry W. Smith/epa/Corbis; p. 47 top right: Steve Pope/epa/Corbis; p. 47 bottom: Shutterstock; p. 49: ChinaFotoPress/Getty Images; p. 50: Shutterstock; p. 51: AP Images/Krista Kennell/Sipa Press; p. 53 top: Will Hart/© NBC/Courtesy: Everett Collection; p. 53 bottom: Shutterstock; p. 54 : epa/Corbis; p. 60 left : Anton Vengo/SuperStock; p. 60 right: allen russell/Alamy p. 61: Shutterstock; p. 63: Shutterstock

Chapter 3: pp. 68, 69, and 92 top left: Shutterstock; p. 72: Karen Neal/ABC via Getty Images; p. 73 left: Colin Young-Wolff/PhotoEdit Inc.; p. 73 right: David R. Frazier/The Image Works; p. 77: Leonard McCombe/Hulton Archive/Getty Images; p. 78: PhotosToGo; p. 79: David Young-Wolff/PhotoEdit Inc.; p. 80: David J. Green-lifestyle themes/Alamy; p. 81: Shutterstock; p. 82; John Minihan/Evening Standard/Getty Images; p. 83: Shutterstock; p. 88: Kellie L. Folkerts/Shutterstock; p. 90: Larry Busacca/Getty Images

Chapter 4: pp. 94, 95, and 120 top left: Shutterstock p. 96: Toshiko Takahashi/Taxi/Getty Images; p. 98: Poncho/Photonica/Getty Images; p. 100: Vasily Smirnov/Shutterstock; p. 102: Shutterstock; p. 103 left: Stephen Coburn/Shutterstock; p. 103 right: Timothy Large/Shutterstock; p. 106: top & bottom right: Shutterstock; p. 106 bottom left: Thinkstock; p. 107: Jan Mammey/Getty Images Royalty Free; p. 109: Graeme Robertson/Getty Images; p. 111: Rhoda Sidney/The Image Works; p. 115: Thomas Kruesselmann/Corbis; p. 116 top: Courtesy of Stalking Resource Center/National Center for Victims of Crime; p. 116 bottom: Shutterstok; p. 117: Shutterstock

Chapter 5: pp. 122 & 123 & 152 top left: Shutterstock; p. 124: ©CBS/ Courtesy Everett Collection; p. 126: Digital Vision/Getty Images Royalty Free; p. 129: Sara De Boer/Retna Ltd./Corbis; p. 130: Shutterstock; p. 133: ©CBS/Courtesy Everett Collection; p. 138 top: Spencer Grant/PhotoEdit Inc.; p. 138 bottom: Shutterstock; p. 141: Bill Aron/ PhotoEdit Inc.; p. 142: David Young-Wolff/PhotoEdit Inc.; p. 145: Esbin-Anderson/The Image Works; p. 148: A. Ramey/PhotoEdit Inc.; p. 150: Lefty Shivambu/Gallo Images/Getty Images

Chapter 6: p. 154, 155, and 180, top left: Shutterstock, p. 158: Copyright © 20th Century Fox Licensing/Merchandising/Everett Collection; p. 160: Lee Snider/The Image Works; p. 162: Tanya Constantine/Photodisc/ Getty Images Royalty Free; p. 163: Mark Peterson/Corbis; p. 165: Robin Laurance/Impact/HIP/The Image Works; p. 166 top: Shutterstock; p. 166 bottom: The Star-Ledger/Mitsu Yasukawa/The Image Works; p. 168: Shutterstock; p. 169: moodboard/Corbis Royalty Free; p. 170: Heidi Gutman/© ABC/Retna (The View); p. 171: Shutterstock; p. 172: Richard Levine/Alamy; p. 176: Michael Newman/PhotoEdit Inc.

Chapter 7: p. 182, 183, and 210, Shutterstock; p. 185 left: Bill Lai/The Image Works; p. 185 right: Louise Gubb/Corbis; p. 187: Cliff Lipson/© CBS/ Courtesy Everett Collection; p. 190: Richard Lord/The Image Works; p. 191: Shutterstock; p. 192: Bruce Glikas/FilmMagic/Getty Images; p. 196: Jim West/The Image Works; p. 198: Shutterstock; p. 199: David Young-Wolff/PhotoEdit Inc.; p. 200: David M. Grossman/The Image Works; p. 203: Monkey Business Images/Shutterstock; p. 205: SW Productions/Getty Images Royalty Free; p. 206 left: Supplied by Karen Seccombe; p. 206 right: Supplied by Karen Seccombe

Chapter 8: p. 212, 213, and 240: Shutterstock; p. 215: Louise Gubb/ CORBIS SABA; p. 218: © Erin Moroney LaBelle/The Image Works; p. 222: Jeff Steinberg/Matt Smith, © PacificCoastNews.com/Newscom; p. 223: Catchlight Visual Services/Alamy; p. 227: Sally and Richard Greenhill/Alamy; p. 229: Shutterstock; p. 230: Kayte M. Deioma/ PhotoEdit Inc.; p 232 top: JACQUELINE PIETSCH/AFP/Getty Images; p. 232 bottom: Supplied by Karen Seccombe; p. 233: Kim Eriksen/Corbis; p. 234: Shutterstock; p. 236: Francis Dean/Dean Dean Pictures/Newscom

Chapter 9: p. 240, 241, and 268: Shutterstock; 242: Alison Wright/ Corbis; p. 244: Library of Congress #LC-DIG-nclc-05129; p. 247 top: Elizabeth Crews/The Image Works; p. 247 bottom: Shutterstock; p. 251: RICHARD B. LEVINE/Newscom; p. 255 left: Kate Mitchell/Corbis; p. 255 right: BananaStock/Jupiter Images/Getty Royalty Free; p. 258: Mike Theiler/epa/Corbis; p. 260: Shutterstock; p. 261: Stock This Way/

Corbis; p. 263: MIKE HUTCHINGS/Reuters/Corbis; p. 266: JupiterImages/FoodPix/Getty Images

Chapter 10: .p. 270, 271, and 298: Shutterstock; p. 272: Sean Sprague/ The Image Works; p. 273: Library of Congress #LC-USZC4-5603; p. 276: Andrew Holbrooke/Corbis; p. 277: Michael Newman/PhotoEdit Inc.; p. 282: ERproductions Ltd./Blend Images/Getty Images; p. 283 left: Sonda Dawes/The Image Works; p. 283 right: Don Mason/Corbis; p. 285 top and bottom: Shutterstock: p. 289: VStock/Alamy Royalty Free; p. 290: Golden Pixels LLC/Shutterstock; p. 294: Caro/Alamy;

Chapter 11: p. 300, 301, and 360: Shutterstock; p. 303: Shutterstock; p. 306: Rob Lewine/Getty Images Royalty Free; p. 309: Splash News/ Newscom; p. 314: Pascal Broze/Onoky/Corbis Royalty Free; p. 316: MBI/Alamy Royalty Free; p. 320: Pixel Memoirs/Shutterstock; p. 321: Mike Goldwater/ Alamy; p. 323: Goodshoot/Thinkstock; p. 325: Bill Olive/Getty Images; p. 328: James Shaffer/PhotoEdit Inc.

Chapter 12: p. 332, 333, and 330: Shutterstock; p.. 335: Stapleton Historical Collection/HIP/The Image Works; p. 337: Kablonk/ Purestock/Super Stock Royalty Free; p. 340: Zurijeta/Shutterstock; p. 341: Shutterstock; p. 344: Denkou Images/Alamy Royalty Free; p. 346: Steven Rubin/The Image Works; p. 348: Bob Daemmrich/ PhotoEdit Inc.; p. 349: axel leschinski/Alamy; p. 352: www.kidsturn.org; p. 354: Tony Savino/The Image Works; p. 356: David Young-Wolff/ PhotoEdit Inc.; p. 359: iofoto/Shutterstock

Chapter 13: p. 362, 363, and 388: Shutterstock; p. 364: Heather Weston/ Workbook Stock/Getty Images; p. 365: Obama For America/Handout/ Reuters/Corbis; p. 369: John Birdsall/ The Image Works; p. 373: ABC-TV/THE KOBAL COLLECTION/D'AMICO, BOB; p. 376: Francis Dean/Dean Pictures/The Image Works; p. 377: Daily Express/ ZUMApress.com/Newscom; p. 378: Jupiterimages/Brand X Pictures/ Getty Images Royalty Free; p. 381: COLUMBIA/THE KOBAL COLLECTION; p. 383: Eric Audras/PhotoAlto/Corbis Royalty Free; p. 384: Thinkstock

Chapter 14: p. 390, 391, and 418: Shutterstock; p. 393 top: Shutterstock; p. 393: bottom: Supplied by Karen Seccombe; p. 395: Corbis; p. 397 top: Liquidlibrary/Thinkstock; p. 397 bottom: Shutterstock; p. 401: Queerstock, Inc./Alamy Royalty Free; p. 405: Michael Newman/ PhotoEdit Inc.; p. 409: Billy E. Barnes/PhotoEdit Inc.; p. 410: Shutterstock; p. 412 left: Colin Young-Wolff/PhotoEdit Inc.; p. 412 right: David Young-Wolff/PhotoEdit Inc.; p. 415: Mary Anne Fackelman-White House via CNP/Newscom; p. 416: ALAN ODDIE/PhotoEdit Inc.

Chapter 15: p. 420, 421, and 446: Shutterstock; p. 422: Armando Gallo/Retna Ltd./Corbis; p. 423: 20th Century Fox Licensing/ Merchandising/Everett Collection; p. 425: Jeff Greenberg/PhotoEdit Inc.; p. 428: Newscom; p. 430: Ellen Senisi/The Image Works; p. 432: Oscar Abrahams/beyond/Corbis; p. 437: Bob Daemmrich/ PhotoEdit Inc.; p. 440: Reproduced with permission of Her Majesty the Queen in Right of Canada 2007; p. 443: Tom Grill/Tetra Images/Corbis Royalty Free; p. 444: Les Stone/ZUMA Press/Newscom.